THE ENCYCLOPEDIA
OF DOGS

THE ENCYCLOPEDIA OF DOGS

THE CANINE BREEDS
by Fiorenzo Fiorone

Thomas Y. Crowell Company
New York   Established 1834

COLLABORATORS AND CONSULTANTS

Edited under the direction ot
PAOLO LECALDANO

Consultants

Professor CESARE CONCI, *Director of the Civic Natural History Museum of Milan*

Professor DANILO MAINARDI, *Director of the Institute of Zoology of the University of Parma*

FIORENZO FIORONE, *Dog Expert*

MARCO VALCARENGHI, *Director of the Ente Nazionale della Cinofilia Italiana (E.N.C.I.)*

BRUNA CASONI, *Consultant to the E.N.C.I.*

Dr. FABIO CAJELLI, *Official Judge of the E.N.C.I.*

Count R. GATTO, *Official Judge of the E.N.C.I.*

Dr. GINO GRANATA, *Official Judge of the E.N.C.I.*

Dr. OTTERINO SCHREIBER, *National President of the National League for the Propagation of the Dog*

LYDIA CATTANEO MARCHIORI, *President of the Milan Branch of the National League for the Propagation of the Dog*

Dr. MINO DE CHIRICO, *National Counselor of the National League for the Propagation of the Dog*

Collaborators

Dr. PAOLO ARBANASSI

Dr. FRANCO ATTANASIO

Professor ETTORE CAMESASCA

Dr. EUGENIO CRAVERI

MARIGOLD FREYTAG

DECIO FRUGIS

Dr. SERGIO FRUGIS

Dr. EDOARDO MAYER CHELLINI

Dr. CARLO PALUMBO

Dr. NINO RAVENNA

Dr. LUIGI SACHERO

SALLY ANNE THOMPSON

Editorial Staff: FRANCESCO FRANCONERI, RITA COLOMBO PAGANI, SERGIO NEGRINI, ANGELO DEL PIANO, LUISA BARONCHELLI, and MARCELLO ZOFFILI

Graphics: GIORGIO FRIGERIO, ANGELO CARA **Technical Adviser:** SANDRO DONETTI

Color Plates: Volfgango Peretti Poggi; Drawings: Tino Chito

First published in Italy under the title *Enciclopedia del Cane*

Copyright © 1970 by Rizzoli Editore
Translation copyright © 1973 by Rizzoli Editore

Published simultaneously in Canada by Fitzhenry & Whiteside Limited, Toronto.

Printed in Italy

ISBN 0-690-00056-1

Library of Congress Cataloging in Publication Data

Fiorone, Fiorenzo.
 The encyclopedia of dogs.

  1. Dog breeds. I. Title.
SF429.A1F5413   636.7   73–6979
ISBN 0–690–00056–1

Contents

Preface 7

Glossary 10

The Dog 11

Variations of the Word "Dog" 18

A Panorama of the Dogs of Today 19

Various Classifications of the Dog 32

Official Subdivisions of Dog Breeds 34

Definition of a Standard 36

CATEGORY I

*SHEPHERD DOGS, GUARD DOGS, DEFENSE AND
WORK DOGS*

Group 1

Shepherd Dogs 38

Group 2

Guard Dogs, Defense Dogs, and Work Dogs 88

CATEGORY II

HUNTING DOGS

Group 3

Terriers 146

Group 4

Dachshunds 172

Group 5

Hounds for Larger Game 180

Group 6

Hounds for Smaller Game 210

Group 7

Setters (Exclusive of British Breeds) 266

Group 8

English Hunting Dogs 314

CATEGORY III

PET DOGS

Group 9

Pet Dogs 358

CATEGORY IV

GREYHOUNDS

Group 10

Greyhounds 420

Index 445

The present work has been carried out with the collaboration of the
Fédération Cynologique Internationale, Thuin, Belgium,
and with thirty-five member organizations which include:

Société Centrale Canine pour l'Amélioration des Races de Chien en France, Paris
Union Cynologique Saint-Hubert, Brussels
Raad van Beheer op Kynologische Gebied in Nederland, Amsterdam
Real Sociedad Central de Fomento de las Razas Caninas en España, Madrid
Ente Nazionale della Cinofilia Italiana (E.N.C.I.), Milano
Société Cynologique Suisse, Berne
Société Canine de Monaco, Monte Carlo
Österreichische Kynologen Verband, Vienna
Norsk Kennel Klub, Oslo
Svenska Kennelklubben, Stockholm
Suomen Kennellitto-Finska Kennelklubben, Helsinki
Fédération Cynologique de la République Fédérative Populaire de Yugoslavie, Belgrade
Clube Português de Canicultura, Lisbon
Verband für das Deutsche Hundewesen, Dortmund
Section Canine du Saint-Hubert, Luxemburg
Ceskoslovensky Myslivecky Svaz, Prague
Zwiazek Kynologiczny w Polsce, Warsaw
Ellinikós Kynologikós Organismós, Athens
Brasil Kennel Club, Rio de Janeiro
Dansk Kennelklub, Copenhagen
Magyar Ebtensyésztők Országos Egyesűlete, Budapest
Kennel Club, London
Kennel Club de Chile, Valparaiso
Kennel Club Argentino, Buenos Aires
Perkumpulan Kynologi Indonesia, Jakarta
Cuba Kennel Club, Havana
Kennel Club Uruguayo, Montevideo
Federación Canina de Venezuela, Caracas
Asociación Canófila Mexicana, Mexico City
Club Canino Colombiano, Bogotá
Société Centrale Canine Marocaine, Rabat
South African Kennel Union, Capetown
Japan Dog Federation, Tokyo
Kennel Club Peruano, Lima
Kennel Club of India, Nilgiris

and with the American Kennel Club, New York City
and the Société de Vénerie Saint-Hubert, Paris

PREFACE

We do not know how long the dog has been extolled in legend, literature and art. Perhaps from the very beginning, since the dog has been man's best friend from the dawn of time.

Nor is this simply rhetoric. *Canis familiaris,* as will often be noted in the course of this work, has been man's chosen companion and guard, at work and at leisure, and his qualities have been so recognized for thousands of years. Xenophon called him an invention of the gods; Socrates made an oath on his head; Plutarch immortalized Melampitos, the dog that followed his master into the water; Alexander the Great declared: "If I were not a man I would like to be a dog," and he so mourned the loss of one of his favorite dogs that he built a city in its honor. Zoroaster claimed that the intelligence of the dog rules the world.

We ourselves, as inheritors of the biblical tradition, are not far from believing that when man was created by God and God saw that he was sad, He presented him with the dog, which, according to Buffon, possesses not only beauty, vivacity, strength, and agility, but also that inner gift that enables him to understand his master's every whim.

Throughout history man has taken great (and not entirely disinterested) care of the dog, and the successive progress of our knowledge has led to the present state of dog breeding. The basic tenet of breeding is the safeguarding of the pure breed, based on rational use. This is an indispensable basis, so that the dog is afforded living conditions in keeping with his nature, which will improve from generation to generation through the transmission of special traits.

Actually, what is meant by the term "pure breed"? Zoologically, "pure breed" is understood to refer to domestic animals which, when they reproduce, transmit intact their structural and behavioral characteristics and their abilities to accomplish special tasks. The various kinds of dogs recognized today as pure breeds have been formed throughout history by all sorts of factors, such as those imposed by geography, climate, and social conditions; more recently, others have been created through a series of contributions planned to obtain dogs for specialized tasks. All breeds, therefore, had their origin in crossbreeding, and it is as these fixed breeds that we know them today.

The practical use of raising dogs through selective breedings in order to obtain pure breeds is evident, since the probability of reproducing the qualities of the parents is higher in proportion as the genetic homogeneity is more pronounced.

Selective breeding, therefore, tends by degrees to refine the traits peculiar to each breed so that the physical and psychic characteristics will be transmitted to the progeny, making it better adapted to its own vocation.

The stray dog, lacking commercial value, is thus destined even in the best conditions to be some child's toy. When the child tires of it, or if the family goes on vacation, the animal is abandoned and its troubles begin once more. So, cast out, hungry, and having become vicious, he is truly dangerous; the animal shelters are too few and cannot take in all these strays.

This sad state of affairs would be alleviated if every dog had some commercial value, which is precisely the case with thoroughbreds.

This is why the present *Encyclopedia of Dogs* undertakes to study them in detail and to accord them considerable space. Fiorenzo Fiorone's *The Canine Breeds* is truly destined to be a classic reference book. The work of Fiorone is indispensable and has already brought a great number of devotees to join the many thoroughbred dog fanciers whose ranks will certainly increase as a result of this English edition. According to Giulio Colombo, one of the most active presidents of the National Association of Italian Dog Fanciers, a single book by Fiorone is of more value than ten dog shows.

The number of enthusiastic dog fanciers grows steadily. They wish to be informed, to learn, and to be able to find their way among the great number of breeds, and to be able to attend and appreciate the many dog shows and tests of beauty and performance as genuine connoisseurs.

The *Encyclopedia* is not reserved for experts but is meant for all dog lovers of long-standing or recent enthusiasm, since knowledge of the dog, how to take care of him, and how to appreciate and love him should not be the province of a selected few.

If every dog needs a master, it is also true that every man needs a dog, even if he does not know it. The aim of this book is to lead us to this realization, to reveal this need within each of us, and to provide the means to satisfy it. The richness, the exactness, and the clarity of the information contained in this work impel us to offer our sincere congratulations to the authors and to express our thanks to the editors for having made available to experts, to professionals, and to all dog lovers this most readable and complete encyclopedia.

MARCO VALCARENGHI
Director of the National Association of Italian Dog Fanciers

GLOSSARY

Angulation The angles formed at the juncture of the bones; particularly the shoulder, upper arm, stifle, and hock.

Ankylosis The abnormal adhesion of bones, especially those forming a joint; stiffening of a joint.

Anorchid A male dog without testicles.

Apophysis An outgrowth or projection, especially one from a bone.

Apple head Top of the head rounded or domed, as in the Toy Spaniel.

Belton An intermingling of colored and white hairs, as blue belton, lemon, orange, or liver belton.

Bitch The female of the dog or other canine animal.

Blaze A white spot on the face of the animal, usually between the eyes.

Blenheim A variety of spaniel with white and reddish markings, developed at Blenheim Park, England.

Blue merle Blue and gray mixed with black; marbled.

Bolt To make a sudden start or spring from a "stay" position.

Braccoid The classification name for the "Hound Family" of dogs. See page 33 for an elaboration of this term.

Breeching Long hair or coarse wool on the hindquarters of the dog, especially on a longhaired dog or a sheep dog.

Brindle Striped coat caused by a mixture of black hairs on a light colored base.

Brush tail A bushy, heavily coated tail.

Burr The inside of the dog's ear.

Buttocks The rump or hips.

Canine Of, pertaining to, like, or characteristic of a dog, fox, wolf, or jackal. See page 18 for the origin of this term.

Carenated Keel-shaped; having a prominent central line like the bottom of a ship.

Castrate To remove the testicles from the male dog; emasculate.

Catfoot A short, compact, round foot with well-arched toes.

Cephalic index The ratio of the greatest breadth of the dog's head from side to side, multiplied by 100 from above the root of the nose to the occiput.

Cheekiness Prominently rounded cheeks.

Chicken-breasted A chest with a short protruding breastbone.

Cobby Short in length, compact.

Coursing The sport of chasing game with hounds that follow by sight instead of sound.

Cow hocks A faulty conformation of the hind legs in which the hocks are too close together and the feet too wide; a disqualification.

Crossbreed An animal produced by interbreeding or blending two varieties; hybridize.

Croup The rump of the dog or portion just above the tail.

Crown The highest part of the head.

Cryptorchid A dog whose testicles have not descended into the scrotum.

Culotte The hair or feather at the back of the thighs of the dog (e.g., Collie).

Depigmentation Loss of coloration; it may be partial or complete.

Dewclaw A rudimentary toe in the dog's foot. In most breeds they are removed when the puppy is a few days old.

Dewlap The pendulous skin under the throat of the dog, as in the St. Hubert Bloodhound.

Dish-faced Having the nasal bone higher at the nose than at the stop.

Dock To shorten the tail by cutting.

Dolichocephalic Having a disproportionately long head—the skull and muzzle both being long and the bite even; a skull with a cephalic index below 75.

Down in pastern Overangulation of the pastern joint.

Dry neck Neck with taut skin; neither loose nor wrinkled; no dewlap.

Dudley nose Brown or flesh-colored.

Ectropion A rolling outward of the margin of a part; e.g., an eyelid exposing the inner lining.

Entropion Inversion or turning inward of a part; e.g., the infolding of the margin of an eyelid, so that the lashes rub against the eyeball.

Fall The long overhanging hair covering the face of the toy dog and Bobtail.

Fallow Light yellowish brown.

Fasciculus A small band or bundle of fibers usually of muscle or nerve.

Feather The fringe of hair behind the legs or on the tail.

Femoral-tibial The joining of the thigh and shin bone.

Fiddle front Forelegs out at elbows, pasterns close, and feet turned out; French front.

Flag The bushy part of the tail of the dog, as that of a setter.

Flews The large chop or hanging upper lip of certain dogs, as the Bloodhound.

Flexor-cubital muscle A muscle the action of which is to flex the joint at the elbow.

Flying lips Unsettled lips, not assuming correct position.

Foreface Muzzle.

Gait The manner or rate of walking or running.

Game Collectively, animals, birds, or fish that are hunted or taken.

Graioid The classification name for the "Greyhound Family." See page 33 for further elaboration of this term.

Grizzle Iron-gray; the color produced by the intermixing of black and white hairs.

Gun dog A dog trained to work with its master in hunting and retrieving game.

Harefoot A foot whose third digit is longer than the others.

Harlequin Parti-colored; motley (e.g., German Mastiff, Dachshund, and Pinscher).

Haunch In a dog, it is the part of the body comprising the upper thigh, including the hip and buttock.

Haw The third eyelid or nictitating membrane.

Heterometropia A condition in which the degree of refraction is unlike in the two eyes.

Hock The joint of the hind limb between the stifle and the hind pastern. Corresponds to the ankle in man.

Isabella Fawn color or grayish yellow.

Ischium Hip bone.

Jabot A white stripe down the chest like a shirtfront.

Knuckling A condition characterized by the presence of cocked ankles.

Kyphosis An abnormal curvature of the spine, with convexity backward.

Lack of type Deficiency in traits which define fundamental makeup of a breed.

Layback The receding nose, e.g., the Bulldog; or angle of shoulderblade to the vertical.

Leatherends The skin or flaps of the long, pendulous ears of spaniels, poodles, and some hounds.

Level back One which makes a straight line from withers to tail, but one which is not necessarily parallel to the ground.

Liver Deep reddish-brown color.

Loin Part of the dog that lies between the lower rib and the hipbone.

Lordosis Hollow back, saddle back; curvature of the spine.

Lupoid The classification name for the "Wolf Family" of dogs. See page 33 for an elaboration of this term.

Mantle Dark, shaded portion of the hair on back and sides; e.g., St. Bernard.

Manubrium The portion of the malleus ("hammer" in the ear) that represents the handle.

Mask Dark marking on the muzzle, sometimes extending over the eyes.

Masseter A powerful masticatory muscle passing from the zygomatic arch to the lower jaw.

Mealy Covered or flecked with spots.

Mesomorph A body type in which tissues that originate from the mesoderm prevail. Morphologically there is a balance between trunk and members.

Molossoid The classification name for the "Mastiff Family" of dogs. See page 33 for an elaboration of this term.

Monorchid A dog with only one descended testicle.

Mort A flourish on the hunting-horn at the death of game.

Muzzle Face in front of the eyes.

Nictitating membrane Winking membrane on the inside corner of the eye, exposed in some breeds; haw.

Occiput The lower back part of the head.

Out at elbows with The joint between the upper arm and the forearm is turning off from the body; not held close.

Out at shoulder with Jutting out shoulder-blades loosely attached to body.

Overshot Projection of the upper jaw.

Pack A group of dogs that hunt together.

Pastern The lower section of the leg, between the knee and the forefoot, or between the hock and the hind foot.

Patella Kneecap.

Pedigree The record of a purebred dog's ancestry.

Penciled hair The black lines on the tan toes as seen in the Manchester Terrier and Gordon Setter.

Pily A coat which contains both soft and coarse hair.

Puppy A dog under twelve months old.

Purebreed A dog whose parents are of the same breed, and who are themselves descended from purebred dogs of the same breed.

Retrieval The act of bringing back shot game by the dog to its master.

Ringtail Having a tail curled in a near circle over the back.

Roach back A back which arches over the spine from behind the withers to over the loins.

Roan Of a color consisting of bay, sorrel, or chestnut, thickly interspersed with gray or white.

Ruff A natural appendage or growth resembling a collar of projecting or peculiar hair around the neck.

Saber tail A tail curved slightly upward at the tip.

Saddle back Mark covering the whole or most of the back and flanks.

Scapula The shoulderblade.

Screwtail A naturally short tail, twisted into screw form.

Second thigh Inner thigh just above the knee on the hindquarters of the dog.

Set-on Insertion or attachment of tail or ears.

Smooth coat Short, close-lying hair.

Spaying Sterilization of the female dog by the surgical removal of her ovaries.

Spitz A breed of dogs with a tapering muzzle.

Splayfoot Toes spread well apart.

Sternum Breastbone.

Stifle Stifle joint: the joint and area around it; corresponds to the knee in man.

Stop The depression between the cranial and the nasal bones in the face of the dog.

Strabismus Crosseyed condition.

Stud book Breeding records kept by kennel clubs.

Topknot The long fluffy hair on the crown.

Topline The line along the dog's back and loin in profile.

Toy dog One of a group of dogs characterized by very small size.

Tricolor Black, white, and tan; three colors on one coat.

Trumpet The depression on either side of the skull just behind the eye socket, comparable to a human's temple.

Undercoat The soft hair lying below the top coat of double-coated breeds.

Undershot Having a projecting lower jaw.

Underslung Built low to the ground, with short legs.

Upper arm Bone of the forelegs, sloping from shoulderblade to forearm.

Walleye An eye in which the iris is white or light colored.

Well sprung ribs Roundness or curvature of rib cage.

Wheaten Pale yellowish-fawn or mealy color.

Wirehaired Coated with hair of hard, crisp, wiry texture.

Withers Topmost point of the shoulderblades, just behind the junction of the neck with the trunk.

Wry mouth Misalignment of upper and lower jaw.

Xiphoid Shaped like a sword.

THE DOG

In the course of the seventy million years which separate us from the beginning of the Tertiary, that is, from the geological era that saw the triumph of mammals over reptiles, numerous dogs made their appearance on earth. These dogs were of very different shapes: Some resembled bears, others hyenas, others again looked more like cats, some were very tiny, others were veritable giants. There must have been altogether, at least seventy different kinds. Only some of them managed to survive through 700,000 centuries. Most have disappeared, along with the bear-dogs, hyena-dogs and cat-dogs. It is almost impossible to establish for the dog a line of descent that would offer every guarantee of accuracy. This is not because of a lack of points of reference, but it is by no means easy to make a selection from a multitude of animals which bear some resemblance to our domestic dogs.

Which is, then, the most ancient dog mentioned in world history? Most paleontologists agree that the *Cynodictis* is the ancestor of the dog. It lived throughout the Eocene in Europe and in Asia sixty to forty million years ago (in Europe it was found in Quercy, France) and also during the early Oligocene. In North America it was found from the early Oligocene to the early Miocene, some twenty-five million years ago, in a form showing some greater evolution called *Pseudocynodictis* (properly known as *Hesperocyon*), closely related to the European *Cynodictis*. It appears from these studies that the *Cynodictis* must have been represented by various species, some having characteristics specific to the Viveridae (another carnivorous family to which belong, for example, the mongoose and the civet cat), while others presented the typical features of the carnivorous species.

It probably had a long and flexible body, relatively short limbs supplied with five functional digits with partially retractile claws. It presented very primitive characteristics, particularly in respect to a skull devoid of an ossified tympanic bubble. However, the brain case was sufficiently developed: the occipital apophysis and the zygomatic arches presented features justifying the assignment of *Cynodictis* to more recent times than its predecessors.

We are not aware of any European descendants of *Cynodictis*; they may be found, however, on the American continent in the Oligocene formations of the White River (North and South Dakota, Nebraska, Wyoming, Colorado) and the John Day River (Oregon).

These are the animals we have already mentioned, the *Pseudocynodictis* which presented a higher degree of evolution than the European *Cynodictis*: their dental arrangement was identical to that of the *canis* species, their tympanic bubble was voluminous, well ossified and completely welded to the skull.

At about the same time, that is, during the period from the early Oligocene to the early Miocene which represents the duration of some one million years, another dog lived in North America—the *Daphoenus*, which resembled the bizarre crossing of a cat and a dog because, in the general outline of its skeleton it resembled the feline species, whereas its head revealed a kinship with the dog and the wolf: according to some scientists the *Pseudocynodictis* heralds the wolf; others believe that *Daphoenus* is its forerunner; a third theory, on the contrary, maintains that both these species became extinct without leaving descendants. A third ancestor has always lived in North America: the *Mesocyon*, a canine of which several kinds are known, that had paws with almost no resemblance to those of the feline species and that already seemed to be quite well adapted to the purpose of running (yet the five functional fingers persisted). The *Mesocyon* could serve as a link between the *Daphoenus* and the present types.

Thus we are now approaching our present dog. Many paleontologists believe indeed that the *Mesocyon* is the immediate ancestor of the two other canines of the Tertiary era: *Cynodesmus* and *Tomarctus*; *Cynodesmus*, assuredly a product of higher evolution that all his predecessors, may be considered as the Greyhound of those times, the racer *par excellence*. The *Tomarctus*, whose skull was very much like those of the present-day canine breeds, was also a good racer and had the appearance of a badger with a thick auburn coat and a very thick tail.

The genuine *Canis* (a name which designates not only the domestic dog but also the wolf, the jackal, the fox, and all the species pertaining to the genus *Canis*) appeared in Europe, Asia, and Africa during the Pliocene, ten million years ago, and in North America only in the Pleistocene, scarcely a million years ago.

The passage of these animals from the Old to the New World should not surprise us since it took place from Asia, which then had a land bridge to North America. Nevertheless, as far as dogs were concerned, these im-

Photo: McCutcheon.

portant migrations did not affect the southern hemisphere. At this period animals were continually migrating back and forth across vast areas in search of better living conditions. Thus the dog was born in Europe, evolved in America, returned to Europe, and reappeared in America at a relatively recent period. The same phenomenon occurred with other animals that had no fixed habitat for enormous spans of time.

Innumerable survivors of Pleistocene dogs returned to Europe. These descendants of ancient animals were closely related to the dog, among them *Canis falconeri*, a large and powerful though not too ferocious wolf, a carrion feeder. His appearance was comparable to the wolf, but his habits were more like those of the hyena. We may also note *Canis arnensis* as being closer to the jackal, in looks as well as habits. Fossils attributed to

GRAY FOX

Twelve genera and thirty-five species make up the family Canidae, whose origin is very ancient. Today these carnivores live on every continent, even in Australia which, although the Dingo originated there, for a time had none. It is thought that this animal was brought there at a very early period by the aborigines. Since the Canidae live in the deserts, forests, and on the steppes and are accustomed to the most extreme climates, they owe their great diffusion to the ready adaptability of their physical structure that makes it possible for them to survive in every kind of habitat. Their behavior differs from one species to another. There are dogs that are nomadic, whereas some are unwilling to leave their place of birth; others that hunt only by night; still others that hunt only by day, alone or in packs. All possessed highly developed learning abilities, even the wild species whose actions were conditioned by prudence and judgment.

him have been found in France, Germany, and Great Britain. The wolf that Linnaeus named *Canis lupus* made its appearance about 500,000 years ago and was a carnivore only a little smaller than today's wolf. Much larger, even gigantic, remains have been discovered in more recent strata, going back to the last glaciation, about 40,000 years ago.

One supposes—but this is only one of many theories —that the domestic dog is no other animal than a wolf that has been tamed. This theory is not without foundation, even though it seems strange today to think that a wolf and a Cocker Spaniel, for example, are members of a single genus with a common lineage.

In reality, however, as far as the characteristics of the skeleton are concerned, the differences are extremely slight and can be easily identified by the dentition (most evident when one compares the teeth of the wolf with those of the short-muzzled breeds like the Boxer, the Bulldog, and the Pekingese). These can be attributed to mutations produced by different diets.

It has been claimed that in fairly recent times countless crossbreedings have occurred between dogs having wolf blood and those with jackal blood. But whatever his ancestors, whether they came from a single or multiple source, in more recent or very remote periods, at some point there appeared on earth an animal we call the dog. At first, naturally, he lived in a wild state and was later domesticated.

Even today the domestication of animals offers many mysteries. Explanations of how completely different

JACKAL

Photo: E.P.S., Popper.

COYOTE

Photo: E. Heiniger.

NORTHERN DOGS

Photo: C. Ray (Photo Res.).

animal species evolved on account of their association with man are many and varied. Countless theories are constantly offered concerning the dog.

It is evident that in nature a certain association in effort occurred, either gradually or spontaneously, between man and animals. Both found a common advantage in working together in the carrying out of definite tasks even without special training efforts on the part of man. Some animal species understand that it is sometimes very useful to them to be close to man and for this reason not only do they not avoid him, but even seek him out.

The domestication of the dog probably started through a voluntary association of this kind. As both

man and dog were living on game, they met on the hunting grounds and the dog noticed that man, being intelligent and better armed, won the prey. Gradually the dog became resigned to letting man carry off the prey and at the same time regarded him as his most fearsome adversary. However, in time, this feeling began to change and the dog found certain advantages in the situation. As the savage human groups were used to eating on the spot or in their shelters after having cut the kill into pieces, it must often have happened that remains of the kill were left on the ground and furnished food for the wild dogs. The dogs therefore became accustomed to associating man with sated hunger, with an endured suffering and a satisfied feeling.

There still exist areas of the world where it is possible to find environmental conditions such as they were when the first friendly contacts occurred which led to the collaboration between man and the dog. In the Far North, in the American forests, in the deserts of Africa and Australia dogs are found which appear to have not yet entirely crossed the boundary which separates freedom and a wild state from disciplined living with man. It is through observing these situations, doubtless similar to those which took place many thousands of years ago, that scientists have been able to develop their theories on the domestication of the canines. Whoever regards the association of man and dog as it exists today in the snowy polar wastes or in Indian villages can verify the extent of the need for mutual aid that impelled these two beings to friendship, with man offering shelter, food, the warmth of a fire, and the power of his superior intelligence, and the animal accepting the role of intermediary between his friend and yet unconquered nature.

Photo: McCutcheon, Barnaby's.

Variations of the word "dog".

The comparative study of words that mean "dog" in various European languages leads us to identify its original form *k'uon*. After entering the western Asiatic languages the *k* became *sh* or *s*—*shvan* in Sanskrit, *shun* in Armenian, and in the Western languages where the *k* took on the sound of *k* or *h* such as *kyon* in Greek, *ku* in Erse, *hunds* in Gothic, and *canis* in Latin.

Herodotus mentions that the ancient Medes designated the dog by the word *spaka*, which evidently gave rise to the Russian word for dog, *sobaka*, and the Turkish word *köpek*.

In addition we find words corresponding to the Indo-European *k'uon* (which denotes the antiquity of this term) in languages belonging to extremely remote language families, such as the ancient Chinese *k'iuan* (in modern form *k'ou*), the Siberian-Ostiak *canac*, and the East African *kunano*. It is interesting to observe that in the Bantu languages of black Africa the predominant word for dog is *bua*, evidently of onomatopoeic origin, roughly similar to the barking or baying of a dog.

In all the Romance languages we find variations of the Latin *canis*, modified by the phonetic laws of each language and giving us the French *chien*, the Italian *cane*, the Rumanian *câine*, the Portuguese *cão*, the Old Spanish *can*, etc.

In Spanish, up to 1400, the word *can* was used, but another word, *perro*, originally an insult, found its way into use and has supplanted the older form.

The Old Gothic *hunds* is easily recognizable in the modern Germanic languages such as *Hund* in German, *hund* in Swedish, *hond* in Dutch, etc.

English, like Spanish, at the end of the Middle Ages supplanted the original word for "dog"—*hound*—with *dog* (from the Old English *docga*), while *hound* is only used in certain meanings and in the names of certain breeds.

Modern Greek has also changed the preferred word for "dog," using *skili*, which in Ancient Greek meant "little dog" or "puppy" instead of *kyon*, although this word is still understood but rarely used, much like the English word *hound*.

The most ancient writings that have come down to us in which mention is made of the dog have been the Sumerian, from ancient Mesopotamia from about 3500 B.C. The Sumerian word for dog was *nug*, and it was probably from this that Tamil, a pre-Indo-European language of southern India obtained its word for dog—*nay*, and perhaps the Japanese also got their word *inu*. Finally we find a curious echo of prehistory in the ancient Egyptian word for dog, *uhor*, mentioned in hieroglyphics written thousands of years ago, while in Basque, an extremely ancient language of unkown origin and still spoken in the French and Spanish Pyrenees, the word for dog is *hor*.

The dog's distrust lessened and, instead of fleeing the approach of man he began to seek out his presence and to lurk around areas where man was in the habit of hunting or resting. Man, on his part, whether by reciprocity or curiosity, but also perhaps because the presence of these animals waiting for food around his fires alleviated the danger of his nightly rest, encouraged the dogs by being less hostile and indifferent to them. One may imagine that he made a friendly gesture by throwing a piece of meat to the dog, who first snatched it as a thief, then accepted it as a guest, and finally as a friend. Up to this point the dog was merely a witness to man's activities, following him at a certain distance, but he soon realized the advantages of such an association and decided to take a chance on participating voluntarily in man's hunting pursuits. In this way man was able to observe the dog's abilities and finally decided to use him in tasks other than hunting. The dog developed a love for man, and defended him from attacks by other men and animals. He learned to respect and then to protect the species which man had begun to raise: reindeer, sheep, and cattle. He came to live in the lake villages which man had learned to build, surrounded by water for protection against wild animals. With the enormous variety that existed among breeds, the dog gradually assumed roles more adapted to the needs of man. He became specialized in different kinds of hunting, in pulling sleds, in combat activities, in fights against other dogs or against other animals, and guarding the flocks which remained his foremost charge, and he learned to keep his master company. The friendship between dog and man was one of the keystones in the development of civilization.

When the dog began his association with man, different canine species already existed. The criteria which enable us to recognize the different types of primitive breeds are numerous and well preserved, and the fossil remains show a pronounced tendency at an early date to wide variation.

Present breeds exhibit distinctive and highly diverse characteristics. The causes for this evolution are to be found not only in the natural tendency to variation on the part of the *Canis familiaris* but also in the effects of prehistoric domestication, that is, in man's intervention. For man has worked diligently over the centuries to fix different psychic and physical traits in dogs. The cultivation of these traits has been profitably employed in developing the working and sporting breeds of today. The dog's inclination toward fidelity and affection did not take long to develop.

Those who support the theory that today's domestic dog comes from a single primitive stock recognize among the causes of diversification the natural mutations resulting from different anatomical elements, the effects of climate and environment, as well as domestication. All these influences, singly or together, combine to explain the many conformations of the dog.

A panorama
of the dogs of today

Today the classification of canine breeds can still be based on the four groups as determined by Mégnin (see page 33) even though, in the last seventy years, numerous breeds came to be added to those known at that time while others gradually became modified to a degree where it becomes difficult to classify some of them. Thus, several morphological types have evolved and have become intermingled to such an extent that it is no longer possible to differentiate them absolutely. If, for example, one observed the Bedlington Terrier, he would assume that it belongs with the lupoids with all the other terriers; yet its head and above all its drooping rectangular ears are typical of the braccoids. This is why, according to the conclusions of Dhers and Roger, it is classified in our panorama among the lupoids, but we have also indicated its appurtenance to a subtype: the lupo-braccoids. If one should carry further the study of this breed and of many others, he would have to create subtypes of subtypes; thus, always in the case of the Bedlington, the elongated foot—"rabbit's foot"—is typical of a racer and presents a clear contrast with the "catfoot" of the terrier, which is round, suitable for digging; but this is not all, the structure of the hind leg as a whole shows all the features of a racing dog (angulation, musculature, general shape) which are those of the graioid group. Accordingly, the Bedlington should belong to the category of lupo-bracco-graioids. Which means that three or four fundamental types have contributed to the emergence of this breed such as it is today.

This confirms the difficulties encountered in trying to establish a morphological identification of the various breeds of recent development. However, we have endeavored to afford an identification as precise as possible in the large colored plates appearing on the following pages. These provide as complete a picture as possible of the breeds officially recognized today.

The letters accompanying the name of each breed indicate the type to which it belongs: L—lupoids, M—molossoids, B—braccoids, G—graioids. In doubtful cases ML would indicate a dog of the molosso-lupoid type, LB—the lupo-braccoid, and MB—the molosso-braccoid type.

German Shepherd Dog (L)

Belgian
Groenendael Shepherd (L)

Belgian
Tervueren Shepherd (L)

Belgian
Malinois Shepherd (L)

Belgian
Laekenois Shepherd (L)

Beauce Shepherd (L)

Briard (L)

Pyrenees Shepherd (L)

Pyrenees
Smooth-Faced Shepherd (L)

Portuguese
Mountain Dog (L)

Catalonian Shepherd (L)

Lapponian Herder (L)

Dutch Shorthaired
Shepherd (L)

Dutch Coarsehaired
Shepherd (L)

Dutch Longhaired
Shepherd (L)

Mudi (L)

Puli (L)

Pumi (L)

Bergamese Shepherd (L)

Norwegian Sheepdog (L)

Valée Shepherd (L)

Lapland Spitz (L)

Västgötaspets (L)

Bearded Collie (L)

Rough Collie (L)

Smooth Collie (L)

Bobtail (L)

Shetland Sheepdog (L)

Welsh Corgi Cardigan (L)

Welsh Corgi Pembroke (L)

Croatian Shepherd (L)

Doberman (L)

Canaan Dog (L)

Austrian Shorthaired Pinscher (L)

Medium-Sized Japanese Dog (L)

Ainu Dog (L)

Akita Dog (L)

San Shu (L)

Atlas Dog (L)

Norbottenspets (L)

Eskimo (L)

Greenland Dog (L)

Samoyed (L)

Alaskan Malamute (L)

Siberian Husky (L)

Smooth-Coated Fox Terrier (L)

Wirehaired Fox Terrier (L)

Airedale Terrier (L)

Irish Terrier (L)

Bedlington Terrier (L)

Cairn Terrier (L)

Dandie Dinmont Terrier (LB)

Kerry Blue Terrier (L)

Lakeland Terrier (L)

Manchester Terrier (L)

Norfolk Terrier (L)

Norwich Terrier (L)

Scottish Terrier (L)

Sealyham Terrier (L)

Skye Terrier (L)

Soft-Coated
Wheaten Terrier (L)

Welsh Terrier (L)

West Highland
White Terrier (L)

Australian Terrier (L)

Silky Terrier (L)

Czech Terrier (L)

German Hunting Terrier (L)

Basenji (L)

Karelian Bear Dog (L)

Norwegian Elkhound
(Gray) (L)

Norwegian Elkhound
(Black) (L)

Jämthund (L)

Small Black Elkhound (L)

Finnish Spitz (L)

Lundehund (L)

Harlequin Pinscher (L)

Kromfohrländer (L)

Pinscher (L)

Great Spitz (L)

Small Spitz (L)

Small Smooth-Coated
German Terrier (L)

Schipperke (L)

Shiba Inu (L)

Japanese Spitz (L)

Italian Spitz (L)

Smooth-Coated
Chihuahua (L)

Longhaired
Chihuahua (L)

Continental Toy Spaniel
With Upright Ears (LB)

Chow Chow (L)

Tibetan Spaniel (L)

Small Black and Red
English Terrier (L)

Yorkshire Terrier (L)

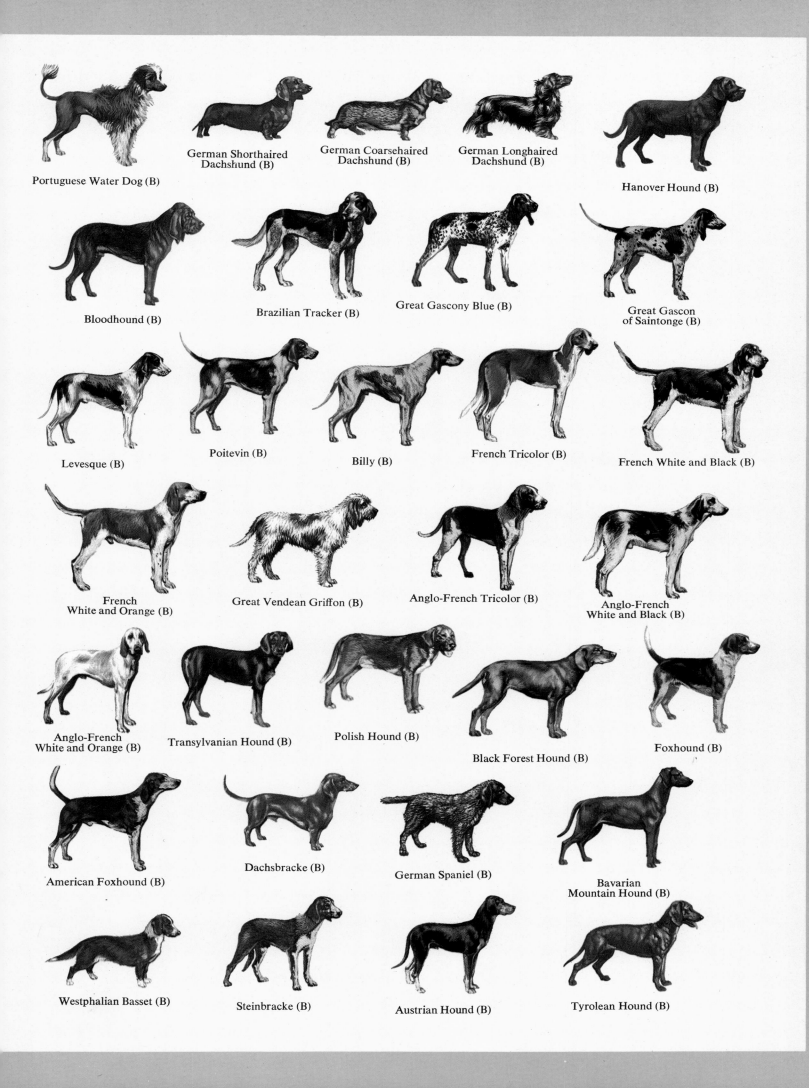

Portuguese Water Dog (B)

German Shorthaired Dachshund (B)

German Coarsehaired Dachshund (B)

German Longhaired Dachshund (B)

Hanover Hound (B)

Bloodhound (B)

Brazilian Tracker (B)

Great Gascony Blue (B)

Great Gascon of Saintonge (B)

Levesque (B)

Poitevin (B)

Billy (B)

French Tricolor (B)

French White and Black (B)

French White and Orange (B)

Great Vendean Griffon (B)

Anglo-French Tricolor (B)

Anglo-French White and Black (B)

Anglo-French White and Orange (B)

Transylvanian Hound (B)

Polish Hound (B)

Black Forest Hound (B)

Foxhound (B)

American Foxhound (B)

Dachsbracke (B)

German Spaniel (B)

Bavarian Mountain Hound (B)

Westphalian Basset (B)

Steinbracke (B)

Austrian Hound (B)

Tyrolean Hound (B)

Austrian Wirehaired Hound (B)

Finnish Hound (B)

Small Gascony Blue (B)

Ariègeois (B)

Artois Hound (B)

Porcelaine (B)

Nivernais Griffon (B)

Vendean Griffon Briquet (B)

Small Blue Gascony Griffon (B)

Tawny Brittany Griffon (B)

Norman Artesien Basset (B)

Blue Gascony Basset (B)

Vendean Griffon Basset (B)

Tawny Brittany Basset (B)

Modern Harrier (B)

Somerset Harrier (B)

Beagle Harrier (B)

Beagle (B)

Otter Hound (B)

Hellenic Hound (B)

Italian Shorthaired Segugio (B)

Italian Coarsehaired Segugio (B)

Dunker (B)

Haldenstover (B)

Hygenhund (B)

Drever (B)

Hamiltonstövare (B)

Schillerstövare (B)

Smålandsstövare (B)

Swiss Hound (B)

Lucerne Hound (B)

Bernese Hound (B)

Jura Hound (B)

St. Hubert
Type Jura Hound (B)

Swiss Coarsehaired
Hound (B)

Small Swiss Hound (B)

Small Bernese Hound (B)

Small Lucerne Hound (B)

Small Jura Hound (B)

Basset Hound (B)

Black and Tan
Coonhound (B)

Balkan Hound (B)

Istrian Coarsehaired
Hound (B)

Istrian Shorthaired
Hound (B)

Posavatz Hound (B)

Bosnian Coarsehaired
Hound (B)

Yugoslavian Tricolor
Hound (B)

Yugoslavian
Mountain Hound (B)

Kurzhaar or
German Setter (B)

Drahthaar
(Coarsehaired) (B)

Langhaar (Longhaired) (B)

Stichelhaar
(Wirehaired) (B)

Large Münsterländer (B)

Small Münsterländer (B)

Pudelpointer (B)

Weimaraner (B)

Gammel
Dansk Honsehund (B)

Burgos Setter (B)

Spanish Hound (B)

Ariège Setter (B)

Blue Auvergne Setter (B)

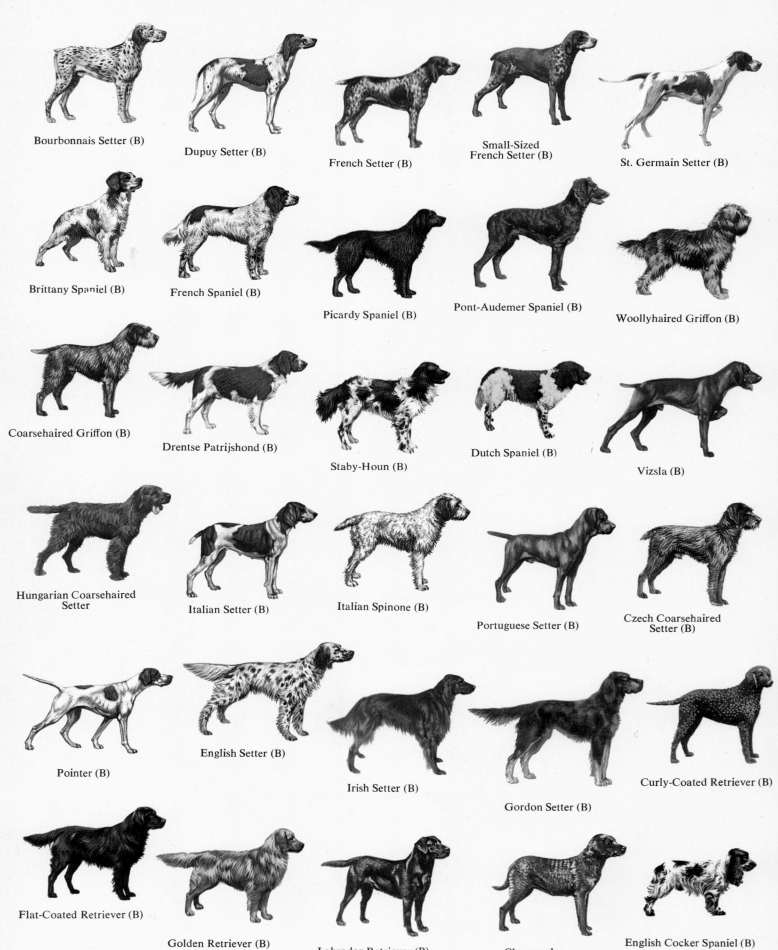

Bourbonnais Setter (B)

Dupuy Setter (B)

French Setter (B)

Small-Sized
French Setter (B)

St. Germain Setter (B)

Brittany Spaniel (B)

French Spaniel (B)

Picardy Spaniel (B)

Pont-Audemer Spaniel (B)

Woollyhaired Griffon (B)

Coarsehaired Griffon (B)

Drentse Patrijshond (B)

Staby-Houn (B)

Dutch Spaniel (B)

Vizsla (B)

Hungarian Coarsehaired
Setter

Italian Setter (B)

Italian Spinone (B)

Portuguese Setter (B)

Czech Coarsehaired
Setter (B)

Pointer (B)

English Setter (B)

Irish Setter (B)

Gordon Setter (B)

Curly-Coated Retriever (B)

Flat-Coated Retriever (B)

Golden Retriever (B)

Labrador Retriever (B)

Chesapeake
Bay Retriever (B)

English Cocker Spaniel (B)

Clumber Spaniel (B)

Field Spaniel (B)

Irish Water Spaniel (B)

English Springer Spaniel (B)

Sussex Spaniel (B)

Welsh Springer Spaniel (B)

American
Cocker Spaniel (B)

American Water Spaniel (B)

Curlyhaired Bichon (B)

Little Lion Dog (B)

Curlyhaired Poodle (B)

Ropehaired Poodle (B)

Continental Toy Spaniel
with Hanging Ears (B)

Bolognese (B)

Maltese (B)

Dalmatian (B)

Shih Tsu (B)

Tibetan Terrier (B)

Lhasa Apso (B)

Havanese Bichon (B)

Picardy Shepherd (ML)

Bouvier des Flandres (ML)

Ardennes Bouvier (ML)

Komondor (M)

Kuvasz (M)

Maremma Shepherd (M)

Tatra Shepherd (M)

Slovakian Chuvach (M)

Charplaninatz (M)

Karst Shepherd (M)

Boxer (M)

Hovawart (ML)

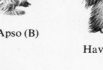

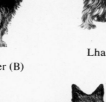

Rottweiler (M)

Riesenschnauzer (M)

Brazilian Guard Dog (M)

German Mastiff (M)

Leonberg (M)

Spanish Mastiff (M)

Pyrenean Mastiff (M)

Great Pyrenees (M)

Bordeaux Mastiff (M)

Neapolitan Mastiff (M)

Japanese Fighting Dog (M)

Serra da Estrela Dog (M)

Castro Laboriero Dog (ML)

Rafeiro do Alentejo (M)

Appenzeller
Cattle Dog (ML)

Bernese Cattle Dog (ML)

Entlebucher
Cattle Dog (ML)

Great Swiss
Cattle Dog (ML)

St. Bernard (M)

Newfoundland (M)

Landseer (M)

Bulldog (M)

Bullmastiff (M)

Mastiff (M)

Tibetan Mastiff (M)

Border Terrier (ML)

Bull Terrier (ML)

Staffordshire
Bull Terrier (M)

Rhodesian Ridgeback (M)

Affenpinscher (M)

Schnauzer (M)

Dwarf Schnauzer (M)

Belgian Griffon (M)

Small Brabançon Griffon (M)

Small Brussels Griffon (M)

French Bulldog (M)

Pekingese (MB)

Japanese Spaniel (MB)

King Charles Spaniel (MB)

Cavalier King Charles Spaniel (MB)

Boston Terrier (M)

Carlin (M)

Great Portuguese Podengo (G)

Cirneco dell'Etna (G)

Medium-Sized Portuguese Podengo (G)

Small Portuguese Podengo (G)

Ibizan Podenco (G)

Hairless Dog (G)

Mexican Hairless (G)

Afghan Hound (G)

Borzoi (G)

Deerhound (G)

Greyhound (G)

Irish Wolfhound (G)

Whippet (G)

Spanish Greyhound (G)

Hungarian Greyhound (G)

Pharaon Hound (G)

Saluki (G)

Slughi (G)

Small Italian Greyhound (G)

Photo: S. A. Thompson.

THE CANINE BREEDS

by Fiorenzo Fiorone

VARIOUS CLASSIFICATIONS OF THE DOG

Man has been trying since ancient times to arrange the various breeds of dogs in some order by setting up a classification based on the aptitudes and later on the most judicious use of each breed. The following table is an example of this endeavor. Established during the Roman era it already envisages several types of dogs.

```
        ┌                ┌ Sagaces (which track the game)
        │  Venatici      ┤ Celeres (which pursue the game)
        │                └ Pugnaces (which attack the game)
CANES ──┤  Pastorales    { (Shepherd dogs)
        │
        └  Villatici     { (Watch dogs—guarding houses, farms, fields, etc.)
```

The classification by the Englishman John Keyes appeared in 1576. He was a medical doctor who later became Queen Elizabeth's first physician. He went to Padua to pursue his studies and there met Konrad von Gesner, a Swiss naturalist who prompted him to edit a table of dogs known in England. Von Gesner wanted to include it in his *Historia animalium*. Keyes wrote his work in Latin—even the author's name was latinized (Caius)—and gave it the title *De Canibus Britannici*; six years later an English translation appeared. His classification is reproduced below. It is not possible to establish a connection with the modern breeds for all the varieties of dogs it mentions.

This was the first attempt at a systematic classification based on practical principles of utilization of the dog. It is interesting to note that the dogs of the "gentle" kind are shown as the exclusive property of the gentry, while those pertaining to the "homely" kind are assigned to guard rural dwellings and flocks. The dogs of the "currish" kind are companions of persons of lower social rank; they seem to be reserved for the most humble tasks and to clownish entertainments (whence they derive the appellation "toy").

This classification, which indicated that some kinds of dogs could be bred exclusively by persons belonging to certain social categories (whence the two designations "country" and "degenerate"), was adopted and remained in force in England for a very long time. Even in the last century the first specimens of bull terriers still belonged exclusively to persons engaged in boxing; thus they came to be called boxers' dogs.

Two centuries later the great Buffon, in his *Ordre des Règnes de la Nature*, based his organization of canine varieties on the various types of ears classified by shape, position, and stiffness.

In the nineteenth century many naturalists dealt with canine classification: Cornevin adopted as norms for the breakdown of breeds the shape and peculiarities of the skull, the position of the ears, and the kinds of hair. Dechambre, in turn, classified dogs according to head profiles and limb characteristics. By subdividing breeds according to straight-lined, concave-lined and convex-

```
                      ┌                      ┌ Hounds  ┌ Leverarius—harriers—hounds
                      │  Venatici            │         ┤ Sanguinarius—bloodhounds
                      │  (furred game)       │         └ Terrarius—terriers
                      │                      └ Hunting { Agaseus—gazehounds—pointers
Gentle Kind ─────────┤                                 { Leporarius—greyhounds
(Sporting dogs)       │
                      │                      ┌ Comforter ┌ Lorarius—lymners
                      │  Aucupatorii         │           ┤ Vertigus—tumblers
                      └  (feathered game)    │           └ Canis furax—stealers
                                             └ Fowling { Index—setters
                                                        { Aquaticus—spaniels

Homely kind—country                          ┌ Canis pastorales—shepherds
                                             ┤ Canis villaticus—mastiffs
                                             └ Canis cabernarius—cattle dogs—bouviers

Currish kind—degenerate                      ┌ Admonitor—wapps
(Toys)                                       ┤ Vernerpator—turnspets, bassets
                                             └ Saltator—daancers
```

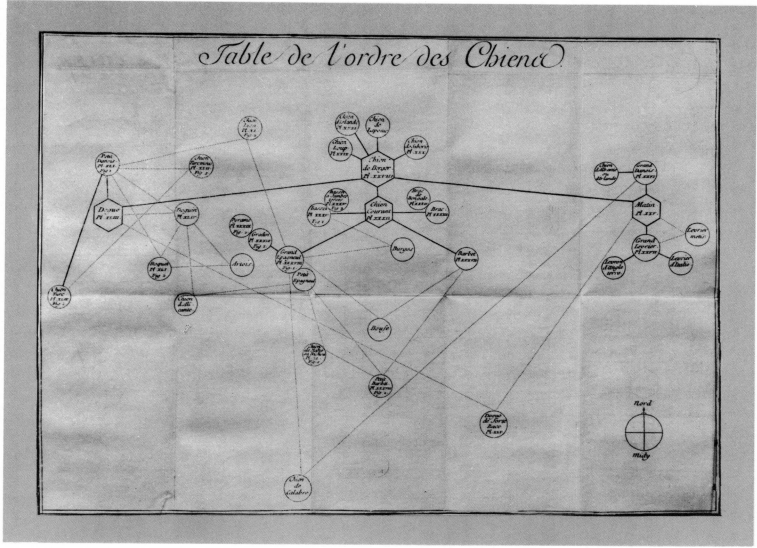

TABLE OF DOG ORDERS, BY BUFFON (courtesy of Dr. F. Méry)

lined, while also taking the coats into account; and Stonehenge has established seven subdivisions by considering the use and the aptitude of the dogs, criteria still used in shows today, even though breeds have become far more numerous than they were a hundred years ago.

We owe to Pierre Mégnin a special method of classification. In 1897 he perfected a classification established in 1800 by Cuvier, the founder of comparative anatomy, and subdivided the known breeds into four broad morphological types:

LUPOIDS The head has the shape of a horizontal pyramid; the ears are straight; the nose is elongated and narrow; the lips are small and tight, the upper lips do not extend beyond the base of the lower gums.

BRACCOIDS The skull is somewhat rounded, the head having a prismatic shape with muzzle as broad at the base as it is at the tip and separated from the forehead by a generally well-marked depression; drooping ears; long, hanging lips, the upper lips stretching beyond the level of the lower jaw.

MOLOSSOIDS The head is bulky, globular; the ears small and drooping; the muzzle short; the lips long and thick; the body massive; such dogs are often large. The hind paws generally have five toes as do the front paws.

GRAIOIDS The head has the shape of an elongated cone; the skull is narrow; the ears are small, extended backwards and straight; the nose is long and thin in a straight-line prolongation of the forehead; the tip of the nose is protruding and angular over the mouth; the lips small, short, and tight. The body is streamlined, the limbs long and delicate, the belly concave.

The criteria of this classication are used to this day for a scientific description of a breed.

The classication of breeds used in national and international dog shows held under the regulations of the International Cynological Federation is the one seen in the table on the following page. All breeds are subdivided into ten groups based on aptitude criteria. We shall refer to the official standard for the description of all these breeds and shall follow the order of this classification.

OFFICIAL SUBDIVISIONS OF DOG BREEDS

SHEPHERD DOGS, GUARD DOGS, DEFENSE AND WORK DOGS

Group 1

Shepherd Dogs

a) Submitted to work tests

1 German Shepherd Dog
(Deutscher Schäferhund)
2 Belgian Sheepdog
(Chien de berger Belges):
Longhaired (Groenendael, Tervueren and other colors)
Shorthaired (Malinois and other colors)
Coarsehaired (Laekenois and other colors)
3 Beauce Shepherd
(Berger de la Beauce)
4 Briard
(Berger de la Brie)
5 Pyrenees Shepherd
(Berger des Pyrénées)
6 Pyrenees Smooth-Faced Shepherd
(Berger des Pyrénées à face rasée)
7 Picardy Shepherd
(Berger Picard)
8 Bouvier des Flandres
9 Portuguese Mountain Dog
(Cão da Serra de Aires)

b) Not submitted to work tests

10 Ardennes Bouvier
(Bouvier des Ardennes)
11 Catalonian Shepherd
(Perro de pastor Catalan)
12 Lapponian Herder
(Lapinporokoira)
13 Dutch Shepherd
Shorthaired (Hollandse herdershond kortharige)
Coarsehaired (Hollandse herdershond ruwharige)
Longhaired (Hollandse herdershond langharige)
14 Komondor
15 Kuvasz
16 Mudi
17 Puli
18 Pumi
19 Bergamese Shepherd
(Pastore Bergamasco)
20 Maremma Shepherd
(Pastore Maremmano-Abruzzese)
21 Norwegian Sheepdog
(Norsk Buhund)
22 Tatra Shepherd
(Owczarek podlhalanski)
23 Valée Shepherd
(Polski owcaarek nizinny)
24 Lapland Spitz
(Lapplandska spetz)
25 Västgötaspets
26 Slovakian Chuvach
(Slovesky čuvac)
27 Charplaninatz
28 Karst Shepherd
(Krašky ovčar)
29 Croatian Shepherd
(Hrvatski ovčar)
30 Bearded Collie
31 Rough Collie
32 Smooth Collie
33 Bobtail (Old English Sheepdog)
34 Shetland Sheepdog
35 Welsh Corgi Cardigan
36 Welsh Corgi Pembroke

Group 2

Guard Dogs, Defense and Work Dogs

a) Submitted to work tests

37 Boxer
Tawny
Striped
38 Doberman
39 Hovawart
40 Rottweiler
41 Riesenschnauzer
Black
Pepper and Salt
42 Brazilian Guard Dog
(Fila Brasiliero)
43 Canaan Dog
Collielike
Dingolike

b) Not submitted to work tests

44 German Mastiff
(Deutsche Dogge)
Tawny and Striped
Blue
Harlequin and Black
45 Schnauzer
Black
Pepper and Salt
46 Leonberg
47 Austrian Shorthaired Pinscher
(Österreichischer kurtzhaariger Pinscher)
48 Spanish Mastiff
(Mastín Español)
49 Pyrenean Mastiff
(Mastín de los Pirineos)
50 Great Pyrenees
(Chien des Pyrénées)
51 Bordeaux Mastiff
(Dogue de Bordeaux)
52 Neapolitan Mastiff
(Mastino Napoletano)
53 Hokkaido Dog
(Kyushu)
54 Ainu Dog
(Hokkaidoken)
55 Japanese Fighting Dog
(Tosa)
56 Akita Dog
(Akita Inu)
57 San Shu Dog
Medium-Sized
Small-Sized
58 Atlas Dog
(Aïdi)
59 Serra da Estrela Dog
(Cão da Serra da Estrela)
Shorthaired
Longhaired
60 Castro Laboriero Dog
(Cão de Castro Laboriero)
61 Rafeiro do Alentejo
62 Portuguese Water Dog
(Cão de Agua)
Wavyhaired
Curlyhaired
63 Appenzeller Cattle Dog
(Appenzeller Sennehund)
64 Bernese Cattle Dog
(Berner Sennehund)
65 Entlebucher Cattle Dog
(Entlebucher Sennehund)
66 Great Swiss Cattle Dog
(Grosser Schweizer Sennehund)
67 St. Bernard
(St. Bernhardshund)
Shorthaired (Kurzhaariger St. Bernhardshund)
Longhaired (Langhaariger St. Bernhardshund)
68 Norbottenspets
69 Eskimo
70 Newfoundland
71 Greenland Dog
(Grünlandshund)
72 Samoyed
73 Landseer
74 Alaskan Malamute
75 Siberian Husky
76 Bulldog
77 Bullmastiff
78 Mastiff
79 Tibetan Mastiff

HUNTING DOGS

Group 3

Terriers

80 Smooth-Coated Fox Terrier
81 Wirehaired Fox Terrier
82 Airedale Terrier
83 Bedlington Terrier
84 Border Terrier
85 Bull Terrier
White
Varicolored
86 Miniature Bull Terrier
87 Cairn Terrier
88 Dandie Dinmont Terrier
89 Irish Terrier
90 Kerry Blue Terrier
(Irish Blue Terrier)
91 Lakeland Terrier
92 Manchester Terrier
93 Norfolk Terrier
94 Norwich Terrier
95 Scottish Terrier
96 Sealyham Terrier
97 Skye Terrier
With Upright Ears
With Hanging Ears
98 Soft-Coated Wheaten Terrier
99 Staffordshire Bull Terrier
100 Welsh Terrier
101 West Highland White Terrier
102 Australian Terrier
103 Silky Terrier
104 Czech Terrier
(Cešky)
105 German Hunting Terrier
(Deutscher Jagdterrier)
106 Basenji

Group 4

Dachshunds
(*Deutsche Dachshunde*)

107 German Dachshund
Shorthaired
(Kurzhaariger Teckel)
Longhaired
(Langhaariger Teckel)
Coarsehaired
(Rauhhaariger Teckel)
108 German Dwarf Dachshund
Shorthaired
(Kurzhaariger Zwergteckel)
Longhaired
(Langhaariger Zwergteckel)
Coarsehaired
(Rauhhaariger Zwergteckel)
109 Kaninchen Dachshund
Shorthaired (Kurzhaariger Kaninchenteckel)
Longhaired (Langhaariger Kaninchenteckel)
Coarsehaired (Rauhhaariger Kaninchenteckel)

Group 5

Hounds for Larger Game

110 Hanover Hound
(Hannoverischer Sweisshund)
111 St. Hubert Bloodhound
(Chien de St. Hubert)
112 Brazilian Tracker
(Rastreador Brasileiro)
113 Karelian Bear Dog
(Karjalankarhukoira
Karelsk bjornhund [Swedish])

French Smooth-Coated Breeds

114 Great Gascony Blue
(Grand bleu de Gascogne)
115 Great Gascon of Saintonge
(Grand Gascon Saintongeois)
116 Levesque
117 Poitevin
118 Billy
119 French Tricolor
(Chien français tricolore)
120 French White and Black
(Chien français blanc et noir)
121 French White and Orange
(Chien français blanc et orange)

Longhaired French Breeds

122 Great Vendean Griffon
(Grand griffon vendéen)

Anglo-French Breeds

123 Great Anglo-French Tricolor
(Grand anglo-français tricolore)
124 Great Anglo-French White and Black
(Grand anglo-français blanc et noir)
125 Great Anglo-French White and Orange
(Grand anglo-français blanc et orange)
126 Transylvanian Hound
(Erdelyi Kopo)
Long-Legged
Short-Legged
127 Norwegian Elkhound (Gray)
128 Norwegian Elkhound (Black)
129 Polish Hound
(Ogar Polski)
130 Great Portuguese Podengo
Shorthaired
Coarsehaired
131 Jämthund
132 Swedish Gray Dog
(Grähund)
133 Black Forest Hound
(Slovensky Kopov)
134 Foxhound
135 American Foxhound

Group 6

Hounds for Smaller Game

136 Dachsbracke
137 German Spaniel
(Wachtelhund)
138 Bavarian Mountain Hound
(Bayerischer Gebirgsschweisshund)
139 Westphalian Basset
(Westfalischer Dachsbracke)
140 Steinbracke
141 Austrian Hound
(Osterreichischer Bracke-Brandlbracke)
142 Tyrolean Hound
(Tiroler Bracke)
143 Austrian Wirehaired Hound
(Steirischer Rauhhaariger Hochgebirgbracke)
144 Finnish Spitz
(Suomenpystykorva)

145 Finnish Hound
(Suomenajokira)

Smooth-Coated Medium-Sized French Breeds

146 Small Gascony Blue
(Petit bleu de Gascogne)
147 Small Gascon of Saintonge
(Petit Gascon Saintongeois)
148 Ariègeois
149 Artois Hound
(Chien d'Artois)
150 Porcelaine

Longhaired Medium-Sized French Breeds

151 Nivernais Griffon
152 Vendean Griffon Briquet
(Briquet griffon Vendéen)
153 Small Blue Gascony Griffon
(Petit griffon bleu de Gascogne)
154 Tawny Brittany Griffon
(Griffon fauve de Bretagne)
French Bassets
155 Norman Artesien Basset
156 Blue Gascony Basset
(Basset bleu de Gascogne)
157 Vendean Griffon Basset
from 15 to 16 inches
from 13 to 15 inches
158 Tawny Brittany Basset
(Basset fauve de Bretagne)

Medium-Sized Anglo-French Breeds

159 Anglo-French Tricolor
(Anglo-Français tricolore)
160 Anglo-French White and Black
(Anglo-Français blanc et noir)
161 Anglo-French White and Orange
(Anglo-Français blanc et orange)

Small-Sized Anglo-French Breeds

162 Small Anglo-French
(Petit Anglo-Français)
163 Modern Harrier
164 Somerset Harrier
165 Beagle Harrier
166 Beagle
167 Otter Hound
168 Hellenic Hound
(Ellinikós ichnilátis)
169 Cirneco dell'Etna
170 Italian Shorthaired Segugio
171 Italian Coarsehaired Segugio
172 Dunker
173 Haldenstover
174 Hygenhund
175 Lundehund
176 Medium-Sized Portuguese Podengo
Shorthaired
Coarsehaired
177 Small Portuguese Podengo
178 Drever
179 Hamiltonstövare
180 Schillerstövare
181 Smålandsstövare
182 Swiss Hound
(Schweizer laufhund)
183 Lucerne Hound
(Luzerner laufhund)
184 Bernese Hound
(Berner laufhund)
185 Jura Hound
(Jura laufhund)
186 St. Hubert Type Jura Hound
(Jura laufhund type Saint-Hubert)
187 Swiss Coarsehaired Hound
(Rauhhaarlaufhund)
188 Small Swiss Hound
(Schweizer Niederlaufhund)
189 Small Bernese Hound
(Berner Niederlaufhund)
190 Small Lucerne Hound
(Luzerner Niederlaufhund)

191 Small Jura Hound
(Jura Niederlaufhund)
192 Basset Hound
193 Black and Tan Coonhound
194 Rhodesian Ridgeback
195 Balkan Hound
(Balkanski gonic)
196 Istrian Coarsehaired Hound
(Istrski resati gonic)
197 Istrian Shorthaired Hound
(Istrski kratkodlaki gonic)
198 Posavatz Hound
(Posavaski gonic)
199 Bosnian Coarsehaired Hound
(Basanski ostrodlaki gonic-barak)
200 Yugoslavian Tricolor Hound
(Jugoslavenski drobojni gonic)
201 Yugoslavian Mountain Hound
(Jugoslavenski planinski gonic)

Group 7

**Setters
(Excluding the British Breeds)**

Setter Breeds

202 Kurzhaar or German Setter
(Deutscher kurzhaariger Vorstehhund)
203 Drahthaar (Coarsehaired)
(Deutscher drahthaariger Vorstehhund)
204 Langhaar (Longhaired)
(Deutscher langhaariger Vorstehhund)
205 Stichelhaar (Wirehaired)
Deutscher stichelhaariger Vorstehhund)
206 Large Münsterländer
207 Small Münsterländer
208 Pudelpointer
209 Weimaraner
210 Gammel Dansk Honsehund
211 Burgos Setter
(Perdiguero de Burgos)
212 Spanish Hound
(Sabueso Español)
Large Mountain Type
Light Type
213 Ibizan Podenco
Coarsehaired
Longhaired
214 Ariège Setter
(Braque d'Ariège)
215 Blue Auvergne Setter
(Braque de Auvergne)
216 Bourbonnais Setter
(Braque du Bourbonnais)
217 Dupuy Setter
(Braque Dupuy)
218 French Setter
(Braque Français)
219 Small-Sized French Setter
(Braque Français de petite taille)
220 St. Germain Setter
(Braque Saint-Germain)
221 Brittany Spaniel
(Épagneul Breton)
White-Orange
Roan-Maroon
White-Black
222 French Spaniel
(Épagneul Français)
223 Picardy Spaniel
(Épagneul Picard)
224 Pont-Audemer Spaniel
(Épagneul de Pont-Audemer)
225 Woollyhaired Griffon
(Griffon à poil laineux — Boulet)
226 Coarsehaired Griffon
(Griffon à poil dur — Korthal)
227 Drentse Patrijshond
228 Staby-Houn

229 Dutch Spaniel
(Wetterhoun)
230 Vizsla
(Hungarian Shorthaired Setter)
231 Hungarian Coarsehaired Setter
(Drotszörüvizla)
232 Italian Setter
White-Orange
Roan-Maroon
233 Italian Spinone
White-Orange
Roan-Maroon
234 Portuguese Setter
(Perdigueiro Português)
235 Czech Coarsehaired Setter
(Cěský fousek)

Group 8

English Hunting Dogs

Setter Breeds
236 Pointer
237 English Setter
238 Irish Setter
239 Gordon Setter
Retriever, spaniel, cocker
240 Curly-Coated Retriever
241 Flat-Coated Retriever
242 Golden Retriever
243 Labrador Retriever
244 Chesapeake Bay Retriever
245 English Cocker Spaniel
Black
Tawny
Varicolored
246 Clumber Spaniel
247 Field Spaniel
248 Irish Water Spaniel
249 English Springer Spaniel
250 Sussex Spaniel
251 American Cocker Spaniel
252 Welsh Springer Spaniel
253 American Water Spaniel

Category III

PET DOGS

Group 9

254 Affenpinscher
255 Harlequin Pinscher
(Harlekinpinscher)
256 Kromfohrländer
257 Pinscher
258 Great Spitz
Gray-Wolf (wolfsfarbig)
Black (schwarz)
White (weiss)
Tawny-Maroon (braun)
259 Small Spitz
Gray-Wolf (wolfsfarbig)
Black (shwarz)
White (weiss)
Tawny-Maroon (braun)
Orange (oranje)
260 Shorthaired Dwarf Pinscher
(Zwergpinscher)
261 Dwarf Schnauzer
(Zwergschnauzer)
Black
Pepper and Salt
262 Schipperke
Miniature (up to 6½ lbs)
Small-Sized (from 6½ to 11 lbs)
Large (from 11 to 20 lbs)
263 Belgian Griffon
(Griffone Belge)
264 Small Brabançon Griffon
(Griffon brabançon)

265 Small Brussels Griffon
(Griffon Bruxellois)
266 Curly-Coated Bichon
(Bichon à poil frisé)
267 Little Lion Dog
(Bichon petit chien lion)
268 French Bulldog
(Bouledogue Francais)
269 Giant Poodle
(Grand Caniche)
White, Black, Maroon, Gray
270 Medium-Sized Poodle
White, Black, Maroon, Gray
271 Miniature Poodle
White, Black, Maroon, Gray
272 Continental Toy Spaniel With Hanging Ears
(Phalène)
273 Continental Toy Spaniel With Upright Ears
(Epagneul nain Continental a oreilles droites—Papillon)
274 Shiba Inu
275 Japanese Spitz
276 Bolognese
277 Maltese
278 Italian Spitz
(Volpino Italiano)
279 Chihuahua
Shorthaired
Longhaired
280 Mexican Hairless
(Xoloitzcuintli)
281 Dalmatian
282 Chow Chow
Black
Other Colors
283 Pekingese
284 Shih Tsu
285 Tibetan Terrier
286 Lhasa Apso
287 Tibetan Spaniel
288 Havanese Bichon
289 Japanese Spaniel
(Chin)
290 King Charles Spaniel
291 Cavalier King Charles Spaniel
292 Boston Terrier
293 Carlin
294 Black and Tan Toy Terrier
295 Hairless Dog
296 Yorkshire Terrier

Category IV

GREYHOUNDS

Group 10

297 Afghan Hound
(Tazi)
298 Borzoi
(Russian Greyhound)
299 Deerhound
300 Greyhound
301 Irish Wolfhound
302 Whippet
303 Spanish Greyhound
(Galgo Español)
304 Hungarian Greyhound
(Magyar Agàr)
305 Pharaon Hound
306 Saluki
(Persian Greyhound)
307 Slughi
(Arabian Greyhound)
308 Small Italian Greyhound
(Piccolo Levriero Italiano)

DEFINITION OF A STANDARD

A standard is the description of characteristics peculiar to a breed. Each standard is therefore a delineation of the corresponding breed. It is established by the cynophile authorities of the various nations according to a precise blueprint approved by the World Cynophile Congress held at Monaco and confirmed since 1934 by the I.C.F. (International Cynophile Federation). Yet it is hard to find exactly comparable standards from country to country. However, there are also rare exceptions such as, for example, the standard of the German Shepherd, as well as some others, which has been adopted by different countries in its original form.

The standards have been established on the basis of the data of Official Cynophilia according to the following plan:

GENERAL CHARACTERISTICS General behavior and aptitudes.

HEIGHT AND WEIGHT In the international type model these features appear following the coat. We felt that it would be appropriate to list them at the outset, not only because height at the withers is a stable measurement with which the dimensions of the other parts of the body are always compared but also because, by providing these two items of information before the others, we enable the reader to know at once whether the dog described is large, medium-sized, small, or very small.

HEAD General formation and according to type: nose, muzzle, jaws, teeth, stop, skull.

EYES

EARS

NECK

FOREQUARTERS Shoulders; arms; forearms; carp and meta-carp; foot.

HINDQUARTERS Hip; leg; ankle; tarsi; metatarsi; foot. According to international norms forequarters were to be described after the *neck* and the hindquarters after the *body*. In this study, even though individually treated, they are mostly grouped under the same heading: fore and hind, so that all four limbs are described as a whole. In certain cases, however, they are described separately whenever special features exist affecting the forequarters.

BODY Chest; thorax; ribs; back; waist; rump; belly; flank.

TAIL According to international norms it should be described after the hindquarters, but since it is in fact a prolongation of the upper line of the body we have preferred to treat it immediately after the section describing the latter.

COAT Hair, color, skin.

GAIT

ANATOMICAL DEFECTS OF THE TYPE

DEFECTS CAUSING DISQUALIFICATION

SCALE OF POINTS

TYPE MEASUREMENTS

Finally, it should be noted that in the beginning the standards did not always adequately set down all the characteristics of a given breed. Some describe the dog in great detail; others, on the contrary, are too sketchy or inadequate; this is due to the too frequent changes in the criteria and the official texts which occurred before normalization. In our work we have endeavored to avoid either subtracting or adding anything so as not to jeopardize the official character of the standards submitted. These standards are the result of complex and laborious translations. We have merely introduced minor stylistic improvements so as to make the presentation of the texts as uniform and as understandable as possible.

The domestic dog, the species that Linnaeus called *Canis familiaris*, today comprises more than 300 official breeds of the family Canidae (which includes wolves, foxes, and jackals). All belong to the order Carnivora, a subclass of placental animals which include man. The place of the dog in the animal kingdom is as follows:

Kingdom Animalia

Subkingdom Metazoa

Phylum Chordata

Subphylum Vertebrata

Class Mammalia

Subclass Placentalia

Order Carnivora

Family Canidae

Genus *Canis*

Species *familiaris* (domestic dog)

Photo: M. Pedone.

SHEPHERD DOGS,
GUARD DOGS,
DEFENSE AND WORK DOGS

Group 1

SHEPHERDS

It is not difficult to imagine that, in far-off times, when sheepherders had to protect their flocks from attacks by men and animals, it was natural for them to attempt to solve this problem with the help of the dog. The dog was already being used as an auxiliary in the hunt and as a watchdog for the bivouac and the home, and had proved his courage, intelligence, and fighting ability. Sheepherders needed a type of dog which· besides these qualities, combined strength and speed and the ability to withstand long journeys and bad weather. For night visibility it was preferable for the dog to have a light-colored coat. Domestication and selection had already produced such dogs from times of remote antiquity, but it is difficult to establish the origin of modern breeds of Shepherds. It would seem, however, that they originated in Asia.

Quite probably the first sheep dogs from Asia arrived in Europe, brought by Phoenician merchants who used them as a means of exchange. According to some authors they either came to Europe with the Roman Legions returning from expeditions in the East, or were introduced by a Tartar tribe which established itself in Moldavia and penetrated into Hungary, or even that they were brought by the Mongols.

If these last hypotheses are true insofar as the Hungarian Shepherd (the Kuvasz) is concerned, they are less probable for the Italian or Spanish breeds: in fact, it is known that large shepherd dogs with light-colored coats existed in the Roman countryside well before the arrival of the barbarian hordes. Lucian G. M. Columella, author of farm treatises, living in the second century A.D., reported as follows: "Sheepherders wish to have white dogs in order to avoid confusing them with wild animals, since, when the wolf attacks in the twilight, it is important that there be a color difference between the dog and the wolf; otherwise the sheepherder might strike his dog, thinking he was killing a wolf. The first duty of the sheepherder's dog is to chase off the wolf, to pursue him for a long time and, when he flees with his prey, to force him to release it so that he in turn may regain possession of it and bring it back."

Whitehaired breeds of dogs existed not only among the Romans but in Mesopotamia and neighboring regions.

In Maremma and the Roman countryside similar dogs are still extant. These are the representatives of the present breed, called Maremma-Abruzzi. It can be considered that this Italian Shepherd breed resembles in its coat and physical and psychological characteristics (with the exception of variations due to climatic differences) the Hungarian Kuvasz breed, the Polish Tatra Shepherd, the Czech Chouvach, and the Pyrenees. It can be concluded that all these breeds have kept almost intact the original characteristics that mark their common origin.

Following the many migrations which took place in the past, the dogs that came from the East, and afterwards their descendants, underwent partial modifications (such as different-colored coats) but nevertheless kept certain typical traits which classified them still within the same group.

In our day the Shepherds, in addition to their traditional duties, have taken on many other tasks as a result of their exceptional intelligence. For this reason the official kennel associations divide the breeds of this group into two categories: those which undergo special championship tests pertaining to work, and those which, on the contrary, are judged exclusively according to the perfect conformity of their physical characteristics with established standards.

1 GERMAN SHEPHERD DOG

Deutscher Schäferhund

GERMANY

This breed has succeeded, perhaps more than any other, in attaining an extraordinary popularity throughout the entire world. It is fitting that we begin our study of the breeds originally employed for the protection of flocks with this dog, inasmuch as this breed offers one of the outstanding examples of how man has been able to put the shepherd dog's unusual qualities to use in the performance of the most varied tasks.

The German Shepherd, often familiarly referred to as Wolf Dog or Police Dog is especially adapted to pastoral life. He has developed into an excellent watchdog and has proved his worth in the pursuit of smugglers, as a help to the wounded, and, in general, fulfills the role of a perfect companion.

The German Shepherd, pride of German breeding, has spread over all the continents. He is also referred to as the Alsatian Shepherd.

According to certain authorities, he is supposed to have descended from the crossing of wolves with domestic dogs, going back to a relatively recent era.

Other authorities think, with probable justification, that the German Shepherd comes originally from Würtemburg and Thuringia where his ancestors were used to guard the flocks from very ancient times. Others of this opinion believe that his origins should be sought in the dog of the Bronze Age, 6000 or 7000 B.C., and which the naturalist Jaitteles called *Canis familiaris matris optimae*. This dog, originating in Asia, progressively spread through Europe.

According to information we now have, as well as the study of the wild forms that have survived through the centuries (in the Indian wolf of our day some have recognized a direct descendent of the ancient wolf of the Bronze Age) allow us to state that, among the representatives of the group which constituted the stock of the race, the tendency to variation has been limited, and all members share common affinities with representatives of the wild canines.

In the case of the German Shepherd, its physical aspect has retained many of the characteristics of the ancient stock, as is shown, for example, by comparison of the physical characteristics of the skull.

In any case, the history of this breed becomes more certain as one approaches the modern era. The presence in Germany of shepherd dogs with a light-colored coat is mentioned in the seventh century B.C. However, around 1600, the light coat was abandoned, perhaps because in the meantime the function of these dogs had changed.

In 1895 the selection which, within a short time, would result in fixing the characteristics of the true breed of German Shepherds began, starting with certain examples of these ancient German dogs. This was essentially the work of von Stephaniz, an enthusiastic dog fancier, who worked with the collaboration of very competent German breeders. The breeding area included Württemberg, certain parts of Hesse, Thuringia, and Bavaria. During this period the Verein für Deutscher Shäferhund was founded, the association which gave its support to the development and perfecting of the breed by attracting the attention of breeders and dog fanciers throughout the world. With the passing years the development of its physical characteristics was accompanied by a notable diversification in the use of this dog. Its character, particularly its power of attention, its faithfulness and its courage, its physical strength, and the acuteness of its

senses have made the German Shepherd capable of carrying out the most varied tasks, at the same time, through atavistic instinct, performing excellent duty as a sheep dog.

It is a most vigilant herder and a brave defender of the animals entrusted to it by man.

In Germany today the society of Schäferhund (shepherd dog) has 150,000 members.

In France the Société du Chien Berger Allemand includes a great number of dog fanciers.

In Italy, where there are many German Shepherds, there also exists a like organization, the Società Amatori Schäferhund.

Qualities of intelligence are accorded considerable importance in this breed, as a fine-looking though frightened and slow-witted dog is always less appreciated than a dog physically less beautiful but having a temperament enabling him to properly fulfill the tasks assigned to him.

This is why representatives of this breed are given official tests in defense and tracking, enabling judges to form a precise evaluation of each subject as to courage, temperament, and the ability to learn the various tasks for the best use to man.

GERMAN SHEPHERD DOG

GENERAL CHARACTERISTICS The average height at the withers is approximately 23½ inches; as a working dog the desirable height for males is 23½-25½ inches; for females 21½-23½ (differences either above or below these figures may diminish the value of the dog, either as a working dog or stud). The height should be measured strictly, along the bony structure and with the hair well down. The measurement should be made along a vertical line from the ground to the withers, tangent to the elbow. The build of this breed is slightly long, robust and muscular; the structure is solid and the skeleton is lean. The proportion between height and length, and the angulations of the bone elements, must be in such a relationship as to guarantee easy trotting and ruggedness. The coat should be highly weather-resistant. A pleasing appearance is desirable, but such appearance should never compromise the utilitarian function of the dog. The sexual characteristics should be well marked. A dog who fulfills the requirements of the standard should give the impression of strength and vigor, of intelligence and agility, and should also be well proportioned with no excess or deficiency. The general behavior of the dog and his movements should indicate complete physiological soundness—a quality which makes the German Shepherd particularly well fitted to carry out his tasks as a working dog continuously and willingly. His natural exuberance should be tempered by obedience and by the pleasure he takes in carrying out any task, adapting himself with good will to every situation. In the defense of his master and his master's property the German Shepherd should show courage and hardiness and should attack decisively when so ordered. At

the same time he must be an agreeable companion in familiar company, vigilant, faithful and friendly toward children and other animals. He should also be at ease in the presence of strangers, and in such behavior he will give an impression of self-confidence and natural nobility.

ANGULATION AND GAIT The German Shepherd is a trotter, and consequently his gait is diagonal (which means that he has two diagonally opposite feet on the ground while the other two diagonally opposite feet are off the ground). His limbs should be harmonious and angulated in such a way as to make it possible for him to move his hind legs as far forward as the midpoint of the trunk, and to extend the forelegs to the same degree, without noticeable displacement of the backline. The proper proportion between height and length and an adequate and well-proportioned length of the limbs permit a trot that covers a lot of ground, stays close to the ground, and gives the impression of easy movement with minimum effort. In a dog that trots with his head pushed forward and with his tail slightly raised, the movement is homogeneous and tranquil; as he moves, his back describes a gently waving line which extends harmoniously from the point of the ears to the tip of the tail, following the nape and the back.

BEHAVIOR AND CHARACTER The chief qualities of an outstanding dog are: a well-balanced nervous system, readiness, lack of inhibition, vigilance, faithfulness, incorruptibility, together with courage, combativity, and cleverness in defense. These are the characteristics which together make the German Shepherd such a fine working dog and, particularly, a watchdog.

Photo: E. Petraroli.

GERMAN SHEPHERD DOG

companion, guard dog, and sheep-herder.

HEAD The head is in good proportion to the body, not stocky, but rather lean and moderately wide between the eyes. The forehead, seen from in front and in profile, is only slightly rounded, with or without a medial furrow which is moderately well defined. The cheeks are moderately curved but not too filled out. The upper part of the head, seen from above, narrows gradually from the eyes to the tip of the nose, with a slanting stock, which must not be too pronounced. The muzzle is powerful, the lips are well drawn, lean, close-fitting, and the bridge, which is straight, is positioned approximately on the same line as the prolongation of the forehead. The teeth are very strong, with the incisors meeting in a scissors bite; the jaws must never be undershot or overshot.

EARS Of medium size, wide at the base, set on high and pointed; they are carried erect and slightly forward. While it is undesirable for the ears to be of the button type, dogs with hanging ears or clipped ears are to be eliminated (puppies up to the age of 4-6 months, and sometimes older, do not carry their ears completely erect).

EYES Of medium size, almond-shaped, slightly slanting and never bulging; the color should be as dark as possible and the expression should be one of liveliness and intelligence.

NECK Robust, of medium length, with well-developed muscles, without loose skin or dewlap. The neck is carried erect when the dog is excited, normally being carried horizontally.

TRUNK The chest is deep but not too broad. The ribs are never flat nor barrel-shaped. The belly is moderately drawn up. The back (including the lumbar region) is straight and well developed; it must not be too long between withers and croup: the length of the trunk is greater than the height at the withers. Dogs with square body outline or high on their legs should be rejected. The loins are broad and robust, the croup is long and slightly hollowed.

TAIL Thickly feathered, the tail reaches at least to the hocks and sometimes forms a slight hook to one side, although this is not desirable. In repose the tail is carried down and slightly curved; when excited or in movement, the dog raises the tail, which becomes more curved, without however going beyond the vertical. It must not, moreover, lie on or curl up on the back. Docked tails are inadmissible.

FOREQUARTERS The shoulders are long, sloping, flat, close to the body and not thrown forward; with the upper arm they form nearly a right angle. The upper arm and the shoulder should both be well muscled. The forearm, seen from any side, should be straight. The pastern is solid but not too straight; the elbows should turn neither in nor out, nor should they be too close to the body.

HINDQUARTERS The thighs are broad, and strongly muscled. The femur is rather long and, seen from the side, oblique in relation to the tibia, which should be of proportional length. The tarsus and metatarsus are solid and robust.

FEET Round, short, well closed, arched. The pads are very hard. The nails are short and strong, generally dark in color. Sometimes dewclaws are present; since the dewclaws can cause wounds or be harmful to the gait, they should be removed as early as possible.

COLOR Black, iron gray, ash gray; solid color or with regular brown markings, yellow, and the various shades thereof to whitish gray. There may also be a black saddle or black shading on a gray or light brown

Photo: S. A. Thompson.

GERMAN SHEPHERD DOG

Photo: S. A. Thompson.

background; among the valid colors for the German Shepherd is included the so-called "wolf color," that is, the original color of the wild dog. Small white spots on the chest are acceptable. The undercoat is invariably little colored, except in black dogs. Puppies change color from birth until they get their final coat.

COAT (a) **Coarsehaired variety:** the top coat is as dense as possible. Each single hair should stand straight and close to the body. On the head the hair is short, as also on the inside of the ear, the forward side of the legs, the feet and the toes, while on the neck the hair is longer and denser. On the hindquarters and buttocks the hair is longer, down to the pastern or the metatarsus: the thighs are moderately trousered. The length of the hair varies from one dog to another, and thus there are many types within the single variety. (b) **Longhaired variety with coarse hair:** The coat is longer than on the preceding variety, not always completely straight, and especially not close to the body. The individual hairs are noticeably longer, particularly inside the ears and behind them, on the back part of the forearm and often in the lumbar region: they form tufts at the ears and fringes from the elbow to the pastern. The trousers are long and dense. The tail is densely feathered with light fringe below. This quality of hair is undesirable, because it is not very suitable as protection against the weather (the opposite of normal short hair); nevertheless, dogs which have a good undercoat are admitted to stud. (c) **Longhaired variety:** the hair is noticeably longer than in (b); often it is parted on the back. The undercoat is absent or present only in the lumbar region. Dogs in this group often have too narrow a chest and a muzzle which, besides being too long, is also too thin and weak. For all these reasons, they are less adapted to use as working dogs, besides being less protected against bad weather: they are therefore to be excluded from stud.

FAULTS All characteristics which have a negative influence on the dog's ability to work, his resistance; appearance not corresponding to the dog's sex; cryptorchidism and monorchidism disqualify from show and stud; details of character different from those required, such as weakness of the nervous system, apathy, timidity, excess excitability, lack of vitality or of willingness to work; soft and spongy build; light coat; white and albino dogs are to be excluded from show

and stud; dogs are also to be considered faulty if they exceed the dimensions indicated, either by being too high or too low on their legs; excess lightness or heaviness, especially a lack of physical consistency in the dog; saddleback, angulations too

straight and, in general, all defects of build which diminish either the extent or endurance of the gait; muzzle too short, too obtuse, too light, too pointed or too long and weak; defects in the teeth, in particular overshot or undershot condition and weakness or

wear in the teeth; coat too soft, short or too long; absence of undercoat; hanging ears or ears constantly carried badly; curled tail, tail excessively curled or carried badly to one side; flipped ears or docked tail; short tail at birth. ●

GERMAN SHEPHERD DOG

2 BELGIAN SHEEPDOG
Chien de berger Belge

BELGIUM

Toward the end of the last century the situation of the Belgian Sheepdog breeds became rather confused in Belgium: there were numerous dogs of all types, sizes, and uncertain origins, often mediocre as drivers of flocks and even dangerous to passersby. In a country like Belgium, where there is a great interest on all levels in the selection and improvement of breeds of domestic animals, the lack of attention given to the sheep dog is rather paradoxical.

Nevertheless, dog fanciers took resolute steps forward. Under the guidance of Reul—of the veterinary school of Cureghem—they succeeded in regrouping in a small number of breeds and varieties those dogs which, more than others, had preserved characteristics considered as fundamental, as well as the qualities needed for efficient help in the field. A group of Belgian Shepherd breeds was established (Groenendael, Malinois, Tervueren, Laekenois) and certain of their variations.

The Groenendael is capable, through its attractive, aesthetic form and its glossy long thick black coat, of holding its own even with today's best luxury dogs. The same thing happened with this breed as with many other shepherd dogs; its intelligence, its spiritual and physical qualities have extended its use into fields quite different from those originally intended. This

courageous, affectionate, and vigilant sheep dog has therefore proved to be an excellent protector and watchdog and has been profitably employed in police activities and in warfare. It is the most widespread among the Belgian Shepherd breeds. It was created by Nicolas Rose, owner of the Château de Groenendael, south of Brussels, and stems from the mating of Petite, a black bitch with white spots on her chest, with the male Piccard d'Uccle, a specimen which had been directly acquired from a sheepherder and which had physical characteristics similar to those of Petite. At first it was decided to call the breed Rose, as a gesture to the breeder. But to give such a name to a dog as black as coal seemed wrong, and it was therefore named for the Château—Groenendael.

The Tervueren, which differs from the Groenendael because of its tawny gold coat splotched with black, is considered more robust, and many breeders use it to reinforce the blood of the allied breed. In general it has characteristics in common with the other Belgian Sheepdogs.

In the northwestern regions of the country we find the Malinois, a country dog that, although not rough or coarse, is quite robust and therefore suitable for many different kinds of work. It is smaller than the German Shepherd, but possesses many of its physical characteristics.

The Laekenois has a coat of tawny gold with long rough hair. It is named for the Château de Laeken, where Queen Marie-Henriette often visited, as this was her favorite breed—an element which contributed to the dog's popularity.

Photo: Fotostampa.

BELGIAN GROENENDAEL SHEPHERD

GENERAL CHARACTERISTICS A medium-sized dog, harmoniously proportioned, intelligent, rustic, accustomed to life in the open, built for resistance to seasonal weather changes and to atmospheric changes which are common in the Belgian climate. His fine proportions and proud carriage of the head give the Belgian Sheepdog an elegant robustness which is the hallmark of well-bred working dogs. He is a born sheep dog and an excellent guard dog; in addition, when necessary he proves to be a stubborn and courageous defender of his master. The lively and questioning expression reveals his nature as an intelligent, vigilant and attentive dog.

SIZE The desirable average for males is 24½ inches and for females 23 inches, with tolerances of ¾ inch shorter and 1½ inches taller.

HEAD Well formed, long (but without exaggeration), lean. The skull and muzzle are nearly the same length: at most the muzzle may be slightly longer, and this gives a greater perfection to the overall appearance. The skull is of medium width, in good proportion to the length of the head; the forehead is flat rather than rounded; the medial furrow is not pronounced. Seen in profile the skull is parallel to the imaginary line prolonging the muzzle. The supraorbital ridges are not prominent, and the muzzle is well chiseled below the eyes. The muzzle is of medium length, tapering toward the tip of the nose. The jaws are long. The nose is black, with nostrils well open. The bridge is straight; seen in profile, it is parallel to the prolongation of the skull. The stop is moderate. The lips are thin, well closed and strongly pigmented; the red of the inner lips should not be visible. The cheeks are lean and flat, although muscular. The teeth are strong and white, regular, strongly set in well-developed jaws. The jaws meet in a scissors bite (the incisors of the upper jaw should fit closely over the lower, but without losing contact). A pincers bite is acceptable, the reason being that it is generally preferred by shepherds and flock handlers.

EYES Of medium size, neither protruding nor deep-set; the shape is slightly almondlike, brownish in color and preferably dark. The eyelids are black. The expression is straightforward, lively and intelligent, as well as curious.

EARS Sharply triangular, rigid and straight, set on high; the length is in good proportion, and the ears are well rounded at the base.

NECK Slightly long, very muscular and without dewlap; it broadens gradually toward the shoulders. Its movement is easy.

FOREQUARTERS The bone structure is compact throughout; the muscles are lean and strong. The scapula is long and sloping, close to the body; with the humerus it forms an angle which allows for easy movement of the elbow. The upper arms should move exactly parallel to the longitudinal axis of the body. The forearms are long and very muscular. Wrists are clean, with no trace of rickets; the pasterns are short and strong. The feet are rather rounded, with well-arched and well-closed toes; the pads are thick and elastic, the nails heavy and dark.

BODY Powerful but not heavy. The length from the point of the shoulder (scapular-humeral) to the outer point of the buttock is approximately equal to the height at the withers in males; it may be slightly more than the height in females. Seen from the front, the chest is not very wide, nor is it narrow. The chest is not wide, but it is deep and well let down, as in all dogs with a high degree of ruggedness. The rib cage has well-sprung ribs in the upper part. The back line is straight, broad, and powerfully muscular. The belly is of moderate development, neither hollowed nor tucked up; it continues the bottom line of the brisket in a graceful curve.

TAIL The croup is slightly sloped, broad, but not excessively so. The tail is of medium length, well set on and strong at the base. In repose it is carried down, with the point slightly curved at the level of the hocks; in action the dog raises it, thus accen-

BELGIAN GROENENDAEL SHEPHERD

Photo: Fotostampa, S. A. Thompson.

TERVUEREN

GRAY BELGIAN SHEPHERD

LAEKENOIS

tuating the curve toward the point. The tail, nevertheless, must never form a hook or incline to either side. **HINDQUARTERS** Must be without heaviness. The movement of the legs is in the same plane as that of the forelegs. The legs are penpendicular to the ground. The thighs are broad and strongly muscular. The second thigh is approximately perpendicular to the haunch. The legs are long, broad, muscular, properly angulated at the hocks but not excessively. The hocks are quite close to the ground, broad and muscular. Seen from behind, they should be perfectly parallel. The metatarsi are solid and short. Dewclaws are undesirable. **FEET** slightly oval in shape, with arched toes which are well closed; the pads are thick and elastic, the nails are heavy and dark. **COAT** Since this varies among Belgian Shepherds insofar as concerns length, direction and aspect, the coat has been adapted to distinguish the different varieties of the breed. In all, however, the hair should be abundant, thick and of good texture; it should, moreover, form a good protective covering with the undercoat, which is woolly. **Color** The following are allowed: fawn, black, grizzle, and the entire range of fawn and the range from gray to black. A little white is acceptable on the chest and on the tips of the feet. The skin is elastic, well fitting over the entire body. The lips and eyelids and nose are strongly pigmented.
GAIT Free and vigorous. The Belgian Shepherd is always in movement and seems tireless, permitting him to cover a maximum of ground. Because of his exuberant temperament, he has a marked tendency to move in a circle rather than in a straight line.
FAULTS Nose, lips eyelids: traces of depigmentation. Teeth: slight overshot condition. Light eyes; shoulders too straight; weak hind limbs; straight hocks; splayed feet; tail carried too high or forming a hook; tail to east or west; lack of undercoat.
DISQUALIFICATIONS Decided overshot or undershot condition; hanging ears; tail absent or docked either from birth or surgery; white markings on parts of the body different from those stipulated by the standard.
AVERAGE MEASUREMENTS The following figures refer to a male dog

whose height at the withers is 24½ inches:

Height at the withers	24½
Length of the body	24½
Length of the back	16
Body circumference behind elbows (minimum)	29½
Height at brisket	12¼
Distance from ground to lowest point of belly	12¼
Length of head	9½-10
Length of muzzle	5

VARIETIES

(a) **Longhaired:** Hair long and smooth, more abundant and longer around the neck and on the chest, where it forms a collar and jabot. Short hair on the head, on the outside of the ears and on the lower part of the leg (except on the back edge of the forearm, which has long hair extending from the elbow to the wrist). The thigh has very long and very thick hair forming a culotte. The tail has long thick hair, forming a flag. The hair around the base of the ears is erect and frames the head; the opening of the outer ear is protected by bushy hair. Dogs belonging to this variety are called *Groenendael*, if the coat is solid black; *Tervueren*, if the hair is a warm fawn color well filled with black and, so far as possible, a black mat. **Faults** Woolly coat, curly, wavy; hair too short. In Groenendaels, red tints in the black top coat; gray culottes. In Tervuerens, absence of blackening or blackening in the form of black spots.

(b) **Shorthaired:** very short hair on the head, on the outer side of the ears and on the lower part of the legs, short on all the rest of the body. It is bushier on the tail, where it is tufted, and around the neck where it forms a small collar, which originates at the base of the ears ad extends to the throat. The edge of the thighs, moreover, is fringed with longer hair. Dogs belonging to this second variety are called *Malinois*, if the coat is fawn tinged with black and if, so far as possible, they have a black mask. **Faults** Long hair where the coat should be short; hard hair scattered among the short hairs; wavy coat; in Malinois dogs the coat is faulty if it is a washed-out fawn color or puffy gray, or if there is a total absence of black

tints, or such blackening is in the form of localized black spots. Too much black is not desirable.

(c) **Coarsehaired:** Characterized by harshness and by the dryness of the coat which, moreover, is tangled. The length of the coat is almost equal on all parts of the body and measures on the average 2¼ inches. The hair on the muzzle and around the eyes should never be so long as to give the head the appearance of the typical

head of Berbets or Briards. However, the presence of feathering on the muzzle is obligatory. The tail should not have a flag. Dogs of this variety are called Laekenois, if they have hard, fawn hair, with traces of black, especially in the muzzle and the tail. **Faults** Hair too long, bristly, curly, wavy or short; tufts of fine hair in the hard hair; excessive length of hair around the eyes or on the lower extremity of the head; tufted tail. ●

3 BEAUCE SHEPHERD
Berger de la Beauce

FRANCE

Also known as the French Shorthaired Shepherd, Beauceron, and Red Stocking (because of reddish spots at the bottom of its legs), the Beauce Shepherd somewhat resembles the Doberman, and many authorities see in this ancient French breed the origin of the modern German guard dog.

The Beauce Shepherd itself is said to descend from a much more ancient stock with rough coat and fierce appearance from which was selectively bred the present breed. In 1897 a breed such as we now know it was presented for the first time in French dog shows. It aroused the interest of many dog fanciers and since then breeding has considerably increased.

Regarding the mental capacity of this dog, Boulet d'Elboeuf (the creator of the Griffon which bears his name) has observed: "The intelligence, the obedience, and the activity of the Beauce are proverbial. He is also a faithful guard and a brave defender, and his herding instinct seems to be inborn, transmitted from his ancestors through the centuries. . . ."

Photo: Kuellenberg, Buzzini, DIM.

BEAUCE SHEPHERD

GENERAL CHARACTERISTICS A big dog, robust and powerful, muscular but not heavy.

SIZE Height: males 25-27½ inches; females 24-26¾. The minimum may be lowered for juveniles.

HEAD Long, wth a flat or very slightly domed skull. The medial furrow is not prominent; the occipital protuberance is visible. The stop is not pronounced, lying at midpoint between occiput and tip of nose. The bridge is not arched except very slightly toward the extremity. Muzzle long, but neither very narrow nor very pointed. The nose is black. The lower lips are slightly let down, not heavy. The teeth are white and well adapted to their purpose.

EYES Set horizontally, the eyes are dark in black-and-tan dogs and vary according to coat color in others.

EARS Set on high; if clipped, they are carried erect and slightly forward, with no divergence. Natural ears are acceptable provided they are set on high. At equal scores, dogs with clipped ears are to be preferred.

NECK Well muscled and well set into the shoulders.

BODY The chest is broad, deep, and well let down. The back is straight, the loins muscular. The croup slopes slightly and only in the direction of the root of the tail.

TAIL Not docked; it is carried low and reaches at least to the hocks; hanging straight, it may be slightly curved or hooked at the end.

FOREQUARTERS The shoulder is long and slanting. The forelegs are straight and well boned. **HINDQUARTERS** The thigh is very well muscled, straight and vertical. The hocks are very slightly angulated, the metatarsus is vertical. **FEET** Strong, rounded, with black nails and hard pads. Double dewclaws on the hind legs. Dogs otherwise well qualified as to type but lacking dewclaws can take only a mention.

COAT Rather rough, short, dense, and close-lying. Length of hair on the dorsal ridge is 1-1½ inches, rarely slightly longer; it is short on the head. There is light feathering on the tail and the back of the thighs. **Color** Black, gray, gray with black-and-tan markings (which the French call "red stockings"), fawn, fawn and black. A white spot on the chest is tolerated but objectionable. For a true working dog, the darker coats are preferred.

FAULTS Slanting eyes, almond-shaped eyes, small eyes; overly flat ribs or overly rounded ribs; horizontal croup; badly carried tail; harefeet (heavy penalty); lack of pigmentation on lips, nose, eyelids; white spot on chest.

DISQUALIFICATIONS Height above or below standard; narrow or pointed muzzle; thick and pendulous lips; thin lips; light-colored nose; walleyes, except for fawn-and-black-coated animals; tail and thighs wholly without feathering; mousetail, weak, docked or rudimentary tail; lack of tail; lack of dewclaws on hind limbs; short or fine hair on body; wavy, curly, unruly hair on muzzle. ●

4 BRIARD
Berger de la Brie
FRANCE

This breed is considered very ancient. Its selection, although continued for centuries in a practical manner by the shepherds, has nevertheless permitted the breed to preserve perfect homogeneity through the centuries. Proof of this is that very old prints show the ancient Briard to be almost identical with that of today.

While certain writers attribute its origins to a remote cross between the Beauceron and the ancient Water Spaniel, others, on the contrary, see its origins in the shepherd dogs which came from the East. This, moreover, is admitted as far as the Italian Shepherds are concerned, and especially the Bergamese Shepherds, with which the Briard shares many points in common and from which it probably derives. French literature begins to make frequent mention of the Briard from the thirteenth century on. For example, Albéric de Trois-Fontaines speaks of it in his *Chronique*.

The Briard is a valuable aid to man in sheepherding, an excellent guard dog, an elegant walking companion, and a valiant protector of the house and children, with whom he likes to play and willingly endures their teasing.

BRIARD

GENERAL CHARACTERISTICS A supple, muscular and well proportioned working dog of exceptionally vigorous movement.

SIZE Males from 24¼ inches to 26¾ inches; females 22 to 25 inches. The minimum is not applicable to young dogs.

HEAD Strong and fairly long, with a pronounced stop midway between the dome of the skull and the tip of the nose. The guard hairs of the head form a beard, moustache and eyebrows. Muzzle neither narrow nor pointed; nose, square rather than round, with tip invariably black. Very slightly rounded forehead. The bridge of the nose is straight. The teeth are strong and white with perfect closing.

EYES Set horizontally, well open, rather large and dark; calm, intelligent expression.

EARS Set high, preferably cropped and erect; rather short and flat if uncropped. At equal ratings, preference to cropped dogs.

NECK Muscular, standing well out of shoulders.

BODY Chest broad and deep, well let down; back, straight; rump, slightly sloping to tail.

TAIL Not docked, well covered, curled at the tip. It is carried low, centered, reaching the hock.

FOREQUARTERS AND HINDQUARTERS Well muscled, strongly boned, and providing an even stance. The hocks are not too near the ground and are well articulated, with the legs nearly vertical beneath the hocks. The feet are strong and rounded, midway between cat and hare feet, with black nails, hard pads, tight toes. Double dewclaws required for winning; single dewclaw merits only mention.

COAT Long, flexible dry hair, not unlike that of a goat. All plain colors admissible except white, but the darker the color the better.

FAULTS Pointed muzzle, small eye, almond shaped or light in color. Rump too straight or overslanted. White spot on brisket. Stripe of white hairs on brisket incurs heavy penalty. Tail very short or carried over the back and spiraled. White nails.

DISQUALIFICATIONS Size surpassing minimum limit; lack of dewclaws; head or legs with short hair; tail missing or docked; light nose; wall eyes; curly hair; white hairs on leg tips; coat of a Great Dane. ●

BEAUCE SHEPHERD

BRIARD

5 PYRENEES SHEPHERD
Berger des Pyrénées

FRANCE

Two breeds of shepherds live in the Pyrenees Mountains. Both are very useful. One of them, the Great Pyrenees, is capable of defending the flocks against all kinds of enemies, including bears, while the other, the Pyrenees Shepherd, is small, light, and used for herding flocks. His origin is under discussion: some think that he is indigenous to the Pyrenees while others think he is descended from the Briard. J. Dhers, an outstanding authority on the breed, contests this and states: "The Pyrenees Shepherd is indigenous and not a crossbreed. All theories of crossing with the Briard must be set aside, at least insofar as his origin is concerned. Moreover, on the Spanish slope and on the plains and valleys below the southern slope of the Pyrenees lives a dog which somewhat resembles the small sheep dog. However, nobody ever had the idea that this is a descendent of the Briard, which he most resembles in size. I am speaking of the Catalonian Shepherd . . ." As is the case with all breeds of ancient origins, it is difficult to establish his ancestry. One must remember, in any case, that he descends from Eastern Shepherds that were modified according to their different habitats.

PYRENEES SHEPHERD

48

Photo: Fotostampa, DIM.

GENERAL CHARACTERISTICS A medium-sized sheep dog of great nervous energy. The wide-awake facial expression, the intelligent, alert nature, and the great liveliness of movement combine to make this working dog unusually interesting.

SIZE Height: males 15½-19½ inches; females 15-19½ inches. There is a tolerance of about 1 inch for dogs that are especially well built and highly typical to their breed.

HEAD The general shape of the head recalls that of the brown bear. The skull is moderately developed, almost flat, with the medial furrow barely evident. The skull is well rounded on the sides; the occipital protuberance is not pronounced. The forepart of the skull slopes gently down to the muzzle; the stop is not accentuated. The muzzle is straight, rather short, and very slightly tapering toward the nose —the shape best described as conical. The tip of the nose is black. The lips should not be thick and should fit well over the gums; the commissure is not visible. The inner lips and the hard palate should be black or strongly shaded with black. Dogs with such a palate are to be preferred. The teeth are strong and should be well proportioned to the overall dimensions.

EYES Expressive, well open, dark brown in color, neither bulging nor deep-set. Walleyes are acceptable in harlequins and slate grays, of which they are almost invariably a characteristic. Delicate eyelids, with black eye rims, are required, whatever the color of coat.

EARS Rather short, moderately wide at the base, and set on neither too close nor too widely separated. The ears are generally clipped. Unclipped ears, if well set on and well carried, do not constitute a fault. Natural prick ears are invariably an indication of crossbreeding.

NECK Rather long, quite muscular, well set on the shoulders.

BODY Structure is lean, with a long but well-sustained back, short and slightly curved loins, in which the curvature appears to be much more than it actually is when the coat is thicker on the hindquarters and rump than over the loins. The rump is short and quite sloping. The flank is barely let down, the ribs are lightly sprung. The brisket is at the level of the elbows, rarely lower.

TAIL Well feathered, not very long, set on rather low, slightly curving up at the tip. When the dog is alert, the tail is raised and more curved. It is often docked, and some dogs are born with a rudimentary tail.

FOREQUARTERS Lean, sinewy, with a pronounced wrist joint. The shoulders are broad and moderately sloping. The point of the shoulder blade is distinctly above the backline. **HINDQUARTERS** The thigh is well muscled but barely let down; the hocks are broad, lean, moderately bent, often slightly closed, especially in dogs born and reared in the mountains. The feet may or may not have dewclaws; (dogs having them are preferred, since dewclaws are an ancient characteristic of shepherd breeds). Dogs with only moderately long hair are not feathered about the hind limbs. **FEET** Lean, slightly flat, of an accentuated oval shape. The pads are dark-colored, the nails small but hard, and covered with hair which also grows between the toes.

COAT Long or moderately so, but always dense and either flat or only slightly wavy; thicker and woollier on the rump and buttocks. The texture of the coat is between that of goat's hair and sheep's wool. The hair is shorter and less dense on the muzzle, while on the sides and cheeks it is brushed back toward the neck. The hair must not cover the ears. **Color** Fawn, more or less dark, with or without a mixture of black hairs, and sometimes with a little white on the chest and feet; more or less light gray, often marked with white on the head, chest, and feet; harlequin of various shades. Black dogs or black with white markings are seldom found. A certain brightness of color is preferable. **Skin** Fine, often spotted, no matter what color coat.

FAULTS Sharply domed skull, rounded forehead; head too short, too long, or too narrow; accentuated stop; square muzzle, excessively long muzzle; coarse jaws; defective dentition; overshot jaw; too small or too round eyes, light color or surly expression; ears set on too low; coarse muscling or cloddiness; saber tail or straight tail; dewclaws on forelimbs; excessive feathering on head, especially if eyes are covered or if muzzle has Griffon-like mustache; black coat with tan markings on head and legs (the so-called *bas rouge*); insufficient pigmentation of lips, nose, eyelids; bad gait. **DISQUALIFICATIONS** Natural prick ears. ●

PYRENEES SHEPHERD

Photo: Buzzini.

6 PYRENEES SMOOTH-FACED SHEPHERD

Berger des Pyrénées à face rasée

FRANCE

GENERAL CHARACTERISTICS Considered as a whole, this dog has the same physical characteristics as the Longhaired Pyrenees Shepherd, except that the smooth-faced variety is less nervous than the other and is generally more tractable, less suspicious of strangers, and a gayer, livelier animal.

SIZE Height: males 16-21 inches; females 16-20½ inches.

HEAD Covered with fine, short hair (whence the breed's name). The muzzle is a little longer than in the longhaired variety.

BODY The body is slightly shorter than in the longhaired variety; otherwise the proportions are the same.

TAIL Can be long and hooked at the end or docked. Many puppies are born with a short tail.

FEET Often more compact and more arched than in the longhaired variety.

COAT Short and fine on the head; on the body the hair is somewhat longer (the maximum length of 2½-3 inches grows only on the neck and withers). Hair along the center of the back may be 1½-2 inches long. The hair on the feet is short, with a slight fringe on the forefeet and a culotte on the hindquarters. **Color** Harlequin black, salt and pepper; fawn in various shades with or without mingling of black hairs and sometimes with white markings. A gray mantle is sometimes, though rarely, encountered.

FAULTS Faults and disqualifications are the same as for the longhaired variety. ●

PYRENEES SMOOTH-FACED SHEPHERD

7 PICARDY SHEPHERD

Berger Picard

FRANCE

Since time immemorial the Picardy Shepherd has guarded the flocks in the region of Pas-de-Calais, by the Somme, in the north of France. His origins are obscure because the breed is so old: one supposes that he shares common origins with the Dutch and Belgian Shepherds. His appearance prevents him from being confused with other breeds. The principal feature of the Picardy Shepherd is the long and shaggy coat.

GENERAL CHARACTERISTICS A medium-sized dog of rustic yet elegant appearance, vigorous, well structured, muscular; face and expression are intelligent and wide-awake and somewhat resemble those of the Griffon.

SIZE Height: males 23½-25½; females 21½-23½.

HEAD The head must not be heavy, but rather in good proportion to overall size. The skull is broad but not excessively so. The eyebrows are fairly thick, but not to the point of shielding the eyes. From in front, the forehead must not look flat but rather vaulted, with a slight furrow between the sinuses. The muzzle is strong, not too long and should not be pointed. The tip of the nose is black, the bridge straight. Mustache and beard are present but light. There must be no cheekiness, but neither should the cheeks be flat. The feathering on the cheeks should be as long as the hair on the body. The stop is not accentuated and should lie halfway between the occiput and the tip of the nose. The lips are lean and closed. The jaws are powerful and close evenly; not undershot nor overshot.

EYES Medium size, not protruding, more or less dark depending on color of coat, and in no case lighter than hazel; walleyes are objectionable. The expression must be neither surly nor suspicious.

EARS Of medium size, set on rather high, carried erect; large at the base, at which point they are something like the ears of a sheep. The tips are lightly rounded. Admissible if they are carried very close together. The length

PICARDY SHEPHERD

PICARDY SHEPHERD

is about 4 inches and should never exceed about 5½ inches, even in the largest males.

NECK Strong, well muscled, of good length and carried erect in action. It stands out well from the shoulders, giving a proud carriage to the head.

FOREQUARTERS Shoulders long and sloping, muscular without being overloaded and allowing great agility of movement. The legs are straight and vertical, the structure lean. The joints are evident, without however any suggestion of malformation. The pastern is very slightly sloped, thus giving elasticity to the pace and facilitating a sudden halt.

BODY The chest well let down but without exaggeration. The brisket must not be below elbow level. Circumference of the body just aft of the elbows is equal to the height at the withers plus 20 percent. The length of the body is scarcely more than the height at the withers. The ribs are well sprung for one third of the rib cage, then they flatten gradually to the rear. The back is straight, the loins are solid, the belly is only slightly tucked up. The croup merges gradually into the buttocks. The skeleton of the hindquarters is visible but not exaggeratedly so.

TAIL At rest the tail should reach the hocks. It should hang straight down, with a very slight curve at the end. In action the dog may carry it somewhat higher, but never over the back.

HINDQUARTERS The thighs are well muscled and long, especially in the upper part. The stifle is robust. The dog should not be too high in the rump nor "seated," that is, underslung. There should be no lack of harmony between thigh and croup, and the whole should dissolve into a graceful curve. The hind legs must be solid, well made for sustaining the rear part of the dog elastically but without weakness. The bone structure should be evident but not excessive. The hocks are moderately angulated, not too obtuse, too acute, nor too high (good angulation is absolutely necessary). The metatarsi are robust, lean, perpendicular to the ground when the dog stands erect. The legs, moreover, must be vertical when viewed from any angle.

FEET Short and rounded, well closed and well arched. The nails should be short and strong and dark in color. Dewclaws and extra toes are not acceptable. Dogs with dewclaws, however, are not disqualified but only penalized. The pads are strong and moderately elastic.

COAT Hard, of moderate length, not flat or curly. Harsh and crisp to the touch. It is about 2 or 2½ inches long over the whole body, including the tail, and about 1½ inches long on the head. The undercoat is fine and dense. **Color** Gray, gray-black, gray with black highlights, gray-blue, gray-red, light or dark fawn, or various combinations of these colorings. Large white markings are objectionable.

Slight white marking on chest and feet is tolerated.

FAULTS Height more than ¾ inch above standard maximum; over- or underaccentuated stop; hair too short or too long; eyebrows absent or too prominent; forehead insufficiently or excessively vaulted; excessive furrow between sinuses; cheekiness or flaccid or unmuscled cheeks; muzzle too long, weak or massive; muzzle pointed or too blunt; tip of nose closed or with flesh markings; heavy lips, with falling commissure; arched bridge; lack of mustache or beard (note that hair on the head should be about 1½ inches long and that the mustache and beard must be neat); slight overshot condition or lack of 2 premolars disqualify from C.A.C. competition and stud books; lack of 4 premolars makes dog ineligible for classification as excellent; caries; broken canines; eyes not meeting above specifications; ears too large, ears too similar to those of Belgian Shepherd; ears set on too low and too close together; long, weak neck or short and coarse neck, neck rising too abruptly from shoulders, neck with loose skin; excessive (Greyhound type) length of shoulders or shoulders too straight (like Bouvier), shoulders impeding easy movement; weak bone structure, excessively heavy bone structure; weak joints, knotty joints; pastern too straight or too sloping, with foot too far forward; body too heavy or too light, too long or too high on the shanks or too close to the ground; ribs too flat or too sprung; Bouvier build; croup too straight or too falling (these faults carry various penalties depending on the severity of the fault, and if exaggerated they lead to disqualification; this rule holds too for the hindquarters and the feet); mousetail, excessively feathered tail; tail too short, crooked or carried badly; body hair less than 1½ inches, not sufficiently harsh; coat flat or curly; white spot on chest of "shirtfront" type; white on all toes.

DISQUALIFICATIONS **Height:** below minimum, even for juveniles, or more than 1½ inches above maximum; **Head:** untypical, disproportionate, with too little or too much hair, flat or excessively domed skull, dishface or downface; muzzle too big for skull, pendulous lips, black tip of nose, lack of pigmentation on lips, nose, eyelids; lack of more than 4 teeth; exaggerated overshot condition; **Eyes:** walleyes, slant eyes, nonuniform eyes, light eyes, pained expression, shifty expression; **Ears:** carried not according to type. **Forequarters and body:** accentuation of faults described above; **Tail:** carrying of tail over back or too low as result of operation, tail rudimentary or lacking; **Hindquarters:** faulty overall structure; double dewclaws on all 4 legs; **Coat:** less than 1½ inches or more than 2½ inches; flatness, curliness, softness or woolliness; **Color:** black, white, harlequin, spotted, excessively white on chest; wholly white feet, white elsewhere than stipulated above. ●

8 BOUVIER DES FLANDRES
FRANCE—BELGIUM

Many discussions have taken place in French and Belgian dog-fancying circles concerning the origin of the Bouvier des Flandres. The Belgians claim that it is of Belgian origin, while the French consider it uniquely French. The latter are probably right. During World War I the French recruited many Bouvier des Flandres for their own medical services. Few survived and, in 1918, when breeding had almost ceased, the Royal Society of St-Hubert (Belgium) decided to restore the crossing of the Bouvier des Flandres breed with the Belgian or Roulers breed which, although different among themselves, in a single breed was named Bouvier des Flandres and established as characteristic of the Belgian Shepherd. This gave rise to interminable discussions which only increased the confusion. Robin, a professor at the Veterinary School of d'Alfort and outstanding dog expert, not only claims the origins of the Bouvier des Flandres for France (which he designates simply as the "French Bouvier") but he clearly separates the two breeds, attributing different stock characteristics to each. In any case, the Bouvier des Flandres, which, according to Dechambre's belief is a cross between a Griffon and the old type of Beauceron, is a dog of exceptional qualities.

He has no equal as a guard dog and represents an exceptional breed encouraged by special clubs which have established and popularized his merits. The surly appearance given to him by his rough coat is in striking contrast to his good nature, and he is so useful that he can accomplish all sorts of different tasks, sometimes in curious circumstances. He is sometimes even used to turn a wheel in the butter-churning process.

BOUVIER DES FLANDRES

GENERAL CHARACTERISTICS A compact, short-coupled, powerfully built dog with well-boned and muscular limbs, giving an impression of great strength without heaviness.

WEIGHT AND SIZE Males 24½-27 inches; females, from 23-25½ inches; the ideal is the average of these two measurements, i.e., 25½ inches for males, 24½ inches for females. Weight, males approximately 77-88 lb; females 60-77 lb.

HEAD The basic impression is one of massiveness, which is accentuated by the beard and moustache. Head should be proportional to height and build, and should feel clean-cut to

the touch. The nose extends the muzzle to a slightly convex tip. Nose should be well developed, rounded on exterior lines, invariably black, with wide nostrils. The muzzle is broad and strong, with straight bridge sloping gently toward nose. The muzzle length is about ⅔ that of the skull; circumference of muzzle just below eyes should be approximately equal to length of head. Cheeks are lean and flat, the underarm areas are strong and equal in size. Teeth are strong and white, with the upper incisors meeting the lower in a scissors bite. The stop is only slightly accentuated and more apparent than real. **Skull** Well developed, flat, somewhat longer than

Photo: Buzzini, S. A. Thompson.

MAREMMA SHEEPDOG

wide. The upper line of skull and that of muzzle should be parallel. Proportion of skull to muzzle length is 3:2. The frontal groove is barely marked.

EYES Free and alert in expression, neither protruding nor sunken. Optimal shape is slightly oval, with axes aligned horizontally. Color should be as dark as possible in relation to color of coat. Light eyes or eyes with a wild expression should be severely penalized. Eyelids are black and must be without a trace of discoloration. The haw must never be visible.

EARS Cropped to a triangular shape, very erect and mobile and set high on the skull. Cropping in proportion to the size of the head is highly recommended.

NECK Should be carried free and easy; it should be strong and well muscled, widening gradually toward the shoulders. Slightly shorter than head. The nape is powerful and slightly arched. No dewlap.

FOREQUARTERS Should be heavily boned, well muscled, and perfectly straight. **Shoulders, upper arms** Shoulders are relatively long, muscular, but not overly so, moderately slanting. The shoulder blade and humerus are approximately equal in length. **Elbows** Parallel and close to body; out-at-elbow appearance is a defect. In action, elbows must remain parallel to the centerline of the body **Forearms** Must be perfectly straight when viewed from front or side, and they must be parallel to each other and perpendicular to the ground. They should be well muscled and strongly boned. **Carpus** Exactly aligned with the forearms. The pisiform bone must alone form a protuberance at the rear of the carpus. The carpus is also characterized by a strong bone structure. **Metacarpus** Strongly boned, quite short and sloping forward only slightly. **Forefeet** Short, round, compact, with toes arched and close. The nails are strong and black. The pads are thick and very tough.

BODY Short, broad-backed, and powerful. The length from sternum to ischium should be approximately equal to the height at the withers. The chest should descend to the level of the elbows; it must never be cylindrical, even though the ribs are barreled. The chest depth (i.e., the distance from the sternum to the last rib) should be about 70 percent of the height at the withers. **Ribs** The first ribs are slightly arched, the others are well sprung and slanted toward the rear, thus providing the desired chest depth. Flat-sided animals should be severely penalized. **Flanks** The flank, located between the last rib and the haunch, must be very short, especially in males. The abdomen rises only very slightly toward the hindquarters. **Back** Short, broad and muscular, free of any weakness yet remaining flexible. **Loins** Short, broad, well muscled, they must show flexibility without any suggestion of weakness. **Croup** Should follow as closely as possible the horizontal line of the back and mold imperceptibly into the curve of the buttocks. Wide but not excessively so in the male, rather better developed in the female. A sunken or slanted croup is a serious fault. **Genitals** Well developed.

TAIL Should be docked during the first week and in adults should measure about 4 inches. The tail must be aligned with the spinal column. It is carried gaily when the animal is in motion. Some individuals are born tailless and should not be faulted for that condition.

HINDQUARTERS Powerful, with pronounced musculature, the hindquarters must move in the same planes as the forequarters. **Thighs** Broad and well muscled. Their action must be parallel to the median line of the body. The femur should be neither too straight nor too sloping. The buttocks are well let down and firm. The patella lies on an imaginary line starting from the highest part of the haunch (known as the iliac crest) and leading to the ground. **Legs** Moderately long, muscular, neither too straight nor too inclined. **Hocks** Rather close to the ground, wide and muscular. Seen from the rear they must be straight and perfectly parallel when in the "stay" position. In movement, they should neither close in or out but remain perfectly perpendicular. **Metatars** Robust, lean, tending to the cylindrical. They should be perpendicular to the ground when the dog is in the "show" position. No dewclaws. **Hind feet** Round, compact, with toes close together and curved. The nails are strong and black, the pads are thick and tough.

COAT Abundant; top coat and thick undercoat make a protective covering ideally adapted to the sudden violent weather changes in the Bouvier's native Flanders. The top coat should be crisp to the touch, dry and dull, neither too long nor too short (about 2½ inches). It should be slightly touseled without being either woolly or curly. It is shorter on the skull and nearly smooth on the outer ears. The inner ear openings are protected by moderately long hair. The top coat is especially close and wiry on the upper part of the back shorter on the lower limbs, but still rough and wiry. A flat-lying top coat is undesirable since it is indicative of a lack of undercoat. The moustache and beard are ample and composed of rough hairs, which are shorter and rougher on the upper part of the jaw. The upper lip must have a moustache and the chin should be adorned with a rough beard to give the gruff expression so characteristic of the Bouvier. **Undercoat** A fluffy mass of fine and close hairs grows under the top coat and with it forms a waterproof covering. **Color** From fawn to black; pepper and salt; gray and brindle. A white star on the chest is allowed. **Skin** Closely adhering to the body, with little slack. Visible mucous areas are invariably dark.

GAIT Free, easy, and proud. The walk and the trot are the most habitual movements, although amblers are found.

FAULTS Long-bodied structure. Overshot or undershot condition of teeth. Light eyes. Low ears. Flat, excessively long or barreled and short ribs. Falling croup. Soft, woolly, or silky coat, too long or too short. Washed-out color.

DISQUALIFICATIONS Flecked nose. Walleyes, wild expression. Monorchidism or cryptorchidism. Chocolate brown coat or excessive white. ●

9 PORTUGUESE MOUNTAIN DOG

Cão da serra de aires

PORTUGAL

In the opinion of some authorities the Portuguese Mountain Dog is descended from a pair of Briard Shepherds imported at the beginning of this century by the Count of Castro Giumaraes. This Portuguese breed is well represented today and has its own distinct characteristics. Experts who maintain that the Briards have contributed to the betterment of the ancient Pyrenean breed are probably right, above all regarding the instinct for guarding the flocks. It is also thought that the Briard does not adapt easily to the particular climate of the Serra de Aires Mountains.

In its native regions this dog is called "the monkey dog" because of its unusual aspect. It is used to guard and herd sheep, cattle, and even other domestic animals, such as horses and pigs. This dog is outstanding for the exceptional cleverness with which it herds the animals in its charge and by the assured manner with which it chases and brings back runaways and strays.

PORTUGUESE MOUNTAIN DOG

GENERAL CHARACTERISTICS A medium-sized dog with fairly long body, exceptionally intelligent and very lively, with conspicuous qualities of seriousness and adaptability to pasture conditions. This dog is dedicated to the shepherd and the flock entrusted to him; he is suspicious of strangers and is a good guard dog at night.

WEIGHT AND SIZE Weight, 26-40 lb. Height: males 16½-19 inches; females 15½-18 inches.

HEAD Strong, broad, neither long nor round. The tip of the nose is well set off, slightly raised, with wide, rounded nostrils; the muzzle is basically cylindrical, terminating in a vertical plane. Black is the preferred color for the nose; in any case, it should be darker than the coat. Viewed in profile, the bridge of the muzzle is slightly hollowed. The muzzle is short, measuring only about two thirds the length of the skull; its breadth is in good proportion to length and shape. The lips are well fitting but not overlapping; they are fairly thin, immobile, and almost straight. The jaws are of normal development, with a perfectly level mouth. The teeth are white and solid. The stop is well defined. The upper longitudinal cranial-facial axes are divergent. The skull is somewhat longer than broad, convex on the two axes, more so laterally. The supraorbital ridges are not prominent; the medial furrow is pronounced; the skull between the ears is approximately flat; the occipital protuberance is visible.

EYES Lively, with a docile yet intelligent expression; they are neither protruding nor deep-set. They should preferably be dark, round, of medium size and horizontal. The eyelids are either black or at least darker than the coat.

EARS Set on high, the ears are hanging but without folds (when they are unclipped); clipped, they are erect. They are triangular, of medium length, finely textured and smooth.

NECK Harmoniously coordinated with head and body, the neck is straight, slightly above the horizontal, of regular dimensions and free of any trace of dewlap.

FOREQUARTERS Strong and evenly separated. The legs are vertical when viewed from both front and side. The shoulder and the upper arm are powerful, of medium length, well muscled. The shoulder angulation is well bent, the wrists are lean and not prominent. The pasterns are of medium bone and length and only very slightly sloping. **FEET** Rounded, not flat; the toes are close and rather long, with pronounced arching. The nails are long, strong and black, or at least darker than the coat. The pads are thick and tough.

BODY A prominent chest, well let down, broad and receding. The thorax descends to a point slightly below elbow level; it is of medium width and depth. The ribs are not greatly sprung, the rib cage viewed from the front is oval. The backline is slightly saddle-backed. The belly is slightly drawn up. The back is long, the loins are short and curved, broad and well filled out. They are well muscled and well joined to the back and croup. The croup is of medium length and width and slightly hollowed. Belly and flanks are of normal volume and slightly on the rise.

TAIL Set on high, pointed, reaches the hocks when relaxed. Carried between the legs or slightly curved at the tip. In action the tail is curved or rolled up.

HINDQUARTERS Strong, the legs normally separated, vertical and straight whether viewed from behind or the side. Thighs of medium length and breadth, well muscled. The legs are long, muscular, and only very slightly off the perpendicular. The hocks are rather lower than high, of normal breadth, strong and lean; the hock angulation is well open. The metatarsus is of normal thickness and medium length, but strong and only very slightly sloped. Simple or double dewclaws are allowed. **FEET** Rounded, not flat; long, close toes are well curved, with strong, black nails or at least darker than the coat. Thick, tough pads.

COAT Very long, smooth or slightly waved, forming a long beard at the chin, a mustache, and heavy eyebrows which, however, must never cover the eyes. The hair is also long on the trunk and the limbs, including the space between the toes. It is of medium coarseness and rather like goat hair, dense and evenly distributed over the entire body. There is no undercoat or down. **Color** Admissible colors are yellow, chestnut, brown, gray, fawn, and wolf gray with dark, light, and medium shades, together with black more or less marked with tan, with or without an admixture of white hairs but never with actual white markings except for a small one on the chest. **Skin** The skin should not fit too tight. Lips, nose, eyelids, and inner lips should preferably be pigmented.

GAIT A light, controlled gait, predominantly a trot. When work calls for a vigorous run, the dog responds enthusiastically.

FAULTS Pointed nose, straight bridge in profile, pendulous or overlapping lips, poorly defined stop; light eyes or small eyes not round or slanting;

trunk with excessive sag in topline or belly line of Greyhound type; straight or too hollowed croup; tail set on low; short tail or tail normally carried rolled over back; white nails; soft coat or coat with white markings over chest.

DISQUALIFICATIONS Long, narrow head, Roman nose, bad jaw closure; flat, round or narrow skull; ears set on low; docked tail, lack of natural tail; short, curled or flocked hair; white hair on feet; dwarfism.

MEASUREMENTS (for a typical female)

Length of skull	4 in
Breadth of skull	3½ in
Bridge	2½ in
Length of trunk	7½ in
Breadth of trunk	3½-4 in
Height of trunk	8¼ in
Scapular-ischial length	7½ in
Length of tail	10 in

Height at withers	17½	in
Height of forequarters	10	in
Height at croup	17¾	in
Diameter of pelvis (at ileum)	3¾	in
Diameter of pelvis (at ischium)	3	in
Body index	87.5	in
Thoracic index	63.83	in
Total cephalic index	52.94	in
Weight	31	lb

SCALE OF POINTS

General appearance	20
Head	15
Eyes	10
Ears	5
Trunk	10
Limbs	10
Tail	10
Coat	15
Gait	5
	100

10 ARDENNES BOUVIER
Bouvier des Ardennes

BELGIUM

The Ardennes Bouvier, quite rare even in its place of origin, possesses characteristics which should correspond to the official standards reproduced here; however, the firm establishment of the points has always been questioned by certain experts.

This country dog, accustomed to life in the open air and to hard work, has a rough and severe appearance, quite sufficient to keep strangers at a distance. On the other hand, he is obedient and affectionate with his master.

ARDENNES BOUVIER

GENERAL CHARACTERISTICS A fine, intelligent country dog, tireless in his work as guardian of the flock.

SIZE Average height: under 23½ inches at the withers. Females are invariably slightly smaller.

HEAD Massive, rather short. The tip of the nose is broad and black. The lips fit closely over the gums. The muzzle is short and broad and feathered with bristly mustache and beard. The jaws are wide and powerful, well adapted to the Bouvier's life. The stop is not pronounced. The skull is broad and flat, with the hair lying smoothly. The bridge is parallel to the profile of the forehead.

EYES Dark; yellow eyes or walleyes are inadmissible.

EARS Natural; flat ears are not acceptable. Prick ears preferred. Semierect and button ears acceptable.

NECK Short and stocky.

BODY The thorax is broad and deep, reaching the elbow. The ribs are well sprung, the backline straight; back, loins, and croup are broad and powerful and of medium length. The belly is not tucked up.

TAIL Most of these dogs are born tailless; if present, the tail should be docked at the first vertebra.

FOREQUARTERS Straight, parallel, exceptionally well boned; shoulders close on the body. **HINDQUARTERS** Parallel, slightly angulated with the well-boned hocks let down. **FEET** Round and close; dewclaws not permitted on hind legs but should be left on forelegs.

COAT Both long hair and short hair are not acceptable. The coast must be rough and wiry, about 2 inches long, except for being slightly shorter on the head and legs. The undercoat is very dense in winter to protect the dog from rough winter weather; in summer it is much less dense. **Color** For this breed all colors are acceptable.

SCALE OF POINTS

General appearance and color	25
Head and neck	20
Body	15
Limbs	20
Tail	10
Coat	10
	100

11 CATALONIAN SHEPHERD
Perro de pastor Catalán

SPAIN

This dog is quite common in Catalonia where it is called "gos d'Atura." The breed certainly has an origin similar to that of the other European Shepherds, as patently proved by its physical characteristics. It is logical, moreover, to imagine that this type of longhaired shepherd, after spreading through Europe, was able to emigrate to Spain, especially in the Pyrenees area where sheepherding has always been a main activity.

The Catalonian Shepherd is used in herding flocks, and has shown himself to be an excellent aid in this work. He is able easily to prevent animals from entering cultivated areas or from straying. He can inspire obedience in the meanest bull or the wildest colt. Because of his judgment, force, and stubbornness he can enforce such obedience that he has only to show himself at the edge of a cultivated field and no animal dares to enter it. Often a single sheepherder, aided by only one or two dogs, can herd a very large flock safely, rapidly, and with remarkable economy of movement.

Outstanding as a guard or army dog because of his coat and small size, the Catalonian Shepherd is also an excellent companion to man.

GENERAL CHARACTERISTICS A sedate, intelligent shepherd dog of medium size, well formed, with a fine coat that resists heat and cold. His expression is gentle, but the breed is inclined to be of nervous temperament.

WEIGHT AND HEIGHT Average weight: males about 40 lb; females 35 lb. Height: makes 17½-19½ inches; females 17-19 inches.

HEAD The skull is well divided for the first third, starting from the muzzle; the remainder, up to the occiput, is crested, with a pronounced occipital protuberance. The head is broad and rounded at the base. The tip of the nose, the lips, and the hard palate are black. The muzzle is straight, rather short, its shape that of a truncated cone. The lips fit closely together, the jaws are powerful, the teeth are strong and healthy.

EYES Wide open, close together, expressive; the color is dark amber, with black eye rims.

EARS Set on high, the ears are of medium length, pointed and clad in long hair. They are carried down against the head (hanging ears), and are generally clipped.

NECK Solid, rather short, well muscled, vigorous, with strong, free movement.

BODY The chest is well developed, the ribs moderately well sprung. The bony structure is robust. The back is straight and of medium length. The loins are broad, strong, rather short and slightly high on the leg. The croup is slightly raised, rather short; the belly is slightly tucked up.

TAIL Well set on, rather low; long and hanging, sometimes short; when short, the maximum length is 4 inches. Tailless dogs and dogs with docked tails are acceptable.

FOREQUARTERS AND HINDQUARTERS The shoulder is sloping, the legs and feet are lean and rather short. The feet are oval, with hard black pads; dewclaws on the hind legs.

COAT Long and wavy; long and silky on the feet and legs; much longer and coarser on the rest of the body, almost becoming bristly on the rump and the ridge over the spine. **Color** On feet, muzzle, and rump more or less burnt cream; on the rest of the body a mixture of black and white with somewhat more of the former, which means that the overall color is grayish or silver. On some dogs the mixture is composed of more or less dark fawn; one of the two shades dominates in certain parts or in the entire coat. Black, cream, and white tricolor is occasionally found. No white spot is acceptable, no matter how small. ●

CATALONIAN SHEPHERD

PASTURAGE IN THE ABRUZZI ▶

Photo: M. Pedone.

12 LAPPONIAN HERDER
Lapinporokoira
FINLAND

The northern Scandinavian possesses, in this dog, a truly irreplaceable helper for herding reindeer. The Lapponian Herder is extremely valuable in keeping the great reindeer herd together and guarding it tirelessly and safely. His courage is so great that he does not hesitate to attack wolves and bears.

Breeders of this dog concentrate especially on the short-haired type—quicker, lighter, and longer-winded—although it is not presently recognized by the Swedish Kennel Club.

LAPPONIAN HERDER

GENERAL CHARACTERISTICS A medium-sized Spitz used for herding reindeer, the Lapponian Herder is longer than high, strong-boned, and muscular. It must not have a heavy overall appearance. The coat is especially well adapted for its work in the severe arctic winters.

SIZE Height at the withers: males, 19-22 inches; females, 17-19 inches.

HEAD Nose well developed, black. Bridge of nose is straight. Muzzle short and thick, not full, and tapering slightly toward the nose. Ears should be erect, pointed forward, well separated, fairly broad at the base, and short in appearance. Skull broad, domed, stop accentuated.

EARS Preferably erect, pointed forward, well separated, fairly broad at the base, and short in appearance. The inside of the ears is covered with dense hair, particularly at the base; such hair continues to cheeks. Slack ears are not desirable.

NECK The neck is strong and of moderate length, the hair dry.

BODY The chest is deep and broad, the back is straight and strong. The croup is strong, not abrupt. The belly is slightly raised.

TAIL Of moderate length and dense hair, the tail is not tightly rolled but is held rather in a loose curl. When the curl is tightened the tail turns on flank, not back. The movement of the tail may also be circular.

FOREQUARTERS AND HINDQUARTERS The forelegs are strong and powerfully muscled. The shoulders are oblique, the pasterns firm; slackness in them is a fault. The angulation of the hindquarters is strong, and the thighs are broad and muscular. **FEET** Compact and protected by a dense growth of hair. Dewclaws are not desirable on the hind legs.

COAT The top coat is of moderate length, the hairs are straight, rather stiff and rough. The coat is often denser and longer on the shoulder front, chest, and behind the thighs. A soft or wavy coat is a fault. **Color** The ideal color is black tinged with reddish. Light spots are often found above the eyes and a lighter color (preferably brownish or grayish) than the dominant color of cheeks, underbody, and legs. White markings on throat, chest, and legs allowed.

CHARACTER The Lapponian Herder is an obedient dog, friendly, vigorous, and a willing worker. It is also noted for its unusual readiness to bark. ●

13 DUTCH SHEPHERD
NETHERLANDS

The Netherlands, where sheepherding is a prominent activity, also has its own breeds of shepherds. Their anatomical conformation relates them to the shepherd dog of neighboring Belgium, whose origin they are thought to share. Today the Dutch

Shepherds form a separate breed divided into three varieties, differing solely by the nature of the coat, described as short hair, coarse hair, or long hair.

The longhaired variety is practically extinct in its place of origin, while the shorthaired is definitely widespread. It is particularly characterized by the light and dark shadings of its coat. The coarsehaired variety has not found much favor among Dutch breeders, and for this reason is somewhat scarce. This lack of popularity is probably due to local aesthetic standards. The Dutch Shepherds are used for herding only in their own country. Only a few specimens are found in neighboring Belgium. In the other countries of Europe and elsewhere they are practically unknown. They are obedient dogs, docile, undemanding, always on guard, most useful, and hardy with respect to fatigue and bad weather.

GENERAL CHARACTERISTICS A medium-sized dog, not too heavy; muscular, strong, symmetrical, always attentive and always in movement, given its vivacious temperament. The Dutch Shepherd has an intelligent expression and shows great aptitude for working with sheep.

SIZE Height at the withers: males 23-25 inches; females 21½-24½ inches. For the longhaired variety (and only for these) the minimum is reduced to 21½ inches for males and 21 inches for females. The ratio between the height at the withers and the length of the body is 9:10.

HEAD In good proportion to the body without being coarse, it gives the impression of leanness. Of moderate length, rather narrow (but not of the Greyhound type), more or less conical in shape. The muzzle is a little longer than the skull. The bridge is straight and parallel to the skull line; the stop is barely perceptible. The head of the wirehaired variety is squarer than for the shorthaired. The tip of the nose is invariably black. The lips are well closed over the gums. The teeth are strong and regular and meet in a scissors bite.

EYES Dark, of medium size, with almond-shaped rims, slightly slanted, not wide apart.

EARS In proportion to the head they are rather small, as stiffly erect as possible, with the outer ear held forward when alert. They are set on high and tend toward each other at the tips, which must be neither rounded nor pointed.

NECK Not too short, without dewlap, well integrated with the shoulders.

BODY The trunk is solid, the ribs slightly sprung; the chest is deep and not too narrow. The belly is only slightly drawn up. The withers are high, the back short, straight and powerful. The loins are not too narrow, nor should the croup be too short or too falling.

TAIL In repose the tail is carried

DUTCH SHORTHAIRED SHEPHERD

DUTCH COARSEHAIRED SHEPHERD

57

Photo: M. Pedone, E. Münch.

KOMONDOR

low with a slight curve, the tip not reaching the hocks. In action it is carried high but not rolled and without tending to either side.

FOREQUARTERS AND HINDQUARTERS The shoulders should be well joined to the body, the shoulder blade sloping and the upper arm of good length. The limbs are solid, muscular, and well boned; they are straight when viewed from any angle. The hind legs are solid and muscular, with good bone; the angulation at the stifle is moderate. The hock is moderately bent. Dewclaws are absent. **FEET** Close, with well-arched toes; nails preferably black. The pads are soft and elastic, preferably black.

GAIT Normal, not jerky or jumpy.

COAT Shorthaired variety (Korthaar): A rather hard coat over the entire body, not too short, with a woolly undercoat. Similar quality on the head; the collar is visible; the thighs and tail are well feathered. Wavy hair is not desirable. **Color** Yellow, chestnut, brown, gold and silver streaked. The streaks should be sharp and distributed well over the entire body, as well as on the back of the thighs and tail. The streaking must involve the hair from root to tip. Too much black in outer coat is a fault. The mask should be black. Yellow, chestnut, brown and yellow-gray can be found only in dogs born after November 17, 1935, and descending from dogs registered with the N.H.S.B. **Wirehaired variety (Ruwhaar):** Wiry hair over the entire body, hard and as little waved as possible. Close, woolly undercoat except on the head. Moustache and beard on the muzzle formed by rather harsh hair. The eyebrows are of stiff hair which does not cover the eyes. On the skull, cheeks and ears the hair is shorter. It is abundant and uniform around the tail, while on the back part of the thighs it forms a well-developed culotte. **Color** Yellow, red-brown, ash blue, streaked, gray-blue, salt and pepper. Yellow, red-brown, and ash blue permitted only in dogs born after November 17, 1935, and descended from dogs registered with the N.H.S.B. **Longhaired variety (Langhaar):** Long, rather stiff hair lying close all over the body. The collar, the back parts of the thighs, and the tail are profusely covered with hair that is neither curly nor wavy. Undercoat woolly and abundant. Head, ears, feet, inner and outer sides of hind limbs covered with short, dense hair. Abundant fringe, longer above, less so below down to the wrists on the back part of the forelimbs. Long, profuse hair forming a culotte on the back of the thighs but not reaching the hocks; hocks and feet clad in short hair. Fringe on the ears objectionable. **Color** Chestnut- gold- or silver-streaked.

DISQUALIFICATIONS Height less than minimum prescribed; overshot or undershot jaws; walleyes; soft or spoonlike ears; short or rolled tail; white streaks or markings; too much white on feet and toes; nose other than black; bad coloring, bad distribution of streaking, too much black. ●

14 KOMONDOR
HUNGARY

The Komondor, the large Hungarian Shepherd dog whose origins probably go back to the Asiatic descendents of the Tibetan dog, has been working for more than a thousand years as an attentive and tenacious sheepherder.

In the past no great importance was attached to the preservation of the pure strain of a working breed, nor was much attention paid to the appearance of a shepherd dog. In spite of this the Komondor, because of generations spent in difficult working conditions in the open air, developed high psycho-physical qualities.

In 1920 standards were established for this breed which definitely set up the different points, and, when entered in different shows, the breed became popular even outside the country. In America especially it has attained great popularity not only as a shepherd dog but as a companion.

GENERAL APPEARANCE A big dog, well muscled and of well-boned structure, with a heavy white coat of unusual appearance.
CHARACTERISTICS An excellent watchdog because of its distrust of strangers. As a herding dog the adult Komondor is serious, brave, and faithful, ready to defend its master from any danger; this readiness to do battle limits its herding activities to guarding, to the exclusion of driving the

Photo: S. A. Thompson.

KOMONDOR

herd. In its native land it lives outdoors during the greater part of the year, unprotected from the elements. Because of the long hair, the Komondor appears to be rather more robust than it actually is.

WEIGHT AND SIZE Height at the withers: males, 25½ inches and upward; females, 23½ inches and upward. Weight: males, 110-132 lb; females, 88-110 lb. Size is important but other qualities, including symmetry and movement, are not to be sacrificed for size.

HEAD Like a huge, hairy ball emerging from the rest of the body. It is broad but well proportioned to the body, in spite of the long, thick coat. The nose is black, cut at a right angle and of the same color as the eyelids and lips. Straight bridge of the nose. The lips adhere to the dental arches, with a visible commissure. The jaws are very broad and of medium length. Both upper and lower jaws are very muscular. The teeth are strong and regular, with a scissors bite. The stop is accentuated. The skull is convex and longer than the muzzle. The frontal arch is broad, with the eye sockets well developed.

EYES Medium in size and almond-shaped, not too deeply set. The iris is dark brown, the edges of the lids gray.

EARS Inserted at the level of the skull, the ears are long and rather V-shaped. They hang down and remain motionless even when the dog is excited or when he is attacking.

NECK Muscular, of medium length, and moderately arched, the neck holds the head erect. The neck should be held at an angle of approximately 35° from horizontal. No dewlap is permissible.

FOREQUARTERS The long, tangled hair makes an accurate evaluation of the limbs rather difficult. They seem to be columns holding up the body. The shoulders are moderately sloping. The chest is powerful and deep, proportionately wide and superbly muscular. The bones are strong and massive, with ample articulations. The feet are large, rather compact, with heavy pads which are elastic and slate-gray in color. The toes are well arched, the claws are black or gray and very strong. The upper arms are closely joined to the body, without loose elbows.

BODY Square or slightly rectangular. The withers are readily observable. The upper line of the back is broad and strongly muscular. The rump is wide, of medium length, slightly sloping toward the tail. The belly is slightly drawn up at the rear.

TAIL Insertion point low. The tail hangs down with its tip curved slightly upward. When the dog is excited the tail rises, possibly as high as the level of the back. The tail is not to be docked.

HINDQUARTERS Covered with thick hair which is almost invariably matted or tangled, the hindlegs seem to form a unit with the rump. They hold up the body with a rather rigid angulation. The legs are characterized by a strong, steely bone structure and highly developed muscles. The thighs are long, the legs are straight when viewed from the rear. The stifles are well bent. Dewclaws must be removed. The hindfeet are longer than the forefeet, but are not soft.

COAT The Komondor is characterized by a heavy, weather-resisting double coat. The outer coat is somewhat coarse and may be wavy or even curly; the undercoat is woolly, soft, and very dense. The long strands of the outer coat tend to cord, and even when freshly combed the Komondor may appear corded. When corded, the cords should ideally be strong, heavy, and feltlike to the touch. Too curly a coat is undesirable; a straight or silky coat is a serious fault; and short, smooth hair on head and legs is disqualifying. The only acceptable color for the coat is white. The hair is longest at the rump, loins, and tail. It is of medium length on the back, shoulders, and chest. The shortest hair is about the eyes, ears, neck, and on the feet. In very young pups sickness or improper diet can cause loss of hair on the body, belly, and limbs; this may become particularly serious on the hindquarters. At birth the pup has a fine, white, shiny coat, either curly or wavy. After weaning, the puppy's coat is displaced by a thicker one. The juvenile coat gives something of the appearance of a small bear to the Komondor puppy until its regular coat has developed. **Color** white **Skin** deeply colored, almost invariably slate-gray. The nose, lips, and edges of the eyelids are also slate-gray or sometimes black. Gums and palate should also be dark. Any pale or pinkish coloring is undesirable. Both under- and overgrooming are to be avoided.

GAIT The Komondor has a light, easy, and well-balanced gait, characterized by a long, confident stride. During the day it likes to lie down, but invariably so as to be able to watch its territory. At night it is constantly in motion.

DISQUALIFICATIONS Blue-white eyes. Color other than white. Undershot or overshot bite. Bobtail. Flesh-colored nose. Short, smooth hair on head or legs.

MEASUREMENTS AND PROPORTIONS

in relation to the height at the withers:

	Ideal (%)	Tolerated (%)
Body length	104	100-108
Depth of body	45	50-56
Width of body	28	30
Circumference of body (behind the elbows)	116	120
Length of head	41	—

Measurements in relation to length of head:

Length of muzzle	42	—
Length of ears	60	—

15 KUVASZ
HUNGARY

Some authorities place the appearance of the Kuvasz, an excellent sheep dog, in Hungary at the time it was occupied by semi-barbarians. Others believe that the Kumans introduced the breed into the Carpathian Basin. The Kumans were nomadic shepherds of Turkish origin who arrived in Hungary in the thirteenth century under the pressure of the Mongol hordes. The origins of the Kuvasz should therefore be traced to the ancient shepherd dogs from the Orient, the shepherd dogs of Tibet, which are also the forerunners of the Maremma Sheepdog, the Great Pyrenees, and other white shepherds bred in Europe.

The name of the breed is derived from the Turkish word *Kavas*, meaning "guard," an unmistakable reference to the fame that this proud and brave dog acquired centuries ago.

GENERAL CHARACTERISTICS A big dog whose pleasing appearance reveals both nobility and power. The various parts of the body are well proportioned, neither excessively long nor excessively compact. The body outline is roughly square. The muscles are lean, the bone structure strong without coarseness. Joints are lean. The regular positioning of the limbs, the deep chest, the slightly hollowed croup allow the Kuvasz to work tirelessly. The teeth are very strong. The coat is rough and wavy in a way that is characteristic of the breed. The Kuvasz is always white.

WEIGHT AND SIZE Height at the withers: males 28-29½ inches; females 26-27½ inches. Weight: males 88-115 lb; females 66-93 lb.

HEAD The most attractive feature of the Kuvasz, the head denotes nobility and power. The nose is pointed and black, as are the inner lips and eye rims. The bridge is long, broad and straight. The lips fit closely to the gums and have a sawtoothed closure. The muzzle tapers from base to nose, but must not be too pointed at the tip. The forehead medial furrow continues to the muzzle. The teeth are well developed, regular and strong; the jaws close in a scissors bite. The stop is gently sloping and broadly curved. The skull is long but not pointed, of medium width with a broad occiput. The ears are set on fairly high, close to the rather flat skull. The supraorbital ridges are of moderate development.

EYES Obliquely set, almond-shaped, dark brown. The lids fit closely to the eyeball. Frequently the expression is one of considerable fierceness.

EARS Set on rather high but on the sides of the skull, the ears are horizontal at the base and hang down on either side of the head, with the upper third lying slightly away from the head. On the alert, the dog raises the ears slightly, but they are never pricked. The outer ear has the form of a blunt V.

NECK Set at an angle of from 25-30 degrees with the horizontal. It is of medium length, or sometimes rather short, and is powerfully muscled. The nape is short. There is no dewlap.

FOREQUARTERS The rib cage is well let down but is not too broad or rounded, thus facilitating the oblique

KUVASZ

Photo: S. A. Thompson.

KUVASZ

used as a guard dog for large animals, an activity which led to the development of its abundant courage. This courage has been of special service in the boar hunt. Today he is often employed as a guard dog or, since his short hair makes his presence acceptable inside the house, as a pet.

GENERAL CHARACTERISTICS A medium-sized sheep dog of vigorous temperament. The head is rather long and narrow, with prick ears. The tail is carried low. The body is long, with the backline sloping gently toward the rear. On the head and feet the hair is short, dense, occasionally a little longer and curled or wavy and glossy. The color is a glossy white or black, but may be brindle.

WEIGHT AND SIZE Average weight is 18-29 lb. The height at the withers is 13½-18½ inches.

HEAD Decidedly elongated, with a pointed nose. The muzzle is straight at its root but tapers toward the nose. The lips fit closely to the gums. The jaws are long, strong, and muscular. The teeth are regular and strong, meeting in a scissors bite. The stop is not greatly accentuated. The skull is slightly domed, the medial furrow is slight, the supraorbital ridges are not greatly developed.

EYES Oval in form, set slightly oblique. The eyelids fit well over the eyeballs. The eyes are dark brown.
EARS Set on high, erect, pointed, with shape of an inverted V. The movement of the ears is rapid and vivacious.

NECK Quite high-set, at an angle of 50-55 degrees, of medium length, slightly curved and very muscular.

FOREQUARTERS The shoulders are sloping. The forearm is of medium length, almost vertical. The back edge of the shoulder blade is set rather behind the plane of the chest. The forelimbs are set rather back, but they support the trunk well. The elbows are close to the body. The forearm is of medium length, the pastern rather long and sloping. The feet are tightly closed, with elastic pads; the nails are well developed and very hard. The position of the forelegs is regular, with occasionally slightly less distance between them than the normal.

BODY The withers are well defined. The chest, of medium width, is raised in the center. The ribs are rather flat and not greatly sprung. The back is short and straight. The loins are of medium length and well placed. The croup is short, hollowed, and of medium breadth. The belly is slightly drawn up.

TAIL The tail is set on at medium height. It is carried down and may be docked to an inch or two.

HINDQUARTERS Remarkable for their position, being set very far back on the body. The hocks are set very low beneath the thigh and long upper leg. The joint between leg and hock is tight. The metatarsus is at an angle, and the hind feet are equipped with strong nails. Dewclaws are not desirable.

COAT The head and legs are covered with a fairly short, smooth and glossy coat. The hair on the ears is rough and of fair length. On the rest of the body the hair is 2-3 inches long, dense, wavy and glossy, and in various places forms a tuft. The longest hair is found below the elbows and on the back side of the legs. **Color** Lustrous white or black, although coats of black on white or white on black marked with scattered spots of more or less uniform size are found fairly frequently. The color of the hair on the legs follows invariably the basic color of the body. **Skin** Highly pigmented, the free surfaces black; soles and nails are slate gray. The skin of white or bicolored dogs is also dark.

GAIT The Mudi's motion is rapid and lively, with brief and sudden movements. He runs in a wide-springing gallop.

FAULTS Short hair on ears; light brown eyes; excessively long coupling; short hair on limbs.

DISQUALIFICATIONS Overshot or undershot condition, if the space between upper and lower teeth, measured between the incisors, is more than 2 mm (roughly 1/12 inch); other than prick ears; short, smooth hair on body; long hair on the head; long hair with tendency to mat; speckled nose; defects of skin pigmentation.

MEASUREMENTS AND PROPORTIONS (expressed as percent of height at withers):

Length of trunk	103
Depth of thorax	40
Width of thorax	30
Circumference of thorax (behind the elbows)	105
Length of head	42

In addition to the above figures, the length of the muzzle is 40 percent of the length of the head; the length of the ears is 45 percent the length of the head. ●

positioning of the rather long shoulder blade. The elbows fit close to the body, but not under the rib cage. The legs are straight up and down. The long forearm is lean and well muscled. The pasterns are long and lean. The joints are also lean. The feet are compact, with little hair growing between the tightly closed toes. The pads are elastic. The positioning of the forelimbs is regular, with medium width between them.

BODY The withers are long and distinctly raised above the backline. The back is of medium length. The loins are short, the croup slightly hollowed, broad, and very well muscled. The abundant coat often shows an upward curve to the croup. The chest is deep, well let down but not excessively broad. At the center of the chest the heavily muscled sternum stands out noticeably. The belly is fairly well drawn up.

TAIL Set on quite low, a continuation of the croup. It hangs down approximately to the height of the hocks, the tip is curved slightly upward, without however forming a ring. When the Kuvasz is excited or alerted, the tail is held above loin level.

HINDQUARTERS Angulations are given in the Hungarian standard as follows: coxal-femoral, 90 degrees; femoral-tibial, 110-120 degrees; tibial-tarsal, 130-140 degrees. The thigh and hind limb are very muscular. The hock is broad, long, and important to the success of the dog. The hock is vertical, the metatarsus long and more sloping than the pastern. The hind feet are longer than the forefeet but just as strong. The pads are tight and elastic, the nails are well developed and slate gray in color. Dewclaws must be removed.

COAT The head, ears, and feet are clad in short, straight, dense hair which may be perhaps ¾ inch on the head. The back parts of the hindquarters also have short hair, as do the backs and sides of the forelimbs. There is rather long hair on various parts of the body, including particularly the neck, which has a considerable mane and ruff down to the chest. The tail is covered with abundant

wavy hair. The longest hair is on the lower half of the tail, where it may be as long as 6 inches. The coat is quite rough and wavy, rather stiff, and never feltlike. The undercoat is woolly and much finer. The coat of puppies may either be glossy and wavy or smooth and dense. **Color** Invariably white; ivory is presently accepted. **Skin** Highly pigmented, slate gray. The nose, the eye rims, and the lips are black. The soles are black or slate, the hard palate should be dark. The belly is of uniform dark pigmentation. The tongue is bright red. Speckled skin is still permitted.

GAIT Slow and dignified. At the trot the Kuvasz has a sideward movement and is capable of continuing the trot for 15-18 miles without undue exhaustion.

FAULTS Short bridge; excessively domed skull; supraorbital ridges insufficiently developed; eyelids and lips pendulous; yellow eyes, suspicious, diffident expression; ears close against head or thrown back; long neck; broad chest; shoulders loose. Yellowish coat or with yellowish markings; light gray skin coloring; weak or soft constitution.

DISQUALIFICATIONS Height at withers less than 25½ inches in males or 23½ in females (entails removal from stud books); weight above 132 lb not desirable; accentuated overshot or undershot condition; excessive accentuation of stop; prick ears; tail rising above loin level; hard or tangled coat; coat of colors other than white.

MEASUREMENTS AND PROPORTIONS (in percent of height at withers):

	acc. to standard	often
Length of body	104	108-110
Depth of chest	48	52- 58
Width of chest	27	—
Circumference of body	120	125-130
Length of head	45	—

Besides the above, the length of the muzzle is 42 percent that of the head, but it often is as much as 50 percent; length of the ears, 50 percent. ●

16 MUDI
HUNGARY

The Mudi was spontaneously stabilized between the end of the last century and the beginning of the present one and has only recently been recognized by official kennel clubs. He was

MUDI

RETURNING HOME ▶

Photo: M. Pedone

17 PULI
HUNGARY

The Puli ("leader" in Hungarian) has been helping Hungarian sheepherders for more than a thousand years. When the Magyars arrived in what is now Hungary, they brought with them their formidable sheep dogs, of which there were several varieties, some huge, like the Komondor and the Kuvasz; others smaller like the Puli of today. Except for the color of coat, the Puli of today and the Puli of those times are similar to the Tibetan Terrier, which many authors mention as the breed's stock.

Besides being an accomplished sheep dog, the Puli has shown his proficiency in retrieving from water, to the extent that he is sometimes called the "Hungarian Water Dog." In past centuries, besides being a guard for livestock and the home, he was also used in hunting. Unlike the Hungarian Whitehaired Shepherds used mainly for night work, the Puli was almost always a daytime worker, probably because of his dark coat which seemed to attract the attention of the sheep.

The official standard of the breed, first published in 1925, has undergone periodic modifications, the last in 1955.

GENERAL CHARACTERISTICS A lively, agile, intelligent, undemanding dog of medium size. He has a solid physique, lean and muscular throughout. The outline of the body and limbs is square. Examination of the individual parts of the body is difficult, since the Puli is completely covered with a thick, long wavy coat that tends to mat. The head gives the impression of being round because of the long hair which comes down over the eyes concealing the true shape. The shaggy tail, long and curled up about to the loins, makes it seem that the hindquarters slope upward. The precise body lines are hard to follow, as a glance will show; even the individual parts are difficult to see clearly because of the Puli's unique coat.

WEIGHT AND SIZE Weight: 28½-33 lb in the male; 22-28½ lb in the female. Height at the withers: optimal, males, 15¾-17½ inches; acceptable, 14½-15¼ inches minimum, 17¾-18½ inches maximum; optimal, females, 14½-16 inches; acceptable, 13½-14 inches, minimal; 16½-17½ inches maximum.

HEAD Small, fine. From the front it appears round, whereas in profile it seems elliptical. The nose is relatively large; it is black, like the eye rims and lips. The bridge is shorter than the skull, its length being 35 percent that of the head. The lips fit closely over the gums. The bridge is straight, the muzzle rounded. The jaws are equally developed, with strong, regular teeth; and the jaws meet in a scissors bite. The lower canines are set slightly forward of the upper. The other teeth meet precisely. The stop is accentuated. The skull is rounded, the supra-orbital ridges are pronounced.

Photo: S. A. Thompson.

PULI

EYES Horizontal, coffee brown in color, with a lively, intelligent expression.

EARS Set on at medium height. They are hanging ears and do not stand erect even when the dog is alert. The outer ear is the shape of a broad, rounded V.

NECK Of medium length, muscular. The lines of the neck are not apparent because of the coat. It is set at an angle of 45 degrees. A too distinct neck is a certain fault.

FOREQUARTERS The shoulder blade is well joined to the rib cage. The scapula and arm are joined at right angles. The arm is of medium length, muscular, and parallel to the longitudinal axis of the body. Its lower edge, joined to the forearm, must not be either twisted or pushed back beneath the body. Upper arm and forearm form an angle of 120 to 130 degrees. The forearm is long and straight, vertical, and provided with fine muscling. The areas beneath it are well formed; they must be short and muscular. The pastern is at a 45-degree angle with the horizontal. The forefeet are short, rounded, compact. The nails are well developed and tight, slate gray in color. The pads are full and elastic. The forelegs are evenly positioned and moderately separated. **BODY** The withers should lie only slightly above the backline. The spinal column lies in a gently sloping arch. The lowest point of the lower line of the trunk marks the bottom of the rib cage, which is of medium breadth, long and deep. The forelimbs are well joined, the ribs well sprung. The body is of medium length and the loins are short. The croup too is rather short and slightly hollowed, but because of the way the tail lies over the loin this is barely visible. The belly is moderately drawn up. A wide pelvis is desirable, especially in females.

TAIL Carried over the loin. Its long hair mingles with the rump hair so that the tail is virtually invisible.

HINDQUARTERS The thighs and limbs are long and extremely well muscled. The pelvis and the femur form a right angle, while the femur joins the tibia at an angle of 100-110 degrees. The hock is lean, as indeed are all parts of the hindquarters. Like the wrist, the hock is at a reduced angle to the horizontal, and as a result the hind feet are longer. The nails are stronger than those on the forefeet, compact, slate gray. The pads are full and elastic. The hind legs are set wider apart than the forelegs.

COAT Heavy in texture, with a fine undercoat. The proportion between top coat and undercoat determines the coat's quality. Much top coat and little of the fine undercoat combine to form a sparse, open coat, whereas much more fine undercoat and less heavy top coat combine to produce excess matting. The proper proportion yields a coat of "tight" matting, which is the kind to be sought. The so-called corded coat is composed of uniform, falling hair, tightly waved. The small strands of such a coat tend to mat rather less and to form long "ropy" strands. The longest hair is on the rump, loins, and thighs (3-7 inches); the shortest hair is on the head and feet. In some specimens the coat hangs down almost to ground level when the dog stands erect. After whelping or following sickness, or because of improper feeding, there may be a partial or total loss of hair on the foreside of the trunk, on the belly, on the lower chest, and on the forelimbs. The original coat of many Pulis cannot be judged except with difficulty. "Porcupine" grooming is not desirable, nor is the total lack of combing. **Color** Today breeders are producing Pulis which are black, black with reddish or white ticking, as well as several varieties of gray. **Skin** Slate gray, richly pigmented. The Puli's skin shows extraordinary variations in every range of color. The areas which have no hair—the nose, the lips, the eyelids—are black. The hard palate is uniformly black or speckled with pigmented spots against a dark background. The tongue is bright red. The nails and pads can be either black or slate gray. A lack of pigment 2 inches in diameter is acceptable on the chest, and white hair between the toes is also acceptable. Larger areas of white are not allowed.

GAIT The pace is not long; the gallop is in short, jumpy steps, irregular, but fast and quite characteristic of the breed.

FAULTS Height outside optimal limits given above; excessively long bridge; light eyes; bad insertion of neck into shoulders; excessively long trunk, going beyond limits of the square; horizontal rump; relaxed tail; smooth top coat or open with excessive undercoat (that is, little matting).

DISQUALIFICATIONS Height above 19½ or less than 13½ inches for males or above 18½ and under 12¼ for females; obvious overshot or undershot condition; straight ears; tail carried straight; lack of tail; short hair; spots or markings excessively big; chocolate color in skin pigmentation; other defects of skin color.

MEASUREMENTS AND PROPORTIONS

(expressed as percent of height at withers):

Length of trunk	100
Height of rib cage	45
Width of rib cage	33
Circumference of thorax	125
Length of head	45

In addition to the above measurements, note that the length of the bridge is equal to 35 percent of the length of the head. The length of the ear is equal to 50 percent of the length of the head. ●

18 PUMI
HUNGARY

The Pumi, considered with the Komondor, Kuvasz, and Puli a national breed by the Hungarian Kennel Union, was formed around the seventeenth and eighteenth centuries through crossing the Puli with straight-eared shepherds imported from France and Germany. Today he is also used for hunting and guard work.

GENERAL CHARACTERISTICS A dog of medium size, vigorous, with many characteristics of the terrier. The head is rather long, with the muzzle even more developed. The ears are semierect. The coat is of medium length, free from matting. The tail is erect. The eyes and muzzle are barely visible because of the long coat, particolored but never brindle.

WEIGHT AND SIZE Weight: 17½-28½ lb. Height at withers 13-17½ inches.

HEAD The shape of the head is imparted largely by the elongated muzzle. The bridge is straight. The muzzle narrows gradually from the skull to the nose, which is pointed. The tip of the nose is also narrow. The lips fit closely over the gums. The teeth are regular and the jaws meet in a scissors bite. The teeth are well developed and strong. The stop is not pronounced. The occiput is rather narrow but slightly domed. The forehead is slightly rounded and long. Development of the supraorbital ridges is moderate.

EYES Slightly oblique, dark brown in color. The eyelids are close-fitting over the eyeballs.

EARS Set on quite high, semi-prick ears, that is, erect with the tips bent slightly forward. The ears are of medium size and well proportioned, like an inverted V, and mobile.

NECK Inserted at an angle of 50-55° degrees from the horizontal. It is of medium length, slightly curved and well muscled.

FOREQUARTERS As a consequence of its square silhouette the Pumi gives an impression of standing high on its limbs. The shoulder is sloping. The upper part of the foreleg is short. Separation of the limbs is medium, the legs perpendicular to the ground. The pastern is sloping. The feet are strong and closed, the pads elastic, the nails very hard.

BODY The chest is deep and well let down. The ribs are rather compact and somewhat flat. The withers are pronounced and long. The topline of the back slopes decidedly toward the rump. The back is short. The loins are of medium length, well formed and firm. The croup is short and moderately hollowed. The belly is moderately drawn up. The plane of the chest is straight and moderately broad.

TAIL Set on high, carried straight out or slightly lowered; should be docked to two thirds of its length.

HINDQUARTERS Remarkable for the way they set back from the body. The thighs and the legs are long, the hock is short, the metatarsus sloping. The hind feet are rounded and compact, with hard nails. Dewclaws are not desirable.

COAT The body is covered with a plaited coat of medium length which should not, however, become matted. There is also an undercoat. There is shorter hair on the muzzle and legs. The hair on the ears is of medium length, dense, hard and stiff; elsewhere, on the other hand, the hair is harder and shorter (about 3 inches) or longer and plaited. The Pumi's coat should never have the characteristics of the Puli's, and a smooth coat is not admissible. The hair of the chest, thorax, and forelimbs is often shorter than that on the rump and the hind limbs. **Color** Many colors occur; dove gray, silver gray, and slate gray are common. Black, light gray, white, and chestnut are also found. The Pumi must not be mottled or have markings of any kind. **Skin** Highly pigmented slate gray. Nose, lips, etc., black or slate gray. The hard palate should be of a solid dark color. The tongue is bright red. The nails are gray.

GAIT The Pumi is extremely lively and is constantly in motion, his action fast, his run springy, stepping in sudden spurts of high-spirited energy.

FAULTS Commonest faults are persistent traits of Puli ancestry. A Puli coat or ears are disqualifying. True prick ears are not desirable. Carrying the tail straight is to be discouraged. Short bridge and light eyes are serious faults.

DISQUALIFICATIONS Overshot or undershot jaws, if the discrepancy exceeds 2 mm (i.e., 1/12 inch); short, smooth hair or hair tending to mat; insufficient pigmentation of skin; speckled coat.

MEASUREMENTS AND PROPORTIONS (expressed as percent of the height at the withers):

Length of trunk	100
Height of thorax	43
Width of thorax	30
Circumference of thorax (behind the elbows)	115
Length of head	44
Length of muzzle	60

PUMI

Photo: S. A. Thompson.

19 BERGAMESE SHEPHERD

Pastore Bergamasco

ITALY

This magnificent shepherd has the qualities which are necessary for a superior sheep dog: he is strong and brave, docile with his master, highly intelligent and, if the animals entrusted to him seem to be in peril, he does not hesitate to employ his force and his scorn of danger.

Unfortunately, the specimens of this breed existing today which can be considered pure are in very small number, a most regrettable fact. Since few Italian sheepherders employ purebred specimens to aid them in their labors, it can only be hoped that a number of dog lovers will become interested in the preservation of this attractive dog of such good qualities and intelligence. Certainly in the last years considerable progress has been made in this regard, but one can and should do more in favor of the Bergamese Shepherd, since from an aesthetic point of view and psycho-physical characteristics he is truly of great importance.

The Briard represents one of the great successes of French kennelmen; and although certain French dog fanciers claim that the Bergamese comes from the Briard, everything indicates that, on the contrary, the latter is the stock of the handsome French Shepherd. In effect, if the plausible hypothesis of the Eastern origin of the group of European Shepherds is correct, one cannot explain how the ancient Asiatic Shepherd would be able to arrive in France before reaching Italy, geographically closer if one considers the communication lines existing at the time of the migration of the canine breeds towards the West.

One thing remains clear: the Briard and the Bergamese Shepherd of Italy possess many similarities, and one might think that the breeding of the Bergamese, carried out on a grand scale and according to all the necessary criteria, could give the same brilliant results in Italy as the Briard did in France.

GENERAL CHARACTERISTICS Scientifically, the Bergamese Shepherd is classed in the lupoid group, according to the method of Pierre Megnin. His practical classification is that of shepherd dog. Of Italian origin. A medium-sized dog, of rustic appearance, with abundant hair on all parts of his body; of robust but well-proportioned build, the Bergamese Shepherd is of good character, decisive, courageous and yet not arrogant. The general conformation is mesomorphic, with the body outline lying within a square, harmonious insofar as form is concerned (heterometric) and also as far as its various profiles are concerned (halloidic). It is a dog whose job is the guiding and custody of the flock. However, its qualities of intelligence, moderation and patience make it a perfect guard dog and companion, suitable for the most varied uses.

WEIGHT AND HEIGHT Weight: males 70-84 lb; females 57-71 lb.

Height at the withers: males, ideally 23½ inches, with 1 inch tolerance above or below. For females, the ideal height is 22 inches with 1 inch above or below being acceptable.

HEAD Dolichocephalic, its length reaching 4/10 of the height at the withers. The length of the muzzle may be as great as the length of the skull. The total cephalic index is 50. The upper longitudinal axes of the skull and of the muzzle are parallel. Overall, the head is large and parallelepiped in shape. The skin should not be thick, but well fitting to the underlying tissues; it should not be wrinkled. Skull broad and slightly domed between the ears; it is also broad and rounded at the forehead. Its length is equal to the length of the muzzle. Its width should not be greater than half the total length of the head; total cephalic index: 50. The frontal sinuses are well developed, both longitudinally and transversally; the supraorbital ridges are well marked. The medial furrow is marked, the occipital protuberance should be clearcut and prominent. **Muzzle** Tapering gradually toward the end, the sides are slightly convergent, thus avoiding a pointed muzzle; the muzzle is, rather, truncated or blunt, with the forepart rather flat. The height of the muzzle should not be less than half its length. **Nose** On the same line as the bridge, with the upper side rounded, humid, fresh and voluminous; it has large and well-opened nostrils. Seen in profile, the nose should not extend beyond the forepart of the muzzle. The color must be black. **Bridge** Straight. The width of the bridge measured at the midpoint should be approximately half of its length. **Stop** Well joined but accentuated, because of the development of the apophyses of the nose and the forehead, of the sinuses and of the supraorbital ridges. **Lips** Thin, beginning beneath the nose, and describing an arc of 120° with an extremely long thord; the lips are not overly developed and barely cover the teeth of the lower jaw; consequently the lower profile of the muzzle is not given by the lip but by the mandible. Because of this conformation the commissure is not descending. The cut of the mouth is long, so that the commissure meets the perpendicular drawn from the outside corner of the eye. **Jaws** Well developed, meeting in a scissors bite. The jaw itself is well developed. The teeth are white, regularly set, complete in development and number. **Eyes** Large and set low; they are neither deep-set nor protruding. The iris is brown, with the darkness of the color varying with the coat; the eyes are oval, nearly circular; the eyelids fit close. Since the position of the eyes is subfrontal, a straight line joining the two corners of the eye opening lies at an angle of 15° to the median plane of the head. The pigmentation of the eyelid is black; the eyebrows are not very long (and this serves to lift up the hair hanging from the forehead). The expression is attentive, calm and intelligent.

EARS Soft, thin, folded, triangular in the second two-thirds of their length. They hang down on either side of the face. They should be mobile and, when the dog is on the alert, they are slightly lifted at the base. The major width of the auricle varies from 2½ to 3 inches, the length 4½-5 inches; the length should not exceed half the total length of the head, and it is desirable that it should be shorter. The base of the ear is inserted above the level of the zygomatic arch; the base is broad and arrives behind at the attachment point of the head, and before it reaches to the midpoint of the skull. The hair on the ears is slightly waved, soft, and finishes in a pointed fringe.

NECK Strong, with a slight arch at the nape, and shorter than the head (measured from the nape to the forward edge of the withers). Extended it does not surpass 8/10 of the total length of the head. The circumference of the neck at its midpoint should be at least twice the length of the neck. There should be no dewlap; the hair should form a thick collar.

FOREQUARTERS Shoulders Strong, massive. The scapula is a little longer than ¼ of the height at the withers (6-6¾ inches): its angle is from 45-55° from the horizontal. In respect to the median plane of the body, when the dog is standing in a normal position, the upper edges of the scapulae should not be more than ¾ inch from each other. **Arm** Well joined to the trunk: in its upper two-thirds it should be like the shoulder, muscular and strong; its horizontal inclination is between 60 and 70°, in such a way that the scapular-humeral angle is about 115 to 125°. In its lower part, the arm is free of the trunk, and therefore the underarm should be above. The tangential plane to the arm should be parallel to the median plane of the body. The length of the arm is 30 percent of the height at the withers. **Forearm** Vertical; its length is at least equal to that of the arm. The elbows should be on planes which are parallel to the median plane of the body, that is, they should not be either closed (close to the trunk) nor open. The point of the elbow should lie on the perpendicular falling from the back angle of the scapular. The hair, from the elbows down, should be abundant, long and thick, with a tendency to form flocks, on both sides and both edges of the forearm. **Wrist** It should follow the vertical line of the forearm and be very mobile, lean, and with the pisiform bone well protruding. **Pastern** It should be lean and very mobile. Seen from the front, its direction should be in the same vertical plane passing through the forearm. Seen in profile, it should be somewhat bent forward. **Foot** Oval (harefoot), with the toes well closed and arched, well feathered, including between the toes. The pads are lean and black. The nails are strong, curved, and dark.

BODY The length of the trunk, measured from the point of the shoulder (scapular-humeral angle, external) to the point of the buttock (posterior point of the ischium), is equal to the height at the withers (this means that the trunk outline lies within a square). **Chest** Large and open. Its breadth between the lateral limits (upper-forward edges of the arms) should be ¼ of the height at the withers. **Rib cage** Should be broad, let down to the elbows, well sprung. Its circumference, measured behind the elbows, is ¼ more than the height at the withers; measured at the rib arches, it is about 4 inches less. Its diameter should be 30 percent of the height at the withers. The depth and the height of the rib cage should be 50 percent of the height at the withers. **Back** Broad, with a straight upper line: only the withers lie above this straight line. The length of the back is about 1/3 of the height at the withers. **Loins** Well joined to the backline and to the croup; well muscled in their breadth. The length is equal to 1/5 of the height at the withers; the width of the loins is about equal to their length. Seen in profile, they are slightly filled out. **Belly** Its lower line ascends very slightly from the profile of the stern, thus it is little drawn up. The flanks should be short, that is, equal in length to the lumbar region: any hollow should be minimum. **Croup** Should be broad, robust, muscular; toward the tail it is the prolongation of the convexity of the loins, and is inclined to the horizontal at about 30°. The width between the two haunches should be 1/7 of the height at the withers; the length is equal to 1/3 of the height at the withers. **Sexual organs** In the male there should be a perfect and complete development of the testicles. **Tail** Set on in the last third of the croup, thick and robust at the root, it tapers to the point. It is covered with abundant "goat hair" and slightly waved. Its length is from 60 to 65 percent of the height at the withers, and when the dog is in normal stance it easily reaches the hock; if it is shorter, however, so much the better. In repose the tail is carried hanging for the first two-thirds and slightly curved in the bottom third. When the dog is in action, the tail is carried gaily.

HINDQUARTERS Thigh Long, broad, covered with muscles, with the back edge slightly convex. Its length is more than 33 percent of the height at the withers and its breadth is ¾ of its length. The direction of the thigh is inclined on the horizontal plane from the top to the bottom and from the back to the front. The vertical plane passing through the thigh should be parallel to the median plane of the body. **Leg** With strong bone, lean muscles and with the furrow between the tendon and bone above the hock well marked. Its length should be about 1/3 of the height at the withers, and its angle 55° to the horizontal. **Hock** The dif-

BERGAMESE SHEPHERD

ference from the point of the hock to the ground should not be less than 25 percent of the height at the withers. The sides of the hock should be broad. Seen from behind, the vertical line passing through the point of the hock should coincide with the line drawn from the point of the buttock to the ground. **Metatarsus** Robust and lean. Its length is about 15 percent of the height at the withers, considering the metatarsus itself. That is measured without the hock (tarsus) and without the foot; if measured at the point of the heel, its length is equal to the length of the hock. Its direction must be vertical. **Foot** Like the forefoot and with all the requirements of it.

COAT **Hair** Soft and very long, strong and wavy flocks, rather harsh ("goat hair") particularly on the fore-half of the body, while from the mid-point of the thorax and over all the posterior part of the body, and over all the members, either it tends to flocking or is already flocking, depending on the age of the dog; the flocks should start at the summit of the back line, falling on the lateral part of the trunk; on the muzzle the hair is less harsh and falls over the eyes, covering them. On the legs, the hair should be distributed uniformly on all parts, in soft flocks, hanging straight without forming a fringe. The undercoat is so short and thick that it conceals almost entirely the skin; it should be, moreover, oily to the touch. **Color** Solid gray, or in spots with all the gradations of gray from the lightest shade to black, possibly with isabella or light fawn nuances. Solid black is allowed, provided it is opaque. Solid white is not allowed. White markings are allowed if they are not more than 20 percent of the total surface of the coat. **Skin** Fitting close to the body, it should be thin all over, especially on the ears and on the forelegs. There must be no dewlap; the head must be without wrinkles. The pigment of the lips and eyelids and of the nose should be black. The pigment of the nails and of the pads and of the toes should be very dark.

GAIT Dogs of this breed are very resistant in the field and are good at trotting.

FAULTS **General Characteristics** Common overall appearance. lymphatic, lacking in harmony; light bone. **Stature** Not lying within the limits specified by the standard, taking into account the tolerances given above (disqualification). **Head** Convergent cranial-facial axes (a very serious fault). Total cephalic index over 50. **Nose** Lower than the vertical line of the forepart of the muzzle; small, with nostrils not well opened; spongy in appearance; deficient in pigmentation; with toal depigmentation (disqualification). **Muzzle** Out of proportion. **Bridge** Short, narrow, with exaggeratedly convergent lateral lines, convex (arched); highly convex (disqualification); concave (disqualification). **Lips** Heavy or deficient in development, flaccid, thick, fleshy; excessively accentuated commissure, falling or lacking. **Jaws** Delicate jaws; overshot jaw (fault), undershot jaw (if due to deficient length of mandible: disqualification; if for dental deviation: (fault); jaws excessively curved. **Teeth** not regularly aligned or deficient in number; horizontal erosion of teeth. **Skull** Small, round, short, too narrow at the parietals, flat, supraorbital ridges flat, sinuses underdeveloped; stop not sufficiently accentuated; lack of medial furrow, lack of occipital protuberance. **Eye** Small (microphthalmic) or prominent; light iris; wall eye (serious fault); totally depigmented iris is a disqualification; eyes almond-shaped and slanted, in lateral ultralateral or frontal position; ectropism; eyes too close together. Shifty glance, suspicious expression; cross eyes, bilateral cross eyes being a disqualification. Partial depigmentation of the eyelids, or total depigmentation thereof (disqualification). **Ear** Thick, too large, too long, narrow insertion, folded back on itself longitudinally, not folded back on itself transversally; inserted on the zygomatic arch rather than above it, or inserted underneath or behind it; curled; with bristly hair; not pointed at the tip. **Neck** Thin, or too short and heavy; with dewlap, flat at the sides or cylindrical; deficient arching of the upper line; not well melded with the shoulders. **Shoulder** Short, straight, lacking in muscle, not free in movement. **Arm** Not in the position or at the angle required by the standard; insufficient muscular development; weak bone. **Forearm** Not of length or angle required by standard; delicate or spongy bone; round bone; elbow turned out or in; low armpit. **Wrist** With evident hypertrophy of the carpal bones; spon-

BERGAMESE SHEPHERD

Photo: Fotostampa.

gy; pisiform bone not sufficiently prominent. **Pastern** Of a length not specified by the standard; too straight, too bent, out of vertical. **Foot** (forefoot) Round, with open toes, broad, splayed, deficient in arching of toes; carried out or in, that is, not in vertical; fleshy pads, lack of pigmentation in nails or pads. Bad position of pads in feet which are too long or too splayed. **Body** Of dimensions not meeting standard, and particularly: longitudinal diameter greater than height at the withers. **Chest** Narrow, badly let down, deficient muscling, manubrium of sternum situated too low. **Rib cage** Of dimensions not specified by the standard; carenated; xiphoid appendage curved inward; short stern, insufficiently open. **Ribs** Not well sprung, that is, flat; spaces between ribs not broad; short and insufficiently sprung false ribs, or open and low. **Back** Saddleback (lordosis); carp back (kyphosis); hock too low. **Loins** Flat, narrow. **Belly** Too drawn up or insufficiently drawn up. **Flanks** Very hollowed. **Croup** Narrow, too short, too hollowed or too straight. **Sexual Organs** Monorchidism (disqualification), cryptorchidism (disqualification). Incomplete development of one or both of the testicles (disqualification). **Tail** Not of proper length. Lack of tail (disqualification); short tail, either natural or artificial (disqualification); set on too low or too high; not thick at the root; carriage not as specified in standard, that is, in repose lower part not hanging; curled on back in action; flaccid, hanging, set on too low. **Thigh** Short, deficient in muscling, narrow, carried deviated to the stifle, too straight or too sloping. **Leg** Light bone, short, too sloping or insufficiently sloping. **Hock** Insufficiently broad; forward angulation too open because of deficient sloping of the tibia (too straight), or with abnormal distension to the rear of the metatarsus; or too closed because of exaggerated slope in front of the metatarsus (out of vertical). **Metatarsus** Of a length not specified by the standard, out of vertical, with simple or double dewclaws. **Foot** (hind foot) As for forefoot. **Hair** Of length, texture, or color not according to specifications of standard, and specifically not goat hair, woolly, soft, uniform; short in the forearm or leg, short on the muzzle, sparse on the tail; with white markings which cover more than 20 percent of the total area (disqualification). **Skin** Thick, overabundant; dewlap, wrinkles on the head, traces of depigmentation on the nose and the eyelids, total depigmentation of the nose (disqualification), depigmentation of the edges of the two eyebrows of both eyes (disqualification); depigmentation of the vulva or vent. **Gait** Ambling (disqualification).

DISQUALIFICATIONS **Height at the Withers** Not falling between regulation limits, taking into account the tolerances. **Head** Too small. **Nose** Total depigmentation. **Bridge** Decidedly arched or concave. **Eye** Total depigmentation bilaterally of the eyelids, bilateral cross eyes, wall eye. **Jaws** Undershot because of insufficient length of the mandible. Overshot to the extent that the appearance of the muzzle is harmed. **Sexual Organs** Cryptorchidism, monorchidism; evident deficiency of development of the testicles. **Tail** Carried over the back; lack of tail, short tail. **Color** White on more than 20 percent of the total area of the coat. **Skin** Total depigmentation of the nose and total depigmentation, bilateral, of the eyelids. **Gait** Ambling.

SCALE OF POINTS FOR JUDGING IN SHOW General Rule If in a judgment formulated during a show, a specific item concerning essentially the *type of breed* is rated as zero, the dog cannot be further considered (disqualification), even if other points are excellent.

SCALE OF POINTS

Stature and general appearance	13
Skull and muzzle	18
Eyes and ears	6
Rib cage	10
Loins and croup	7
Legs	20
Tail	6
Hair and color	15
Expression and character	5
	100

RATINGS

Excellent: not less than	92
Very good	86
Good	80
Fairly good	72

BERGAMESE SHEPHERD

20 MAREMMA SHEEPDOG
Pastore Maremmano-Abruzzese
ITALY

Almost everything we have said in the introduction to the sheep dog group applies directly to the origins of the Maremma Sheepdog. Today it is spread throughout the countryside of Tuscany and Emilia, in the Marches, Abruzzi, in Apulia and Latium. This great dog with the luxurious white coat is regularly employed and well cared for by sheepherders with the result that the pure strain has been preserved.

Some years ago it was customary to distinguish between the Maremma and the Abruzzi dogs. In spite of the slight differences which distinguished them, the two types were classed together for the publication of a single standard.

The physical qualities are excellent, and contribute to making him unexcelled as a guard dog, although his principal function, even today, is as a helper in pastoral work. He is attentive and indomitable in this area—courageous to the point of standing his ground even before wolves which, impelled by the rigors of winter, sometimes roam around the sheep folds.

Imported and officially recognized in England from 1936, it was only after 1945 that he gained (and continues to gain) great popularity as a show dog and pet.

MAREMMA SHEEPDOG

Photo: Prato

MAREMMA SHEEPDOG

GENERAL CHARACTERISTICS The Maremma is classified scientifically as belonging to the lupoid group (according to Pierre Mégnin). As a working dog he is classed as a sheep dog. Italian origin. His full name is Cane da Pastore Maremmano-Abruzzese, and he is a large, strongly built dog; in spite of his rustic appearance, he is at the same time majestic and distinguished, robust and courageous, with a very intelligent expression. His character is docile, but he becomes fierce when he is at work as guardian of the flock and of his master's property. His hair is abundant, long and white. The general conformation is that of a heavy mesomorph, with the body longer than the height at the withers, harmonious as to form (heterometric), and relatively harmonious in outline (halloidism).

WEIGHT AND HEIGHT Weight: Males 77-99 lb; females 66-88 lb.

Height at the withers: males 25½-29 inches; females 23½-27 inches.

HEAD Dolichocephalic; the total length of the head is about equal to 4/10 of the height at the withers; the length of the muzzle is less than 1/10 of the length of the cranium. The width of the skull measured from one cheekbone to the other is rather more than half of the total length of the head, but the cephalic index should not be more than 52.5. The direction of the upper longitudinal axes of the skull and of the muzzle is slightly divergent. Overall, the head is large, shaped like a blunt wedge, and is reminiscent of the head of the brown bear. **Skull** The length of the skull is 1/10 more than the length of the muzzle, and its width from cheek to cheek is more than half ot the total length of the head; the lateral walls of the skull are therefore somewhat rounded. Seen in profile, the skull is

also somewhat rounded and rather wide between the eyes; it narrows toward the facial region. Its upper longitudinal axis diverges slightly from the axis of the nasal bridge. The sinuses are not pronounced. The medial furrow is not pronounced. The occipital protuberance is not accentuated. **Muzzle** The sides of the muzzle tend to converge, but the forward part of the muzzle has a rather flat surface. The muzzle should be, in height or depth, 5/10 of its length (measured at the level of the commissure). The suborbital region should be rather chiseled. **Nose** Wet and cool; it is positioned on the line of the nasal bridge, with a large border, and nostrils which are large: seen in profile, the nose should not extend beyond the front vertical line of the lips; its forward face is on the same vertical plane as the forward face of the muzzle. Pigmentation black. **Bridge** Straight (for its length and

direction in relation to the cranial axis, see HEAD). Its width, measured at the midpoint, should be 22 percent of the total length of the head, and about 55 percent of the length of the nasal bridge itself. **Stop** Should not be pronounced. **Lips** The upper lips, seen from in front, are shaped like a semicircle with a very narrow chord. The lips are not high, and thus they barely cover the lower teeth: the commissure, because of the slight development of the lips, is not pronounced. Consequently, the lower lateral profile of the muzzle is described by the lips only in their lower-lateral-forward part, while farther back, toward the commissure, it is delineated by the mandible and by the commissure itself. The pigment of the lip edges should be black. **Jaws** Robust, with normal development and meeting in a perfectly level bite: the back part of the upper incisors should fit snugly over the front side of the lower in-

67

Photo: S. A. Thompson.

clsors. The upper line of the lower jaw is nearly straight; the teeth should be white, regularly aligned, and complete in development and number. **EYES** The eyes are not large, considering the overall size of the dog. They should neither be deep-set nor protruding. They are ocher or dark brown in color. The eyelids should fit fairly close to the eyes. The eye slit is almond-shaped. Pigmentation of the eyelids should be black. The direction of the axes of the lids (that is, the straight line which passes between the two corners of the eye opening) determines a 30° angle with the median plane of the head.

EARS Considering the size of the dog, the ears are rather small; they are V-shaped, set on considerably above the zygomatic arch, and are covered with hair. The tip should be sharply pointed and never broadly rounded. Ear length in an average-sized dog should not be more than 4¾ inches when the dog is completely in repose, the ears hang down at the sides of the head, but whenever the dog is alerted, the ears are very mobile and should rise to a semierect position: this is indicative of the Maremmano's talents as a guard dog and is a specific trait of the breed. The ears may be clipped to a certain extent, if the dog is to be used as custodian of a flock.

NECK Strong, with long, thick hair which forms a collar; there should be no dewlap. The length of the neck measured from the nape to the edge of the withers should not be more than 8/10 of the length of the head, and is almost 3.2/10 the height at the withers.

FOREQUARTERS The shoulders should be long, sloping, strongly muscled, and very free in movement. The length is about ¼ of the height at the withers, while the slope varies from 50 to 60° from the horizontal. The points of the scapulae are relatively vertical in respect to the medial plane of the body, and are therefore fairly well apart. **Upper Arm** Well joined to the body in the upper two-thirds, with strong muscles, sloped at 55 to 60° from the horizontal. Its length at the withers and its direction are nearly parallel to the medial plane of the body. **Forearm** Well boned, vertical. Its length is slightly more than the length of the humerus, and measures slightly less than ⅓ of the height at the withers. The height at the elbow is 52.87 percent of the height at the withers. The elbows, which are normally close to the body and covered with soft, loose skin, should lie on a plane which is parallel to the medial plane of the body. The point of the elbow should lie on a perpendicular from the scapular. **Wrist** The wrist lies on the vertical of the forearm; lean, smooth, with no visible bone relief, except at its back edge, where the pisiform bone protrudes. **Pastern** Seen from in front, the pastern follows the vertical line of the forearm; it is lean with a minimal amount of subcutaneous cellular tissue. Its length should not be less than 1/6 of the height of the entire member at the elbow. Seen in profile, it should be slightly extended. **Foot** Large, rounded, with toes well closed, and covered with short, dense hair. The pads are lean and hard: the nails are strong and arched. The pads are strongly pigmented, as are the nails: the pigment should be black (brown in the nails is acceptable).

BODY The length of the body, measured from the point of the shoulder (outer scapular-humeral angle) or from the manubrium of the sternum to the point of the buttock (posterior point of the ischium), is 1/18 greater than the height at the withers. **Chest** Broad and well open, with well developed pectoral muscles; the width between the lateral limits (the upper and forward edges of the arms) should be 25 percent of the height at the withers. The sternum should be level with the point of the shoulders. **Ribcage** Broad, descending to the level of the elbow, deep, well rounded at the midpoint of the height. The cross diameter, which is greatest at half the height, diminishes slightly toward the bottom, so that the stern region is still broad. The ribs are well sprung, oblique, with well extended interrib spaces; the last false ribs are long, oblique and well open. The sternum is long: in profile its outline is that of a semicircle with a very broad chord, which ascends toward the abdomen. The circumference of the rib cage should be about ¼ greater than the height at the withers, and its diameter should be at least 32 percent of the height at the withers, while the depth of the rib cage should be 50 percent. In a dog 27 inches high the rib cage should have the following dimensions: circumference (behind the elbow) 32.6 inches; circumference on the rib arches, 28.7 inches; depth, 13.4 inches; height, 12.8 inches; cross diameter, 8.25-8.67 inches. The thoracic index, therefore, should not exceed 8 (and should be preferably less). **Back** The withers are slightly raised above the backline, with the points of the scapulae set well apart. The upper outline of the back is straight. The length is about 32 percent of the height at the withers. **Loins** Well incorporated into the backline, slightly convex as viewed in profile, the muscles are well developed in their breadth. The length is 1/5 of the height at the withers; the width is almost equal to the length. **Belly** Its lower line, from the stern forward, rises very slightly toward the flanks, in such a way that the belly is slightly drawn up. The flanks should be of a length which is almost equal to that of the lumbar region; the hollowing of the flank should be minimal. **Croup** Broad, robust, muscular; the cross diameter btween the haunches should be 1/7 of the height at the withers. Its length is ⅓ of the height at the withers (more precisely, 33.3 percent of such height). Its slope, from the haunch to the set-on of the tail, is 20° from the horizontal, and thus the dog's croup is hollowed. **Sexual organs** The male should have perfect and complete development of the testicles. **Tail** Set on low, because of the hollowed croup: when the dog is standing in normal position, the tail passes the hock. In repose it is carried hanging down, while when the dog is excited it is carried at the backline, with the tip slightly curved. It is well feathered with dense hair, but there should be no fringe.

HINDQUARTERS **Thigh** Long, broad, covered with powerful muscles, with the back edge slightly convex. Its length is ⅓ of the height at the withers. Its outer face, from one edge to the other, should be ¾ of its length; therefore, in a dog 26¾ inches high at the withers, the breadth of the thigh should be 6-7/10 inches; its direction is slightly sloping from above to below and from the back forward, and, in respect to the vertical, it should be parallel to the medial plane of the body. **Leg** Well boned, and well equipped with lean muscles. The length of the leg is slightly less than the length of the thigh, and is 32.5 percent the height at the withers. Its slope is about 60° from the horizontal. **Hock** Its height is 30.9 percent of the height at the withers; this means that in a dog 26¾ inches high, the height of the hock should

Photo: M. Pedone.

PASTURE IN SARDINIA

be about 7¼ inches. The sides of the hock are very broad; its forward angulation is quite closed; seen from behind, the backline which goes from the hock to the ground should be on the vertical and on the prolongation of the buttock line. **Metatarsus** Robust and lean; its length depends on the height of the hock. Seen from behind as well as in profile, it should always be vertical. There should be no dewclaws. **Foot** Like the forefoot, but slightly more oval in shape.

COAT Hair Very abundant, long, rather harsh to the touch, close to the body. A slight wave is permitted: around the neck, the coat forms a rich collar. It is short on the muzzle, on the skull, on the ears, on the forward edge of all four limbs, on the back edge of which it forms a slight fringe. The undercoat is abundant and only a winter coat. The texture of the hair is semivitreous. The length of the hair on the body may be as much as 3 inches. **Color** Solid white. Ivory, pale orange, pale lemon shadings are acceptable if not excessive. **Skin** Close-fitting and rather thick all over; the neck has no dewlap. Lips, nose and eyelids should be black, as should the pads of the feet and the nails. (Brown nails are acceptable.)

GAIT The pace is long, as is the trot.

FAULTS General Characteristics Undistinguished overall appearance, light bone, lack of symmetry. **Height** Deficient or excessive. **Head** Convergent cranial facial axes (a very serious fault). Nose lower than the line of the bridge; protruding on the vertical of the forepart of the nose; small; nostrils not well open; deficient pigmentation. Total depigmentation is a disqualification. **Bridge** Short, narrow, with the sidelines exaggeratedly convergent; convex (arched): a pronounced arch or hollow constitutes a disqualification. **Lips** Over- or underdeveloped. Conjunction of the upper lips decidedly in the shape of an inverted V. **Muzzle** Short, exaggerated convergence forward of its sides, that is, a decidedly pointed muzzle. **Jaws** Thin; overshot condition if it harms the general appearance of the muzzle; undershot condition if due to lack of length in the mandible is a disqualification; if it is the result of bad direction of teeth, it is a fault. Curved lower jaw. Irregular teeth, teeth lacking; horizontal erosion of the teeth. **Skull** Small, short, flat on top, or exaggeratedly rounded; broad at the zygomatic arches; masseters overly developed; underdeveloped sinuses; or (a very serious fault) overly developed, to the point where the stop is pronounced. Convergence of the cranial-facial longitudinal axes. **Eyes** Too small, or prominent; light eyes; walleyes (disqualification). Eyes set too high; round; ectropion; suspicious expression; cross eyes. Partial depigmentation of the eyelids, or (disqualification) total depigmentation. Total bilateral depigmentation of the eyelids (disqualification). **Ears** Too long or too short; semierect or rose ears. Set on low; rounded tips, covered with excessively long hair, not mobile. **Neck** Thin, too short; presence of dewlap. **Pastern** Short, thin, spongy; too long, too extended or straight; out of vertical. **Foot** (Forefoot) Fat; splayed, broad, too big, crushed; deficiency of arching in the toes; foot carried in or out, that is, not vertically. Toe pads fleshy, thin soles; deficiency of coloring in nails and pads. Bad positioning of pads. **Body** Too long; longitudinal diameter equal to the height at the withers. **Chest** Narrow; insufficiently let down; poor muscular development; manubrium of sternum positioned too low.

Rib cage Too low, too shallow and of insufficient circumference; narrow; carenated. Xiphoid appendage curved inward; short stern; rib arches not sufficiently open. Ribs not sufficiently sprung; interrib spaces not broad; false ribs short and closed. **Back** Short, interruption of the backline at the eleventh vertebra. Saddleback (lordosis); carp back (kyphosis). **Loins** Long, flat, narrow. **Belly** Drawn up; long and hollowed flank. **Croup** Narrow; deficient in length; horizontal. **Sexual Organs** Monorchidism (disqualification), cryptorchidism (disqualification). Incomplete development of one or both testicles (disqualification). **Tail** Too long or too short; lack of tail or brachyurism, either congenital or artificial (disqualification); tail set on high. Tail curled over the back (disqualification), or with decided fringes. **Thigh** Short, or with badly developed muscles, that is, flat; deviated from the stifle; too straight or too sloped. **Leg** Light bone; short; insufficiently sloped. **Hock** High; not broad; open or closed angulation; out of vertical. **Metatarsus** Long, thin; out of vertical; dewclaws (a very serious fault). **Foot** (hindfoot) As for the forefoot. **Hair** Strongly waved; curly (disqualification); short; lack of winter undercoat; hair too harsh or too soft. **Color** Other than solid white; isabella coat (disqualification); isabella or ivory markings, even if very small, with sharp edges, disqualify. Ivory or pale orange tints in abundance. **Skin** Thin or too thick, over abundance; dewlap; traces of depigmentation on the nose and on the edges of the eyelids; lack of coloring, even if seasonal; total depigmentation of the nose (disqualification). Total depigmentation of the two edges of one or both eyes, or total depigmentation of the edges of the eyelids or both eyes (disqualification in both cases). Depigmentation of the vulva and the vent. **Gait** Short, jumpy, ambling.

DISQUALIFICATIONS Height More than 30 inches at the withers and more than ¾ inch less than the minimum height required by the standard. **Head** Decidedly convergent cranial-facial axes. **Nose** Totally depigmented. **Bridge** Concave or exaggeratedly arched. **Jaws** Undershot condition; accentuated overshot condition if it harms the general appearance of the muzzle. **Eyes** One or both eyes walleyed. Total depigmentation of the eyelid of one or both eyes. Bilaterally cross eyed. **Tail** Curled over the back; lack of tail or brachyurism, either congenital or artificial. **Sexual Organs** Monorchidism, cryptorchidism. Incomplete development of one or both testicles. **Hair** Curly. **Skin** Total depigmentation of the nose; total depigmentation of the edges of the eyelids of both eyes or of one eye alone. In judging if any characteristics vital to the type of the breed is graded zero, the dog cannot be considered, but will be disqualified even if the other characteristics are all graded excellent.

SCALE OF POINTS

Height and general appearance	15
Skull and muzzle	20
Eyes and ears	5
Rib cage	10
Loins and croup	7
Forequarters and hindquarters	20
Tail	8
Coat and color	15
	100

RATINGS

Excellent: at least	92
Very good	86
Good	80
Fairly good	72

NORWEGIAN SHEEPDOG

21 NORWEGIAN SHEEPDOG
Norsk Buhund
NORWAY

Traveling in Scandinavia, one often notices representatives of this breed close to the small chalets and mountain farms. They are excellent guard dogs and also very capable in herding sheep and excellent for hunting. No game is able to escape from their acute hearing, their keen sense of smell, and their keen eye.

The Buhund is an ancient breed, according to the authority Mark Watson, who claims that, as far back as A.D. 874 the first Norwegian colonists brought it with them to Iceland where it became the source of many Icelandic breeds.

This is one of the rare Scandinavian dogs which has been successfully established in other regions, such as England and Australia, where a considerable number have been bred.

GENERAL CHARACTERISTICS The Norwegian Sheepdog is a typical Spitz of less than middle size, lightly built, with a short, compact body, fairly smooth-lying coat, erect, pointed ears, tail carried curled over the back, and with a courageous and energetic character.

SIZE Males, ideal height 18 inches; females slightly smaller.

HEAD Lean, light, rather broad between the ears, wedge-shaped, narrowing toward the stop. Skull and back of head almost flat; marked but not sharp stop; nose short rather than long, tapering toward· the point seen from above and from the side, with straight bridge; lips tightly closed. Underbite and nose any other color than black are disqualifying traits.

EYES Not protruding, color dark brown, lively with a fearless, energetic expression.

EARS Placed high, erect, the height greater than the base; sharply pointed and very mobile.

NECK Medium length, lean, without loose skin, good carriage.

BODY Strong and short, but rather light; chest deep, with good spacing of ribs; straight line of back, good loins, strong couplings; slightly drawn up.

TAIL Placed high, short and thick, with dense but not long coat; tightly curled, not too much on one side.

HINDQUARTERS AND FOREQUARTERS Legs are lean, straight, and strong; elbows tightly placed; hindlegs only little angulated, straight when seen from behind. **FEET** rather small, slightly even in shape, with tightly closed toes.

COAT Close and harsh, but smooth; on head and front of legs, short, close and smooth, longer on chest, neck, shoulders and back of legs, and inside of curl. The coat consists of longer and harsh top hair, with a soft and woolly undercoat. **Color** Wheaten (biscuit color), black, red (if the red is not too dark), wolf sable; should be self color but small symmetrical markings such as white chest, blaze on head, narrow ring on neck, and white on legs are permissible. ●

22 TATRA SHEPHERD
Owczarek podlhalanski
POLAND

During his long migration from the East, the sheep dog also established himself in Central Europe as far as Yugoslavia. He gave birth to new breeds which in turn were perfectly adapted to the climate and nature of these regions. In this way sheep dogs were developed that were tenacious guard dogs, expert in lead-

Photo: S. A. Thompson.

THE DISOBEDIENT SHEEP

ing herds, robust, faithful to their master, but dangerous to an adversary. The Tatra, Valée, Karst, and Croatian Shepherds, etc. (which will be found in the following pages) continue to aid man today in his toil, and to attract the attention of international dog lovers.

TATRA SHEPHERD

GENERAL CHARACTERISTICS Rectangular build, male slightly shorter than female. An impression of stamina and activity. The expression of the eyes is intelligent, alert. The temperament is well balanced.

SIZE Height at the withers: male, not less than about 25½ inches; female, not less than about 23½ inches.

HEAD Of good proportions, with a gently tapering muzzle. In profile the skull is slightly domed, with a distinct stop. The topline of the muzzle is wide, the black nose is of medium size with wide nostrils. Cheeks are clean-cut, with tight-fitting lips having dark edges. Teeth strong and level, with scissors bite, although it may be of pincer type.

EYES Expressive, slightly slanting, of medium size. The iris is dark brown, the edges of the lids dark.

EARS Of medium length, triangular in contour, fairly thick, densely coated, and lying close with the inner edge to the head.

NECK Without dewlap, muscular, of medium length, the neck is deepset on the body. The neckline lies above the backline, with considerable ruff.

BODY Long and massive, with deep, wide, muscular chest. The ribs are sloping and rather flat. The back's contour may be slightly concave; the back itself is wide, the hips are wide and strong, well knit. The rump is slightly sloping.

TAIL Carried below the line of the back, reaching the hocks. It may also be slightly curved at the tip, but never excessively.

FOREQUARTERS The forelegs are muscular, with strong but not heavy bones. The scapula is sloping and lies close. Observed from the side and front, the forearm is perpendicular. **HINDQUARTERS** The hindlegs must be set at the correct angle, slightly protruding toward the back. **FEET** Perpendicular, relatively large and oval in shape. The toes are not splayed, the pads are hard and strong. The nails are strong and blunt, dark in color.

COAT Closely lying on head and muzzle, short and soft; on the neck and body the hair is long and thick, straight or slightly wavy, rough to the touch. The entire tail sports a distinct feather. The thighs are covered profusely with hair. From the elbows and hocks, fore- and hindlegs covered with short thick hair down to the feet. **Color** white, may also be light cream.

FAULTS Weak build, insufficiently compact. Muzzle too narrow or shallow. Dewlap. Back too long or too short. Protruding brisket. Barrel chest. Falling away of rump. Tail constantly raised. Steep slant to shoulders. Stiff hindquarters. Weak pasterns. Visible haw ("bear eyes"), light eye. Curly hair on head. Loose, curly, or woolly coat on body, neck or legs, too soft, without undercoat. Poor pigmentation of nose, lips, and eyelids. Multicoloring (cream markings permissible). Nervous, cowardly, or aggressive character. ●

Photo: M. Pedone.

23 VALÉE SHEPHERD
Polski owcaarek nizinny

POLAND

VALÉE SHEPHERD

GENERAL CHARACTERISTICS A medium-sized dog, short, strong, muscular, with a profusion of long hair and a brisk, free gait. Resistant to adverse conditions, it has a lively disposition, is self-possessed, alert, intelligent, observant, and with an excellent memory.

SIZE Height-to-length ratio, 9:10. Height at the withers: males, 17-20 inches; females, 16-18 inches.

HEAD Well proportioned, medium-sized, not too heavy; has profuse hair on forehead, cheeks, and chin, which makes the head seem larger than it actually is. The skull is of moderate width, slightly domed, and with a distinct stop. The frontal furrow and occipital bone are prominent. The length of the muzzle with a level nose is equal to or slightly shorter than the length of the skull. The nose is large, invariably black, blunt, with wide nostrils. The lips are tight-fitting, with dark edges. The jaws are strong, teeth are strong, neither undershot nor overshot.

EYES Medium in size, with a lively, keen expression; oval in shape, not bulging, dark brown in color, with dark eyelids.

EARS Medium in size, active, heart-shaped, wide at the top, and set at a moderate height, hanging, with the fore edge held close to the cheek.

NECK Strong, muscular, of moderate length; it is without dewlap and is carried rather level.

BODY Chest deep, not excessively wide; the ribs are well sprung, neither flat nor too rounded. The belly is slightly arched. The back is level and well muscled. The loins are broad, the shoulder distinct. The buttocks are broad and slightly curved.

TAIL Short or rudimentary from birth or docked very short.

FOREQUARTERS The shoulder is wide, of medium length, tightly sloped and well muscled. The forelegs are straight when viewed from any angle. **HINDQUARTERS** Wide, muscular thighs, with distinct pasterns. **FEET** Oval, with close toes, slightly arched; the pads are hard, the nails short and dark.

COAT The entire body is covered with a profusion of thick, shaggy hair over a soft, thick undercoat. The hair falling from the forehead covers the eyes in a characteristic manner. The hair may be slightly wavy. All colors and markings are acceptable.

FAULTS Round, apple-shaped head. Concave or convex bridge. Bad teeth. Lack of pigmentation. Erect ears. Slackness in bony structure. Long tail. Crooked or badly set legs. Ribs badly sprung. Stiff or rolling movement. Weak coat, curly hair. Laziness, cowardice, nervousness. ●

24 LAPLAND SPITZ
Lapplandska spetz

SWEDEN

The Lapland Spitz was admitted to the breeds recognized by the official kennel clubs in 1944 only when the FCI approved the breed characteristics presented by the National Association of Swedish Dog Fanciers.

In any case he was already well established through Sweden. His excellent psycho-physical qualities enable him to assist man in hunting as well as in many other activities. Today, however, he is principally used for protecting houses and property. He is affectionate, gentle with children, well disciplined and faithful to his master. However, he is suspicious and vigilant with strangers.

LAPLAND SPITZ

Photo: A. Wintzell.

25 VÄSTGÖTASPETS
SWEDEN

GENERAL CHARACTERISTICS A medium-sized dog, rather tall, with very strong jaws, prick ears, and either a ring or docked tail.

SIZE Height: males 17½-19½ inches; females 15½-17½ inches.

HEAD The head is roughly conical, with a straight bridge and dark nose which should ideally be jet black. The lips fit well over the gums. The muzzle is rather short and actually practically a cone, broad at the base and narrowing to a point at the nose. The teeth are well adapted and close in a scissors bite. The stop is well defined. The skull is domed and broad between the ears. The ridge above the eyes is rather prominent.

EYES Dark brown, rather large and well spaced. They are horizontally set, not obliquely.

EARS Broad at the point of insertion, well spaced from each other, short, erect and pointed; in some specimens the point tips slightly.

NECK Of medium length, lean and powerful. The dog has a dewlap.

BODY The body is longer than the height at the withers. The back is straight, the belly only slightly drawn up.

TAIL Well curled up onto the back, resplendent in its thick feathering, and normally long. A natural short tail or a docked tail is acceptable.

FOREQUARTERS AND HINDQUARTERS The forequarters seem to be short in comparison with the rest of the body. The forearms are very strong and vertical. The hindquarters are also vertical, with only the hock and stifle slightly angulated. **FEET** Rather long and powerful, with close toes, well arched, with hair between them.

COAT Abundant, brush type, thick and wiry. The undercoat is fine, thick, and waterproof. The hair is short on the head, muzzle, and front of the limbs; however, the hind part of the limbs and neck have exceptionally thick hair. **Color** Dark brown, black, brown-white. Solid colors are preferable, although not required. A white spot on the chest is also allowed, as are a white collar, white chest, markings on the feet and on the nape. ●

This dog so much resembles the Welsh Corgi that one could imagine that the two dogs had the same ancestry, if the Official Swedish Dog Association had not definitely defined the Västgötaspets as a completely indigenous breed. Information at our disposal does not enable us to establish the origin of this remarkable sheepherder, endowed as he is with remarkable strength and energy, which make him an excellent drover. In this last respect he shows a special affinity to the Corgi by his way of keeping the herd together. The official standard published here was ratified by the Swedish Kennel Club on October 20, 1948.

Photo: M. Pedone.

When the dog is on the alert the tail tends to rise, but it never rises above the point of forming a right angle with the backline. A docked tail is disqualifying.

FOREQUARTERS AND HINDQUARTERS The shoulder is long, set at an angle of 45 degrees from the horizontal. The arm must be a little shorter than the shoulder and form an obtuse angle with it. The upper arm fits close to the body, although it is wholly free in its action. The forearm, as viewed from the front, should be sufficiently inclined to permit free movement toward the rear part of the rib cage; seen from the side, the forearm should be straight. The hindquarters are quite well angulated at the stifle and the hock. The thigh is muscular, and the leg between hock and heel is only a trifle longer than the foot itself. The legs and feet should be exceptionally strong-boned. **FEET** Of medium size, short, oval, turned neither inward nor outward, with solid pads and close, well-arched toes.

COAT Of fair length, hard and dense. The undercoat is fine and tight. **Color** Preferably gray, with the top coat dark on the back, nape, and shoulders, extending down toward the ribs. Areas of light gray or yellow gray are found on the muzzle, throat, chest, and feet, up to about the half-way point of the leg. Acceptable but not preferable is a clean reddish yellow, with clearer areas corresponding to those mentioned above for the gray coat. A gray-brown mantle, or a mantle of brown-gray, brindle, or blue-gray marked is permitted but not desirable. White markings on the muzzle, throat, chest, belly, buttocks, feet and legs are also tolerated but not desirable. White markings over 30 percent of the total color are a disqualification. ●

26 SLOVAKIAN CHUVACH
Slovenski čuvač
CZECHOSLOVAKIA

The Czechs consider this the youngest of their native breeds: its standard was confirmed by the FCI in 1964. The Chuvach comes from the Slovakian Mountains where for centuries he has watched over the flocks. Thanks to Professor Hruza of the Brno Veterinary School, it has been possible to raise thoroughbreds and to obtain fixed characteristics. The Chuvach is impressive in appearance, calm, sure of himself, and courageous. His thick coat protects him from storms in the mountain pastures where he lives. He is faithful, affectionate to his master, and is often used as a shelter guard. In his land of origin he is supposed to stem from the Hungarian Kuvasz.

VÄSTGÖTASPETS

GENERAL CHARACTERISTICS A low-slung dog, long in the body, small and muscular. His carriage and expression indicate vigilance, courage and energy.

WEIGHT AND SIZE Weight: 20-31 lb. Height: 13-16 inches; the ratio between height and length should be 2:3.

HEAD Broad, lean, with a nearly flat skull. Viewed from above the skull narrows toward the muzzle, but the nose, seen in profile, is in no sense pointed. The tip of the nose is very black. The lips fit closely over the gums; the muzzle is a little shorter than the skull. The stop is accentuated.

EYES Of medium size, oval, and dark brown.

EARS Of medium size, pointed, well pricked, rigid to the tips, highly mobile, with very fine hair.

NECK Long, carried proudly, with a very muscular nape.

BODY The chest is broad and deep, the ribs quite well sprung. Viewed from in front, the rib cage is egg-shaped, whereas from the side it is elliptical. It is let down to about 40 percent of the forearm. As the dog is examined in profile the lowest point of the rib cage lies immediately behind the rear edge of the forearm. The sternum is slightly prominent. Straight back, very muscular, with a short, powerful croup, broad and almost hardly sloping.

TAIL The tail must never be more than 4 inches long. It is usually carried straight out or slightly lowered.

VÄSTGÖTASPETS

SLOVAKIAN CHUVACH

GENERAL CHARACTERISTICS A mountain dog of Slovak origins, tall, with a thick white coat splendidly adapted to the weather conditions of the Tatra region and the Liptovsky, Beskids and Carpathian mountains. His strength, courage, and lively personality make him a valuable ally to the mountain people. Cuvac in Slavonic means "to listen"; the dog earned this name by his vigilance—a guard dog always on the alert. The Cuvach is also a very faithful dog, ready to fight off any intruder and to watch over the animals entrusted to his care. Among the enemies in the Tatra region are the wolf and the bear. The Cuvach is readily distinguishable from these by his white coat. (See the description of the Maremmano sheep dog: "The sheep dog should be white, so that when the wolf attacks the flock at dawn and the dog fights to defend the sheep, if the shepherd comes to his aid he will not attack the dog instead of the aggressor.") He is a good companion for the shepherd in the mountain pastures, and has earned a good reputation as a guardian even if he is basically a sheep dog.

WEIGHT AND SIZE Weight: males 77-110 lb; females 66-88 lb. Height at withers: males 23½-27½ inches; females 21½-25½ inches.

HEAD The skull is big, rather elongated, broad between the ears and straight when viewed from in front. The medial furrow is rather shallow. The stop is not greatly accentuated. The upper longitudinal cranial-facial axes are parallel. The bridge is long, practically half the length of the head. The muzzle is broad at the base, narrowing toward the nose. The tip of the nose is brown-black in winter and black in summer. The lips are of medium dimensions, not pendulous, and fit closely over the gums. The edges of the lips are black. The jaws are well developed and powerful, with strong teeth closing neatly in a scissors bite.

EYES Set horizontally, the eyes are oval and dark-colored, with a lively expression. The lids are black and fit closely over the eyeballs.

EARS Set on high, they are hanging ears, rounded at the tips, mobile, with fine hair over the upper half. They are carried down, and in this position they extend to mouth level.

NECK The neck is set on horizontally and carried high when the dog is excited. The length equals the length of the head. It is a strong neck, particularly in the male, and free of dewlap.

FOREQUARTERS The shoulder is long and sloping. The foreleg is muscular, slightly angulated at the elbow. The scapular-humeral angle is almost 90 degrees. The forearm is straight, muscular, and long. The wrist is strong; the pastern is strong, short, and bent frontward. The feet are compact, with strong, well-arched toes with hair between them. The nails are strong and gray. The pads are robust and black.

BODY The chest is deep, reaching a point slightly below the elbow; it is well rounded in front. The ribs are well sprung and inclined toward the stern. The back is solid and straight, rising slightly toward the withers. The loins are strong and broad and very well muscled. The croup is broad and slightly descending. The belly is only slightly drawn up.

TAIL Set on low, it is extremely well feathered and reaches below the hocks. When excited the dog carries it curved up to the level of the rump, but normally it is carried down.

HINDQUARTERS The thigh, quite wide, is nevertheless elongated and is very muscular. The hind leg is sloped, well muscled, rather long in relation to the thigh and the metatarsus. The hock is well boned, unusually large, and forms an obtuse angle with the rest of the leg. The metatarsus is short, strong and vertical. Dewclaws are rarely found but are to be considered a fault when present. The foot is slightly longer than the forefoot but of similar form and structure.

COAT Length is 2-4 inches. Thicker and coarser on the neck; on the back it is gently waved, and toward the rump there are successive wavy stretches that overlap. On the head and ears the hair is short. The neck has something of a mane. The hair on the hindside of the legs is longer and slightly fringed, on the foreside short and smooth. On the chest and tail the hair is very thick. In winter the thick undercoat grows to two thirds the length of the top coat, making the whole coat softer and limiting its tendency to become wavy. **Color** White. On the neck and ears a slight yellow shading is permitted but not required. Yellow spots or large yellow markings are not acceptable. **Skin** The skin is pinkish, as is the inside of the lips. Outer lips and nose are black.

GAIT Normally the Cuvac trots easily and agilely over all kinds of terrain and in any weather.

FAULTS Steep forehead, short nose, pendulous or salivating lips; walleyes; flat feet; drooping coat, with hair parted on back; mane on head; ropy hair on flanks, ears or tail; depigmentation of lips or nose; spotted skin; ugly disposition.

NORMAL MEASUREMENTS FOR 2-YEAR-OLD MALE

Weight	78	lb
Height at withers	25¼	in
Length of head	10¼	in
Skull	5½	in
Muzzle	4½	in
Width of head	5¼	in
Width of chest	10	in
Depth of chest	16	in
Length of body	29	in
Circumference of body (behind elbows)	29	in
Circumference of belly	22	in
Scapular-humeral angle	107°	
Humeral-radial angle	155°	
Coxal-femoral angle	90°	
Femoral-tibial angle	110°	
Tibial-tarsal angle	100°	

27 CHARPLANINATZ
YUGOSLAVIA

This breed is of ancient origin. It was very widespread in Roman Illyria on the Adriatic and is descended from the shepherds that migrated, stopping in different places, from the East to the West. They became indigenous breeds when certain of their characteristics became fixed, with changes caused by acclimatization or by selective breeding. Its extraordinary strength and especially its strong teeth make it an excellent shepherd and an indomitable adversary of the wolf.

The standard of this breed was officially established about 1930 by the Yugoslavian Kinoloski Savez FNR.

GENERAL CHARACTERISTICS A compact dog of medium size and strong bone. The abundant coat makes him seem even more robust than he actually is. Its body outline is neither square nor excessively rectangular.

WEIGHT AND SIZE Weight: 55-77 lb. Height at withers: males 21½-23½ inches; females 19½-21½. The height measured at the croup is slightly less.

HEAD Should not suggest the head of either the German Shepherd or the Leonberg. The tip of the nose is unusually developed but not protruding; it is black. The bridge is as straight as possible. The lips are closed, lean and dry, well fitting over the gums and without pockets. The muzzle is of medium length (4-5 inches), broad with broad bone, narrowing slightly toward the tip but without becoming pointed. The nose, indeed, is rather blunt. The jaws are very strong and of equal length. Dentition is complete, the teeth very strong, especially the canines. The jaws meet in a scissors bite. The stop is not particularly accentuated. The skull is strong and lean. Seen from in front and in profile the forehead is slightly convex and broad between the ears. It narrows gradually as it joins the muzzle, which is strong. The length of the skull is 8-10 inches. The face is a little cheeky, but with flat cheekbones. The medial furrow is scarcely perceptible. Cheek muscles are well developed but not exaggerated. A black mask is desirable.

EYES Not prominent; almond-shaped, dark, and with lids well pigmented. The expression of the eyes is melancholy, often serious but never vicious.

EARS Set on high, V-shaped, carried obliquely. They are of medium length, reaching to the inner corner of the eye.

NECK Inserted low and carried straight or only very slightly arched, the neck is moderately long, well muscled, without dewlap.

BODY The chest is well developed, the rib cage ample in length, depth, and width. The ribs and croup are well arched. The depth of the chest is about 9-11 inches; the circumference of the body measured behind the elbows is 26-32 inches. The back is moderately long, wide, and straight. The withers are high and long. The loins are broad, slightly curved, strong, musclar, and of moderate length. The croup is of medium length, broad and straight, not falling. The muscling of the belly is well developed, with the depth of the flanks in good proportion to the rest of the body.

TAIL Set on high and of medium length; it is carried low and curved in repose. When the dog is in motion the tail is carried at the level of the back.

FOREQUARTERS AND HINDQUARTERS The shoulders are broad and of medium length, set obliquely and close to the body. The angle between the scapula and the humerus is correct. The shoulders must not stand out from the body. The forearm is well boned and well muscled and almost vertical. The wrist is strong, the pastern slightly oblique. The forefeet are round, with well-closed and arched toes. The nails are black, the pads hard. The foot should be turned neither in nor out. The hindquarters are moderately angulated, but the hock must never be without a slight deflection. The thigh is long and well muscled. The hind legs are long and robust. The hock is very strong, the metatarsus is short and vertical (duck feet are never acceptable). Dewclaws must be removed. The hind feet are similar in all respects to the forefeet.

COAT The hair is more than 4 inches long, dense, and evenly distributed over the body; the undercoat is very dense. **Color** Iron gray (dark or light). A white spot on the chest and white markings on the feet are permitted but not desirable. **Skin** Dark in pigmentation; lips and nose dark.

FAULTS Light eyes are penalized; white, yellow, or brown coat is disqualifying. ●

CHARPLANINATZ

Photo: A. Wintzell, S. A. Thompson, J. Jaros.

CHARPLANINATZ

28 KARST SHEPHERD
Krašky ovčar

YUGOSLAVIA

GENERAL CHARACTERISTICS A medium-sized dog, strong and robust, with ears hanging flat against the head. The hair is long and abundant, iron gray in color. The build is harmonious, with exceptionally well developed muscles and a strong constitution. A fairly vivacious animal, he is known for his courage and capability. He is never vicious, has a good character, and is very loyal. A good house dog, a good guard dog, obedient, suspicious of strangers and not easily won over, he is always ready to defend his master if attacked. The outline of the body is roughly rectangular, the length being slightly more than 100 percent of the height at the withers (26-27 inches). The female may be slightly longer.

WEIGHT AND HEIGHT Weight: males 66-88 lb; females 55-77 lb. Height: males 21½-23½ inches (ideal height 22½ inches); females 20½-22 inches (ideal height 21¼ inches). A tolerance of ½ inch over the maximum is allowed but penalized in scoring.

HEAD The head is of noble aspect and of good size in proportion to the body. Viewed in profile, the head is deep, and the skull line is at a slightly different angle from the ridge. Seen from above, the head is broad at ear level, narrowing gradually toward the tip of the muzzle. The tip of the nose is broad, well developed and black, protruding slightly beyond the muzzle. The muzzle itself is of medium length (about 4½-5 inches), deep and broad at the base, narrowing gradually toward the nose. The bridge is straight and broad. The black lips are rather thick and drawn tight over the bone. The teeth are exceptionally strong, especially the canines; the incisors are well developed. The jaws close in a scissors bite. Dentition is complete. The skull is slightly longer than the muzzle, the head muscular and lean, seen from any angle, and slightly rounded; the profile slightly convex. The stop is not accentuated. The length of the skull is equal to its width at ear level, broadening toward the level of the supraorbital ridge. The length of the head from the occiput to the tip of the nose is 9¾-10¼ inches. The supraorbital ridges are strongly accentuated. The dome of the skull is moderately accentuated, the occipital protuberance being only slightly developed.

EYES Almond-shaped, a little oblique downward, chestnut or dark brown in color. The space between the eyes is moderately broad. The Karst Shepherd has a frank, serene, confident expression, with perhaps just a touch of melancholy.

EARS Set on moderately high and lying flat against the head, V-shaped, their fore edge turned outward. The ears are of medium length; extended, they reach to the inner corner of the eye.

NECK The top line of the neck is straight or very slightly arched; the throat line is straight. The neck is set on obliquely and is carried proudly. It is of medium length (about 10 inches), deep, broad, well muscled. At the top it is oval in cross section and inserted into the shoulders with powerful muscling. The skin is thick and tightly fitted to the neck, with no dewlap. The hair is dense and long, forming a rich collar and mane.

FOREQUARTERS AND HINDQUARTERS The forequarters are straight, whether viewed from the front or in profile, and they should be well proportioned to the rest of the body. The shoulder is of medium length, wide, oblique, well muscled, and close to the body. The upper arm is proportionally long and more oblique than the shoulder; it is strongly muscled but not excessively so and is kept close to the rib cage. The scapular-humeral angle is almost 90 degrees. The forearm is quite long, straight, of strong bone and muscle. The humeral-radial angle is not too big; the elbows are close to the chest. The wrist is strong, well joined to both forearm and pastern. The latter is broad, of medium length and slightly oblique. The forefeet are oval in shape, compact, with well-arched toes, strong and dark-colored. The pads are strong and black or very dark. **HINDQUARTERS** Viewed from the side, the angulations are rather closed. Seen from behind, the limbs are straight and all round in good proportion. The thigh is long, broad, well filled out and muscular. The coxal-femoral angle is fairly acute. The leg is moderately long, sufficiently oblique, strong with good muscling all the way down. The femoral-tibial muscle is slightly obtuse. The stifle is strong, with a robust patella. The hock is very strong at the angulation and is moderately open. The metatarsus is strong, short and straight. Dewclaws, if present, must be removed. **FEET** Compact and rounded, with well-arched toes; nails are dark-colored, as are the pads and the soles.

BODY A well-developed chest, well let down, with the lower extremity reaching the level of the elbow, and broad. The ribs are broad and moderately well sprung. The chest is well developed, with the sternum sufficiently well rounded. Depth of the chest is 10-11 inches; the circumference of the body behind the elbows is 27½-31 inches. The back line is

CHARPLANINATZ

KARST SHEPHERD

Photo: Fotostampa.

straight and horizontal, or very slightly sloping toward the rump. The withers are long, moderately broad and high, and well set into the neck. The back is of medium length, straight, broad and muscular. The croup is of medium length and sloping, broad and very well muscled. The belly is tight and fairly well drawn up; the flanks are short and moderately hollowed.

TAIL A saber tail, of medium length, reaching at least to the hocks. It is set on high, thick at the root, and tapers to the tip. It is richly clad in long hair which forms a flag. At rest, the tail is carried low; in movement or when the dog is excited the tail is carried as high as the back line or slightly higher. The tip is often slightly hooked upward.

COAT The coat is thick and flat, with an abundant undercoat. The head and foreparts of the limbs are covered with short hair, as is the forward edge of the ears. The back part of the ears has longer, softer hair. The upper part of the neck has a mane of long, fairly harsh and very thick hair; the lower neck has even longer and softer hair that forms a collar extending to the margin of the head. The body is also covered with long hair. On the lower part of the chest and on the belly the hair is softer than elsewhere. On the back parts of the hind limbs the hair, which is also long and soft, forms fringes; the equivalent on the back part of the forelimbs is harder. The longest hair is on the withers, where it is at least 4 inches long. **Color** Iron gray, preferably with dark shading, particularly on the withers. Toward the belly and on the feet the color nuance goes into light gray or sandy, with the darker shade on the back sides of the limbs. The dark mask on the head is surrounded by light gray or sandy gray hair. A white spot on the chest is acceptable but undesirable. **Skin** Fairly thick, elastic, tight-fitting, without wrinkles. The pigmentation of the skin is dark. Lips, nose, and eyelids are dark.

FAULTS Minor Faults: Small, narrow or long head, different from norm; shallow head, arched profile without medial furrow; insufficient development of the jaws; excessively hollow or full cheeks; level bite; slightly undershot condition; irregular incisors; pronounced supraorbital arches, pronounced cheekbones; flaccid lips; lack of stop or excessively accentuated stop; ears set on too high or too low, ears insufficiently close to cheeks; eyes too open, too light, or too close together; narrow chest, shallow chest, "tuna" chest; slight saddleback; height to croup slightly more than height to withers; hollow croup; tail shorter than normal. Dewlap, wrinkled skin, or insufficiently pigmented skin; insufficient pigmentation of lips, nose, eyelids, nails, pads; lack of mask; small defects in verticality of limbs; hocks shorter than normal; splayed feet, harefeet; white spot on chest; all other small constitutional faults. **Major faults:** Narrow head, light or coarse head; muzzle too long or too sharp; overaccentuated stop; walleyes; square rather than rectangular body outline; height at croup obviously higher than at withers; prick ears; saddleback; screwtail or ringtail; wavy or woolly hair on hocks; light pigmentation on lips, nose, eyelids, pads; all other serious constitutional faults.

DISQUALIFICATIONS Incomplete dentition; advanced overshot or undershot condition; excessively large head in proportion to rest of body; atypical head; disproportion among various parts of body; below minimum height standard; excessive saddleback; short hair; coat of any color except light gray, bicolors or multicolors with sharp division between the different colors; grave lack of pigmentation on lips, nose, eyelids; bow or cow hocks; tail too short; tail with ankylosis of caudal vertebrae; all other serious faults of degeneration. ●

KARST SHEPHERD

29 CROATIAN SHEPHERD

Hrvatski ovčar

YUGOSLAVIA

GENERAL CHARACTERISTICS A dog which might be said to be at the lower limits of the medium-sized group. Vivacious, attentive, modest, and responsive to training. The basic color is black. The short hair on head and limbs is characteristic of the breed. The sheepherding instinct is very well developed; nevertheless the dog can well be used as a guard dog.

SIZE Height: for both males and females 15¾-19½ inches. The length of the body is greater than the height at the withers (which means that the body outline is rectangular).

HEAD Relatively light and somewhat conical. The length of the muzzle bears the ratio to the length of skull of 9:11. The total length of the head is about 8 inches. The muzzle is lean; in profile the bridge is straight. The muzzle itself, conical, is an extension of the upper part of the skull. The lower jaw is in good proportion to the bridge, and thus the muzzle seems neither blunt nor too pointed. The nose is invariably black and is not prominent compared to the bridge. The lips are delicate, tight-fitting, and elastic; the corners of the mouth are closed. The visible part of the inner and outer lips is black. The teeth are well developed and meet in a scissors bite; a level bite is acceptable but not desirable. Dentition should be complete. The stop is not pronounced. The skull narrows in conformity with the muzzle. The supraorbital ridges are not greatly developed. The cheeks are rounded, but the head, viewed overall, is compact. The skull, seen from above, is oval. The occipital protuberance may be marked.

EYES Of medium size, almond-shaped, the color ranging from chestnut brown to black, with a lively, alert expression. The eyes are not oblique. The lids, well fitting, are dark in pigmentation.

EARS Triangular, prick or semiprick, set on somewhat on the side. Prick ears are to be sought. Clipping of the ears is not permitted.

NECK At a fairly high angle to the back line. Both the upper and lower neck lines are straight. Moderately long, deep, well muscled, well rounded without being extremely strong, the neck has skin free from wrinkles, with no dewlap, and covered with thick hair.

FOREQUARTERS The shoulder is not very oblique; it is well muscled, of moderate length. The forelimbs are straight and, viewed from in front, parallel. The angulations are rather open, with rather sharp vertical orientation of the limbs. The legs themselves are of medium length. The upper arm is relatively short, the forearm long, fine-boned and well muscled. The wrist is lean and not distinguishable from the rest of the forearm. The pastern is slightly sloped. The foot is small, rather elongated; the toes are close, with black or gray nails; the pads are robust.

BODY The body is of medium proportions; the ribs well sprung. The chest is not pronounced, merging into the foreneck line. The back is short, well muscled; the lumbar area is also short, well muscled. The withers are not prominent, and the neck seems to flow into the backline. The rump is of moderate length and slightly sloping. It is muscular and visibly broad.

TAIL Set on fairly high, well feathered and normally carried low or even with the back line. When the animal is excited the tail is carried above the back. Puppies may be born without tails; if not, the tail should be docked so as not to exceed 1½ inches in the adult dog.

HINDQUARTERS The angulations are moderately obtuse. Viewed from behind, the limbs are parallel. The thigh is fairly broad and muscular. The leg is rather long, the hock quite low; the latter is lean, well developed, with a wide angulation. The hind feet are similar to the forefeet except in length, which is rather greater. Dewclaws must be removed.

GAIT The preferred gait is the trot; the length of the pace is moderate.

COAT On the back, the coat is 2¾-5½ inches long. The face is invariably covered with short hair. The outer side of the ear is covered with short hair, with somewhat longer hair on the inner side. The back of the forelegs has a fringe of rather long hair down to the wrist; the hind legs have culottes down to the hocks. The hair is quite soft, wavy, or even curly, but it must never be woolly. The undercoat should be thick. **Color** The background is black. A few white markings are allowed. White markings on the head, body, or tail are not permitted, although they are allowed on the throat, chest, and brisket. White on feet or toes is undesirable but tolerated.

DISQUALIFICATIONS Loss of more than 2 premolars (the fifth tooth); light or albino eyes; any other pigmentation of the nose than black; entirely woolly coat or excessively long coat; white markings on the head, body, or tail; long hair on the face; any type of ears other than those mentioned above; white spots on the limbs should be penalized in scoring; undershot or overshot jaws; height more than 19½ or less than 15¾ inches. ●

CROATIAN SHEPHERD

THE DOGS AT WORK

Photo: M. Pedone.

30 BEARDED COLLIE

GREAT BRITAIN

Despite its name, this dog is quite different from the famous Longhaired Collie, also from Scotland. Although not in great evidence today, it appears that this breed was popular when the Romans invaded Britain, despite a lack of documentation. Its presence in Scotland in the sixteenth century is historically certain. Many writers of this period have alluded to the great sheepherding qualities of the Bearded Collie as well as admiring his resistance to winter weather. Obviously the severe life led by this breed for centuries brought about the natural selection which even today still produces specimens of exceptional quality.

GENERAL CHARACTERISTICS Alert, lively, self-confident and good-tempered, the Bearded Collie is an extremely active dog. It has a long, lean body, with none of the stumpy quality of the Bobtail. Though strongly made, it is gracefully built and does not have too heavy an appearance. The face has an inquiring expression.

SIZE The ideal height at the shoulder is 21-22 inches for males, 20-21 inches for females.

HEAD Broad and flat, with ears set high. The foreface is fairly long, with a moderate stop. The nose is large and black, except in brown or tawny individuals, in which a brown nose is acceptable. The eye sockets are slightly raised and surmounted by rough eyebrows. The teeth are large and white, the bite never overshot or undershot.

EYES Consistent in color with the coat, eyes are set rather wide apart. Big and bright, they have arched eyebrows, not so long, however, as to cover the eyes.

EARS Medium-sized, drooping, and covered with rather long hair. A slight lift at the base indicates alertness.

NECK Of fair length, the neck should be muscular and slightly arched.

BODY Fairly long, with a level back. The ribs are flat, the loins are strong. The rib cage is deep and long, the shoulders flat.

TAIL Set low, the tail should be moderately long and have abundant hair. It is carried low when the dog is quiet, with an upward swirl at the tip. It is carried gaily when the animal is excited, but not over the back.

FOREQUARTERS The Bearded Collie has straight legs that are well boned and with flexible pasterns which, however, show no weakness. The forelegs are covered with shaggy hair. Observed from the front they are straight.

HINDQUARTERS Very muscular hindlegs at the thighs, with well-bent stifles and hocks. The feet are oval, the soles well padded, with close, arched toes and with hair between the pads.

COAT Must be double, the undercoat being soft and furry, the outer coat harsh, strong, and flat. It has no woolliness and is free from any tendency to curl. Sparse hair on the nose ridge, slightly longer laterally, barely covering the lips. Fairly long beard.

COLOR The Bearded Collie may be slate-gray or reddish fawn, black, gray of any shade, brown, and sandy, with or without white markings.

FAULTS Narrow skull. Muzzle too long or too short. Body too barreled or too short. Rib cage barreled or rounded. Tail short or stubby. Hindquarters excessively closed or cowlike. Lack of hair on legs. ●

BEARDED COLLIE

Photo: S. A. Thompson, T. Fall.

31 ROUGH COLLIE

GREAT BRITAIN

The impossibility of establishing the origins of the Long-haired Collie is due to the fact that from the eighteenth century on this breed was considered solely as a work breed. Its purity was respected without its being thought necessary to keep pedigrees. When the Collie began to attract the attention of dog lovers at the beginning of the last century, it was principally spread throughout northern Scotland. It was not as tall as the dogs we see today and had a shorter head. The breed was carefully bred up to 1860, when it was presented at the first official dog show organized on English soil.

Numerous hypotheses have been made concerning the antecedents of the Scotch Shepherd: some see the Newfoundland as its ancestor, others the Gordon Setter, the Deerhound, or the Scottish Terrier. Certainly the modern Collie represents long and careful selective breeding; and one can state that the definite fixing of its important points, such as height and weight, was not achieved until 1885. Since then breeders have been careful to preserve and refine this dog's numerous and valuable characteristics.

His world-wide fame in America, Europe, and Australia is certainly due to his beauty and to his exceptional psycho-physical qualities. These enable him not only to accomplish the work for which he was developed, that is, as a sheepdog, but also to be trained as a police dog, guard dog, hunting dog, and show dog. Films and TV shows featuring Lassie are examples of this last-named activity and have greatly contributed to making this breed popular in the countries where it was little known, if at all.

ROUGH COLLIE

GENERAL CHARACTERISTICS The Rough Collie's natural talent for sheep dog work requires it to have a physical structure characterized especially by strength and activity, wholly free from any trace of cloddishness or coarseness. One of its chief points for judging is expression, and this is refined by a perfect balance of skull and foreface; of size, shape, and positioning of eye, and of correct positioning and carriage of ears. The basic impression of the Rough Collie at first sight should be one of great handsomeness, of unshakable dignity, of total harmony of the parts. All of these qualities are to be considered in judging, and in considering size and weight they must not be sacrificed in an effort to achieve ideal dimensions.

WEIGHT AND SIZE Height at the withers: males, 22-24 inches; females, 20-22 inches. Males should weigh 45-65 lb, females 40-55 lb.

HEAD The characteristics of the head in the Rough Collie are of supreme importance and must be considered at all times in proportion to the overall size of the dog. When viewed either head-on or from the side, the head has the form of a blunted wedge with smooth contours. The skull should invariably be flat, and the sides of the head should taper smoothly and gently from the ears to the tip of the black nose. Cheekbones should not be unduly prominent, nor should the muzzle appear pinched. In profile the top of the skull and the surface of the muzzle are seen to lie in two straight, parallel lines of equal length, which are divided by a slight but definitely perceptible stop. The center of balance of the

ROUGH COLLIE

Photo: Palnich, S. A. Thompson.

BORDER COLLIE

length of the head is at the midpoint between the inside corners of the eyes; this point, incidentally, is also the center of an ideally positioned stop. The muzzle is smooth and well rounded, blunt but not square. The underjaw is strong and clean-cut. The depth of the skull from the brow to the underpart of the jaw must not be excessive (the fault is known as a deep trough). The nose must always be black, no matter what the coloring of the coat. The teeth should be of good size, and the lower incisors should fit snugly behind the upper incisors. A very slight space in the bite is not to be considered as a serious fault.

EYES In the Rough Collie the eyes are one of the most important features, for it is the eyes that give the face the sweet and gentle expression for which the dog is justly famous. They should be of medium size, set rather obliquely. They are almond-shaped and dark brown, except in the case of blue merle Collies, in which one or both eyes or part of one or both may be blue or blue-flecked. The expression

must be intelligent, with an alert look when listening.

EARS The Rough Collie's ears are small, not too close together and well centered on the skull. In repose they should be carried thrown back, but when on the alert they should be brought forward and carried semi-erect, which means with approximately two-thirds of the ear standing erect and the top third tipped forward naturally below the horizontal.

NECK Muscular and powerful, the Rough Collie's neck is of fair length and well arched.

FOREQUARTERS The shoulders should be sloped and well angulated. The forelegs should be straight and muscular, neither in nor out at the elbows, and with a moderate amount of bone.

BODY The Rough Collie's body should be a trifle long in comparison with its height. The back should be

firm, with a slight rise over the loins. The ribs must be well sprung, the chest deep and fairly broad behind the shoulders.

TAIL Should be long, with the bone reaching at least to the hock joint. It is to be carried low when the animal is quiet, but with a slight upward swirl at the tip. It may be carried gaily when the dog is excited, but even then it must not be carried over the back.

HINDQUARTERS The hind legs must be muscular at the thighs, clean and sinewy below. The stifles must be well bent, and the hocks must be well let down and powerful. **FEET** These should be oval, with soles well padded, toes arched and close together. The hind feet are slightly less arched.

COAT Should fit snugly to the outline of the dog, and the hair must be very dense. The outer coat is straight and harsh to the touch, but the undercoat is soft, furry, and exceptionally close, so much so as almost to con-

ceal the skin completely. Both mane and frill should be abundant, the mask or face should be smooth, as also the ears at the tips. The ears should have rather more hair toward the base. The forelegs should be well feathered, and the hindlegs above the hocks should be profusely covered. They should be smooth below the hocks. The hair on the tail is very profuse. **Color** There are three recognized colors for the Rough Collie—sable and white, tricolor, and blue merle. Sable: any shade from light gold to rich mahogany or shaded sable; light straw or cream color is highly undesirable. Tricolor: predominantly black, with rich tan markings about the legs and head; a rusty tinge in the topcoat is highly undesirable. Blue merle: predominantly clear, silvery blue, splashed and marbled with black. Rich tan markings are to be preferred, but their absence should not be counted as a fault. Large black markings, slate color, or a rusty tinge of either the topcoat or undercoat are highly undesirable. White markings: all the above may carry the typical white Collie markings to a greater or lesser degree. The following

Photo: S. A. Thompson.

markings are favorable: white collar, full or part; white shirt, legs, and feet; white tail tip. A blaze may be carried on muzzle or skull or both.

GAIT Movement is a distinct characteristic of this breed. A sound dog is never out at elbow, yet it moves with its front feet comparatively close together. Plaiting, crossing, or rolling are highly undesirable. The hind legs from the hock joint to the ground should be parallel when viewed from the rear. The hindlegs should be powerful and full of drive. Viewed from the side the action is smooth. A reasonably long stride is desirable, and this should be light and appear quite effortless.

FAULTS Length of head apparently out of proportion to body; receding skull or unbalanced head to be strongly condemned. Weak, snipy muzzle; domed skull; high-peaked occiput, prominent cheekbones; dish-faced or Roman-nosed; undershot or overshot mouth; missing teeth. Round or light-colored and glassy or staring eyes are highly objectionable. Body flat-sided, short or cobby; straight shoulder or stifle; out at elbow; crooked forearms; cow hocks or straight hocks; large, open or hare feet; feet turned in or out; long, weak pasterns; tail short, kinked, or twisted to one side or carried over the back; a soft, silky, or wavy coat or insufficient undercoat; prick ears, low-set ears; nervousness. ●

SMOOTH COLLIE

32 SMOOTH COLLIE
GREAT BRITAIN

A close relative of the Scotch Rough Collie, the Smooth Collie, after some years of relative obscurity, today is winning

ROUGH COLLIE

Photo: A. Roslin-Williams, S. A. Thompson.

well-deserved popularity, especially in England. The breed was achieved by crossing the old black-and-white Longhaired Collie with the Greyhound. Through the years the characteristics of the Greyhound have been diluted (to the point that today they are scarcely noticeable) while the physical as well as mental qualities of this excellent shepherd remain.

33 BOBTAIL
Old English Sheepdog
GREAT BRITAIN

The Bobtail owes his name to the short tail typical of his breed. In France, as in the other non-English-speaking countries, he is called the Old English Sheepdog. It is certain that the breed is very ancient, although today it is more widespread in the New World than the Old, where, as in Italy, it is most popular as a luxury dog and pet. His almost complete absence of tail, his special bark, his way of advancing, swinging to and fro like a bear, his affectionate nature, and his great intelligence explain the admiration accorded him in the most elegant circles. But it was as sheepherder's clever helper that this old English breed received esteem and confidence over the centuries.

It is not easy to trace the origins of this charming dog, as he has similarities to the Russian Owtchar, whose characteristics are not certain, although several representatives of this breed arrived in England on ships from the Baltic. It also resembles the French Briard, and therefore the Italian Bergamese. In England some authorities recognize the Poodle and the Deerhound as the Bobtail's ancestors.

The breed's characteristics were established about a century ago, while it was being successfully developed in southern England and Scotland. In this region it is supposed that it was the ancestor of the Bearded Collie.

An old tradition has it that the Bobtail's tail was cut in order to distinguish work dogs, exempt from tax, from luxury dogs, for which a tax had to be paid. Many Bobtails are found today with a short tail, and perhaps this characteristic is on the way to becoming hereditary.

BOBTAIL

GENERAL CHARACTERISTICS A strong, compact dog of great symmetry, absolutely free of legginess, profusely coated all over, very elastic in a gallop but in walking or trotting has a characteristic ambling or pacing movement. His bark should be loud, with a peculiar **pot cassé** ring in it. All around, he is a thickset, muscular, able-bodied dog with a highly intelligent expression, free of all Poodle or Deerhound traits.

SIZE Males, 22 inches and upward; slightly less for females. Type, symmetry and character of the greatest importance and on no account to be sacrificed to size alone.

HEAD The skull is capacious and rather squarely formed, giving plenty of room for brain power. The parts over the eyes should be well arched, and the whole well covered with hair. Jaws fairly long, strong, square and truncated; the stop should be defined to avoid a Deerhound face. Nose invariably black, large, and capacious. The teeth are strong and large; they should be evenly placed and level.

EYES In the old English Sheepdog dark eyes or walleyes are to be preferred.

EARS Small and carried flat to side of head, moderately coated.

NECK The neck should be fairly long, gracefully arched, and well coated with hair.

BODY Rather short and very compact, ribs well sprung, brisket deep and capacious. The loin should be very stout and gently arched.

TAIL Puppies requiring docking should have the operation performed within a week of birth, preferably within four weeks of birth. Tail should either be wholly absent or never exceed 1½ to 2 inches in grown dogs.

FOREQUARTERS The forelegs should be dead straight, with plenty of bone, holding the body well from the ground, without approaching legginess. They should be well coated all around. The shoulders should be sloping and narrow at the points, the dog standing lower at the shoulders than at the loin. **HINDQUARTERS** Should be round and muscular, hocks well let down and the hams densely coated with a thick, long jacket in excess of that of any other part of the body. **FEET** Small, round, with toes well arched and pads thick and round. The pads should also be fairly hard.

COAT Profuse and of good, hard texture, not straight but shaggy and free from curl. The undercoat should be a waterproof pile when not removed by grooming. Quality and texture of coat to be considered above mere profuseness. **Color** Any shade of gray, grizzle, blue, or blue merle, with or without white markings. Any shade of brown or sable is to be considered distinctly objectionable and not to be encouraged.

FAULT Excessive length and narrowness of head. ●

BOBTAIL

Photo: R. Kinne (Photo Res.), T. Fall.

34 SHETLAND SHEEPDOG
GREAT BRITAIN

In the Shetland Islands off the coast of Scotland small animals seem to be the fashion, from ponies to small sheep with silky fleece and black muzzles. It is therefore logical that the sheepherders in this region, when they wanted to find a sheep dog for their miniature sheep, tried to get a breed of small stature, which still possessed the typical sheep dog qualities. This gave rise to the Dwarf Scotch Shepherd.

Was this the result of methodical selective breeding on the Collie, or a cross with another breed? Clara Bowring, an English author, claims that it is most likely that the Shetland descends from Rough Collies brought into the islands and then crossed with different dogs such as the Yakkin, an island dog not officially recognized, which arrived in Scotland on whaling ships.

The Shetland's appearance is that of a miniature Collie. The Scotch Dwarf is quite able to herd the miniature sheep he guards, and also to take care of very large flocks. He has a pleasant nature. He is intelligent, stubborn, very faithful, attached to his master, and perfectly happy when he is raised in the open. In official tests he has frequently shown excellent herding ability for sheep or larger animals.

SHETLAND SHEEPDOG

GENERAL CHARACTERISTICS To enable the Shetland Sheepdog to fulfill its natural bent for herding sheep, its physical makeup should follow the lines of strength and activity. It must be free from cloddiness and with no trace of coarseness. Although the desired type is similar to that of the Rough Collie, there are marked differences that must be noted. The expression, which is one of the identifying marks of the breed, comes from a perfect balance of skull and foreface, size, shape, color and placement of eyes, correct positioning and carriage of ears, with all these harmoniously blended to produce the look of alert, gentle intelligence which is characteristic of the Shetland Sheepdog. The dog should show affection toward and be responsive to his master; he may be reserved toward strangers but not belligerent. He should have instant appeal as a dog of great beauty, intelligence, and alertness. His action must be lithe and graceful with extraordinary speed and jumping power for his size. The outline must be symmetrical, with no part seeming out of proportion to the whole. An abundant coat, mane, and frill, with shapeliness of head and sweetness of expression all combine to make up the ideal Shetland Sheepdog that will inspire and win admiration.

SIZE Ideal height at the withers:

males 14½ inches; females 14 inches. In judging, any height at the withers which is more than 1 inch in excess of these dimensions is to be considered a serious fault.

HEAD The Shetland's head should be refined and noble. Its shape when viewed from above or in profile is that of a long, blunt wedge tapering from ear to nose. Width of skull necessarily depends on the combined length of skull and muzzle, and the whole must be considered in relation to the overall size of the individual specimen. The skull should be flat, of moderate width between the ears and with no prominence of the occipital bone. Cheeks should be flat, merging smoothly into a well-rounded muzzle. Skull and muzzle must be of equal length, and the central point of combined skull and muzzle length should be the inner corner of the eye. In profile the topline of the skull should be parallel to the topline of the muzzle except that the skull line is high because of the stop, which is slight but nevertheless well defined. The jaws should be clean and strong, with the underjaw well developed. Lips should be tight, and the teeth should be sound and level with an evenly spaced scissors bite.

EYES An important feature, since the eyes give expression to the dog. They

should be of medium size, set obliquely; they are almond-shaped. Except in the case of merles, the eye color is dark brown; blue is permissible in the merle.

EARS Small, moderately wide at the base, set on fairly close together high up on the skull. In repose the ears should be thrown back, but when the dog is on the alert the ears should be brought forward and carried semierect, with tips dropping forward.

NECK The neck should be muscular, well arched, and of sufficient length to carry the head proudly.

FOREQUARTERS The shoulder blade should slope at an angle of 45 degrees from the withers, forward and downward to the shoulder joint. At the withers the shoulders are separated only by the vertebra, but they must slope outward to accommodate the desired spring of ribs. The upper arm should join the shoulder blade as nearly at a right angle as possible. The elbow joint should be equidistant from the ground and the withers. The forelegs should be straight when viewed from the front; they must be clean and muscular, with strong bone. The pasterns are strong and flexible.

BODY Measures slightly longer from the withers to the root of the tail than the height at the withers, but most of the length is due to the proper angulation of the shoulders and the hindquarters. The chest should be deep, reaching to the point of the elbow. The ribs should be well sprung and tapering at their lower half to permit free play of the forelegs and shoulders. The back should be level, with a graceful sweep over the loins, and the rump should slope gradually to the rear. The feet are oval, with a strong sole. The toes are well arched and close.

TAIL The Shetland's tail is set on low. As it tapers, the bone must reach at least to the hock joint. The tail is abundantly feathered and ends with a slight upward sweep. It is carried raised when the dog is moving, but it never reaches the level of the back.

HINDQUARTERS The Shetland's

thighs are broad and muscular, with the thigh bones set into the pelvis at a right angle, balancing the right-angled insertion of the shoulder blade. The stifle should have a distinct angulation; the hock joint must be clean-cut, angular, and well let down with strong bone. Viewed from the rear the hocks should be straight.

COAT The coat must be double, with the top coat made up of long, straight, harsh hair and the furlike undercoat composed of short, close hair. The mane and frill must be very abundant; the forelegs should be well feathered. Hair should be profuse above the hocks, fairly smooth below. The face has smooth hair. The variety known as "smooth-coated" is barred. **Color** Tricolor dogs should be deep black on the body, with no ticking whatsoever; rich tan markings are preferable on the tricolor. Sables may be clear or shaded, and of any color from gold to deep mahogany, with the color rich in tones in the shaded area. Wolf sable and gray are undesirable colors. In blue merles, clear silvery blue is desirable, splashed and marbled with black. Rich tan markings are preferred, but their absence is not to be held a fault. Heavy black markings or a slate or rusty tinge to either top or undercoat is highly undesirable; the general effect should be blue. White markings are acceptable in blaze, collar, chest, frill, legs, stifle, and tip of the tail. Tan markings may be shown on some or all of the following: eyebrows, cheeks, legs, stifles, under tail. The white markings are preferred, no matter what the color of the dog, but the lack of such markings shall not be held a fault. Black and white, black and tan are also acceptable colors. Patches of white as overmarkings on the body are highly undesirable. The nose is invariably black, regardless of other coloring.

FAULTS Domed or receding skull, lack of stop, large drooping or prick ears, overdeveloped cheeks, weak jaw, snipiness, missing teeth; crooked forelegs, cow hocks; kinky tail, short tail, tail carried over back; predominance of white; pink or flesh-colored nose; blue eyes in dogs other than merles; nervousness; full or light eye; undershot or overshot jaw. ●

SHETLAND SHEEPDOG

COLLIE AND SHETLAND SHEEPDOG ▶

Photo: R. Kinne (Photo Res.), T. Fall, S. A. Thompson.

WELSH CORGI CARDIGAN

35 WELSH CORGI CARDIGAN

GREAT BRITAIN

Although it is one of the oldest English breeds, it was only recently that the Welsh Corgi Cardigan was admitted to the official kennel classification. His origins seem to be clouded in mystery, which is understandable if one remembers that he was raised by the Celts three thousand years ago. Probably he belongs to the same stock as the German Basset.

The Celts, who brought him to England, valued him for his intelligence and vigilance. They admitted him to their homes, used him for hunting, and even made him a guard dog for their children.

Only much later, although several centuries ago, did the Cardigan begin to work with the flocks, above all as a drover, for which he is especially valued today, as well as pet and guard dog.

Through the years the original characteristics of the breed have been modified and reinforced by crossing with other British dogs, including the Collie, to the point where the standard defined by the Welsh Corgi Association was approved by the English Kennel Club in 1934.

GENERAL CHARACTERISTICS Expression should be as foxy as possible; alertness essential; the body to measure 36 inches from point of nose to tip of tail.

SIZE AND WEIGHT Height, as near as possible to 12 inches at shoulder. Weight, males, 22-26 lb, females, 20-24 lb.

HEAD Should be foxy in shape and appearance. Skull, fairly wide and flat between the ears, tapering toward the eyes, above which it should be slightly domed. Muzzle, about 3 inches long (or, in proportion to skull, as 3:5) and tapering toward the snout. Nose black (except in blue merles), slightly projecting and in no sense blunt, with nostrils of moderate size. Underjaw clean-cut and strong but without prominence. Teeth strong, level, and sound.

EYES Medium size, but giving a sharp and watchful expression, rather widely

Photo: S. A. Thompson.

WELSH CORGI CARDIGAN

WELSH CORGI PEMBROKE

set, with corners clearly defined; preferably dark in color but clear. Silver eyes permissible in blue merles.

EARS Rather large (in proportion to size of dog) and prominent, moderately wide at the base, carried erect, set about 3½ inches apart and well back so that they can be laid flat along neck.

NECK Muscular, well developed, and in proportion to the dog's build, fitting into well-sloped shoulders.

BODY Chest should be moderately broad, with prominent breastbone. Body should be fairly long and strong, with deep brisket, well-sprung ribs, and clearly defined waist.

TAIL Moderately long and set in line with body (not curled over back) and resembling that of a fox.

FOREQUARTERS Front should be slightly bowed, with strong bones. Legs short and strong. Shoulders strong and muscular. **HINDQUARTERS** Strong, with muscular thighs. Legs strong and short. **FEET** Round and well padded and rather large. Dewclaws removed.

COAT Short or medium hair, of hard texture. **Color** Any color except pure white.

FAULTS Overshot or undershot mouth, high-peaked occiput, prominent cheeks, low flat forehead, expressionless eyes, crooked forearms, splayed feet, tail curled over back. Silky coat. ●

36 WELSH CORGI PEMBROKE

GREAT BRITAIN

Although of more recent vintage than the Cardigan, the Pembroke is nevertheless a very old breed. It was brought to England by Flemish weavers, summoned in 1107 by King Henry I to introduce their craft into Wales. This breed is related to the Nordic dogs, such as the Samoyed, the Norwegian Elkhound, and other breeds of the same stock. The old Pembroke began to resemble the Cardigan about the middle of the last century as the two breeds were crossing among themselves. Taller, and shorter in body than the related Cardigan, the Pembroke is much esteemed today as a pet and guard dog.

GENERAL CHARACTERISTICS Low-set, strong, sturdily built, alert and active, giving an impression of substance and stamina in a small space; outlook bold, expression intelligent and workmanlike. The movement should be free and active, elbows fitting closely to the sides, neither loose nor tied. Forelegs should move well forward without too much lift, in unison with thrusting action of hindlegs.

WEIGHT AND SIZE Males, 20-24 lb; females, 18-22 lb. Height at shoulder: 10-12 inches:

HEAD The head should be foxy in shape and appearance, with alert and intelligent expression, skull should be fairly wide and flat between the ears; moderate amount of stop. Length of foreface should be in proportion to the skull as 3:5. Muzzle slightly tapering. Nose black. Teeth level, or with the inner side of the upper front teeth resting closely on the front of the lower.

EYES Well set, round, medium size, hazel in color and blending with color of coat.

EARS Pricked, medium-sized, slightly pointed. A line drawn from the tip of the nose through the eyes, if extended, should pass through or close to the tip of the ear.

NECK Rather long.

BODY Of medium length, with well-sprung ribs. Not short-coupled or terrierlike. Level topline. Chest broad and deep, well let down between the forelegs.

TAIL Short, preferably natural.

FOREQUARTERS Legs short and as straight as possible. Ample bone carried down to the feet. Elbows should fit closely to the side, neither loose nor tied. **HINDQUARTERS** Strong and flexible, slightly tapering. Legs short. Ample bone carried right down to the feet. Hocks straight when viewed from behind. **FEET** Oval, the two center toes slightly in advance of two outer ones, pads strong and well arched. Nails short.

COAT Of medium length and dense, not wiry. **Color** Self colors in red, sable, black and tan, or with white markings on legs, chest, and neck. Some white on head and foreface is permissible. ●

WELSH CORGI PEMBROKE

Photo: S. A. Thompson, J. Cooke (Photo Res.).

Group 2

GUARD DOGS, DEFENSE DOGS, AND WORK DOGS

It may seem arbitrary to have classified in this group of guard dogs, defense dogs, and work dogs only fifty breeds of the three hundred recognized breeds, especially since it must be remembered that all dogs, through atavistic instinct, guard the home and property of their master, react when they see him attacked, and can always be useful in one way or another.

In the second group of canine breeds, the official kennel clubs have listed the dogs that have notably exercised guard and defense duties traditionally since ancient times, while those classified as work dogs are those that have in the past, and today as well, in their own areas, been helpful to man in activities other than pastoral life and hunting.

In this second group we will also find dogs that in shows must undergo trials connected with their work, and dogs that are classified solely according to the function of physical and mental characteristics required by different standards.

Among the guard and defense breeds we find primarily mountain dogs and descendents from the ancient Mastiffs.

The Tibetan Mastiff is also considered to be the stock for mountain dogs. Aristotle has described for us a gigantic dog, fearful because of its strength and ferocity; and Marco Polo, who saw some at the Court of the Great Khan, remarked: "They were terrifying." It is from this dog (which migrated to the West as did the Eastern sheep dogs, ancestors of the present-day breeds) that the Pyrenees, the St. Bernard, the Bernese, the Newfoundland, and so many more descend.

The other large group of guard dogs, the Mastiffs, have different origins which, in turn, are difficult to trace because of their antiquity. They are less homogeneous than the mountain breeds which include dogs that, at first sight, seem to be very different from each other. Some are large with a long muzzle, while others have somewhat twisted legs and a flat muzzle. Dogs such as the German Mastiff, the Boxer, the Bulldog, the Neopolitan Mastiff, and still others whose history and standards are given in the following pages, are in any case dogs whose appearance has influenced the choice of tasks to which man has assigned them over the centuries.

Certain highly specialized German guard and defense breeds belong to the Pinscher family. They are definitely more modern than those mentioned above (or indeed very modern, such as the Doberman, as recent as the second half of the last century).

Then we finally come to the working breeds among which, besides extremely specialized dogs such as the Portuguese Water Dog or the St. Bernard, we find the important group of Nordic breeds. Among them are the most ancient dogs known to man, such as the Malamute, the Siberian Husky, the Samoyed, and the Eskimo dog. If these had not existed and been characterized by an unbelievable attachment to man, and by a sense of duty which we might call stoical, whole regions of the world would have remained unexplored and the human race, now living for centuries in the great North, would have been forced to halt—who knows for how long a time?—before the rigors of unconquered nature.

37 BOXER
GERMANY

The Boxer is not an old breed. His breeding dates from the end of the last century and his appearance from the middle of the same century. At that time a group of Bavarian dog lovers were seeking to attain through a cross between a dog known as a "Bullenbeisser" with the English Bulldog, through selective breeding, a new breed wherein the physical characteristics of elegance and uniformity would be combined with courage, balance, intelligence, and power. In a fairly short time quite satisfactory results were obtained. The ancestor, the Bullenbeisser (bull biter) was a fighter—an aggressive dog much used in Germany and the Netherlands for hunting boar, deer, and even bear. He was used for herding as a secondary operation. He is descended from the German dogs of the Middle Ages called "Saupacker"—dogs for capturing bears and bulls, themselves descended from English Mastiffs that migrated as far as Germany and whose fossil form appears to be *Canis familiaris decumanus.*

The beginnings of the Boxer as a show dog took place in Munich, Bavaria. The grand design of dog breeding has spread to the continent and the astute Bavarians, as Rowland Johns writes in *Our Friend the Boxer*, thought that they would be successful with their dog if they succeeded in improving the breed through a cross. They knew all about the English Bulldog, and that since 1835 it had been exempted from fighting bears and bulls. They decided to introduce some of these qualities into the dog they were engaged in selecting. The Bulldog was then very similar to the modern English Terrier, although much heavier.

The first concrete result was obtained in 1890 when a Munich Boxer was crossed with a White-Striped Boxer. From this cross we get the specimens with the strongly developed lower jaw, erect ears, and a stronger bone structure. Cross breeding was continued between related dogs to eliminate the excess of white coloring and to obtain the desired tawny speckled color. It should be noted that the Bullenbeisser already had a tawny or speckled, although not very elegant, color, and was of a robust constitution, massive, with imposing teeth.

Rowland Johns wrote in 1894 that the crosses had their firm supporters in Robert Koenig and Hopner, whose efforts to make the breed popular were not immediately successful. At the Munich show of 1895 there was only one entry in the category: the dog Flocki, son of Tom and of Alt. After this modest beginning, thanks to the qualities of Flocki, the breed convinced the experts to such a degree that the first Boxer club was founded in 1896.

"Three months later a show for Boxers only took place with Koenig as judge. This called to the attention of these pioneers the need for eliminating all bulldog characteristics which could lessen the ideal type of Boxer. Thus they wished to eliminate the white color, stabilize the tawny and speckled shade, although permitting white on the thorax and paws. They kept other Bulldog points, such as the prognathism, the break of the frontonasal line referred to as the "stop," from the hollow of which the unusually flat muzzle rises. These characteristics have come down today in all good specimens."

The first entry was presented at the Munich Dog Show of 1895 and aroused much curiosity and interest. Breeding started and achieved a considerable number. The ancestor of the Boxer as we see him today was Meta von der Passage, mother of a numerous and homogeneous progeny and particularly of Hugo von Pfalzgau, a sire that played an essential role in the breed's development. Hugo sired the champion Kurt von Pfalzgau, father of the famous Rolf Walhall. The latter inherited the great qualities of his ancestors and gave an impulse to breeding which increased after World War I and brought the breed to worldwide fame.

The careful selective breeding which has been carried on during the last decades has given splendid results in beautiful defense and guard dogs and companions. The harmony of form, together with intelligence and character, make the Boxer an ideal dog. In many countries he is used as a police dog. In short, the Boxer is a most popular and well-distributed breed.

BOXER

GENERAL CHARACTERISTICS The Boxer is a medium-sized, smooth-haired, sturdy dog having a square structure and heavy bones. The muscular system is rather lean, strongly developed and very prominent. The movements are lively and full of strength and nobility. The Boxer should appear neither heavy nor clumsy, neither too lean nor overgrown.

WEIGHT AND SIZE Height: males measuring about 24 inches at the withers should weigh more than 66 lb; females 23 inches at the withers should weigh about 55 lb. Height at the withers: in Boxers height is measured with the dog standing erect and the measurement taken with a straight-edge from the withers, along the elbow down to the ground. Males 22½-25 inches; females 21-23½ inches. Males should not go under the minimum nor females over the maximum.

HEAD The Boxer's head is what gives him his character. It has to be in good proportion to the body and should appear neither too light nor too heavy. The upper part of the head is as slender and angular as possible, without salient cheeks. The muzzle is as broad and massive as possible. The beauty of the head depends on the harmonious proportion between the muzzle and the upper part of the head. From whatever direction one views the head—whether from in front, from above, or from the side—the muzzle must always be in the proper proportion to the upper part of the head, that is, it must never seem too small. It has to be lean, showing neither wrinkles nor dewlap. Wrinkles naturally appear on the upper part of the head whenever the ears are set up. Descending on both sides from the root of the nose, they are always slightly marked. The dark mask is limited to the muzzle and must stand out clearly against the color of the head so that the face does not look grim. The muzzle should be developed strongly in all three dimensions; thus it should be neither pointed nor slim, neither short nor low. Its form is influenced by (1) the form of both jaws; (2) the position of the teeth in the jaws; (3) the condition of the flews. In front, both jaws do not end in a vertical plane; the lower jaw undershoots the upper and has a slight upward curve. The upper jaw has a broad connection to the upper part of the head and tapers only slightly toward the end. Thus, in front both jaws are very broad. The canine teeth should be set as far apart from each other as possible. The incisors should be in a row, and those in the middle should not protrude. In the upper jaw they are set in a line curving slightly forward, while in the lower jaw they should be in a straight line. Teeth must be strong and healthy and regular. The shape of the muzzle is completed by the flews. The upper lip is thick and padded. It fills out the frontal space, the cavity formed by the projection of the lower jaw, and rests on the fangs (canines) of the lower jaw. These fangs, therefore, must stand far apart and be of good length so that the front surface of the muzzle is broad and squarish and, when viewed from the side, forms an obtuse angle with the topline of the muzzle. Too much protrusion of the overlip or underlip is undesirable. The chin should be perceptible when viewed from the side as well as from the front without rising above the bite line ("overrepandous"), as in the Bulldog. The Boxer must not show teeth or tongue when the mouth is closed. Excessive flews are not desirable. The top of the skull is slightly arched, not rotund, flat, nor noticeably broad, and the occiput must not be

BOXER

too pronounced. The forehead forms a distinct stop with the topline of the muzzle, which must not be forced back into the forehead as in a Bulldog. It should not slant down ("downfaced"), nor should it be dished, although the tip of the nose should lie somewhat higher than the root of the muzzle. The forehead shows just a slight furrow between the eyes. The cheeks, though covering powerful masseter muscles compatible with the strong set of teeth, should be relatively flat, not bulged, maintaining the clean lines of the skull. They taper into the muzzle in a slight, graceful curve. The nose is broad and black, very slightly turned up; the nostrils broad, with the nasolabial line running between them down through the upper lip, which, however, must not be split.

EYES Dark brown, not excessively small, protruding, nor deepset, are encircled by dark hair and should have an alert, intelligent expression. How the expression mirrors the dog's mood, along with the mobile furrowing of the skin at the forehead, gives the Boxer's head its unique appeal.

EARS Set on extremely high, at the highest points of the sides of the skull. They should be cut rather long, without too broad a shell, and must be carried erect.

NECK Round, of ample length, not too short; strong, muscular, and clean throughout, without dewlap; distinctly marked nape with an elegant arch running down to the back.

FOREQUARTERS The shoulders are long and sloping, close-lying, and not excessively covered with muscle. The upper arm is long, set almost at a full right angle to the shoulder blade. Viewed from the front, the forelegs must be straight, parallel to each other, and characterized by strong, firmly joined bones. The elbows neither press too closely against the chest nor visibly stand off from it. The forearm is straight, long, and firmly muscled. The pastern joint is clearly defined but not distended; the pastern itself is strong and distinct, slanted slightly but standing nearly perpendicular to the ground. Dewclaws may be removed as a safety precaution. Forefeet should be compact, turning neither in nor out. The toes are tightly arched ("catfeet"), with tough pads.

BODY On the Boxer the brisket is extremely deep, reaching down to the elbows (its depth is equal to half the height at the withers). The ribs extend far to the rear; they are well arched out but must not be barrel-shaped. The chest is of fair width, and the forechest is well defined. The loins are short and muscular; the belly lightly tucked up, its line blending into a graceful curve to the rear. The withers should be clearly defined as the highest point of the back. The back itself is short, straight and muscular, with a firm topline.

TAIL Set on high rather than low. The tail should be clipped and carried upward.

HINDQUARTERS Should be strongly muscled and with angulation balanced with that of the forequarters. The thighs are broad and curved, the breech musculature hard and strongly developed. The rump is flat, broad, and slightly sloped. The pelvis is long and in females is markedly broad. The upper and lower thighs are both long, the

Photo: M. Pedone.

BOXER

BOXER

leg is well angulated with a clearly defined hock joint that is well let down. In standing position the leg below the hock joint should be practically perpendicular to the ground; a slight rearward slope is permissible. Viewed from the rear, the hind legs should be straight, the hock joints turning neither inward nor outward. The metatarsus should be short, clean and strong, and supported on powerful rear pads. The rear toes are slightly longer than the front toes but similar in all other respects. Dewclaws if present may be removed.

COAT Short and glossy, lying smooth and tight to the body. **Color** Fawn and brindle. Fawn in various shades from light tan to dark deer red or mahogany, with preference to the deeper colors. The brindle should have clearly defined black stripes on a fawn background. White markings on fawn or brindle dogs are not to be rejected and are often very attractive; such markings, however, must be limited to one third of the ground color and are not desirable on the back of the torso proper. On the face, white may replace part or all of the otherwise essentially black mask. Such white markings, however, should be of a distribution such as to enhance and not detract from true Boxer expression.

CHARACTER AND TEMPERAMENT These are of supreme importance in the Boxer. He has long been known for his attachment to his master and his fidelity to the entire household. Vigilant and of undaunted courage as a guard dog, with family and friends his disposition is basically playful; with children he seems to have infinite patience. Deliberate and wary with strangers, he will show curiosity and, above all, if threatened, fearless courage and tenacity. Normally the Boxer responds to friendly overtures when honestly rendered. His intelligence, loyal affection, and adaptability to discipline make him a highly desirable companion.

FAULTS Head not typical, plump or bulldoglike appearance, lightness of bone, lack of balance, lack of noble bearing; lack of expression, somber face, unserviceable bite, Pinscher or Bulldog head, sloping muzzle topline, lightness of muzzle in relation to skull, snipiness, visibility of teeth or tongue when mouth is closed, driveling, split in upper lip, poor ear carriage, light ("bird of prey") eyes; dewlap; excessive breadth of chest, excessive shallowness or depth of chest, looseness or excessive musculature of shoulders, chest hanging between shoulders, elbows tied in or bowed out, turned feet, hare feet, hollow flanks, hanging stomach; rump too rounded, too narrow or falling off; low-set tail, raised rump, steepness or stiffness or slight angulation of hindquarters, light thighs, bowed or crooked legs, cow hocks, overangulated hock joints ("sickle hocks"), high hocks, bad positioning of hindquarters; roach back, swayback, thin or lean back, narrowness of loin, weak union with rump; stilted or inefficient gait; pounding, paddling, or flailing out of front legs; rolling or waddling gait, tottering hock joints, crossing over or interference in front or rear, lack of smoothness in gait; character faults such as lack of dignity and alertness, shyness, cowardice, treachery and viciousness (which does not include belligerence toward other dogs). ●

Photo: S. A. Thompson.

38 DOBERMAN
GERMANY

As the famous expert Setgast wrote, "Dog breeds so well adapted to defense and guard duties are very rare. The Doberman's physical qualities and his character have established him within a short time in the forefront. He is distrustful of strangers and prefers always to stay by his master. Ever vigilant, he darts his glance around incessantly as if to warn his master of possible danger. He is fearless. At a moment of danger his muscular body stiffens, his aspect becomes fierce, his eyes light up, and, at his master's first command, he attacks his adversary."

It is surprising to realize how selective breeding has established this breed in so short a time.

The Doberman's origin, such as we know it, is recent; the breed has existed for only several decades, and, if we go back further than the middle of the last century, we find specimens with little affinity among themselves. However, we know little about the Doberman's origins. The French tend to think that he derives from the Beauceron, and it is true that there is a clear resemblance between the two breeds. But most German dog fanciers trace the Doberman to different ancestors. Some claim that

he comes from Thuringia, from the town of Apolda, where a bailiff named Doberman (whence the name) was supposed to have successfully bred this dog from crosses among several breeds including the old German Shepherd and the German Pinscher. At first the breed was called "Belling," which appears to be the surname of the Apolda bailiff, though others claim that the Belling is another, different dog. Others consider that the old German Shepherd was the main influence in the Doberman's creation, through crossing it not only with the Pinscher but also with the Weimar Pointer. Still others credit the crossing of the Black and Tan Terrier with the Rottweiler, but this hypothesis is denied by Otto Goller, himself quite successful in Doberman breeding. It is said that Goller was the real selective breeder who definitely established the breed. In any case, it is probable that contributions of English blood were made, with the aim of refining the dog that at first was too heavy. Crosses were made with Black and Tan Terriers, plentiful in Germany. It appears that it was only in 1900 that the Doberman acquired its present slender, well-built form.

We have already mentioned his physical qualities and aptitude. He also has a great capacity for learning and is easy to train. Constitutionally robust, he appears to be tireless and ready at any moment to give his life for his master.

DOBERMAN

DOBERMAN

GENERAL CHARACTERISTICS The Doberman Pinscher is a dog of medium size and strong, muscular structure. In the elegant line of his body, in the proud and erect carriage, fine temperament, and resolute expression, the Doberman represents virtually the ideal of the normal-bodied dog. His outline is almost square, especially in the male. The Doberman is a faithful and fearless guard dog of solid and sensitive constitution. Training is relatively easy because of the dog's intelligence and natural aptitude for guard duty, his scenting ability, willingness to work, and obedience. He is a splendid house dog, both as companion and guard, and is thus a multipurpose dog.

SIZE Height at the withers: males 26-28 inches, the ideal being about 27½ inches; females 24-26 inches, the ideal about 25½ inches; length of head, neck, and legs in proportion to the length and depth of body.

HEAD The head must emerge markedly from the neck. Viewed from

above and in profile the head is a long truncated cone. The skin fits tightly over the bone structure and the flat muscles, providing a fine, lean structure. The nose is black. The muzzle is long and broad, with close-lying, tightly fitting lips. There should be a full complement of shining white teeth (42), meeting in a scissors bite. Viewed from front and in profile, the skull is flat. The top profile of the head and muzzle is formed by two parallel lines set off by the stop. The lines of the muzzle and forehead ascend from the nose to the top of the skull, then descend to the nape in a gentle curve. Viewed from front, the top of the skull is flat, that is, not curving toward the ears.

EYES Oval in form and of medium size, the eyes should be as dark as possible. For brown and blue dogs, a lighter shade is permissible, provided however that the eyes and nose are proportionately darker.

EARS Set on very high, carried erect

and clipped to a suitable length in proportion to the size of the head.

NECK The neck should be of a harmonious length in proportion to the body and the head. It should be lean and well muscled. Starting from the shoulders and withers, it should mount with a pleasing curve to the nape. The neck is carried erect, with great distinction.

FOREQUARTERS Viewed from any angle the forelegs must appear straight and perpendicular to the ground. They should be strongly built. The long bone of the upper arm meets the shoulder blade virtually at a right angle. The shoulder blade fits tightly against the body and is well muscled. It extends beyond the point where foreribs and spine are joined. The articulation of the elbow, formed by the juncture of forearm and humerus, is tight to the body. The wrist should turn neither inward nor outward. The forefeet are well arched, compact and catlike.

BODY The back is short, firm, of suf-ficient width and muscular at the loins, extending in a straight line from the withers to the slightly rounded croup. The withers should be strongly marked, especially in the male; the height and length of the withers determines the angle of the back line down to the croup. The loins are well muscled. The croup, formed by the sacral vertebrae, is rounded but not hollow. The gently arched ribs terminate beyond the articulation of the elbow, at which point, however, the position of the shoulder blade and humerus should be clearly apparent. The depth of the chest should be in good proportion to the length of the torso, and in any event it must not be less than half the height at the withers. The chest is of good width and with the forechest well defined. The belly is well tucked up, extending in a curved line from the brisket to the pelvis. (The female may be slighter longer in the body, affording room for the dugs.)

HINDQUARTERS The thigh is of good breadth, powerfully muscled and forming a robust stifle at the juncture with the hind leg. The angulation of the stifle is approximately 130 degrees. The hocks are strong, parallel, and set at a widely obtuse angle to the metatarsi, which are perpendicular to the ground. The feet are compact, arched catfeet, as on the forelegs. Dewclaws must be removed.

COAT Smooth-haired, short, hard, thick and close-lying. Invisible gray undercoat on neck permissible. **Color** Black, red blue, and fawn (the type of fawn known as Isabella) are accepted. Rust markings, sharply defined, appear above each eye and on the muzzle, throat and forechest, on all legs and feet and below the tail around the vent. Coloring of the nose should be solid black on black dogs, dark brown on red ones, dark gray on blue dogs, dark tan on fawns.

GAIT Free, balanced and vigorous, with good reach in the forequarters and good driving power in the hindquarters. In trotting, there is strong rear-action drive. Each rear leg moves in line with the foreleg on the same side. Rear and front legs are thrown neither in nor out. Back remains strong and firm. When moving at a fast trot, a properly built dog will single-track.

FAULTS Excessively arched nose, round skull, protruding cheecks, too little or too much stop, short or coarse head; pointed muzzle, loose lips, fewer than 42 teeth, overshot or undershot jaw; bulging or excessively deep-set eyes, light eyes; ears set on too high or too low; short, heavy neck, dewlap; short, straight shoulder; deviated elbow articulation; cow hocks; long, open or soft feet; large belly; light bone structure; excessively long back; hollow or roach back; hollow croup; carinate breast bone; flat ribs, shallow torso; insufficient chest development; one or both testes undescended; bad angulation of hindquarters; hocks turned inward or outward; long, soft or wavy hair; excessively light tan, not clearly defined and not pure, solid tan; white spots; visible undercoat; unsure, unrelaxed or jumpy gait; ambling gait; timidity, nervousness, cowardice. ●

Photo: A. Wintzell.

39 HOVAWART
GERMANY

This breed, which goes back to olden times, has been recently restored. It was mentioned in the *Sachsenspiegel* of Eike von Repgow around 1220, and the reproductions of that time show the dog to be similar to its present appearance. Writings of the Middle Ages indicate that it was used to guard the courtyard. It is mentioned again in 1473, with stress on its excellence as a guard. But through the centuries the Hovawart was neglected. Fifty years ago breeders renewed the breed through the use of subjects living in the Harz Mountains and the Black Forest. It is an easy dog to train, although only as an adult, since the Hovawart retains its puppy nature for a long time.

HOVAWART

GENERAL CHARACTERISTICS A robust working dog of medium weight, the Hovawart is strong and highly weather-resistant, a good runner and jumper, brave, attentive and quick to react. It is a splendid guard dog. Sexual characteristics should be clearly evident. His voice is deep, full, and powerful.

WEIGHT AND HEIGHT Weight: males 66-88 lb; females 55-77 lb. With variations of no more than 10 percent from these figures, dogs are conditionally suitable for breeding but open to penalties in showing; variations in excess of 10 percent exclude dogs from breeding and from show. Height at withers: males, 23½-27½ inches; females 21½-25½ inches. With variations from these figures no greater than 5 percent more or less, the dog is conditionally suitable for breeding but liable to penalties in show. Variations of more than 5 percent are grounds for exclusion from breeding and from showing.

HEAD Strong, with a broad, convex forehead. The muzzle is straight, neither too long nor too short. Maximum muzzle length should be equal to the distance from the occipital bone to the stop. Tight lips, well-formed muzzle. Teeth should be strong, with a scissors bite. A pincer (level) bite is allowed but is counted a fault in show, and dogs with a level bite are only conditionally eligible for breeding. Overshot and undershot jaws are disqualifying for show and breeding. The scalp must be tight-fitting.

EARS In proportion with the size and shape of the head. They should be triangular and set on high; they should cover the meatus. Ears too wide apart call for penalties and are condition-ally eligible for breeding. Exaggeration of this condition is a disqualifying fault for both show and breeding.

NECK Strong, moderately long, well clad but without mane.

FOREQUARTERS Straight, strong, well fringed. The angle of shoulder blade and humerus should be a right angle if possible. Free, elastic joints. Hard pads on the forefeet.

BODY Longer than the height at the withers. Broad torso, deep and rugged. Loose skin or dewlap disqualifying for both breeding and show. Straight back (saddle back is disqualification from breeding and show). Gently sloping croup, not too long.

TAIL Reaches beyond hocks but not to the ground. Well feathered, carried low in repose and high when the dog is excited or on attack.

HINDQUARTERS Well angulated and strongly muscled. Broad hocks, no dewclaws. A straight stern is a penalty fault and conditionally eligible for breeding. A high rump is disqualifying in both show and breeding.

COAT Long, not woolly, slightly wavy; dense, not curly; curly coat is penalty fault, and when exaggerated disqualifies from show and breeding. Parting of the coat is to be penalized and affects eligibility for breeding. **Color** Black, black and tan (small white ticking permissible), flaxen (with a dark shade preferred). Eyes, nose and nails to be of a color consistent with the basic coloring of coat, but not too light. ●

HOVAWART

40 ROTTWEILER
GERMANY

His origins are very old and the theories about his descent are numerous. The Germans, who have studied the question for some time, maintain that the breed is entirely German and that it was developed by butchers.

In any case, it is probably an ancient drover and not a dog used originally for guard or defense, although today he is expert in both.

Although a fancier such as Strebel claims that the Rottweiler descends from the Bavarois Bouvier, many others do not share his opinion. In ancient times this dog was prevalent in all the regions which, from the Swiss canton of Argovie, extend to the Nacker and Rottweil to the south of Württemberg, where the Romans had established an important military center. There they had brought a Mastiff (a distant descendent of the famous Tibetan Mastiff) which worked as a guard and a herder. It is said that this dog is the ancestor of the Rottweiler. It is certain that, since the herds of Argovie supplied vast zones in southern Germany, the breed which worked as a drover could have reached Germany and been bred there.

GENERAL CHARACTERISTICS The Rottweiler is a robust dog, above medium size, neither clumsy nor light, neither spindle-shanked nor like a Greyhound. His frame is compact, strong, and well proportioned and clearly shows self-confidence, great determination, agility, and endurance. Yet he is a good-natured dog, with remarkably alert reactions to his master and to his surroundings. He is a wonderful companion, especially with children, as a guard as well as a working dog. Psychologically he is outstanding for his superior learning capacity. With his unsuspicious nature and high degree of self-assurance, the Rottweiler reacts quietly and calmly in all circumstances. In the field he is a willing retriever and a good tracker.

SIZE Height at shoulders: males 23½-27 inches; females 21½-25 inches. In both sexes the height should be in harmony with the basic body structure.

HEAD Of medium length, with a broad skull. Viewed in profile, the fore-

Photo: E. Münch, S. A. Thompson.

head line is moderately arched. The occipital bone is well developed but not overly protruding. The stop is pronounced. The distance from the tip of the nose to the corner of the eye should not be longer than from the upper part of the head at the eye corner to the occipital bone. The scalp is tightly fitted, forming a slight wrinkle only when the dog is alerted—ideally, a head without wrinkles. The lips are black and firm, close-fitting to the teeth. The corners of the mouth are closed. The nose is invariably black; the bridge straight, broad at the root, and moderately tapered. The tip of the nose is well formed, broad rather than round, with relatively large nostrils. The teeth are strong and dentition is complete (42 teeth). The jaws meet in a scissors bite.

EYES Medium-sized, almond-shaped, dark brown, eyelids well fitting. The expression shows fidelity and gentleness.

EARS As small as possible, pendant, triangular, standing well away from each other and set on high, and carried well forward, thus closing the ear opening.

NECK Powerful, fairly long, well muscled, lean; the skin fits tightly. No dewlap.

FOREQUARTERS The shoulders are long and well set. The upper arm lies close to the body but without being constricted. The lower arm is strongly developed and well muscled. The pasterns are slightly springy and strong. The forefeet are round, very compact, and with arched toes. The pads are tough, the nails short, black and strong. Viewed from the front, the forelegs are straight and not set too close. The lower thighs, seen from the side, are also straight.

BODY The chest is deep and broad, with plenty of heart and lung room, and well developed in front. The ribs are well sprung. The back is straight, powerful, and rigid. The loins are short, powerful, and deep. The belly is not drawn up. The rump is broad, of medium length and slightly rounded; it must be neither straight nor fall away too much.

TAIL The tail should be docked at birth if very long. It should be short and strong and carried horizontally.

HINDQUARTERS The upper thigh is fairly long, broad, and well muscled; the lower thigh long, powerful, and extensively muscled. The hock joint is well angulated and not steep. The hind feet are somewhat longer than the forefeet; they are equally compact, the toes strong and well arched. There should be no dewclaws.

COAT Consists of both top coat and undercoat. The top coat is bristly, of medium length, rough, dense and close. The undercoat must not be visible through the top coat. The hair is a little longer on the forelegs, hind legs, and tail than on the rest of the body. **Color** Black, with well-defined, deep tan markings on the cheeks, muzzle, throat, chest, and legs as well as above the eyes and under the tail. The tan markings range from light tan to mahogany.

FAULTS General appearance too light in weight, with Greyhound traits; too high above hindquarters; overweight; too long, too short, or too thin in the body; head too narrow and long or too short and heavy; light or flesh-colored nose; concavity or convexity of nasal bridge; open lips or commissure; long or pointed muzzle with cheeks too pronounced; teeth damaged by distemper; overshot or undershot jaw; lack of premolars; flat forehead, with resulting lack of definition of the stop; exaggerated occipital protuberance; loose or wrinkled skin on head; head, muzzle, or expression like those of a hunting dog; light eyes, small eyes, eyes half-closed or too open; sharp expression of eyes; cow eyes. Ears set on too low; heavy, long, or thin ears; lack of substance to leather; ears flopping backward, carried too much on the side or with one ear carried differently from the other; neck excessively long, too thin, or lacking in muscle; loose skin on neck or dewlap; weak bone or muscle; straight or badly placed shoulders; forelegs too close together or not perpendicular to the ground; weak or rigid wrist; toes open, weak or too rigid, with nails light-colored or indrawn; flat ribs; excessively long back; saddleback or roach back; depression in croup; body too heavy or awkward; loins drawn up excessively; tail set on too high or too low, tail too thin or too long; flat thighs on hindquarters; narrow hocks, cow hocks, bowed hocks; still or excessively angulated metatarsus; dewclaws; soft coat, coat too short or too long, lacking in density or wavy; lack of undercoat; colors different from those listed above; tan markings badly delimited or lacking in purity; white markings; reversal of sexual characteristics; timidity, cowardice, gun-shyness, viciousness. ●

ROTTWEILER

ROTTWEILER

41 RIESENSCHNAUZER
GERMANY

The breed's origins are similar to those of the average Schnauzer and the Dwarf Schnauzer. Milia Pozzi Tarlarini states that after the average type was fixed, work was then begun on the formation of Giant and Dwarf Schnauzers. In the case of the Giant Schnauzer, the size and color derive from contributions of German Mastiff blood. It is also thought that they are a result of crossbreeding with the Bouvier des Flandres.

The selection was slow and patient, and when at last the Giant Schnauzer's characteristics were successfully attained, it was found that he was also a good herd dog and a leader of sheep. He then became popular as a "butcher's dog"—useful for guarding livestock. In Bavaria he is used as a guard dog in breweries, and today he is recognized everywhere as an excellent defense dog.

Photo: S. A. Thompson.

A GROUP OF FRIENDS IN THE ENGLISH COUNTRYSIDE

GENERAL CHARACTERISTICS The Riesenschnauzer or Giant Schnauzer is a larger and more powerful version of the Standard Schnauzer, which it should resemble as nearly as possible. Robust and powerful, this breed is squarely built, that is, the proportion of body length to height at the withers is very nearly 1:1. Calm but with considerable temperament, he is endowed with great courage, intelligence, constancy, and absolute fidelity to his master. He can take all kinds of weather, owing to his rough wiry coat, sturdy hindquarters, and powerful gait that can cover wide stretches of ground. Everything about the Schnauzer inspires respect, deserved also by the Giant because of his great size.

SIZE Height at the withers: males 25½-27½ inches; females 23½-25½ inches. The ideal height is the median between the maximum and minimum figures. Excessive size would hurt the Giant Schnauzer's efficiency as a working dog, just as falling below the minimum would also have a negative effect. Besides proper height, good proportions among the various parts of the body must also be taken into account, with preference given to animals of good line and litheness as opposed to coarseness and heaviness.

HEAD Strong, rectangular, elongated, narrowing slightly from the ears to eyes to tip of nose. Length of the head should be about half that of the back from the withers to the root of the tail. The head conforms to the sex and substance of the individual. The bridge is parallel to the topline of the skull; the stop is not pronounced, but it is emphasized by the eyebrows. The skull, from occiput to stop, is moderately broad between the ears. The top of the skull is flat, the occiput not pronounced. The cheeks are flat but well muscled, free of cheekiness. The muzzle is strong and well filled under the eyes. It is equal in length to the skull. Its shape is that of a moderately blunt wedge. The nose is large and black. The black lips fit tightly without overlapping. The teeth should be complete (42), and the jaws should meet in a scissors bite.

EYES Oval, dark-colored, well directed to the fore; visible haws are a fault.

EARS Should be cropped to equal length and set on high. Uncropped ears are of button type and V-shaped.

NECK Powerful, well arched, of moderate length, set well into the shoulders. The skin should fit tightly at the throat, with no dewlap.

FOREQUARTERS The shoulders should be sloping, strongly muscled, yet flat. The forearm is well angulated. The forelegs are straight and vertical when viewed from any side, with good bone and strong pasterns. It is a fault if the forelegs are too close together. Catfeet, with rugged pads, the toes well joined, the nails dark. Hair on the feet is short.

BODY The Giant should exhibit the kind of strength typical of the Standard Schnauzer. The chest is medium in width, the ribs well sprung but not suggesting a barrel chest; it is oval as viewed from the front and deep at the brisket. The brisket descends at least to the elbows and rises to a moderately tucked-up belly. The body is short-coupled, the loins well developed but short, in keeping with the desired compactness of build. The back is short and straight, but not without a slight, elegant curve made by the harmonious configuration of a strong first dorsal vertebra, straight topline, and a gently rounded croup to the root of the tail. As mentioned above, the length of the body is approximately the same as the height at the withers.

TAIL Set on moderately high and carried high when the dog is animated. It should be docked to the second or third joint, but never beyond (i.e., 1½ to about 3 inches at maturity).

HINDQUARTERS Must be well angulated if they are to give the Giant all the power needed in a working dog. The hindquarters are strongly muscled, in balance with the forequarters. The thighs are slanting and well bent at the stifles; the second thighs are approximately parallel to an extension of the upper neckline. The metatarsi are short and vertical in normal position and, viewed from the rear, are parallel. Feet are as described for the forequarters.

COAT Hard, wiry, and quite dense; perfection of such a coat should be one of the chief objectives of the breeder. The undercoat is soft. When seen against the grain, the outer coat stands slightly off the back, lying neither smooth nor flat. On the head the hair must be coarse and without undercoat. The hair of the beard and eyebrows must be long and coarse, the hallmark of the Giant Schnauzer. A goat's beard is to be avoided, however. **Color** Black or salt and pepper (see description of the Standard Schnauzer, #45, of which many other details also apply to the Giant). ●

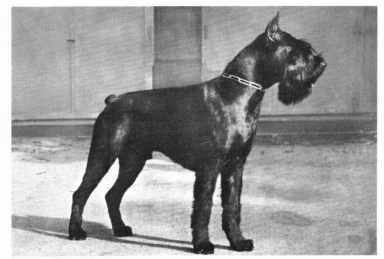

RIESENSCHNAUZER

96

Photo: S. A. Thompson.

42 BRAZILIAN GUARD DOG

Fila Brasileiro

BRAZIL

BRAZILIAN GUARD DOG

Among the more than 300 officially recognized dog breeds there is one that has won adherents in many countries. This is the Cão de Fila, or Brazilian Fila. Its origins, as with many breeds, are obscure. It is thought to have derived from cross-breeding of dogs that came to Brazil with the Portuguese or Spanish Conquistadors—Bloodhounds, Mastiffs, and English Bulldogs. These were bred according to the work the dog was meant to do. In the Fila are found characteristics of all three breeds.

The sad look certainly reminds one of the Bloodhound, from which the Fila has inherited its keen scent. Its powerful physique recalls the Mastiff, which demands respect by its very presence, and to this quality is added an almost savage courage and innate vigilance. Finally, the Bulldog has given him the old impetuous and implacable nature. He does not, however, kill his victim when he catches him, but holds him until the arrival of his master. This behavior of the Fila is of even greater importance when we consider that formerly it was used to capture fugitive slaves, whom he located by his excellent scent, and returned them alive to their masters. The dog is extremely useful in guarding livestock. He can control the herd on his own, and a timely nip can bring the most obstinate steer to heel.

It is clear that such dogs cannot feel at home in the city. They are meant to stay in the country where they can freely use their strength and where their strong constitution is not limited in its development. Sidewalks, no matter how wide, do not permit these dogs the freedom they need. Although it has a rather frightening appearance and is always ready to attack, the Fila has a docile nature and is devoted to his master. On the other hand, he is suspicious of strangers and does not permit the slightest familiarity. As a magnificent guard dog he has a successful show record worldwide.

GENERAL CHARACTERISTICS The Fila Brasileiro is a breed typical of the Mastiff group. He is a dog of impressive bearing, with strong bone and muscle. The body is longer than it is high, well proportioned and symmetrical.

HEAD Invariably big and heavy compared to the rest of the body—a massive, square head, typically brachycephalic (short, broad skull). The tip of the nose is broad, well developed, and takes up much of the front part of the upper jaw. It is black, except in chocolate, brown, or chocolate-and-brown-spotted dogs, in which case the nose may be brown. The upper lips are heavy and pendulous, overlapping the lower lips and imparting a typically square Mastiff look. The lips are firm at the point of the maxillaries and loose on the sides, with sawtooth edges. The muzzle is strong and broad, shorter than the skull, but always in good proportion to it. Deep throughout its length, the muzzle ends in a nearly vertical plane. The teeth are strong and white, with well-spaced canines. The upper incisors are broad at the roots and pointed. The jaws close in a scissors bite. The stop, viewed from the front, is practically nonexistent and becomes a furrow that continues longitudinally almost to midskull. Viewed in profile, however, the stop is well defined by the prominent supraorbital ridges. The skull, large and broad, narrows abruptly at the start of the muzzle. The occiput is prominent.

EYES Dark, medium size, slightly almond-shaped, set well apart and deep in their sockets. Because of the loose skin the Fila's eyelids are often drooping; this should not be considered a fault since it contributes to the dog's characteristic pensive expression.

EARS Large, V-shaped, set on far back, although the exact position on the skull depends on the quality of the skin. On the alert, the ears are lifted high by the scalp, possibly reaching the level of the occiput; in repose the skin is down and the ears drop back to reveal the under surface of the leather. Mastiff ears (dropped to the sides of the head), folded, and rose ears also occur in the breed.

NECK The Fila has an extraordinarily thick neck, with very strong muscles. It is rather shorter than long; the nape is harmoniously curved. There should be a moderate dewlap.

BODY Powerful. The skin is thick and loose. The ribs are well sprung, the chest broad and well let down, the brisket at least down to the elbow. The pectoral muscles are well in evidence. The shoulders are well angulated. The points of the scapulae do not join, and the distance between them causes the withers to be low and flat. The back is strong, fairly straight, but gently rising toward the croup, which is slightly higher than the backline. From the forepart of the ilium the croup slopes gracefully into the base of the tail. The belly is only slightly drawn up.

TAIL The root of the tail is very broad and tapers rapidly to a point at the tip. When down, the tail reaches the hocks. It is slightly curved at the end. When the dog is excited, the tail is raised and the curve is accentuated. The tail must never be carried over the back or curled.

FOREQUARTERS Well set into the trunk, well spaced out by the breadth of the chest. The legs are straight and perpendicular to the ground. The forearm is well boned, the pasterns slightly sloped. **HINDQUARTERS** Less strongly boned, the hindquarters are slightly higher than the forequarters, with not very pronounced angulations. The hocks are only slightly bent. **FEET** Well arched toes, well directed forward. Black nails, although the nails may be white if the toes are spotted with white.

COAT Short, soft, dense and smooth. **Color** All colors and shades thereof are allowed. In self-colored or streaked coats, white markings are common on the chest, throat, feet and tip of the tail. **Skin** Thick and elastic, loose especially on neck and trunk.

GAIT The pace is long, measured, and elastic, seemingly heavy, somewhat feline. Typical also of the Fila are certain rolling and waddling movements. In walking, the dog's tail, which is raised, moves rhythmically from side to side in time with the body movements. When the tail is down, the movement of the hindquarters should be equally apparent in the croup and in the ribs. The trot is easy and elastic, with great drive in the hind legs, and covers a lot of ground. In movement the Fila usually holds his head lower than the backline.

DISQUALIFICATIONS Undershot jaw showing teeth when mouth is closed; one or both testes undescended; cropped ears or docked tail; wholly white coat; flesh-colored nose.

FAULTS Major: small head; skimpy upper lip; bulging eyes, traces of albinism; tight-fitting skin; rigid gait (i.e., without waddle); timidity, cowardice. **Serious:** undershot or overshot condition; light bone; shallow chest; croup lower than withers; short pace; friendliness to strangers. **Minor:** Any variation from standard.
In deciding quality of breed, the judge should prefer a dog with several light faults to one with fewer but more serious faults. ●

43 CANAAN DOG

ISRAEL

The Canaan dog is an indigenous breed of Israel where it is used as a guard, defense, and shepherd dog. It has proved a useful auxiliary to the Israeli army as guard dog and messenger during the conflicts of recent years. When it was imported into the United States it aroused the interest of local dog fanciers and is widely bred in California. The breed is recognized by the F.C.I. and the American Kennel Club.

GENERAL CHARACTERISTICS A medium-sized, well-proportioned dog. Alert, sharp, distrustful of strangers, aggressive but not quarrelsome, vigilant not only against human invaders but also against animals (in the great shepherd dog tradition), extraordinarily devoted to its master, and docile. When well kept the Canaan Dog is firmly attached to its home and shows no tendency to stray. Can serve as guard dog, as shepherd, as guide for the blind, or as a search dog in the mines.

WEIGHT AND SIZE The weight range is 40-55 lb. Height: 19½-23½ inches, with males considerably taller than females. The Israeli standard gives a "coefficient of robustness" of 20-25.

HEAD Well proportioned, not at all heavy or clumsy but at the same time lacking the excessive delicacy of the Greyhound, for example. The head is rather long, with the length exceeding the breadth and depth by a considerable margin. It is blunt and wedge-shaped, not too broad in the frontal region, although it gives an impression of breadth because of the low setting on of the ears. The skull is not domed, nor is it flat. It is approximately equal in length to the muzzle or perhaps a trifle longer. The stop is very slightly accentuated. The foreface is longer than it is broad or deep. It is better if the preorbital depression is absent or only slightly marked. The angle be-

Photo: S. A. Thompson, MARKA.

CANAAN DOG

44 GERMAN MASTIFF
Deutsche Dogge

GERMANY

If the larger dogs are almost always thickset and rather heavy, this is certainly not the case with the German Mastiff. Although a giant among the breeds, he is pleasingly nimble and remarkably agile.

Opinions about his origin are far from agreement. Even his name varies from country to country. The Italians and English call him a Dane or Great Dane, although he certainly does not come from Denmark. Today in France it is known as Dogue Allemand, in Italy as Alano Tedesco, in Germany as Deutsche Dogge, all of which mean German Mastiff. According to the most plausible theories, the German Mastiff was bred by Germans through crossing Mastiffs and Greyhounds.

As Greyhounds were spread throughout the Mediterranean and then into Gaul by Phoenician merchants, some Mastiffs from Assyria and India also must have reached Europe in this way. Having arrived in France and England, these Mastiffs spread through the north of Germany, giving birth to the *Canis familiaris decumanus*, which was probably the ancestor of the German Mastiff, whose descendents during the Middle Ages were doubtless the German Saupacker.

Another hypothesis indicates its Asiatic origin as having arrived with the Alans, a Scythian people who used the Mastiff for the hunt and protection. When they arrived in Germany these Mastiffs became "civilized" through crossbreeding with Greyhounds, so as to achieve a sturdy dog of great size that would also have speed and form. According to others, the Pointer also contributed to the German Mastiff of today.

According to Mégnin, the large dogs that came with the Alans produced, after many crossbreedings, not only the German and Bordeaux Mastiffs but also other large-sized breeds of various countries.

Even outside Germany the German Mastiff is one of the most popular guard and defense dogs. In England, France, the United States, and Italy specialized breeders have joined German breeders in producing specimens of great value.

---

tween the topline of the muzzle and the line between nose and lower jaw is rather acute (from 40 to 50 degrees). The nose is preferably dark, but lack of pigment has been allowed to date (especially in harlequins); the size of the nose is in good proportion to the rest of the dog. The lips should not be too thick; they should be tight to the jaws; pendulous not desirable. Good pigmentation desirable but not mandatory. Teeth should comprise a complete set, including the premolars. A scissors bite is preferred but a level bite is not a fault. Overshot or undershot jaw is a fault.

EYES Slanting slightly; the darker the better. Unpigmented corners normal in harlequins, permissible but not desirable with other colors.

EARS Prick ears are the desired type, with a relatively broad base and rounded tip. The ears are set on low and wide apart; not high and long as are the ears of the Alsatian, for example. Button ear and all ear types intermediate between prick and drop ears permissible but not desirable.

NECK Well arched, free of clumsiness. It is of medium length, well in proportion to body and head, well muscled, without flabbiness of skin or dewlap.

FOREQUARTERS The forelegs should be straight when viewed from front. The bones are slighter than in most breeds of comparable size. The shoulders are well angulated and slope back well. The forearm is straight and sufficiently long to ensure the square shape of the body outline. The muscles are well developed. The angle formed by shoulder blade and humerus is 100-110 degrees. The elbow is of medium angular opening. The wrist is fairly strong, the pastern is straight, not too short, not knuckled. The forefeet are nearly catlike, with hard pads and color varying with color of coat.

BODY The body is generally strong but not too massive or clumsy. The topline is straight, with a slight slope from withers to croup. The withers are well accentuated; they are the highest point of the body. The back is short and firm, of sufficient width and extending in a straight line from withers to croup. The brisket is deep and of medium breadth. The croup should be neither too short nor too slender, nor should it fall off. The chest is deep, reaching at least to the level of the elbows, without excessive breadth. The belly is well tucked up, the flanks short but well muscled.

TAIL Carried curled over the back when the dog is alerted. It is set on very high and is very bushy.

HINDQUARTERS Proportional to the forelegs, that is, sufficiently long to ensure the square shape of the basic

body frame. The thigh should be strongly muscled, broad but not corpulent. The coxal-femoral angle should be between 110 and 120 degrees. Viewed from behind, the legs must be straight, with no tendency to cow hocks or bow hocks. The femoral-tibial angle may vary from 100 to 110 degrees. It should be free in its movement and not overly angulated (as, for example, in the German Shepherd). The hocks should be broad, with the angulation approximately 120 degrees. The heel bone should be a straight continuation of the metatarsus, which should be well let down. The description of the forefeet applies equally to the hind feet.

COAT Medium-long, straight and harsh, with an undercoat varying with the season. Smooth and long hair are allowed but are less desirable. Legs should be well feathered. The tail is plumed; a mane is desirable in the male. **Color** Sandy to red-brown, white or black; large white markings permissible, even desirable, with all colors. Harlequin of all kinds as well as dark and white masks are also permissible. Boston Terrier markings are frequently found. Gray and black-and-tan are not desirable in order to differentiate the Canaan from similar European sporting breeds. **Skin** Of medium thickness, tight to body. Pigmentation of skin conforms to color of coat.

GAIT A short, fast, natural trot is the characteristic gait of the Canaan dog in action.

FAULTS Aside from failure to meet the requirements of the official standard, all defects in body structure which conflict with that of the typical Canaan dog. ●

CANAAN DOG—Dingo variety

BODY Square or rectangular. When the length is greater than the height, this is due to the shortness of the legs and not to the length of back or loin. Chest let down, not too narrow; ribs well rounded; withers well developed; loin arched, belly slightly tucked up.

HEAD Well proportioned, not too heavy or coarse, occasionally with more accentuated stop. Often the length of the skull tends to increase in proportion to the length of the muzzle. The head, although reminiscent of the Collie's, is closer to that of the Dingo.

EARS Rarely erect or semi-erect, most commonly of button type, with all the stages intermediate between erect and lightly pendulous ears.

NECK Straight, occasionally short. ●

GENERAL CHARACTERISTICS The German Mastiff (also called the Great Dane) is a dog of noble appearance, robust and exceptionally well built, proud, powerful and elegant. It has been called "The Apollo of Breeds." Its fine head is highly expressive, and it never shows any signs of nervousness, not even in its most emotional manifestations. Standing still, the dog looks like a noble statue. A nervous or frightened dog, no matter what its other esthetic qualities may be, should not be given any rating higher than "insufficient." Its character is friendly, affectionate with the family, especially with children, suspicious of strangers.

SIZE The minimum height at the withers is 31½ inches for males and 28 inches for females. It is desirable, however, that the height be in excess of this minimum limit.

HEAD Long, narrow, important, highly expressive, well chiseled (particularly in the suborbital region), with a very pronounced stop. The nose should be large and black in solid-colored or streaked dogs; in the case of harlequin German Mastiffs further details are given below under the heading COLOR. (A nose medially furrowed is excluded from all awards.) The muzzle should be full, with abundant lips, the forward profile of which should form a right angle with the point of the nose; the commissure is well marked. Seen in profile, the forehead should be de-

cidedly set off from the bridge. Forehead and bridge should be parallel. Seen from in front, the head appears narrow, the nasal bridge rather broad, the masseters are only slightly visible, and never pronounced. The lower jaw should be neither protruding nor regressive. The teeth are highly developed and strong, white and closing in a good scissors bite; the position of the teeth is correct if the inner side of the upper incisors barely touch the outer side of the lower incisors, like the blades of a scissors (scissors bite). Any deviation from such scissors dentition is to be considered a fault and to be judged accordingly. Generally speaking, to establish the position of the upper jaw in relation to the lower jaw judges must base their decision on the latter, because of its great mobility. The length of the head should if possible be divided into two equal parts: first, from the tip of the nose to the stop; the second, from the stop to the occipital protuberance (which is not accentuated). The head, seen from any angle, should appear well formed in its outward lines, and at the same time it should harmonize fully, as to expression and dimensions, with the overall dimensions of the body.

EYES Well closed, of medium size, round, dark, with a lively and intelligent expression; the eyelashes are well developed.

EARS Set on high, not too far apart, long and pointed, but always in good

GERMAN MASTIFF ▶

Photo: T. McHugh (Photo Res.), MARKA.

GERMAN MASTIFF

proportion to the size of the head, and in such a way that they are carried firm and erect. In dogs whose ears are not carried according to the standard, the rating of the dog shall be lowered (dogs with hanging ears or excessively docked ears shall not be rated "excellent"; dogs with natural ears shall be excluded from awards).

NECK The neck is set on high, it is long, lean, muscular, vigorous, with well fitting skin and without dewlap. The neck tapers slightly toward the head, with a fine, clean, elegantly arched line and with a well marked nape.

FOREQUARTERS The scapula should be long and sloping, forming an angle of about 90° with the upper arm: this permits a greater amplitude of pace. The upper arm should be strong and muscular; the elbows should be turned neither in nor out, and the articulation should be vertical. The forearm is robust and, seen either from in front or in profile, it runs in a straight line from the elbow to the feet. The pastern, seen from in front, is on the same straight line to the feet; in profile, the pastern is seen to be slightly sloped forward. The feet are rounded, turned neither in nor out. The toes are short, well arched and compact (catfeet). The nails are short, robust and if possible, dark.

BODY The thorax has plenty of room, with a well developed rib cage with the brisket down to the elbows. The withers should mark the highest point of the robust back. The backline slopes very slightly, but is straight, robust, and clean. The back is short. In the ratio between height and length, the build should, if possible, be square in outline; in females a slightly longer back is permitted. The loins are slightly rounded and robust. The croup is full, slightly hollowed, and slopes gently to the insertion of the tail. The belly is well drawn up toward the loins and is well supported, forming a graceful lower line to the body.

TAIL Of medium length, the tail should reach and slightly surpass the point of the hock. The root is set on high and is thick, tapering gradually to a fine and elegant tip. In repose the tail should hang straight; when the dog is excited or in movement, the tail is slightly curved (saber tail) and raised, but not to the point where it rises above the backline.

HINDQUARTERS The thigh is broad and muscular, the legs are long and strong. The ideal solid position of the hindquarters is achieved when the articulations of the haunch, the stifle and the hock do not have too open an angulation. Seen from behind, the hindquarters should appear absolutely straight, not deviating inward or outward. The feet are similar to the forefeet.

COAT Hair Very short and dense, close fitting and glossy. **Color** (a) **Streaked coat:** The color ranges from a light golden yellow to a deep golden yellow, with transverse black streaks which are continuous and very evident. The more intense and glossy the background color, the more de- cided are the streaks and to so much greater an extent does the color of the coat approach the ideal. Small white spots on the chest or toes are not desirable, nor are light-colored nails or eyes. (b) **Fawn coat:** Ranging from light golden yellow to deep golden yellow; a black mask is desirable, as are black nails. Golden yellow is always the preferable color. (c) **Blue coat:** The color should be, if possible, pure steel blue, with no yellow or black tone. In blue dogs lighter eyes and white spots are more tolerable. (d) **Black coat** A glossy black, dark eyes. (e) **Harlequin coat (white-black):** The background color should be pure white, if possible with no spotting, with black markings with irregular borders distributed over the entire body (permissible, but not desirable, are a few small gray or brown spots). The eyes should be dark. Permissible but not desirable, lighter eyes or eyes of a different color. The nose should be black, but spotted or flesh-colored noses are admissible. Dogs with white coats with large black markings are judged as black Great Danes; the same is true for Great Danes whose black coat extends over the whole body, leaving only the color, legs and the tip of the tail white.

GAIT Ample, slightly springy.

FAULTS Head Forehead descending or noticeably ascending. Bridge concave, convex or puglike, with stop either lacking or insufficiently accentuated. Bridge too narrow, or inserted wedgelike in the skull; skull excessively rounded ("apple head"), muscling of the cheeks excessively accentuated. Pointed muzzle, or lips to flaccid and hanging down over the lower jaw; so-called "flying lips," which give the illusion of a full, deep muzzle which in reality is not there. A short, but important, head is preferable to a long, light and expressionless head. The lower incisors in front of the upper (undershot), or touching beneath the upper dental arch (overshot), or with the upper in-

GERMAN MASTIFF

GERMAN MASTIFF

GERMAN MASTIFF IN GERMANY ▶

Photo: A. Roslin-Williams, S. A. Thompson, Fotostampa, J. L. Stage (Photo Res.).

ENGLISH BRED GERMAN MASTIFFS

GERMAN MASTIFF

cisors meeting the lower in a pincers bite. This last position can be the cause of premature wearing down of the teeth. All deviations from the scissors bite are irregular, and those dogs which show them should be penalized in ratings. Distempered teeth are also faulty, since cavities or decay underneath are to be assumed: in this case the teeth appear to be corroded and have a brownish color. This fault is not, however, transmittable; dogs with distempered teeth should not be rated "excellent." Tartar on the teeth is to be discouraged. **Eyes** Well open, light, penetrating, amber yellow, light blue, darker blue, or of other color; eyes too far from each other or half-closed; lower eyelids falling, thus revealing the haw. For the color of the eyes, see further details below under COLOR. **Neck** Short, stocky; flaccid skin, over abundant and loose; dewlap. **Forequarters** Straight shoulder or shoulder not carried close to body; one of the causes of the former fault is the insufficient sloping of the scapula; a cause of the latter is bad elbow position. Elbows turned inward or outward; the former position is generally caused by narrowness and insufficient height of the brisket, and this causes the forelegs to be too close to each other and consequently the dog, in trying to establish support, turns outward the lower part of the legs. Elbows turned out cause the turning in of the feet and toes. A noticeable curving of the wrist region is an indication of weakness (yielding of the joints), and is generally accompanied by toes which are very long and open. Deviation from a straight line is also a defect in the legs, with the wrist turned in or out (French position). Swelling of the foot joints is also bad. Such swelling of joints in most cases is caused by bone disease (rickets). Open toes, crushed toes, long toes (harefeet), turned in or out. Nails excessively long. **Body** Chest narrow or of insufficient depth; flat ribs, with the sternum protruding excessively (chicken-breasted). Saddleback or roach back. Height of hindquarters greater than height of forequarters (the dog is thrown forward); penalties are also incurred by a long back, since this has a bad effect on the gait (rolling gait). Excessively hollowed croup, falling belly, and, in females, dugs not well drawn up. Male dogs having one or both testicles not evident are excluded from prize awards. Tail too thick, too long, set on low, carried above the backline; hooked or curled, deviated laterally. Dogs with these faults should not be rated "excellent." Broken or docked tail (docking the tail to meet the standard for length is prohibited). Brush tails (excessive fringe) are not desirable; it is prohibited to shave the tail. **Hindquarters** When the stifle is deviated outward, there is an inward deviation of the hock, and the dog takes the position known as "cowhocked," while at the same time the feet turned outward. The contrary position is that in which the hocks are very wide apart (barrel hocks). The defect known as "straight hindquarters" occurs when the angulations of the haunch, knee and hock are too obtuse, in such a way as to form a line which is almost straight. An excessively accentuated angulation is objectionable, and this occurs when the bones of the hindquarters are too long in proportion to those of the forelegs. **Feet** Presence of the fifth toe with characteristics of the dewclaw; for the rest, as given under forequarters. **Hair** Too long, disorderly and dull (generally caused by bad nutrition, worms, and lack of care). **Color** (a) **Streaked coat:** Gray-blue or isabella background color, washed-out streaking, white stripe on the forehead, white collar, white feet, white tip on tail. Dogs of this type are not to be awarded prizes. (b) **Fawn coat:** The colors gray-yellow, blue-yellow, isabella, dull yellow are to be rated low. White spots are to be judged as for the streaked dogs. (c) **Blue coat:** Blue-yellow or blue-black color. Light eyes, wall eyes. (d) **Black coat:** Yellowish black, brown-black, blue-black. Light eyes. White marks are permissible. Dogs with black mantle are to be judged with black Great Danes. (e) **White-black coat (Harlequin):** Blue gray or speckled background. Watery eyes, red or bleary eyes. The following are to be excluded from awards: (1) white dogs with no black marks (albinos), and dove-gray dogs; (2) the so-called porcelain coats, which have evident blue-gray yellow or even streaked markings; (3) the so-called gray-streaked, which have a gray background. **Gait** Short step, narrow gait or gait lacking in freedom of movement; ambling gait. ●

Photo: S. A. Thompson, Fotostampa.

45 SCHNAUZER
GERMANY

Dogs have always been known as the companions of horsemen. Some breeds, especially the Schnauzer, have a genuine predilection for the horse.

When Europe, especially Central Europe, was covered with great forests, and travelers had to make their trips by stagecoach, the Schnauzer invariably was a member of the party. By day he ran beside the horses, almost under their hooves, from time to time running ahead of them to inspect the route and barking furiously if he noted anything suspicious. At night he slept beside the coachman.

This dog's origins are confused and may be traced back to the oldest terriers. The Schnauzer is, moreover, a true terrier and, in Italy, France, and some other countries he is classed with guard dogs, at which work he is expert. Nevertheless, he can still be included among the terriers, as suggested by its name, Schnauzer-Pinscher ("Pinscher" is German for terrier). Although rarely used against burrow-living animals, it shows great aptitude in hunting rats, skunks, and martens.

Originally found in Württemberg, Bavaria, and Baden, the breed has long been prevalent in northern Switzerland and France. It was shown in Germany in 1879 under the name of Coarsehaired Pinscher.

His many qualities (he is vigilant, strong, hardy, dynamic, faithful, and intelligent) make him a particularly useful dog for guard and personal defense. He is also much esteemed as a companion because of his happy nature and amusing aspect, with his moustache, formed by long muzzle hairs, and his long eyebrows.

GENERAL CHARACTERISTICS The Schnauzer is a coarsehaired dog, of medium size, more robust than delicate, square in outline, with the height at the withers approximately equal to the length of the trunk. The ideal male is slightly shorter than the female. The typical features of the Schnauzer insofar as character is concerned are an enterprising temperament and a serene, easygoing nature. His friendly disposition is shown in his willingness to play and in his gentle way with children. He is exceptionally affectionate toward his master but highly suspicious of strangers; as a guard dog he is faithful but not unduly noisy. The Schnauzer has a highly developed sense of smell. His prudence, his tractability to training, his absolute fidelity, his inexhaustible attentiveness, his courage, constancy and resistance to both weather and sickness are his chief qualities, which go far to make the Schnauzer possibly the best of all breeds as a guard dog and pet.

SIZE Height: 18-19½ inches, with males slightly smaller than females. Smaller dogs are deficient.

HEAD Long and powerful, narrowing gradually from the ears to the eyes and from the eyes to the tip of the nose. The length of the head is about half the length from the withers to the root of the tail. Thus the head length is always important in judging, and it should always be in keeping with the sex of the dog and in good proportion to the dog's development. The nose is full and black. The bridge and the plane of the forehead are parallel. The lips should fit closely; they must be black in both varieties. The muzzle is wedge-shaped. The muscles of the jaws should be strongly developed, but not to the point that they cause widening of the masseters, since such widening would disturb the rectangular outline of the head (including beard). The teeth should be normal, very strong, sound, and white, closing in a scissors bite. The stop should be well accentuated and must be visible between the eyebrows. The forehead should be flat and free of wrinkling.

EYES Dark, oval, directed straight ahead; the lower lid fits closely, and the haw should never be visible.

EARS Set on high, of equal size and shape.

SCHNAUZER

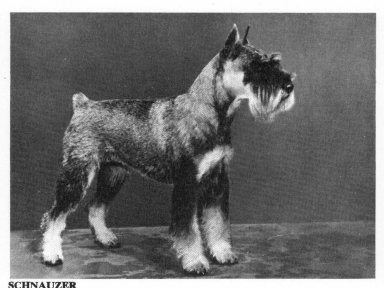

SCHNAUZER

Photo: A. Wintzell.

SCHNAUZER

NECK Elegant and of good thrust. The meeting with the shoulders should be robust and in harmony with the overall physique of the dog. It should not be too long, too short or too thick. The nape is strong and beautifully arched. On the throat the skin should be well fitting and without folds (dry neck).

BODY Of medium size, with flat ribs; in cross section it is oval. When the ribs are properly sprung the brisket reaches below the elbows. So far as possible, the beginning of the sternum should extend forward to give proper shape to the chest. The total length of the trunk is approximately equal to the height at the withers; this means that the back is short, solid and slightly dipped behind the withers, that is, that the backline is not straight like a taut string but describes an elegant, slightly rising line from the withers, along the top line, over a slightly falling rump to the root of the tail. The belly is moderately tucked up. The distance from the last false rib to the middle of the trunk should be short, to enhance the compact appearance of the dog. Dogs that are too low or too high on their limbs, light or with Greyhound characteristics are deficient.

TAIL Set on high and carried in various ways, according to the temperament of the individual dog. It is cut at the third (and never after the fourth) joint. Dogs born with short tails must have at least one joint apparent.

FOREQUARTERS The shoulders are slanted and well angulated with the

forearm; the muscling is flat but robust. The forelegs should be straight as seen from any angle. Only slightly angulated shoulders (as in terriers) and legs set too close together are faults. **HINDQUARTERS** The thighs are well slanted and muscular. The hocks should be well angulated. **FEET** Short and round, with well-closed and arched toes (catfeet). The nails are black, the pads strong and solid.

COAT The Schnauzer is a coarse-coated dog, the hair strong, hard and dense. As seen against the grain it should be raised from the body, that is, neither flat nor close-fitting nor too short, but rather held up by the undercoat. The hair forms a characteristic rigid beard and bristly eyebrows which slightly shade the eyes. On the forehead and ears the hair is shorter than elsewhere; it is coarse, however, over the entire head. Bristly, wavy hair, curled or tangled, is a fault. **Color** The coat should be salt and pepper or solid black. The ideal for the breeder is a medium shade of bright salt and pepper distributed evenly over the body, with a gray undercoat. All shades, from dark iron gray to silver gray, are permissible. All color tones, however, must set off the Schnauzer's expression by providing a dark mask in harmony with the general coloring, without being either too light or too dark. Faded or dull colors, lack of salt-and-pepper quality, or white markings are faults. Other faults include the mixing of such colors as rust, brown, red, yellow, spots and streaking; a dark streak on the back or a black saddle. ●

46 LEONBERG
GERMANY

Opinions are mixed concerning the origins of the Leonberg. Some hold that he descends from the ancient Tibetan Mastiff; others, that he is a product of selective breeding performed by Essig, a resident of Leonberg, Württemberg. He is supposed to have crossed specimens obtained at the St. Bernard hospice with Newfoundlands and perhaps also with Great Pyrenees. He had great difficulty in fixing the characteristics of the new breed and only in 1949 was the official standard published, clearly indicating the differences between this dog and the St. Bernard.

GENERAL CHARACTERISTICS The Leonberg is a big dog, extremely muscular yet elegant and well proportioned, with a lively temperament.
SIZE Minimum heights for males and females, respectively, are 30 and 27½ inches.
HEAD The upper part of the head is moderately domed, but it must never even approach the length and depth of the St. Bernard's head. It must appear generally longer than it is wide. The nose is less obviously open than in the St. Bernard. The lips should be well fitted and not pendulous as in the St. Bernard, and there must be no slavering. The skin on the head and muzzle must always be close-fitting, and there should be no wrinkles on the forehead. The muzzle is moderately deep, sufficiently well proportioned and never pointed. The cheeks are not greatly developed.

The teeth are very strong, with good adaptation between lower and upper jaws. The stop is not pronounced, the bridge is proportionately broad, continuous and slightly arched.

EYES The eyes range from light brown to brown (yellow eyes are objectionable). They are of medium size, with a friendly, intelligent expression. They must never have a terrier-like shape nor should they be "pigeyes" or like the Bulldog's. The lids close well over the eyes without showing the haw, which is of a light color and not red, like the haw in the St. Bernard.

EARS The ears are set on high but not too far back; they are as wide as they are long, rounded at the tips and well feathered with long hair.

NECK Moderately long, without dewlap.

Photo: S. A. Thompson.

LEONBERG

BODY Slightly longer than the St. Bernard's, with strong loins, a deep chest, with no barreling of the ribs. A strong back is a prime requisite in the Leonberg.

TAIL Bushy, the tail is always carried "at half mast," not too high and never curled over the back.

FOREQUARTERS The forelegs are straight, normally positioned, not too close together and well articulated. The shoulders are sloped, the elbows close to the body and slightly above the lower edge of the brisket. **FEET** Well closed and quite rounded; hare-feet are not acceptable. The toes are almost invariably webbed. Generally the Leonberg loves the water and is a good swimmer. **HINDQUARTERS** The thighs are well muscled. The articulation of the stifle is well formed, with strong hocks well tendoned and tending to be slightly angulated rather than straight. Dewclaws are considered a fault and if present should

be removed about the 14th day after birth.

COAT Of medium softness, perhaps slightly harsh, without being bristly. The hair is quite long and fits closely to the body, always letting the form of the body be seen despite the fairly thick undercoat. The hair is always smooth but possibly with a slight wave. Tangled or curly hair is a fault. There is a very evident mane on the neck and chest. **Color** Light yellow, golden yellow to reddish brown, with a black mask which is highly desirable without being imperative. There may be dark or even black points on the coat. Particularly in the south of Germany there are dogs whose coats may be sandy, silver gray (wolf gray) or yellow-red with dark points (wolf yellow). White is absolutely inadmissible and should be completely eliminated in breeding. A small white star on the chest is allowed, as is a little light or white hair on the toes. The color of the tail is the same as the rest of the coat. ●

pronounced cheekbones. The nose is large and dark-colored, ranging from black to yellowish black or dark leather in dogs with brown coats. The muzzle is short but powerful; it should not be pointed, too broad, or rounded off. The stop is well accentuated. The teeth almost invariably close in a pincers bite, but a scissors bite is preferred. Teeth set at an angle or irregular or an overshot or undershot bite are faults.

EYES The eye rims are rather round, large, slightly protruding; the supra-orbital ridge is darker in color.

EARS May be variously shaped—button, bat, prick or rose (the last being rare). Button ears are commonest and are to be preferred.

NECK Varies from short to medium length, sturdy at the base.

BODY The withers are pronounced; the back and loins are short, ample, well muscled; the loins are slightly arched. Roach back or saddleback are faults. The croup must be neither horizontal nor too sloping. The chest is deep, broad, and well let down. The ribs are well sprung and barrel-shaped. The forepart is rounded. The muscles are taut and robust. Seen

from the front the dog should give a general impression of considerable breadth.

TAIL Set on high and usually carried up over the back in a ring. It is short, coarse and bristly. It may be docked.

FOREQUARTERS The shoulder is well sloped. The forelegs are straight, of medium length. The elbows fit close to the body. The wrist is strong, with a short pastern, set rather obliquely. The feet are compact, with well-closed, arched toes and tough pads. **HINDQUARTERS** Well angulated, with fairly long hind legs. The hocks are broad and strong, with short, muscular metatarsi.

COAT Short, or with short topcoat and undercoat like that of the Smoothhaired Fox Terrier. **Color** For the most part light yellow, pale yellow, fawn, reddish, black and tan, streaked. Almost always there are white markings which may be large on the muzzle, collar, throat, the forepart of the chest and feet, and often on various points of the legs and the tip of the tail. Harlequin markings, pure white and glossy black are objectionable. ●

47 AUSTRIAN SHORT-HAIRED PINSCHER

Österreichischer kurtzhaariger Pinscher

AUSTRIA

GENERAL CHARACTERISTICS A small or medium-sized dog, short and compact, with a vivacious personality. The Pinscher is a courageous guard dog.

WEIGHT AND SIZE Weight: 26-40 lb. Height: 13½-16 inches, with a height of about 15½-16 inches preferred.

HEAD The head is pear-shaped, with the wider part at the top, and with

AUSTRIAN SHORTHAIRED PINSCHER

Photo: Fotostampa.

LEONBERG

48 SPANISH MASTIFF
Mastín Español

SPAIN

The Spanish Mastiff, also locally called "Mastí de Extremadura" or "Mastín de la Mancha," is a powerful and brave country dog, used as a guard dog for property and for cattle and sheep. When trained he can become an excellent hunting dog for boar and other large game. His strength and size make him a very useful dog in warfare.

It is customary to snip his tail and ears to help him combat his natural enemies—an unfortunate custom, since the tail completes his aesthetic line and the ears protect his hearing from the rain.

GENERAL CHARACTERISTICS In appearance the Spanish Mastiff should be robust, stocky, symmetrical, and in no sense obese. The gait should give an impression of power and agility.

WEIGHT AND SIZE Weight: 110-132 lb. Height: 25½-27½ inches. Females are generally shorter and lighter than males.

HEAD Well built and in good proportion. The skull is broad, slightly rounded, long, with a rather long muzzle. The nose is black. The lips are full, especially the lower lips, which form two pendulous pouches at the commissure; these pouches are rounded, wet, very black with pink at the edges. The jaws are powerful; the molars are large and sound. The other teeth should be small and white, except for the canines, which are large and well set for taking prey. The stop is not pronounced but should be well defined.

EYES Small and intelligent; the lachrymal pouch is loosely attached and falls in a pronounced manner, showing a great deal of haw.

EARS Small, stout at the base, hanging; they are pointed at the tips.

NECK Strong, muscular and flexible, with abundant, loose skin, which forms two large pouches at the throat; these pouches are identical and well divided by a deep furrow; they are soft to the touch.

FOREQUARTERS Strong, muscular, well-formed shoulders. The legs are well shaped, strong but not coarse, with the muscles and tendons very much in evidence. The forearms are straight and moderately long, stout at the joint and less so at the extremities. The forefeet are not very large or long; the toes and knuckles are well defined.

TAIL Strong and flexible, with long, thick hair forming a flag; it is moderately thick and is carried low, with a slight curve at the end when the dog is in repose. It is carried high and proudly when the dog is animated, but it should never curl over the back.

HINDQUARTERS Long and well positioned, forming almost a right angle with the body; strong and well muscled in the upper part, fine and well shaped in the lower. Vertical and parallel, with no tendency to cowhocks. **FEET** Without dewclaws; they set well on the ground and are short, with well-shaped toes.

COAT Not long, but fine and thick, soft to the touch, with a short fringe behind and on the back part of the forelegs. **Color** Varies widely in this breed, the commoner colors being: reddish, wolf gray, fawn, white and black, white and golden yellow, white and gray, grizzle. In dark coats the hair should be of a lighter shade at the roots. **Skin** Rosy white.

FAULTS Nose mottled or not black; muzzle too pointed; badly adapted jaws ill equipped for seizing; excessive saddleback; short tail or tail carried over back; weak or crooked legs; cow hocks; excessively long or woolly hair.

SCALE OF POINTS

General appearance	15
Head	12
Eyes	5
Ears	4
Neck, shoulders	10
Body, chest	20
Limbs	10
Tail	4
Coat, color	10
Size	10
	100

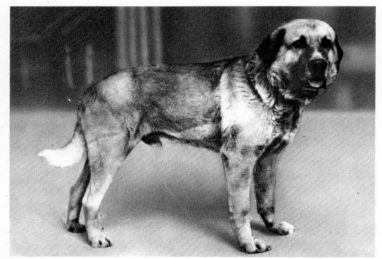

SPANISH MASTIFF

PYRENEAN MASTIFF

49 PYRENEAN MASTIFF
Mastín de los Pirineos

SPAIN

This breed is also known as Mastiff of Navarra and Mastiff of Leon, and since the dog originated on the southern slopes of the Pyrenees, he is often confused with the Great Pyrenees, a quite different French breed.

GENERAL CHARACTERISTICS The general appearance should be that of a strong, wholly symmetrical dog of fine looks, with legs and feet well to the ground and of an elegant gait. On sand and mud he should leave a clear, well defined but not deep track (a deep track would be symptomatic of heaviness or weakness).

WEIGHT AND SIZE The weight ranges from 121-155 lb. Height at the withers varies from 27½-31½ inches. Females, of course, are normally of lesser weight and height than males.

HEAD Large, long and strong. The skull is broad and slightly rounded, with a pronounced occipital protuberance. The forehead is almost flat. The nose is black, the lips heavy and pendulous. The hard palate is black and well streaked. The muzzle is long, the jaws long and powerful in the bite. The molars are large and sound, the other teeth small and white, except for the canines, which are large, sharp and well adapted to seizing prey.

EYES Small and dark; they have an intelligent expression. The haw is visible, revealed by the fall of the lower eyelid.

EARS The ears are small, sturdy at the base, pointed at the tips and hanging.

NECK The neck is slender, supple and strong; it is well defined at the head and shoulders, to which it is harmoniously coupled. The skin is loose, forming two dewlaps at the throat which are identical and separated by a deep furrow.

FOREQUARTERS Strong, well boned, shapely, with perfect muscling and neat tendons. The shoulders are powerful and well set; the forearms are not excessively long, strong at the elbow, fixed at the extremities. They are straight and lithe. The forefeet are not large or long; the toes are close and well arched.

BODY Long but without exaggeration, robust, supple, not massive; it is lower at the withers than at the rump and well sprung in the ribs. The outline of the body has well-defined curves which set off the muscles well (the Pyrenees Mastiff must be both handsome and strong). The chest is broad and well let down. The croup is high and free of weakness.

TAIL Strong and supple, not set on too high, with good feathering. It is moderately long and is carried low with a slight curve at the end when the dog is in repose. It is raised and carried proudly when the dog is excited.

HINDQUARTERS Long, well positioned, forming almost a right angle with the body; strong and well muscled in the upper part, fine and well shaped in the lower. Vertical and parallel, with a slight tendency for the hocks to turn in. The feet are without dewclaws; they set well on the ground, are not long and have well-shaped toes.

COAT Thick, dense, rough to the touch, the coat should not be long nor woolly. It is slightly longer at the throat, on the neck, the lower belly, and on the back part of forelegs and thighs. **Color** White with two large golden or gray markings covering the sides of the head and the beginning of the neck. Many dogs have a similar marking on the croup, reaching to the root of the tail, with other markings on the back and ribs. White and black are less desirable, as is speckled white. The hair of the markings is white at the roots and colored after the first third, in such a way that by passing the hand over the dog against the grain the hair is white. The borders of the markings are not sharp and thus the markings do not stand out against the white background but merge gently into the other color. **Skin** White or pink.

FAULTS Mottled nose or nose not black; excessively pointed muzzle; jaws poorly adapting to seizing; saddleback; short tail or tail carried above the back; weak or crooked legs; cow hocks; long or woolly coat; overall coat basically dark (since white should predominate).

SCALE OF POINTS

General appearance	15
Head	12
Eyes	5
Ears	4
Neck, shoulders	10
Body, chest	20
Limbs	10
Tail	4
Coat, color	10
Size	10
	100

THE GUARDIAN OF THE SHIP ▶

Photo: Barrachina, M. Pedone.

50 GREAT PYRENEES
Chien des Pyrénées
FRANCE

GREAT PYRENEES

This dog is considered a close relative to the Hungarian Kuvasz and the Maremma of the Abruzzi marshes. As his name indicates, he is prevalent in the Pyrenees region, particularly Andorra, where he still justifies his role as faithful defender of the flock, guarding it even against the dangerous bears of that area. Shepherds consider him an excellent guide and a drover of great experience, and use it when sheep have to traverse difficult snowy mountain passes. Moreover, when well trained, he makes a brilliant first-aid dog, as useful as the St. Bernard. He has also been used successfully as an avalanche dog.

GENERAL CHARACTERISTICS A huge dog, strong, muscular, yet elegant.

WEIGHT AND SIZE Weight: 100-120 lb. Height: males 27-31½ inches; females from 25½-28½ inches.

HEAD All things considered, including the overall size of the dog, the head is not excessively large. It resembles the head of the brown bear with the ears dropped. The skull is slightly domed. The muzzle is broad, of good length and slightly pointed at the tip, which is black. The stop is not pronounced. The lips are not pendulous, fitting fairly close to the lower jaw. The lips, like hard palate, are either black or profusely spotted with black. The teeth are evenly closed.

EYES Rather small, intelligent, amber brown in color; they are set slightly oblique and have a gentle expression. The eye rims are black.

EARS Set on at eye level, the ears are small, triangular, rounded at the tips; they hang flat against the sides of the head.

NECK Rather strong, quite short; there is no dewlap.

BODY The chest is broad and moderately deep. The ribs are moderately sprung, the flanks fairly high. The croup is gently descending. The haunches are rather prominent.

TAIL Of sufficient length, with a tuft of long hair. At rest the tail is carried low, the tip slightly curved; when the dog is alert the tail is carried on the back—"making a wheel" is the expression used by the mountaineers of the Pyrenees to describe the distinct change in position of the tail.

FOREQUARTERS Straight and strong legs, moderately sloping shoulders.

HINDQUARTERS Well-muscled thighs, broad, lean hocks, fairly angulated. Double dewclaws on the hind legs and sometimes also on the front. **FEET** Rather short, compact, with well-arched toes.

COAT The outer coat is made up of abundant white hair, rather long and soft and lying flat, longer about the neck, where it may be slightly wavy; on the tail and back of the thighs it is more abundant, finer and woollier, forming culottes. **Color** White, sometimes white, light yellow, or gray markings or (better) badger, wolf gray; such markings are found on the head, ears, and base of the tail. A few markings on the body should not be penalized.

FAULTS A general impression of heaviness, without distinction, or suggesting a similarity with the St. Bernard, the Newfoundland, or the Leonberg; weight and height below the minima; excessively massive head; too large a skull; bulging forehead; accentuated stop; pendulous lips; bad dentition; overshot jaw; insufficient pigmentation on lips, nose, eyelids; round eyes, light eyes, protruding eyes; drooping eyelids; flesh-colored nose or eyelids; long ears, curled ears; tail badly feathered or carried wrong; hocks with insufficient angulation; short or curly hair; colors different from those given in the standard (which would imply cross breeding).

DISQUALIFICATIONS Absence of double dewclaws on the hind legs. ●

GREAT PYRENEES

51 BORDEAUX MASTIFF
Dogue de Bordeaux
FRANCE

As Varrone has been singing the praises of this dog since the first century A.D., this appears to confirm the theory of French dog lovers that this Mastiff, even if it does not belong to a distinctly French breed, is certainly one of the oldest breeds of France. The British writers believe that he comes from crossbreeding Mastiffs and Bulldogs.

Studies on the origin of this dog are quite varied. Some writers trace his ancestry to the Greek Mastiffs used by the Romans in their wars, and in the arena. According to others, the Bordeaux Mastiff is descended from the great Mastiffs that entered Europe with the Alans, an Oriental tribe who settled to the north of the Gironde estuary. Besides the Bordeaux, the German and English Mastiffs would also be descended from this stock. Others think that the Bordeaux originate from the Mastiffs employed by the Celts on wild cattle hunts and that the Aquitanian dogs were their descendents.

The President of the Society of Bordeaux Mastiff Fanciers, Boogazerdt, thinks that the Burgos Mastiff from Spain is the ancestor of the Bordeaux Mastiff who was obtained by crossbreeding the above dog with the English and German Mastiff.

Scholars such as Kell and Tschudy seem more plausible in their claims that the ancestors of this dog should be looked for among the Assyrian and Indian Mastiffs introduced into Gaul and England by the Phoenicians. Nowadays the Bordeaux Mastiff is not so prevalent in France as it was half a century ago. He is an excellent companion in spite of his surly disposition, and is also an excellent guardian of property.

BORDEAUX MASTIFF

GENERAL CHARACTERISTICS This is not a giant among dogs, but he is a massive animal, well built though rather low in stature, very muscular and well balanced overall. The huge head, furrowed by wrinkles, is typical of the breed. The muzzle is square, truncated and short, with a black or red mask. The general appearance is that of an athlete demanding and getting respect—compact, muscular and proud.

WEIGHT AND SIZE Weight: for the larger variety called Dogues, males over 100 lb; females 88 lb; for the medium variety, called Doquins, males 84-100 lb; females 77-88 lb. Height at withers: males 23-26 inches; females proportionately smaller.

HEAD Tremendous, with a characteristic expression and appearance. The skull is broad and short, and its circumference is approximately the same as the height at the withers in males. The stop is abrupt, forming a right angle; the medial furrow is deep. The muzzle is large, short, and slightly hollowed; it is square, with prominent cheeks, which are well developed and have an under structure of heavy bone encased in muscle. The jaws are very powerful, broad and square. The lower jaw is undershot by well over ¼ inch. The teeth are very strong, especially the canines, which are only slightly curved. The nose is broad, dark in those dogs with a dark mask, lighter in those with a reddish mask. It is vertical or slightly regressive when the head is held horizontally.

EYES Oval, set as far apart as possible, large, not bulging; the supra-orbital ridges are pronounced.

EARS Small and hanging. The front

BORDEAUX MASTIFF

BORDEAUX MASTIFF

Photo: E. Munch, Fotostampa, Buzzini.

of the ear base is slightly raised. The ears are a little darker than the rest of the coat and slightly rounded at the tips.

NECK Very strong and muscular, quite robust at the juncture with the shoulders.

BODY The chest is powerful, broad, deep, let down below the elbows. The circumference of the body behind the elbows should be some 10-12 inches more than the height at the withers. The ribs are solid asd well sprung. The back is broad and muscular. The loins are short. The withers are high enough to dominate the dorsal line, which should be straight from beginning to end. The croup should not be rounded or raised but sloping evenly to the point of insertion of the tail.

TAIL Thick at the root, not reaching farther than the hocks, carried low. It is deeply set on, without flag or rough hair below. When the dog is excited, the tail stands at a right angle to normal.

FOREQUARTERS The shoulders are well sloped, protruding slightly from the withers. Together with the forelegs they form an angle slightly more than 90 degrees. The legs are heavy, exceptionally muscular, vertical, although in particularly broad-chested dogs they are slightly sloped from top to bottom and from inside outward. **HINDQUARTERS** Elongated, with thighs well let down and muscular. The hocks are short and angulated. The hindquarters are not as broad as the forequarters. **FEET** Strong, with closed toes and regularly separated nails.

COAT Fine, short and soft. **Color** Mahogany, fawn, golden, black-speckled. A solid-colored dark coat with warm tones is the most desirable. A definite red or black mask is required. Limited white markings are acceptable.

FAULTS Small head, not in good proportion to the height; long, narrow, Great Dane head; absence of medial furrow; total lack of wrinkles; narrow nose, flesh-colored or mottled nose, nose color contrasting with coat; narrow, pointed, excessively projected or excessively recessed muzzle; Roman nose; soft, bony or underdeveloped cheeks; overshot or not properly undershot jaws; teeth visible, yellow, decayed, badly set or underdeveloped; lack of stop; small, round eyes, too deep-set, too light, too close. vicious, blind or walleyes; conjunctivitis; ears set low, long ears, excessively thick ear cartilage; prick ears, ears carried forward, pointed, shell ears; long or weak neck; flat ribs; undersized false ribs; saddleback, flat back, narrow or weak back; falling belly, paunchy or excessively drawn-up belly; tail too long, trumpet tail, tufted tail; knotty or sinuous tail; lack of tail, even if accidental; weak shoulders, badly muscled shoulders; shoulders too short, straight or flat; elbows turned outward or inward; weak forearm; pasterns turned excessively outward; harefeet, splayed feet; white nails in dark dogs; weak thighs, flat thighs; hocks too straight, causing elevated croup; hocks turned outward or inward; dewclaws; white hair on muzzle; entirely white coat (white is acceptable on chest and feet); heavy, harsh, curly, wavy, excessively long hair; dull coat. ●

52 NEAPOLITAN MASTIFF
Mastino Napoletano

ITALY

The first dog show in Naples took place in 1946 and was marked by the presence of a group of eight magnificent Mastiffs. The interest of experts was marked by the fact that they belonged to a breed shown for the first time. These were Neapolitan Mastiffs. They were new only to the official dog world, since they have been prevalent in Campania since ancient times.

They may be the descendents of Mastiffs raised by the Greeks and then by the Romans, the fighting Mastiffs of Roman wars and circuses, and also doubtless descendents of the great dogs which Alexander so esteemed in Greece and which later arrived in Italy.

Each one of these theories should be considered as well as our own hypothesis that the Mastiffs could have reached Italy on Phoenician ships in even more ancient times.

All this concerns only where the dog came from, since, according to all theories, his ancestor would be the Tibetan Mastiff. Some naturalists believe, however, that the Mastiff is of European origin, but one thing is certain: as well as the White-Coated Shepherd there also existed a large dog with a dark coat in southern and central Italy during the Roman era. Columella described him: "The guard dog for the house should be black (or dark) so that during the day a prowler can see him and be frightened by his appearance. When night falls the dog, lost in the shadows, can attack without being seen. The head is so massive that it seems to be the most important part of the body. The ears fall toward the front, the brilliant and penetrating eyes are black or gray, the chest is deep and hairy, the hind legs are powerful, the front legs are covered with long thick hair, and he is short-legged with strong toes and nails."

It seems quite probable that the great Neapolitan Mastiff is none other than the descendent of the guard dogs Columella described. Just as the Maremma Shepherd has been preserved for centuries in the Roman countryside, so may the ancient house guardian have disappeared from his place of origin but may have survived around Naples and farther to the south.

As mentioned above, the breed was presented to the official dog world in 1946. One writer, P. Scanziani, today considered to be the reconstructor of the Neapolitan Mastiff, became particularly interested. From 1949 on he began, in his kennels at Rome, to gather the best subjects for breeding and obtained splendid results. The breed was fixed and recognized by the E.N.C.I. which adopted the standards proposed by Scanziani and recently modified. Thanks to the ten-year effort by du Tessin, an ardent dog lover, it is now able to present a very ancient breed which had been completely forgotten for centuries. Today the Neapolitan Mastiff is raised in various parts of Italy and is exported all over the world.

NEAPOLITAN MASTIFF

GENERAL CHARACTERISTICS The scientific classification of the Neapolitan Mastiff puts him in the molossoid group (according to the classification of Pierre Mégnin). A rectilinear, shorthaired breed,, according to the classification of Déchambre. The dog is further classified as a guard and defense dog, police dog and tracking dog. Origin Italian, more specifically Neapolitan. This dog is a guard dog par excellence, as well as a fine defense dog; of large size, the Neapolitan Mastiff is strongly built, vigorous, of rustic but at the same time majestic appearance, robust and courageous, intelligent in his expression, and having good mental balance, with a docile, unaggressive character; a matchless defender of its master and his property. The general conformation is that of a heavy mesomorph, with a body longer than the height at the withers, of harmonious proportions (heterometric), and relatively in respect to outline (halloidism). The skin is not adherent to the underlying tissues, but abundant, with loose connective tissue in all parts of the body, and especially on the head, where it forms wrinkles and folds, and on the neck, where it forms a dewlap.

WEIGHT AND SIZE Weight: 110-150 lb. Height: males 25½-28½ inches; females 23½-27 inches, with a tolerance of ¾ inch above or below the standard.

HEAD Brachycephalic, massive, with a broad, short skull. The total length of the head is about 35 percent of the height at the withers; the length of the muzzle should be 1/3 of the total length of the head. In a dog 27½ inches high at the withers, the skull should be 5½ inches long and the muzzle 2¾ inches. Total length of the head: 8¼ inches. The width from cheek to cheek is greater than half the total length of the head, and is approximately equal to its length. The total cephalic index lies in a ratio of approximately 66. The directions of the upper longitudinal axes of the skull and the muzzle are parallel. The skin is abundant, with wrinkles and folds. **Nose** On the same line as the nasal bridge. Seen in profile, the nose should not protrude over the forward vertical line of the lips, but the foreface is on the same vertical plane of the forepart of the muzzle. The nose should be generous, with large and well open nostrils, wet and cool. The pigmentation varies with the color of the coat: black in black-coated dogs, dark in others, brown in dogs having a mahogany coat. **Nasal Bridge** Straight. For its length and direction relative to the axis of the skull, see HEAD. Its width, measured at the midpoint of its length, should be about 20 percent of the total length of the head, and about 50 percent of the length of the nasal bridge. **Lips and Muzzle** The lips are thick-textured, full and heavy. The upper lips, seen from the front, are shaped like an inverted V; they are full and consequently the forepart of the muzzle is well developed as to height, and is

also well developed in breadth. Moreover, because of the fact that the sides of the muzzle are parallel, the forepart should be flat, giving origin to the square aspect of the muzzle. The lower lateral profile of the muzzle is provided by the lips, while the lowest point is provided not by the lips but by the commissure. The commissure is pronounced and the mucous area is well visible, that is, the area between the folds of the upper and lower lips should be visible. The forward-lower lateral profile of the muzzle is a semicircle with a well-closed chord. The length of the muzzle is determined by the length of the bridge, and the height must not be less than half its length. The opening of the mouth is sufficiently long so that the commissure should meet the perpendicular from the outer corner of the eye. **Jaws** Robust, well developed and meeting in either a scissors or a pincers bite. The jaws are very robust, essentially curved in profile, especially in the back part. The body of the lower jaw should be well developed in front, never minimal, in such a way as to form practically a support for the lower lips at the point where they meet. The teeth are white, regular, and complete both as to development and number. **Stop** Should be approximately at a 90° angle at the sinus and a 120-130° angle with the forehead. **Skull** Its length should be equal to 2/3 of the total length of the

head and equal to the width from cheek to cheek. The zygomatic arches are pronounced and are noticeably extended to the outside, thus providing adequate insertion for the masseter and temporal muscles. It is spheroid in form, as seen from the front; seen from the side it is close to this form, except that in its upper part—that is, between the insertion points of the ears—it is flat. The sinuses are highly developed. The medial furrow or metopic is pronounced. The occipital protuberance is pronounced.

EYES The eyelids should be normally close-fitting (neither ectropionic nor entropionic). The eyes, set in a subfrontal position, are well separated from each other and rather rounded, in spite of the oval appearance given by the abundant skin surrounding them. They are fairly deep set. The pigmentation of the eyelids is black, blue or brown, depending on the coat. The color should correspond to that of the coat, except that it is generally darker.

EARS Small in comparison to the size of the dog, triangular, set on well above the zygomatic arch; if not clipped they hang flat, adhering to the cheeks and the parotid region; in length they should not extend beyond the edge of the throat. The ear rises abruptly at the insertion

point and then falls with equal suddenness. In clipping, the ear is almost completely amputated and docked to the point where it forms a nearly equilateral triangle.

NECK Short, stocky, extraordinarily muscular; its length from the nape to the forward edge of the withers is about 28/10 of the height at the withers, and its circumference at its midpoint is approximately 8/10 of the height at the withers. The topline, in the forward third, is slightly convex; the lower side of the neck has much loose skin, which forms a dewlap which should be neither too abundant nor undivided. The dewlap begins at the lower jaw and reaches approximately to the midpoint of the neck.

FOREQUARTERS Shoulder Should be long, slightly sloped, with long muscles, well developed and well separated from each other and free in their movements. Its length is about 3/10 of the height at the withers. Its slope is 50-60° from the horizontal. In respect to the medial plane of the body, the points of the scapulae are fairly separated from each other, tending rather to be vertical to that plane. **Upper arm** Well joined to the body in its upper ¾, it should have, like the shoulder, strong, clean and well developed muscles. Its slope is 55-60° from the horizontal and its length is approximately 30 percent of the height

at the withers. Its direction is almost parallel to the median plane of the body. **Forearm** Straight, vertical and exceptionally well boned. Its length is almost equal to the length of the upper arm. The height of the foreleg, at the elbow, is 5.2/10 of the height at the withers. The elbows, covered with abundant and loose skin, should lie on a plane which is parallel to the median plane of the body, and therefore they should not be too close to the body, thus eliminating the underarm cavity (the so-called closed elbows), and should not be turned out ("open elbows"). The point of the elbow should lie on the perpendicular from the caudal angle of the scapula. **Wrist** The wrist should lie on the vertical of the forearm, it should be broad, lean, smooth, with no visible points of bone, except on the back edge, where the pisiform bone is protruding. **Pasterns** The pasterns should be flat from forward to back and, seen from the front, should follow the vertical line of the forearm. Seen in profile, the pasterns should be somewhat extended, about 70 to 75°. Their length should not be less than 1/6 of the height of the entire leg to the elbow. **Foot** Oval (harefoot), with close, arched toes; the pads are lean and hard, and dark in color. The nails are strong, curved and dark.

BODY The length of the body exceeds the height at the withers by

NEAPOLITAN MASTIFF

10-11 percent, measured from the point of the shoulder (outer scapular-humeral angle), or from the manubrium of sternum, to the point of the buttock (back point of the ischium). **Chest** Broad, well open, with exceptionally well developed pectoral muscles. Its width, which varies with the width of the rib cage, should be 40-45 percent of the height at the withers. The manubrium of the sternum should be positioned at the same level as the point of the shoulders. **Rib cage** Broad, descending to the level of the elbow or slightly below; well rounded at the midpoint; its cross diameter diminishes slightly toward the sternum. The ribs are long, well sprung, oblique; the interrib spaces are extended; the last back ribs are long, sloping and well open. The circumference of the rib cage should be about ¼ more than the height at the withers, while, measured at the rib arches, it is about 2½ inches less; its cross diameter should be at least 32 percent of the height at the withers, its depth should reach 50-55 percent, also in reference to the height at the withers. The thoracic index should be not more than 8, and it is desirable for it to be lower. The sternum region is long: its profile is a semicircle with a very broad chord, which ascends slightly toward the abdomen and tends toward a straight line. **Back** The backline is straight, and only the withers rise above it. The back is broad and its length is about 32 percent of the height at the withers. **Loins** Well let into the backline; slightly rounded as seen in profile, with well developed muscling in their width. Length of the loins is a little less than ½ of the height at the withers; the width approximates the length (in a ratio of 14.5:16). **Belly and flanks** The line of the belly is nearly horizontal. The flanks should be approximately equal in length to the lumbar region. The belly is voluminous, and the hollow of the flank should be minimal. **Croup** The croup, which prolongs toward the rear the

rounded line of the loin, should be broad, robust, muscular, and consequently the cross diameter between the two haunches should be 5/10 of the height at the withers. The haunches should be sufficiently prominent to reach the upper line of the loins. Its length is equal to 3/10 of the height at the withers; it is hollowed and its slope, considering the line which joins the outer forward angle of the ileum to the ischiatic tuberosity is about 30° from the horizontal. **Sexual Organs** Perfect, complete and equal development of the testicles.

TAIL The tail is thick at the root, robust and slightly tapered toward the tip. In repose the tail should be carried as a saber tail, that is hanging for the first ⅔ of its length and slightly curved in the lower third. It is never carried straight up or curled over the back, but horizontal or very slightly above the backline when the dog is in action. Its length is equal to or slightly more than the distance to the hock. It is docked to about ⅔ of its length.

HINDQUARTERS **Thigh** Long, broad, covered with heavy muscles, prominent, but clearly separated from each other; the back edge tends to be straight. The length should not be less than ⅓ of the height at the withers, and it should be 3 percent of the height at the withers, and have a slope of about 60 degrees; from back forward it forms with the coxal approximately a right angle. In respect to the vertical, it should be parallel to the median plane of the body. **Leg** Strongly boned with good muscling. Its length is slightly less than the length of the thigh and its slope, from fore to aft, is about 50-55°; the femoral-rotular-tibial angle is about 110-115°. The furrow between the tendon and bone above the hock is well marked and evident. **Hock** The sides of the hock can scarcely be too broad. Because of the slope of the tibia its forward

angle is open. The distance from the sole of the foot to the point of the hock is about 2.5/10 of the height at the withers. Seen from behind, the backline from the point of the hock to the ground should be on the vertical and on the prolongation of the buttock line. The forward angle, that is the tibial-metatarsal angle, is open, as already mentioned, and is about 150-145°. **Metatarsus** Robust and lean, almost cylindrical in form; its length is about ¼ of the height at the withers; seen from behind as well as in profile, it should lie on the vertical. Any dewclaws, either simple or double, should be removed. **Foot** Less oval than the forefoot, not so large, but otherwise with the same characteristics as the forefoot.

COAT **Hair** The hair should be dense, equal in length, smooth throughout, fine, short, no longer than 6/10 inch; there should be no sign of a fringe, in no part of the body, legs or tail. The texture is hard. **Color** Permissible colors are: black, lead, mouse gray, streaked, sometimes with small white spots on the chest or on the tip of the toes. **Skin** Abundant over the entire body and particularly on the head, where it forms numerous folds or wrinkles, and along the lower side of the neck, where it forms a dewlap. The pigment of the lips, nose and eyelids should be black or brown, depending on the darkest markings of the coat. The color of the nails and the pads should be dark.

GAIT The gait is one of the characteristics of the breed; it is a slow, free, bearlike gait. The trot is slow, with long steps, covering a good deal of ground. The Mastiff rarely gallops.

FAULTS **General Characteristics** Undistinguished overall appearance, lightness, weak or spongy bone, lack of symmetry. Height insufficient or exaggerated. **Head** The upper cranial-facial axes divergent or convergent (a very serious fault). **Nose** Above or below the bridge; protruding on the vertical line of the foreface of the muzzle, with traces of depigmentation; nostrils not well open; small, with insufficient pigmentation. **Nasal bridge** Too long or too short, narrow, with lateral lines converging, upper profile not straight. **Lips and Muzzle** Muzzle too long or too short; lips underdeveloped or overdeveloped, falling below the commissure, flaccid; fold of the commissure too accentuated, too falling, inverted or lacking. Lip profile falling back. Forward convergence of the lateral walls of the muzzle, that is, pointed muzzle and consequently with the foreface of the muzzle not flat. The upper and lower lips meet in a semicircle. **Jaws** Thin or weak; overshot (if it harms the outer appearance of the muzzle), undershot (if resulting from shortness of the lower jaw: disqualification; if resulting from crooked teeth: fault). Lower jaw too curved. Irregular teeth, incomplete dentition; horizontal erosion. **Skull** Small, short, rounded, narrow at the sides, that is, at the sides of the zygomatic arches and the parietals; domed; flat supraorbital ridges, underdeveloped chewing muscles; lack of occipital protuberance, exaggerated occipital protuberance; underdeveloped sinuses. Stop flat or insufficiently accentuated. Exaggerated convergence of the cranial-facial axes. **Eyes** Smaller prominence, eyes too light in relation to coat; eyes not in subfrontal position; ectropion, entropion; eyes too close together; cross eyes. Partial depigmentation of the eyelids. **Ears** Too long or too short; set on low; tip of ear narrow and pointed; ears carried badly or badly docked; hair on ears not short. **Neck** Weak, long or too short, flat on the sides, without dewlap or with exaggerated, undivided dewlap, deficient in arching of upper neck line, lacking in separation from nape and not well fused with shoulders. **Shoulder** Straight, heavy, short; with underdeveloped muscles, not free in movement; points of the scapulae too close together. **Upper Arm** Too slanted or too straight; short, defi-

cient in muscular development, weak bone. **Forearm** Weak or spongy bone; round bone, off vertical; divergent or convergent elbow; underarm cavity low. Height from ground of the elbow less than half of the height at the withers or much more than such height. **Wrist** With noticeable hypertrophy of the wrist bones, spongy, small; pisiform bone minimal. **Pastern** Short or too long, weak, too extended or straight, out of vertical. **Foot** Round (catfoot), broad, crushed, fat, splayed, deficient in arching of toes, carried in or out, that is, not in vertical; toe pads fleshy, soles insufficiently tough, deficiency of pigmentation in nails and pads. Pads out of place; pads too long. **Body** Longitudinal diameter equal to the height at the withers; too long. **Chest** Narrow, insufficiently let down, insufficient muscular development, manubrium of sternum positioned too low. **Rib cage** Lacking in height, depth, too large or too small in circumference, xiphoid appendage curved in, short stern region; rib arches insufficiently open. **Ribs** Improperly sprung, interrib spaces not broad; back ribs short, insufficiently sprung, not open and low. **Back** Short, saddleback (lordosis), roach back (kyphosis); break in the backline at the eleventh vertebra, withers not sufficiently raised. **Loins** Long, flat, narrow. **Belly and Flanks** Belly drawn up; flanks very curved and long. **Sexual organs** Incomplete development of one or both of the testicles; (see **Disqualifications** below). Monorchidism and cryptorchidism. **Croup** Narrow, short, insufficiently hollowed, horizontal. **Thigh** Short, deficient in muscular development, narrow, deviated in the region of the stifle, too straight or too slanted. **Leg** Weak bone, furrow between tendon and bone above hock not evident, short, too straight or too sloping. **Hock** High, not broad; angulation of hock too open or too closed because of forward deviation of the metatarsus, out of vertical. **Metatarsus** Long, weak, out of vertical; dewclaws. Faults of foot, same as for forefoot. **Tail** Too long or too short. Tail lacking or brachyurism from birth; set on too high or too low, not thick at the root, carried above the loin, curled over the back, straight up, lateral deviation, flaccid, hanging, mousetail. **Hair** Not sufficiently short, or hard. **Color** Partially white coat. **Skin** Close-fitting to the body in every part, insufficiently loose, lack of wrinkles on the head, lack of dewlap. **Character** Timidity, fractiousness; fierceness or tendency to bite (disqualification).

DISQUALIFICATIONS Height at the Withers: More than 29½ inches; more than 1-1/5 inch less than the standard minimum height. **Head** Accentuated divergence of the upper cranial-facial longitudinal axes. **Nose** Total depigmentation. **Nasal Bridge** Decidedly arched or hollowed. **Jaws** Accentuated overshot or undershot condition. **Eye** Walleye; total bilateral depigmentation of the eyelids; bilateral strabismus (cross eyes). **Neck** Lack of dewlap. **Sexual organs** Monorchidism, cryptorchidism. **Tail** Lack of tail, short tail from birth; carried curled over back. **Color** Extensive white markings; partially white coat.

SCALE OF POINTS

General appearance and stature	30
Skull, muzzle	20
Eyes, ears	10
Rib cage	15
Loins, croup	10
Forequarters, hindquarters, feet	20
Tail	10
Coat and color	15
Expression, character	20
	150

RATINGS

Excellent: score not less than	140
Very good	130
Good	110
Fairly good	100

Photo: M. Pedone.

53 HOKKAIDO DOG
Kyūshū
JAPAN

HOKKAIDO DOG

The cradle of this breed is the Japanese island of Hokkaido, more precisely the departments of Mie, Aichi, Kochi, Toyama, Yamanashi, Iwate and Akita. This Japanese dog of medium height is also called the Kyushu or Ochi dog.

He is a capable guard and hunting dog and an excellent companion. Of relatively ancient lineage, he used to be raised mainly for hunting and, because of his remarkable physique and intelligence, he was principally employed in mountainous regions.

GENERAL CHARACTERISTICS A well-constructed, well-formed, and well-muscled dog, robust and patient. The height at the withers is 10/11 of the total length. The appearance is simple but distinguished. The Hokkaido Dog has a sensitive temperament, and is

TERRITORIAL DEFENSE

greatly attached to its master; it is docile and makes a fine guard dog.

SIZE Height: males 19½-21 inches; females 16½-19 inches. These limits should be observed insofar as possible, but higher figures can be ac-

cepted in the case of dogs otherwise in outstanding form.

HEAD The forehead is broad, with the medial furrow accentuated; the cheeks are well formed. The stop is rather prominent. The muzzle is straight, the tip of the nose is dark.

The lips are not thick. The muzzle, which should be neither too long nor thick, is rather pointed. The teeth are solid, and the jaw must not be overshot.

EYES Small, triangular; dark brown. ●

54 AINU DOG
Hokkaidoken

JAPAN

This breed originated on the island of Hokkaido and is trained for hunting larger game; he is also a tenacious guard dog. The indigenous Ainu value it highly since they know it to be capable of fighting, with impetuous and surprising courage, bears weighing over 650 lbs. He has an extraordinary sense of orientation and is able to find his way home under the most difficult circumstances. In 1937 Japan took measures to protect this breed and at the same time gave it its present official name. In spite of this it continues to be known as the Ainu dog. (A more exact term would be "dog of the Ainu.")

AINU DOG

GENERAL CHARACTERISTICS A strong, muscular, well-formed dog, lean and built for country life. Impetuous and fast in action. The forequarters are more important in judging this breed than the hindquarters. There are marked differences between male and female. The Ainu Dog is very faithful, obedient, with a marked tendency to return to its master's house under all conditions.

SIZE Height: males 16-19½ inches. The height is 10/11 of the overall length. Females are slightly smaller and longer.

HEAD The length of the head, which is equal to its width, is ¼ the height at the withers. The length of the muzzle is 2/3 the length of the head. The nose is dark, the bridge straight. The lips are closed, of dark pigmentation and well fitting. Good solid teeth (caries or irregular teeth are a fault). The jaw must not be overshot. The

dental arrangement, with a total of 42 teeth, is:

	I	C	Pr	M
Upper	6	2	8	4
Lower	6	2	8	6

The skull is relatively broad and slightly rounded. The forehead is broad, the cheeks well formed. The medial furrow and the stop are well defined but not accentuated.

EYES Triangular in shape, with corners slightly raised. The pupil is deep black, with a dark brown iris. The expression is lively and daring.

EARS Well set on, erect at right angles to the brow. They are pointed and turn neither in nor out.

NECK Stout, robust, with a slight but not exaggerated dewlap.

FOREQUARTERS The shoulder is moderately sloping. The forelegs are straight and lean. The elbows are

close to the body. The pasterns are slightly sloping. If the scapula and humerus are not well angulated the pastern is vertical, and the dog has an appearance of being "thrown forward"; if, one on the other hand, the scapula and humerus are acutely angulated, the pastern is too sloping and the dog "sits on its haunches"). The forefeet are well closed and rounded, with hard pads. The nails are strong and should be dark-colored.

BODY Deep, quite broad chest. The circumference of the body behind the elbows is 13/10 of the height at the withers. Viewed in profile, the brisket is at the halfway point between ground and withers. The ribs are well sprung. The back is straight and powerful; the loins are strong and relatively broad. The belly is fairly drawn up in relation to the well-developed thorax. No genital abnormality.

COAT Harsh and straight over a

soft, dense undercoat. **Color** Reddish, white, black, salt and pepper, red and black, black-brown.

GAIT Agile, lively, light and energetic.

FAULTS Minor: slight overshot condition; **Serious:** excessive overshot condition; lack of more than 5 teeth; monorchidism; ambivalent sex characteristics; timidity.

DISQUALIFICATIONS Naturally flat ears; cryptorchidsm.

SCALE OF POINTS

General appearance	20
Character	10
Head	20
Back, loins	10
Thorax, belly	10
Legs	10
Coat	10
Gait	10
	100

55 JAPANESE FIGHTING DOG
Tosa

JAPAN

The origins of this powerful fighting dog are rather recent, since they go back only to the Meiji era (1868–1912), and the Tosa dog is the result of careful selective breeding between the local Kochi breeds (on the island of Shikoku) to which has been added the blood of European dogs, like the Bulldog, the St. Bernard, the Bull Terrier, and the German Mastiff. Certain important characteristics were successfully bred: strength, aggressiveness, courage, as well as a patient nature tempered by great prudence, all of which made the Tosa an excellent fighting dog and also perfectly adapted to be a watchdog and pet.

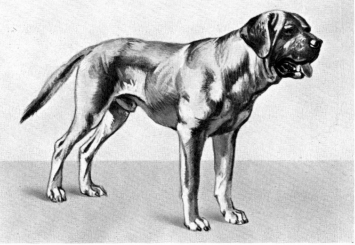

JAPANESE FIGHTING DOG

GENERAL CHARACTERISTICS A massive dog with hanging ears and a short, flat coat. The muzzle is square. This is a fighting dog, solidly built for its work. The tail is thick at the root and hangs down to the hocks.

WEIGHT AND SIZE Weight: males more than 82 lb; females more than 66 lb. Height: males at least 23½ inches; females at least 21½ inches.

HEAD A broad skull, with a muzzle of medium length. Bridge is straight, the tip of the nose big and black. The jaws are powerful, with solid teeth and exceptionally strong incisors. The jaw must not be overshot. The stop is well defined but not accentuated.

EYES Reddish brown, rather small, with a penetrating expression.

EARS The ears are relatively small, the leather rather thin; they are set on high and lie close to the sides of the head along the cheeks.

NECK Extraordinarily muscular, with a dewlap.

BODY The chest is broad and deep, with exceptional spring of rib. The withers are high and well developed. The back is straight, the loins broad and powerful. The croup is slightly curved in front. The belly is well drawn up, genital development must be faultless.

TAIL Set on high, tapering to the tip. Carried low, it reaches the hocks.

FOREQUARTERS The shoulders are well directed to the rear. The forearm is straight, strong, and moderately long. The pastern is solid and slightly sloped. The feet are close, with tough pads and hard, solid nails which are dark in color. **HINDQUARTERS** The thighs are well muscled, the metatarsus strong. The hock is only slightly bent. The feet, pads, and nails are approximately as described above for the forequarters.

COAT Short, strong, dense, covering the entire body. **Color** Reddish fawn, solid. Fawn markings on a white or other background are acceptable provided such markings have a reddish tint.

GAIT Steady, sustained.

DISQUALIFICATION Cryptorchidism.

FAULTS Major: Accentuated overshot condition; lack of more than 5 teeth; monorchidism. **Minor:** Weak build; any degree of overshot jaw.

SCALE OF POINTS

General appearance	20
Character	20
Head	20
Back, loins	10
Thorax, belly	10
Legs	10
Coat	5
Gait	5
	100

115

56 AKITA DOG
Akita Inu
JAPAN

This breed is prevalent in the Akita region of Japan and is used as guard and companion. Formerly it was used in the northeastern section of the country for hunting larger game. From the time of the Tokugawa to the Taisho era (1603–1925) he was often used for fighting because of his particularly strong physique and courageous nature. Today the breed is protected by the Japanese government which forbids its being employed for fighting.

AKITA DOG

AKITA DOG

GENERAL CHARACTERISTICS A solidly built dog, well proportioned, with an imposing appearance of great distinction; Prudent, docile, intelligent without sacrificing an impetuous temperament.

SIZE Height: males 25-27½ inches; females 23-25 inches. These limits should be observed insofar as possible. Dogs of greater height are not disqualified if they are outstanding in other respects.

HEAD The skull is large, with a broad forehead; the medial furrow is well marked. The stop is well defined. The cheeks are well formed. The muzzle is strong and pointed, the bridge straight and short. The teeth are solid and must meet in a bite free from overshot effects. The nose is large and black (white dogs may have a pink nose). The lips are rather thin and well fitted over the gums.

EYES Small, somewhat triangular set neither too close nor too far apart, deep brown. The dark color is to be preferred in every case of otherwise equal scoring.

EARS Relatively small and thick, the ears are triangular, erect, and carried sligthly forward. They are spaced rather wide apart, with tips slightly rounded.

BODY Deep chest, ribs fairly well sprung. The back is straight and flat, the withers long and high. The loins are broad and very strong. The belly is well drawn up. Genitals must have no imperfection.

TAIL The tail is stout and strong, reaching the hocks when straight. It is carried over the back in a ring which can be shifted from one side to the other. Sometimes the tail is a screwtail, at others a spiral curl; in either case the curl should be a complete turn.

FOREQUARTERS The shoulders are sloping and well developed. The forearms are straight and well boned, elbows snug to the body. The pasterns are slightly bent. The feet are large, with close toes. The nails are hard; they should be dark in color. The pads should be hard and rugged. **HINDQUARTERS** Long thighs, short legs; hocks strong, lean, elastic, and well directed. Details of feet, metatarsi, and nails for the hind legs are approximately the same as for the forelegs.

COAT Hard, neither long nor short. The undercoat is fine and dense. **Color** Salt and pepper, reddish salt and pepper, black pepper, streaked, white, or white with markings.

GAIT Vigorous, energetic.

DISQUALIFICATIONS Hanging ears; cryptorchidism; short or naturally hanging tail.

FAULTS Major: Excessively overshot jaw; monorchidism; uncurled tail; long hair, excessively thick hair; timidity. **Minor:** Nose of a color not indicated in standard (except in white dogs, which may have pink nose). Slight overshot condition; short hair.

SCALE OF POINTS

General appearance	20
Character	10
Head	20
Back and stern	10
Thorax and belly	10
Legs, feet, pads	10
Coat	10
Gait	10
	100

◄ **IN WINTER**

Photo: M. Beebe (Photo Res.), A. Wintzell.

AKITA DOG

57 SAN SHU DOG

JAPAN

This dog is of medium build and around 1912 became fixed as a breed through crossbreeding the old Aichi and the Chow. It was therefore possible to create a less compact dog possessing physical and mental qualities desirable in a pet. Today the breed is prevalent throughout Japan, although its place of origin is still the region of Aichi (Honshu). He is also very useful for guard work.

GENERAL CHARACTERISTICS A well-formed dog, robust and solidly built. Seen in profile, the body outline is square. The height at the withers is 10/11 of its overall length. Erect ears. Tail carried curled over back. This dog is of a very sensitive disposition and is a good guard dog.

SIZE Height at the withers: males 19½-21½ inches; females 17½-19½ inches.

HEAD The skull is relatively large and rather flat between the ears. The forehead is slightly rounded. The medial furrow, which is very apparent, goes from the occiput to the stop. The muzzle is robust, short and wedge-shaped. The cheeks are well formed. The teeth are strong and meet in a good bite, with no overshot effect. The stop is well defined. The tip of the nose is black, the bridge straight. The lips are not thick and are black in color.

EYES Dark-colored, with almond eye rims; rather deep-set. The corner of the eye is slightly drawn up.

EARS Very small and triangular. They are set on high and somewhat close together and are carried slightly forward.

NECK Heavy and powerful.

MINIATURE SAN SHU

This variety is smaller than the one described above. The height at the withers is 15½-17½ inches for males, 14½-16½ for females. The muzzle is pointed, the limbs not so stiff as in the larger breed. The tail is a sickle tail. The other characteristics are the same as for the standard variety. ●

58 ATLAS DOG

Aïdi

MOROCCO

We know very little about this Moroccan breed. Dog fanciers of Morocco credit it with great qualities as a guard and defense dog.

GENERAL CHARACTERISTICS A solid farm dog, known for strength and mobility. He is muscular, sensitive, powerfully built, free of all coarseness. The coat is thick and serves as protection against both sun and the cold mountain climate where he lives. The coat also protects him in battles he has to wage against jackals and other predators. His expression is lively, straightforward and decisive, as befits a guard dog ever on the alert. In some regions the ears are clipped and the tail is docked, but this is not desirable in a working dog.

SIZE Height: 20½-24½ inches.

HEAD A bear's head, lean and in good proportion to the overall physique. The general shape is that of a blunt wedge. The cheekbones are not pronounced and serve to join the skull smoothly to the muzzle. The nose is black or brown, according to the color of the coat, quite wide and with well-open nostrils. The muzzle is wedge-shaped, like the entire head, and noticeably shorter than the skull, to which it stands in a ratio of 5:6. The stop is not pronounced and is definitely slanted. The jaws are strong and equipped with firmly planted teeth which are white and regular. The jaw must not be overshot. The lips are lean, well closed, with black or brown edges varying according to the color of the coat. The skull is flat and broad, with a slight medial furrow. The occipital protuberance is scarcely apparent.

EYES Of medium size, their darkness depending on the color of the coat. They are slightly slanted; the eyelids are dark, and in light-colored dogs they appear penciled. The expression is vivacious, attentive and probing.

EARS The ears are of medium length, set on obliquely, so that the skull appears capacious. The tips are slightly rounded, and the ears are carried half-hanging and turned forward when the dog is on the alert. At rest they are sometimes carried slightly back.

NECK Powerful, well muscled, free of any sign of dewlap.

BODY The chest is broad, deep and well let down, reaching almost to the elbows. The withers are definitely raised. The back is broad, very muscular and of medium length; the loins are exceptionally powerful, very muscular and slightly arched. There is a slight slope in the back from croup to forequarters, but with no suggestion whatever of hollowness or roach back. The belly is drawn up slightly, but with no Greyhound quality. The iliac bones are very pronounced.

TAIL Long, reaching at least to the hocks, set on at the prolongation of the loin; it is carried low and curved when the dog is in repose. It is richly feathered, which marks the purity of breed. In action the tail is carried gaily, but it should never be curled over the back.

FOREQUARTERS The shoulders are well directed. The forearms are straight, solid and fairly muscular. The pasterns are short and almost straight. **HINDQUARTERS** The thighs are muscular, well let down, but without coarseness. The angulations of the lower thighs and the hocks are widely obtuse, and thus the croup is raised and the back seems to slope toward the withers. Dewclaws are inadmissible. **FEET** Noticeably round, with solid pads and strong nails, the color of which varies with the color of the coat.

COAT Extremely dense, fairly long (about 2-2½ inches), except on the face and ears, where it is finer. On the neck and under the throat the hair forms a mane, especially in males. Haunches and tail have culottes and a flag which is both dense and long.

Color Variable, including sandy, fawn, white, red, grizzle, black and white, white and more or less speckled tan, tricolor, etc. A good and generous distribution of markings is one in which the saddle and head markings are separated by a scarf, with a blaze widening toward the muzzle (St. Bernard markings). Nose and lips are black.

FAULTS Cobby appearance; narrow skull; short ears or long ears; lack or excess of stop; shifty expression, vicious or vacuous expression; dudley nose, lack of pigmentation on eyelids; legs not vertical.

DISQUALIFICATIONS Hawk eyes; short hair; curled tail; insufficient flag; pointed muzzle: prick ears, cryptorchidism, monorchidism. ●

SAN SHU DOG

ATLAS DOG

THE MASTER'S BOOTS ▶

Photo: Kuellenberg, R. Kinne (Photo Res.).

59 SERRA DA ESTRELA DOG

Cão da Serra da Estrela

PORTUGAL

In far-off times this dog inhabited the high Serra da Estrela range. It is therefore difficult to define his origins although there is reason to believe that this may be one of the oldest breeds of the Iberian Peninsula. He is an outstanding guard dog and also a great friend to the shepherds of the mountains as he protects their flocks against wolves. He is sometimes used for hauling.

Specimens of this breed are numerous throughout Portugal, although the best breeders today are those who live on the slopes of the Estrela range.

GENERAL CHARACTERISTICS This Portuguese dog is of a breed related to the Mastiff. A country dog, compact in structure, he is known for his great vitality and good character. His expression is calm, alert and expressive. Unfriendly to strangers, he is quite the contrary with people he knows, very docile with both its master and those who are close to him. Well proportioned, with perfect conformation; the overall harmony is noteworthy and indicative of longstanding purity of breed. His temperament is exceptionally vigorous and combative.

WEIGHT AND SIZE Weight: males 88-110 lb; females 66-88 lb. Height at the withers: males 25½-28 inches; females 24½-27 inches.

HEAD Strong, huge, well set on, with well-developed jaws; the hair is smooth on the skull and cheeks. The head is long and slightly oval, and in good proportion to the body, the skull in good proportion to the muzzle. The skull-forehead interface is well developed and slightly rounded. The occiput is not domed; the stop at the midpoint between the tip of the nose and occiput. The overall harmony of the head is exceptional. The bridge is long and tapers a bit toward the nose, although the muzzle must never be pointed; for most of its length it is straight, with only a slight convexity near the nose. The nostrils are straight and well open, always darker in color than the coat and preferably black. The jaws are clean-cut, the lips are big but neither heavy nor pendulous. The bite is good. The inner and outer lips are black, as is the hard palate. The teeth are strong, white, well inserted and well adapted.

EYES The oval eyes are set horizontally. They are of medium size, well open, and neither protruding nor deep-set. The color is almost always dark amber, their expression calm and intelligent. The eyelids are black, the eyebrows somewhat accentuated.

EARS The ears are small in comparison with the other features (about 4½ inches long and a little less than 4 inches broad); they are thin, triangular and rounded at the tips. They are set on only moderately high, hanging and slightly inclined backward, close to the head, leaving a portion of the inner side visible at the base. Clipped ears are acceptable but natural ears are preferable.

NECK Short, straight, and thick and well set into the shoulders. The dewlap is not pronounced.

BODY The ribs are well sprung without, however, giving the trunk a cylindrical shape. The chest is broad and well let down. The circumference at the brisket is 30½ inches in males, 27½ inches in females; width, 8 and 7 inches for males and females respectively; depth, 11½ and 10 inches, respectively. The back is straight, and short coupling is preferable. The loins are broad, short, well muscled and well joined to the croup, which should be slightly inclined. The lower belly should not be large but should be in good proportion to the rest of the body. The lower line should rise gradually from stern to groin.

TAIL Long, not docked; it should reach the hocks when down, as it is when the dog is standing still. It is heavy and scimitar-shaped, set on at a normal height, well feathered. In the longhaired variety the tail is fringed and has a slight upward curve at the end. In movement the tail is carried level and falls naturally when the dog is still. In action the tail rises slightly above the horizontal and curves upward.

FOREQUARTERS AND HINDQUARTERS The legs are practically vertical when the dog is in good stance. The forelimbs, the pasterns, the metacarpi are well boned and approximately cylindrical in cross section. The muscling is solid throughout. The articulations are strong, the angulations are regular and permit great ease of movement. The hocks are slightly let down, evenly open and well directed. The metatarsus is vertical. The feet are in good proportion to the other dimensions; they are strong and neither too round nor too long. They should not be flat. In type they should be midway between catfeet and harefeet. The toes are large, well joined, with abundant hair between them and around the pads. The pads are thick and tough. The nails are dark and preferably black. The hind limbs may have one or two dewclaws each.

COAT Heavy, thick, not too hard, somewhat like goat's hair. It is smooth or slightly wavy, and very abundant in both longhaired and shorthaired varieties. Normally the hair is not evenly distributed over the body. On the head and the lower limbs, below wrist and hock, it is shorter and denser, also shorter at the tip of the ears than at the base and finer and softer. The hair is longer on the tail, which is well feathered, heavy, and fringed in longhaired dogs. There may be a collar of long hair about the neck, and long hair may also be found on the buttocks and the back part of the forearm, especially in the longhaired variety. The undercoat is short, fine, abundant and normally lighter in color than the top coat; such a coat is found more often among the longhaired dogs. **Color** The only permissible colors are fawn, wolf, and yellow, either solid or with markings.

GAIT The dog moves with an easy, relaxed gait.

DISQUALIFICATIONS Excessive size or insufficient size, acceptance being granted to a discrepancy of plus or minus 1½ inches from the standard; head too narrow, too long, too pointed; overshot jaw; light or speckled nose; walleyes or eyes of unequal size; ears badly set on, too large, too fleshy or round; docked, rudimentary or innately defective tail; albinism; coat varying from natural type.

SCALE OF POINTS

	M	F
Head: skull, ears, eyes, bridge, mouth, stop	20	20
Neck, withers, shoulders, forequarters	15	13
Trunk, loins, upper and lower lines of trunk	15	15
Croup, pelvis, hindquarters	13	15
Tail: carriage, shape, set-on	5	5
Feet, toes, nails	5	5
Coat: texture, color, density	7	7
General appearance, harmony of proportions, gait, physique, sexual characteristics	20	20
	100	100

60 CASTRO LABORIERO DOG

Cão de Castro Laboriero

PORTUGAL

This typical Portuguese breed gets its name from the village of Castro Laboriero. It has spread through the area which includes the Peneda and Soajo Mountains between the Minho and Lima rivers. Its origins are lost in the past. This dog is a Mastiff type. Loyal and docile with his master, he proves an ideal watchdog, capable not only of facing but of attacking wolves which still infest the mountains. He is therefore much used for the protection of livestock.

GENERAL CHARACTERISTICS A vigorous dog, of pleasing lines; of noble carriage, the expression severe and rustic, a "mountaineer" dog. The gait is free, easy and nervous; although not aggressive, this breed is often openly hostile. It barks in a characteristic way, loudly, beginning with variable tones, which in general are quite low, ending with sharp, prolonged barking. **Weight and Size** Weight: males 66-88 lb; females 44-66 lb.

HEAD Of normal size, light rather than massive, very lean, but not excessively so, well supplied with skin, but without wrinkles. The nostrils are pronounced, big, straight and well open, invariably black. The bridge is long, strong, straight throughout its entire length; it tapers toward the tip of the muzzle, without however being narrow or pointed. The mouth is well cut; the lips are regular, neither falling nor fleshy, well adapted with a commissure which is not highly visible.

SERRA DA ESTRELA DOG

CASTRO LABORIERO DOG

Photo: F. Jovane.

The inside of the mouth, the hard palate and the edges of the lips are strongly pigmented with black. The teeth are sound, white, strong, well adapted and solidly set in the jaws, which are powerfully muscled. The stop is not pronounced, and is positioned farther from the occiput than from the nose. The cranial-frontal region is of regular development and slightly raised. The medial furrow is minimal. The profile is close to a straight line. The occipital protuberance is not pronounced.

EYES Slanting, neither deep-set nor prominent; they are almond-shaped, of medium size, perfectly equal and well open; they have a rather severe expression. Light brown in dogs with light coats, they are dark brown or nearly black in dogs with dark coats.

EARS Of medium size (4¾ inches wide), not thick, nearly triangular but rounded toward the tips, set on rather high. They fall naturally and parallel to each other at the sides of the head, and when the animal is on the alert the ears are turned forward.

NECK Straight, well built, short and of proportionate thickness. It is well inserted into the shoulders, and is carried proudly. There is no dewlap.

BODY The chest is ogival in shape, high, broad and normally deep. The back is horizontal and of normal length. The loins are strong, broad, short and well muscled: they are well joined to the croup, which slopes gently to the tail. The belly is not of great volume, and is slightly drawn up; there is a noticeable difference in level between the xiphoid region and the pubic region: this means that the lower line of the body is appreciably sloped from the stern to the groin.
TAIL The tail is not docked, and when the dog is in repose it reaches the hock. It is long and thick, very hairy on the underside, a saber tail, well set on and rather high, hanging well between the buttocks, which are feathered with abundant hair. When the animal is excited, the tail rises above the backline and is held upward, toward the front and a little on one side; it is never carried down.

FOREQUARTERS AND HINDQUARTERS
The forelegs are properly vertical as seen from in front and from behind; in profile, the forelegs are correct, but in the hindquarters the line of the hock, in its lower part, slopes slightly forward from the vertical (slightly underneath itself, as seen from behind). The legs are well boned and covered with powerful muscles, especially on the upper arm and the thigh, which is well supplied with abundant muscular masses. The forearms and pasterns are practically cylindrical. The joints and angulations are well developed; the angulations are of regular opening, with the scapula-humeral almost straight, and the tibial-tarsial moderately obtuse; the forearms are straight, with a gradual tapering from above down, as far as the pastern, which should be neither too long nor too bent. **Feet** In good proportion to the size of the dog and rather more rounded than long (tendency to catfoot); large toes, naturally arched, which are turned neither inward nor outward and are well joined. The pads are thick and hard; the nails are well set, black or dark gray, smooth and hard, of regular dimensions. Simple or double dewclaws may be present.

COAT Heavy, resistant, rather hard to the touch, rather dull, smooth, well distributed over practically the entire body, and very abundant. The commonest type has short hair (about 2 inches); dogs with hair either longer or shorter than this are rare. Generally the hair is shorter and more abundant on the head and ears (where it is finer and softer), and also at the extremities (elbows, hocks); it is abundant and long on the tail, especially on the underside; it is thicker at the midpoint, and also on the buttocks, which are especially well feathered; there is no undercoat.
Color Wolf color is common in its light, medium and dark variants; the dark shade is commonest. Exceptionally one may find these three shades in different parts of the body: dark wolf on the head, back and shoulders; medium wolf on the chest, croup and thighs; and light wolf on the belly. The preferred color is the so-called "mountain color," as it is called locally, and considered by the breeders in the Portuguese countryside as the dog's the genetic trait, that is, a composite coat like that of the wolf: grayish with more or less deep tones, tending to black; brown or reddish hairs are found on the entire body or on a part of it.

GAIT The Cão de Castro Laboreiro moves easily and rhythmically. The legs move parallel to the sagittal plane of the body. The dog seems to prefer a normal pace, occasionally an ambling gait, unless some outside influence obliges him to move at the trot or gallop.

DISQUALIFICATIONS Dog too big or too little: head too large (bony or fleshy); head too narrow, long and pointed; nose not black; overshot or undershot condition; walleyes or eyes of unequal size; ears set on badly, too large, too fleshy or rounded; congenital or acquired deafness; trumpet tail, docked tail; lack of tail; coat with markings or otherwise varying noticeably from the standard; albinism.

SCALE OF POINTS

	M	F
Head: carriage, skull, ears, eyes, bridge, mouth, stop nose	20	20
Neck, withers, shoulders, forelegs	15	13
Chest, loins, upper and lower lines of body	15	15
Croup, pelvis, hind legs	13	15
Tail: carriage, shape, insertion	5	5
Coat: texture, color, density	7	7
Feet, toes, nails	5	5
General appearance, harmony of build, gait, stature, sexual characteristics (male or female)	20	20
	100	100

Photo: M. Pedone.

RAFEIRO DO ALENTEJO

61 RAFEIRO DO ALENTEJO

PORTUGAL

GENERAL CHARACTERISTICS A large dog of powerful build, a sober farm animal of fairly but not excessively long, stout configuration.

WEIGHT AND HEIGHT Weight: males 88-110 lb; females 34½-44½ lb. Height: males 26-29 inches; females 25-27½ inches.

HEAD A bearlike head, in good proportion to the overall body structure. The skull is broad, with a slight medial furrow above and between the eyes. The stop is not accentuated. The upper longitudinal axes of muzzle and skull are divergent. The occipital protuberance is not very pronounced. The muzzle is rounded, with a straight profile, not so long as the skull and moderately broad. The lips are slightly rounded in front, well cut and overlapping; they are thin, solid, and give a slight curve to the lower profile. The jaws are strong, well muscled and well opposed. The nose is oval, its tip blunted from above to below and from forward back, and dark in color.

EYES The eyes are not deep-set, their expression calm. They are horizontal and rather small and elliptical, with dark lids.

EARS Set on medium high, folded and hanging down at the sides of the head. When the dog is alert they are raised only at the base and folded vertically. They are triangular in shape, rather small with a narrow base. In length they are equal to the furrow.

NECK Well set into the shoulders, straight, short and strong, with a moderate dewlap.

FOREQUARTERS Strong, vertical as viewed from both front and profile. The shoulders are strong, of moderate length, well developed, muscular and slightly sloping. The angulation is open. The forearm is vertical and long, strong and muscular. The pasterns are strong, of medium length and slightly sloping. The feet must not be flat; they are well closed and long, with stout toes that are barely arched. The color varies with the color of the coat. The pads are thick and tough.

BODY Short-coupled, strong, muscular, fairly long and large. Its lower line is slightly sloping from fore to aft and from the bottom to the top. The chest, though ample, is not prominent. The brisket is approximately at the level of the elbows. The stern is nearly horizontal. The back is long and straight or slightly hollowed. The loins are of moderate length and straight, broad and well filled out and well muscled. The croup is of moder-

ate length, in good proportion to the size of the dog, broad and high, slightly hollowed. The belly and flanks are in good proportion to the rest of the body; they must not be like those of the Greyhound. They follow the line of the stern.

TAIL Set on moderately high, the tail is slightly curved at the end and is of good length. When the dog is at rest it is carried between the hocks and reaches below them. It may curl moderately when the dog is in action.

HINDQUARTERS Strong, well separated, vertical as viewed from behind as well as in profile. The thigh is long, broad and muscular, though not too plainly so. The hind legs are moderately inclined, of medium length and muscular. The hock is of moderate height and length and is lean; normally angulated. The metatarsus is strong, of medium length and slightly sloping. Single or double dewclaws may be present. The feet are similar to the forefeet.

COAT Preferably short or moderately long, the coat is heavy, dense, and evenly distributed over the body to the toes. **Color** Black, wolf, tawny or yellow, mixed with white; bicolored, roan or dappled; very often streaked or grizzled. **Skin** Thick and quite close-fitting; inner and outer lips black.

GAIT Rather heavy, slow and rolling.

FAULTS Generally poor appearance, skinniness or obesity; excessively light build; pointed nose or vertically cut forenose; long bridge; lack of dewlap; excessively hollow croup; tail set on too high or too low or curled when dog is in repose; bad-looking coat.

DISQUALIFICATIONS Long, narrow head; excessively long muzzle or bridge arched in profile; overshot or undershot jaws; flat or narrow skull; light eyes, eyes of different size; ears set on too high or too low, round or excessively large ears; short, docked or absent tail; hair too short; lack of black pigmentation on nose, lips or mouth (albinism).

SCALE OF POINTS

General appearance	20
Head	15
Eyes	5
Ears	5
Neck	10
Trunk	10
Legs	15
Tail	10
Coat	10
	100

RAFEIRO DO ALENTEJO

Photo: F. Jovane.

62 PORTUGUESE WATER DOG

Cão de agua

PORTUGAL

Among the many tasks accomplished by different dog breeds, the duties of the Portuguese Water Dog are certainly most unusual. This dog is a specialist not only in retrieving game birds or rabbits, but also fish. He is an expert diver and swimmer and observes attentively the moves of his master. When he sees a fish escape from the net or hook, he jumps in, catches it, and brings it back to land, and will also bring back a hawser or other boat accessory that falls into the water. As a liaison between the shore and the boat he is a tenacious watchdog, able to swim considerable distances, and a valuable aid to fishermen and boatmen. Of uncertain origin, he was widely prevalent in the past, although today he is rare except in the Algarve region. Impetuous and quarrelsome, he is happy with those he knows.

PORTUGUESE WATER DOG

PORTUGUESE WATER DOG

GENERAL CHARACTERISTICS A medium-sized dog, very well proportioned, rugged and massive. Viewed in profile, the skull is slightly longer than the muzzle. Its constant use as a water retriever accounts for his extraordinary muscular development. Formerly used throughout Portugal, it is almost limited today to the region of Algarve, where fishing traditions continue very much as in the past.

WEIGHT AND SIZE Weight: males 42-55 lb; females 35-48½ lb. Height: males 20-22½ inches; females 17-20½ inches.

HEAD The head is well proportioned and massive. Viewed in profile, the skull is slightly longer than the muzzle. The curve of the skull is rather more accentuated at the back than in front. The occiput is well defined. Viewed from the front the skull is domed, with a slight concavity in the middle. The forehead is furrowed for two thirds of the length of the parietal bones; the frontal bones are prominent. The muzzle tapers from base to nose. The stop is well defined and lies slightly farther back than the inner corner of the eyes. The nose is wide, with well-open nostrils, which are finely pigmented. Nose color varies with coat color. The lips are rather thick, especially in front. The inner mouth is well blacked, the powerful jaws are neither undershot nor overshot. The teeth are not visible when the mouth is closed; the canines are strongly developed.

EYES Medium-sized and are set well apart. They are slightly oblique, quite round, and neither deep-set nor protruding. The color of the eyes may be either brown or black. The finely textured eyelids have black rims. The haw is not visible.

EARS Heart-shaped, thin in texture and set on well above eye level. Except for a small opening at the back, the ears are held close to the head. The tips should not reach below the top of the neck.

NECK Short and straight, well rounded and carried proudly. It is strongly muscled, without mane and without dewlap.

FOREQUARTERS The forelegs are strong and straight. The shoulder is sloping and very well muscled. The upper arm is strong and of regular length, the forearm long and extremely well muscled. The carpus is well boned, wider in front than at the side. The pastern is long and powerful. The forefeet are round and rather flat. The toes should not be too long and should not be knuckled up; they are webbed to their tips with a soft membrane well covered with hair. Black nails are preferred, but nails of other colors are permitted in conformity with color of coat. Normally the nails are held slightly off the ground. The central pad is very thick, the others normal.

BODY The brisket is wide and deep, reaching to the elbow. The ribs are rather long and well sprung. The withers are broad and not especially prominent. The back is short and well coupled. The belly is drawn up in a graceful line. The rump is well formed, with only a slight slope; the hips are barely apparent.

TAIL Not docked; it is thick at the base and tapers gradually to the tip. It should be set on neither too high nor too low. Extended, it should not reach below the hock. When the dog is on the alert the tail should be held in a ring, the forepart of which does not lie beyond the rear limit of the loin. The tail is used actively in both swimming and diving.

HINDQUARTERS The thighs are powerful and of normal length, strongly muscled and with the thigh bone set parallel to the medial body line. The second thigh is long and strongly muscled, decidedly inclined from front to back. Tendons are well developed. The metatarsus is long. There are no dewclaws. The hind feet are similar in all respects to the forefeet. The legs are regularly positioned. It is not a fault if the forelegs are held so that they lie slightly forward of the perpendicular and if the hind legs, from the hock down, are also held slightly forward.

COAT Thick coat distributed evenly over the entire body except for the underarm and groin, where it is thinner. There are two kinds of coat—one with fairly long, wavy hair growing rather loose and with a slight sheen, the hair on the top of the head being erect and the hair on the ears longer than the leather; and a second type with shorter hair made up of compact, cylindrical curls, very thick and not particularly glossy. In the latter variety the hair on the top of the head is similar to the rest of the coat, while on the ears it is sometimes wavy rather than curly.
Color Black, white, and various shades of brown; also combinations of black or brown with white. A white coat does not indicate albinism provided nose, mouth, and eyelids are black. **Skin** In animals with black, white, or black and white coats the skin has a decidedly bluish color. There is no undercoat.

DISQUALIFICATIONS Oversize or undersize; very long, narrow, flat or pointed head; funnel-shaped muzzle or excessively pointed muzzle; flesh-colored or discolored nose, wholly or in part; light eyes, eyes differing from each other in form or size, sunken or bulging eyes; ears set on otherwise than noted above, excessively big or small ears, folded ears; docked or rudimentary tail, total lack of tail, heavy tail, tail droopy in action or held perpendicularly; dewclaws on hind legs; coat differing from types described above; albinism; undershot or overshot jaws; deafness, either hereditary or acquired.

SCALE OF POINTS

	Male	Female
Head, how held; muzzle, stop, nose, mouth, eyes, and ears	20	20
Neck, withers, shoulders, forelegs	10	7
Brisket, loins, upper and lower body line	15	15
Croup, pelvis, hind legs	10	13
Feet, toes, nails	10	10
Tail, how carried; form, setting	5	5
Coat, texture, color, density	5	5
General aspect, harmony of form, movement, body development, sexual development	25	25
	100	100

123

Photo: T. Fall, R. Kinne (Photo Res.).

63 APPENZELLER CATTLE DOG

Appenzeller Sennenhund

SWITZERLAND

The Swiss Cottage Dogs (which include the three following breeds) are of very ancient origin. Some naturalists believe that these are local breeds, indigenous, and trace them back to the Bronze Age (*Canis familiaris inostranzewi*) with the addition of wolf blood). On the other hand, Tschudy, Keller, and Kraemer think that the Tibetan is the ancestor of the present Cottage Dogs. As maintained in the case of the St. Bernard and the Rott-weiler, the Romans may have introduced herds into their Swiss colonies which would naturally be accompanied by their shepherd dogs. On a pottery lamp from Roman times discovered at Vindonissa, a sheep dog is shown exactly like the present Bernese Cottage Dog. Moreover, the Bernese and Appenzeller Cattle Dogs resemble the light Tibetan with brownish-black coat while the St. Bernard resembles the heavy Tibetan.

The Appenzeller Cattle Dog is an unbelievably vital breed that is greatly attached to his master and his work. He is used for driving livestock and sheep through the mountains. At night he proves to be most vigilant, and even when he does not go into the pastures with the livestock he still acts as a watchdog for the house and property. He has a more boisterous nature than the Entlebucher, a related breed, and needs open air and plenty of space.

Photo: M. Pedone

APPENZELLER CATTLE DOG

GENERAL CHARACTERISTICS A muscular but not massive dog, a fine herder and guard dog.

WEIGHT AND SIZE The weight from 48-55 lb. Height at the withers: males, 19-23 inches; females, slightly smaller.

HEAD The head should not be narrow and round, but broad and flat. The stop is not prominent. The nose is black. The muzzle tapers gradually toward the nose, but it must not do so exaggeratedly, and the degree of tapering should be less than in the German Shepherd.

EYES Small, brown, vivacious.

EARS Small, set on high, hanging.

NECK Short and wide towards the shoulders.

BODY The chest is of the broad type, fairly well let down but not excessively so.

TAIL The tail is strong and covered with hair of medium length. It is carried curled over the back when the dog is in movement.

FOREQUARTERS AND HINDQUARTERS Straight, lean, muscular. The feet are small and of moderate length. There are dewclaws on the hind legs. The hindlegs are slightly longer than the forelegs.

COAT Short, thick and glossy. **Color** Black with spots ranging from yellow to fawn and with symmetrical white markings. There should always be markings above the eyes. A white star is desirable. White normally appears on the chest, neck, muzzle, feet and the tip of the tail. Wherever the yellow or fawn spots appear, they are invariably located between black and white areas.

FAULTS Rounded forehead; excessively long, thin or curved muzzle; stop too pronounced; light eyes; short, pointed ears, ears lying away from head or carried badly; colors or markings other than those specified above. ●

Photo: E. Münch.

APPENZELLER CATTLE DOG

Photo: Comet.

64 BERNESE CATTLE DOG

Berner Sennenhund

SWITZERLAND

Also referred to as cattle dogs or stable dogs, the Sennenhund does valuable work throughout Switzerland. His task is different from the shepherd's usual work, for the cattle dog, and not only the Swiss type, is above all a dependable and hardy stable guard.

In the pasture where he tends the herds he is a real tyrant that can frighten and round up animals when they stray or enter another's pasture. His truly difficult task is not within the scope of the ordinary shepherd dog, even if he is very brave, since he is accustomed to the timid submission of the sheep. The cattle dog knows how to make himself obeyed by direct methods; he nips the muzzle, the ears, the hindquarters, and especially the hocks, jumping as high as possible with surprising agility.

The Sennenhund is prevalent in the hill area. He does not bite but has a vigilant and energetic nature and a well-developed instinct for guarding property. He is perfectly able to distinguish between his master's possessions and those of a neighbor. Unlike the related breeds, in particular the Appenzeller and the Entlebucher, he must be properly trained in order to accomplish his tasks. He is very robust and almost insensible to cold. His fidelity is legendary and his affection is always directed to one person —his master. He always distrusts strangers. Among cattle dog breeds this is the one that has been most successful abroad. In America, for example, he is much sought after, but only as a luxury and show dog.

BERNESE CATTLE DOG

GENERAL CHARACTERISTICS A strongly built animal and an excellent guard dog.

SIZE Height at the withers: males 25-27½ inches; females 23-26 inches.

HEAD Short and massive, with a flat skull. The stop is not pronounced. The nose has open, black nostrils. The muzzle is rather long.

EYES Dark, with a lively and intelligent expression.

EARS Set on high and V-shaped, hanging close to the cheeks.

BODY The body is powerful in every respect. The chest is broad, deep, well let down. The back is straight and broad. The loins and haunches are muscular. The belly is moderately tucked up.

TAIL The tail is fluffy, not curled or rolled; it is very well feathered, with slightly wavy, but not curly, hair.

FOREQUARTERS AND HINDQUARTERS The legs are solid and straight, excellent in the way they support the powerful body. The feet are round.

COAT The hair is abundant, long and smooth. **Color** Glossy black, with tan markings. There may be white on the chest, bridge, feet, and the tip of the tail.

FAULTS Excessively massive or heavy head, undershot jaw, walleyes; bulging eyes; heavy, gun dog-type ears; long body; tail carried above the backline; harefeet. ●

65 ENTLEBUCHER CATTLE DOG

Entlebucher Sennenhund

SWITZERLAND

Native of the region of Entlebuch, that is to say the valley of the Little Emme and the Enteln, in the canton of Lucerne, he is skilled at maintaining order in the herds. To accomplish this task he uses his great agility in avoiding the angry reaction of the cattle when he makes them obey. The Entlebucher adapts easily to the most varied milieux. He is attentive and very intelligent and eager to work. He is docile with people he knows and very good with children.

BERNESE CATTLE DOG

GENERAL CHARACTERISTICS A rather small dog, less than the average size, with all parts in good proportion. It is an extremely agile dog of a pleasing, intelligent appearance. A good herd dog, it is also a faithful guard dog and an excellent companion.

SIZE Height at the withers: 16-19½ inches.

HEAD Proportionate to the body, with a flat skull. The jaws are powerful and well formed. The stop is not pronounced and is clearly off center. The tip of the nose is black.

EYES Rather small, brown and lively.

EARS Small, set on high, V-shaped. They hang down against the cheeks, carried slightly forward when the dog is alert, typical of all pasture dogs.

NECK The neck is short and well set into the shoulders.

BODY The chest is broad and well let down, the brisket is deep. The overall impression is of greater length than height, although this is largely due to the depth of the brisket.

TAIL This breed is born short-tailed.

FOREQUARTERS AND HINDQUARTERS The forelegs and hind legs are straight and robust. The shoulders are long and sloping. The hocks are well bent, the feet rounded and close. Dewclaws preferably absent.

Photo: S. A. Thompson, E. Münch.

ENTLEBUCHER CATTLE DOG

COAT Short, thick, close, hard and glossy. **Color** As with Swiss pasture dogs generally, the color is black with tan markings ranging from light to dark on eyes, cheeks and all four legs. Regular, symmetrical white markings on the head, neck, chest and feet are a good feature. There are also tan markings between the black and white of the feet.
FAULTS Bulging forehead; long, thin or curved muzzle; overshot or undershot jaws; light eyes; short, pointed ears; hair too long or too soft; colors other than those prescribed by the standard; an excess of white color. ●

66 GREAT SWISS CATTLE DOG

Grosser Schweizer Sennenhund

SWITZERLAND

This cattle dog is an excellent leader of herds, endowed as he is with a mild temperament and great self-control. As it stands today, the breed stems directly from the great dogs which followed old Swiss confederation bands in the wars of the Middle Ages. These dogs underwent a difficult period in 1849 when a Zurich burgomaster ordered them to be suppressed on the pretext that they were dangerous to game. This ordinance, however, provoked the indignation of the peasants, who kept these dogs as faithful pets and valuable helpers, one of the rare examples of man's gratitude to the dog that the centuries have shown us, a gratitude which helped to maintain a valuable breed whose troubles have been intimately connected with the history of the Swiss people. Besides his use as a herd dog, this great cattle dog is very valuable as a guard and defense dog and also for hauling, although the latter task has been replaced by the no less important one of faithful companion.

GENERAL CHARACTERISTICS A large dog, robust and lively, black with brilliant russet and white markings, attractive and well balanced in symmetry and coat. This is an intelligent dog, courageous and faithful, admirably suited for duties as a guard, companion, defender, and gun dog. He has endurance and can cover a lot of ground, walking or trotting.

SIZE Height: males 25½-27½ inches; females 23½-25½ inches.

HEAD The skull is flat, with a slight medial furrow. The head is robust in proportion to the body, but it should never be heavy. The length from occiput to eyes is about equal to that from eyes to tip of nose. The bridge is straight, with possibly a slight rise just before the tip of the nose. The cheeks are normal, neither sunken nor exceptionally filled out. The jaws are of medium length, strong and not tapering to a point when viewed either from above or in profile. The lips are well fitting and lean. The teeth are strong, the jaws closing in a scissors bite. The stop is slightly accentuated.

EYES Of medium size, neither deep-set nor protruding. The color ranges from hazel to brown, with an attentive, intelligent and faithful expression. The lids adhere closely to the eyeballs.

EARS Of medium size, triangular and set on rather high; at rest they hang flat and close to the head, becoming slightly raised and turned forward when the dog is excited. They are well furnished with hair, both outside and inside.

NECK Strong and muscular, of medium length, with no dewlap.

BODY The rib cage, as viewed from in front, is neither flat nor barrel-chested. The chest is broad, fairly deep and well rounded. The withers are high and long, the back moderately long, robust, and straight. The loins are broad and strong. The croup is long and broad, descending in an attractive, somewhat rounded curve. The belly and groin are neither full nor drawn up. The length of the trunk,

GREAT SWISS CATTLE DOG

GREAT SWISS CATTLE DOG

Photo: Kino Blatter, H.P.F., K. Wolfram.

67 ST. BERNARD

St. Bernhardshund

SWITZERLAND

measured from the point of the shoulder to the point of the buttocks, should be slightly more than the height at the withers, in a ratio of about 10:9.

TAIL The tail is rather stout and reaches the hocks. At rest it is carried down; when the dog is in movement or excited it is carried up and slightly curved, never curled or carried over the back.

FOREQUARTERS The shoulders are long, strong and sloping, forming an obtuse angle with the upper arm; they are muscular and set close to the body. The forearm is short and straight as seen from all sides. **HINDQUARTERS** The thighs are broad, strong and well muscled. The femur is quite long and, seen in profile, inclined toward the long leg. The hocks are broad and strong. **FEET** Short, round, with well-closed and arched toes. The nails are short and strong. Dewclaws on the hind legs should be removed shortly after birth.

COAT The top coat is hard and 1-2 inches long. There is an undercoat as well. **Color** The base color is black, with bright, symmetrical russet and white markings. The russet color occurs between the black and white. Russet markings on eyes ("four

eyes"), on the forelimbs and on both sides of the chest and on the feet. The inner side of the hind legs are similarly colored, as is the underside of the tail and the inner side of the ear, which also has a black edge. White markings are found on the head (muzzle and as a blaze from nose to forehead), chest, feet and tip of tail. White is permitted on the muzzle and as a collar. The nose and lips should invariably be black.

FAULTS (a) Structural faults: Any divergence from standard in size and proportion; ambivalent sexual characteristics; sponginess, excessive fineness or heaviness of bone; insufficient muscling; obesity; excessive heaviness or lightness of the head; defects of teeth; pendulous lips or eyelids; too open eyes; too square or too long-lined build; saddleback; bad angulation of forelegs or hind legs; splayed feet; coat too long or too fine. (b) **Esthetic faults:** Light eyes, bad carriage of tail and ears; dull or impure coloring, unsymmetrical markings. (c) **Temperamental faults:** Lack of temperament, timidity or, on the contrary, viciousness. Structural and temperamental faults are to be judged more severely than esthetic faults because they hamper the capabilities of the dog as a working animal. ●

A colossus of the dog family, living symbol of strength and sacrifice, the St. Bernard dog arouses the deepest admiration in many who appreciate his extraordinary intelligence, strength, and fidelity.

The history of the famous dog is linked to the refuge of St. Bernard, founded shortly before A.D. 1000 by a young noble, Bernard de Menthon, for the purpose of sheltering travelers or saving unfortunates overtaken by storms and buried under the snow. After Bernard's death many monks followed his example, but it was only during the middle of the seventeenth century that the coenobites of St. Bernard decided to use for their task dogs capable of confronting the snows and difficulties of the high Alps.

The monks, according to certain writers, themselves created

the breed which bears the name of the refuge by crossing German Mastiffs with Pyrenean mountain dogs, but this hypothesis has not been proved by the information at our disposal. Everything seems to indicate that the St. Bernard goes back to the Tibetan Mastiff. Keller writes concerning the latter: "From the plateau of Tibet the domestic animals spread to Nepal, to India, and at the same time, to China. The Assyrian Babylonian culture knew him for a while. It appears that the Pharaonic Egypt did not, although he was present in the year of Alexander, and it was just after the departure of Alexander from India that the dog appeared in Greece as a present from King Porus. The breeding of the Mastiff began in Greece as well, and later it was followed by the Romans. Roman colonists, crossing the Alps into Switzerland, took the Mastiff with them, as well as to other parts of central and western Europe." Numerous contemporaneous reports prove that the Romans, founders of numerous colonies in Switzerland, brought their Mastiffs with them. In time specimens raised in the Alps underwent changes and attained their particular variety.

Around 1820 the breed faced extinction, being difficult to maintain. Partly from this and partly because the monks cared more about the hardiness of the stock than its aesthetic qualities, the dogs were not successful as show dogs, in today's parlance.

Dog fanciers, however, maintained the breed's purity and continued with its breeding, based exclusively on its aesthetic qualities. Their efforts in this field were crowned with success.

For a very long time there have been two kinds of St. Bernard, the long-haired and the short-haired. The monks concentrated on the breeding of stock with short hair for a good reason: the long hair offers more space for the snow to gather and form icicles so heavy as to impede the movements of the animal; some dogs died in this way, immobilized by the ice.

Modern means of communication and the present network of routes allow travelers to cross the Alpine passes safely, and the importance of the St. Bernard's life-saving role has lessened. Nevertheless this dog can still be useful to man. The monks of the ancient refuge now use him as an avalanche dog, and once more the St. Bernard is able to maintain his legend.

GENERAL CHARACTERISTICS Powerful, proportionately tall, strong and muscular in every part, with powerful head and most intelligent expression. In dogs with a dark mask the expression appears more stern but never ill-natured.

SIZE Males at least 27½ inches, females 25½ inches. Females are of finer, more delicate build.

HEAD Like the whole body, very powerful and imposing. The massive skull is wide and slightly arched, the sides sloping in a gentle curve into the very strongly developed high cheekbones. Occiput only moderately developed. The supraorbital ridge is very strongly developed and forms nearly a right angle with the horizontal axis of the head. Deeply imbedded between the eyes and starting at the root of the muzzle, a furrow runs over the whole skull. It is strongly marked in the first half, gradually disappearing toward the base of the occiput. The lines at the sides of the head diverge considerably from the outer corner of the eyes toward the back of the head. The skin of the forehead, above the eyes, forms rather noticeable wrinkles, which converge toward the furrow. Especially when the dog is in action, the wrinkles are more visible without in the least giving the impression of morosity. Too strongly developed wrinkles are not desired. The slope from the skull to the muzzle is sudden and rather steep. The muzzle is short and does not taper; the vertical depth at the root of the muzzle must be greater than the length of the muzzle. The bridge of the muzzle is not arched but straight; in some dogs it may be slightly broken. A rather wide, well-marked, shallow furrow runs from the root of the muzzle over the entire bridge of the muzzle to the nose. The flews of the upper jaw are strongly developed, not sharply cut, but turning in a beautiful curve into the lower edge, and slightly overhanging. The flews of the lower jaw must not be deeply pendant. The teeth should be sound and strong and should meet in either a scissors or an even bite, the scissors bite being preferable. The undershot bite, although sometimes found with good specimens, is not desirable. The overshot bite is a fault. A black roof of the mouth is desirable. The nose is very substantial, broad with wide-open nostrils, and, like the lips, always black.

EYES Set more to the front than the sides; they are of medium size, dark brown, with an intelligent, friendly expression; they are set moderately deep. The lower eyelids as a rule do not close completely and form an angular wrinkle toward the inner corner of the eye. Eyelids that are too deeply pendant and conspicuously show the lachrymal glands or a very red, thick haw are objectionable, as are eyes that are too light.

ST. BERNARD

ST. BERNARD

ST. BERNARD

EARS Of medium size, set rather high, with very strongly developed burr at the base. They stand slightly away from the head at the base, then drop with a sharp bend to the side and cling to the head without a turn. The flap is tender and forms a rounded triangle, slightly elongated toward the point, the front edge lying firmly to the head, whereas the back edge may stand somewhat away from the head, especially when the dog is at attention. Lightly set ears, which at the base cling closely to the head, give it an oval and too little marked exterior, whereas a strongly developed base gives the skull a squarer, broader and much more expressive appearance.

NECK Set high, very strong and, in action, carried erect; otherwise horizontally or slightly downward. The junction of head and neck is distinctly marked by an indentation. The nape of the neck is very muscular and rounded at the sides; this makes the neck appear rather short. The dewlap of throat and neck is well pronounced; excessive development of the dewlap, however, is not desirable.

BODY The chest is very well arched, moderately deep, not reaching below the elbows. The back is very broad, perfectly straight as far as the haunches, from there sloping gently to the rump and merging imperceptibly into the root of the tail. The belly is distinctly set off from the very powerful loin section and only slightly drawn up.

TAIL Starting broad and powerful directly from the rump, the tail is long and very heavy, ending in a powerful tip. In repose it hangs straight down, turning gently upward in the lower third only (this is not considered a fault). In a great many specimens the tail is carried with the end slightly bent. In action all dogs carry the tail more or less turned upward. However it may not be carried too erect and by no means rolled over the back. A slight curling of the tip is admissible.

FOREQUARTERS The shoulders are sloping and broad, very muscular and powerful. The withers are strongly pronounced. The forearms are very powerful and extraordinarily muscular. The forelegs are straight and strong. **HINDQUARTERS** Well developed. Legs very muscular with hocks of moderate angulation. Dewclaws are not desired; if present, they must not obstruct gait. **FEET** Broad, with strong toes, moderately closed, and with rather high knuckles. The so-called dewclaws, which sometimes occur on the inside of the hind legs, are imperfectly developed toes. They serve no purpose and are disregarded in judging. They may be removed.

COAT Very dense, shorthaired, lying smooth, tough, without however feeling rough. The thighs are slightly bushy. The tail at the root has longer and denser hair, which gradually becomes shorter toward the tip. The tail appears bushy, not forming a flag. **Color** White with red or red with white, the red in various shades; brindle patches with white markings. The colors red and brown-yellow are of entirely equal value. Necessary markings are: white chest, feet and tip of tail, noseband, collar or spot on the nape; the latter and blaze are very desirable. Never of one color or without white. Faulty are all other colors, except the favored dark shadings on the head (mask) and ears.

FAULTS All deviations from the standard, such as swayback and a disproportionately long back, hocks too bent, straight hindquarters, upward-growing hair in spaces between the toes, out at elbows, cow hocks and weak pasterns.

LONGHAIRED ST. BERNARD (Langhaariger St. Bernardshund) The long-haired type completely resembles the shorthaired except for the coat which is not shorthaired but of medium length, plain to slightly wavy, never rolled, curly or shaggy. Usually, on the back, especially from the area of the haunches to the rump, the hair is wavier, a condition, by the way, that is slightly indicated in the shorthaired dogs. The tail is bushy with dense hair of moderate length. Rolled or curly hair on the tail is not desirable. A tail with parted hair or a flag tail is faulty. Face and ears are covered with short and soft hair; longer hair at the base of the ears is permissible. Forelegs only slightly feathered; thighs very bushy. ●

ST. BERNARD

131

Photo: H.P.F., MARKA, S. A. Thompson.

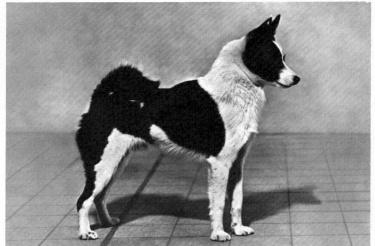

NORRBOTTENSPETS

68 NORRBOTTENSPETS
SWEDEN

GENERAL CHARACTERISTICS A small dog, compact but light in build, very much of the Spitz type, with good carriage and attentive expression.

SIZE Height at the withers should be about 16 inches.

HEAD Viewed from above and in profile, the head should be wedge-shaped, the skull flat or very slightly curved and with a pronounced stop. The muzzle should taper steadily and be lean, with thin lips very tight over the gums. The jaws meet in a scissors bite. The tip of the nose is black.

EYES The eyes are of moderate size, dark, with a vigilant and constantly alert expression.

EARS Of medium size, erect, with the tips held forward. The ears are highly mobile, and when the dog is on the alert they should approach each other.

NECK Relatively long and slightly curved, lean and muscular and carried proudly. The nape is noticeably curved outward.

BODY The outline is square; the body itself is compact, with a well-developed chest. The back is straight, strong and flexible.

CROUP Well developed, relatively broad and moderately sloped. The belly is only slightly tucked up.

◄ SLED DOGS IN HARNESS

Photo: McCutcheon, A. Wintzell.

FOREQUARTERS AND HINDQUARTERS
The shoulders are set well back. The forearm is relatively long, the elbows directly back. The hindquarters are robust and lean, with a fairly good angulation and with straight legs as seen from the front. The pastern is moderately angulated and springy. The feet are small, compact and very springy. There may be dewclaws, although they are not desirable. The dog should move freely, with great ease, giving an impression of vigor and springiness.

TAIL Set on high, curved, generally carried on the side, and when down the tip reaches mid-thigh. The tail joints should not reach below the hock. A docked tail is permissible but not desirable.

COAT Thick and of medium length. It is composed of a soft undercoat and by a rougher top coat. On the head and front of the legs the hair should be short and flat; on the body it should be of medium length; on the neck, the back of the thighs and tail it should be somewhat longer. **Color** All colors are permissible, although the preference goes to white as base color, with russet or yellow markings. Each color area should be distinct from the others. ●

ESKIMO

69 ESKIMO
CANADA

Between 60° and 72° north latitude, in the areas which include Lapland, Siberia, Kamchatka, Alaska, Greenland, and Iceland, there live a great number of valiant sled dogs, immortalized in so many stories. Among them are many breeds, some of which are recognized by international dog associations. The Eskimo is one of these. He is excellent for hauling and also for hunting bears. He can stand temperatures of 60° to 70° below zero. He is raised in North America and his origins go back to the dogs introduced by the Eskimo tribes of eastern Siberia, and from there to the northernmost parts of the New World.

GENERAL CHARACTERISTICS A large sled dog, very wolflike in appearance, always alert, with a courageous, penetrating expression.
WEIGHT Males 66-110 lb; females 55-88 lb. Other conditions being equal, the most powerful-looking dogs are to be preferred.
HEAD Broad, well proportioned, strong, with a rather flat skull and a wedge-shaped muzzle. The nose is black or brown, as are the lips. The muzzle is broad, of medium length, and it must not have a foxlike look. The jaws are powerful. The head of the female is a little less robust than the male's.
EYES Moderately small, deep-set and slanted with a suggestion of the Mongoloid.

EARS Short and broad, the shape being an equilateral triangle. They are set on rather low on the skull, quite far apart; they are always carried erect and slightly forward, slightly rounded at the tips and fairly rugged. They are well covered with hair, both outside and in. The ears may be a bit longer in females and set on a little higher.
NECK Short, strong, very muscular.
BODY The chest is deep, broad and very muscular. It is well let down, with well-sprung ribs. The back is long and straight.
TAIL Stout, extremely well feathered and carried curled up over the back.
FOREQUARTERS Big and strong, with very good bone and prominent muscles. The forelegs are straight, not too long, and there is a slight spring in the pastern. **HINDQUARTERS** The thighs and hind legs are strongly developed. The stifle is moderately bent. The stern, considered as a whole, should be powerful and muscular and capable of strenuous effort. **FEET** Broad, long and slightly flat (this doesn't mean that they are truly flat or splayed). They are robust, well protected by abundant hair between the toes and with sturdy nails. The small, compact foot has a clear advantage on the snowy and icy terrain where these dogs work.
COAT The hair is evenly distributed over the entire body, forming a dense, thick coat. The hair varies from 2 to 6 inches. The longhaired variety has a rough coat 5-8 inches long. Both varieties have a thick, woolly undercoat. **Color** All colors are acceptable. ●

SLED RACE IN ALASKA

70 NEWFOUNDLAND
CANADA

The bravery and devotion of the St. Bernard is also characteristic of the Newfoundland to whose generous endowment of intelligence many people have owed their lives. This magnificent giant dog still carries out his innumerable exploits, and one wonders how many shipwrecked victims he has saved from icy northern waters.

Much has been written about the origin of the stock, but without any agreement. Some claim that the British brought this dog to Newfoundland. He makes an excellent helper to man in the codfish industry, as well as being a faithful guard and lifesaving dog.

Others maintain that the breed was developed through crossbreeding Labradors with Scandinavian sled dogs brought to Newfoundland by Norwegian fishermen before the English came in 1622. One must observe that this hypothesis is uncertain. The Newfoundland shares a few common traits with the Scandinavian sled dogs but rather resembles the Tibetan Mastiff.

In any case, it is interesting to realize that there still exist two varieties that resemble each other in general appearance but differ in size and physical traits. One variety lives in the interior of the island, still in a semi-wild state, while the other, the domesticated one, is used for fishing and also for hauling. (It is fascinating to watch these dogs, so well trained that they are able to catch large fish and carry them to the shore.) This variety lives on the coast.

The first variety is more massive and its coat is uniformly black. The second is lighter in movement, of a more docile nature, and also black; it is the type most like the handsome and imposing examples we admire at dog shows.

NEWFOUNDLAND

GENERAL CHARACTERISTICS A water dog, used for lifesaving; should have an exceptionally gentle and docile nature. The dog should impress one with its strength and great activity. He should move freely on his legs with the body swung loosely between them, so that a slight roll in gait should not be objectionable. Bones massive throughout, but not to give a heavy, cumbersome appearance.

WEIGHT AND SIZE Considerable size and weight are desirable so long as symmetry is maintained. A fair average height at the shoulder is 28 inches for a male and 26 inches for a female, and fair average weights are respectively, males, 140-150 lb; females, 110-120 lb.

HEAD Broad and massive, the occipital bone well developed; there should be no decided stop. The muscles should be short, clean-cut, and rather square in shape and covered with short, fine hair. Mouth should be soft and well covered by the lips.

EYES Small, dark brown; rather deeply set but not showing any haw; should be set rather wide apart.

EARS Small, set well back, square with the skull, lie close to the head, and covered with short hair without a fringe.

NECK Strong, well set on the shoulders and back.

BODY Well ribbed up with broad back and strong muscular loins. Chest should be deep and fairly broad; well covered with hair, but not to such an extent as to form a frill.

TAIL Of moderate length, reaching down a little below the hocks. It should be of fair thickness and well covered with hair, but not forming a flag. When the dog is standing still and not excited, it should hang downward with a slight curve at the end; but when the dog is in motion it should be carried up, and when he is excited straight out with only a slight curve at the end. Tails with a kink or curled over the back are very objectionable.

FOREQUARTERS Legs should be perfectly straight, well covered with muscle, elbows in, but well let down; feathered all down. **HINDQUARTERS** Should be very strong. The legs should have great freedom of action, slightly feathered. Slack loins and cow hocks are a defect. Dewclaws are objectionable and should be removed. **FEET** Should be large and well shaped. Splayed or turned-out feet are objectionable.

COAT Should be flat and dense, rather coarse, oily, and water-resistant. If brushed the wrong way it should fall back into place naturally. **Color** (a) Dull jet black: a slight tinge of bronze or white on chest and toes is not objectionable; (b) other than black: should in all respects have the same remarks enumerated in (a), but the colors most desirable are white, black, and bronze. Beauty in markings is important. Black dogs that have only white breast and white to tip of tail must be exhibited in the "black" classification.

FAULTS Weak or hollow back, slack loins or cow hocks. Dewclaws. Splayed or turned out feet. Tails with a kink or curled over the back. ●

NEWFOUNDLAND

71 GREENLAND DOG
Grünlandshund

COUNTRIES OF FAR NORTH

This polar Spitz is extremely hardy and well adapted to the rigors of the Arctic. He is used for pulling sleds.

The FCI has recently defined its characteristics by publishing a standard detailing the traits which make this breed different from other Arctic dogs to which it is connected through common origin.

SIZE 23½ inches and up for males, 21½ inches and up for females.

HEAD The skull is broad and slightly domed. The stop is pronounced but not exaggerated. The bridge should be straight and broad from the base to the tip of the nose. The muzzle is wedge-shaped, strong, broad at the base and tapering toward the tip but not pointed. The nose must be black in summer but it can be flesh-colored in winter. The teeth are extremely strong; the jaws meet in a scissors bite.

EYES Preferably dark, although they may be lighter depending on the color of the coat. They are slightly oblique, neither deep-set nor protruding. The expression is frank and open, with no hint of viciousness.

EARS Rather small, triangular and rounded at the tips; they are carried decidedly erect.

Photo: E. Münch

GREENLAND DOG

72 SAMOYED
COUNTRIES OF FAR NORTH

As Cardano wrote in his study on the Samoyed, this is one of the oldest dogs known to man, being descended without mixture from the dog that accompanied the Samoyed tribes during their migrations. He is a typical Siberian breed, with prehistoric origins.

Its thousand-year association with man has domesticated this dog to a unique degree. He is an exceptional guard dog, a task that has always been entrusted to him.

Many consider him the most beautiful dog in the world. He was introduced into England less than a hundred years ago, and since then has always been a leading contender in dog shows.

NECK Very strong and rather short.
BODY The height at the withers is slightly less than the length of the body. Above all the body must be strong and well muscled. The chest is very broad, the back is straight. The loins are straight and broad, the rump is slightly falling. The belly is not drawn up.
TAIL Stout, rather short, set on high and carried curled over the back.
FOREQUARTERS The forelegs are perfectly straight, seen from in front. The muscles are strong, the legs extremely well boned. The elbows work freely but are close to the body.
HINDQUARTERS The hind legs are perfectly straight, viewed from behind. The angulation of both stifle and hock is slight. The hocks are broad and powerful, with strong muscle and good bone. **FEET** Rather large, strong and rounded, with sturdy pads and nails.

COAT The coat is double, with a dense undercoat; the top coat is close, straight, rough, not curly or wavy. The hair is rather short on the head and legs, long on the body, abundant and long on the lower part of the tail, with a good flag. **Color** Coats of any color are allowed, both solid and parti-colored, with the sole exception of albino, which is disqualified. ●

GENERAL CHARACTERISTICS The Samoyed is above all a working dog. As such he should be handsome, alert and strong, with great agility, dignity and grace. Since his work is done in cold climates, the coat must be heavy and weather-resistant, well groomed and of good quality. The male carries more of a ruff than the female. He must not be long in the back, since a weak back would make him practically useless for his work, yet a close-coupled body would also put him at a great disadvantage as a draft dog. Breeders should aim at the happy medium, with a body not long but muscular, allowing freedom, with a deep chest and well-sprung ribs, strong neck, straight front and especially strong loins. Males should be masculine in appearance and behavior without unwarranted aggressiveness; females should be feminine without any weakness of structure or apparent softness of temperament. Females may be slightly longer in the back than males. Both should give an impression of great endurance but should be free from coarseness. Because of the depth of chest required, the legs should be moderately long. A very short-legged dog is undesirable.

WEIGHT AND SIZE Weight: males 44-66 lb; females 37½-55 lb. Height: males 21 inches and up; females 18 inches and up.

HEAD Powerful, wedge-shaped, with a broad, flat skull. The muzzle is of moderate length, rather pointed but not excessively. The jaws are strong, with well adapted teeth. The hair on the head is short and smooth. The tip of the nose should preferably be black, but a brown nose is acceptable. The lips are black.

EYES Dark, set well apart. They are deep, with a lively, intelligent expression.

EARS The ears must not be too long.

Photo: S. A. Thompson.

SAMOYED

They are slightly rounded at the tips. They are set well apart and are covered with hair both outside and inside.
BODY The chest is broad and deep, the ribs well sprung to allow good heart and lung room. The back is of medium length, broad and well muscled.
TAIL The tail is long and imposing. It is carried over the back when the dog is alert and is often carried down at rest.
FOREQUARTERS The forelegs are straight and muscular, with good bone. **HINDQUARTERS** The hind legs are extremely muscular, with well-developed upper thighs. The stifles are well bent (approximately 45°). The hocks should be well developed and sharply defined. **FEET** Large, long and somewhat flat. They are harefeet, slightly spread but not splayed. The toes are arched, the pads thick and tough, with hair between the toes.

COAT The body should be well covered with a soft, short, thick undercoat, close and woolly, with longer, harsh hair growing through it to form the top coat. The coat should form a ruff around the neck and shoulders, framing the head. **Color** Pure white, white and biscuit, cream or all biscuit. These are the only permissible colors, any others constituting disqualification.

SCALE OF POINTS

General appearance	20
Coat	15
Head	10
Weight and size	10
Chest and ribs	10
Stern	10
Back	10
Feet	5
Legs	5
Tail	5
	100

GENERAL CHARACTERISTICS The Landseer should give the impression of a big dog, powerfully but harmoniously built. It is set on higher and better-proportioned legs than the Newfoundland (especially the male). The movement of the muscular legs must be such as to permit an ample, easy gait.

SIZE Height at the withers: males 28½-31½ inches; females 26½-28½ inches. Small variations from these figures are admissible.

HEAD Large and massive, with a well-developed occiput; of noble aspect, with moderately developed cheeks that flow smoothly into the muzzle. Nose and lips are black, the lips lean, with the upper lips slightly overlapping the lower, which are tight and dry. The length of the muzzle is equal to its height when measured perpendicularly in front of the stop. The bite is the scissors kind. The stop is pronounced, but less so than in the St. Bernard. The skin on the head is free of wrinkles and is covered with short, fine hair.

EYES Of medium size, moderately deep-set, brown or dark brown. Light brown is acceptable. The expression is friendly. The eye rim is almond-shaped; the haw is not visible. Decidedly light eyes (sulphur, gray) constitute a fault, as do eyes set too close together.

EARS Of moderate size and set close to the eyes, the ears are triangular, slightly rounded at the tips and set on high but not too far back. They reach the inner corner of the eye when extended. They hang flat and close to the sides of the head. They are covered with fine, short hair with a fringe of longer hair on the back side of the base.

NECK Not too round, but somewhat oval in cross section, the neck is muscular and thick. The nape is slightly arched, symmetrical, and the length of the neck from the top of the skull to the withers is 75-80 percent of the length of the head measured from the occiput to the tip of the nose. The dewlap must not be too apparent, nor should there be loose skin about the throat.

BODY The body as measured from the withers to the set-on of the tail should be about twice as long as the head. The back is straight, ample and powerful from withers to croup. The shoulders are well muscled. The chest is broad and well let down, and there is a good, robust spring of rib. The croup is of good size, well rounded by layers of lateral and posterior muscles. The belly is only slightly drawn up, and between belly and the muscular loins there should be a clearly visible hollowing of the flanks. Faults in the back include weak back or saddleback, weak loins, the last false ribs too short, with the belly too drawn up.

TAIL Sturdy, reaching the hocks when carried down, covered with thick, ruffled hair which, however, is not a flag. At rest the tail is carried down, with a slight curve at the tip. In movement it should be carried straight out and slightly ascending. A tail curled over the back is objectionable.

FOREQUARTERS The shoulders are covered by a robust mass of muscle, extending down to the humerus. The forearm is exceptionally well boned and properly angulated, standing vertical and well muscled. The elbows are close to the brisket, rather high and turned to the rear. The entire leg down to the wrist is lightly fringed. **HINDQUARTERS** Powerful, moving freely, with robust bone; the thighs are exceptionally broad and well developed. The hind legs should be moderately fringed. Cow hocks or insufficient angulation are faults. Dewclaws are not admissible and must be removed at birth. **FEET** Large and well-formed catfeet. Toes separated or turned outward are disqualifying. The toes should be webbed almost to the tips.

COAT Except on the head the coat should be as long as possible, smooth and dense, soft, with a mingling of undercoat (which should be less dense than on the Newfoundland). A top coat which is slightly wavy on the back and thighs should not be penalized. When brushed the wrong way the coat should return to its normal condition automatically. **Color** The base color is white with markings on the trunk and croup. The neck, chest, belly, legs and tail should be white. The head is black. To conform to type, a part of the muzzle should have a white streak across it; this streak should be symmetrical and not too broad. Smoky markings against a white background are not faulty, but they should be eliminated through selective breeding. ●

SAMOYED

LANDSEER

Photo: S. A. Thompson, E. Münch.

74 ALASKAN MALAMUTE
UNITED STATES

This breed owes its name to a tribe of Indians who established themselves in northwest Alaska. These Malamute Indians were clever hunters and fishermen who used these animals as sled dogs and valuable aids in hunting. The dog is considered the finest-looking of the northern dogs.

When the white man came to occupy Canada and the neighboring regions, he also made use of the Malamute for mail delivery in remote areas. When sled racing became popular the Malamute proved to be an excellent racer who still wins, to this day, a whole series of prizes, especially in the long-distance runs. He is very clean, odorless, and attached to his master. Like other northern dogs, the Malamute does not bark.

ALASKAN MALAMUTE

GENERAL CHARACTERISTICS The Alaskan Malamute is a powerful and substantially built dog with deep chest and strong, compact body, not too short-coupled, with a thick, coarse guard coat long enough to protect a dense, woolly undercoat 1-2 inches deep when the dog is in full coat. Stands well over pads, and this stance gives the appearance of much activity, showing interest and curiosity. The head is broad, ears wedge-shaped and erect when alerted. The muzzle is bulky with only slight diminishing in width and depth from root to nose, not pointed or long but not stubby. He moves with proud carriage, head erect and eyes alert. Face markings are a distinguishing feature. These consist of either cap over head and rest of face solid color, usually grayish white, or face marked with the semblance of a mask. Combinations of mask and cap are not unusual. The tail is plumed and carried over the back, not like a fox brush, nor tightly curled, but rather like a plume waving. Malamutes are of various colors, but are usually wolfish gray or black and white. Their feet are of the "snowshoe" type, tight and deep, with well-cushioned pads, giving a firm and compact appearance. Forelegs are straight with big bone. Hind legs are broad and powerful, moderately bent at stifles, without cow hocks. The back is straight, gently sloping from shoulders to hips. The loin should not be so short or tight as to interfere with easy, effortless motion. Endurance and intelligence are evident in body and expression.

The Malamute has a "wolflike" appearance from his stance, but his expression is soft and indicates an affable disposition. In temperament he is an affectionate, friendly dog, not a "one-man" dog. He is a loyal, devoted companion, playful on invitation, but generally impressive by his dignity as an adult. It is important in judging the Alaskan Malamute to consider, above all else, his function as a sledge dog for strenuous hauling. This breed is designed primarily as the working sledge dog of the north woods for pul-

ALASKAN MALAMUTE

Photo: A. Wintzell, McCutcheon.

ling heavy freight, and therefore he should be heavy-boned, powerfully built and compact, with sound legs, good feet, deep chest, powerful shoulders, a steady, balanced and tireless gait, along with all the other physical qualities needed for doing his job well. The Malamute is not meant to be a racing sled dog to compete in speed trials with the smaller northern breeds. Because of the nature of his work, any characteristic, including temperament, which conflicts with this purpose is a serious fault indeed. Other faults under this provision include splay feet, any sign of unsound or weak legs, cow hocks, bad pasterns, straight shoulders, lack of angulation, stilted gait or any unbalanced gait lacking in strength and steadiness, ranginess, shallowness, heaviness, lightness of bone, poor overall proportion, etc.

WEIGHT AND SIZE There is a natural range in size in the breed. The desirable freighting sizes are: males 25 inches at the shoulder—85 lb; females 23 inches at the shoulder—75 lb. However, size consideration should not outweigh that of type, proportion, and functional attributes, such as shoulders, chest, feet and movement. When dogs are judged equal in type, proportion and functional attributes, the dog nearest the desirable freighting size is to be preferred.

HEAD The head should indicate a high degree of intelligence, and is broad and powerful as compared with other "natural" breeds, but should be in proportion to the size of the dog so as not to make him appear clumsy or coarse. The skull should be broad between the ears, gradually narrowing to eyes, moderately rounded between the ears, flattening on top toward the eyes, rounding off to cheeks, which should be moderately flat. There should be a slight furrow between the eyes, the topline of skull and topline of the muzzle showing but little break downward from a straight line as they join. The muzzle should be large and bulky in proportion to size of skull, diminishing but little in width and depth from junction with skull to nose; lips closefitting; nose, black; upper and lower jaws broad with large teeth, front teeth meeting in a scissors grip, but never overshot or undershot.

EYES Brown, almond-shaped, moderately large for this shape of eye, set obliquely in skull. Dark eyes preferred.

EARS The ears should be of medium size, but small in proportion to head. The upper halves of the ears are triangular, slightly rounded at tip, set wide apart on outside back edges of the skull, with the lower part of the ear joining the skull on a line with the upper corner of the eyes, giving the tips of the ears the appearance, when erect, of standing away from the skull. When erect, the ears point slightly forward, but when the dog is at work the ears are sometimes folded against the skull. High-set ears are a fault.

NECK Strong and moderately arched.

BODY The chest should be strong and deep; body should be strong and compactly built but not short-coupled. The back should be straight and gently sloping to the hips. The loins should be well muscled and not so short as to interfere with easy, rhythmic movement with powerful drive from the hindquarters. A long loin, which weakens the back, is also a fault. No excess weight.

TAIL Moderately set and following the line of the spine at the start, well furred and carried over the back when not working—not tightly curled to rest on back—or short-furred and carried like a fox brush, a wavingplume appearance instead.

FOREQUARTERS Shoulders should be moderately sloping; forelegs heavily boned and muscled, straight to pasterns, which should be short and strong and almost vertical as viewed from the side. The feet should be large and compact, toes tight-fitting and well arched, pads thick and tough, nails short and strong. There should be a protective growth of hair between toes. **HINDQUARTERS** Must be broad and powerfully muscled through thighs; stifles moderately bent, hock joints broad and strong, moderately bent and well let down. As viewed from behind, the hind legs should not appear bowed in bone but stand and move true in line with movement of the front legs, and not too close or too wide. The legs of the Malamute must exhibit unusual strength and tremendous propelling power. Any indication of unsoundness in legs or feet, standing or moving, is to be considered a serious fault. Dewclaws on the hind legs are undesirable and should be removed shortly after pups are whelped.

COAT The Malamute should have a thick, coarse guard coat, not long and soft. The undercoat is dense, 1-2 inches in depth, oily and woolly. The coarse guard coat stands out, and there is thick fur around the neck. The guard coat varies in length, as does the undercoat; however, in general, the coat is moderately short to medium along the sides of the body, the length increasing somewhat around the shoulders and neck, down the back and over the rump, as well as in the breeching and plume. Malamutes usually have shorter and less dense coats during the summer months. **Color and markings** The usual colors range from light gray through the intermediate shadings to black, always white underneath, parts of legs, feet, and part of mask markings. Markings should be either caplike and/or masklike on face. A white blaze on forehead and/or collar or spot on nape is attractive and acceptable, but broken color extending over the body in spots or uneven splashings is undesirable. One should distinguish between mantled dogs and splash-coated dogs. The only solid color allowable is the all-white.

SCALE OF POINTS

General appearance	20
Head	15
Body	20
Legs and movement	20
Feet	10
Coat and color	10
Tail	5
	100

GENERAL CHARACTERISTICS The Siberian Husky is a medium-sized dog of a vivacious nature and a pleasing appearance, with agile, easy movement. Its body is strong, the chest broad and deep. The shoulders are powerful, the legs are strong and of medium bone. The coat is abundant and soft. The tail is carried curled up over the back when the dog is in action and is carried down in repose. The head is finely chiseled and often resembles the head of a fox. The expression of the eyes is bold, yet gentle and intelligent. The characteristic gait of the Husky is easy and regular, quick and elastic. Females are generally smaller than the males by about 2 inches and lighter by about 10 lb. Huskies are powerfully built dogs without heaviness, and elegant in outline. They should be of medium bone and have a muscular back (never let down because of excess length); height at the withers should never be more than 23½ inches. The salient breed characteristics of the Siberian Husky include the following: medium size, moderate bone, well-balanced proportions, ease and freedom of movement, proper coat, pleasing head and ears, correct tail, good disposition. Any appearance of excessive bone or weight, constricted or clumsy gait or long, rough coat should be penalized. The dog must never appear so heavy or coarse as to suggest a work horse, nor must he be so light or fragile as to suggest a sprint-racer. In both sexes the Siberian Husky appears capable of great endurance. In addition to the faults already noted, obvious structural faults common to all breeds are as undesirable in the Siberian Husky as in any other breed, even though they are not specifically mentioned here.

WEIGHT AND SIZE Height at withers: male 21-23½ inches; female 20-22 inches. Weight: male 45-60 lb; female 35-50 lb.

HEAD Medium in proportion to body; a trifle rounded on top and tapering gradually to the eyes, the width between the ears medium to narrow. Muzzle medium long, the distance from nose to stop about the same as from stop to occiput. Skull and muzzle are

75 SIBERIAN HUSKY
UNITED STATES

The Husky comes originally from Siberia, from the Kolyma River region which extends to the Bering Strait, and was imported into Alaska for the first time in 1909 for use in the sled races. The Husky is noted for his cleverness and his extraordinary endurance. Because of his lively intelligence and docile and affectionate nature he is very popular in the United States and especially in Canada. The standard published here was proposed by the Siberian Husky Club in 1940 and approved by the American Kennel Club.

SIBERIAN HUSKY

Photo: S. A. Thompson.

finely chiseled. Lips dark and close-fitting, the jaws strong and the teeth meeting in a scissors bite. The nose is preferably black; brown permissible in specimens with reddish coats; flesh-colored nose and eye rims allowed in white dogs. Temporarily pink-streaked nose in winter is permissible but not desirable. Excessive heaviness or width of skull constitutes a fault, as does bulk, snipiness or coarseness of muzzle. The neck should be strong, arched and fairly short.

EYES Set a trifle obliquely, their expression keen but friendly, interested and even mischievous. Color of eyes may be either brown or blue; one brown eye and one blue eye permissible but not desirable. The Husky's expression has been compared to that of the fox, and an alert expression of the fox type is admirable when it does not indicate malice or excessive craftiness.

EARS Medium-sized, set high and carried erect. When at attention they are practically parallel to each other. They are moderately rounded at the tips and well furred on the inner side. The base of the ear is broader at the point of insertion.

BODY Moderately compact but never cobby. Chest deep and strong but not too broad, the ribs well sprung and deep. Shoulders powerful and well laid back. Back is medium length and strong, the backline level. Loins taut, lean, and very slightly arched. In profile the length of the body from the point of the shoulder to the rear point of the croup is slightly longer than the height of the body from the ground to the top of the withers. A well-furred brush carried over the back in a sickle curve when the dog runs or stands at attention, trailing out behind when working or in repose. When carried up, the typical tail does not curl to either side of the body nor does it snap flat to the back. The tail hair is usually of medium length, although length varies somewhat with overall coat length.

FOREQUARTERS AND HINDQUARTERS The legs are straight and well muscled, with bone substantial but not heavy. Hindquarters are powerful with good angulation. Well bent at stifles. Dewclaws on the rear legs, if any, are to be removed. **FEET** Oval in shape, medium size; compact and well furred between the toes. Pads tough and deeply cushioned. Briefly, a typical snowshoe foot, somewhat webbed between the toes.

COAT The coat of the Siberian Husky is double and medium in length, giving a well-furred appearance, but it is never so long as to obscure the clean-cut outline of the dog. The undercoat is soft and dense and of sufficient length to support the outer coat. The guard hairs of the outer coat are straight and somewhat smooth-lying, never harsh nor standing straight off from the body. It should be noted that the absence of the undercoat during the shedding season is normal. Trimming of the whiskers and fur between the toes and around the feet to present a neater appearance is permissible. Trimming of the fur on any other part of the dog is not allowed and should be severely penalized. **Color** All colors and white and all markings are allowed. The various shades of wolf and the silver grays, tan and black with white points are most usual. A variety of markings, especially on the head, are common to the breed, including many striking and unusual patterns not found in other breeds. The caplike mask and spectacles are typical.

FAULTS Head clumsy or heavy; head too finely chiseled. Muzzle either too snipy or too coarse; muzzle too short or too long; insufficient stop; any bite other than scissors. Ears too large in proportion to the head; too wide-set; not firmly erect. Eyes set too obliquely; set too close together. Neck too short and thick; neck too long. Straight shoulders; loose shoulders. Chest too broad; "barrel ribs"; ribs too flat or weak. Weak or slack back; roached back; sloping topline. Weak pasterns; too heavy bone; too narrow or too wide in the front; out at the elbows. Straight stifles, cow hocks, too narrow or too wide in the rear. Soft or splayed toes; paws too large and clumsy; paws too small and delicate; toeing in or out. A snapped or tightly curled tail; highly plumed tail; tail set too low or too high. Short, prancing or choppy gait; lumbering or rolling gait; crossing, crabbing. Long, rough, or shaggy coat; texture too harsh or too silky; trimming of the coat, except as permitted above.

DISQUALIFICATION Males over 23.5 inches and females over 22 inches. ●

SIBERIAN HUSKY

139

Photo: H. Bading (Photo Res.), W. Prather (Photo Res.).

BULLDOG

76 BULLDOG
GREAT BRITAIN

Adapted by man to fighting, the Bulldog can perhaps be defined as being handsome in his ugliness. He is the result of long selection processes which resulted in the formation of a breed whose principal characteristics present marked anomalies. Although he has a surly and forbidding appearance, the Bulldog is one of the most peaceful of dogs, very faithful, clean, intelligent, robust, who only uses his fighting qualities when directly attacked. The term "bulldog" was used in the middle of the seventeenth century when this dog was used in the arena for fighting bulls. The origins of this breed go back to the ancient Mastiff of Asiatic blood which, once established in England, became the *pugnax Britanniae* which the Romans brought back to Rome to fight their own "pugnaces," that is, the Greek Mastiffs.

The Bulldog that we know today is unquestionably of British origin. Numerous documents discovered in Great Britain indicate the ancient presence in this area of a dog very much like the Bulldog of today. He was used as a fighting dog and performed in the ring. Tron writes, regarding these cruel combats: "Each town and village had its own ring (from the thirteenth to the eighteenth century). The spectacles were frequent and scheduled in advance. The dogs destined to fight against bulls were carefully selected; beauty or symmetry was not considered, only limitless courage, instinct for attack, and extreme ferocity. Because of this severe selective process a dog was bred that was so bloodthirsty that he would not be stopped by pain." Toward the

end of the last century a movement was formed against this kind of combat and a law was passed in Parliament forbidding it.

Since that time the breed has at times been forgotten, but its characteristic beauty had brought it back. Breeders favor the development of intelligence and reducing its ferocity while increasing its faithfulness. Today the Bulldog is one of the most affectionate dogs extant and is above all a great friend to children.

BULLDOG

140

Photo: S. A. Thompson.

GENERAL CHARACTERISTICS The Bulldog is a smooth-coated, thickset dog, rather low in stature, but broad, powerful, and compact. The head is strikingly massive in proportion to the rest of the body. The face is extremely short, the muzzle very broad, blunt and inclined upward. The body is short and well knit, the limbs stout and muscular. The hindquarters are high and strong but rather lightly made compared with the heavy foreparts. The dog should give an impression of determination, strength and activity, similar in that way to the Ayrshire Bull. His makeup gives him a peculiarly heavy, awkward gait; he seems to walk with short, quick steps on the tips of his toes, its hind feet not lifted high but appearing to skim the ground; he runs with the right shoulder advanced, in a sort of canter.

HEAD The skull should be very large, measuring in circumference at least the height of the dog at the shoulders. From the front, it should appear very high from the corner of the lower jaw to the apex of the skull and also very broad and square. The cheeks must be well rounded and extended sideward beyond the eyes. In profile, the head should appear very high and very short from back to front. The forehead should be flat, neither prominent nor overhanging the face; the skin there and around the head should be very loose and well wrinkled. The projections of the frontal bones should be very prominent, broad, square and high, resulting in a wide, deep stop. From the stop a deep, broad furrow should extend up to the middle of the skull, reaching the apex. The face, measured from the front of the cheekbone to the nose, should be as short as possible, with skin deeply and closely wrinkled. The muzzle should be short, broad, and turned upward and very deep from the corner of the eye to the corner of the mouth. The nose should be large, broad, and black; never liver or brown. The top of the nose should be deeply set back, almost between the eyes. The distance from the inner corner of the eye (or from the center of the stop) to the extreme tip of the nose should not exceed the length from the tip of the nose to the edge of the lower lip. The nostrils should be large, wide and black, with a well-defined vertical straight line between them. The flews, known to Bulldog fanciers as the "chop," should be thick, broad, pendant, and very deep, hanging completely over the lower jaw at the sides (but not in front). They should join the under lip in front and quite cover the teeth. The jaws should be broad, massive, and square, the lower jaw projecting considerably in front of the upper and turning up. Viewed from the front, the various properties of the face must be equally balanced on either side of an imaginary line down the center of the face. Teeth: The jaw should be broad and square and have 6 small front teeth between the canines in an even row. The canine teeth (tusks) should be wide apart. The teeth, large and strong, should not be seen when the mooth is closed. Seen from the front, the underjaw should lie centrally under the upper, and should also be parallel to it.

EYES As seen from the front, the eyes should be situated low down in the skull, as far from the ears as possible. The eyes and stop should be in the same straight line, at right angles to the furrow, with eyes as far apart as possible, provided their outer corners are within the outline of the cheeks. They should be quite round, of moderate size, neither sunken nor prominent, and very dark—almost, if not quite, black, showing no white when looking directly forward.

EARS Set on quite high, i.e., the front inner edge of each ear (as viewed from the front) join the outline of the skull at the top corner of such outline, so as to place them as wide apart and as high and as far from the eyes as possible. They should be small and thin; the shape termed "rose ear" is correct, folding inward at the back, the upper or front edge curving over outward and backward, showing part of the inside of the burr.

NECK Should be of moderate length (rather short than long), very thick, deep, and strong. It should be well arched at the back, with much loose,

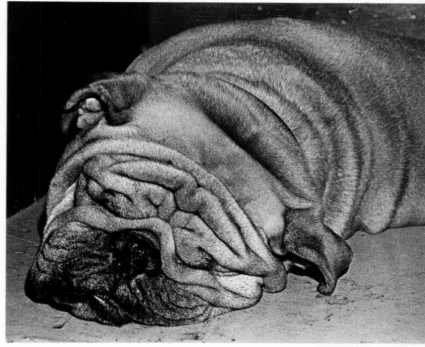

BULLDOG

thick, and wrinkled skin about the throat, forming a dewlap on each side, from the lower jaw to the chest.

FOREQUARTERS The shoulders should be broad, sloping, and deep, very powerful and muscular, seeming as if "tacked on" to the body. The brisket should be capacious, round, and very deep from the top of the shoulders to the lowest part where it joins the chest, and be well let down between the forelegs. It should be large in diameter and round behind the forelegs (not flat-sided, the ribs being well rounded). The forelegs should be very stout and strong, set wide apart, thick, muscular, and well-developed forearms presenting a rather bold outline, but the bones of the legs should be large and straight, not bandy or curved.

BULLDOG

Photo: J. Cooke (Photo Res.).

They should be rather short in proportion to the hind legs, but not so much so as to make the back appear long, nor impede the dog's activity so as to cripple him. The elbows should be low and stand well away from the ribs. The pasterns should be short, straight, and strong.

BODY The chest should be very wide, laterally round, prominent and deep, making the dog appear very broad and short-legged in front. The body should be well ribbed up behind, with the belly tucked up and not pendulous. The back should be short and strong, very broad at the shoulder, and comparatively narrow at the loin. There should be a slight fall to the back close behind the shoulders (its lowest part), from where the spine should rise to the loins (the top of which should be higher than the top of the shoulders), then curving again more abruptly to the tail, forming an arch—a distinctive characteristic of the breed—termed "roach back."

HINDQUARTERS The legs should be large and muscular, and longer in proportion than the forelegs, so as to elevate the loins. The hocks are slightly bent and well let down, so that they are long and muscular from the loins to the point of the hock. The lower part of the leg should be short, straight, and strong. The stifles should be round and turned slightly outward away from the body. The

hocks thus approach each other and the hind feet to turn outward. **FEET** The hind feet, like the forefeet, should be round and compact, with the toes well split up and the knuckles prominent. The forefeet should be straight and turned very slightly outward, of medium size and moderately round. The toes, compact and thick, being well split up, make the knuckles prominent and high.

TAIL Known also as the stern, the tail should be set on low, jutting out rather straight, then turning downward. It should be round, smooth and devoid of fringe or coarse hair, moderate in length, rather short than long, thick at the root, and tapering quickly to a fine point. It should be carried down (without a decided upward curve at the end), and the dog should not be able to raise it over the back.

COAT Fine-textured, short, close and smooth; it should be hard only from the shortness and closeness, not wiry. **Color** Should be whole or smut, i.e., a whole color with a black mask or muzzle. The only colors, which should be brilliant and pure, are whole colors—namely, brindles, reds, fawns, fallows, etc., white, and also pied (i.e., a combination of white with any other of the foregoing colors). Dudley, black, and black with tan are extremely undesirable. ●

77 BULLMASTIFF
GREAT BRITAIN

In order to obtain the best possible qualities for a guard dog British breeders decided at a certain time to add to the already excellent qualities of the English Mastiff special features of other large breeds. There were numerous attempts: crossbreedings of the Bulldog-Mastiff–German Mastiff, the Bulldog-Mastiff–Wolfhound, and the Bulldog-Mastiff–German Mastiff-Wolfhound. But the results were unsatisfactory until S. S. Moseley, considered the true creator of the Bullmastiff, was able to fix the characteristics of the new breed by using only the Bulldog and the English Mastiff. The Bullmastiff was recognized officially in 1924 and today is a faithful and dependable friend, very gentle with children. He is esteemed everywhere as a guard dog.

GENERAL CHARACTERISTICS The temperament of the Bullmastiff combines high spirits, reliability, activity, endurance, and alertness. He is a powerfully built, symmetrical dog, showing great strength but not cumbersome.

WEIGHT AND SIZE Height at shoulder: Males, 25-27 inches; females, 24-26 inches. Weight: males, 110-130 lb; females, 90-110 lb. It must be borne in mind that size must be proportionate to weight and that soundness and activity are most essential.

HEAD The skull should be large and square, viewed from every angle, with fair wrinkle when interested, but not when in repose. The circumference of the skull may be equal to the dog's height; it should be broad and deep, with good cheeks. The muzzle short, the distance from the tip of the nose

BULLDOG AND HER PUPPY

BULLMASTIFF

to the stop should be not more than one-third the length from the tip of the nose to the center of the occiput, broad under the eyes, and nearly parallel in width to the end of the nose; blunt and cut off square, forming a right angle with the upper line of the face, and at the same time proportionate to the skull. Underjaw broad to the end. Nose broad with wide-spreading nostrils when viewed from the front; flat, not pointed or turned up in profile. Flews (chaps) not pendulous and not hanging below the level of the bottom of the lower jaw. Stop definite. Mouth should be level, slight undershot allowed but not preferred. Canine teeth large and set wide apart, other teeth strong, even, and well placed. Irregularity of teeth a definite fault.

EYES Dark or hazel, and of medium size, set apart the width of the muzzle with furrow between. Light or yellow eyes are definite faults.

EARS V-shaped, or folded back, set on wide and high, level with occiput, giving a square appearance to the skull, which is most important. They should be small and deeper in color than the body and the point of the ear should be level with the eye when alert. Rose ears are a fault.

NECK Well arched, moderate length, very muscular and almost equal to the skull in circumference.

FOREQUARTERS Chest wide and deep, well set down between forelegs, with deep brisket. Shoulders muscular, sloping and powerful, not overloaded. Forelegs powerful and straight, well boned and set wide apart, presenting a straight front. Pasterns straight and strong. Feet not large, with rounded toes, well arched (cat feet), pads hard. Splay feet are a decided fault.

BODY Back short and straight, giving a compact carriage, but not so short as to interfere with activity. Roach back and swayback a fault.

TAIL Set high, strong at root and tapering, reaching to the hocks, carried straight or curved but not hound-fashion. Crank tail is a fault.

HINDQUARTERS Loins are wide and muscular, with fair depth of flank. Hindlegs strong and muscular, with well-developed second thighs, denoting power and activity, but not cumbersome. Hocks moderately bent. Cow hocks a decided fault.

COAT Short and hard, giving weather protection, lying flat to the body. A tendency to long, silky, or woolly coats should be penalized. **Color** Any shade of brindle, fawn, or red, but the color should be pure and clear. A slight white marking on chest permissible but not desirable. Other white markings a definite fault. A dark muzzle is essential, toning off toward the eyes, with dark markings around the eyes, giving expression. Dark nails desirable. ●

78 MASTIFF
GREAT BRITAIN

This powerful guard dog is considered a traditional English breed. Some authorities consider that it is a breed indigenous to the British Isles, although it appears that it has Eastern origins like other ancient breeds. Its ancestry must be looked for among the Assyrian Mastiffs, themselves descended from the Tibetan Mastiffs, which were brought into Europe by the Phoenicians as they spread their culture there. Theories on the origins of the very famous English breed are varied. Many claim that it descends from the Epirus Mastiff brought to England by the Roman legions. But even if this were true the ancestors of the Mastiff would not have changed much; in fact, the Greek Mastiff comes from Asiatic breeds and therefore from the Tibetan Mastiff.

In England as elsewhere the Mastiff was used for many things in ancient times—hunting, warfare, and guarding people and property. Today, civilized and somewhat modified from his ancestors, he is essentially a guard and defense dog, tasks which he habitually fulfills. He has abandoned the bloodthirsty exploits

of his ancestors and has become a good friend of man. But he is still wary of strangers and can be terrifying when he is provoked to attack.

Dog fanciers have great respect for him and for his aesthetic as well as his physical qualities and great intelligence.

GENERAL CHARACTERISTICS Large, massive, powerful, symmetrical and well-knit frame. A combination of grandeur and good nature, courage and docility. The head, in general outline, gives a square appearance when viewed from any angle. Breadth greatly to be desired and ratio of head breadth to overall length of head and face should be 2:3. Body massive, broad, deep, long, powerfully built, on legs wide apart and squarely set. Muscles sharply defined. Size a great desideratum, if combined with quality. Height and substance important if both points are proportionately combined.

HEAD Skull broad between the ears, forehead flat but wrinkled when attention is excited. Brows slightly raised. Muscles of the temples and cheeks well developed. Arch across the skull of a rounded, flattened curve, with a depression up the center of the forehead from the median line between the eyes halfway up the sagittal suture. Muzzle short, broad under the eyes, and of nearly equal width to the tip of the nose; truncated squarely, thus forming a right angle with the upper line of the face, of great depth from the point of the nose to under jaw. Lower jaw broad to the end. Nose broad, with widely spreading nostrils when viewed from the front, flat (not pointed or turned up) in profile. Lips diverging at obtuse angles with the septum and slightly pendulous so as to show a square profile. Length of muzzle to whole head and face in ratio of 1:3. Circumference of muzzle measured midway between eyes and nose is in ratio of 1:3 to circumference of head measured before the ears. The canine teeth should be healthy, powerful, and wide apart; the incisors should be level or with the lower projecting beyond the upper, but never so much as to become visible when the mouth is closed.

EYES Small, wide apart, divided by at least the distance of two eyes. The stop between the eyes well marked but not too abrupt. Color hazel brown, the darker the better, showing no haw.

EARS Small, thin to the touch, wide apart, set on at the highest points of the sides of the skull, so as to continue the outline across the summit and lying flat and close to the cheeks when in repose.

NECK Slightly arched, moderately long, very muscular, measuring in circumference about 1 or 2 inches less than the skull before the ears.

FOREQUARTERS Shoulder and arm slightly sloping, heavy and muscular.

BULLMASTIFF

Photo: S. A. Thompson, T. Fall, R. Kinne (Photo Res.).

MASTIFF

Legs straight, strong, and set wide apart; bones large. Elbows square. Pasterns upright. **FEET** Large and round, with toes well arched; nails black.
BODY Chest wide, deep, and well let down between the forelegs. Ribs arched and well rounded. False ribs deep and well set back to the hips. Girth should be one-third more than the height at the shoulder. Back and loins wide and muscular, flat and very wide in the female, slightly arched in the male. Great depth of flanks.
TAIL Set on high up, reaching to the hocks or a little below them; wide at the root and tapering to the end. It

hangs straight in repose but forms a curve with the end pointing upward (but not over the back) when the dog is excited.
HINDQUARTERS Broad, wide, and muscular, with well-developed second thighs, hocks bent, wide apart and quite squarely set when standing or walking. The feet are large and round, toes well arched; nails black.
COAT Short and close-lying, but not too fine over the shoulders, neck, and back. **Color** Apricot or silver, fawn, or dark fawn-brindle. In any case, muzzle, ears and nose should be black, with black around the orbits and extending upward between them. ●

79 TIBETAN MASTIFF
GREAT BRITAIN

The Tibetan Mastiff is the direct descendent that we have continually mentioned in connection with the numerous canine breeds existing today. This is a breed which has remained unchanged for thousands of years, as proved by bones unearthed from different eras, and from pictures as well. In ancient times predators were larger than they are now. Therefore, to defend the herds, it was necessary to use dogs as big as their enemies. This is how the Tibetan Mastiff was developed, and although today this dog is smaller, probably through adaption to different tasks, the proportions between the different parts of the body are the same, as well as the general structure and psycho-physical qualities.

Although the breed in its present form has been regenerated by the English and is considered to be typically English, it still exists in the Orient, where it originated. There, it is not unusual for this dog to be given the task of guarding an entire village, as the male population is often obliged to go far from the village to care for the livestock, to hunt, or to work in the fields. The Tibetan Mastiff then defends the women and children who remain in their houses, and his presence alone is enough to keep away prowlers and wild animals. When necessary, he does not hesitate to attack, whether his adversary be man or animal, showing his great courage and devotion to duty.

GENERAL CHARACTERISTICS A powerful, heavy-boned dog, docile and aloof. A good guard dog.

SIZE Height at shoulder: males, 25-27 inches; females, 22-24 inches.

HEAD Broad, massive head and smooth face. Perfectly level mouth, powerful jaws. Muzzle, of Mastiff type but lighter than that of the English Mastiff.

EYES Brown, medium size.

EARS Pendant, medium length, heart-shaped, smooth, side placement with forward carriage when at attention.

NECK Powerful.

BODY Compact but not cloddy, heavily bodied, well ribbed up, deep brisket, strong-loined.

TAIL Tail set on high, curled over back to one side, very thick and bushy.

FOREQUARTERS AND HINDQUARTERS Shoulders strong and well laid. Forelegs feathered, strong, straight, massively boned, with strong pasterns. Hind legs have hocks well let down, well-bent stifle, heavy feathering on buttocks. **FEET** Smooth, large, strong and compact.

COAT Long, straight coat with thick heavy undercoat. **Color** Black and tan, golden.

GAIT Slow and deliberate.

EXPRESSION Solemn but kind. ●

MASTIFF

TIBETAN MASTIFF

Photo: S. A. Thompson, T. Fall, M. Pedone.

HUNTING DOGS

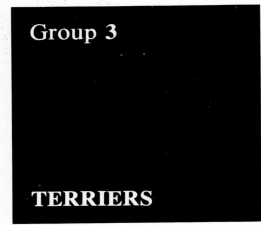

Group 3

TERRIERS

It is considered that the terrier is an English dog, and the small number born outside the British Isles only confirms the fact. The word "terrier" comes from the Latin *terra* (earth) and refers to dogs that hunt *in* the earth, which is precisely what terriers do. The description of their activity left to us by John Keyes (to whom we owe the classification of English breeds) is classic: ". . . there also exist dogs for hunting the fox or the badger; we call them "terrars" because they go down into the ground to frighten, excite, and bite the game until they tear it to pieces with their teeth, under the very ground· or drag it out from winding recesses, dank dens, and narrow caves, or they cause it such fear that they force it out of its refuge to flee to another safe from attack, whereupon the fox, badger, or other game finds itself caught in the traps and snares placed to catch it next to the hole made by the terrier . . ."

Although famous, Keyes's description, written in 1570, is not the first one we possess on terriers. Pliny the Elder tells how the Roman legionaries who invaded Britain in 55 B.C. encountered there ". . . little dogs who pursued their prey even under the ground." This statement by the ancient naturalist has often been quoted as definitive proof that terriers came from Great Britain, a hypothesis nevertheless widely contested. Today experts consider that the ancestors of most of the present terrier breed were brought to the British Isles before the present era. Certainly completely identical dogs also lived in continental Europe or in other parts of the world. Several circumstances particularly favored the evolution of the varieties that were established in Great Britain. Terrier breeds developed elsewhere were scarce and isolated as, for example, the Tibetan Terrier and the German Jagdterrier.

Up to relatively recent times, terriers were bred principally by persons of modest circumstances, since their small size and hardy nature made them easy dogs to keep, and also since they were useful for tasks other than hunting. They might be called "people's dogs" and, since for centuries the style or type of dog or horse was decreed by the nobles, the terriers passed through a very long period practically without notice, although mentioned by John Keyes and several other English, French, or German chroniclers. Nor is it possible to say exactly when the attention of the wealthier classes and of dog fanciers was directed to these valorous little dogs. Some experts claim that a well-defined breed—the Skye Terrier—already existed in the sixteenth century. Others hold that terriers were crossbred in a more or less haphazard fashion. It has been only in the past 150 years that, in certain areas of Scotland and England, breeders have undertaken to improve local breeds and to create new ones through careful selective breeding.

The terriers we know today are very different from their rough working ancestors. The fact that one breed or another has enjoyed popularity at various times has decreased the importance of its hunting ability, while emphasizing, according to the caprice of style, sometimes the coat and its color or the shape of the ears or the tail. In spite of these human whims, however, a good terrier, whatever the breed, still possesses the basic psycho-physical qualities which surprised the Roman legionaries when they crossed the Channel 2,000 years ago. And, although the modern dog world considers the ability of a dog for a specific task, it nevertheless has placed certain terriers in the class of nonsporting dogs or toys or, in the case of the Schnauzer, as a guard and defense dog.

80 SMOOTH-COATED FOX TERRIER

GREAT BRITAIN

The Fox Terrier cannot be said to be of recent origin. Although it is true that the Reverend Rosselyn Bruce, in his study of the evolution of the breed, admits that there is no information about it until 1850. Until that time every fox-hunting dog, whether wirehaired or smooth-coated, large or small, white or reddish, was called a Fox Terrier. However, among all these dogs, the one today called the Fox Terrier is the most classic type and for this reason is the oldest. Fanfani, a reputable expert on the breed, is also of this opinion.

In the past, however, this dog had neither his present elegance nor appearance. If we have no precise information beyond the middle of the last century, we still have a representation on a canvas of 1796 by Francis Sartorius the Elder showing a typical Black and Tan Fox Terrier, as well as a memoir by Peter Beckford, who claims to have owned black-and-white and white-and-tan fox dogs at the end of the eighteenth century. These are still the fundamental colors of the Fox Terrier.

Many, and sometimes quite unusual, statements have been made about the ancestry of the Fox Terrier, but no one can offer precise information. Among his ancestors there were no doubt Cheshire and Shropshire Terriers, that is to say, the white English Terriers and also Beagles. In any case, the true development of the breed began in 1850 when breeders vied with each other to produce ever better specimens. During the first years it was a question only of the smooth-coated breed, the wirehaired breed appearing around 1870.

As far as the Smooth-Coated Fox Terrier is concerned, English breeders were successful in obtaining the utmost in regard to his typical points and beauty, although in their breeding they completely overlooked the preservation of his hunting ability, important in a dog which has always been a hunting breed and should remain so. However, chance came to the aid of English breeders since, after a remote period of struggle against game, the Smooth-Coated Fox Terriers still preserve some of their excellent hunting ability, resulting from a long period of natural selection which preceded their anatomical selection.

The French were the first to introduce the Smooth-Coated Fox Terrier to continental Europe, followed by the Germans and Belgians. The breeders of these countries immediately concerned themselves with fixing hunting abilities in these dogs.

An excellent dog for terrier work, the Smooth-Coated Fox Terrier has also been used as a pointer for partridge and snipe, and for boar hunting in Maremma, while in Germany he is used as a retriever. The Smooth-Coated Fox Terrier is versatile, intelligent, and today is again making progress, after the interruption of the war and postwar periods. He surely deserves his title as "the little athlete" of the dog world.

GENERAL CHARACTERISTICS The dog must present a generally gay, lively, and active appearance; bone and strength in a small compass are essentials, but this must not be taken to mean that a Fox Terrier should be cloddy or in any way coarse. Speed and endurance must be looked to as well as power, and the symmetry of the Foxhound taken as a model. The terrier, like the hound, must on no account be leggy, nor should he be too short in the leg. He should stand like a cleverly made hunter, covering a lot of ground, yet with a short back. He will then attain the highest degree of propelling power, together with the greatest length of stride compatible with the length of his body.

WEIGHT Not an absolute criterion of a terrier's fitness for his work: general shape, size, and contour are the main points, and if a Fox Terrier can gallop and stay and follow his fox up a drain, it little matters whether he weighs a pound more or less. Roughly speaking, 15-17 lb for a female and 16-18 lb for a male are the appropriate weights for a dog in show condition.

SMOOTH-COATED FOX TERRIER

WIREHAIRED FOX TERRIER

HEAD The skull should be flat and moderately narrow, gradually decreasing in width to the eyes. Not much stop should be apparent, but there should be more dip in the profile between the forehead and the upper jaw than is seen in the Greyhound. The cheeks must not be full. The jaw, upper and lower, should be strong and muscular and of fair punishing strength, but not in any way resembling the Greyhound's. There should not be much falling away below the eyes. This part of the head should, however, be moderately chiseled out, so as not to go down in a straight line like a wedge. The nose, toward which the muzzle must gradually taper, should be black. Teeth as nearly as possible level, i.e., the upper on the outside of the lower teeth.

EYES Should be dark, small, and rather deep-set, full of fire, life, and intelligence; as nearly as possible round.

EARS Should be V-shaped and small, of moderate thickness and dropping forward close to the cheek, not hanging by the side of the head like a Foxhound's.

NECK Should be clean and muscular, without throatiness, of fair length, and gradually widening through its length to the shoulders.
BODY Chest deep and not too broad. Back should be short, straight, and strong, with no appearance of slackness. Loin should be powerful and very slightly arched. The fore ribs should be moderately arched, the back ribs deep, and the dog should be well ribbed up. Short back, straight and robust, with no sign of weakness.
TAIL Should be set on rather high and carried gaily, but not over the back or curled. It should be of good strength.
FOREQUARTERS The shoulders should be long and sloping, well laid back, fine at the points and clearly cut at the withers. **HINDQUARTERS** Strong and muscular, quite free from droop or crouch; the thighs long and powerful; hocks near the ground, the dog standing well up on them like a Foxhound, and not straight in stifle. **FEET** Should be round and compact, not large. The soles hard and tough. The toes moderately arched and turned neither in nor out.
COAT Straight, flat, smooth, hard, dense, and abundant. The belly and underside of the thighs should not be bare. **Color** White should predominate; brindle, red, or liver markings are objectionable. Otherwise this point is of little or no importance. ●

81 WIREHAIRED FOX TERRIER

GREAT BRITAIN

It often happens that even dog lovers say that the Wirehaired Fox Terrier is a variety of the Smooth-Coated breed. Actually they are two completely different breeds, although the general conformity is identical: they differ only by the length and quality of their hair. Specimens from crossbreeding between these two types of Fox Terrier are not mentioned today in the *Book of Origins* in any of the world's countries.

GENERAL CHARACTERISTICS The Wirehaired Fox Terrier should be alert, quick of movement, keen of expression, hopeful and ready for any activity. Character is revealed by the expression of the eyes and the carriage of ears and tail. In general appearance, the dog should be balanced, and balance may be defined as the correct proportions of a certain point or points in relation to others. It is the keystone of the terrier's anatomy. The chief points for consideration are the relative proportions of skull and foreface, head and back, height at withers, and length of body from shoulder point to buttocks, the ideal proportion being achieved when the last two measurements are equal. It should be added that, although the head measurements can be taken with absolute accuracy, the height at withers and length of back are approximate and are included here for the information of breeders and exhibitors rather than as a hard-and-fast rule. The movement or action is the crucial test of conformation. The terrier's legs should be carried straight forward while traveling, the forelegs hanging perpendicular and swinging parallel to the sides. The principal propulsive power is furnished by the hind legs, perfection of action being in the terrier's long thighs and muscular second thighs well bent at the stifles, which admit of a strong forward thrust of the hocks. Seen from in front, the forelegs should form a continuation of the straight lines of the chest, the feet being the same distance apart as the elbows. When he stands still it is often difficult to determine whether the dog is slightly out at shoulder, but when he moves, any imperfection, if it exists, becomes more apparent, since the forefeet have a tendency to cross, "weave," or "dish." However, when the dog is tied at the shoulder, the feet tend to move wider apart, with a sort of padding action. When the rocks are turned in (cow hocks), the stifles and feet are turned outward, resulting in a serious loss of propulsive power. When the hocks are turned outward, the tendency of the hind feet is to cross, resulting in an ungainly waddle.

WEIGHT, SIZE AND PROPORTIONS
Bone and strength in a small compass are essential, but this must not be taken to mean that a terrier should be cloddy or in any way coarse, speed and endurance being requisite as well as power. The Wirehaired Fox Terrier must on no account be leggy, nor must he be too short in the leg. He should stand like a well-made, short-backed hunter, covering a lot of ground. According to present-day requirements, a full-sized, well-balanced male should not exceed 15½ inches at the withers, the female being proportionately smaller, nor should the length of back from withers to root of tail exceed 12 inches; to maintain the relative proportions, the head should not exceed 7¼ nor be less than 7 inches. A male with these measurements should scale 18 lb in show condition, a female weighing some 2 lb less, with a tolerance of 1 lb either way.

HEAD The topline of the skull should be almost flat, sloping slightly and gradually decreasing in width toward the eyes. In a well-balanced head there should be little apparent difference in length between skull and foreface. If, however, the foreface is noticeably shorter, it amounts to a fault, the head looking weak and "unfinished." On the other hand, when the eyes are set too high in the skull, too near the ears, it also amounts to a fault, the head being said to have a "foreign appearance." Although the foreface should taper gradually from eye to muzzle and should dip slightly at its juncture with the forehead, it should not "dish" or fall away quickly below the eyes, where it should be full and well made up, but relieved from "wedginess" by a delicate chiseling. Well-developed jawbones, armed with a set of strong white teeth, should impart an appearance of strength to the foreface. An excessive bony or muscular development of the jaws is objectionable, since it is partly responsible for the full and rounded contour of the cheeks to which the term "cheeky" is applied. Nose should be black. Both upper and lower jaws should be strong and muscular, the teeth as nearly as possible level and capable of closing together like a vise,

WIREHAIRED FOX TERRIER PUP

Photo: A. Roslin-Williams, S.E.F.

WIREHAIRED FOX TERRIER

with the lower canines locking in front of the upper and the points of the upper incisors slightly overlapping the lower.

EYES Should be dark in color, moderately small, not prominent, full of fire, life, and intelligence; as nearly as possible they should be round and not too far apart. Anything approaching a yellow eye is most objectionable.

EARS Should be small and V-shaped and of moderate thickness, the flat neatly folded over and drooping forward close to the cheeks. The topline of the folded ear should be well above the level of the skull. A pendulous ear, hanging dead by the side of the head like a hound's, is uncharacteristic of the terrier, while an ear which is semierect is even more objectionable.

NECK Clean, muscular, of fair length and free from throatiness; it should present a graceful curve when viewed from the side.

BODY The back should be short and level, with no appearance of slackness, the loins muscular and very slightly arched. The brisket should be deep, the front ribs moderately arched, the back ribs deep and well sprung. The term "slackness" is applied both to the portion of the back immediately behind the withers when it shows any tendency to dip and to the flanks when there is too much space

between the back ribs and hipbone. When there is little space between the ribs and hips, the dog is said to be "short in couplings," "short-coupled," or "well ribbed up." A terrier can scarcely be too short in back, provided he has sufficient length of neck and liberty of movement. The female may be slightly longer in couplings than the male.

TAIL Should be set on rather high and carried gaily but not curled. It should be of good strength and substance and of fair length (a three-quarters dock is about right) since it affords the only safe grip when handling working terriers. A very short tail is suitable neither for work nor show.

FOREQUARTERS When viewed from the front, shoulders should slope steeply downward from their juncture, with the neck toward the points, which should be fine. When viewed from the side they should be long and well laid back and should slope obliquely backward from points to withers, which should always be clean-cut. A shoulder well laid back gives the long forehand which, in combination with a short back, is so desirable in terrier or hunter. The chest should be deep and not broad, a too narrow chest being almost as undesirable as a very broad one. Excessive depth of chest and brisket is an impediment to a terrier when going to ground. Viewed from any direction, the legs

should be straight, the bone of the forelegs strong right down to the feet. The elbows should hang perpendicular to the body, working free of the sides, carried straight through in traveling. **HINDQUARTERS** Should be strong and muscular, quite free from droop or crouch. The thighs should be long and powerful, the stifles well curved and turned neither in nor out, the hock joints well bent and near the ground, the hocks perfectly upright and parallel with each other when viewed from behind. The worst possible form of hindquarters consists of a short second thigh and a straight stifle, a combination which causes the hind legs to act as props rather than as instruments of propulsion. The hindlegs should be carried straight through in traveling. **FEET** Should be round, compact, not large; the pads should be tough and well cushioned, the toes moderately arched and turned neither in nor out. A terrier with well-shaped forelegs and feet will wear his nails down short by contact with the road surface, the weight of the body being evenly distributed between the pads and the heels.

COAT The principal difference between that of the smooth and wirehaired varieties is that, whereas the former is straight and flat, that of the latter appears to be broken, the hairs tending to twist. The best coats are of a dense, wiry texture, like coconut matting, the hairs growing so closely and strongly together that

when parted with the fingers the skin cannot be seen. At the base of these stiff hairs is a shorter growth of finer, softer hair, the undercoat. The coat on the sides is never quite as hard as on the back and quarters. Some of the hardest coats are crinkly or slightly waved, but a curly coat is very objectionable. The hair on the upper and lower jaws should be crisp and only sufficiently long to impart an appearance of strength to the foreface, thus effectually differentiating them from the smooth variety. The hair on the forelegs should also be dense and crisp. The coat should average in length from ¾ to 1 inch on shoulders and neck, lengthening to 1½ inches on withers, backs, ribs, and quarters. These measurements are given rather as a guide to exhibitors than as absolute requirements, since the length of coat varies with different specimens and seasons. The judge must form his own opinion as to what constitutes a "sufficient" coat. **Color** White should predominate; brindle, red, liver or slate blue are objectionable. Otherwise, color is of little or no importance.

FAULTS Nose white, cherry, or spotted to a considerable extent with either of these colors; prick ears, tulip or rose ears; excessively undershot or overshot jaws. (Old scars or injuries that are caused by work or accident must not prejudice a terrier's chance in the show ring, unless they interfere with his movement or with his utility for work or stud.) ●

Photo: S. A. Thompson.

149

AIREDALE TERRIER

82 AIREDALE TERRIER
GREAT BRITAIN

Only a short time ago dog fanciers grouped the Airedale with the defense breeds. Actually he is a valuable aid to man not only as a guard dog but also for hunting. The Airedale has a keen sense of smell, and for working in swamps few dogs are his equal. His wiry coat and his oily undercoat enable him to resist wetness and freezing, and since he is extremely hardy and courageous he is used in some countries to hunt boar, deer, and bear.

Workmen in Leeds, on the banks of the Aire, in Yorkshire, England, were the first breeders of this dog. They used him as a ratcatcher, as well as for hunting beaver and otter; as a hound, Pointer, and water dog. In the early 1800s the Otter Hound was much employed in these regions for otter hunting, as they were very good swimmers and able to follow their prey in the water. On land, however, they were of little use when the otter escaped them by many ruses, finally taking refuge in its lair under the water level along the river banks. It was then decided to breed a dog capable of pursuing the otter into the lair itself. In the same region there had existed for some time a particular type of dog, the working terrier, much used in crossbreeding with other dogs. It was therefore a matter of course to cross this animal with the Otter Hound to obtain a new breed. The result was the Airedale.

GENERAL CHARACTERISTICS Keen expression, quick movement, on the tiptoe of expectation at any movement. Character is revealed by the expression of the eyes and the carriage of the ears and tail. The various parts of the dog should be in proportion, giving a symmetrical appearance. In movement the legs should be carried straight forward, the forelegs being perpendicular and parallel with the sides. The propulsive power is furnished by the hind legs, perfection or action beind found in the terrier possessing long thighs and muscular second thighs, well bent at the stifles, which give strong forward thrust. When approaching, the forelegs should form a continuation of the straight lines of the front, the feet being the

AIREDALE TERRIER

Photo: S. A. Thompson.

same distance apart as the elbows; when stationary it is often difficult to determine whether a dog is slightly out at shoulder, but when he moves the defect, if it exists, becomes most apparent, since the forefeet have a tendency to cross. When, on the contrary, the dog is tied at the shoulder, the feet tend to move wider apart. When the hocks are turned in (cow hocks), the stifles and feet are turned outward, resulting in a serious loss of propulsive power. When the hocks are turned outward, the hind feet tend to cross.

WEIGHT AND SIZE Weight must be considered in relation to type and size. For males the ideal weight is 45 lb, for females slightly less. All other considerations being equal, preference is to be given to males weighing a pound or two more than 45 lb over those weighing a pound or two less. Height at the shoulder: males 23-24 inches; females 22-23 inches. In some countries a tolerance of ½ or ¾ inch is permitted.

HEAD The skull should be long and flat, not too broad between the ears and narrowing slightly to the eyes. It should be well balanced, with only little apparent difference in length between skull and foreface. The skull should be free from wrinkles, the stop barely visible, the cheeks level and free from fullness. The foreface must be well filled up before the eyes, not dish-faced or falling away quickly below eyes; a little delicate chiseling should keep appearance from wedginess and plainness. Upper and lower jaws should be deep, powerful, strong and muscular, as strength of foreface is highly desirable in the Airedale, but there must be no excess development of the jaws to give a rounded or bulging appearance to the cheeks (cheekiness). The lips must fit tightly, be strong and level, closing in a vise The nose should be black. Teeth should bite.

EYES Should be dark in color, small, not prominent, full of terrier expression, keenness and intelligence.

EARS Should be V-shaped, with a side carriage, small, but not out of proportion. The top line of the folded ear should be above the level of the skull. A pendulous ear, hanging limp by the side of the neck like a hound's, is a fault.

NECK Should be clean, muscular, of moderate length and thickness, gradually widening toward the shoulders, and free from throatiness.

BODY Back should be short, strong, straight and level, with no appearance of slackness, loins muscular, ribs well sprung. In a well-ribbed-up or short-coupled dog there is a little space between ribs and hips. When the dog is long in couplings some slackness will be shown here.

TAIL Should be set on high and carried gaily, but not curled over the back. It should be of good strength and substance and of fair length.

FOREQUARTERS Shoulders should be long, well laid back and sloping obliquely into the back, shoulder blades flat. Forelegs should be perfectly straight, with plenty of bone. Elbows should be perpendicular to the body, working free of the sides. **HINDQUARTERS** Should be long and muscular with no droop. Thighs long and powerful with muscular second thigh, stifles well bent, not turned in or out. Hocks well let down, parallel with each other when viewed from behind. **FEET** Should be small, round and compact, with good depth of pad, well cushioned, and the toes moderately arched, not turned in or out.

COAT Should be hard, dense and wiry, and not too long as to appear ragged. It should also lie straight and close, covering the body and legs; the outer coat of hard, wiry, stiff hairs; the undercoat should be a shorter growth of softer hair. Some of the hardest coats are crinkly or just slightly waved; a curly coat is objectionable. **Color** The head and ears, with the exception of dark markings on each side of the skull, should be tan, the ears being of a darker shade than the rest. The legs up to the thighs and elbows also should be tan. The back is nearly covered by a black or dark grizzled saddle. ●

BEDLINGTON TERRIER

83 BEDLINGTON TERRIER
GREAT BRITAIN

Certain writers have considered the Bedlington to be the product of crossbreeding between the Dandie Dinmont, the Otter Hound, and the Whippet, while others believe that he derives from the Rabbit Dog prevalent in England and Scotland during the eighteenth century. Two characteristics incline us toward the first hypothesis: in the first place, the Bedlington's foot is like that of the rabbit, altogether different from other Terrier breeds in that respect. In the second place, the structure of the entire rear leg is characteristic of a racing dog because of its angulation and musculature as well as in general conformation. Certainly the Bedlington represents a little marvel, since he resembles at least three fundamental types according to Mégnin's morphological division of types: "graioid," according to his legs and Greyhound type; "braccoid" according to his triangular ears, which lie at the side of the skull; "lupoid" by its type of structure and by the marked length of skull.

The first reports on the Bedlington go back to 1882. Until 1885 the breed was known as the Rotbury Terrier and sometimes also as the Fox Terrier of the northern counties. Joseph Ainsley, a mason from Bedlington, gave his city's name to the breed, since this was the name recognized by the Kennel Club.

GENERAL CHARACTERISTICS A graceful, lithe, muscular dog, with no sign of either weakness or coarseness. The entire head should be pear- or wedge-shaped, and the expression in repose mild and gentle, though not shy or nervous. When roused, the dog's eyes should sparkle and he should appear full of temper and courage. Bedlingtons are capable of galloping at great speed and should have the appearance of being able to do so even when in repose. This action is very distinctive. Rather mincing, light and springy in the slower paces, the dog may have a slight roll when in full stride. When galloping, the Bedlington must use the whole body, rather like a Greyhound.
WEIGHT AND SIZE Height at the withers: male, slightly above 16 inches; female, slightly below 16 inches. Weight: 18-23 lb.
HEAD Skull narrow, but deep and rounded, covered with profuse silky topknot, which should be nearly white. The jaw is long and tapering. There must be no stop, and the line from nose to occiput must be straight and unbroken. Well filled up beneath the eye. Close-fitting lips without flew. The nostrils must be large and well defined. Blues and blue-and-tans must have black noses; livers and sandies must have brown noses. Dentition is level or pincer-jawed, the teeth large and strong.
EYES Small, bright, and well sunk. The ideal eye seems triangular in shape. Blues should have a dark eye; blue-and-tans have lighter eyes with amber lights; and livers and sandies have a light hazel eye. The eyes are among the most characteristic features of these unusual dogs.
EARS Moderate in size, filbert-shaped, the ears are set on low and hang flat to the cheek. They should be covered with short, fine hair and should have a fringe of whitish, silky hair at the tip.
NECK The Bedlington's neck is long and tapering, deep at the base; there

151

Photo: A. Wintzell.

BEDLINGTON TERRIER

84 BORDER TERRIER
GREAT BRITAIN

This is the smallest of the terriers, and he takes his name from his region of origin, the border between England and Scotland. He was already known by the end of the nineteenth century, and was employed for hunting in burrows. We know little of the formation of this breed except that the Border Terrier began to grow more popular in England only after a group of fanciers made him known outside his place of origin. The breed was officially recognized in 1920 by the British Kennel Club.

In spite of his small size this dog is especially hardy and of remarkable vitality. He is able to follow a racing horse and to hunt foxes in their lairs.

BORDER TERRIER

should be no tendency to throatiness. The neck should spring well up from the shoulders, and the head should be carried rather high.

BODY Muscular, yet markedly flexible; flat-ribbed and deep through the brisket; well ribbed up. The chest should be deep and fairly broad. The back should be roached, and the loin should be markedly arched. Muscular galloping quarters which are also fine and graceful.

TAIL Of moderate length, thick at the root and tapering to a point and gracefully curved. Should be set on low and must never be carried over the back.

FOREQUARTERS The forelegs should be straight but wider apart at the chest than at the feet. Pasterns long and slightly sloping without weakness. Shoulders flat and sloping. **HINDQUARTERS** Muscular and of moderate length. The hindlegs, by reason of the roached back and arched loin, have the appearance of being lower than the forelegs. The hocks should be strong and well let down. **FEET** Long hare feet with thick, well-closed-up pads.

COAT Very distinctive. Thick and linty, standing well out from the skin but not wiry. There should be a distinct tendency to twist, particularly in the head and face. **Color** Blue, blue and tan, liver, or sandy. Darker pigment to be encouraged. ●

GENERAL CHARACTERISTICS The Border Terrier is essentially a working terrier. It should be able to follow a horse and must combine activity with gameness.

WEIGHT Males, 13-15½ lb; females, 11½-14 lb.

HEAD Like that of an otter, moderately broad in skull, with a short, strong muzzle. A black nose is preferable, but a liver or flesh-colored nose is not a serious fault. Teeth should have a scissors grip, with the upper teeth slightly in front of the lower, but a level mouth is quite acceptable. An undershot or overshot mouth is a major fault and highly undesirable.

EYES Dark, with keen expression.

EARS Small, V-shaped, of moderate thickness and dropping forward close to the cheek.

NECK Of moderate length.

BODY Deep and narrow, fairly long. Ribs carried well back, but not oversprung, since a terrier should be capable of being spanned by both hands behind the shoulder.

TAIL The Border Terrier's tail is short and fairly thick at the base, then tapering; it is set high and carried gaily, but it must never be curled over the back.

FOREQUARTERS Forelegs straight and not too heavy in bone. **HINDQUARTERS** Should be racy, the loin strong. **FEET** Small, with thick pads.

COAT Harsh and dense, with close undercoat. The skin must be thick. **Color** Red, wheaten, grizzle and tan, blue and tan. ●

85 BULL TERRIER
GREAT BRITAIN

In times past the English were enthusiastic spectators at fights between dogs and bulls, this being the reason that the Bulldog was created. It was noticed however, that the Bulldog, although very brave in close combat, lacked agility, so it was decided to breed an animal that would combine the power and ferocity of the Bulldog with agility and speed. The Bulldog was crossbred with the old White English Terrier, very prevalent throughout the island.

The first Bull Terriers were massive and of different sizes, although this mattered little to the breeders, who wished above all to obtain dogs capable of taking part in the goriest contests possible. When the law forbade fights between dogs and bulls, dogs were pitted against each other, and the Bull Terrier played a heroic role in this questionable sport until it, too, ceased.

BEDLINGTON TERRIER

Photo: S. A. Thompson, A. Roslin-Williams.

According to Captain Brown, an outstanding student of this breed, the points of the Bull Terrier were fixed about a century ago. The development of the old Bull Terrier into the Bull Terrier of today was sudden rather than gradual, which was without precedent in the history of other canine breeds. The phenomenal change in the characteristics of the Bull Terrier is attributed to James Hinks, the famous breeder who refined the former type by crossing it with Dalmations and White English Terriers. After a famous dogfight he was able to prove that his more elegant champion was also invincible in combat. The success and propagation of the Hinks type of Bull Terrier were immediate.

When dogfighting was outlawed, the breed was used for rat-catching, and then breeders cultivated it further by modifying its instinctively combative character. By the end of the nineteenth century the Bull Terrier was already a guard dog, faithful and well mannered to the extent that his sobriquet of "gladiator" was replaced by that of "gentleman."

BULL TERRIER

GENERAL CHARACTERISICS The Bull Terrier is the gladiator of the canine family and must be strongly built, muscular, symmetrical, and active, with a keen, determined and intelligent expression. He must be full of fire and courageous, but of even temperament and amenable to discipline. Irrespective of size, the dogs should look masculine, the bitches feminine. Males should have both testicles visibly and fully descended into the scrotum. The moving dog should appear well knit, smoothly covering the ground with free, easy strides and with a typical jaunty air. Forelegs and hindlegs should move parallel when viewed from in front or behind, the forelegs reaching out well, the hindlegs moving smoothly at the hip and flexing well at the stifle and hock, with great thrust.

HEAD Long, strong and deep to the end of the muzzle, but not coarse.

From the front it should appear egg-shaped and completely filled. Skull almost flat from ear to ear. Profile curving gently downward from the top of the skull to the tip of the nose. Nose black, bent down at the tip. Nostrils well developed. The underjaw should be strong. Teeth should be strong, sound, clean, large, and perfectly regular. The upper front teeth should fit in front of and closely against the lower. Lips should be clean and tight.

EYES The eyes should appear narrow, obliquely set and triangular, well sunk; in color the eyes should be black or as dark brown as possible, so that they appear black to the observer. They should have a piercing glint.

EARS The ears should be small, thin, and placed close together. The dog should be able to hold them stiffly erect, and in that position they should point straight up.

NECK The neck should be very muscular, long, arched, tapering from the shoulders to the head. It should be free of any trace of dewlap or of any other defect tending to induce a guttural variation in the natural voice.

FOREQUARTERS The shoulders should be strong and muscular but without loading. The shoulder blades should be flat, wide, and attached closely to the chest wall; they should have a very pronounced backward slope of the front edge from bottom to top.

BODY Should be well rounded with marked spring of rib, with great depth from withers to brisket. The back should be short, with the topline level behind the withers and arching slightly over the loin. Underline from brisket to belly should be a graceful upward curve. The chest should be broad when viewed from the front.

TAIL Should be short and set on low. It should be carried horizontally, except when the dog is excited, when it should rise almost to the vertical. Thick at the root, it should taper to a fine point.

HINDQUARTERS The hind legs should be parallel when viewed from behind. The thighs must be muscular, with the second thigh well developed. The stifle joint should be well bent and the hock well angulated, with the bone to the foot short and strong. **FEET** Should be round and compact, with well arched toes.

COAT Short, flat, even, and harsh to the touch, with a fine gloss. The skin should fit the dog tightly. **Color** For white, the coat should be pure white. Skin pigmentation and markings on the head should not be considered faults. Other than white, the color (preferably brindle) should predominate. ●

BULL TERRIER PUPPIES

153

Photo: C. M. Cooke, S. A. Thompson.

86 MINIATURE BULL TERRIER

GREAT BRITAIN

MINIATURE BULL TERRIER

The standard for the Miniature Bull Terrier is identical to that of the Bull Terrier except for weight and size. The height at the withers should not exceed 14 inches, the weight should not be above 20 lb. ●

87 CAIRN TERRIER

GREAT BRITAIN

It appears certain that the Cairn is the most ancient Scottish breed, and perhaps the ancestor of all the others, although it made its official entry into the Kennel Association only in 1909. In any case, it is certain that the Cairn already existed during the time of Mary Queen of Scots and her son, James VI.

The Cairns of that day were only 10 inches high and were either black or sable. Those that had the smallest white spot were put aside, as it was considered a sure risk in crossbreeding. The Cairn's role was to kill the fox within his lair and other animals that sought refuge in the rocky fissures typical of the region, called "cairns" in Gaelic.

Some modifications were later made on the original type of Cairn Terrier with the intention of improving his appearance and making him more acceptable to the general public. This breed has enjoyed and maintained great popularity. It is the most numerous breed among the terriers, according to the entries in the *Book of English Origins*. The breed is also very prevalent in the United States and Canada. The Cairn is a gay and lively dog, of little trouble in the house. He makes an excellent pet and still remains a typical burrow hunter, thanks to his natural gifts which he has never lost.

GENERAL CHARACTERISTICS This terrier should impress one with his fearless and gay disposition. Active, game, hardy, shaggy of aspect, the Cairn is strong and compactly built. Should stand well forward on forepaws. Strong quarters, deep in ribs, very free in movement. Coat tough enough to resist rain. Small head, but in proportion to body. A generally foxy appearance is the chief characteristic of this working terrier.

WEIGHT Ideally, 14 lb.

HEAD Skull broad in proportion; strong jaw but level and not too long or heavy, and should be neither undershot nor overshot. A decided indentation between eyes; hair should be full on forehead. Muzzle powerful but not heavy. Teeth are large.

EYES Set wide apart; medium in size; dark hazel, rather sunken, with shaggy eyebrows.

EARS Small, pointed, well carried and erect, but not too closely set.

NECK Well set on but not short.

BODY Compact, straight-backed; well sprung, deep ribs; strong sinews. Back medium in length and well coupled.

TAIL Short, well furnished with hair but not feathery; carried gaily but should not turn down toward back.

FOREQUARTERS Sloping shoulder and a medium length of leg; good, but not too large, bone. Forelegs should not be out at elbows. **HINDQUARTERS** Very strong. **FEET** Forefeet larger than hind feet, may be slightly turned out. Pads should be thick and strong. Thin and ferrety feet are objectionable.

COAT Very important. Must be doublecoated, with profuse, hard, but not coarse, outercoat, and undercoat which resembles fur and is short, soft and close. Open coats are objectionable. Head should be well furnished. **Color** Red, sandy, gray, brindled or nearly black. Dark points, such as ears and muzzle, very typical.

FAULTS Muzzle undershot or overshot. Eyes: too prominent or too light. Ears: Too large or round at points; they must not be heavily coated with hair. Coat: silkiness or curliness objectionable; a slight wave permissible. Nose: flesh or light-colored most objectionable. In order to keep this breed to the best old working type, any resemblance to a Scottish Terrier will be considered objectionable. ●

CAIRN TERRIER

88 DANDIE DINMONT TERRIER

GREAT BRITAIN

In Sir Walter Scott's novel *Guy Mannering*, one of the characters is a strange country gentleman, rough but with a heart of gold, named Dandie Dinmont. To describe him, the author took his inspiration from a real person, a cabinetmaker of Hyndlea, named James Davidson, who was also a breeder and huntsman and who owned two terriers (Pepper and Tarr) of very curious build. Scott's successful book was responsible for giving these terriers the name of their engaging master.

However, James Davidson was not the creator of this breed, which, although neglected, had existed for a long time. It is probably a very old variety raised by gypsies, then very numerous in southern Scotland. As far as its origins are concerned, some think that it goes back to the Otter Hound bred with the old type of Scottish Terrier, whereas others consider that it comes from the Skye and the Bedlington. It also appears that the coursing Flanders Basset, brought from France by the troops of William the Conquerer, also contributed to the breed.

WEIGHT AND SIZE Weight: The ideal weight for males in good working condition is 18 lb. Height at shoulder: 8-11 inches. Length from the top of the shoulder to the root of the tail should not be more than twice the height and should preferably be 1 or 2 inches less.

HEAD Head strongly made and large, not out of proportion to the dog's size, the muscles showing extraordinary development, more especially the maxillary. Skull broad between the ears, getting gradually less toward the eye and measuring about the same from the inner corner of the eye to back of skull as from ear to ear. The forehead well domed. The head is covered with very soft silky hair, which should not be confined to a mere topknot; the lighter in color and silkier the better. The cheeks, starting from the ears, taper gradually toward the muzzle, which is deep and strongly made; it is about 3 inches long. The ratio of muzzle length to skull is 3:5. The muzzle is covered with hair of a little darker shade than the topknot; it is of the same texture as the feather of the forelegs. The top of the muzzle is generally bare for about an inch from the back part of the nose, the bareness coming to a point toward the eye; it is about 1 inch broad at the nose, which is black. The in-

Photo: Fotostampa, S. A. Thompson.

CAIRN TERRIER

side of the mouth should be black or dark-colored. The teeth should be very strong, especially the canines, which are of extraordinary size for such a small dog. The canines fit well into each other, so as to give the greatest available holding and punishing power. The teeth are level in front, the upper very slightly overlapping the lower. Undershot or overshot jaws are equally objectionable.

EYES Set wide apart, large, full, round but not protruding, the eyes are bright, expressive of great determination, intelligence and dignity; they are set low and prominent in front of the head. Their color is a rich dark hazel.

EARS Pendulous, set well back, wide apart and low on the skull, hanging close to the cheek, with a very slight projection at the base, broad at the junction of the head and tapering almost to a point, the forepart of the ear coming almost straight down from its junction with the head to the tip. Ear color should be in harmony with the body color. In pepper-colored dogs they are covered with soft, straight, dark hair, which in some cases is almost black. In mustard-colored dogs the hair should be a shade darker than the skin, but not black. All should have a thin feather of light hair starting about 2 inches from the tip, of nearly the same color and texture as the topknot, which gives the ear the appearance of a distinct point. The animal is often 1 or 2 years old before the feather shows. The cartilage and skin of the ear should not be thick, but very thin. The length of the ears is 3-4 inches.

DANDIE DINMONT TERRIER

DANDIE DINMONT TERRIER

155

Photo: S. A. Thompson, A. Roslin-Williams, R. Kinne (Photo Res.).

NECK Very muscular, well developed and strong, showing great power of resistance, being well set into the shoulders.

BODY Long, strong, and flexible; ribs well sprung and round, chest well developed and well let down between the forelegs; the back rather low at the shoulders, having a slight downward curve and a corresponding arch over the loins, with a very slight gradual drop from top of loin to root of tail; both sides of backbone well supplied with muscle.

TAIL Rather short, perhaps 8-10 inches, and covered on the upper side with wiry hair of a darker color than on the body. The hair on the underside of the tail is lighter in color and not so wiry, with a nice feather about 2 inches long, shortening as it nears the tip; rather thick at the root, getting thicker for about 4 inches, then tapering off to a point. It should not be twisted or curled in any way but should come up with a curve like a scimitar. When the dog is excited, the tail is perpendicular to its root. It should be set neither too high nor too low. In repose it is carried gaily, a little above the level of the body.

FOREQUARTERS The forelegs are short, with immense muscular development and bone, set wide apart with the chest coming well down between them. Bandylegs are objectionable. The hair on the forelegs of a pepper dog should be tan, varying according to the body color from rich tan to pale fawn; in a mustard dog they are a darker shade than the head, which

is a creamy white. In both colors there is a nice feather about 2 inches long, somewhat lighter in color than the hair on the forepart of the leg.
HINDQUARTERS The hindlegs are a little longer than the forelegs and are set rather wide apart, but not spread out in an unnatural manner; the thighs are well developed, and the hair is of the same color and texture as on the forelegs, but with no feather or dewclaws. **FEET** Flat feet are objectionable. The nails should be dark, but in all these dogs the nails correspond to color of the body. The feet of a pepper dog should be tan, varying according to the body color from rich tan to pale fawn; in a mustard dog they are a darker shade than the head. Hind feet should be much smaller than the forefeet.

COAT The hair should be about 2 inches long. From the skull to the root of the tail it is a mixture of hard and soft hair, which is crisp to the touch. The hard hair should not be wiry; the coat is what is termed "pily" or penciled. The hair on the underpart of the body is lighter in color and softer than on top. **Color** Pepper or mustard. The pepper ranges from dark bluish black to light silvery gray, the intermediate shades being preferred; the body color comes well down the shoulder and hips, gradually merging into the leg color. The mustards vary from a reddish brown to a pale fawn, the head being a creamy white, the legs and feet a shade darker than the head. The nails are dark, as in dogs of other colors. (Nearly all Dandie Dinmont Terriers have some white on the chest, and some have white nails). White feet are objectionable. ●

IRISH TERRIER

89 IRISH TERRIER
IRELAND

This terrier is probably the modern form of a very ancient terrier called "madah" in southern Ireland. Before the Christian era there were three types of dogs in Ireland, one for land hunting, an attack dog used against large, dangerous animals, and a burrowing dog. Modern breeds stemming from these ancient dogs are the Irish Water Spaniel, the Irish Wolfhound, and the Irish Terrier. According to old Celtic legend these dogs are of Eastern or, more precisely, Egyptian origin, brought to Ireland about 2000 B.C.

For a long time the size and color varied from one specimen to another. But after 1870 the genetic points were defined and from then on breeding not only preserved a rare variety but perfected it as well.

The Irish Terrier is essentially considered a pet, but in his country of origin as well as several other European countries his excellent hunting abilities are put to good use.

GENERAL CHARACTERISTICS Dogs that are very game are often surly or snappish, but the Irish Terrier is an exception. He is remarkably good-tempered, especially with people, but it must be admitted that he is a little too ready to resent interference from other dogs. There is a heedless, reckless courage about the Irish Terrier which is characteristic, and because of it he has earned the nickname of "daredevil." Off duty, these dogs are quiet and affectionate, but in the "set on" they can demonstrate the courage of a lion and are capable of fighting to the last gasp. They develop an extraordinary devotion to their masters and have been known to track them for incredible distances when required. The Irish Terrier must present an active, lively, lithe, and wiry appearance, with plenty of substance; at the same time he must be free from clumsiness, since speed, endurance, and power are all essential to his work. The dog should be neither cloddy nor cobby but should be framed rather on "lines of speed," with a graceful racing outline.

WEIGHT AND SIZE The most desirable weight in show condition is: male, 27 lb; female, 25 lb. Height at the shoulder is approximately 18 inches.

HEAD Long; skull flat and rather narrow between ears, becoming slightly narrower toward the eye; free from wrinkles; stop barely visible except in profile. The jaw must be strong and muscular but not too full in the cheek and of a good punishing length. The foreface should not dish or fall away quickly between or below the eyes, where it should be well made up and relieved of wedginess by delicate chiseling. The hair should be crisp and only sufficiently long to impart an appearance of additional strength to the foreface. Lips should be well fitting and externally almost black. The nose must be black. The teeth should be even, strong, and free from discoloration, with the upper teeth slightly overlapping the lower.

EYES A dark color, small, not prominent; full of life, fire, and intelligence. A light or yellow eye is a fault.

EARS Small and V-shaped, of moderate thickness, set well on the head and dropping forward closely to the cheek. The top of the folded ear should be well above the level of the skull. The ear must be free of fringe, and the hair thereon must be shorter and darker than the body.

NECK Should be of fair length, gradually widening toward the shoulders, well carried and free of throatiness. There is generally a slight frill at each side of the neck, running nearly to the corner of the ear.

BODY Chest deep and muscular, but neither full nor wide. Body moderately

IRISH TERRIER

Photo: S. A. Thompson, A. Roslin-Williams.

long. Back should be strong and straight, with no appearance of slackness behind the shoulders; the loin muscular and slightly arched; ribs fairly sprung, rather deeper than round; the back is well ribbed.

TAIL Generally docked to about ¾ length. Should be free of fringe or feather, but well covered with rough hair, set on rather high and carried gaily, but not over the back or curled.

FOREQUARTERS The shoulders must be fine, long, and sloping well into the back. The legs moderately well set from the shoulders, perfectly straight, with plenty of bone and muscle; the elbows working freely clear of the sides; pasterns short and straight, hardly noticeable. The forelegs should be moved straight forward when traveling. The hair on the legs should be dense and crisp. **HINDQUARTERS** Should be strong and muscular, the thighs powerful, the hocks near the ground, stifles moderately bent. The hind legs should be moved straight forward when traveling, the stifles not turned outward. The hair on the legs should be dense and crisp. **FEET** Should be strong, tolerably round and moderately small, the toes arched and turned neither in nor out; black nails a definite preference. Pads must be sound and free from cracks or horny excrescences.

COAT Hard and wiry, with a broken appearance, free of softness or silkiness, not so long as to hide the outline of the body, particularly in the hindquarters; straight and flat, no shagginess, and free of lock or curl. At the base of these stiff hairs is an undercoat of finer and softer hair. **Color** Should be whole-colored, the most preferable colors being a bright red, red wheaten, or yellow red. White sometimes appears on chest and feet and is more objectionable on the latter than on the former, as a speck of white on chest is frequently to be found on all self-colored breeds. ●

KERRY BLUE TERRIER

90 KERRY BLUE TERRIER
Irish Blue Terrier

IRELAND

This Irish breed originated in the mountains of Kerry County, a chain which traverses the extreme southwestern part of the island. It was only toward the middle of the last century that these dogs became known outside of Kerry County. It is also certain that the Kerry and the Irish Terrier descend from the same ancestor, although the Irish Terrier, being bred in the neighboring counties of the St. George's Channel, doubtless was influenced by English dogs, while the Kerry, isolated in his mountains, was protected from chance crossbreeding. It was only later, when it was desired to make the Kerry a fighting dog, that he was crossbred with the Bedlington and the Bulldog.

Although bred to hunt badgers and foxes, he adapted readily, as he is a good swimmer, to otter hunting. He is also an effective guard dog for sheep and larger livestock. In some regions he is also used to guard pigs. In World War II he was frequently used by the British Army, as his dark blue coat made him particularly effective for night work.

Because of his characteristic coat and color, the Kerry Blue is generally considered a pet dog, especially in continental Europe.

KERRY BLUE TERRIER

GENERAL CHARACTERISTICS Disciplined gameness. The Kerry Blue Terrier is a compact, powerful terrier displaying gracefulness and an attitude of alert determination with definite terrier style and character throughout. The typical Kerry Blue should be upstanding, well knit and well proportioned, showing a well-developed and muscular body.

WEIGHT AND SIZE The most desirable weight for a fully developed male is 33-37 lb; females should weigh proportionately less, but 35 lb is the most desirable weight to aim for. Ideal height: males 18-19 inches at the shoulder; females slightly less.

HEAD Well balanced, long, proportionately lean, with a slight stop and flat over the skull. Foreface and jaw very strong, deep and punishing; nose black, with nostrils duly proportioned. Teeth level, with upper teeth closing just over the lower; dark gums and palate.

EYES As dark as possible; small to medium in size, with a keen terrier expression.

EARS Small to medium, V-shaped; carried forward but not so high as in some terrier breeds.

NECK Strong and reachy, running into sloping shoulders.

BODY Short-coupled, with good depth of brisket and well-sprung ribs. Chest must be deep, the topline level.

TAIL Set on high to complete a perfectly straight back and carried erect.

FOREQUARTERS Shoulders as flat as possible with elbows carried close to the body while the dog is standing or in action. Legs straight, bone powerful. Front straight, neither too wide nor too narrow. **HINDQUARTERS** Large and well developed, stifle bent and hocks close to the ground, giving perfect freedom of action behind. **FEET** Round and small, with black nails.

COAT Soft and silky, profuse and wavy. **Color** Any shade of blue, with or without black points. A shade of tan is permissible in puppies, as is also a dark color up to the age of 18 months. A small white patch on chest should not be penalized.

FAULTS Hard or woolly coat; solid black after 18 months; over 19 inches in height; bumpy cheekbones; teeth undershot or excessively overshot; rose ears; snipy foreface; light or full eyes; roach or hollow back; close, stilted, or cow-hocked hind action. ●

Photo: B. Moruzzi, Palnic.

uted to the formation of a single breed and that the Lakeland stock is derived from the old English Black and Tan Rough Terrier.

GENERAL CHARACTERISTICS Smart and workmanlike, with gay, fearless demeanor.

WEIGHT AND SIZE Average weight of males is 17 lb, of females 15 lb; height should not exceed 15 inches at the shoulder.

HEAD Well balanced; skull flat and refined. The jaws are powerful, and the muzzle should be broad but not too long. The length of the head from the stop to the tip of the nose should not exceed the length from the occiput to the stop. Nose black. Teeth even, closing in a scissors bite, the upper teeth fitting closely over the lower.

EYES Should be dark or hazel.

EARS Moderately small, V-shaped, and carried alert. They should not be placed too high or too low on the head.

NECK Reachy.

BODY Chest reasonably narrow, back strong and moderately short and well coupled.

TAIL Well set on, carried gaily but must not curl over the back.

FOREQUARTERS Shoulders well laid back; forelegs straight, well boned.

HINDQUARTERS Strong and muscular, thighs long and powerful, well-turned stifles, hocks low to the ground and straight. **FEET** Small, compact, round and well padded.

COAT Dense and weather-resistant, harsh, with good undercoat. **Color** Black and tan, blue and tan, red, wheaten, red grizzle, liver, blue or black. Small tips of white on feet and chest not disqualifying. Mahogany or deep tan is not typical.

FAULTS The true Lakeland expression is determined by the head, ears, and eyes. Too long a head, ears set on top of the head, and slanting eyes are faults. ●

LAKELAND TERRIER

91 LAKELAND TERRIER
GREAT BRITAIN

Also called Fell Terrier, Patterdale Terrier, Colored Working Terrier, Westmoreland Terrier, and Cumberland Terrier, this breed originated in the Lake district of England, the region that inspired the writings of Wordsworth and Coleridge. The origins of this breed are thus lost in an aura of romanticism, as its pedigrees stop in 1921, when the Lakeland Terrier Club was founded.

Authors who lived in the preceding period report that burrow dogs living in this area were called Patterdale Terriers, while other similar terriers existing in Fell, Westmoreland, and Cumberland were known by the names of the areas they lived in.

Lee writes that these dogs are excellent fox and badger hunters, clever at catching them in the rocky crevices of that region and the tunnels and rock piles called "borrans" by the local inhabitants. It is probable that all these types of dogs contrib-

92 MANCHESTER TERRIER
GREAT BRITAIN

Much has been written concerning a probable crossbreeding between the early Manchester (also more exactly called the Black and Tan Terrier) and the Small Italian Greyhound. This theory seems logical because of the obvious Greyhound characteristics in the structure of this breed.

Manchesters have been separated into two types since the club was founded in 1879: a large-sized one, with characteristics similar to those of today's Manchester and employed for burrow hunting and ratcatching, and a smaller one favored as a pet, the ancestor of the Toy Terrier, now called the Black and Tan Toy Terrier.

Today the Manchester Terrier does not enjoy the popularity he deserves. Even in England he seems to be disappearing, which is unfortunate, since he is an intelligent, faithful, and active dog. The breed is of excellent appearance, needs little space, and is endowed with a short and finehaired coat that needs little special care.

GENERAL CHARACTERISTICS Compact in appearance with good bone and free from any resemblance to the Whippet.

Photo: S. A. Thompson, A. Roslin-Williams, T. Fall.

WEIGHT The most desirable weight is: males 18 lb; females 17 lb.

HEAD Long, flat in skull and narrow; level and wedge-shaped, without showing cheek muscles; well filled up under the eyes, with tapering, tight-lipped jaws. Mouth should be level.

EYES Small, dark and sparkling, oblong in shape, set close to head, not prominent.

EARS Small and V-shaped, carried well above the topline of the head and hanging close to the head above the eyes.

NECK The neck should be fairly long and tapering from the shoulder to the head and slightly arched at the crest, free from throatiness.

BODY Short with well-sprung ribs, slightly roached and well cut up behind the ribs.

TAIL Short and set on where the arch of the back ends, thick where it joins the body and tapering to a point, carried not higher than the level of the back.

FOREQUARTERS The shoulders should be clean and well sloped, the chest narrow and deep. The forelegs must be quite straight, set on well under the dog and of a length proportionate to the body. **HINDQUARTERS** The hind legs should be neither cow-hocked nor with the feet turned in; they should be well bent at the stifle. **FEET** Small, semi-harefooted and strong, with well-arched toes.

COAT Thick, smooth, short and glossy, dense and not soft. **Color** Jet black and rich mahogany tan distributed as follows: on the head, the muzzle to be tanned to the nose, with the nose and nasal bone to be jet black; there should be a small tan spot on each cheek and above each eye, the underjaw and throat to be tanned with a distinct tan V. The legs from the knee down to be tanned with the exception of the toes, which should be penciled with black, with a distinct black mark (thumb mark) immediately above the feet. ●

MANCHESTER TERRIER

NORFOLK TERRIER

NORFOLK TERRIER

NORWICH TERRIER

93 NORFOLK TERRIER
GREAT BRITAIN

GENERAL CHARACTERISTICS The Norfolk Terrier is one of the smallest of terriers, but a demon for its size. Lovable disposition, not at all quarrelsome, and with a hardy constitution. His temperament is steady and fearless. A small, low, keen dog, strong with good substance and bone.

HEIGHT The ideal height is 10 inches at the withers.

HEAD Skull wide, with good width between the ears and slightly rounded. Muzzle strong, about one third shorter than the length from the top of the occiput to the bottom of the stop; the stop is well defined. The mouth should be tight-lipped, with clean, strong jaws and rather large, strong teeth. The jaws meet in a scissors bite.

EYES Dark, intelligent, full of expression, bright and keen.

EARS Neatly dropped, slightly rounded at the tips, they are carried close to the cheek.

NECK Of medium length and strong.

BODY Comparatively short and compact, with well-sprung ribs.

TAIL Docked at medium length, not excessively gay in carriage.

FOREQUARTERS Clean, powerful shoulders, with strong, straight legs. **HINDQUARTERS** Sound and well muscled, good turn of stifle, hocks well let down and straight when viewed from the rear, with great power of propulsion. **FEET** Round, with thick pads.

COAT Hard, wiry and straight, lying close to the body. It should be longer and rougher on the neck and shoulders and in winter it almost forms a mane. Hair on the head, ears, and muzzle is short and smooth. **Color** All shades of red, red wheaten, black and tan or grizzle. White marks or patches are undesirable, but do not disqualify.

FAULTS Overshot or undershot mouth; long, narrow head. In general, trimming is not desirable. Honorable scars from fair wear and tear should not be penalized. ●

94 NORWICH TERRIER
GREAT BRITAIN

In 1870 a Cambridge breeder obtained a small and very lively red terrier which he called the Norwich Terrier. A person named Hopkins also bred a terrier with similar black and red or gray coat which he called the Trumpington Terrier. The two breeds were then combined to produce the Norwich.

GENERAL CHARACTERISTICS The Norwich Terrier is one of the smallest of the terriers, but a demon for its size. Lovable disposition, not quarrelsome, and has a hardy constitution. In general appearance a small, low, keen dog, compact and strong, with good substance and bone.

WEIGHT AND SIZE Ideal weight is 11-12 lb; Ideal height is 10 inches at the withers.

HEAD The Norwich has a "foxy" muzzle, which is strong and about one third shorter the length from the top of the occiput to the bottom of the stop, which is well defined. Skull wide, with good width between the ears, and slightly rounded. The mouth is tight-lipped, the jaws clean and strong. The teeth are strong, rather large and close-fitting.

EYES Dark, full of expression, bright and keen.

EARS May be either erect or dropped, but in the latter case they should be neat and small and correctly dropped.

NECK Short and strong, well set on clean shoulders.

BODY Short and compact, with well-sprung ribs.

TAIL Docked at medium length, not excessively gay in carriage.

FOREQUARTERS Clean and powerful shoulders, with short, powerful and straight legs. **HINDQUARTERS** Sound and strong, with great powers of propulsion. **FEET** Round, with thick pads.

COAT Hard, wiry and straight, lying close to the body. It is longer and rougher on the neck and shoulders, and in winter it forms almost a mane. Hair on the head, ears, and muzzle is short and smooth, except for slight eyebrows and slight whiskering. **Color** Red, including red-wheaten, black and tan, or brindle. White marks or patches are undesirable but not disqualifying.

FAULTS Light bones; long, weak back; a mouth overshot or undershot; a long narrow head; square muzzle; yellow or pale eyes; a full eye, soft expression; soft, wavy, curly, or silky coat. Trimming is not desirable and should be penalized. Honorable scars from fair wear and tear should not be penalized. ●

NORWICH TERRIER

Photo: T. Fall, Thurse R. Kinne (Photo Res.)

95 SCOTTISH TERRIER

GREAT BRITAIN

Toward the end of the nineteenth century there lived, in the pleasant Scottish city of Aberdeen, a certain Mr. Van Best, who was long considered the leading breeder of a special terrier that was most efficient in burrow hunting. When this dog became popular throughout the rest of Scotland and Great Britain he was referred to as the Aberdeen Terrier. He kept this name through various changes of fortune until 1887, and from then on became known as the Scottish Terrier.

The first pedigrees go back to that year, which indicates the beginning of the selective breeding which has made the present Scottish Terrier a much finer dog than the one bred by Van Best.

Nevertheless, this dog still preserves special aptitudes for hunting wild animals, his powerful dorsal muscles enabling him to penetrate underground passageways with great speed.

GENERAL CHARACTERISTICS The Scottish Terrier is a sturdy, thickset dog of a size suitable to go to ground, placed on short legs, alert in carriage and suggestive of great power and activity in small compass. The head gives the impression of being long for a dog of his size. The body is covered with a close-lying, broken, rough-textured coat. With its keen, intelligent eyes and sharp prick ears, the dog looks willing to go anywhere and do anything. In spite of his short legs, his construction is such that he is a very agile and active dog. The movement of the dog is smooth, easy and straightforward, with free action at the shoulder, stifle, and hock.

WEIGHT AND SIZE The ideal dog in show condition should weigh 19-23 lb and measure 10-11 inches at the withers.

HEAD Without being out of proportion to the size of the dog, it should be long, the length of the skull enabling it to be fairly wide and yet retain a narrow appearance. The skull is nearly flat, the cheekbones do not protrude. There is a slight but distinct stop between skull and foreface, just in front of the eye. The nose is large, and in profile the line from the nose toward the chin appears to slope backward. The teeth are large, and the upper incisors closely overlap the lower.

EYES Should be almond-shaped, dark brown, fairly wide apart and set deeply under the eyebrows.

EARS Neat, of fine texture, pointed and erect.

NECK Muscular, of moderate length.

BODY The body has well rounded ribs which flatten to a deep chest and are carried well back. The back is proportionately short and very muscular. In general the topline of the body should be straight and level; the loin should be muscular and deep, thus powerfully coupling the ribs to the hindquarters.

TAIL Of moderate length, giving a general balance to the dog. It is thick at the root, tapering toward the tip; it is set on with an upright carriage or with a slight bend.

FOREQUARTERS The head is carried on a muscular neck of moderate length, showing quality, set into a long, sloping shoulder. The brisket is well in front of the forelegs, which are straight and well boned to straight pasterns. The chest should be fairly broad and hung between the forelegs, which must not be out at the elbows nor placed under the body. **HINDQUARTERS** Extraordinarily powerful for the size of the Scottish Terrier, with big and wide buttocks, deep and muscular thighs, well-bent stifles. The hocks are strong and well bent and turned neither inward nor outward. **FEET** Of good size and well padded, with well arched toes, close-knit.

COAT Short, dense, soft undercoat and a harsh, dense, wiry outercoat. The combination of the two coats gives the dog remarkable weather resistance. **Color** Black, wheaten, or brindle of any color. ●

SCOTTISH TERRIER

161

SKYE TERRIER

96 SEALYHAM TERRIER
GREAT BRITAIN

This breed was born about a century ago in the small Welsh town from which it got its name. It was recognized in 1910 by the International Kennel Association.

A Captain Edwards, naturalist and avid hunter, attempted in 1845, through a series of crossbreedings, to create a new terrier which would combine the small stature required for underground burrowing with highly developed qualities of zeal, courage, and strength.

By crossbreeding the regular Flanders Basset with the Welsh Corgi and then with other breeds such as the Dandie Dinmont, he obtained a dog which, while possessing the desired qualities, still presented a serious drawback: the coat was too nearly like a fox's. Edwards remedied this by crossing the dog with a variety of Bull Terrier with snipped tail, and V-shaped ears. He again used the Flanders Basset and other breeds until he obtained a terrier that, over the years, has proved an excellent hunter, not only for burrows but also over the ground where his work often resembles that of a hound. Like other terrier breeds, the Sealyham is almost everywhere looked upon as a pet.

SEALYHAM TERRIER

GENERAL CHARACTERISTICS Those of a freely moving and highly active dog.

WEIGHT AND SIZE Males should not exceed 20 lb; females should not exceed 18 lb. Height at shoulder should not exceed 12 inches.

HEAD The skull is slightly domed and wide between the ears. The jaw is powerful and long, with a punishing and square jaw. The nose is black. The teeth are level and square, strong, with the canines fitting well into each other; for the dog's size, the canines are long.

EYES Dark, well set, round, and of medium size.

EARS Medium size, slightly rounded at the tip and carried at the side of the cheek.

NECK Fairly long, thick and muscular, and set strongly on sloping shoulders.

BODY Of medium length, level, with well-sprung ribs. Body very flexible, chest broad and deep and well let down between forelegs.

TAIL Carried erect.

FOREQUARTERS Forelegs short, strong and straight. **HINDQUARTERS** Remarkably powerful for the size of the dog. Thighs deep and muscular, well bent at the stifle. Hocks strong, well bent and turned neither inward nor outward. **FEET** Round and catlike, with thick pads.

COAT Long, hard and wiry. **Color** Mostly all white, white with lemon, brown or badger pied markings on head and ears.

FAULTS Light or small eyes; nose white, cherry, or spotted to a considerable extent with either of these colors; prick, tulip, or rose ears; much black coloring objectionable; defective teeth; much undershot or overshot mouth; soft and woolly coat. ●

Photo: S. A. Thompson, A. Roslin-Williams.

SKYE TERRIER

SOFT-COATED WHEATEN TERRIER

97 SKYE TERRIER

GREAT BRITAIN

The Skye was being written about as far back as 1600. He was then called the Scottish Terrier but was quite different from the present breed. He gets the name from the island where he originated, located in the Hebrides.

According to legend, a Spanish vessel was shipwrecked on the reefs surrounding the island and some Maltese dogs survived by swimming ashore. These were crossbred with the local terriers and produced the Skye. According to some authorities the breed came from a cross between the Scottish Terrier and the Dandie Dinmont. In former days the Skye was used in wolf hunting, but later, because of his winsome appearance, his great intelligence, and his splendid coat, he became popular as a toy dog and pet.

GENERAL CHARACTERISTICS A hardy and active dog, giving a general impression of strength with graceful and lively movement characterized by straight action fore and aft. The dog must not be leggy nor too close to the ground.

WEIGHT Males 35 lb; females somewhat less.

HEAD Moderately long, with a flat skull which is not too wide between the ears. The stop is well defined, the jaws strong and punishing. The foreface should not be longer than the skull. Hair abundant all over head and of the same color as the body hair. Cheekbones not prominent. The head in general is powerful but in no way coarse. The teeth are large and level, neither undershot nor overshot.

EYES Dark hazel, not too large, well placed, not prominent.

EARS Small, thin, held to the front, the ears are covered with hair and sport a fringe.

NECK Moderately long and strong, but not throaty.

BODY Compact and not too long, with powerful, short loins and strong, muscular thighs, hocks well let down.

TAIL Well set on, not too thick, well covered with hair and carried gaily, but not over the back. A curled tail is objectionable.

FOREQUARTERS Sloping and fine but muscular. Chest deep, with well sprung ribs. Forelegs perfectly straight when viewed from any angle, good bone and muscle. **HINDQUARTERS** Well developed, with powerful muscle. Stifles well bent, hocks turned neither in nor out. **FEET** Small, not spreading. Nails black.

COAT Abundant and soft, wavy or curly; but if curly, curls must be large and loose. **Color** A good, clear wheaten.

DISQUALIFYING POINTS Overshot or undershot mouth; any color other than wheaten. ●

SKYE TERRIER

GENERAL CHARACTERISTICS A one-man dog, distrustful of strangers but not vicious.

WEIGHT AND SIZE Weight: male 25 lb; height: male 10 inches; overall length 41½ inches. Female slightly smaller in same proportions of height and weight.

HEAD Long, with powerful jaws. The nose must be black. The teeth close and level.

EYES Hazel, preferably dark brown, of medium size, close-set and full of expression.

EARS Prick or drop ears. Prick ears should be gracefully feathered, not large, erect at outer edges and slanting toward each other at inner edge from peak to skull. Drop ears should be larger, hanging straight and lying flat and close at front.

NECK Long, gracefully arched and slightly crested. It should be carried high and proudly.

BODY Long and low; back level, ribs well sprung, giving a flattish look to the sides.

TAIL When hanging, the upper part of the tail is pendulous while the lower half is thrown back in a curve. When raised it is a prolongation of the incline of the back, neither rising higher nor curling up.

FOREQUARTERS Shoulders broad and close to body, chest deep; legs short and muscular. **HINDQUARTERS** Hindquarters and flanks are full and well developed. Legs short and muscular, without dewclaws. **FEET** Large and pointing forward.

COAT The Skye's coat is double, with a close, soft, short woolly undercoat and top coat which is made up of long hair, straight, flat, free from crisp and curl. Hair on head shorter and softer, veiling the forehead and eyes. On ears the hair is overhanging within, falling down and mingling with the side locks; it surrounds the ears like a fringe and permits their shape to appear. The tail is gracefully feathered **Color** Dark or light blue-gray; fawn, cream with black points. Any color is permissible so long as the nose and ears are black. ●

98 SOFT-COATED WHEATEN TERRIER

IRELAND

The Irish hold their terrier in great esteem, as he has many uses: guard dog, defense dog, herd leader, and hunter of destructive game. He is little known outside of his region of origin (County Kerry) perhaps because he may be considered less attractive than other Irish Terriers.

Photo: S. A. Thompson, T. Fall, H.P.F.

SOFT-COATED WHEATEN TERRIER

99 STAFFORDSHIRE BULL TERRIER

GREAT BRITAIN

We previously mentioned, in speaking of the Bull Terrier, an ancient variety from which the breeder, James Hinks, obtained the present dog. Although it has practically disappeared, the old type of Bull Terrier is still esteemed around Staffordshire, although he is not recognized by the official kennel associations,

as is the modern Bull Terrier. However, all writers agree that the Staffordshire is the ancestor of the modern Bull Terrier, and many claim that the great resemblance between the two is due to crossbreeding.

In the case of the Staffordshire we can observe the effects of style changes even within the domain of dog breeding. Although practically forgotten for a long period, this dog was again accepted in shows while many breeders devoted themselves to the "new" older breed.

The Staffordshire is an able ratcatcher and has preserved the qualities of great courage, intelligence, and tenacity. He is also gentle with children.

STAFFORDSHIRE BULL TERRIER

GENERAL CHARACTERISTICS Courageous, intelligent, tenacious, although of an affectionate nature, particularly toward children. Smooth-coated, he is of extraordinary strength for his size and although muscular, he should be active and agile.

WEIGHT AND SIZE Weight: male 28-38 lb; female 24-34 lb. Height at shoulder: 14-16 inches, varying with weight.

HEAD Short, deep, with broad skull and very pronounced cheek muscles. A well-defined stop, short foreface and black nose. The mouth should be level, i.e., the incisors of the lower jaw should fit closely within the upper incisors, and the lips should be tight and clean. Either undershot or overshot condition is to be severely penalized.

EYES Preferably dark, but may vary in relation to coat color. Round, of medium size and set to look straight ahead.

EARS Rose or half-pricked, not large. Full drop or prick ears to be penalized as a fault.

NECK Muscular, rather short. It should be clean in outline and should show a gradual widening toward the sturdy shoulders.

BODY Should be close-coupled, with a level top line and wide front. The brisket should be deep, the ribs well sprung; relatively light in the loins.

TAIL Medium length, set on low and tapering to a point which is carried rather low. It should not curl much. Its general appearance may be likened to that of an old-fashioned pump handle.

FOREQUARTERS Legs straight and well boned, set rather wide apart, without looseness at the shoulders and showing no weakness at the pasterns, from which point the feet turn out a little. **HINDQUARTERS** The hindquarters should be well muscled, the hocks well let down and the stifles well bent. Legs should be parallel when viewed from behind. **FEET** The feet should be well padded, strong and of medium size.

COAT The coat should be smooth, short, fitting close to the skin. **Color** Red, fawn, white, black or blue; or any of these colors with white. Any shade of brindle with white. Black and tan or liver not desirable.

FAULTS To be penalized according to severity: light eyes, pink eye rims; tail too long or badly curled; nonconformity to weight and height limits; full drop or prick ears; undershot or overshot mouth.

DISQUALIFYING FAULTS Pink or Dudley nose; badly undershot or overshot mouth; badly undershot mouth in which the lower incisors do not touch the upper. ●

Photo: S. A. Thompson, T. Fall.

Photo: S. A. Thompson.

WELSH TERRIER

100 WELSH TERRIER
GREAT BRITAIN

Although certain writers consider the breed of recent development, since it was presented for the first time in 1885, the Welsh Terrier is really only a variety of the old black and red coarsehaired terrier developed by the Welsh through rigorous selective breeding. At the same time, some English breeders achieved a similar variety by crossbreeding Airedales and Fox Terriers. A kind of rivalry arose between the Welsh and the English, the former being unable to have their Welsh Terrier officially recognized, whereas the new English variety practically disappeared. The Welsh Terrier is lively and gay and is very prevalent throughout all of Great Britain, especially as a pet.

WELSH TERRIER

GENERAL CHARACTERISTICS The Welsh Terrier has a gay, volatile disposition and is rarely shy. Affectionate, obedient, easily controlled, he is an eminently suitable dog for town. His size and color make him an ideal house dog—size being in his favor wherever accommodations are limited, while color precludes the need for the frequent bathing required by white terriers. The Welsh is game and fearless, although definitely not pugnacious; he is capable of holding his own when necessary, however. He is ideally constituted to be a perfect town or country companion. Normally hardy and robust, Welsh Terriers need no pampering. As working dogs they are second to none, easily accepting training to all sorts of game and adaptable to working with gun or ferrets. They are generally excellent water dogs.

WEIGHT AND SIZE The average weight is 20-21 lb; height should not exceed 15½ inches.

HEAD The skull should be flat and rather wider between the ears than the Wirehaired Fox Terrier. The jaw should be powerful, clean-cut, rather deeper and more punishing, characteristics which give the head a more masculine appearance than that usually found in a Fox Terrier. The stop is not overly defined; there is a fair length from stop to tip of nose. The nose is black. The mouth should be level, the teeth strong.

EYES Small and well set in, of a dark color, expressive and indicative of great keenness. A round, full eye is undesirable.

EARS Should be V-shaped, small, not too thin, and set on fairly high. They should be carried forward and close to the cheek.

NECK Of moderate length and thickness, slightly arched and sloping gracefully into the shoulders.

BODY The back should be short and well ribbed up; the loin strong, with good depth and moderate width of chest.

FOREQUARTERS The shoulders should be long, sloping, and well set back. The legs should be straight and muscular, with ample bone and with powerful, upright pasterns. **HINDQUARTERS** Should be strong, with muscular thighs and of good length, with the hocks well bent, well let down and with ample bone. **FEET** Small, round, and catlike.

COAT Should be wiry, hard, very close and abundant. A single coat is not desirable. **Color** The preferred color is black and tan, or black grizzle and tan; the coat should be free from black penciling on toes. Black below the hocks is a fault.

FAULTS White, cherry or spotted nose; prick ears; tulip or rose ears; any appreciable amount of black below the hocks. ●

101 WEST HIGHLAND WHITE TERRIER
GREAT BRITAIN

Around 1600 King James I of England wrote to a Scottish noble, requesting him to send several Argyle Terriers to the French Court. At this time the terriers from this part of Scotland already enjoyed the reputation of being the very best.

For centuries they were carefully bred and selected for the preservation of two important qualities: their superb courage and their decisiveness in charging into burrows. Argyleshire is on the border of the region where the Cairn originated, and it is probable, even certain, that the original stock is the same for both breeds. Fanfoni believes this for two reasons: first, the identical physique of the two breeds, and second, the Kennel Club's decision of November 18, 1924, forbidding the breeding of Cairns with West Highland White Terriers, which was previously authorized and even widely practiced. The essential difference which exists today between the two breeds is in the color, which must be absolutely white in the case of the West Highland White, whereas the Cairn must never be white. The natural history of this region has been the cause of a curious

WEST HIGHLAND WHITE TERRIER

Photo: S. A. Thompson, Thurse, A. Roslin-Williams.

similarity: in Argyleshire many white-coated animals exist, the result of unknown mutations, not found in other regions, such as foxes, hares, woodcocks, and others. One might imagine that a simple mutation of the color came about in the case of the dog and that this feature was carefully selected thereafter, since it was easier to recognize the dog during the somber days in the north of Scotland when he left the burrows of the animals he was hunting.

This breed of ancient origin was recognized by the Kennel Club only in 1907. In this case too, the general rule was confirmed, wherein the more recent the breed the sooner it is recognized, although the oldest breeds remain forgotten for a long time until they suddenly spring forth and attain fame.

GENERAL CHARACTERISTICS This is a small, game, hardy-looking terrier, possessed of no small amount of self-esteem, with a varminty appearance; strongly built, deep in chest and back ribs; level back and powerful quarters on muscular legs, exhibiting in a marked degree a combination of strength and activity. Movement should be free, straight and easy all around. In the front the legs should be freely extended forward by the shoulder. The hind movement should be free, strong and close. The hocks should be freely flexed and drawn close in under the body so that, when moving off the foot, the body is pushed forward with some force. Stiff, stilted movement behind is very objectionable.

SIZE Height at the withers should be about 11 inches.

HEAD The skull should be slightly domed and, when gripped across the forehead, should present a smooth contour. There should be only a very slight tapering from the skull at the level of the ears to the eyes. The distance from the occiput to the eyes should be slightly greater than the length of the foreface. The head should be thickly coated with hair and carried at a right angle or less to the axis of the neck. On no account should the head be carried in the ex-tended position. The foreface should gradually taper from the eye to the muzzle. There should be a distinct stop formed by heavy, bony ridges, immediately above and slightly over-hanging the eye, with a slight indenta-tion between the eyes. The foreface should not dish or fall away quickly below the eyes, where it should be well made up. The jaws should be strong and level. The nose must be black and should be fairly large, form-ing a smooth contour with the rest of the muzzle, and not to project for-ward, for that gives a snipy appear-ance. The mouth should be as broad between the canine teeth as is con-sistent with the sharp, varminty ex-pression required. The teeth should be large, the lower canines should lock in front of the upper canines. The upper incisors should slightly overlap the lower. When the mouth is closed, there should be a keen bite.

EYES Should be widely set apart, medium in size, as dark as possible. Slightly sunk in head, sharp and and intelligent.

EARS Small, erect and carried firmly, terminating in a sharp point. The hair should be short and smooth and should remain untrimmed. The ears should be free from any fringe at the top. Rounded, broad, large, or too thick ears are very objectionable, as are ears too heavily coated with hair.

NECK Should be sufficiently long to allow the required proper set-on of head, muscular, gradually thickening toward the base and allowing the neck to merge into nicely sloping shoulders, thus giving freedom of movement.

BODY Compact with level back and broad, strong loins. The chest should be deep and the ribs well arched in the upper half, presenting a flattish appearance from the side. The back ribs should be of consider-able depth to allow free movement of the body.

TAIL 5-6 inches long, covered with hard hair, without feather, as straight as possible, carried jauntily but not gaily nor over the back. A long tail is objectionable, and on no account should the tail be docked.

FOREQUARTERS The shoulders should be sloped backward. The shoulder blades should be broad and lie close to the chest wall. The joint formed by the shoulder blade and the upper arm should be placed forward because of the obliquity of the shoulder blades, bringing the elbows well in and allowing the foreleg to move freely, parallel to the axis of the body, like the pendulum of a clock. Fore-legs should be short and muscular, straight and thickly covered with short, hard hair. **HINDQUARTERS** Strong, muscular and wide across the top. Legs should be short, muscular and sinewy. The thighs very muscular and not too wide apart. The hocks bent and well set in under the body so as to be fairly close to each other when standing, walking or trotting. Cow hocks detract from the general ap-pearance. Straight or weak hocks are undesirable and are a fault. **FEET** The forefeet are larger than the hind ones; they are round, in good propor-tion to the rest of the body, strong, thickly padded and covered with short, hard hair. The hind feet are smaller and thickly padded. The undersurface of the pads and all nails should pre-ferably be black.

COAT The top coat consists of hard hair, about 2 inches long, free from any curl. The undercoat, which resem-bles fur, is short, soft and close. Open coats are objectionable. **Color** Pure white, double-coated only. ●

102 AUSTRALIAN TERRIER

AUSTRALIA

Probably the result of crossbreeding between terriers imported from England, the Australian Terrier is descended, according to some experts, from the Yorkshire, Skye, Norwich, and Cairn. The breed was presented for the first time at a show in Melbourne in 1903. Shortly afterwards it was introduced in Great Britain and in 1933 was officially recognized by the Kennel Club.

He is an excellent rat hunter, according to breeders. The breed is not well known in Europe because no practical use has been found for it. The Australian Terrier has become a luxury dog, like so many other terriers.

Photo: S. A. Thompson.

AUSTRALIAN TERRIER

GENERAL CHARACTERISTICS A rather low-set dog, compact and active.

WEIGHT AND SIZE Average weight, 10-11 lb; average height, approximately 10 inches.

HEAD Head long, skull flat, full between the eyes. There is a soft-hair topknot, a long powerful jaw. The nose is black. Teeth are level.

EYES Small, keen, dark in color.

EARS Small, set high on skull, pricked or dropped toward front, free of long hair.

NECK Tends to be long in proportion to the body, with a decided frill of hair.

BODY Rather long in proportion to height; well ribbed up, with a straight back.

TAIL Docked.

FOREQUARTERS Legs should be perfectly straight, well set under the body, slight feather to the knee. **HINDQUARTERS** Good, strong thighs, hocks slightly bent. **FEET** Clean, small, well padded, with no tendency to spread. Black nails.

COAT Straight hair from 2-2½ inches long, hard in texture. **Color** (1) Blue or silver-gray body, tan color on legs and face (the richer the tan the better). Blue or silver topknot; (2) clear sandy or red with soft topknot.

FAULTS Flesh-colored nails or nose, white on feet, white breast, curly or woolly coat, all-black coat (puppies excepted), overshot or undershot mouth.

103 SILKY TERRIER
AUSTRALIA

This breed was recognized by official kennel clubs only in 1962, and the first breed standard published during the same year was modified in 1967. This dog is also known as the Sydney Terrier and is probably the result of crossbreeding of Skyes with Yorkshires. He resembles the Yorkshire in the color of his coat.

Lively, active, and hardy, he has the characteristics of a rodent hunter although today he is generally considered a pet, like so many other terrier breeds.

SILKY TERRIER

GENERAL CHARACTERISTICS A compact, moderately low dog, of medium length, of light but consistent build well adapted to hunting and killing rodents. He should have the characteristics of a terrier, combining liveliness, activity and solidity. His silky hair, straight and well divided, gives the dog a pleasant and neat appearance.

WEIGHT AND HEIGHT Weight: 9-11 lb. Height, approximately 9 inches.

HEAD Of medium length, with the distance from the tip of the nose to the stop shorter than from the stop to the back of the occiput. The head should be strong and typical of the terrier, moderately broad between the ears, with a flat skull not rounded between the eyes. Long hair on the forehead and cheeks is not desirable; the head should have a dense, silky growth of hair which, however, must not conceal the eyes. The nose should be black. The jaws are strong, the teeth regular, with upper incisors fitting well over the lower.

EYES Small, round, as dark as possible, with a lively and intelligent expression.

EARS Small, V-shaped, thin, set on high and carried erect, free of any long hair.

NECK Of medium length, fine and slightly crested; it should be well covered with long, silky hair.

BODY Moderately long, in good proportion to the overall size of the dog. The chest is of average depth and breadth. The ribs are well sprung and extend to strong loins. The back is straight.

TAIL Docked; carried straight and not too gaily.

FOREQUARTERS Light shoulders, set well back, well adapted to the forelegs with good angulation. Elbows turned neither inward nor outward. The forearms are lightly boned and round, straight and set well under the body, with no weakness in the pasterns.

HINDQUARTERS Well-developed thighs; the second thigh should be well bent and the hocks should be well angulated. Viewed from behind, the hocks must be well let down and parallel. **FEET** Small catfeet, with good pads, well-closed toes, with black or very dark nails.

COAT Fine and glossy, of silky texture. It should preferably be 5¼-6 inches long at the base of the ears to the root of the tail. There should not be long hair on the legs, pasterns or metatarsi. **Color** Blue and tan, or gray-blue and tan, as richly hued as possible. The blue on the tail should be very dark. The distribution of blue and tan should meet the following requirements: foreknot gray-blue if possible; tan around the base of the ears, on the muzzle and on the sides of the cheeks; blue from the base of the skull to the tip of the tail, on the forelegs, down to the pasterns, on the hind legs, on the thighs down to the hocks; the tan on the metatarsi follow a line which includes the second thigh, stifle and hock down to the feet on the back of the leg; tan also around the vent.

GAIT Free and straight, with no indication of weakness in shoulders or elbows; viewed from behind, the dog's gait should appear neither too closed nor too wide. No bending at the pasterns. The hindquarters should have good propulsion, with great flexibility at the stifle and the hock.

FAULTS Major: skinniness, rusticity, lack of solidity; overweight or underweight; nose not black; overshot or undershot jaw; sheeplike neck; white nails; curly, woolly, wavy, short or harsh coat; any color of coat besides blue and tan or gray-blue and tan (except in puppies); tan or bronze in blue areas of coat; sooty or dark shade in tan areas.

104 CZECH TERRIER
Český
CZECHOSLOVAKIA

Czech breeders, when they undertook to cross different terrier breeds, endeavored to develop a dog with short legs, very active, courageous, stubborn, and also easy to train. The first breeder who succeeded in definitely fixing the characteristics of the new breed was Franta Horák, of Klanovice.

Although Czechoslovakian breeders have classed him among burrow hunting dogs, connoiseurs consider him very good at rat hunting. He is a good house dog, and he gets along easily with other domestic animals.

In cities he has been adopted as a pet for his attractive appearance and his pleasant nature. He is also a very good guard dog, faithful, and particularly vigilant with children.

The breed was recognized by the FCI in 1963 and spread rapidly through the eastern and northern countries of Europe.

GENERAL CHARACTERISTICS Thanks to its size, the Czech Terrier has fine natural qualities as a going-to-ground and open-field terrier. Although his legs are short, he is an agile, rugged dog, tenacious in his battles against game and rodents, but not unduly aggressive. An especially attractive quality of the breed is its ability to adapt to new conditions; it is thus a fine house dog and pet and gets on well with children. A rare quality of this terrier is the pastel coloring of the coat, which is silken in its splendor.

WEIGHT AND SIZE The weight varies from 13-20 lb. Height at the withers, 10½-14 inches.

HEAD The head is long but in good proportion to the overall length of the dog. The nose is well developed and of good shape; in gray-blue dogs it should be black, in gray-brown or light brown dogs it should be liver. The bridge is straight. The lips should be relatively fleshy but not excessively so; they should fit neatly over the gums. The jaws are robust, closing in either a scissors or pincers bite. The stop is apparent but not accentuated. There is a decided angle formed by the intersection of forehead and bridge. The skull is not broad between the ears and should taper moderately toward the supraorbital ridges. The cheekbones are lightly accentuated. The medial furrow is not pronounced; the occipital protuberance is accentuated. The muscles of the lower jaw should not be too prominent. Overall, the head has the shape of an obtuse parallelepiped, long and blunt.

EYES Of medium size, rather deep-set, friendly. They are almost concealed behind the overhanging brows.

Photo: S. A. Thompson, A. Wintzell.

In gray-blue dogs, the eyes are black; in gray-brown or light-brown dogs, the color ranges from light to dark brown.

EARS Of medium size, hanging in such a way as to cover the opening entirely. They are set on relatively high and hang close against the cheeks. They are triangular, with the shortest side of the triangle at the fold of the ear.

NECK Of medium length, carried on a slant and relatively robust. The skin at the throat is fairly loose, but without forming a dewlap.

FOREQUARTERS The shoulders are muscular, with the scapula well placed and mobile. The elbows are fairly loose, but they must turn neither inward nor outward. The forelegs are well boned and vertical. Their movement is straight ahead and parallel to the body axis. The feet should be rather big, with well-arched toes and strong nails. The pads are full and well developed.

BODY Of moderate length, the rib cage approximately cylindrical and not very let down. The ideal circumference of the body immediately behind the elbows is 15½-18 inches. The ribs are well sprung. The back line is straight and the croup is moderately rounded. The loins are very muscular, their length in good proportion to the trunk, broad and fairly raised. The belly, observed at the most distant point from the back ribs, is ample and moderately drawn up. The groin is full, the croup is well developed, muscular and fairly hollowed.

HINDQUARTERS Should be robust and well boned, with muscular thighs. The hind legs, proportionately shorter, are slanted toward the rear, so as to permit good angulation of the hindquarters. The hocks are rather high and robust. The hind feet are smaller than the forefeet. The hind legs are parallel, their movement free and easy.

TAIL 7-8 inches long and rather robust. It should not be set on very high. In repose it is carried downward, with the tip slightly raised. When the dog is excited, the tail is carried curved, horizontal or slightly raised.

COAT Should be clipped, depending on the season and the working requirements. On the forepart of the head the hair should not be clipped, thus forming a thick beard and prominent eyebrows. On the legs, chest and belly also the hair should not be clipped. The dividing line between

SILKY TERRIER

clipped and unclipped areas should be skillfully tapered, not abrupt. In a dog prepared for showing, the hair on the neck and back should not be

longer than ⅔ inch. When it is cut, the coat is lighter, finer and moderately wavy; As it grows out it becomes darker, wavier and almost curly. Over the entire body the hair should be dense and with a silky gloss. **Color** Czech Terriers are bred in two distinct basic colors: gray-blue (black at birth) and light coffee brown (chocolate at birth). In both colors, yellow, gray or white shadings are permitted, normally on the head (cheeks, muzzle), on the neck, on the chest, on the belly and feet and under the tail. Sometimes the tip of the tail and the collar are white. The basic color, however, must cover most of the coat. **Skin** In gray-blue dogs, the skin is gray, whereas in light coffee-brown dogs it is flesh-colored.

GAIT The movement of the forelegs is easy and straightforward. The normal step and the trot are such that the dog can easily keep up with his master. The run is slow but enduring. The build and movement of the legs are of prime importance in judging the Czech Terrier.

FAULTS Nose of another color than those specified; short or pointed muzzle; weak teeth; overshot or undershot jaw; large or cow eyes; light eyes in gray-blue dogs; entropion or ectropion (inversion or eversion) of the eyelids; ears too long, too small,

oddly shaped or carried otherwise than prescribed above; forelegs not straight; body circumference more than 20 inches; back too short, too long, saddlebacked or humpbacked; tail turned or carried over back; defective position of hind legs; hair too soft or too hard; white markings covering more than 20 percent of the body; white shading on head; faulty movement; weak bone structure.

MEASUREMENTS

	M	F
Average weight	17½ lb.	15½ lb.
Heigth at withers	12 in.	11 in.
Length of head	8¼	7¾
Length of skull	4¾	4¾
Breadth of skull	4	3½
Length of bridge	3½	3
Diameter of rib cage	6	5½
Depth of chest	6½	6¼
Length of trunk	17	15¾
Circumference of trunk (behind elbows)	17¾	17¼
Circumference at loin	17	16½

ANGULATIONS

	Degrees
Scapular-humeral	100
Humeral-radial	135
Coxal-femoral	100
Femoral-tibial	120
Tibial-tarsal	135

CZECH TERRIER

Photo: S. A. Thompson, J. Jaros.

GERMAN HUNTING TERRIER

GERMAN HUNTING TERRIER

105 GERMAN HUNTING TERRIER

Deutscher Jagdterrier

GERMANY

This breed was created by Germans, who evidently crossbred a variety with British Terriers, and marks a return to the old type of coarsehaired English Terrier. Recently admitted to competition by official kennel clubs, although he is not really a recent breed, the German Hunting Terrier is a dog of such aggressive character that some observers believe he has a cruel instinct. However, it is his lively and combative nature that impels him, despite his small size, to take on the fox or the boar with the same assurance as when hunting rodents in their burrows.

He is an excellent hunter and certainly cannot be grouped with the terriers that are classed as nonsporting dogs. The Association of Deutscher Jagdterrier has published a special ruling for the work tests assigned to this breed, and accepts for breeding only specimens that obtain good results in these tests.

GENERAL CHARACTERISTICS A fighting dog, both on and beneath the ground, and a good gun dog on land and water; he is also a good tracker and retriever of small game. His smallness makes him a good companion in town and in the car. He needs, however, ample exercise in the field, being a natural-born hunting dog of rugged constitution, not easily subject to sickness.

WEIGHT AND SIZE Weight: males 19½-22 lb; females 16-18 lb. Height at withers should not be more than 16 inches.

HEAD The skull is flat and wider between the ears than the Fox Terrier's. It narrows between the eyes and continues with a minimum stop. The muzzle is a little shorter than the skull from the occiput to the stop. The muzzle is powerful, with pronounced cheeks; there must be nothing of the Greyhound in the muzzle. The lower jaw is robust, with a well-chiseled chin. The teeth are exceptionally strong and the jaws close in a scissors bite. The nose is black or brown in basically brown dogs.

EYES Small, dark, deep-set, with a determined expression. The eyelids are close-fitting.

EARS V-shaped, set on high, not too small, carried lightly against the sides of the head.

NECK Powerful, not excessively long, rather arched, broadening at the point of insertion into the shoulders.

FOREQUARTERS The shoulders are long and sloping; the legs are straight and well muscled; the pastern is slightly slanted. The bone is robust rather than delicate. Catfeet are not desirable. The forefeet are frequently larger than the hind feet.

BODY The chest is deep and well sprung. The back is strong and straight, of moderate length. The loins and croup are strongly muscled.

TAIL Well set onto the long croup and carried horizontally; it should not be carried high.

HINDQUARTERS Long, well angulated and muscular. The hocks are low, the bones strong.

COAT Smooth, close, hard and rough, never short. **Color** The principal colors are black, black mixed with gray, or dark brown with lighter markings, brown-red-yellow on the brows, muzzle, chest, legs and vent. The mask may be either dark or light. A little white on chest and toes is allowed.

FAULTS Lack of premolars; overshot or undershot jaw; straight, tulip, or rose ears; tail carried vertically; forequarters or hindquarters too vertical; short back (the dog should have a rectangular rather than a square outline); fine, excessively short hair, woolly or open coat; lack of hair on belly.

GAIT Rigid, rather like that of a wader. ●

106 BASENJI

SOUTH AFRICA

This very ancient breed, originating in the Congo, began to be specially bred by English breeders after World War II. An indication of the breed's extreme antiquity can be gathered by the fact that it is depicted, crouched beside the seat of his master, in many Egyptian tombs of the Fourth Dynasty, about 3600 B.C.

After the decline of the Egyptian empire with no further mention of this breed, it was thought to be extinct, but toward 1870 these dogs were rediscovered in territory that Europeans were beginning to explore between the Sudan and the Congo. The natives took great care of them and esteemed them highly as hunting dogs. Here is what Arbanassi, a dog expert, writes about them: "After his 'rediscovery' he became an object of study on the part of scientists and immediately aroused the interest of dog fanciers, especially the English living in Egypt and the Sudan. Eventually he arrived in Europe where breeding started."

"We can in no way say that the Basenji is a wild dog. It is

Photo: S. A. Thompson.

true that he lived for thousands of years without contact with other canine breeds, but he never returned to his savage state.

"Nor can we compare him to the Dingo, the dog that man brought to Australia over a land route a very long time ago and which became wild and remained so for tens of thousands of years. This has nothing in common with the Basenji, that was crossbred by the Egyptians and then by the natives of the Sudan and the Congo."

The Basenji never barks. The strange sound he makes is something between a laugh and a Tyrolese yodel. The Basenji is considered to be the ancestor of the terrier breeds.

He presently lives in different areas of central Africa. There are two types, that of the plains and the type that lives on forest-covered heights. The variety presently bred in Great Britain is thought to have originated in the Kwango region of the Central Congo.

BASENJI

GENERAL CHARACTERISTICS The Basenji never barks. Its general appearance is that of an agile, attentive and well-balanced dog.

WEIGHT AND HEIGHT Weight: males 23½ lb; females 20 lb. Height at withers: males 17 inches; females 16 inches.

HEAD Of medium size, not coarse but well chiseled, narrowing at eye level. His carriage is distinguished. The skull is flat; the muzzle tapers from the eyes to the tip of the nose and is slightly shorter than the skull. The teeth are well adapted. When the ears are held erect, wrinkles are formed on the forehead and skull, giving the dog a surprised expression, peculiar to the breed. Exaggeration of this wrinkling, however, is to be avoided since it would give the dog a Bloodhound appearance at the expense of the head detail. The nose should preferably be black, but if slightly pink, this does not call for a penalty in a dog otherwise perfect.

EYES Dark hazel in color, although many dogs have yellow or light blue eyes. The eyes should be small, almond-shaped, and deep set with a penetrating expression.

EARS Pointed, of fine texture, carried erect. The ear opening should always be forward.

NECK Of good length, issuing cleanly from the shoulders. The nape is prominent and muscular; the throat is rather full.

BODY The chest is well let down and of moderate breadth. The trunk is short and straight, with well-sprung ribs which leave ample heart room. The loins are short, and the belly is very slightly drawn up.

TAIL Set on high and forming one or two rings, held close against one side of the croup.

FOREQUARTERS The shoulders are closely fitted to the body and slanted. The forelegs are straight, clean-boned, with well-defined tendons. The pasterns are quite straight, though unlike those of the Fox Terrier.

HINDQUARTERS Robust and muscular, with long thighs. The hocks are well let down and should not be turned either inward or outward.

COAT Short and of a silky texture. **Color** Sorrel with white markings, with feet and tail also white; there are also dogs with white-black coats or white-black marked with tan. Sometimes the sorrel coloring is very deep; in that case, the white markings are very small. Dogs with cream coats are disqualified from both show and stud. **Skin** Very loose.

GAIT In movement the Basenji projects his forelegs in a free movement more or less like the trot of a thoroughbred horse. This light and tireless gait is characteristic of the breed. ●

BASENJI

Photo: S. A. Thompson, Fotostampa.

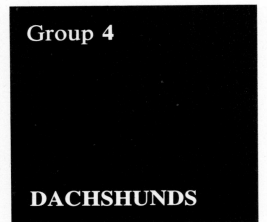

Group 4

DACHSHUNDS

The fourth group in the classification of dog breeds combines the three types of German Dachshunds having a single standard, although each constitutes a separate breed.

107 GERMAN DACHSHUND

Teckel

GERMANY

The Dachshund is the finest burrow dog. When the subterranean refuge into which the fox or the badger has slipped has an opening too small for a Basset, the Dachshund sets to work speedily and masterfully to enlarge it. Thereupon he attempts to penetrate it by getting in full length and then moving forward by a process of stretching and contracting. It is possible to attribute to these exercises, which have been going on for centuries and over generations, the peculiar physical structure of the Dachshund that brought about the slight but constant modification of his shape. One might even call it an anomaly that developed from the Dachshund's peculiar burrowing method. Selective breeding by man has done the rest.

The funerary monuments of ancient Egypt depict dogs only slightly different from today's Dachshund, although this is not enough to conclude that this is an Egyptian breed. Also, in Peru and Mexico, statuettes have been found of dogs very much resembling the Egyptian kind. This would seem to prove, as has often been claimed, that the quality of "Basset activity" has occurred in different regions and not always with dogs. One may surmise that the Dachshund was formed, or at least perfected, in Germany in very ancient times.

He is often considered a pet because of his intelligence and affectionate nature, but in Germany and also in England he is used for hunting in burrows. He has a keen sense of smell and the habit of penetrating bravely into the burrow, a tendency which sometimes causes him to be the victim of his own tenacity. The Dachshund is also capable of attacking larger game, which he often succeeds in holding until the hunter's arrival. This seems difficult to believe, considering his appearance and size. However, as often happens, appearances are deceptive.

GERMAN DACHSHUND

Photo: S. A. Thompson.

GERMAN DACHSHUND AND WIREHAIRED DWARF DACHSHUND

GENERAL CHARACTERISTICS Low to the ground, short-legged, long-bodied but sturdily built and strongly muscled, with a bold and challenging head carriage and intelligent expression. In spite of shortness of limb in comparison to body length, the Dachshund is not crippled, clumsy, or restricted in movement, nor is he tucked-up and weasel-like in appearance.

HEAD Lengthy as viewed from above and in profile, tapering symmetrically to the nose, clean and sharply chiseled. Forehead only slightly arched and almost without stop (the less stop the more typical), sloping to the finely formed, lightly arched bridge of the nose. Eyebrows strong and prominent. Nasal cartilage and bridge of nose long and narrow. Lips tightly stretched, well covering the jaw, which should be neither too deep nor too snipy; the corners of the mouth lightly indicated. Wide nostrils. The jaws open widely, cleft to behind the eyes, with strongly developed

GERMAN DACHSHUND

GERMAN DACHSHUND

Photo: S. A. Thompson, E. Bennet (Photo Res.).

GERMAN DACHSHUND AND GERMAN SHORTHAIRED DWARF DACHSHUND

GERMAN LONGHAIRED DACHSHUND

teeth and jawbone. Powerful canine teeth closing in either a scissors or pincers bite.

EYES Medium size, oval, set obliquely, with a clear, lively, yet friendly expression, not sharp. Color, lustrous dark red-brown to black-brown for all coat colors. Glass (blue), fish (silver gray) or pearl eyes in gray or dappled dogs are not bad faults but are not desirable.

EARS Set high but not too far forward, of moderate length but not too long, nicely rounded, not narrow, pointed or folded, and very mobile; the forward edge lies close to the cheek.

NECK Of pleasing length, muscular, clean, showing no dewlap, slightly arched in the nape, carried proudly.

TEETH Normally the adult Dachshund has 42 teeth (12 incisors, 4 canines, 16 premolars, 10 molars. The number of molars may vary). Breeders recognize four different types of dentition, only two of which are permissible: (a) pincers type, in which the upper and lower incisors meet perfectly; (b) scissors type, in which the outer face of the lower incisors closes contiguous with the inner face of the upper teeth; and (c) and (d), overshot and undershot types, both of which are irregular and disqualify the dog for stud.

FOREQUARTERS Muscular, compact, deep, long and broad, suitable for strenuous work underground. The shoulder blade (scapula) is long and set obliquely, lying closely over the well-developed rib cage; strongly and flexibly muscled. The upper arm (humerus) is of equal length and set at right angles to the shoulder blade, strong of bone and firmly muscled, set close to the ribs but free in movement. The lower arm (radius and ulna) is short, with a very slight inward bend; the fore and outer muscles are strong and flexible. The forearm is approximately of such length that the height from the ground to the breastbone is a third the distance from the ground to the top of the withers. When the dog is standing, the wrists should be slightly closer to each other than the shoulder joints. The pasterns should be neither too straight nor too sloping as viewed in profile. The feet are tight and well arched, with firm pads. Four of the

Photo: S. A. Thompson.

five toes are used in the tread. They are closely set, with a pronounced arch to each toe. They have strong nails and firm pads.

BODY The withers must be long and high, the back level over the rib cage with a slight arch over the loins. Breastbone strong and prominent enough to show a cavity at each side. Viewed from the front, the rib cage should be oval; from above or in profile it is roomy, providing ample space for the full development of heart and lungs. Widely ribbed to the loins, gradually leading up from the line of the belly. With the correct length and angle of the shoulder and upper arm, the foreleg should cover the lowest point of the breastbone. The belly is moderately tucked up.

TAIL Set on in such a postion that it continues the line of the spine, straight and without deviation.

HINDQUARTERS The rump is long, broad, round and fully muscled. The pelvis should not be too short; it should be quite strongly developed and set at a moderate slope. The thigh bone should be strong, of good length and set at right angles to the pelvis. The buttocks should be well rounded, the stifle broad and powerful. The second thighs are short compared with those of other dogs; they are set at right angles to the upper thigh and are strongly muscled. The tarsal bones are broad in placement, with the hock very prominent. The metatarsi are long and independent in movement from the second thigh; they are inclined slightly forward. The hind feet have four closely set and nicely arched toes, like those of the forefeet, the whole foot resting on the pad, not just on the toes. Short nails. The legs should be absolutely straight when seen from behind.

SPECIAL CHARACTERISTICS OF THE DACHSHUND VARIETIES The Dachshund is bred in three different kinds of coat: (1) Smooth-coated; (2) Wirehaired; and (3) Longhaired. All three must correspond in the same degree to the foregoing standard of points. Particular points required for each:

SMOOTH-COATED DACHSHUND

COAT Short, dense, lustrous, lying smoothly, showing no bare patches. Special faults of the coat are: too fine, thin hair; leather ends to the ears; bare patches, or too coarse and altogether too profuse a coat.

TAIL Finely tapered, fully but not profusely coated. Somewhat longer hair on the underside is indicative of a good coat and is not a fault. A bushy tail is a fault, also a tail partly or completely bare.

COLOR (a) **Dachshunds of solid color:** red, red-yellow or yellow, with or without black streakings. A clear color is, however, preferable, and red better than red-yellow or yellow. Dachshunds with much dark shading belong to this category and not to that of "other colors." Nose and nails black; red also permissible but not desirable. (b) **Bicolored Dachshunds:** jet black or brown (chocolate), or gray or white, but all with tan or yellow markings (brand) above the eyes, on the sides of the muzzle and lower lips, on the inner margins of the ears, on the chest, on the inner and back sides of the legs, on the paws, around the vent and from there to between one-third and one-half of the underside of the tail. Nose and nails in black dogs should be black; in chocolate (brown) dogs, brown or black, in gray or

GERMAN SHORTHAIRED DWARF DACHSHUND

HARLEQUIN DACHSHUND

white dogs, nose and nails should be gray or flesh color, but the latter is not desirable; in white dogs, black is preferable. In Dachshunds of solid color as well as in bicolor Dachshunds (in which white is not one of the two colors), white is not desirable but small, isolated patches do not completely disqualify. (c) **Dachshunds of mixed coloring** (dapple, tiger-brindle): The coat color of dapples is a light brownish, gray or white ground, with dark irregular markings (large patches not desirable) or darker gray, chocolate, red-gold or black. It is desirable that neither the dark nor the light color predominates. The color of the tiger-brindle is red or yellow with darker striping. Nose and nails are the same as for the solid color or bicolored Dachshunds. (d) **Dachshunds of other colors.** Any not already mentioned.

FAULTS Black or white without tan points is not permissible. Too heavily marked tan points are not desirable.

WIREHAIRED DACHSHUND
GENERAL APPEARANCE Similar to the smooth-coated.

COAT Except for the muzzle, eyebrows and ears, the whole body is evenly covered with a close, thick, wiry coat and undercoat. The muzzle carries a beard. The eyebrows are bushy. On the ears the hair is shorter than on the body, almost smooth, yet in keeping with the rest of the coat.

TAIL Hair coarse but lying closely and tapering finely without a tuft. The entire coat must so lie that, seen from a distance, the wirehaired variety resembles the smooth.

FAULTS A soft coat in general, whether short or long, or long on any particular part of the body; long, unruly, curly or wiry coat; feathered tail.

COLOR All colors are permissible. White marks on the chest are allowed but not desirable. For the rest, similar to the smooth-coated.

LONGHAIRED DACHSHUND

The only difference from the smooth is the longer, silky coat.

COAT The soft, sleek, shining coat is longer under the throat, on the underside of the body and particularly on the ears and the back of the legs,

where it constitutes a definite feathering, reaching its greatest length on the underside of the tail. The hair must extend beyond the lower edge of the ears. Short hair here, so-called "leather-ends," is not desirable. Too profuse hair on the feet ("fins") is ugly and unserviceable for work.

TAIL Carried in a graceful continuation of the back. Here the coat reaches its greatest length and constitutes a complete "flag."

FAULTS Too heavy a coat of equal length all over the body is incorrect, also too wavy or rough, coarse hair, lack of the "flag" on the tail or fringe on the ears, definite hair-parting on the back, hair too long between the toes.

COLOR OF COAT, NOSE, NAILS Exactly the same as that of the smooth.

DISQUALIFICATIONS Overshot or undershot condition; monorchidism, cryptorchidism; the following defects in tail: broken tail, deviated joint(s), knottiness; xiphoid appendage deviated; short chest; shoulders away from body; pasterns turned outward. Various other defects disqualify a dog from ratings higher than *Good* or from a rating of *Excellent*. ●

177

Photo: S. A. Thompson, A. Wintzell.

GERMAN DACHSHUND

Photo: R. Kinne (Photo Res.).

108 GERMAN DWARF DACHSHUND

Zwergteckel

GERMANY

109 KANINCHEN DACHSHUND

Kaninchenteckel

GERMANY

GERMAN DWARF DACHSHUND

KANINCHEN DACHSHUND

179

Photo: S. A. Thompson, A. Roslin-Williams, Hartman.

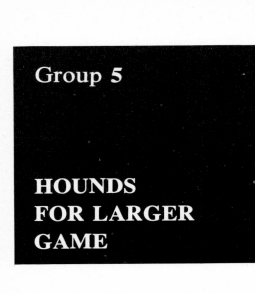

Group 5

HOUNDS FOR LARGER GAME

After terriers and German Dachshunds, the hunting-dog category includes hounds for hunting larger game. Hounds, or pursuit dogs, possess an exceptional physical resistance; they hunt their prey alone or in packs, according to breed, aided by scent and sometimes by sight and hearing. More than any other breed, hunting dogs, especially those that hunt by scent, have preserved the atavistic instinct of common effort, the pack, still typical today with many wild dogs. Hounds almost always bear witness to the particular psychic qualities which make them live together as a group, whereas other dogs have developed their individuality, sometimes even to the disadvantage of their gregarious instincts. Foxhounds, Beagles and Harriers are all dogs that work in packs, as are all the numerous breeds employed in the hunts of today.

Almost all these hounds can be considered today as specialized for hunting. Nevertheless there are some that aid man in other ways. Among them are the Bloodhound, a dog recognized for police work; the Basset, an esteemed pet and show dog; and the Cirneco de l'Etna, used in Italy for hunting, although considered in other parts of the world a rare luxury dog.

HANOVER HOUND

110 HANOVER HOUND
Hannoverischer Schweisshund

GERMANY

A descendent of the St. Hubert Hound, he has the same melancholy expression due to the characteristic skin folds around his head. In the fifth century one of his ancestors was designated as a lead dog because of his exceptionally keen scent, whose task was to go ahead of the pack to rouse the game. In Germany he was assigned the hunting tasks given to the Bloodhound in England and to the St. Hubert Hound in France and Belgium.

By crossing the old German hound with the lighter Harz (Harzerbracke) Hound, breeders of the Jaegerhof, Harz, Solling and Hanover attained in 1800 the Hannoverischer Schweisshund, greatly esteemed for his hunting qualities.

GENERAL CHARACTERISTICS A medium- to small-sized dog, of robust build, rather long and low. The head and tail are rarely high. The expression is grave.

HEAD Of medium size, with a broad, flat skull, slightly domed, wider in its upper part. The skin on the forehead is slightly wrinkled. The muzzle is in good proportion to the skull. The occipital protuberance is barely apparent. The nose is comparatively more ample than in any other breed and may be black, brown or reddish. The muzzle narrows at the border

Photo: J. Fields (Photo Res.), S. A. Thompson.

HANOVER HOUND

with the skull. Seen from the side, the bridge appears either nearly straight or slightly arched; it must never be concave. The stop is not pronounced. The cheekbones are pronounced and should be clearly visible. The forepart of the muzzle is rounded off at its lower half. The lips are heavy and pendulous, with a well-pronounced fold at the commissure.

EYES Clear, set well up into the frontal area. The haw should not be visible. The expression of the eyes is serious. The wrinkles in the skin on the supraorbital ridge form a triangle.

EARS A little longer than average, very broad, rounded at the tips and set on low. They hang flat and close to the head. When the dog lifts his head they do not fall back in folds.

NECK Long, strong, broadening toward the shoulders. The skin is thick and loose, but the dewlap must not be excessive.

BACK Long, broad and slightly hollowed toward the loin area. The croup slopes.

CHEST, BRISKET AND BELLY The chest is broad, the rib cage is deep, with the brisket down to the level of the elbows. The belly is slightly drawn up.

TAIL Long, reaching at least to the midpoint of the metatarsus. It is thick at the root and tapers to the tip. It is almost straight, with the hair longer and more bristly on the lower part, without, however, forming a flag or fringe. For the most part it is carried low and between the hind legs.

FOREQUARTERS More robust than the hindquarters. The shoulders are sloping, highly mobile and with good muscles. The forearm is straight or gently curved, with powerful muscling. The pastern is well boned and straight.

HINDQUARTERS The thighs are massive, the muscles well developed. The hind legs are long, sloping and covered with dense hair. The metatarsus is nearly straight, neither sloping nor turning in or out. **FEET** Strong, round, with well-closed, arched toes. The nails are strong, the pads are rugged.

COAT Short, dense, smooth and elastic, with a dull, silky appearance. **Color** Gray-brown, with a dark brown mask (on the cheeks and lips and around the eyes and on the ears); brown-red, yellow-red, yellow-ocher, dark yellow and speckled brown. The darkest colors are found chiefly on the muzzle, around the eyes and ears, and as streaking on the back.

FAULTS Narrow, bulging forehead; excessively square or pointed muzzle; excessively narrow bridge, the same width as the forehead forward of the stop; ears too long, thin or curled; weak forelegs, curved forearm, pasterns and feet as in the German Dachshund; short or thin tail, tail carried too high and too curved; any white or light yellow markings on the coat. ●

111 ST. HUBERT BLOODHOUND

Chien de Saint-Hubert

BELGIUM

Already famous in ages past for his exceptional sense of smell and hunting qualities, this hound, raised by the monks of the St. Hubert Monastery, is of very ancient origin. According to Tschudy, the original breed arose in England where certain racing hounds were put in contact with the brownish-black Mastiff. These gave birth to a breed which was transplanted to the Ardennes, where it became the raw material for the St. Hubert Bloodhound. Of course, not everyone agrees with this theory; most experts lean toward a continental origin.

It is certain that for centuries the monks of the monastery founded by St. Hubert (the nobleman who had the vision of the deer with the cross between its horns) bred a particular type of hound, while another very similar hound caught the attention of English hunters, who called it the "Bloodhound." The two breeds were long considered distinct though very similar. Since a short time ago the St. Hubert Hound and the Bloodhound have a single standard accepted by the FCI, and the uniform breed is called the St. Hubert Bloodhound and declared to be Belgian.

English specimens today, however, are more numerous than Belgian. The Bloodhound is patently the St. Hubert bred in England. Some time ago he was called the "Falbot," a name that was kept for some time, and then he was called the Bloodhound (a reference to selective breeding, in the same way that "blood horse" means "pure blood"). His always surprising keenness of scent has resulted in his being employed in police work. He is a superb tracker, but it must be said that his temperament leaves something to be desired, for he still remains pleasant and affectionate when confronted by his adversary. He is not aggressive but rather timid. Moreover, he does not bark and therefore causes no disturbance even in the most confining quarters.

During the last ten years he has been successfully introduced in North America, where breeding kennels are numerous today.

GENERAL CHARACTERISTICS A heavy, massive dog, with a slow, imposing gait. The tracking hound *par excellence.*

WEIGHT AND SIZE Weight: Mean average for males, 90 lb; for females, 80. Height: males 25-27; females 23-25 inches; averages are 26 and 24, respectively. Greater weights and heights are to be preferred if character and quality are combined.

HEAD The head is one of the more typical features of this breed. It should be well shaped and well developed in all dimensions except width. The skull is very high, with a big occipital protuberance. The supraorbital ridge is not pronounced. The general impression given by the head is one of size and majesty. The skin on forehead and cheeks is deeply wrinkled, more so than in any other breed. The nose is invariably black; the lips are very long and pendulous, with the edge of the lower lip a good 2 inches below the corner of the mouth. The jaws are very long and broad in the forward part; they are hollowed and lean on the cheeks and especially below the eyes.

ST. HUBERT BLOODHOUND

Photo: M. Pedone, E. Münch, R. Kinne (Photo Res.).

ST. HUBERT BLOODHOUND

ST. HUBERT BLOODHOUND

EYES Dark hazel. The lower lid falls away to reveal a dark red inner rim. They are deep-set in the head and consequently appear to be rather small.

EARS Extremely long, exceeding the muzzle length. Set on low, they hang forward against the cheeks in a graceful fold. The leather is thin and covered with short, fine, soft and silky hair.

NECK Long, constructed in such a way as to permit following a scent with nose close to ground without slackening pace. It is exceptionally well muscled, with an abundant dewlap.

BODY The trunk is broad and deep, as is the powerful back, extraordinarily strong for the size of the dog. The flanks are broad, almost coarse, and·the belly is slightly drawn up.

TAIL Carried in an elegant curve slightly above the topline of the back, although it must never be carried over the back. The lower part of the tail is feathered with long hair (about 2 inches), which becomes gradually shorter near the tip.

FOREQUARTERS AND HINDQUARTERS The shoulders are sloping and very muscular. The legs are straight, muscular and well boned. The hocks are well developed and the feet are round (catfeet).

COAT Short and fairly hard on the body, soft and silky on ears and skull. **Color** Black and tan or solid tan, with preference going to the former. Black should be present as a saddle and on the flanks and nape. White is objectionable, but a small amount of white on the chest or feet does not disqualify. ●

ST. HUBERT BLOODHOUND WITH PUPPY

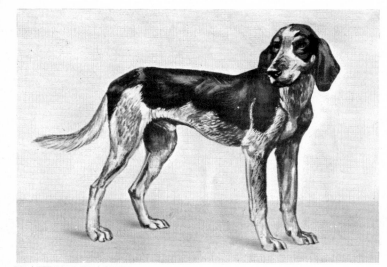

BRAZILIAN TRACKER

KARELIAN BEAR DOG

112 BRAZILIAN TRACKER
Rastreador Brasileiro

BRAZIL

The Brazilian Tracker is the result of selective breeding carried out on the American Foxhound and some of his varieties (Coonhound, Bluetick, Walker Hound). Other factors, such as the Brazilian climate and the special tasks assigned to this ardent hunter of jaguars, have influenced his development. He is capable of pursuing his prey for many hours over the most difficult obstacles, whether rivers, swamps, or the thickest underbrush.

GENERAL CHARACTERISTICS A sturdy country dog, good-natured, lively, not aggressive. An excellent tracker, he has extraordinary talents as a hunting dog.
SIZE Height: males, about 25½ inches; females slightly smaller.
HEAD Triangular, brachycephalic. The stop is not prominent, the muzzle is long, with a straight bridge. The nose is dark, in keeping with the coat.
EYES Dark, almond-shaped, very vivacious, with metallic highlights.
EARS Long, hanging beneath the set-on of the head; they are pendulous, with rounded tips.
NECK Strong, with a slight dewlap.
BODY The chest is broad and deep. The back is straight, long and strong. The belly is not very accentuated and is tucked up to about the same degree as the American Coonhound.

TAIL A saber tail, carried dead center and always gaily.
FOREQUARTERS AND HINDQUARTERS The shoulders are remarkably well boned. The forefeet and hind feet are broad and powerful, with tough, springy pads.
COAT Shorthaired and dense, rather rough to the touch. **Color** (1) Bluetick (azulejo): blue markings on white background, with brown markings on legs; (2) Foxhound or Walkerhound: markings in two or three colors (black, brown) on white background; (3) Black and tan (Coonhound): brown, with head, back, loins and tail black, and chest, belly and outer side of legs dark brown. **Skin** Dark and loose.
FAULTS Curled tail, short or butterfly ears, excessively fine bone, lack of vivacity, excessively pronounced stop, overshot or undershot jaw. ●

113 KARELIAN BEAR DOG
Karjalankarhukoira
Karelsk björnhund (Swedish)

FINLAND

Breeders today tend to strengthen this dog, traditionally a hunter of elk, in order to put him to better use in hunting bear.

GENERAL CHARACTERISTICS The Karelian Bear Dog is medium-sized, of robust build, strong and slightly longer than high; has a thick coat, cocked ears, an introverted nature, and is brave and persistent. His senses, particularly that of scent, are keen, and he is admirably adapted to big-game hunting.
SIZE Height at withers: males 21-23½ inches; females 19-21 inches.
HEAD Shaped like a blunt wedge, fairly broad at the forehead and cheeks. Forehead slightly arched, stop gently sloping, slight protuberance above the eyes. The muzzle is high and its bridge is perferably straight, tapering slightly only toward the nose. Nose black and well developed.
EYES Rather small, brown, with an alert, often fiery expression.
EARS Cocked, pointing slightly outward, medium-sized and fairly blunt at the points.
NECK Muscular, medium-sized, curving, covered with thick coat.

FOREQUARTERS Sturdy, with shoulders sloping somewhat, and muscular. Elbows pointing straight back. Forearm straight, pastern only slightly bent. Paws thick, high and roundish.
BODY Sturdy; the back has well-developed muscles, gently sloping, without bulges or hollows. Chest spacious, extending approximately to the level of the elbow. Abdomen slightly drawn up.
TAIL Of medium length, usually arched; a full arch is most desirable.
HINDQUARTERS The stifle points straight forward, the hock straight back. Thighs look very broad because of the opulent coat, particularly in the upper parts. Front line of leg curving without sudden bends. Hock comparatively straight, hind feet slightly longer and lower than forefeet.
COAT Outer coat straight and stiff, undercoat soft and dense. Outer coat on the neck, back and rear parts of the thighs longer than elsewhere. **Color** Black, preferably slightly brownish or dull, mostly with distinct white markings or spots on the head, neck, chest, belly and legs.
FAULTS Weak bones; snipy muzzle; curly or wavy coat; batlike ears; domed forehead; light eyes or wall-eyes; loose skin under the neck; chest too deep or barrel-like; straight shoulders and hocks; flat feet; straight or whiplike tail; unusual colors; viciousness toward humans. Till now admissible but not desirable are: bob-tail, dewclaws, white color with black markings, wolf-gray color or spots. ●

KARELIAN BEAR DOG

Photo: M. Pedone, S. A. Thompson.

PACK OF FRENCH TRICOLOR AND WHITE AND BLACK DOGS

Photo: Buzzini

114 GREAT GASCONY BLUE

Grand bleu de Gascogne

FRANCE

France possesses more varieties of hounds than any other country. A great number of these breeds have gradually disappeared, but many still remain, even if some of them have been reconstituted. Today their breeding is being sedulously conducted.

The very ancient origin of French hounds must be looked for among the racing dogs (though not among the Greyhounds) who were brought by the Phoenicians and the Greeks centuries before the Christian era to the islands of the Mediterranean, the coasts of southern Europe, and the eastern shores of Gaul and Brittany.

Then came the intervention of the Bloodhound and perhaps other important hounds from the same stock. According to Thomas, the oldest French hound was the St. Hubert (Bloodhound), which, from his birthplace in the Belgian Ardennes, spread to Hainaut, Flanders, Lorraine, and Burgundy as far as the south of France. Tschudy contests this claim and is of the following opinion: The most ancient French running dog does not come from the north but from Egypt.

Among the most ancient French hounds whose origins are consequently difficult to establish, the Great Gascony Blue must be named first of all. Former experts consider him not only the most important of the French hunting dogs, but also of all dogs of this general type. He deserves his status because his blood has been lent to the formation of different breeds. As regards the nearly complete extinction of this breed, perfectly adapted to the wolf hunt, it is because of the disappearance of wolves from the French countryside. There nevertheless exist some excellent packs, used for rabbit hunting. Through crossbreeding with the Saintonge dogs of the Count de Saint Léger, the Grand Bleu then gave rise to the Virelade breed.

His highly developed scent permits the Grand Bleu to raise game. His strong and sonorous voice reaches the hunter even at a great distance, informing him of the progress of the hunt. He has great endurance and runs at moderate speed.

GREAT GASCONY BLUE

GENERAL CHARACTERISTICS A dog of an ancient breed, outstandingly French. The coat and expression present a unique type. The identifying features are the coat and the head, which is aristocratic and decidedly French. **SIZE** Height: Males 25-27½ inches; females 23½-25½ inches.

HEAD Rather strong and elongated in shape. The skin covering the head is fairly slack and forms one or two wrinkles along the cheeks. The stop is barely defined. The nose is black and well developed, with a long, strong, and slightly curved bridge. The lips are fairly drooping, covering the lower jaw.

The commissure of lips is well defined. The skull is slightly domed, with something of a point. The occipital bone is fairly evident.

EYES These have thick lashes and appear rather sunken, deep chestnut in color. The lower eyelid is often falling, revealing a red, mucous area. The expression of the eyes is somewhat sad but sweet and trusting.

EARS Strongly characteristic of the Gascony Blue, the ears are set very low and are thin and curled. If placed along the jaw they should reach at least the tip of the nose and are often longer.

NECK Of medium length, rounded at the upper part and with a dewlap at the lower part.

BODY The chest is well developed in every sense, being long, wide, and deep. The ribs are moderately rounded, the back is rather long but well supported. The loin is slightly flat and not invariably muscled. The flanks are flat and well dropped.

TAIL Well set on, rather thick, fairly long and carried like a sickle.

FOREQUARTERS The forelegs have strong forearms and are well muscled, offering good support. The shoulders are massive and muscular, the elbows well placed. **HINDQUARTERS** Breeders are seeking to improve the hindquarters, which are frequently less developed than the forequarters. The hocks are near the ground, broad and slightly bent; the hips protrude, the rump fairly sloping, the thighs slightly flat. **FEET** Slightly oval in shape, similar to those of the wolf. Lean toes, not too close.

COAT Fairly thick, not very short, and profuse. The skin is black or white, strongly marked with black patches, but never completely white. The palate, lips, genitals, and underlegs are black. **Color** Black markings on an entirely black background give a general impression of blue-slate coloring. Two black spots are usually found on each side of the head, covering the ears, surrounding the eyes and stopping at the cheeks. These spots do not meet on the dome, leaving rather a white space in the center of which there is often an oval black spot, one of the characterisitic markings of the breed. There are two tan marks above the eyes, and other tan marks appear on the cheeks and lips, the inner side of the ear and on the legs and under the tail. Some dogs are speckled black, invariably with tan markings.

FAULTS Short head; short ears set high, insufficiently folded; light eye; pink mucous areas; underdeveloped chest; slender legs; excessively receding croup; lack of tan markings. ●

GREAT GASCONY BLUE

Photo: Buzzini, DIM.

115 GREAT GASCON OF SAINTONGE

Grand Gascon Saintongeois

FRANCE

GREAT GASCON OF SAINTONGE

Among the following French dogs considered the most elegant coursing breeds we find the Great Gascon of Saintonge. The creator of this breed was the Baron Joseph de Caryon Latour de Virelade, who wished to embody in a single hound the excellent qualities of three other breeds: the Saintongeois, the Bleu de Gascogne, and the Ariègeois. By careful selective breeding he was able fully to succeed in this attempt, creating a new type of hound that added muscular force to elegance, keen scent, a sonorous voice, and a manifest instinct for hunting the wolf and the roebuck.

Henri de Caryon, the nephew of the Baron de Virelade, strengthened the breed with a Bordeaux specimen about which we have no information other than that it also descends from the Saintongeois.

GENERAL CHARACTERISTICS A hunter par excellence, the Great Gascon of Saintonge shows the traits of the two breeds from which he was developed. The essence of French breeding is found in both his general appearance and face and in his attitude. Sweet and trustful in demeanor.

SIZE Males, 25-28 inches; females 24-26 inches. Some packs for hare-hunting in southwestern France have been bred to a size several inches smaller for both males and females.

HEAD Fairly lean, long, with a moderate stop. The black nose is open and well developed, the muzzle is long, generally straight but sometimes slightly curved. The lips are pendulous, fairly falling to cover the lower lips. The upper jaw fits exactly over the lower. The skull is long, pointed, rather narrow, but not exaggeratedly so. The dome is pronounced.

EYES Brown, preferably dark brown, sometimes slightly covered.

EARS Set on below the eye line and fairly back, clear the skull well. They are thin, folded, and should be long enough to reach the tip of the nose.

NECK Of medium length and thickness; frequently has a slight dewlap.

BODY The chest is deep and well let down. The terminal ribs, slightly short, may suggest the appearance of a Greyhound. The back is long and well supported, the loin may be a little long, slightly domed and sufficiently muscled. The flank is fairly long but slightly drawn up.

TAIL Long and thicker at the root than at the tip; it is well set on, rounded in shape and elegantly carried.

FOREQUARTERS The shoulders are long, slightly sloping and well muscled. The elbows are well directed. The forearms, wide and strong, are also well directed. **HINDQUARTERS** The haunches are rather horizontal. The thighs are muscular, the hocks near to the ground, the hind legs well directed. **FEET** The Great Gascon of Saintonge's ancestors were hare-footed, the Gascon's forebears were wolf-footed; in this cross the animal has oval feet.

COAT The hair is short and close. The skin is pink under white hair, black under black hair. The palate and scrotum are black. **Color** The root of the coat is white speckled with black and irregularly marked with specks of the same color. Some specimens have a black mantle. Two markings on either side of the head are often found, covering the ears, surrounding the eyes and stopping at the edge of the cheeks. These markings are tan, preferably pale blending with the adjacent speckled white. Two characteristic markings of the same tan and of the shape and size of the eyes are found on the orbital ridge, almost like a reflection of the dog's gaze. The same shade of tan is also found on the inner side of the ears and as specks on the legs. The upper area of the ear often has a few fawn hairs mixed with black, but this mixture should not give a tri-color appearance to the head. Sometimes a characteristic leaf-brown marking, called the "roebuck mark," is found at the back of the thighs above the hocks. A few white and black individuals are found and, much more rarely, some with the coat of the Gascony Blue.

FAULTS Overshot or undershot mouth; light eyes; bad temperament.

DISQUALIFICATION Any other coat than those mentioned above. ●

GREAT GASCONY BLUE

Photo: Buzzini.

GREAT GASCON OF SAINTONGE

116 LEVESQUE

FRANCE

In 1873 Rogatien Levesque created a hound breed. Its ancestors were quite different from each other—a Gascony Blue brood bitch was mated with a Foxhound possessing a strong and rough coat, still a feature of all his descendents. Two litters were bred, then the progeny were crossbred with Virelades, which were interbred among themselves, and finally crossbred with Gascon Saintongeois Vendéens. Perfect homogeneity was attained, and this breed caused a sensation in Paris when a pack of forty was shown.

GENERAL CHARACTERISTICS Excellent gun dog, very French, well typed and well set up, bony and with great energy.

SIZE The Levesque is a very big dog, height: male 25½-28 inches; female 25 to almost 27 inches.

HEAD The head is strong, rather short, with a wide forehead and a prominent orbital arch. The nose is open, well developed and slightly turned up. The muzzle has a marked depression at the stop. The lips are pendulous and wide, giving the muzzle a distinctly square aspect. The skull is well developed and slightly domed.

EYES Light chestnut, fairly large but sunken; the expression is one of sweetness and intelligence. The haw is visible and deep pink in color.

EARS Set on a level with the eye, with slight folds and not extending beyond the muzzle.

NECK Strong, with traces of dewlap; the neck is more or less developed but never excessively so.

BODY The chest is wide and fairly well let down. The ribs are flat. The back is long and well supported. The loin is straight, well formed and well supported. The flank is slightly raised but well furnished in width.

TAIL Long, rather thick at the root, set on high and slightly curved.

FOREQUARTERS The shoulders are long and muscular, especially above the elbows, which are well directed. The forelegs are heavy and strong, especially the forearm, which is well muscled and well directed. **HINDQUARTERS** The haunches are slanting, well developed, protruding, with the tips of the well-muscled buttocks slightly accentuated. The thighs are lean, the hocks are well let down, pow-

erful and slightly bent. **FEET** The feet are strong, rounded and closed.

COAT Invariably white and black, with the black frequently having a purplish-blue gloss, either with a broad black mantle or with large black markings. Both sides of the head and ears are black. The white area has black speckling. When the thigh is black there is usually a "roebuck mark" of gray-tan hairs to the back of the thigh above the hock. A pale speck above each eye. A little pale tan on the cheeks, under the eyes and ears and at the root of the tail, a distinctive

mark of the breed. The hair is short, strong and close. The skin is white with black markings under its surface; black markings on the belly skin. The mask, palate, and scrotum are black.

GAIT The Levesque runs with a supple, long-paced gallop.

DISQUALIFICATIONS Overshot or undershot mouth; tricoloring; lack of type; excessively short ears or ears set on too high and back; light eyes and nose; thin legs; exceeding or failing to meet stated limits of size by 2 inches. ●

LEVESQUE

Photo: Barbier-Petit, Buzzini.

POITEVIN

117 POITEVIN
FRANCE

At the present time this breed no longer maintains its original purity because the dogs descended from the remarkable original specimens have gradually disappeared. Nevertheless the products of their crossbreeding with other dogs also make excellent hounds.

The origin of the breed goes back to 1692. The Marquis François de Larrye, of Poitou, had received from the kennels of the Dauphin of France a dozen Foxhounds he used for hunting wolves which infested the region at that time. He crossbred with his own dogs some magnificent hounds (Céris dogs) which he obtained locally. Thus he got a breed which proved unbeatable in wolf hunting, thanks to its well-developed scent, its voice so well suited to its courage, and to its speed descending into ravines.

During the French Revolution the magnificent Larrye pack was destroyed, although some dogs were saved owing to the efforts of huntsmen and local peasants. Different crossbreedings took place on many occasions, and although the breed re-created by Larrye has been modified on certain points, the dogs' psycho-physical qualities have been preserved.

GENERAL CHARACTERISTICS A very distinguished dog, carrying to a high degree of perfection strength, elegance, and lightness combined with remarkable coloring.

SIZE Height, 24-28 inches.

HEAD Lengthy but not excessively so; not very wide; projecting bones with a slight occipital protuberance. The skull is more flat than domed and drops with a very slight slope onto the forehead, which is slightly curved and not excessively long. A very slight stop. The upper lip covers the lower; the muzzle is rather thin and tapering.

EYES Large, brown, encircled by

black; the eyes have an expressive look.

EARS Of average width, thin, set on rather low on the head; they are not very long and are slightly folded.

NECK Long, slender, without dewlap.

BODY The chest is very deep, proportionately deeper than wide. The ribs are long, the back well muscled and well supported. The loins are muscular and the flanks are slightly drawn up but sufficiently powerful.

TAIL Of average length, thin and well attached on the loins; it is carried elegantly and with a slight curve.

190

Photo: Buzzini

POITEVIN

118 BILLY
FRANCE

This dog is still called the Montambeuf, the Céris of Billy breed. We only know of his origins through the information given by his creator, Hublot du Rivault: the dog was made up of three breeds which were different but related: 1) the Céris, graceful dogs of small stature, white spotted with bright orange, 24-25 inches, very elegant and, above all, hunters of the hare and the wolf; 2) the Montambeufs, large and beautiful dogs wth strong bone and muscle structure, a white and pale orange-spotted livery with a coat of the same color, giving them an extremely noble appearance; very quick, resourceful, great hunters, and remarkable for their gift of discernment, for they would follow only the animals they were meant to attack; 3) the marvelous dogs of upper Poitou, the Larrye, created around 1808 by Émile de Mauvisse, Count of Villars; the most truly remarkable of all the French breeds. These three blood streams were united and fused into one through a series of repeated and painstaking crossbreedings which saw fruition in the Billy breed. Today the Billy is still a hound of exceptional qualities, a very acute scent, a good worker, resourceful and clever. In the woods he makes a good approach towards the game and has a light and harmonious voice. He is rather sensitive to intense cold, and when he is not hunting he is rather quarrelsome with his fellows.

FOREQUARTERS The shoulders are long, flat and sloping, closely set onto the chest. The forelegs are straight and muscular, lean, strong, flat and wide. **HINDQUARTERS** The haunches are slightly sloping, well furnished and of a good length. The thighs are very muscular, the hocks close to the ground, well upright and slightly bent. **FEET** A wolflike foot, rather long, very tough.

COAT Tricolor, with black mantle or large markings, sometimes white and orange; many individuals have the "wolfish" coat. Color of the skin at the scrotum varies from white to black.
GAIT Easy movement, galloping with outstanding ease. The Poitevin jumps well and is capable in the woods.
DISQUALIFICATIONS Black and white coloring; dewlap. ●

BILLY

Photo: DIM, Buzzini.

PACK OF FRENCH WHITE AND BLACK DOGS

Photo: Buzzini

BILLY

GENERAL CHARACTERISTICS A well-built dog, strong and light. In the Billy the forequarters are more strongly developed than the hindquarters.
SIZE Height: Males 24-26 inches; females 23-24½ inches.
HEAD Fairly lean and thin, of medium length, with a rather square nose which is well developed and either black or deep brown-orange in color. The lips are not heavily pendant, the upper one covering the lower one slightly. The commissure of the lower lip is often visible. The forehead is slightly domed, rather narrow, and the stop is well defined. The occipital protuberance is apparent; the muzzle is fairly broad, straight and slightly arched; it is moderately long.
EYES Alert, well opened and dark; edged with black or brown.
EARS Medium in size, set on slightly high, the ears are rather flat and slightly turned.
NECK Of medium length, rather rounded and quite strong. There is a slight dewlap.
BODY The chest is very deep and narrow, the ribs are flat. The back is fairly wide, strong, and slightly arched. The loins are wide and slightly curved. The flanks are rather long, occasionally drawn up but not excessively so.
TAIL Long, strong, in some individuals slightly hairy.
FOREQUARTERS The shoulders are rather long and quite close to the chest. The forelegs are strong, flat, and well directed. **HINDQUARTERS** Characterized by slanting haunches. The thighs are muscular to a moderate degree and the hocks are wide, strong, and slightly bent. **FEET** Well made, close and rather round.
COAT Short, harsh to the touch and frequently rather thick. The skin is white, sometimes speckled with deep brown, or it may be almost black. It is supple and fine in quality. **Color** Completely white or light brown, sometimes white with light orange or lemon markings.
GAIT The Billy is a good galloper.
DISQUALIFICATION Black in coat; excessive slenderness or length of muzzle. ●

119 FRENCH TRICOLOR
Chien Français tricolore

FRANCE

In 1957 three new breeds were added to the official classification of French hounds. These were the French Tricolor, the French White and Black, and the French White and Orange. All are descended from old French dogs reinforced by considerable infusions of English blood: the Foxhound has been employed to this end for more than a hundred years. In time these new hounds lost all traces of their English characteristics, although they kept the Foxhound's robust constitution, the bone structure, and certain psycho-physical traits.

While the breeds where crossbreeding with the Foxhound is evident or indicative—such as the form of the head, length and fixation of the ear, drooping lips, feet and perpendicular measurements—are classed among the Anglo-French hounds, which are described later and which represent a traditional stage, those most closely resembling the original French type are classified according to the color of the coat.

The important question of head structure has not yet been clearly defined as regards French hounds. However, an almost complete standard has been published and approved.

GENERAL CHARACTERISTICS A French hound, elegant, fairly well built, fairly muscular.
SIZE Height: males 24½-28½ inches; females 23½-27 inches.
HEAD Not particularly imposing, elongated, with a slightly domed skull and a rather accentuated occipital protuberance. The nose is black with well open nostrils. The bridge is straight, long, and in some dogs slightly arched. The cheeks are more substantial than in the Poitevin, serving to square the muzzle to a certain extent. The stop is more accentuated than in the Poitevin.
EYES Large and brown, sometimes with black eye rims. The expression is intelligent.
EARS Broader than those of the Poitevin. They are set on at eye level and are slightly voluted. They should not be too soft; when extended along cheek the tips reach to the beginning of the nose or no less than 1 inch from it.
NECK The neck is long and quite strong. It may have a slight dewlap.
BODY The chest is deep, with the brisket at least as far down as the elbow. The ribs are long and not too flat. They are well directed, in harmony with the foreparts. The back is solid and sustained, and the belly is slightly drawn up.
TAIL Quite long, carried with great elegance.
FOREQUARTERS The shoulders are long and set well onto the body. The limbs are straight, broad and well directed. **HINDQUARTERS** The thigh is long and muscular. The hocks are fairly broad and well let down, with a slight angulation. **FEET** Lean.
COAT Short and rather fine. **Color** Tricolor, with a more or less extensive saddle. There are tan markings, preferably bright tan or leather-colored. Undesirable markings are black speckling on the cheeks and lips and tan or blue speckling on the legs and body. Wolf coat is acceptable. **Skin** Rather fine in texture.
GAIT Light and easy.
FAULTS Depigmentation of the nose; overshot or undershot jaw; light eyes; flat or short ears, ears set on too high; weak or badly directed legs; too straight hocks, fat feet; any trace of English-bred dog, especially if apparent in the head; "smoky" head, suggesting cross-breeding of white and black; and generally any color other than the standard. ●

FRENCH TRICOLOR

120 FRENCH WHITE AND BLACK
Chien Français blanc et noir

FRANCE

The White and Black is the most prevalent among the French group. It might be said that, considering also his abilities, he represents the classic type of today's great French hunting hounds. In 1957 the White and Black represented 60 percent of the hunting packs.

Of typically French stock because of his somewhat convex skull, his rather elongated head, the ear attached at the height of the eye, this dog's structure is further characterized by his strong legs which enable him to operate quickly and easily in hunting deer or roebuck.

The improvement in structure and conformation as compared with older breeds is due, in this case, to the English blood, evidently added in small amounts, since careful selection has made it possible to eliminate from the breed any foreign characteristic.

GENERAL CHARACTERISTICS A great hunting dog, distinguished and solidly built, giving a general appearance of good balance.
SIZE Height: males 25½-28 inches; females 24½-27 inches.
HEAD The skull is fairly domed and rather narrow, but without exaggeration. The occipital protuberance is apparent without being excessive, that is, only sufficient to keep the skull from seeming flat. The supraorbital ridge may be fairly prominent (reminiscent of Levesque blood). The head is on the whole quite prominent and rather long, in good proportion to the rest of the body, without being massive or coarse but expressive and well carried. The bridge is preferably slightly arched. The upper lip covers the lower. The stop is not pronounced. The nose is black and well open.
EYES Dark, with an intelligent and trusting expression.
EARS Set on at eye level and slightly voluted. Extended, they should reach the beginning of the nose or at least to within 1 inch of it.

Photo: Studio Pierre, Buzzini.

FRENCH WHITE AND BLACK

NECK Quite long and strong; in some dogs there is a slight trace of dewlap, but never very much.

BODY The thorax is higher than it is broad, and the brisket is down at least to the elbow. The ribs are long and moderately sprung. The back is rather long but well sustained. The loins are muscular and well joined. The belly is slighlty drawn up but allowing good internal room. The haunches are oblique and invariably extended for a good length, at least to the point of the buttocks.

TAIL Thick at the root, quite long, and carried elegantly.

FOREQUARTERS The shoulders are long, lean and sloping. The legs are strong and well directed, with the elbows carried well against the body.
HINDQUARTERS The thighs are long and well muscled; the hocks are broad, powerful, well let down and slightly angulated. The feet are rather long but lean and sturdy.

COAT Shorthaired, dense, rugged.
Color The coat must be black and white, either with an extended saddle or with more or less extended black markings, with black spots or tan markings on the legs alone. Above each eye there is a light tan marking, and there are similar markings on the cheeks, beneath the eyes, on the inner parts of the ears and at the root of the tail. As with the Great Gascon of Saintonge, a "roebuck" marking is often found on the thigh.
Skin White under the white part of the coat and black under the black area. Sometimes more or less dark blue subcutaneous markings are found on the belly and the inner thighs.

GAIT A long, fluid, galloping run.
FAULTS Skull too broad, too round or too flat; brows too prominent; stop overly accentuated; light eyes and nose; overshot or undershot jaw; ears flat, short or badly set on; excessive dewlap; weak or badly directed limbs; fat feet; trace of depigmentation anywhere on the dog; tricolor coat, tan markings too bright, black color continuing from cheeks to lips; any suggestion of English-bred dog in the head; any apparent Poitevin quality in head under the black and white; timidity or cowardice. ●

PACK OF FRENCH WHITE AND ORANGE DOGS

Photo: Barbier-Petit, Buzzini.

FRENCH WHITE AND ORANGE

121 FRENCH WHITE AND ORANGE

Chien Français blanc et orange

FRANCE

One may presume that this breed descends from the Poitevin or the Billy. Too few in number for a standard to be set, it is judged in shows according to the French Tricolor dog's standard, except for color and some other individual points.

122 GREAT VENDEAN GRIFFON

Grand Griffon Vendéen

FRANCE

The origin of this dog must be sought among the "greffiers" (recorders) who, in turn, are descended from the white variety of the St. Hubert crossed with an Italian white and tawny bitch. The progeny were called "The King's White Dogs," the first of the stock being a white dog given by the king to the breeder. The term "greffier" comes from the fact that the owner of the Foxhound bitch was the king's recorder or clerk. A cross-breeding with the Nivernais Griffons and an infusion of setter blood decreased the breed's qualities of endurance.

Although good hunters, these hounds exhaust themselves after a few hours and must give up the chase.

GREAT VENDEAN GRIFFON

FRENCH WHITE AND ORANGE PUPPIES

Photo: Buzzini.

123 GREAT ANGLO-FRENCH TRICOLOR
Grand Anglo-Français tricolore

FRANCE

GREAT ANGLO-FRENCH TRICOLOR

All the present Anglo-French dogs (large, average, and small) were formerly listed under the rather unflattering grouping of "bastards." In time they were defined and classed according to their breeds or origin and distinguished as: a) Anglo-Poitevin; b) Anglo-Gascon-Saintongeois; c) Anglo-French shorthaired, a product of a cross between a Foxhound and a French longhaired hound. Since 1957 the three divisions above have been regrouped into the following breeds: a) Great Anglo-French Tricolor; b) Great Anglo-French White and Black; c) Great Anglo-French White and Orange, the same subdivision having been carried out in France together with the elimination of the long hair. These hounds are energetic and of perfect structure. English blood has made them more robust and given them new vigor. They are used in many packs belonging to the finest hunts and have developed a high degree of homogeneity.

GREAT VENDEAN GRIFFON PUPPY

GENERAL CHARACTERISTICS An intelligent dog, sure of itself, distinguished in physique and gait. It is well proportioned and robust without a sign of coarseness.

SIZE Height: 23½-25½ inches.

HEAD The skull is well rounded and should not be too broad. The stop seems more accentuated than it actually is because of the bushy eyebrows. The head is rather long and not too broad between the eyes. The bridge is broad and straight, the lips well feathered. The nose is big, black, with well open nostrils.

EYES Large, dark and vivacious.

EARS Soft, narrow, fine, covered with long hair, the ears terminate in an elongated oval. They are well turned in and not too long. They are set on low, below eye level.

NECK Light and without dewlap.

BODY The chest is well developed, quite high and not too broad. The ribs are moderately well sprung. The back is solid and short, straight and slightly rising. The loins are well muscled, the flanks slightly drawn up but nevertheless full and broad.

TAIL A saber tail, set on quite high; it is thick at the root and tapers gradually to the tip.

FOREQUARTERS The shoulders are long and sloping. The legs are straight, with a heavy, well-boned forearm. The elbows are carried close to the body. **HINDQUARTERS** The thighs are long and well muscled. The hocks are broad and low, neither open nor closed, but vertical to the ground.

COAT The hair is long but not excessively so. It is bushy, heavy and hard. The undercoat is abundant. The belly and the inner thighs must be hairy. The eyebrows are well developed but must not cover the eyes. **Color** Fawn, hare-haired, white and orange, white and gray, white and hare color, tricolor combining the aforesaid colors. **Skin** Not too fine.

GAIT A soft gait, indicative of a nervous breed.

DISQUALIFICATION Woolly coat. ●

Photo: Buzzini, J. Cooke (Photo Res.).

124 GREAT ANGLO-FRENCH WHITE AND BLACK

Grand Anglo-Français blanc et noir

FRANCE

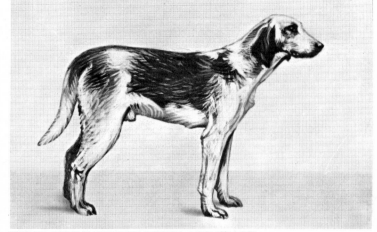

GREAT ANGLO-FRENCH WHITE AND BLACK

It must be said that these dogs should not be considered as mixtures, although they have not yet attained the status of a typically French and homogeneous breed, nor has it been possible to fix an official standard. In this matter we can only quote the Société de Vénerie Saint-Hubert of Paris which, together with the Société Centrale Canine—a society for the betterment of French dogs—controls the qualifications of French hounds: "If we have decided to adopt the term Anglo-French, or Anglo-Poitevin, it is simply that we have not been able to come up with a more appropriate one. However, we do not wish to suggest a 50-50 division of qualities. That would give the Foxhound blood too considerable a quotient.

"In this category we have established only two distinct varieties. These are the Anglo-Gascon-Saintongeois and the Anglo-Poitevin, the groups that we find most numerous today. We have

125 GREAT ANGLO-FRENCH WHITE AND ORANGE

Grand Anglo-Français blanc et orange

FRANCE

GREAT ANGLO-FRENCH WHITE AND ORANGE

not considered it necessary to set standards, as their essential type comes from the French breeds which gave them birth.

"The Anglo-Gascon-Saintongeois are, in our opinion, French dogs whose conformation has been improved by the English strain and which have preserved the essential points of the breeds from which they are derived. They should be judged and classed according to these standards. A judge who encounters such specimens in a dog show, products of too predominant English crossbreeding or of a cross of several French breeds with English blood, should place these dogs in the third category provided for Anglo-French classifications. This is where the Anglo-Poitevins-Saintongeois and other more or less fixed varieties belong, dogs which perform excellently but which cannot be classed as a definite type. In these cases the judge can only judge them on their general conformation."

FOXHOUNDS DURING THE HUNT

126 TRANSYLVANIAN HOUND

Erdelyi Kopo

HUNGARY

The origin of this Hungarian hound goes back to the "Seven Regions Hound" of the nineteenth century, when the Carpathian region was invaded by the Magyars. A Magyar hound was crossbred with a local dog and with Polish dogs of Eastern Europe. A breed was produced which proved good for mounted hunting and well adapted to the terrain and special climate of the Carpathians. Today the Transylvanian Hound is obedient, tireless, easy to train, and courageous. He combines an excellent sense of smell with an exceptional sense of orientation.

GENERAL CHARACTERISTICS A medium-sized tracking hound, friendly, daring and tenacious, with an excellent sense of smell. Requires little care and is easily trained. The shape of the head, the position of the neck, the proportions of the body, the strong and muscular legs and the positioning of the tail are all characteristic of central European tracking hounds. The Transylvanian Hound is bred in two varieties, the long-legged and the short-legged. The difference lies in the size, color and hair. The former often has a black coat and longer, denser hair, while the latter is red-brown. The larger variety is used in hunting wild boar, deer and lynx, while the smaller is adapted to hunting fox and hare. This dog hunts and points in splendid fashion, emitting a sharp cry and barking in response to his master and will defend him if the occasion arises.

WEIGHT AND SIZE Weight: 66-77 lb. Height at the withers: the larger dogs, 21½-25½ inches; the smaller variety, 17½-19½ inches.

HEAD A typical tracking hound's head, rather long but not pointed, with a slightly rounded skull. The skin is free of wrinkles. The forward edge of the nose should not be too rounded. The nostrils are well open, the bridge is straight. The lips are well developed, lean and fit well over the teeth, which are strong and well developed. The jaws close in a scissors bite. The stop is not very evident, nor are the supraorbital ridges.

EYES Of medium size, oval, slightly slanted, dark brown in color. The eyelids are firm.

EARS Set on at medium height; they hang without folds and are widened at the midpoint, tapering to rounded tips. Extended forward, they reach the eyes and cover them but do not reach far beyond.

NECK Carried at medium height, the neck is of average length and is muscular. The skin is wrinkled at the lower part; a slight dewlap is permitted.

FOREQUARTERS The forelegs are like columns holding up the body; they are moderately separated. The feet are round and well closed. The pads are large, long and elastic; the nails are strong and black.

BODY Fairly long, but outline is very nearly square. The chest is broad and long, not deep. The withers are pronounced, and the backline is straight. The croup is not overly muscular and slopes moderately. The stern is not imposing, the belly is only slightly drawn up.

TAIL Set on low, and in repose hangs down, with the last third curved upward. It reaches ½ or 1 inch below the hocks. When hunting, the dog carries his tail curled at the level of the back. The tail should not be docked.

HINDQUARTERS Set rather far back. The thighs are muscular, the legs only moderately so. The hocks are set low and open. The feet are round, with closed toes, big pads and strong nails.

COAT Short, strong, straight and close-fitting. The coat is longer on the larger variant, as well as denser, closer and harsher. It is glossy, with an undercoat. **Color** Large variety: basically black, with white markings often found on the forehead, chest, feet and the tip of the tail. Tan markings may be found on the brows, throat, upper legs and occasionally the lower legs as well. Small variety: Basically brown-red, slightly lighter toward the belly and on the limbs. Small white markings may be found on the forehead, chest, feet and tip of the tail. The head is often peppered with black. **Skin** Dark; bare parts are black. The nose of the smaller variety is often deep reddish brown.

GAIT Should not be too fast; at the gallop the dog is of outstanding endurance. ●

127 NORWEGIAN ELKHOUND (GRAY)

NORWAY

NORWEGIAN ELKHOUND (GRAY)

GENERAL CHARACTERISTICS The Norwegian Elkhound (gray) has a compact and proportionally short body; a thick and abundant, but not bristling, coat; and prick ears. Its tail is tightly curled over the rump.

WEIGHT AND SIZE Approximate weight; males 50 lb; females 43 lb. Average height at the shoulder: males 20½ inches; females 18½ inches.

HEAD Broad between the ears. The forehead and back of the head are slightly arched, with a clearly marked but not imposing stop. Muzzle moderately long, broader at the base and tapering uniformly but not pointed. Bridge of the muzzle is straight; the jaw is strong, with tightly closed lips.

EYES Not prominent, brown and as dark as possible, with a frank, fearless and friendly expression.

EARS Set on high, firm and upstanding; their height slightly more than their width at the base; pointed, extremely mobile.

NECK Of medium length, firm, muscular, well set up.

BODY Short in the couplings. The back is wide and straight from neck to stern. Chest wide and deep, well ribbed up. Loins muscular. The belly is very slightly drawn up.

TAIL Set on high, tightly curled over the back but not carried on either side. The hair on the tail is thick and close.

FOREQUARTERS Legs firm, straight and powerful, well boned. Elbows closely set on. **HINDQUARTERS** Legs straight at the hock and as viewed from the rear. There should be no dewclaws. **FEET** Compact, oval and not turned outward. The toes are tightly closed, the nails are firm and strong.

COAT Thick, abundant, coarse and highly weather-resistant. Short on the head and on the front side of the legs; longest on the chest, neck, buttocks, behind the forelegs and on the underside of the tail. The coat is composed of a coarse, long-haired top coat, soft, woolly undercoat. Around the neck and chest the longer top coat forms a kind of ruff which, together with the prick ears, the energetic eyes and the curled tail, gives the animal its characteristic unique, alert appearance. **Color** Gray of various shades, with black tips on the long hairs of the top coat. Lighter on chest, stomach, legs, and underside of the tail. Any distinctive variation from the gray color is most objectionable, and too dark or too light colorings are discredited. Also, pronounced markings on legs and feet are not desirable. ●

128 NORWEGIAN ELKHOUND (BLACK)

NORWAY

GENERAL CHARACTERISTICS A typical Spitz dog, a little under medium size, light in build with a short, compact body and a dense but not bristling

TRANSYLVANIAN HOUND

NORWEGIAN ELKHOUND (BLACK)

Photo: A. Wintzell, G. Kapocsy

coat. Has prick ears, the tail curled over the back. He has a fearless and energetic disposition.

SIZE Height at shoulder: Males 17¾-19½ inches; females slightly smaller.

HEAD Lean and rather light, comparatively broad between the ears. The head is wedge-shaped, tapering toward the nose. The skull is nearly flat with a distinct but not abrupt stop. The muzzle tends to be short rather than long, tapering both as viewed from above and in profile. The lips are tightly closed.

EYES Not protruding. Brown, preferably dark, with a fearless and energetic expression.

EARS Set on quite high, pricked, slightly higher than their width at the base. They are pointed, not rounded, and very mobile. When the dog is listening the ears are moved forward; in repose they may be relaxed and held back.

NECK Of medium length, firm, with no loose skin and well set up.

BODY Strong and short but rather light. Chest deep, with good spring of ribs. Back straight, loins well developed. The croup is straight, the belly only slightly drawn up.

TAIL Set on quite high, short, cobby with a thick and close coat, but without a flag. It is carried tightly curled over the back but not to either side. A naturally short tail is a fault but does not disqualify.

FOREQUARTERS The forelegs are firm, straight and strong; the elbows are turned neither in nor out. **HINDQUARTERS** The hindlegs are slightly angulated and are straight when viewed from the rear **FEET** Rather small, oval, compact and not turned outward, preferably without dewclaws.

COAT Dense and rough, but lying close to the body. On the head and the front side of the legs the hair is short; on the front part of the neck, the underside of the chest, and on the back of the legs and underside of the tail the coat is longer. It is composed of a long, coarse top coat and a soft, woolly, black undercoat. **Color** Glossy black. A little white in the brisket, forelegs, and feet is acceptable. ●

NORWEGIAN ELKHOUND

129 POLISH HOUND
Ogar Polski
POLAND

GENERAL CHARACTERISTICS A medium-size dog, of vigorous build, strong-boned, of good weight with proportionately long legs. The lines are those of a vigorous, persevering dog, not however given to violence. Its voice on the trail is pure and sonorous, of medium tone; the female voice is higher than that of the male.

WEIGHT AND HEIGHT Weight: males 55-70½ lb; females 44-57 lb. Height at the withers: males 22-25½ inches; females 21-23½ inches.

HEAD Rather heavy, of noble lines, approximately rectangular, of medium length. The length of the skull is equal to the length of the muzzle, which is long and rounded at the tip, but neither pointed nor wedge-shaped. The stop is well defined, the supraorbital ridges are well developed, the forehead is wrinkled. The occipital protuberance is marked. The jaws are strong, quite long and fleshy. The nose is large and dark. The lips are thick, and the lower lip is falling.

EYES Rather large, with a gentle and serene expression; they are slightly slanted, not very deep-set, and are dark brown in color. The lower eyelid is relaxed in older dogs.

EARS Set on rather low, of medium length and hanging; they are rounded at the tips and hang close to the head.

NECK Of medium length and rather thick, especially toward the point of insertion with the shoulders. The dewlap is loose, with considerable wrinkled skin.

BODY The chest is capacious, broad and well let down; the brisket is below elbow level. The ribs are well sprung, long, with a more nearly vertical arrangement than in similar breeds. The loins are broad and high. The croup is long, broad and muscular. The belly is capacious, and nearly as deep as the chest; it encloses the inner organs well. The flanks are short.

TAIL Set on rather low. thick, covered with hair—especially in the lower part—which is longer than elsewhere; the tail hangs below the hock, slightly sloping and curved. When the dog is in action, the tail is raised to the level of the back.

FOREQUARTERS Sloping shoulders, muscular; the forearms are very well boned. The wrists are well defined, of a thickness in proportion to other nearby bone. The toes are well closed, with strong, heavy nails typical of a working dog; the nails are short and dark if the toes are yellow, or lighter if the toes are white. **HINDQUARTERS** The thighs are long and well boned. The tibias are sloping, quite short and well muscled. The metatarsi are lean and neat. The toes on the hind feet are well closed; the nails are heavy and strong, the pads broad and rather thick.

GAIT The Ogar Polski normally travels at a trot, rather slow and heavy.

In the hunt he moves with a heavy gallop.

COAT Head and ears brownish, except for a few spots on the two sides of the head. The ears are rather dark. The feet, belly and thighs are brown. The body is black, dark gray or dark brown. This brown color includes a wide range of tones, from yellow to rust brown or cinnamon, the latter being the desirable color. Also permissible is white striping on the head reaching to the nose, on the belly, on the chest, on the feet and the tip of the tail. There may be a black mantle descending from the head, with distinct points of brown color above the eyes. A wholly black head is a serious fault.

FAULTS Black nose; pointed muzzle; defective teeth; head lacking a distinct occipital protuberance; supraorbital ridges not sufficiently defined; too light eyes; ears too long, too small or standing out from the head; lack of flesh; underdeveloped chest; thin, too short tail or without sufficient hair; twisted tail; splayfeet. ●

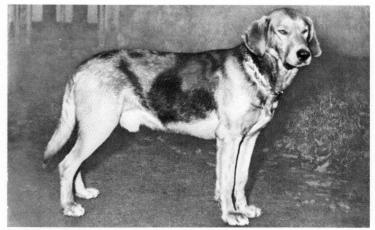

POLISH HOUND

Photo: S. A. Thompson.

GREAT PORTUGUESE PODENGO

He excels in the hunting trials which take place in Scandinavia where he competes with the Finnish Hound, the Greyhound, the Norwegian Sheepdog, and others. The trials consist of the dog's searching out the elk in silence and still maintaining contact with his master. Only when the quarry comes into view or is about to flee should the dog bark in a special way. If he is able to stop the elk by his barking, then he changes the tone of his bark, letting the hunter know that he can approach the quarry which the dog has meanwhile immobilized by his attack. This demands considerable courage, as the furious elk constantly tries to reach the dog with his great horns and powerful hoofs.

The Jämthund is also a very good sled dog and is used in this regard to transport supplies to ski troops. Many of these dogs are trained in military schools, and even when they later belong to private masters they are mobilized in case of military necessity.

130 GREAT PORTUGUESE PODENGO

PORTUGAL

This dog is prevalent in northern Portugal where he is used in a pack or alone for rabbit hunting. There exists no precise information concerning his origins in Portugal, although it is evident that among his ancestors figure those that gave birth to the Greyhound. Over the years these underwent mutations brought about by climate and terrain. The Podengo possesses, in fact, the qualities and abilities of the Greyhound. He is classed in three varieties: the medium, from which came many breeds of average size, the great Podengo, and the dwarf. The great and the medium-sized Podengos are used in certain areas as guard dogs and give excellent results.

GENERAL CHARACTERISTICS A large dog, well adapted for working with sizable game. This variety is practically extinct in Portugal today. It differs from the medium-sized Podengo in the following characteristics:
SIZE 21½-27½ inches.
TAIL May be curved. ●

131 JÄMTHUND
SWEDEN

The Jämthund is very popular in Scandinavia and has been known since ancient times. He is mainly used for elk hunting.

JÄMTHUND

GENERAL CHARACTERISTICS A large elkhound of the Spitz type, with erect ears, a well-curled but not tightly curled tail, carried high over the back. The Jämthund is robust, compact and lean, without heaviness; it should not look long. Courageous and energetic, this breed is at the same time calm and reflective.
WEIGHT AND HEIGHT Weight: a dog 23½ inches high should weigh 66 lb. Height at the withers: males 23-25 inches; females 21-23 inches.
HEAD Long, lean, relatively broad between the eyes. The skull is very slightly rounded. The stop is clearly defined but is not pronounced. The nose is broad, the bridge straight, wide and strong. The lips are close-fitting over the jaws. The muzzle is slightly shorter than the skull, tapering gently and uniformly to the nose. It should not, however, be pointed as seen from either above or in profile. The cheeks are flat. The teeth should meet in a level bite.
EYES Rather small, not protruding, brown and preferably dark brown.

The expression is lively but at the same time calm.
EARS Set on high, very straight, pointed and mobile. They are relatively small, longer than their width at the base. The inner side of the auricle is covered with long hair.
NECK Long, lean and robust; it is carried well.
BODY Robust, slightly longer than the height at the withers. The chest is broad and roomy, with well sprung ribs. The backline is straight and very slightly sloping from withers to croup. The loins are broad, well up, and the belly is slightly drawn up.
TAIL Set on high, of medium length and uniform thickness. It is well feathered but without fringe; it is carried curled up over the back, not too much to the side.
FOREQUARTERS Lean, straight and robust. The shoulders are long and sloping; the elbows are close to the body. **HINDQUARTERS** Straight, but with good flexure at the second thighs and hocks. Seen from behind, the hindquarters should be straight

HUNTING AT ORBETELLO ▶

JÄMTHUND

Photo: E. Münch, S. A. Thompson, A. Wintzell, M. Pedone.

and parallel. **FEET** Robust, not turned out, slightly elliptical, with closed toes.

COAT Long and hard, quite close-fitting, with the tips of the top coat darker than the rest. The undercoat is short, soft, woolly, light in color and preferably white. On the head and front side of the legs the hair is short and smooth; on the chest, neck, tail, buttocks and the back of the forelegs it is longer. **Color** Dark gray, light gray; parts of the muzzle, cheeks and throat are light gray or cream, and these are characteristic of the breed. Varicolor on legs, chest, belly and around the vent is allowed. ●

132 SWEDISH GRAY DOG
Grähund
SWEDEN

This hunter possesses speed and great endurance (as do other Scandinavian Elkhounds, some of which are used in America for hunting raccoons and even mountain lions and lynxes) and is also an excellent pet.

Its origins, as in the case of other neighboring breeds, are very ancient. Some trace it back to the *Canis familiaris palustris* and others to prehistoric dogs whose fossils are preserved. In any case the modifications undergone by these dogs through the centuries are relatively slight.

SWEDISH GRAY DOG

GENERAL CHARACTERISTICS The Swedish Gray Dog should be compact and square in outline, a typical fox-like dog, with good carriage. He should also be attentive, resolute and energetic.

SIZE Height at the withers: males 20½ inches; females 19 inches.

HEAD Wedge-shaped, as seen both from in front and in profile, of harmonious lines; proportionately broad between the ears, the head tapers gradually toward the nose, with a regular development from skull to muzzle, which is proportionately robust. The bridge is straight. The lips are closely fitted together and to the jaws. The muzzle is very slightly shorter than the skull; it appears pointed from above and from the side. The teeth are strong and meet in a scissors bite. The stop is not pronounced but it is well defined. The skull is slightly arched; the skin, which is rather thick, should fit elastically over the underlying tissues.

EYES Brown or, preferably, dark brown. Dogs with yellow eyes can not receive prizes. Protruding eyes are not permitted. The eye opening should be of medium proportions.

EARS Rather high and rigid, pointed and proportionately small; longer than they are wide at the base. They are moderately mobile.

NECK Of medium length, powerful, well carried. The skin is elastic and thick on the underside.

BODY Strong, compact and short. The chest is full, well let down, with well-sprung ribs. The backline is straight from withers to croup; lumbar region is well developed. The croup is well developed, muscular and gently sloped. The belly is moderately drawn up.

TAIL Well set on, strong and proportionately short. It is tightly curled and is preferably carried over the back, to one side.

FOREQUARTERS Heavy, lean and strong, perfectly in vertical, with elbows close to the body. **HINDQUARTERS** Vertical, strongly boned, lean. The stifle and hock are gently but definitely angulated. **FEET** Small, directed well forward, slightly elongated, with well closed toes. Harefeet are objectionable.

COAT The top coat is moderately long, strong and smooth; the undercoat is soft. On the head and the front of the legs it should be short and smooth; it should be longer on the back of the legs and on the thighs. On the neck it forms a collar. It is thick on the tail, without, however, forming a flag. **Color** Various shades of gray, lighter on the chest, belly and legs, on the collar and the lower part of the tail, starting from the root. The ears and the front of the muzzle are dark. The divisions of the various shades should be regular. The top coat should have its black points more or less long, while the undercoat should be completely light gray. Yellowish colors are objectionable, as are those tending toward brown; other undesirable features are reddish legs, light-colored rings around the eyes and white spots. Colors remote from gray are not acceptable.

GAIT Harmonious and ample. ●

Photo: A. Wintzell, McCutcheon.

133 BLACK FOREST HOUND

Slovensky Kopov

CZECHOSLOVAKIA

The Black Forest Hound is the only hound breed from Czechoslovakia. The Black Forest Hound is of ancient origins, although breeding for the purpose of preserving and strengthening certain characteristics was started only during the years following World War II.

He was originally a hound used as a guard dog, and nowadays is principally employed for boar hunting in the Czechoslovakian mountains. He is of an independent nature and needs rigorous training. He is adept at following a blood trail and is helped by his excellent scent and well-developed orientation to his environment.

GENERAL CHARACTERISTICS Invariably black and tan, this dog has a powerful bone structure which serves as a framework for a rather light build. The body outline is elongated, the temperament lively. The hair is of medium length, with a thick undercoat. The Black Forest Hound is single-minded in his work as a tracking hound, and is capable of following a fresh trail for hours, barking in a high voice. An excellent dog for its ancient gifts, it is used mostly in hunting the European wild boar.

SIZE Height: males 17½-19½ inches; females 15¾-17¾ inches.

HEAD The skull is slightly rounded on top; the occipital protuberance is not pronounced. The upper cranial-facial axes are parallel. The nose should invariably be black, well proportioned, with slightly pointed nostrils, which are well open. The lips are close-fitting, thin, not pendulous. The muzzle is straight along its upper edge, not too wide, and of a length in good proportion to the length of the skull. The jaws are regular and robust, with a full complement of well-developed teeth. The stop is sloped at an angle of about 45°.

EYES Dark, fairly deep-set, indicating a dog of lively personality and great courage. They are almond-shaped, with dark lids.

EARS Set on a little above eye level, the ears are rather short and carried at an angle of 135°. The neck is well muscled and should be free of any trace of dewlap.

FOREQUARTERS The shoulders are rather short, well developed and muscular. The scapular-humeral angle is about 100°. The forearm is straight and lean. The pastern is short and gently sloped. The foot is oval, with well arched toes; the nails should invariably be black and strong.

BODY The chest is broad and full moderately let down, with the brisket proportionately broad and deep. The ribs should be well sprung (flatness of chest or thorax is a serious fault). The back is straight, of medium length; the loins are short, rather broad and muscular. The croup is rather short, of medium breadth; it is sloped. The belly is slightly drawn up.

TAIL Set on below the backline, it is proportionately strong; it tapers toward the tail. It reaches the point of the hock. In action it is carried as a saber tail at an angle of 150°.

HINDQUARTERS The thigh is quite broad, proportionately long and muscular. The leg is proportionately long and broad and is well boned. The hock is moderately broad, with an angulation of about 150°. There are no dewclaws. The feet are oval, with toes closed and well arched; the pads are well developed and dark.

COAT From ¾ to 2 inches long, closefitting, thick, of moderate harshness. It is longer on the back, neck and tail. The undercoat is particularly dense during winter and is present the year round. Color Black with tan markings which range from fawn to mahogany on the lips, cheeks, throat, chest, forehead over the eyes and legs. Skin Dark brown to black; it should fit close to the body and be without wrinkles.

GAIT Regular, lively.

FAULTS Height greater than that required by standard; heavy head; pendulous lips; incomplete dentition, bad bite (overshot or undershot); light eyes, eyes too open or too closed; small or pointed ears; dewlap; massive build; flat chest, weak back; tail over back when dog is not in action; toes not well closed; legs out of vertical; hair too short or too long; lack of undercoat; coat of colors other than black; white markings, poorly defined limits of tan markings.

MEASUREMENTS (in ideal type)

Weight	35.27 lb.
Height at withers (male)	18.1 in.
Height at withers (female)	16.9 in.
Length of head	8.66 in.
Length of skull	5.12 in.
Width of skull	4.1 in.
Length of muzzle	3.54 in.
Width of chest	6.5 in.
Height of thorax	8.66 in.
Depth of brisket	12.4 in.
Length of trunk	21.65 in.
Circumference behind elbows	26 in.
Circumference behind last rib	21.25 in.
Scapular-humeral angle	110°
Humeral-radial angle	140°
Coxal-femoral angle	130°
Femural-tibial angle	130°
Tibial-tarsal angle	145°

BLACK FOREST HOUND

205

Photo: J. Jaros.

FOXHOUND

Photo: S. A. Thompson.

134 FOXHOUND
GREAT BRITAIN

Most experts and writers agree that the Foxhound is derived from crossbreeding between the old Norman tracker and different breeds of hounds prevalent since ancient times throughout Great Britain. Although the English have practically always had hunting hounds and have always hunted with them, it was only after the Norman conquest that the mounted hunt with the pack was introduced and became a regular sport. The dogs brought over by the Norman conquerors were unquestionably the Norman hounds used for the mounted hunt. In England this breed was called the Talbot. The purebred Talbot continued to exist although crossbreeds derived from it produced different dogs in different parts of England, according to need, type of terrain, and taste and ideas of hunters and breeders. Thus the Lancashire, Cheshire, and Staffordshire types of Foxhounds were big, heavy, and slow, but of strong voice, while the Worcestershire, Berkshire, and Bedfordshire types were of medium size and faster. The speediest, the "northern hounds," came from Yorkshire and Northumberland. In certain areas the smoothhaired were more numerous while in others the breeds had roughhaired coats.

During the reigns of James I and Charles I a sudden improvement in the speed of certain English hounds occurred. Some writers attribute this sudden modification to the fact that James I of England received a pack of hounds for the mounted stag hunt from Henri IV of France. This pack belonged to one of the French royal hound breeds and these dogs, considered the very best, were generally used as breeders throughout the country. Other commentators attribute this change to repeated and intensive crossbreeding with the Greyhound. However, during the second part of the eighteenth century in England, the fox replaced the stag as a favorite quarry of the hunt and, at the same time, the standards and rules of foxhunting were uniformly applied throughout the country and the Foxhound attained a type defined by precise characteristics which are still constant today.

The English Foxhound is at present a model hound because of his qualities, his beauty, and his hunting abilities. What other dog is capable of trotting ten to twelve miles from the kennel to the rendezvous, then hunting for five or six hours at top speed in pursuit of the quarry through woods or in the open at a speed capable of tiring two purebred horses and then to return the same distance home, still lively, with sparkling eyes and tail high. And this twice a week for eight months each year.

Today 658 hound packs for the mounted hunt are officially recognized. Among these, 369 are composed of Foxhounds—212 in Great Britain, 32 in Ireland, 12 in other European countries (among which is included the Società Romana della Caccia alla Volpe, in Italy) 113 in the U. S. A. and Canada, while 289 are used for hare hunting (Harrier), stag hunting (Staghounds) and otter hunting (Otter Hounds).

FOXHOUND

show quality with no lumber. A shoulder with an excessive amount of fleshy conformation will prevent the hound from running up or down hill at top pace. Legs full of bone right down to the feet, not tapering off in any way. HINDQUARTERS Full and of great muscular proportions. Hocks should be well let down, and the bone of the hind legs (as in the forelegs) should continue all the way down to the foot and not become light under the pastern. FEET With toes close together, never open. ●

HEAD Skull broad.
NECK Long but not thick; a short-necked hound is deficient in pace.
BODY Girth should be deep with plenty of heart room. Back broad. A hound should be well ribbed up, but there should be a fair space between the end of the ribs and the commencement of the hindquarters, otherwise the hound will be deficient in stride with a consequent lack of pace.
TAIL Should be well put on at the end of good quarters, which should never end abruptly (the type that hound experts call "chopped off behind"). A curly stern is unsightly but not detrimental to hunting quality.
FOREQUARTERS Shoulders should

135 AMERICAN FOXHOUND
UNITED STATES

The first reports on the importation of hounds on American soil can be found in a sixteenth-century diary written by one of De Soto's men. He reported how, in these new lands, dogs were used to hunt Indians instead of rabbits and foxes.

In 1650 the Englishman Robert Brooke arrived in America with an entire pack of hounds. These were the dogs that became the true source of present North American hounds. Around 1770 George Washington imported other hounds from Great Britain and in 1785 he received as a present from Lafayette a group of excellent French specimens. The different English and French breeds were crossbred to produce the Virginia hounds, which are today's American Foxhound.

At the beginning of the nineteenth century, hunting clubs were quite numerous throughout the United States and each attempted to improve its own packs through selective breeding and new blood. Imports of English and Irish hounds were frequent. The American hound produced some well defined varieties as, for example, the Walker Hound. Today the American Foxhound Club and the Masters of Foxhounds Association are attempting to make the true American Foxhound homogeneous and different in his characteristics and aptitudes from the numerous other varieties of hounds which have been selectively bred in the New World.

SIZE Height at the withers: Males, not under 22 nor over 25 inches; females, not under 21 nor over 24 inches. Measurements made across the back at the point of the withers, the hound standing in a natural position with his feet well under him.
HEAD Skull Should be fairly long, slightly domed at occiput, with cranium broad and full. **Ears** Ears set on moderately low, long, reaching when drawn out nearly, if not quite, to the tip of the nose; fine in texture, fairly broad, with almost entire absence of erectile power—setting close to the head with the forward edge slightly turning to the cheek— round at tip. **Eyes** The eyes are large, set well apart; soft and hound-like, they have a gentle, pleading expression. The color is brown or hazel. **Muzzle** Of fair length, straight and square-cut; the stop is moderately defined. **Faults** A very flat skull, narrow across the top; excess of dome; eyes small, sharp and terrier-like, or prominent and protruding; muzzle long and snipy, cut away decidedly below the eyes, or very short. Roman-nosed, upturned, giving a dish-faced expression. Ears short, set on high, or with a tendency to rise above the point of origin.
BODY Neck and throat Neck rising

Photo: A. Roslin-Williams.

FOXHOUND

free and light from the shoulders, strong in substance yet not loaded, of medium length. The throat clean and free from folds of skin, a slight wrinkle below the angle of the jaw, however, is allowable. **Faults** A thick, short, cloddy neck carried on a line with the top of the shoulders.

AMERICAN FOXHOUND

Throat showing dewlap and folds of skin to a degree termed "throatiness." **Shoulders, chest and ribs** Shoulders sloping, clean, muscular, not heavy or loaded, conveying the idea of freedom of action with activity and strength. Chest should be deep for lung space, narrower in proportion to depth than the English hound (28 inches girth in a 23-inch hound is good). Ribs well sprung, with back ribs extending well back and a 3-inch flank allowing springiness. **Back and loins** Back moderately long, muscular and strong. Loins broad and slightly arched. **Faults** Very long back, sway-back, roach back; flat, narrow loins.

FOREQUARTERS Forelegs Straight, with fair amount of bone. Pasterns short and straight. **FEET** Foxlike; pad full and hard; toes well arched, nails strong. **Faults** Straight, upright shoulders, chest disproportionately wide or with lack of depth; flat ribs; out at elbow; knees knuckled over forward or bent backward; forelegs crooked; feet long, open or spreading.

HIPS, THIGHS, HINDQUARTERS Hips and thighs are strong and muscled, giving an abundance of propulsive power. The stifles are strong and well let down. The hocks are firm, symmetrical and moderately bent. The feet are close and firm. **Faults** Cow hocks, straight hocks; lack of muscle and propulsive power; open feet.

TAIL Set on moderately high and carried gaily, but not turned forward over the back; with slight curve and very slight brush. **Faults** Long tail, teapot curve or inclined forward from the root; rattail; entire absence of brush.

COAT A close, hard, houne coat of medium length. **Faults** Short, sparse or soft hair.

COLOR Any color is acceptable.

SCALE OF POINTS

Head	**20**	
Skull		5
Ears		5
Eyes		5
Muzzle		5
Body	**35**	
Neck		5
Chest and shoulders		15
Back, loins and ribs		15
Running Gear	**35**	
Forelegs		10
Hips, thighs, hind legs		10
Feet		15
Coat and tail	**10**	
Coat		5
Tail		5
		100

Photo: J. Martin (Photo Res.).

FOXHOUND

Group 6

HOUNDS
FOR SMALLER
GAME

DACHSBRACKE

Photo: Fotostampa.

136 DACHSBRACKE
GERMANY

It was not easy for this dog to take its place among the official German breeds, although thanks to its qualities it was finally recognized by German dog fanciers. It is only since 1896 that these mountain hunting dogs, that have been the pride of their owners for decades, have been known by their present name. The Dachsbracke is a hunting dog adapted to the most difficult terrain. In his work he has proved himself to be tenacious though calm. He is able to endure bad weather and is profitably employed, because of his excellent sense of smell, for rabbit and fox hunting. Today he is used even for following blood trails of stags and boars and for bringing back game. Regarding big game, he shows himself to be a truly dedicated hunter.

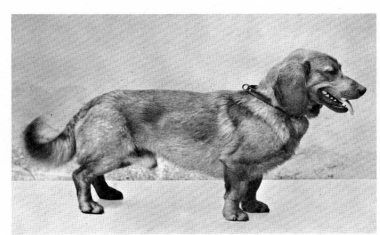

DACHSBRACKE

READY FOR THE HUNT

Photo: J. Jaros, Barbier-Petit.

SIZE The Westphalian Dachsbracke measures 12-14 inches at the withers; the Alpine variety measures 13½-16½ inches.

HEAD The head is in good proportion to the overall size of the dog. The skull is slightly rounded and not overly developed. The stop is moderately pronounced. The bridge is straight or slightly arched. The muzzle and the nose are moderately large. The teeth close well in a pincers bite; the canines are strong. The lips are thin and close-fitting; they should not overlap excessively. The commissure is rather accentuated.

EYES Of medium size, round, with a lively expression. They are light or dark brown, depending on the color of the coat. The lachrymal sac is not highly developed.

EARS Of medium length, broad, rounded at the base, set on high and rather far back, flat, thick, hanging without twisting and close to the cheeks, slightly erect when the dog is on the alert.

NECK Muscular, moderately long and fairly arched. The skin on the neck is slightly loose but should not form a dewlap.

BACK Straight, solid, rather long. The withers are raised and slope rather steeply to the backline. The loins are well filled out, the croup is rounded.

CHEST AND THORAX The ribs are well sprung, the sternum prominent. The rib cage tapers toward the last back ribs. The belly is well tucked up.

FOREQUARTERS Robust and exceptionally well muscled. The body, as in all Dachs- types, is suspended between the forelegs. The forelegs are nearly vertical and often but not always slightly bent at the wrist. **HINDQUARTERS** Slightly lighter than the forequarters, especially in the thighs. They are muscular and well angulated, and the lower leg is vertical. **FEET** The forefeet are more rugged than the hind feet. They are compact, with arched nails and large, robust pads. The toes on the hind feet are smaller, shorter and less arched.

TAIL Of medium length, thick at the root and tapering toward the tip. It is carried either down or with a slight upward curve.

COAT The hair is short, very dense, close-fitting, hard but elastic, with little undercoat. The hair is short on the head, ears and legs, longer on the neck. It is fairly long and harder on the back and the back of the thighs. It is not quite so long around the flanks and is longer and heavier on the upper belly and brisket. The tail has a brush. Wiry, excessively hard hair is a fault.

COLOR (a) **Black:** black with tan, black with grizzle; (b) **brown:** brown with lighter streaking; (c) **reddish:** reddish fawn, reddish peppered with black, yellowish red with lighter marks; (d) **white** (Westphalian Dachsbracke): white with varied tones of red. In the last case the markings are above the eyes and on the muzzle, legs and chest. A white stripe on the bridge is allowed in all reddish dogs, as are a light collar, a star on the chest, and white on the belly, toes and the back of the legs. A little black is acceptable above the eyes and on the muzzle, the edges of the ears, the nape, the back and (in brown and reddish animals) on the tail.

FAULTS Weak muscle and bone; head too large or too small for the rest of the body; head too broad or too narrow; stop too much or too little pronounced; bridge excessively arched; muzzle too pointed or too blunt; badly developed teeth; overshot or undershot jaw; lips too pendulous; ears short, folded, set on too far forward or not sufficiently close to head; hawkeyes; overdeveloped lachrymal sac; dewlap; chest too narrow or too barreled, too pronounced; crooked forelegs; weak hind legs, cow hocks, bowed hocks; open feet, harefeet; curled tail; long, wavy hair; hair on head too long; over or under standard for height. ●

Photo: S. A. Thompson.

137 GERMAN SPANIEL
Wachtelhund
GERMANY

Toward the turn of the century it occurred to some breeders, who were also ardent hunters, to crossbreed certain small or medium-sized dogs, all longhaired and with a particular talent for hunting in the forest. Although we do not know which breeds were employed, one thing is sure: a spaniel was produced which has proved to be truly remarkable for the find: the Wachtelhund.

GENERAL CHARACTERISTICS Except for height and weight, the Wachtelhund is similar to the German longhaired pointer. He is not quite so high on his legs, although he does have a definitely lengthened structure. This little carrier of heavy burdens, in order to maintain his balance in carrying a hare or a fox, needs a proportional length and robust physique. The German Wachtelhund, although an elegant dog in general appearance, should have good bone and muscling, should not be high on the legs, have the look of the Greyhound, nor should he be heavy, awkward, or low. In other words, the Wachtelhund is long in the withers and croup, very short in the backline and loin region, which should be broad enough to give the impression of a long animal. He should have resistance and power to keep going on the longest day of hunting, even on difficult and rocky terrain and in the snow. In a German hunting dog pointing is not a natural trait, but can only be the result of training. Dogs of this breed are above all hunting dogs and coursing dogs, excellent at hunting and rooting out game in all kinds of terrain. These dogs should be able confidently to give tongue after having picked up the scent. If they are silent or noisy after having only sighted the game, if they lack holding power and security in following the scent, and if they are without ability to work in water and have no spirit of the chase—these are serious faults. The male, which is invariably more robust and larger, should be able, with training, to retrieve hare and even fox. An intelligent dog learns easily to avoid game it cannot carry, or it will bark in such a way as to scare off such game. The Wachtelhund should possess to the utmost degree the zest for the hunt; many are pitiless stranglers once they have seized their prey.

SIZE Maximum and minimum measurements for the height at the withers are 15½-19½ inches. For females, the figures are 15½-17½; for males, 18-19½ inches. A dog of exceptional quality should not be penalized for ½ or ¾ inch above or below these limits.

HEAD The skull and the muzzle are of approximately the same length; the upper part of the skull is flat and not very broad. The occipital protuberance is not pronounced. The head is lean, with thin lips, not prominent. Dogs of this breed should not slaver. The stop is almost imperceptible and the medial furrow is either absent or very slight. The nose is brown, mobile, as large as possible at the tip and with nostrils well open. The muzzle is robust, with a broad, well-rounded bridge. A slightly arched nose is an advantage. The cheekbones are not pronounced. The teeth are strong and should preferably meet in a scissors rather than a pincers bite, since the latter causes more wear on the teeth. An undershot jaw is ob-jectionable and considered to be a serious fault.

EYES Should be as dark brown as possible. They are intelligent eyes, highly expressive, of medium size, almond-shaped, and should be slightly oblique. They should not be large, or protruding or deep-set. They should be well closed, with close-fitting lids and with the haw not visible. It is of prime importance for the dog to have excellent eyesight and a correct position of the eyes, which is given by a regular conformation of the skull and permits the dog to work well in fairly heavily wooded terrain.

EARS Wide and set on high; they should hang flat, with no folds, immediately behind the eye. They should not be too long, too thick, too fleshy or too soft. Extended, they should be long enough to reach the tip of the nose. Because of the long, thick hair, often curly, the ears seem to be longer and broader than they actually are.

NECK Robust but elegant and not too short. There should be no dewlap, and the neck should join the trunk with good lines. Since the dog is called upon to retrieve very heavy game, the nape must be of a particularly robust and strong muscling.

BODY The chest should not be too narrow, the cross section of the trunk should be oval; seen in profile, the chest is well let down (the brisket should be at least at elbow level and preferably below), deep (the back ribs are particularly long); the ribs are well sprung but not barrel-like, nor should they be flat. The backline, measured from the beginning of the withers to the root of the tail, is longer than the height at the withers. The withers are high and broad, the back itself is very short and robust, with no depression behind the withers. The loins are short but broad and deep, well muscled toward the groin and slightly arched. The croup is flat and long, so that there is room beneath it for a deep and broad pelvis and broad thighs, on which depend the power and the good shape of the hind legs. The belly and the flanks, from the so-called false ribs back, are moderately drawn up.

TAIL Set on high and is carried either straight or hanging down in repose; it is never carried straight over the back. The dog wags his tail in a lively manner when he has sighted game. The tail should be moderately docked to avoid wounds in the field; the tail is docked before the puppy is weaned; ⅓, or at most ½, of the tail should be docked. The tail has a fine fringe.

FOREQUARTERS The humerus should be very long and should form an angle of approximately 45° with the scapula. In movement it should move along the thorax, but it should not "row," and in repose it should lie with the elbow close to the chest.

The forelegs are straight, robust and strong, and are vertical to the ground. Seen from in front, the outer lines of the forelegs should be perpendicular to the ground, and the pastern should not turn inward nor outward. Seen in profile, the pastern should not be perpendicular to the ground but slightly slanted forward. The legs and especially the joints should be cleanboned, that is, there should be no swelling nor sign of rickets. The pastern should be very strong and solid. It ends in a spoon-shaped foot. Catfeet are objectionable. The toes should be well closed and have tufts of thick hair. The forelegs have a good fringe from the elbow down. **HINDQUARTERS** The thighs are wide and deep, and are trousered with long hair. The hock should be very robust and bent. The point of the hock should be pronounced. The hindquarters should be neither rigid nor under the dog. The hind legs, seen from behind, should be parallel and not turning inward or outward.

COAT The hair is long and rugged, thick and wavy, but it should not be too long or too fine, and definitely not silky. The hair should be either lightly waved (like astrakhan) or smooth and close-fitting. A silky coat is not adapted to hunting and therefore is unacceptable in this breed. On the nape, ears and croup the hair is often curly, while on the muzzle and the upper part of the skull the hair is short and very thick. Often there is a jabot on both sides of the chest. The back of the forelegs and thighs, and the tail also, have a good fringe. The ears are covered with curly hair or with thick, wavy hair that descends below the lower edge. Ears not covered with hair never occur in this breed. There is thick hair between the toes, which, however, should not be too long; if the dog is put to work during the winter, in snow, a little of this hair should be cut from between the toes. **Color** The Wachtelhund is found in two varieties—roan and brown. ●

GERMAN SPANIEL

GERMAN SPANIEL

Photo: Fotostampa.

138 BAVARIAN MOUNTAIN HOUND

Bayerischer Gebirgsschweisshund

GERMANY

When an attempt was made to use the excellent Hanover Hound in the Bavarian Mountains it was immediately noted that he was too heavy. A smaller-sized dog was indicated, capable of overcoming the obstacles of the terrain with greater ease. Breeders came up with the idea of crossbreeding the old Bavarian Hound with the Tyrolean and thus obtained the Bavarian Mountain Hound. This dog possesses a perfect instinct for the chase as well as a remarkable agility.

GENERAL CHARACTERISTICS In general appearance, this is a rather light, lively and muscular dog of medium size. Males should not be over 20 inches at the withers, females not over 18 inches. The body is rather long and up at the rump; the legs are rather short.

HEAD The skull is relatively broad, not steeply domed, not coarse. The cheeks are unusually lean, the jaws neither too long nor too wide. The nose is black or brown. The supraorbital ridges are prominent. The lips are close-fitting over the gums, not pendulous, and the commissure is well in evidence.

EYES Clear, not too large nor too round; the lids are close-fitting. The color is dark brown or brown.

EARS The ears are a little longer than average for dogs of this size, heavy, set on high, hanging flat and close to the head. They are rounded at the tips.

NECK The neck is of moderate length, robust and lean.

BACK Must not be too short, but definitely robust, broad and muscular toward the loins, which are always slightly curved. The croup is fairly level.

CHEST AND BELLY The chest is not too broad but is deep and well let down. The false ribs reach the flanks. The belly is slightly drawn up.

TAIL Long, reaching below the point of the hocks. It is slender and set on low, carried straight out or slightly lowered. The lower part is hairier than the rest.

FOREQUARTERS The shoulders are sloping, the upper arm is long. The forelimbs are well boned but not heavy; they are quite straight and very well muscled. The pasterns are straight but slightly off the vertical.

139 WESTPHALIAN BASSET

Westfalischer Dachsbracke

GERMANY

A product of selective breeding between the medium-sized German Hound and the Dachshund, this dog adds to the specific points of terriers the psycho-physical qualities typical of hounds.

GENERAL CHARACTERISTICS The Westphalian Basset is a hunting dog 12-14 inches high of moderate length and with a robust body. It has a noble head of moderate size, a well-set tail which is carried in a curve at normal gait. The expression of the eyes is melancholy, friendly and attentive.

HEAD From in front, the head is seen to be neat and rather long. The upper part is a little broader at the cheekbones; the cheekbones are not pronounced, and they diminish gradually toward the jawbone. The occipital protuberance is scarcely evident. The stop is not pronounced. The bridge is very slightly arched, the lips are slightly pendulous. The commissure is not pronounced.

EYES Lively, with a likable, friendly expression; light brown in color.

EARS Hanging, of medium length, broad-based, close to the head, rounded at the tips. The nose is dark in dark-coated dogs, lighter in light-coated dogs.

TEETH Strong and regular, closing in either a pincers or a scissors bite. The canines are especially well developed.

NECK Moderately long and quite strong in relation to the head, well set into the shoulders, broadening from the nape down to the withers. The skin is fairly loose, but there is no dewlap.

BODY The back is slightly arched, muscular, of medium length, slightly hollowed behind the withers. The loins are broad and well developed. The croup slopes slightly to the root of the tail.

CHEST AND BELLY The chest, as in the Dachshund, is strongly supported by the forelegs and is not especially let down. The rib cage is long, the belly moderately tucked up.

TAIL Set on moderately high and is a definite prolongation of the spinal column. It is strong at the root and covered with smooth thick hair in the upper part and bristly hair on the lower part. It ends in a bristly tip but with no tuft.

FOREQUARTERS The forelegs are well developed, lean, well boned and well muscled. The elbows are close in to the ribs. Viewed from in front the legs are not curved, but vertical, with the feet straight forward. **HINDQUARTERS** The thighs are high and strongly muscled, quite straight as viewed both from the side and behind. The hind legs are straight. The metatarsus is much more developed than it is in the German Dachshund. **FEET** Robust, with short toes, well closed.

COAT Extremely dense, and raised over the entire body, including the underparts. On the head, ears and the lower legs it is short; longer on the back, the body generally and the underpart of the tail.

COLOR All colors of the German tracking hounds are acceptable, with more or less white as one of the colors. Black and chocolate are not desirable. ●

WESTPHALIAN BASSET

BAVARIAN MOUNTAIN HOUND

IN THE MARSHES

HINDQUARTERS The thighs are very broad and long, with the hind legs proportionately long and oblique. The metatarsus is vertical. The hair at the edges of the buttocks is almost bristly. Viewed from behind, the hind legs should be parallel and perfectly straight. **FEET** Not too strong, but with toes well closed and arched. The nails are well developed and are black or horn color. The feet should not be either round (catfeet) nor long (harefeet), but rather spoon-shaped.

COAT Thick, short, moderately hard to the touch, little gloss, finer on the head and ears, less fine and longer on the belly and thighs.

COLOR Dark red, deer red, chestnut red, yellow red, yellow ocher, pale yellow to blond; gray red, like the winter coat of the Rottweiler, grizzle with darker streaks. In the reddish dogs the base color on the back is more intense. Cheeks, lips, ears, back and tail are dark.

FAULTS Short, telescoped figure; high withers; legs too long or too short; arching of forearm bone, splay-feet, long and flat feet, pasterns and feet turned outward; saddleback; weak loins, short or falling rump; hind legs under body; cow hocks or bow hocks; ribs excessively sprung; narrow head with weak jaws; ears set on low, pointed or curled; light-colored nose, flesh-colored nose; eyes too open or revealing haws; yellow hawk eyes; neck too short and thick; hair too bristly; tail carried high or curled.

DISQUALIFICATIONS Bones showing signs of rickets, light bones, lack of muscle, soft hair, overshot or undershot jaws, harefeet; any color besides those mentioned above, especially black with tan markings as in Dachshunds and Bloodhounds; white markings, but a small white star does not disqualify. ●

Photo: M. Pedone, E. Münch.

STEINBRACKE

FAULTS Faults eliminating dog from rating better than *Good:* feet not compact, nervousness; faults eliminating dog from rating of *Excellent:* incorrect forequarters, narrow chest, forelegs not straight-boned. ●

141 AUSTRIAN HOUND
Österreichischer Bracke-Brandlbracke
AUSTRIA

GENERAL CHARACTERISTICS A medium-sized dog (18-20½ inches at the withers), powerfully built but graceful and long-bodied. The head is carried proudly, the tail down at normal gait but carried higher when the dog is on the scent.

HEAD Of medium size. The forehead is spacious, narrowing toward the muzzle. The skull is well domed. The bridge is straight, the stop is not pronounced. The lips are well developed, the supraorbital ridges are at best moderately accentuated.

EYES Clear, the haw not visible. They are generally brown and have an intelligent expression.

EARS Of medium size, not too big, rounded at the tips, set on high and preferably hanging flat against the sides of the head.

NECK Of medium length, very strong, broadening toward the withers.

BACK Long and gently sloping from the withers. The croup is slightly raised.

CHEST AND BELLY The chest is broad, deep and well let down. The belly is slightly tucked up.

TAIL Long, moderately strong at the root and tapering gently but without coming to a sharp point. It is slightly sloping and quite tufted, although it does not have an obvious brush.

FOREQUARTERS Well developed, with sloping, highly mobile shoulders. Powerful muscling. The forearms are straight and strong, the pasterns generous and straight. **HINDQUARTERS** The thighs are moderately well developed, the legs of medium length, sloping, with straight, strong metatarsi. **FEET** Large and round, with close, arched toes. The nails are strong and arched, the pads large and tough.

COAT Flat, elastic, with a silky gloss to it.

COLOR (a) Black with well-defined tan markings ("brandl"); (b) reddish (fawn, reddish grizzle). A small white marking on the chest is admissible.

TEETH A perfect pincers bite, neither overshot nor undershot. Strong, sharp canines.

FAULTS Forehead too narrow; broad muzzle; curled ears, ears too pointed at tips; weak legs; short, weak or curled tail; tail without harsh hair on underside; height greater than length; any color not described above; lack of pincers bite; weak canines. ●

TYROLEAN HOUND

140 STEINBRACKE
GERMANY

GENERAL CHARACTERISTICS A medium-sized dog with a tricolor coat.

HEAD Light, lean, rather long; there should be no wrinkles.

EYES Clear, with a friendly expression; dark brown in color.

EARS Broad, carried close to the head; they are set on high and slightly rounded at the lower edge.

NOSE Uniformly straight from the stop to the tip.

TEETH Strong, meeting in a scissors bite.

NECK Long, robust, muscular at the nape.

CHEST AND THORAX Of medium breadth, but well let down; the brisket is slightly below the elbows.

BACK, LOINS, CROUP The back is short and straight, the withers are slightly raised, and the croup is moderately hollowed. All three are well developed.

TAIL Set on high, with a brushlike tip.

FOREQUARTERS Exceptionally well boned. The elbows are turned outward. Viewed from in front, however, the forelegs appear absolutely straight. **HINDQUARTERS** The thighs are broad and well filled out; the hind legs are long. **FEET** Long and oval, with abundant hair.

COAT Proportionately long, very dense and hard. **Color** White, the back dark, black and tan.

BONE STRUCTURE Fine but robust.

AUSTRIAN HOUND

Photo: K. Wolfram, S. A. Thompson.

142 TYROLEAN HOUND
Tiroler Bracke

AUSTRIA

This dog is probably descended from the old types of hounds which, from the mixtures of blood and appropriate selective breeding, have given birth to numerous local breeds adapted to various kinds of hunting and terrain.

GENERAL CHARACTERISTICS A small to moderately large dog, with bones of medium weight. Very muscular, with good tendons; the body outline is rectangular (slightly longer than high); the basic line is long and fluid, the backline is horizontal. Lively, resolute, with a fine sense of smell, the Tiroler Bracke is a capable, highly resistant tracker. It is used both as a coursing and a tracking hound.

WEIGHT AND SIZE Weight, 33-49 lb. Height: 15½-19 inches (miniatures, 12-15¼ inches).

HEAD Long, narrow, light-boned. The skull is lean and slightly rounded. The forehead is also slightly rounded, with a medial furrow which is not pronounced. The stop is fairly accentuated. The suborbital areas are finely chiseled. The nasal bridge is narrow and long, hollowed at the root, either straight or slightly arched. The muzzle is of moderate depth. The lips are quite short and close-fitting, moderately developed at the commissure. The teeth are strong, complete in number and closing in a scissors bite. The upper jaw is wider than the lower; the intermaxillary bone is narrow and fairly long. The nose is slightly protruding. The eyes are large, not deep-set; the shape of the eyes is either round or spherical-triangular. The color is dark brown, preferably, although medium chestnut is also permitted. The edges of the eyelids and the haw are pigmented. Medium width between the two supraorbital ridges. Eyes not excessively slanted. The lids must fit closely over the eyes. The occipital protuberance must be well in evidence in males and is desirable in females. The edge of the lower jaw is straight, with a slight curve in the area of the incisors. The depth of the buccal cavity is less than in Bloodhound type and in Pointers and Setters. The depth of the muzzle is moderate. The ears are fairly flat; their length is such that the tip reaches below eye level but does not reach the upper canines. They are broad, set on rather high and of fine cartilage. They hang straight, with no curl, with a longitudinal fold which is apparent but not excessively so. The tips are rounded.

NECK Of medium length, slightly shorter than the head, moderately arched and carried neither high nor low. It is lean and without dewlap.

TRUNK Back straight, long; withers long and prominent. The dorsal-lumbar region is firm, straight and moderately broad. The highest point of the back profile is the withers. The chest is well let down, rather more narrow than broad; the ribs are moderately wide. The brisket is well rounded. The sternum is long, not excessively protruding. The belly is only slightly drawn up (the flanks are of medium height). The legs are set fairly wide apart (the section forms two right angles situated on the shorter side). The croup is slightly hollowed, not excessively sloped, long and broad. The coxal bone is close to horizontal.

TAIL Set on rather high. It is long (when hanging, the tip reaches or slightly surpasses the hock), thin in its first half. It should be straight, slightly raised when the dog is in action. A saber tail is acceptable. A tail which is too high or excessively curved is faulty. Excessive tuft, untidy tail or flag are objectionable.

FOREQUARTERS AND HINDQUARTERS Shoulders long and sloping, muscling flat, upper arm slanted. The forearm is vertical, of moderate length; the shoulder and elbow are both well angulated. The pasterns are neither vertical nor excessively sloped. The feet are strong, with closed, well-arched toes. The pads are tough. The bone is neither coarse nor light. The axes of each segment of the forelegs should lie in a single plane. The thighs are broad, well muscled; the hind legs are long, slightly less muscular than the thighs. The axes of the hind legs should also lie in a single plane. **FEET** Short.

COLOR Basic color: black or red or reddish yellow. White on the muzzle, collar, chest, brisket, tip of the tail. **Tricolored dogs:** black saddle or mantle, brown-yellow or red markings on legs, thorax, belly and head; small white marks and a barely visible collar. **Faults:** obvious speckling, white collar too extended, too much white on legs.

COAT Smooth or wiry, thick, rather coarser than finer; undercoat; belly hairy; tail has good feathering. Flag or excessively bristly tail are to be considered faults.

GAIT Regular, free, fast, with good endurance. ●

AUSTRIAN COARSEHAIRED HOUND

143 AUSTRIAN COARSEHAIRED HOUND
Steirischer Rauhhaariger Hochgebirgsbracke

AUSTRIA

This dog comes from the Hanover, the Austrian, and the Styrian coarsehaired breeds, the latter being responsible for his characteristic rough coat. He is known and appreciated even outside his country of origin. He is an ardent worker and has an excellent disposition.

GENERAL CHARACTERISTICS A dog of medium size. The height at the withers is 15½-20 inches. The muscles are powerful. The tail is generally carried high and sometimes curved. The expression is grave but not vicious. Intelligent.

HEAD Of medium size, slightly

TYROLEAN HOUND

Photo: K. Wolffram.

FINNISH SPITZ

AUSTRIAN COARSEHAIRED HOUND

rounded. The occipital protuberance is well developed. The stop is not pronounced. The nose is black, cut straight at the front. The lips are not pendulous. The teeth are strong and close in a pincers bite. The hair is harsh, shorter than on the body and forming a moustache on the lips. The length of the head from the occiput to the tip of the nose is from 8½ to 9½ inches.

EYES Clear, varying from brown to yellow in color. The expression is intelligent.

EARS Should not be too big. They are flat and are clad in short hair which is less harsh than the body hair.

NECK The neck is strong, not too long and slightly arched.

BACK Fairly broad; it measures 25½-27½ inches from the occiput to the root of the tail, and should never measure less than 25½ inches.

CHEST AND BRISKET Well let down, Body circumference at the brisket is 26-31 inches.

BELLY Moderately tucked up.

TAIL Of medium length, never curled, strong at the root, well feathered; the lower part is tufted, but without forming a flag. It is carried slightly curled.

FOREQUARTERS AND HINDQUARTERS Vertical, muscular. The toes are well closed, the pads should not be too big.

COAT The hair is slightly curled, not obviously so. It is dull, hard and wiry. On the chest and the back of the legs the hair is slightly bristly.

COLOR Reddish and pale yellow. A white mark on the chest is acceptable, but other white markings are not. The "boots" which were allowed by earlier standards are no longer acceptable.

FAULTS Head too lean, ears curled or pointed; weak legs; tail too short, thin or curled upward; curly hair, too long, not consistent in texture; any color other than those prescribed by the standard; overshot, undershot jaws; weak canine teeth. ●

218

Photo: S. A. Thompson, K. Wolfram.

FINNISH SPITZ

FINNISH HOUND

144 FINNISH SPITZ
Suomenpystykorva

FINLAND

The genetic characteristics of this breed were fixed in 1812 in Finland. The breed was officially recognized when the Finnish Kennel Club was recognized by the FCI. The history of this dog is intimately linked to that of the Finnish people. He was bred for centuries, especially in the eastern zone of the country, and is mentioned in the *Kalevala*, the national epic of Finland. As the puppies are very delicate at birth the Finnish Spitz is quite difficult to breed. Each year not more than 150 specimens are inscribed in the *Book of Origins*.

GENERAL CHARACTERISTICS With an almost square body, the Finnish Spitz is a dog of bold bearing in which the entire appearance—and particularly the eyes, ears and tail—suggests a high degree of liveliness. He is characterized by a great eagerness for the hunt, by his courage and fidelity to his master.

SIZE Height at withers: males 17½-19½ inches; females 15¼-17¾ inches.

HEAD Medium-sized and without any loose skin ("dry"), with a slightly arched forehead and a pronounced stop. The muzzle is narrow and dry, tapering evenly as viewed from both above and the side. The nose is pitch black, the lips are tightly closed and thin.

EYES Medium in size, vivacious, preferably dark.

EARS Prick ears, sharply pointed, fine in texture, of an extraordinary mobility.

NECK Muscular, with a rather short appearance in males due to the thick coat; in females it looks somewhat longer.

BODY Back straight and powerful. The chest is deep. The belly is slightly drawn up.

TAIL Curves vigorously from the root forward, downward and backward, finally pressing against the thigh with the tip extending to the middle of the thigh. Uncurled, its length is sufficient to put the tip at the level of the hock joint.

FOREQUARTERS AND HINDQUARTERS Relatively straight shoulders. Strong, straight forelegs. Hind legs strong, hocks comparatively straight. **FEET** Preferably rounded.

COAT On head and legs, but not on back of head or back of legs, the coat is short and close-lying; on the body it is fairly long, the hairs are erect or semi-erect; on the neck and back the hair is stiffer. The top coat on the shoulders, and particularly in males, is considerably longer and coarser. On the back of the thighs and on the tail the hair is long and dense. The undercoat is short, soft, dense and light in color. **Color** On the back, reddish brown or yellowish red, preferably bright. The hair on the inner sides of the ears, on the cheeks, under the muzzle, on the breast and abdomen, inside the legs, behind the thighs and under the tail is of a lighter shade. White markings on the feet and a narrow white stripe on the breast can be permitted; also some black hairs on the lips and sparse separate hairs with black points along the back.

FAULTS Fleshy head, coarse muzzle, ears pointing forward at a sharp angle or ears with tips pointing outward or inward; ears curving backward or with slack points or with long hair on inside of ear; yellow eyes or wall-eyes; elbows turned inward, weak pasterns; slack tail or excessively curled tail; tail too long, soft, or too short; coat close, wavy or curly; muddy coloring; too distinctly defined differences between shades; dewclaws. ●

145 FINNISH HOUND
Suomenajokoira

FINLAND

GENERAL CHARACTERISTICS A medium-sized hound, well balanced, slightly longer than high, strong but not heavy. It is a tricolor dog of unambiguous sexual characteristics, calm, energetic and friendly; developed and used for hunting hare and fox.

SIZE Height at the withers; males 21½-24 inches; females 20½-23 inches.

HEAD Fairly lean, noble. Skull, when viewed from the front, evenly wide, domed at the top. Arches above the eyes clearly visible. Stern slightly convex when viewed from the side; the stop is not pronounced. Muzzle long (distance from tip of nose to inner corner of eye about equal to distance from there to occiput). Base of muzzle hollowed under the eyes, bridge of nose straight and almost evenly broad when viewed from above. Nose well developed, black. Nostrils large and mobile. Jaws powerful, the incisors of the upper jaw close tightly over those of the lower jaw; upper lip thin and nicely arched. Occiput and the hollows behind the ears clearly visible. When the dog is standing in repose, the nose is level with the back or a little higher.

EYES Dark, looking directly forward; the expression is calm and alert.

EARS Set fairly high, rather long and twisted so that the front rim of leather is close to the head, the back rim pointing out and forward with the tip almost directly forward.

NECK Straight, of moderate length, fairly lean.

BODY Chest is fairly long, mobile; brisket reaches to the elbows. Ribs well sprung. Front clearly visible. The belly is slightly raised. The back is of moderate length, straight and muscular. Flanks rather short and strong. The croup is well developed, broad and strong, slightly sloping; its outline continues the line of the back when viewed from the side.

TAIL Sturdy, reaches approximately to the hock, evenly tapering. As a rule it is carried at the height of the back or a little lower.

FOREQUARTERS Shoulders oblique and powerful, well fastened by muscles. Upper arms fairly long. Elbows pointing straight backward. Forelegs straight, strong and sinewy, only slightly bent at the pastern. **HINDQUARTERS** Moderately angulated. Front line of the hind legs evenly arching, without abrupt curves. Thighs broad, long, and well muscled. Knees pointing straight forward. Hock joints well developed. Pasterns sturdy and rather broad. **FEET** Fairly large, oval and compact. Toes pointing straight forward. Pads flexible and protected on the sides by dense hair.

COAT Close, of moderate length, dense and fairly harsh. The hair on the tail similar to that on the body. **Color** Black mantle; warm tan color on head, under the body, on shoulders, thighs and elsewhere on the limbs. White usually on head, throat, chest, lower parts of the limbs and tip of tail (white markings on neck and higher on limbs allowed). Not desirable are somber and "dirty" coloring, colors with abrupt borders, white with multiple spots of another color, rusty brown or faded yellowish-brown color, brown hairs in the mantle.

GAIT Light and springy, with long pace. When hunting, the dog usually gallops. ●

FINNISH HOUND

219

Photo: A. Wintzell, V. I. Iyrväinen, S. A. Thompson.

LARGE AND SMALL GASCONY BLUES

146 SMALL GASCONY BLUE

Petit bleu de Gascogne

FRANCE

This hound is generally used for hare hunting, as the hare leaves few prints and the hounds used for the hunt must have an excellent sense of smell. He is more resourceful and shows more determination than the general run of hounds. This descendant of the Gascony Blue appears to be worthy of his stock. Nowadays he is quite prevalent in southwestern France although relatively rare elsewhere.

SMALL GASCONY BLUE

GENERAL CHARACTERISTICS The Small Gascony Blue is generally used for hunting hare. A dog of great class and distinction, the dogs were bred down to a smaller size to proportion them better to their quarry; except for size the official standard for this dog is basically the same as for the larger breed. Shorter lines are required, along with greater homogeneity and cohesion of characteristics.

SIZE Height: 19-22 inches.

HEAD Finer than that of the Grand Bleu, rather long and light. The nose is black, with well open nostrils. The bridge is long without being pointed and is often slightly arched. The lips are not thick nor are they greatly developed, snugly covering the lower jaw. The skull is lean, rather narrow, sharply domed, with a well-marked occipital protuberance.

EYES Brown, with the eyelids bordered in black; the haw is not visible.

EARS Set on low and long, but they are often thicker and less curled than the ears of the Great Gascony Blue.

NECK Fairly long and lean, with a slight dewlap.

BODY The chest is higher than broad; the brisket is at the level of the elbows. The ribs are gently sprung, the back is fairly long and sustained. The loins are lightly curved and firm. The flanks are flat.

TAIL Long and slender.

FOREQUARTERS The shoulders are quite long and sloping. The legs are strong in relation to the rest of the body. The elbows are vertical. **HINDQUARTERS** The thighs are relatively flat in many dogs, even when well let down. The hocks are well directed. **FEET** Oval and fairly long, with black pads.

COAT The hair is quite heavy, dense and not too short. **Color** Besides blue, the coat may be white with black spots, with variable speckling over the white; tan spots over the eyes, on the head, on the inside of the ears and on the legs, as well as on the blue coat. **Skin** The skin, the lips, eyelids, nose and hard palate are black or veined with black. ●

Photo: Buzzini, E. Barolo.

SMALL GASCON OF SAINTONGE

147 SMALL GASCON OF SAINTONGE

Petit Gascon Saintongeois

FRANCE

148 ARIÉGEOIS

FRANCE

D'Aubigné, a great expert on French hounds, has written: "Among the French hounds of pure breed, the Ariegeois has always been the least known and the least prevalent outside its place of origin and neighboring provinces. Other varieties not better than he have enjoyed periods of popularity and diffusion but not the Ariégeois. His realm is in the southwest where he has been helped by the Gaston Phoebus Club, organized from

ARIÉGEOIS

1912 on pack trials at the Céron Villa, which demonstrated the great qualities of the Ariégeois. His lack of renown is perhaps due to the fact that the Ariegeois is not regarded as a completely pure breed. (As if a perfectly pure breed in the true sense of the word were possible!) It may also possibly be due to the modest statements of the local population who, with great modesty and considerable frankness qualify him as a 'half-dog' or 'half-blood' dog. There are always those who, fearing the pejorative term, would feel that they would somehow suffer dishonor through using a 'half-blood.' The explanation of this term, however, is that the Ariégeois hound has *two* strains of noble blood—that of the Gascony Blue and the Gascon of Saintonge. But there is also a third blood strain, that of the Briquet."

The Ariégeois dog is actually the product of the Briquet and a hunting hound. The crossbreeding was originally occasional, then became habitual, and selective breeding was carefully carried out. The breed improved, and once it became defined its standard was fixed by the Gaston Phoebus Club.

ARIÉGEOIS

GENERAL CHARACTERISTICS A light, slim, distinguished-looking dog, resembling a tracking hound except for size and weight, for the Ariègeois is lighter.

SIZE Height at shoulder: male 21½-23½ inches; female 21-23 inches.

HEAD Lean and long, rather light on the whole, with no wrinkles or throatiness. The skull is rather more narrow than wide, the occipital bone prominent. The muzzle is straight or very slightly curved; the nose is black, with open nostrils.

EYES Dark, well open, but not normally showing the haw because of the drooping eyelid. A gentle, affectionate expression.

EARS Thin, fine, with folds; set on low, not too long.

NECK Light, rather slim, long and slightly arched.

BODY The chest is deep, reaching almost to the elbow; it is a closed type of chest rather than a broad, open one. The ribs are long and moderately rounded. The back is generally robust and the loins are straight, of medium width and well muscled. The flanks are slightly drawn up and flat rather than round.

TAIL Well set on, scimitar-shaped, carried gaily.

FOREQUARTERS The shoulders are well directed, the forelegs straight, with wide forearms; the elbows are turned neither in nor out. **HINDQUARTERS** The rump is horizontal, neither lower nor higher than the hindquarters. The thighs are slightly flat, the hocks are neither too straight nor overly bent. **FEET** Lean and of the type called hare-feet.

COAT The hair is fine and close. Skin fine, supple, not closely adhering to the body. **Color** White and jet black, sometimes speckled or bluish, pale tan on the cheeks and above the eyes. Bright red is not a disqualifying color.

GAIT Medium gait, but thoroughly supple and easy.

DISQUALIFICATIONS Any coat other than those cited above; excessive roundness of the head; wrinkles; dewlap. ●

ARTOIS HOUND

149 ARTOIS HOUND
Chien d'Artois
FRANCE

This hound is considered the most adaptable for small packs for hare hunting. In former times, however, he was used for larger game and he was called the Picard. His white-orange coloration changed as a result of many crossbreedings, and his size also became so modified that he became a better hunter of hares than of larger game. He is usually referred to in France as the Briquet. According to Cornevin, this is a phonetic derivation of "braquet" or "brasquet," which means "small braque." As the Artois Hound shares many comparable points with the Braques it seems logical to suppose that he is the result of crossbreeding a hound with a Braque.

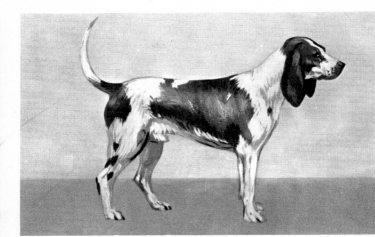

ARTOIS HOUND

GENERAL CHARACTERISTICS A type of French dog of average height, well shaped, muscular and not too long; differs from the Artésien Normand in that he has shorter lines, a noticeably leaner head and much flatter ears.

SIZE Height at shoulders: 20¾-23¼ inches.

HEAD Large, wide rather short, terminating in a slight peak. The skull is very slightly domed, the occipital protuberance scarcely evident. The forehead is wide and straight, slightly elongated. The lips are rather thick, slightly drooping and fairly accentuated. The nose is black, large, with open nostrils which occasionally cause the tip to seem slightly raised.

EYES Full, large, very open, with a sweet and melancholy expression; the eyelids are taut, totally concealing the haw.

EARS Rather thick, wide, almost flat, but fairly long; they are set on at the level of the eye.

NECK Rather long and powerful, with very little dewlap.

BODY The chest is fairly wide and moderately let down; the sides somewhat rounded. The back is of average length and well supported; it is well muscled, particularly at the shoulders. The loins are wide, muscular and slightly arched. The flanks are dropped and very full.

TAIL Rather long, arched, and of the sickle-tail sort.

FOREQUARTERS The shoulders are rather straight and very muscular; the forelegs are strong and upright, with a fairly long pastern. **HINDQUARTERS** Muscular, with the buttocks well attached to the loins, wide and slightly slanting. The thighs are dropped and well furnished, the hocks slightly bent. **FEET** Strong but lean, with fairly closed toes, which should be rather longer than too rounded. Good black pads, tough and compact.

COAT The coat is short, thick and strong. The skin is rather thick. **Color** Deep fawn tricolor, similar to the coat of a hare or badger, with either a mantle or large patches; the head is usually fawn, although it may be charcoal.

GAIT Supple accentuated composed —that is, with nothing of the force and speed of the English gun dog.

FAULTS Too short or insufficiently flat ears; a coat of any color other than specified above is a disqualification. ●

150 PORCELAINE
FRANCE

His origins are very old and much discussed. Swiss dog fanciers claim that the Porcelaine originated in their country, whereas the French are convinced that the dog is theirs. However this may be, it is certain that the breed has long been preva-

Photo: Buzzini

PORCELAINE

lent in France as in Switzerland. Nevertheless, some experts claim that the Porcelaine has been mentioned as a prevalent bloodhound in France since 1845, while in Switzerland it has been noted only since 1880 when the first modern hunting packs were formed.

After the revolutions of 1789 and 1830 surviving specimens were collected in an effort to safeguard the purity of the breed and to increase its number. Many individuals were found along the Franco-Swiss border. Thanks to constant and devoted care on the part of breeders, the breed soon made many friends abroad, especially among the English, who were enthusiastic hunters with hounds.

He is a beautiful dog. His name comes from his coat, which gives off reflective glints like genuine porcelain.

Photo: Buzzini.

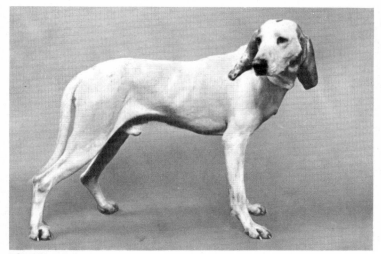

PORCELAINE

NIVERNAIS GRIFFON

GENERAL CHARACTERISTICS A small hunting dog very distinguished; a fine French dog which shows his breeding in every structural detail.

SIZE Height at shoulder: males 22-23¼ inches; females 21¼-22½ inches.

HEAD Should be typically lean and finely chiseled proportionately rather long. The skull is wide at the top, between the ears; the occipital protuberance is rounded. The forehead is flat and furrowed in the middle; the stop is fairly defined but not exaggerated. The muzzle is of good length, neither square nor pointed; the bridge is straight but with a slight rise at the tip. The nose is well developed and coal black. The nostrils are well open. The upper lips cover the lower without drooping. The mucous areas are black.

EYES Of normal development, they should be set deep and well sheltered under the eyebrows. The expression is gentle and intelligent.

EARS Thin, well curled, slightly pointed at the tips. They are as long as the muzzle. The ears ought never be set on above eye level.

NECK Fairly long and slender, with a slight dewlap—not flabby.

BODY The chest should be of average width but well let down, with correspondingly long but not flat sides. The withers should be prominent, the back wide and straight. Loins should be wide, very muscular, well attached and not too long. The belly is slightly drawn up but full.

TAIL Well put on, fairly thick at the root and tapering to the tip. Of average length, never erect, carried slightly curved.

FOREQUARTERS The shoulders should be long, well sloped, well muscled but lean. The forelegs should be fairly long, lean but not too fine, with the tendons fitting closely, straight and upright. **HINDQUARTERS** The haunches should be of good width or spaced apart, slightly projecting, somewhat slanting. The thighs are well let down, the muscles well in evidence, with no excess flesh. The hind legs are powerful, the hocks strong and set low to the ground, normally bent. **FEET** The feet are typically those of a French-bred dog—that is, with rather long toes, slender but close, with hard, tough pads.

COAT Smooth, fine, close and glossy, with no superfluous hair. The skin is fine and supple, mottled with many small black markings. **Color** Very white, with round orange spots, never merging as a mantle, however. These spots are generally found covering the black markings on the skin. The orange spots on the ears are characteristic of the breed.

GAIT Lively and gay, with a light, fluid gallop.

DISQUALIFICATIONS Lack of type; light eye or nose; harsh or excessively thick hair; excessively curved tail; orange spots too bright, bordering on mahogany, grayish or mingled with black hairs; spots concentrated into mantle; paleness of orange markings; absence of spotting undesirable but not disqualifying; too much or little height (an exception is made for otherwise excellent males who are suitable for stud and who may reach a maximum of 24 inches. Common faults limiting usefulness of breed include rickets, lack of compactness, excessive length. ●

much in evidence, and there is a slight beard on the chin.

EYES Preferably dark, occasionally lighter; the expression is vivid and piercing.

EARS Supple, set on at the level of the upper part of the eye. The ears are fairly well covered with hair; they are of moderate width, well shaped, not very long, and slightly twisted at the tips.

NECK Relatively light, lean, and without throatiness.

BODY The chest is let down as much as possible between the elbows. The brisket is not very wide. The rib cage is long and the first ribs are slightly flattened, the last ones more rounded. The back is rather long, the loin is sustained rather than arched. Belly slightly drawn up, but not as in the Greyhound.

TAIL Well set on, of the sickle type; not very long, better furnished at the middle. Occasionally the tip is slightly curved over the back.

FOREQUARTERS The shoulders are slightly on a slant, lean and set close to the body. The forelegs are fairly

strong but rather leaner, although this is concealed by the hair. They are fairly upright, although at rest they may appear slightly retrograde in profile. The pasterns are invariably rather short. **HINDQUARTERS** Fairly strong, with a slanting rump. The thighs are lean and rather flat. Hocks well let down and with a slight angulation. At rest the hind legs may be a little close under the body, but not exaggeratedly so. **FEET** Slightly elongated, but with good solid toes.

COAT Long, shaggy, bushy, fairly harsh, but never woolly or frizzy. The skin is pigmented, with black specks on the body and inner lips. **Color** Preferably wolf gray or blue-gray, with a trace of "gray" or wild-boar gray, or faded black or black, with tan cheeks and tan markings above the eyes, on the inner flanks and feet, or fawn peppered with black and white hairs, giving it a dark shading.

GAIT Supple, never abrupt or jumping.

FAULTS Round skull; short head; light eyes or walleyes; pink or maroon nose or scrotum; jet black, wheaten, or orange coat; tricolor with bright, clearly delimited markings; dewclaws. ●

151 NIVERNAIS GRIFFON
Griffon Nivernais

FRANCE

This dog is derived from the Gray St. Louis Dog, one of the great breeds that formed the celebrated French hunting packs which were scattered after the Revolution. The Nivernais Griffons also enjoyed a period of renown but thereafter they practically disappeared until the end of the last century, when a special club was formed which gathered the survivors and reconstituted the breed according to its original characteristics. The standard was published a few years ago.

GENERAL CHARACTERISTICS A typically rustic, shaggy breed with lean legs and fine muscles built for long, hard work rather than speed. Of a rather melancholy character but not nervous.

SIZE Permissible limits are 20-24 inches, with a tolerance of 1-2 inches

more; the ideal height is 21½-23 inches.

HEAD Lean and light, not small, fairly well eared, rather long. The skull is nearly flat, the forehead slopes gently to a straight bridge with little stop. The eyebrows are accentuated by the bristling hair. The nose is black,

NIVERNAIS GRIFFON

Photo: M. Pedone, Bonora, A. Gonin, Buzzini

VENDEAN GRIFFON BRIQUET

SMALL BLUE GASCONY GRIFFON

152 VENDEAN GRIFFON BRIQUET

Briquet Griffon Vendéen

FRANCE

GENERAL CHARACTERISTICS A medium-sized Griffon, intelligent and decisive, of distinguished bearing and gait. Short and well proportioned, robust without any suggestion of heaviness.

SIZE Height at shoulder: Male 20-22 inches; female 19-21 inches.

HEAD The head is rather short and light, but not exaggeratedly so. The skull is gently rounded and not overly imposing. The nose is black, substantial, with well-open nostrils. The muzzle is broad and straight, the stop well defined and well set off by the face hair and eyebrows. The mouth is covered with an abundant moustache.

EYES Dark, large and bright; the eyebrows are rich and pronounced but do not cover the eyes.

EARS Supple, narrow and fine, covered with long hair. The ears have pointed tips which are turned inward and should not be too long. They must be set on below eye level.

NECK Long and slender, without a dewlap.

BODY The chest is fairly deep and not too wide. The ribs are moderately rounded, the loins straight, well muscled, and well supported. The back is short and solid, straight or, even better, slightly rising.

TAIL The tail is short and set on high, a saber tail, not a sickle. It is thick at the root, tapering progressively toward the end; it is tufted.

FOREQUARTERS The shoulders are long, lean and slanting. The forelegs are straight, with a thick forearm; the elbows are low and held close to the body, with good bone. **HINDQUARTERS** The thighs are long and muscular, the hocks are wide and close to the ground. Cow hocks are never permissible. **FEET** Not too strong, with hard soles, well arched, close toes and solid nails.

COAT Long but not exaggeratedly so, sometimes bushy but always harsh to the touch. The undercoat should be well furnished, the inner thighs should not be bare. **Color** Fawn, hare-haired, white and orange, white and gray, white and hare-haired, tricolored with the foregoing colors.

GAIT A supple gait, symptomatic of a nervous animal.

FAULTS Oversized, undersized; too strong, Bassetlike head; undershot mouth; discoloration of inner lip; excessively long, flat, or short-haired ears; high ear position; cylindrical body; long back; roach back; elbow turning inward or outward; light bone; insufficient thighs; cow hocks; flattened foot; splay feet; excessive tail length; insufficient tail length; deviated tail; insufficient harshness of coat. ●

153 SMALL BLUE GASCONY GRIFFON

Petit Griffon bleu de Gascogne

FRANCE

This dog combines the best psychological characteristics of the two breeds used in his formation, the true Griffon and the Gascony Blue.

GENERAL CHARACTERISTICS A rustic-looking Griffon, solidly shaped, low slung, with a thoroughly French look about him, something halfway between the two breeds from which he was bred—the Griffon and the Gascony Blue.

SIZE Average height: 17-21 inches.

HEAD The occipital protuberance and the stop are barely marked. The skull is slightly domed, not too wide and pointed. The muzzle is straight or very slightly curved and is not as long as the Gascon's. The nose is black. The upper lips are not greatly developed, but they are sufficiently let down to

keep the muzzle from appearing pointed.

EYES Very expressive and bright, golden brown; they are smaller than the eyes of the Gascon and the eyelids are more closed.

EARS Slightly shorter and less draped than those of the Gascon Blue and are often nearly flat but nevertheless set on low, that is, at eye level; they have little hair.

NECK Rather slender with, however, a very slight dewlap.

BODY The chest is well developed and well let down to the level of the elbow. The back is rather long and

well supported. The ribs are rounded, but not exaggeratedly so. The loins are muscular and very sound. The belly is full and well drawn up.

TAIL Of good length, slightly curved and carrying out the curve of the rump; thin at the tip.

FOREQUARTERS The shoulders are fairly slanting, powerful, extremely well muscled. The forelegs are strong and broad, with short pasterns. **HINDQUARTERS** The rump is short, giving something of the appearance of a broad-backed small dog. **FEET** Round and very compact. The sole is full and the nails are extremely solid.

COAT Never woolly or frizzy, but dry and harsh, not too long, nearly flat on the body and slightly wavy on the thighs and chest. A little shorter on the head, where the eyebrows do not quite cover the eyes, although they are quite

bushy. Much shorter on the ears. The skin is black or white, marbled with black specks. **Color** White, with black markings and black speckling, the total effect being something like slate-blue. There are tan markings above the eyes (the French call it being "four-eyed"), and more or less bright tan specks on the cheek, the inner side of the ears, the chest and the legs. The bluish effect may be much less pronounced, with fewer black specks and only black markings on a white base, often with tan markings on the head and on the body parts mentioned above. The slate-blue dogs usually have black inner lips. Some specimens have a large blue-gray mantle, with the tips of the legs white or slightly speckled.

GAIT Regular and of great quality.

DISQUALIFICATION Any coat other than that described above. ●

154 TAWNY BRITTANY GRIFFON

Griffon fauve de Bretagne

FRANCE

Descriptions from the Middle Ages indicate that the anatomy and abilities of this hound, a very old breed, have varied but little through the centuries. The great Tawny Griffon packs of Brittany disappeared after 1885, when the wolf became practically extinct in Brittany, as this dog was especially adapted for wolf hunting.

GENERAL CHARACTERISTICS A dog of medium size, well boned and muscular, giving a strong impression of vigor and rusticity rather than of distinction.

SIZE Height: males 20-22 inches; females 18½-20½ inches.

HEAD The skull is rather long, with a well-defined occipital protuberance. Viewed from the front, the skull has the shape of a flattened arch, but not exaggeratedly so, dwindling in width to the level of the eyebrows, which are not strongly accentuated. The muzzle

TAWNY BRITTANY GRIFFON

Photo: Buzzini

is rather long, straight, and slightly hooked. The stop is fairly oblique, less accentuated than in the Vendée breed. The upper lips are not pendant. The nose is black or dark brown. Nostrils well open.

EYES Dark and bold in expression; the haw is not visible.

EARS Finely set on, at eye level. They are barely long enough to reach the muzzle. The tips are pointed and covered with a finer, softer hair than the rest of the body.

NECK Fairly short and muscular.

BODY The chest is deep and broad, well let down. The dog is well ribbed up, the back is short and wide. The loin is curved by the development of the muscles of the hindquarters. The belly is very slightly drawn up.

TAIL Of good shape, moderate length, well carried, often tufted and tapering to the tip.

FOREQUARTERS The shoulders are sloping, the forelegs are sturdy and straight. **HINDQUARTERS** The thighs are well fleshed out, the hocks and stifles well bent. **FEET** Close, lean and hard.

COAT Very hard, not too long, never woolly or frizzy. **Color** Fawn; the best colors are the golden wheaten and the bright red-brown.

FAULTS Thin, slender in general appearance; wide or narrow skull; eyebrows exaggerated; pointed, short muzzle with pendant lips; ears set on too low; ears too short, too long or covered with frizzy hair; belly too drawn up; thighs too rounded; slack, wide feet; black speckled or white coats to be avoided. ●

155 NORMAN ARTÉSIEN BASSET

Basset Artésien Normand

FRANCE

This is the first of the Basset Hounds that we have presented. A typical disproportion between his legs and his body makes it possible for him to penetrate thickets and brambles with ease.

GENERAL CHARACTERISTICS A long-bodied dog, his length exceeding his height, well standing, well built, showing great breeding.

SIZE Height at shoulders: 10¼-14 inches.

HEAD Dome-shaped, of medium size, with well-formed cheeks, its form not derived from muscular structure (as in the Bulldog) but solely from the skin, which has one or perhaps two wrinkles. On the whole, the head should have a lean appearance. The stop is well defined, but not in excess. The occipital protuberance is sometimes very noticeable. The bridge is of medium length, fairly wide, slightly rounded in front. The nose is black and wide, protruding slightly over the lips; the nostrils are well open.

EYES Large, dark, calm and serious in expression. The haw is sometimes visible.

EARS Set on as low as possible, in any case not above eye level. They are narrow at the base, well draped, supple, fine, very long (reaching to the tip of the muzzle) and pointed at the tips.

NECK Fairly long, with a little throat, but not in excess.

BODY The chest is characterized by a noticeably protruding sternum; the chest is moderately well let down, but wide and rounded. The ribs are well rounded to offset their lack of depth. The back is wide and well supported. The loin is slightly curved and the belly is slightly let down and full.

TAIL Well set on, rather long, robust at the root and tapering to the tip. It is sometimes carried as a saber tail, but never over the back. Tail must not be docked.

FOREQUARTERS The shoulders are rounded, strong and short; they are well muscled. The forelegs are short, big-boned, twisted or half-twisted, provided there is sufficient support to avoid deformation. They often have wrinkled skin on the pasterns. **HINDQUARTERS** The hips are slightly slanted, with a gentle curve at the croup. The thighs are very well fleshed out and muscular, and with the croup they form an almost spherical mass of muscle. The hocks are slightly bent and strong; they are often covered with several folds of skin.

FEET The feet are set upright, with rounded, well-shaped toes which are able to bear the dog's full weight, so that in snow or on wet ground the footprint of the Basset Artésien looks like that of a much larger animal.

COAT Close, short and smooth, without being excessively fine. **Color** Tricolor or white and orange bicolor. The former must be widely marked on the head with fawn and must have a mantle or markings, either black, hare-coated or badger-coated, ending with fawn on the feet.

GAIT Calm and easy; relaxed.

FAULTS Flatness of head; excessive width of forehead; flatness of ears; thick ears or ears set too high; short neck; slack or roach back; forelegs touching at the wrist or upright above fetlock; elbows turned inward or outward; flat ribs; flat feet; splayed toes; excessively long tail or deviated tail; flat thighs; closed hocks; pronounced haw.

DISQUALIFICATIONS Overshot mouth; straight legs. Black speckling not disqualifying but not to be encouraged. ●

NORMAN ARTÉSIEN BASSET

Photo: Buzzini, DIM.

BLUE GASCONY BASSET WITH PUPPIES

156 BLUE GASCONY BASSET

Basset bleu de Gascogne

FRANCE

This hound possesses valuable psychological qualities and a graceful carriage. We know little about his origins but it seems evident that his ancestors were the large Gascony Blue among which certain dogs were subjected to different crossbreeding until the new breed became definitely fixed.

GENERAL CHARACTERISTICS A superior Basset, large, fairly heavy but never too heavy, showing great good breeding.

SIZE Average height, 12-15¼ inches.

HEAD The head is lean and forms an elongated, pointed dome, with the occiput moderately accentuated. The skull is rather more narrow than wide. The forehead is long and has a very slight curve. The lips are accentuated, but not too much so. The muzzle is long and finely formed. The nose is black, with well-open nostrils.

EYES Deep brown, with a beautifully gentle expression not without a certain melancholy. In some specimens the upper eyelids have a slight droop which reveals a little haw.

EARS Set on low, well below eye level and well away from the skull. They are long, thin and folded, when stretched against the length of the jaws, they must reach at least the end of the muzzle.

NECK The neck is rather long, slightly arched; there is a fairly developed dewlap, but never in excess.

BODY The chest is well developed in length, quite wide and not greatly let down. The flanks are rounded, the back is long and well supported. The loins are short and often curved. The belly is slightly drawn up. The genitals are black.

TAIL Well put on and fairly long, sometimes but not invariably slightly curved.

FOREQUARTERS The shoulders are muscular but not heavy. The forelegs are strong and straight, with a typical Basset conformation. **HINDQUARTERS** The thighs are muscular, the hocks broad but sometimes rather straight and close. **FEET** Fairly strong, oval in shape, slightly elongated. The pads are black and strong, with black nails.

COAT Not too fine, well furnished. **Color** Blue or white with more or less extensive black markings, with or without saddle. More or less light tan markings above the eyes. Tan markings also on the cheeks, lips, and inner side of the ears, more or less accentuated. The skin is either black or white with black spots. The palate and inner lips are black.

FAULTS Pointed muzzle; undershot mouth; light eyes; depigmentation of markings.

DISQUALIFICATIONS Any coat other than those described above. ●

BLUE GASCONY BASSET

Photo: Buzzini.

157 VENDEAN GRIFFON BASSET

Basset Griffon Vendéen

FRANCE

As its name indicates, this breed comes from the Griffon Vendéen whose origins we have already discussed. He is proud and attractive in his expression and in the way he carries his tail. He is useful for the hunter of small and larger game, since he is adapted to hunting with the pack as well as to working alone.

VENDEAN GRIFFON BASSET

GENERAL CHARACTERISTICS A dog of a very slightly elongated structure. It has straight legs, and its stern is slightly lifted but not falling back on the loin. The hair is harsh, not silky nor woolly, and covers the whole body. The head is imposing, elongated and domed. Ears are fairly long and set on low, and have long hair.

SIZE Height. 15-16½ inches, with a tolerance of 0.4 inch more for exceptional specimens. The size for females has an upper limit about 0.8 inch less than for the male.

HEAD The skull is domed and elongated; not too wide, well formed under the eyes. The stop is well defined and the occipital bone is well developed. The muzzle is long and square at the tip; the bridge is very slightly hooked. The nose is black, well developed, with open nostrils. The lips are covered with a thick moustache.

EYES Large, dark, without whites, and have a pleasing expression, intelligent and friendly. The haw should not be visible. The eyebrows should fall forward but without covering the eyes.

EARS Fine, narrow and thin, covered with long hair and with elongated oval tips which are well turned inward. Set on below eye level, they should reach the tip of the nose at least.

NECK Long and robust, thicker near the shoulders, without throatiness.

BODY The chest is open, long and deep, the ribs well rounded. The loin is solid, well filled and slightly harped. The flank is rather more full than let down, and the rump is muscular.

TAIL Set on high, thick at the root, tapering regularly to the tip. It is fairly long and tufted and carried straight or slightly curved.

FOREQUARTERS The shoulders are lean and sloping, not turned outward, and close to the body. The forelegs are straight, with well-developed bone. The forelegs must not touch each other at any point. **HINDQUARTERS** The thighs are strongly muscular but not excessively rounded. The hocks are wide and bent; they must never be completely straight. **FEET** Large and close, with a hard sole and solid nails.

COAT Harsh and not excessively long, flat, never silky nor woolly, not too abundantly feathered. **Color** Self-color: more or less dark fawn, hare-haired, gray-white (fawn is not recommended). Bicolor: white and orange, white and black, white and gray, white and tan, white and hare. Tricolor: white, black and tan; white, hare and tan; white, gray and tan. **Skin** Fairly thick, often marked white and black or white and gray in tricolor specimens.

GAIT The three gaits should be effortless.

FAULTS Head flat and short, nose stingy or discolored; light eyes; pointed muzzle; jaws uneven, ears flat and with small amount of long hair; ears set on high; neck too short; height below or above standard limits; slack back, saddleback; forelegs touching at wrists, forelegs bowed; elbows turned outward; flat or fat feet, splayed toes; hocks too bent or too straight, close or open; flat thighs; tail too curved or carried on the hocks; hair silky, woolly or frizzy.

MINIATURE VARIETY

GENERAL CHARACTERISTICS A small, lively, strong dog with a very slightly elongated body. Tail carried proudly. Hair hard and long, but without excess. Head with a good expression; ears well-turned but not too long, set below eye level, and with long hair.

SIZE Height 13½-15 inches, with a tolerance of ⅜ inch lower for minimum.

HEAD Skull slightly domed, neither very long nor very broad, well formed under the eyes. The stop is well defined, the occipital bone fairly well developed. The nose is black, well developed, open and well out. The muzzle is much shorter than in the standard variety. It is, however, very slightly elongated and square at the tip. The bridge is straight. The lips are furnished with a fine moustache.

EYES Fairly large, without white; intelligent expression. The haw should not be visible. The eyebrows fall forward but should not conceal eyes.

EARS Supple, narrow and thin, covered with long hair. The tips are slightly oval, turned inward and not quite long enough to reach the end of the nose.

BODY The chest is fairly deep but not too wide. The ribs are moderately

VENDEAN GRIFFON BASSET

TAWNY BRITTANY BASSET

rounded. The loin is straight, muscled, well supported. The rump is well muscled and fairly open.

TAIL Set on high, fairly thick at the root, tapering evenly to the tip. It is tufted and not very long; it is carried as a saber tail.

FOREQUARTERS Shoulders are lean and sloping, well joined to the body. The forelegs are well boned in proportion to the dog's size; they are straight, with a good forearm and a very slightly marked wrist. **HINDQUARTERS** The thighs are muscled and slightly rounded. The hocks are fairly broad and slightly bent; they must never be straight. **FEET** Not too

strong, with a hard sole, close toes, strong nails.

COAT Harsh but not too long, never silky or woolly, fewer fringes than in the standard variety. **Color** The same as for the standard variety, with fawn also not recommended for the miniature.

FAULTS Too long in the body, head too flat, spotted or miscolored nose, light eyes, snipy muzzle, uneven jaws, flat or badly set ears; scanty hair; bad back; twisted or half-twisted legs, hocks too bent or too straight, flat thighs; tail too long, too curved or carried on the hocks; hair insufficiently curled; silky or woolly. ●

158 TAWNY BRITTANY BASSET

Basset fauve de Bretagne

FRANCE

The origin of this breed is the same as that of the Great Tawny Griffon. This dog underwent numerous crossbreedings with the Vendean Basset in particular. He resembles the breed

230

Photo: Buzzini

TAWNY BRITTANY BASSET

from which he is derived by his head characteristics, the quality of his coat, and the color and tilt of his tail. However, since he hunts in a region of steep cliffs and extensive moors he has been bred to develop certain physical characteristics, especially those of stature, limited to an approximate minimum of 15 and maximum of 17 inches.

GENERAL CHARACTERISTICS In head, coat, color and carriage the Basset Fauve resembles the breed from which he is descended. Since he has to work in thickly wooded country crossed by high hills, he must be a smart, alert dog, perhaps a little dumpy overall, but with a good Basset appearance. With straight or only slightly curved legs, he is a relatively fast dog for his size.

SIZE Height at the shoulders: 13-14 inches.

HEAD The skull is of moderate length, the occiput well defined. Viewed from the front, the skull has the shape of a flattened dome, diminishing in width to the level of the eyebrows, which are not highly accentuated. The muzzle is either straight or very slightly arched and rather long. The lips are quite pendant. The nose is black or dark, with well-open nostrils.

EYES Dark, alert; the haw is not normally visible.

EARS Thin, set on at eye level, not too low; they are of moderate length, barely reaching the nose when measured against the muzzle.

NECK Fairly short and muscular.

BODY The chest is quite wide and well let down, the ribs are rather long and slightly rounded. Since the dog is a Basset, it has a rather long back, but not excessively so; indeed, perhaps not as long as most Basset strains. Broad, sustained loins, muscular and sound. The flank is full.

TAIL Thick at the root, the sickle tail is not very long; it tapers toward the tip.

FOREQUARTERS The shoulders are slightly slanted; the forelegs are straight or slightly curved, well muscled and strong. **HINDQUARTERS** The thighs are muscular, the hocks wide, strong, and moderately bent. **FEET** Lean, close and hard.

COAT The hair is harsh, close, rather short, flat, never woolly, never tousled. The skin is rough to the touch. **Color** Golden wheaten or fawn, more or less dark, with occasionally a white spot on brisket and neck; such marking, however, is not to be encouraged.

GAIT Lively.

DISQUALIFICATIONS Difference in size of 1½ inches more or less than standard; legs excessively curved; head too short; flat ears; long hair; woolly coat; coat other than specified above.

159 ANGLO-FRENCH TRICOLOR

Anglo-Français tricolore

FRANCE

While the Foxhound was used for the English strain in the case of the large Anglo-French hounds, the smaller Harrier was employed for the medium-sized hounds.

These Anglo-French medium hounds were long referred to as "bastards" but subsequently were labeled according to their origin, such as Harrier-Poitevin; Harrier-Porcelaine; Anglo-French dogs born from crossbreeding the Harrier with a short-haired medium-sized hound and also Anglo-French born from crossbreeding the Harrier with a French medium-sized long-haired hound.

Since 1957 they have been regrouped as Anglo-French Tricolor, Anglo-French White and Black, and Anglo-French White and Orange. To date no standard for this dog exists.

160 ANGLO-FRENCH WHITE AND BLACK

Anglo-Français blanc et noir   FRANCE

ANGLO-FRENCH WHITE AND BLACK

161 ANGLO-FRENCH WHITE AND ORANGE

Anglo-Français blanc et orange   FRANCE

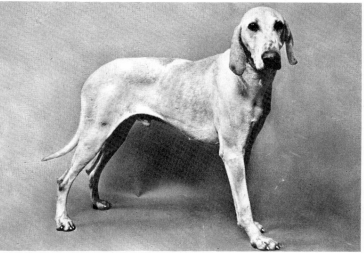

ANGLO-FRENCH WHITE AND ORANGE

Photo: Buzzini, Bonora.

RUNNING HARRIERS

162 SMALL ANGLO-FRENCH

Petits Anglo-Français

FRANCE

These Anglo-French dogs derive from crossbreeding the Beagle or Beagle Harrier with medium-sized French shorthaired hounds. Up to now they have no established standard since they are not sufficiently homogeneous. At shows it has been left to the judges to evaluate the psycho-physical characteristics of these dogs according to their origins. In general they are tri-colors and occasionally white and black or white and orange.

163 MODERN HARRIER

GREAT BRITAIN

The word "harrier" comes from "hare" and denotes the dog selectively bred to take part in mounted hare hunts. Formerly such hunts consisted principally in following the dogs that pursued the quarry and blocked its flights, its doubling back, feints, and other ruses. The dogs were therefore selectively bred to develop their sense of smell, a quality essential to the Harrier.

However, toward the end of the last century, the hare hunt became more and more like the fox hunt; the hounds following the quarry closely in order to force it to flee in a more or less straight line thereby enabling the horsemen to enjoy a good gallop across the countryside. As more hares were caught by this method than by the former manner, the hunters, performing a function merely as horsemen, became less interested in the hunt in itself, and thereby determined the transformation of the Harrier.

Today's Harrier is a very handsome small hound possessing excellent qualities, compact, perfectly balanced, very fast, of good endurance, and with an excellent sense of smell which breeders had developed to the highest degree by the end of the last century. In any case, the modern Harrier hunts not only the hare but, with equal impartiality and spirit, the fox as well.

GENERAL CHARACTERISTICS A strong, light dog, less powerful but more distinguished than the Fox-hound.

SIZE Height: 19-22 inches; an upper limit of 19½-20 inches is preferable.

HEAD Expressive, not so broad as the Beagle's; rather long muzzle, more pointed than square or wedge-shaped. Black nose, rather well developed. The lips cover the lower jaw. The skull is flat, and the occipital protuberance is slightly evident.

EYES Smaller, less rounded, slightly deeper-set than in the case of the Beagle.

EARS V-shaped, almost flat, slightly turned, rather short and set on quite high.

NECK Long and free, but well rooted in the shoulders. Slightly rounded in its upper part.

BODY The chest is more developed in depth than in breadth. The ribs are deep and well sprung, running well back, with plenty of heart room. The back is straight and muscular. The loins are strong and slightly arched. The belly is neither too full nor tucked up. The haunches are strong and well set off.

TAIL Of medium length, lightly tufted and carried well.

FOREQUARTERS AND HINDQUARTERS The shoulders are sloping and muscular, the forelegs well directed. The thighs are long and well let down. The hocks should be neither too straight nor too angulated. **FEET** Neither too closed nor too long.

COAT Smooth in the style of English dogs, that is, flat rather than short. **Color** Normally white as base color, with all shadings from black to orange (tricolor); a black saddle covering the entire upper torso and back also occurs in this breed. **Skin** White with black markings.

GAIT Sure and easy.

DISQUALIFICATIONS Loins long or soft, weak thighs, Dudley nose, undershot jaw. ●

SMALL ANGLO-FRENCH

MODERN HARRIER

Photo: W. Chandoha, A. Roslin-Williams.

MODERN HARRIER

164 SOMERSET HARRIER
GREAT BRITAIN

When fox hunting became popular at the end of the nineteenth century, many owners of hound packs, wishing to follow the style and hunt the fox from horseback, extended their efforts to increase the speed of their dogs through crossbreeding.

As opposed to the older and classic Old English Harrier, the Somerset Harrier has increased his speed to the detriment of purity of blood and his original characteristics.

SOMERSET HARRIER

GENERAL CHARACTERISTICS A strong, well-built dog, very typical, with a highly intelligent expression.

SIZE Height at withers: about 21½ inches.

HEAD Fairly long, with a broad, flat skull. The occipital protuberance is scarcely noticeable, and the stop is not pronounced. The nose is black and fairly large. The bridge is straight. The lips cover the lower jaw but must not be pendulous.

EYES Brown or hazel, rather dark.

EARS Set on extremely low, they are flat, moderately long, thin and soft.

NECK Fairly long, with a slight dewlap.

BODY The chest is broad and well let down. The backline is straight, the ribs robust. The loins are broad and muscular and gently arched. The flanks are fairly well filled out. The haunches are strong and well set off.

TAIL Set on as a continuation of the loins, the tail slightly tufted is carried gaily.

FOREQUARTERS The shoulders are long and sloping. The forelegs are straight and well boned. The pasterns are very slightly bent. **HIND-QUARTERS** The thighs are muscular, the hocks well let down. **FEET** Neither too closed nor too round.

COAT Fairly thick but absolutely flat. **Color** Completely white, white and pale tan, white and orange, white and gray, white and fawn. ●

165 BEAGLE HARRIER
GREAT BRITAIN

Although he is usually classed among the English hound breeds, the Beagle Harrier appears to be of French origin. Baron Gérard actually succeeded in establishing the points of the Beagle Harrier by breeding specimens that possessed the hunting qualities of the two breeds that gave him birth. As his name indicates, the breed is a cross between the Beagle and the Modern Harrier. It was meant to produce a dog which would combine the Beagle's fine sense of smell and inborn hunter's instinct with greater size and increased speed.

..The different conformation of the Beagle and the Harrier at first resulted in somewhat heterogeneous specimens, but finally a homogeneous type was arrived at. Its genetic characteristics are still those defined by the standard of Baron Gérard, who wished to obtain a hound especially adapted for hunting the roebuck.

GENERAL CHARACTERISTICS A gracefully built dog, well balanced and distinguished, of good substance, lighter than the Beagle. The Beagle Harrier is a typical light, elegant hunting dog, with a good solid general appearance, agile and vigorous. Its expression is lively, energetic, friendly and intelligent, mirroring frankness, courage, temperament and speed.

SIZE Height: 17-19 inches.

HEAD Quite noticeably less powerful than that of the Beagle, the Harrier's head is nevertheless sufficiently broad is more or less equal to that of the skull; the muzzle must not be and capacious. The occiput is not prominent. The nose is black and fairly large. The length of the muzzle

BEAGLE HARRIER

Photo: Buzzini.

is more or less equal to that of the skull; the muzzle must not be square; in profile it must be seen to taper, although it is never pointed. The bridge is quite straight, never arched. The lips cover the lower jaw. The stop is not pronounced. The occipital protuberance is barely noticeable.

EYES Smaller and deeper-set than those of the Beagle. They are well open, of dark color, and are of a frank, courageous, intelligent expression.

EARS V-shaped, almost flat, turned against the sides of the head. They are not very long and are set on above eye level.

NECK Long, free and well carried; it must never be weak.

BODY The chest is well let down, fairly open, not very narrow, since there must be good heart and lung room. The sternum is projected well back. The false ribs should be long and sufficiently well sprung to provide ample room. The back is short, well sustained, muscular. The loins are strong and preferably slightly arched, although the chief requisites are breadth and good muscling. The flanks must not be excessively filled out, but at the same time they should not be drawn up: a well-filled-out flank is preferable to one like a Greyhound's. The haunches are well set off, sloping and strong.

TAIL Of medium length, lightly tufted and carried gaily.

FOREQUARTERS The shoulders are long and sloping. The forelegs are straight and vertical. **HINDQUARTERS** The thighs are well let down, muscular, well fleshed out. **FEET** Not too round nor too long. They should never be flat or crushed, but rather well closed. The pads are thick and tough.

GAIT Soft, lively and sure.

COAT Quite thick, not too short, lying flat. **Color** Not very important in the Beagle Harrier. The dog is generally tricolor, with more or less bright tan markings or black speckling. Since there are gray Harriers, the gray and white-gray tricolors must not be disqualified nor even penalized for that reason.

FAULTS Frightened appearance; soft or stupid appearance; head too heavy, with excessive stop; arched bridge, short or square muzzle, pointed muzzle; Beagle-type ears; curled ears, indicative of French-bred type; coarse-appearing body, common or massive body; insufficient depth or breadth of chest; legs not vertical and straight; lack of muscle; jumpy, crooked gait; all other signs and symptoms of temperamental and physical deficiencies which may be detrimental to the good use of the dog. ●

166 BEAGLE
GREAT BRITAIN

The Beagle is the smallest of the English hounds and greatly resembles the Harrier except that his legs are shorter. Just as the Harrier is a small Foxhound, the Beagle is a miniature Foxhound particularly adapted to hunting the hare and wild rabbit which rarely escape his pursuit.

He has a characteristic harmonious voice; in fact, the cry of the pack is almost like a choir, which is why he is referred to in England as the "singing Beagle."

The Beagle is much esteemed by specialists for his small size, sturdy temperament, and exceptional speed. Although there exist other excellent small-sized dogs, for example the well-known French Bassets, Beagles and Bassets are not the same, because they are the products of two different concepts. In the case of the Basset the size and speed were diminished by shortening the legs, resulting in a dog greatly appreciated for his graceful, easy gait and vociferous style. The Beagle, on the contrary, was reduced not only in the length of his legs but in his

Photo: Hollyman (Photo Res.).

BEAGLE

overall size, which resulted in a marvelously proportioned dwarf, well balanced, harmonious, and very speedy.

According to experts the Beagle is a very ancient breed going back ot the third century. The English used him for rabbit hunting, but inasmuch as they favored speed (for them the hunt is above all an occasion to go horseback riding) they were not long in crossing him with the Harrier and finally replacing him with this breed. The Beagle's survival is due only to the perseverance of some breeders.

Queen Elizabeth I possessed numerous packs of these small hounds which she esteemed highly. She herself caused to be bred a special variety of very small proportions, called the "Elizabeth Beagle" as well as the "Pocket Beagle" and "Glove Beagle," since it was so small that it could be put into a pocket.

GENERAL CHARACTERISTICS A compactly built hound without coarseness, conveying the impression of great stamina and activity.

SIZE Maximum and minimum for desirable size are 16 and 13 inches, respectively.

HEAD Fairly long, powerful without being coarse; skull domed, moderately wide with an indication of peak; stop well defined, muzzle not snipy and lips well flewed. Nose black, broad, with nostrils well expanded.

EYES Brown, dark hazel or hazel, neither deep-set nor bulgy and with a mild expression.

EARS Long, set on low, fine in texture and hanging in a graceful fold close to the cheek.

NECK Moderately long, slightly arched, with throat showing some dewlap.

BODY Short between the couplings, well let down in chest, ribs fairly well sprung and well ribbed up. Loins powerful and not tucked up.

TAIL Of moderate length, set on high and carried gaily, but not carried over the back.

FOREQUARTERS Shoulders clean and slightly sloping. Forelegs quite straight, well under the dog, of good substance and round in bone. **HINDQUARTERS** Very muscular about the thighs; stifles and hocks well bent and hocks well let down. **FEET** Round, well knuckled up, strongly padded.

COAT Smooth variety: smooth, very dense and not too fine or short. Rough variety: very dense and wiry. **Color** Any recognized hound color. ●

A BEAGLE PACK

167 OTTER HOUND
GREAT BRITAIN

As we have seen, the Foxhound was employed in England for the fox, the Harrier for the hare and the deer, the Bloodhound for the boar, the Beagle for the hare and especially the wild hare. The Otter Hound is another specialist among hounds, as he chases the otter which lives in burrows whose entrances are below water level. The otter gives birth and raises its young in the dry upper galleries. The otter is an excellent swimmer and lives on fish and is therefore the bane of fish-breeders who see their reserves being depleted. The Otter Hound possesses the necessary abilities to hunt the otter in its natural habitat.

As far as the origins of the Otter Hound are concerned, some hold that he descends from a cross between the Rough-Coated Terrier and the Southerhound or the Harrier and a Rough-Coated Terrier or Griffon. (It appears that some Nivernais Griffons were imported into England for this purpose.) Others believe that the Otter Hound descends from the Bloodhound and from an unknown dog that gave to this breed its characteristic rough coat.

GENERAL CHARACTERISTICS A dog of moderate size, short and square, reminiscent in many traits and general bodily makeup of the Bloodhound, although smaller. The coat is harsh, wiry and disordered. The dog has great resistance to fatigue and rough weather. He has a keen sense of smell.

WEIGHT AND HEIGHT Weight: 66-77 lb. Height: males 23½-25½ inches, females proportionately smaller.

HEAD Of the same general type as that of the Bloodhound; it is well shaped. The skull is domed. The nose is black, the lips are well developed and fairly heavy, hanging down but without the Bloodhound's wrinkles.

EYES Dark, very deep-set, with a serious expression. The haw is visible and deep red in color, so that the eyes seem bloodshot.

EARS Long, hanging in a beautiful fold and covered with long hair.

NECK Muscular and moderately long.

Photo: J. Cooke (Photo Res.), A. Wintzell, R. Kinne (Photo Res.).

OTTER HOUND

The dewlap is abundant. The thick, heavy hair gives an impression of a shorter neck than the Otterhound actually has.

BODY The chest is deep and broad; the back is strong, long and arched; the loins are strong and slightly arched.

TAIL Without a curve (unlike photo) carried gaily.

FOREQUARTERS Of correct form, with good articulation. **HINDQUAR-** TERS Well developed, with hocks low and well bent.

COAT Harsh, bristly, closed at the roots; it covers the entire body. It is slightly less coarse on the muzzle. The woolly undercoat protects the dog from the harshness of the climate and from water. Large bushy eyebrows.

Color Acceptable colors include gray, yellow mixed with gray and black, reddish, black. Tan or black markings are sometimes found. ●

168 HELLENIC HOUND
Ellinikós ichnilátis
GREECE

GENERAL CHARACTERISTICS This dog is scientifically classified as belonging to the braccoid group of dogs, and in practice is considered a hunting dog, specifically a tracking hound. It is of Greek origin. Mesomorphous, shorthaired, with a black coat with tan markings. Strong, vigorous, lively and intelligent, this breed is characterized by an extremely sensitive sense of smell. It is an active hunter, either alone or in the pack. It re-

OTTER HOUND

HELLENIC HOUND

Photo: R. Kinne (Photo Res.), A. Roslin-Williams.

sponds with everything it has on all types of terrain, in both the lowlands and the mountains, and even in rocky areas which are hard for a man to get through. Its voice is resonant and pleasing.

WEIGHT AND SIZE Weight: 37-44 lb. Height: males 18½-21½ inches; females 18-21 inches.

HEAD Long; its total length reaches 4.35/10 of the height at the withers. The width of the skull at the cheeks should not be greater than the total length of the head; therefore the cephalic index must be less than 50. The upper cranial-facial lines are divergent. The length of the skull is equal to or slightly less than the length of the muzzle. The muzzle itself is rectilinear or, in males, very slightly arched. The tip of the nose is located on the muzzle line, overhanging the forward vertical lip line. It is humid, mobile and black. The stop is not very pronounced. The skull is slightly flat, and the occipital protuberance is not notably evident. The jaws are strong, meeting perfectly in either a scissors or a pincers bite. The teeth are strong and white. The lips are well developed. The forehead is quite broad, the medial furrow is not pronounced. The supraorbital ridges are prominent.

EYES Of medium size, neither protruding nor deep-set. They are brown, with a lively, intelligent expression.

EARS Of medium length (approximately half the length of the head), set on high (above the cheekbones). They are flat and rounded at the tips; they hang vertically.

NECK Powerful, muscular and without dewlap. It descends to the shoulders in a graceful line; its length is about 6.5/10 the total length of the head.

BODY The length of the trunk is about 10 percent more than the height at the withers. The backline is straight, slightly rising at the loins; the belly line is slightly rising. The chest is well developed, deep, let down to the level of the elbows. The ribs are only slightly sprung. The withers are slightly higher than the backline, which is straight and long. The loins are slightly arched, short, strong and very muscular. The belly is lean and slightly drawn up. The croup is broad, long, well muscled and slightly hollowed.

TAIL Not long, at maximum length only reaching to the hocks, It is set on rather high, thick at the root and tapering toward the tip. In movement the tail is curved.

FOREQUARTERS The shoulders are sloping, muscular, close to the body.

The forelegs are straight and vertical, viewed both from in front and in profile; they are muscular and strong. The upper arm is oblique, the forearm long and straight, exceptionally well boned. The wrist is lean and not prominent, the pastern is fairly long, strong, quite straight. The feet are round and compact, with strong, closed, well-arched toes. The nails are robust, curved and black. The pads are large, hard and tough. **HINDQUARTERS** Straight and vertical, viewed from behind or in profile; they are robust and muscular. The thighs are long and vigorous. The leg above the hock is slightly slanted, and the hock is bent so as to give a general impression of straightness to the entire leg. The metatarsus is lean, quite long, nearly straight, and without dewclaws. The feet are similar to the forefeet.

COAT Short, dense, rather hard, very consistent and close-fitting. **Color** Black and tan. A small white spot on the chest is allowed. The lips, eyelids, nose and nails are black.

GAIT Swift and light.

FAULTS (disqualifying faults are in italics)

Height at the withers over or under standard (tolerance, ¾ inch above or below); short, broad muzzle, *hollowed or excessively pointed; overshot or undershot jaw; convergence of upper longitudinal cranial-facial axes;* ears too long, too short, pointed, curled, *semiprick;* neck too short, weak or too thick or with dewlap; backline arched or hollowed; belly line too let down or drawn up; flat or narrow loins; short, narrow, nonsloping croup; *monochidism, cryptorchidism;* tail too long, too thick or *curled;* hocks too open or too close; *legs out of vertical;* pasterns or metatarsi too long, too short, weak or not straight; *dewclaws; harefeet; colors different from those specified above for coat, nose, eyes and nails; flesh-colored nose, lips, eyelids.*

SCALE OF POINTS

General appearance	20
Head (skull and muzzle)	15
Eyes	5
Ears	5
Neck	5
Trunk	15
Legs	20
Tail	5
Coat	10
	100

RATINGS

Excellent: points not less than	90
Very good	80
Good	70
Fair	60

169 CIRNECO DELL'ETNA
ITALY

One might conclude from a study of Mediterranean breeds that the Cirneco's origins go back to the Greyhounds of antiquity, as is precisely the case with the Pharaon Hound (now located in the Balearic Islands) with which, except for general dimensions, it shares many common points. The Phoenicians carried on a lucrative trade in Greyhounds which they obtained in Africa and later in Asia and which they brought to the coast of Greece and the Greek islands, then to Sicily and the other islands of the Mediterranean.

Today there does not exist a true type of Greyhound in Sicily, probably owing to the fact that those brought by the Phoenicians to the Sicilian shores became adapted thereafter and then were modified into the present Cirneco. The ancient Greyhounds suffered a progressive loss of stature probably because of scanty food, a lack of great spaces to run in, and repeated interbreedings. Nevertheless the upstanding ears, a characteristic typical of the ancient Greyhound, has remained unchanged.

In its present form the Cirneco dell'Etna is doubtlessly indigenous to Sicily where it has been found since time beyond memory. Numerous archaeological artifacts, as well as carved stones and ancient coins, bear witness to this. At Adrano, where the breed is prevalent today, there has existed since prehistoric

times a temple dedicated to a local divinity which was guarded, according to Aelian (*De Natura Animalium*) by Cirneco dogs that possessed a supernatural instinct which impelled them to attack the sacrilegious and thieves while enthusiastically welcoming the devout.

The Cirnecos are the only dogs now used for hunting on the slopes of Etna. Although they are specialists at hunting the wild rabbit and the hare, they also hunt any kind of feathered game: pheasant, partridge, woodcock, gray partridge, and quail. They work slowly, nose to the ground, following the traces of the game with patience and concentration. They are absolutely silent and are only heard when they are digging or following closely.

GENERAL CHARACTERISTICS Scientifically this dog belongs to the graioid group, according to the classification of Pierre Mégnin. As a working dog it is classed as a hunter and tracker. Origin Italian. The general conformation is subdolichomorphous, with a body outline fitting into a square, harmonious in respect to shape (heterometric), and slightly unharmonious in respect to profile (halloidism). The Cirneco's function is chiefly that of a hunter of rabbits that are found among the volcanic rocky terrain of Italy. Light but robust in constitution, the Cirneco has an excellent nose and great resistance, being especially adapted to rough terrain.

WEIGHT AND SIZE Weight: males 26½-31 lb; females 22-26½ lb. Height: males 18-19½ inches; females 16½-18 inches.

HEAD Dolichocephalic; its total length may be 4/10 of the height at the withers. The length of the muzzle is approximately that of the skull. The width of the skull should not be more than half the total length of the head. The cephalic index, therefore, should not exceed 50. The directions of the upper longitudinal axes of the skull and the muzzle are parallel. A slight divergence is admissible. **Nose** Large, the upper surface slightly rounded, with large, well-open nostrils, wet and cool. It is positioned

CIRNECO DELL'ETNA

on the same line as the bridge and, seen in profile, protrudes from the plane of the forepart of the muzzle. The pigmentation, in fawn, light fawn or fawn-and-white dogs, may be flesh-colored or brown; in dark fawn dogs a dark brown nose is acceptable, but it must never seem black nor should it ever be completely black. **Nasal Bridge** Straight (for its length and its direction in regard to the upper longitudinal axis of the skull see HEAD). The width of the bridge, measured at its midpoint, should be about half its length. **Lips and Muzzle** The lips are of fine and thin texture, not very high, nor very prominent in profile or seen from the front, and consequently the commissure is quite high and not plainly visible. The upper lips, seen from in front, show at their lower edge where they meet, a suggestion of a semicircle, that is, of a semicircle with a very wide chord. The lower lateral profile of the muzzle is determined by the lower jaw. The lateral sides of the muzzle are convergent, consequently the muzzle is rather pointed, and its forepart is small. The edges of both the upper and lower lips should be brown and never black. The suborbital region should be sharply chiseled. **Jaws** Of normal size, and meeting in a perfect scissors bite. The teeth are white, completely developed and complete in number. The lower jaw is very nearly straight. **Stop** Not pronounced and slopes gently. Because of the outline of the forehead and the muzzle, it may be said that the stop is practically nonexistent. **Skull** Flat, slightly oval. Its length is equal to the length of the muzzle. Its width from cheek to cheek should not be more than half of the total length of the head (cephalic index:50). The medial furrow is very slight; the occipital protuberance is not prominent. The skin on the skull and muzzle should be close fitting without wrinkles and stretched over the underlying tissues in such a way as to give a lean and streamlined look to the head. The sinuses are not very large.

EYES Of medium size, oval in shape; they are deep-set with well-fitting lids. The eyes are in a lateral position, and in color may be ocher, amber and gray, not brown or dark hazel. The pigmentation of the edges of the lids is brown, flesh-colored, but never black.

EARS Set on high, above the zygomatic arch; they are triangular, rigid and erect, and in length they reach at most the midpoint of the total length of the head, and it is preferable that they be shorter. The tip of the ear is not rounded, but pointed. The cartilage is thicker at the base. The auricles are close together at the point of insertion.

NECK The length of the neck, measured from the nape to the fore edge of the withers, and while it is extended, is almost equal to the length of the head, that is, 4/10 of the height at the withers. It is well arched, and there is a well-marked distance from the nape to the point of insertion, and the neck must fuse harmoniously with the shoulders at the point where it joins the body. The skin should be well fitting, and the lower line of the neck must be absolutely free of any suggestion of dewlap.

FOREQUARTERS **Shoulder** Long, lean, very free in its movements, with the points close to each other. The scapulae in length should be 1/3 of the height at the withers, and with a slope varying between 50° and 55° from the horizontal. **Upper Arm** Well joined to the body, with long, lean muscles; its direction is parallel to the medial plane of the body. Its length is half the height of the foreleg at the elbow. Its slope from the horizontal is between 60° and 70°, thus the scapula-humeral angle is about 115-123°. **Forearm** Straight and vertical, with light bone, and the elbows should lie in a plane parallel to the median plane of the body. The height of the entire foreleg, from the ground to the elbow, is 56 percent of the height at the withers, and therefore slightly more than half of the height at the withers; consequently, the dog is slightly high on its legs. **Wrist and pastern** Seen from in front, they must follow the straight vertical line of the forearm; the pastern, seen in profile, is slightly extended, and its length is about 1/6 of the length of the foreleg from the ground to the elbow. The wrist is clean-cut and there is no bony growth of cartilage. **FOOT** Oblong (harefoot), with the toes well closed and arched, covered with short, dense hair; the pads are lean and hard, leathery and brown; dogs with fawn or white coats have flesh-colored to brown pads. The nails are strong, curved, with the same color as the pads.

BODY The length of the trunk, measured from the point of the shoulder (scapula-humeral joint) to the point of the buttock (point of the ischium), is equal to the height at the withers. **Chest** Moderately full; its width between the upper arms should be approximately 25 percent of the height at the withers, but no more than that. The manubrium of the sternum is situated at the level of the point of the shoulders. **Rib cage** Let down to the level of the elbow, deep, but the ribs are not greatly sprung. The rib arches should be well open. The sternum is long: in profile it is outlined by a straight line which ascends gently toward the abdomen. A dog 19½-20 inches at the withers should have a thoracic circumference of 23¼ inches, and a depth of 10-6/10 inches; the vertical thickness of the thorax should be 38 percent of the height at the withers. The thoracic index should not be more than 7. The back is long and straight, and its length is approximately 31 percent of the height at the withers. **Withers** Raised and narrow, because the points of the scapulae are close together. **Loins** Well joined to the backline, slightly filled out in profile, without great breadth. Their length is less than 1/5 of the height at the withers. **Belly** Lean, not greatly drawn up, and its lower outline ascends toward the flank very slightly. The flanks should be almost equal in length to the lumbar region. **Croup** Robust and flat. Its slope should be 45° from the horizontal, which means that the croup is hollowed. Its length is ⅓ of the height at the withers, precisely 33.3 percent of that dimension. **Sexual organs** In the male there should be a perfect, complete and uniform development of the testicles.

TAIL The tail is set on low because of the slope of the croup. It is uniformly thick for its entire length, in repose it is carried as a saber tail while at attention it is raised above the croup. Its length should be ½ or ¾ inch more than the height of the foreleg at the elbows; in a dog 19½ inches high at the withers, the tail should be 12 inches long.

HINDQUARTERS **Thigh** Its length should be ⅓ of the height at the withers, which means that is long. It is broad and covered with flat muscling; its rear edge is very slightly filled out, and the point of the buttocks is evident. The direction of the thigh is slanting from above down and from back forward. In respect to the vertical, it should be parallel to the medial plane of the body. **Hind legs** Covered over their entire length with lean muscles, and lightly boned. The external saphenous vein is well defined. The leg is slightly shorter than the thigh, and its slope is 50° from the horizontal. **Hock** The sides of the hock cannot be too broad; its forward angulation is very closed, because of the slope of the tibia (50°). The hock is low because the distance from the ground to the point of the hock should not be more than 27 percent of the height at the withers. Seen from behind, the backline from the point of the hock to the ground should be on the vertical and on the extension of the line of the buttocks. **Metatarsus** Should be lean; its length depends on the height of the hock; seen from behind and in profile, it should be perfectly vertical. There should be no dewclaws. **FOOT** Less oval than the forefoot, but otherwise with all the characteristics of the latter.

COAT **Hair** Very short on the head, ears and legs; longer, smooth and close lying on the trunk and tail. It is of very hard texture. **Color** Solid fawn, with all of its gradations. Fawn with a white line on the head and chest, white on the feet, at the tip of the tail and on the belly. Solid white or white with orange markings are accepted; a white collar is not desired. A fawn coat peppered with lighter or darker hairs is accepted. **Skin** Well fitting in every part of the body, and fine. The pigmentation of the lips, nose and eyelids should never be black, but more or less dark brown, and the color of the pads and nails should also be brown.

GAIT A long pace, with a jumpy trot.

FAULTS **General Characteristics** Undistinguished overall appearance, heaviness, lack of symmetry. **Height** Below or above the standard. **Head** A slight divergence of the upper cranial-facial axes. **Nose** Above the bridge line. Short, badly chiseled muzzle; lips overdeveloped below. Square muzzle. Accentuated commissure. Slight overshot condition not spoiling the general outer appearance of the muzzle. Unsound or incomplete dentition. Skull not flat, and broad at the zygomatic arches. Overdeveloped occipital protuberance. Pronounced stop and accentuated medial furrow; excessively high supraorbital ridges. **Eyes** Small or prominent; brown or dark hazel color; round eyes; eyes not set to the side. Partial depigmentation of the eyelids. Ectropion or entropion. **Ears** Longer than half the overall length of the head; hanging or slanting outward, with a very rounded tip. Thin cartilage; ears set on low or far from each other; hair on ears not short. **Neck** Short, thin or massive, insufficiently arched at the nape; neck with dewlap, not well integrated with the shoulders or lacking in detachment from the nape. **Forequarters** Straight shoulders, short, heavy shoulders or lacking in freedom of movement. Points of the scapulae far apart. Upper arm too slanted or top straight, short, deficient in muscular development. Forearm out of vertical; converging or diverging elbows; spongy bone; absence of furrow between the tendon and bone above the knee. Spongy, small wrist, with evident hypertrophy of the wrist bones; pisiform bone not clearly evident. Pastern out of vertical, short or too long, too extended or straight, thin. Wide foot, crushed foot; insufficiently arched toes. Feet turned in or out; deficiency of pigmentation in feet. **Body** With longitudinal diameter greater than the height at the withers. Narrow or broad chest, little let down; manubrium of the sternum too low. Height, depth and circumference of the rib cage insufficient; narrow or too broad rib cage; carenation; xiphoid appendix curved upward; short sternum, rib arches insufficiently open. Ribs too little or too well sprung; interrib spaces not broad; false ribs short, low and not open, not sufficiently well sprung. Short back, saddleback (lordosis), roach back (kyphosis); break in the backline at the eleventh vertebra. Low hocks. Long, flat loins, badly muscled, narrow or weak. Belly excessively drawn up or too low; flanks very hollowed or long. Incomplete development of one or both testicles (see **Disqualifications below).** Insufficiently hollowed croup, short, rounded, narrow. **Tail** Too long or too short, set on high; thin or not uniform in thickness, flaccid, hanging; very short hair or tufted. **Hindquarters** Short, narrow thigh, insufficient muscular development of thigh; carried away from the stifle, too straight or too slanted. Short legs, insufficiently or excessively sloping, with scant furrow between the tendon and bone above the knee little evident. Hock out of vertical, high, narrow; angulation of the hock open or too closed; deviation forward of the metatarsus (beneath itself in the rear). Metatarsus long, thin, out of vertical; dewclaws. **Feet** As for the forefeet. **Coat** Hair not sufficiently short on the head and legs, short on the body and tail; tufts on the back side of the legs and the underside of the tail. Thick skin, not closely fitting to the underlying tissues; dewlap; depigmentation on the nose and eyelids. **Gait** Ample, not jumping; slow trot in hunt.

DISQUALIFICATIONS Stature below 17½ or above 20½ inches in males; below 15¾ and above 19 in females. Convergence or accentuated divergence of the cranial-facial axes. Totally depigmented nose or black nose. Hollow bridge. Undershot or accentuated overshot condition. Black pigment in edges of eyelids; wall eye. Hanging ears; rounded tips or bat ears. Monorchidism, cryptorchidism. Black nails; black pads. Lack of tail; brachyurism, either congenital or artificial; tail curled on back. Streaked coat, solid brown or liver coat; black or brown markings, presence of black or brown hairs. Black mucous areas.

SCALE OF POINTS

General appearance and stature	20
Skull and muzzle	25
Eyes and eyelids	10
Ears	20
Shoulders	10
Rib Cage	10
Loins and croup	15
Legs and feet	10
Coat and color	15
Tail	15
	150

RATINGS

Excellent: points not less than	140
Very good	130
Good	120
Fairly good	110

CIRNECO DELL'ETNA

CIRNECO DELL'ETNA

170 ITALIAN SHORT-HAIRED SEGUGIO

Segugio Italiano a pelo raso

ITALY

Unlike hunting with a setter or Pointer, hunting with the Segugio has special features. With this type of dog the hunt is aimed at direct contact with the quarry, be it wild boar or smaller animals like fox, hare, or wild rabbit.

In Italy, no doubt because of the terrain, hunting from a stationary position using one or two Segugio hounds is generally preferred. A sport, one may say, considerably less ceremonious than that of earlier times (with hundreds of dogs, many horses, beaters, trumpets, participants in full livery, and many other features) and within anyone's reach.

Italy has had since ancient times a hound which has been unsurpassed for hare hunting. His sense of smell is exceptional. He searches out the track of the game and, once he has found it, never leaves it. Putting his highly developed intelligence to the test, vying in evasive action with his prey, he raises the quarry, follows it closely, and chases it to within firing distance of his master, confidently waiting at his position.

The origins of the Italian Segugio are very old, and we repeat here that all hounds (except northern hounds which descend from other stock) go back to the coursing dogs of ancient Egypt which the Phoenician merchants, starting with Greece, spread along the coasts of the Mediterranean where they were frequently used as a medium of exchange with the local populations.

These racing dogs also arrived quite soon in Italy where they bred with Mastiffs and produced the setter. The original breed was evidently unchanged, or almost unchanged, in all its points. We are able to determine through examination of artifacts going back to the times of the Pharaohs that the famous racing dogs of ancient Egypt were quite similar to the hounds of today and above all to the Italian Segugio. These dogs have, among other peculiarities, low-hanging ears, a sign of their domestication.

Today the Segugio is very prevalent on the Italian peninsula, although the specimens which fulfill the official standard are unfortunately rather rare. This is due to the irrational crossbreeding carried out by those who wanted only to produce a dog to hunt hares without consideration for the purity of the breed. This concept is of course mistaken, since the Segugio's good qualities would be even greater as the breed became more pure.

GENERAL CHARACTERISTICS Scientifically this breed belongs to the braccoid group, according to the classification of Pierre Mégnin. As a working dog it is classified as a tracking dog. Italian origin. The ancient lineage of the breed is shown by the fact that dogs of the same type and stature are depicted in two ancient statues, the *Diana the Huntress* (Naples Museum) and *Diana with Bow and Arrow* (Vatican Museums). In the castle of Borso d'Este there is a painting which shows the perfection of the Italian Segugio. The general conformation is that of a mesomorph, whose body outline is square, harmonious in respect to form (heterometric), and unharmonic in respect to the profiles (halloidism). The Italian Segugio is not a very effusive dog; he is of lively and courageous temperament, strongly built, of perfect symmetry and of well-developed bone, lean, with excellent muscles and with no trace whatsoever of fat. His well-balanced build makes it possible for him to follow game from dawn to dusk. High withers are not required, but they should be slightly above the level of the croup. The dog is used for hunting both on level ground and in the mountains, and on the most difficult terrain. He responds perfectly to these tasks; besides being a dog of great resistance, he is fast and courageous, alone and in the pack. His voice is resonant and highly likable. There are two varieties: a longhaired and a shorthaired type. The principal type characteristics are: head with upper cranial-facial longitudinal axes divergent; stop not pronounced; eyes positioned semilaterally, large, expressive; muzzle with convergent lateral sides, with an arched upper profile; lips not greatly developed, yet sufficient to establish the lower outline of the muzzle; ears set on the zygomatic arch, very wide, flat, long, with sharp points and a very slight internal volute; uniform tail, small, with a root which is neither strong nor robust; long, carried as a saber tail.

WEIGHT AND HEIGHT Weight: 39-62 lb. Height: Males 20½-23 inches; females 19-22 inches.

HEAD Dolichocephalic; its total length is 4.5/10 of the height at the withers; the length of the muzzle should be half the total length of the head; so that the midpoint of the head falls on the horizontal line joining the two inner corners of the eyes. The width of the skull should be less than half the total length of the head, and therefore the total cephalic index should not exceed 44. The directions of the upper longitudinal axes of the skull and of the muzzle are divergent, and if the upper line of the nasal bridge is prolonged it should emerge not only before the occipital protuberance, but on the midpoint of the length of the skull. The head, in every part, should show no wrinkles, and the skin should always be well fitted to the underlying tissues, that is, very smooth and tight: the head, in other words, should show an absolute tightness of skin. **Nose** Seen in profile, the nose protrudes beyond the forward vertical line of the lips; the nostrils are well open and mobile. The pigment of the nose is always black. The opening of the nostrils is slightly lateral, and the two wings are not on the plane of the nasal septum, that is, the forward edge of the wings of the nose does not meet the length of the nasal septum. **Nasal Bridge** Slightly convex (arched); for its length, see HEAD below, as well as for its direction in respect to the cranial axis. Its width, measured at the midpoint of its length, should be 17 percent of the total length of the head, or 34 percent of the length of the nasal bridge itself. **Lips and Muzzle** The upper lips, seen from in front, show a semicircle at their lower edge, that is, a semicircle with a very wide chord. The lips are of fine, thin texture, not very developed as to height, neither in front nor in profile, and therefore the commissure is not accentuated. The lower lateral profile of the muzzle, in spite of the fact that the lips are not high, is nevertheless determined by the lips themselves. The edges of the lips, both upper and lower, should be absolutely black. The sides of the muzzle are convergent, and therefore the forepart of the muzzle, although not flat, is nevertheless decidedly not pointed. The suborbital region should be chiseled, so that it is very lean, as is indeed the entire head. **Jaws** Not robust in appearance, with normal development,

and with the teeth closing in a perfectly even bite. The lower jaw is straight; the body of the jaw is not greatly developed in the front. The teeth are white, regular, and should be complete both as to number and development. **Stop** Not pronounced; consequently, the sinuses are not greatly developed. **Skull** Its length should be equal to the length of the muzzle, and its width should be less than half of the total length of the head (see HEAD). The zygomatic arch should therefore be flat. Seen from above, the skull is an elongated ellipse: its upper longitudinal axis is divergent from the longitudinal axis of the muzzle. Sinuses, as already mentioned, are not greatly developed. The medial furrow is not pronounced. The occipital protuberance should be neat and prominent without exaggeration, in such a way as to be readily visible; longitudinally it should be short. The interparietal crest is not pronounced. The temporal muscle is not highly developed over the parietals, giving the appearance of an extremely lean head.

EYES The eyes should be large, luminous and set in semilaterally: the inner corner of the eyelids should be at an equal distance from the forward edge of the nose and from the extreme outer point of the occipital crest. The eyes are normal, and should be neither deep-set nor protruding. The color should be dark ocher, and the eyelids should be normally close-fitting to the eye. Because of the position of the eyes, they are rather almond-shaped. The pigment of the eyelids should be black.

EARS In this breed the ears have certain characteristic features not found in other tracking hounds. The ears should be hanging, triangular, flat in almost their entire length, and very broad. The apex should end in a tight point, and should never be broadly rounded. The cartilage should be thin, but rather rigid throughout its entire length, and its insertion, which is very rigid, is characterized by a tension which draws the entire ear forward and does not permit it to relax, nor to fold over on itself or to curl. The point of the ears is turned slightly inward, that is, with a very slight internal volute. They are set on at the level of the zygomatic arch, or slightly beneath. The length of the ear is 66-70 percent of the total length of the head, and not less than 30 percent of the height at the withers.

NECK The length of the neck, measured from the nape to the forward edge of the withers, and while the neck is extended, is almost equal to the length of the head, that is, it should be 2/5 of the height at the withers. At its insertion into the head, the neck is well separated from the nape: similarly, it should fuse harmoniously into the shoulders. The neck is very lean and light, and it should give the impression of not being highly muscled; nevertheless, its upper edge is still slightly arched. The throat is entirely free of any suggestion of dewlap.

FOREQUARTERS Shoulders Should be long, lean, very free in movement; the points of the scapulae are very close to each other. Its slope should vary from 45° to 55° from the horizontal. **Upper Arm** Well joined to the body, the upper arm should be like the shoulder equipped with long, lean muscles and should not be excessively filled out with flesh. The scapular-humeral angle is 110°, based on a scapular angle of 45°. **Forearm** Not heavily boned, the forearm is a straight vertical line. The forearm should give the impression of a dry, very lean member. The elbows should be in a plane parallel to the medial plane of the body, and therefore they should turn neither in nor out. The height of the foreleg to the elbow is 56 percent of the height at the withers. **Wrist and Pastern** Seen from in front, the wrist and pastern should continue the straight vertical line of the forearm; they are smaller than the forearm, and should be dry, covered with fine, delicate skin, with a minimum of subcutaneous tissue. The wrist is neat, free of any sign of bony cartilage, with the pisiform bone protruding. The pasterns, whose length should not be less than 1/6 of the entire foreleg to the elbow, when seen in profile, should be rather extended. **Foot** Oval in shape (harefoot), with

ITALIAN SHORTHAIRED SEGUGIO

ITALIAN SHORTHAIRED SEGUGIO

closed, arched **toes**, covered with short, dense hair; the pads are lean and hard, rugged and black. The nails are strong, curved and black.

BODY The length of the trunk, measured from the point of the shoulder to the point of the buttock, is equal to the height at the withers. **Chest** Moderately full; the manubrium of the sternum should be positioned at the level of the point of shoulder. **Rib cage** It reaches below the level of the elbow; it is deep, but the ribs are not greatly sprung. The rib arches, however, should be well open. The sternum region is long: the profile of the sternum is determined by a straight line which ascends toward the abdomen. The circumference of the rib cage should be more than ¼ of the height at the withers, and its height should be 38 percent of the height at the withers. **Withers** Raised over the backline, and narrow because of the closeness of the scapulae. The backline is straight, and its length is about 31 percent of the height at the withers. **Loins** Well fused with the backline, slightly convex when seen

from the side, and with good broad muscles. Its length is a little less than 1/5 of the height at the withers. **Belly** Very lean, but not greatly drawn up, and the croup is considered to be horizontal, since its slope, from the haunch to the set on of the tail, is about 10°. **Sexual Organs** In the male, perfect and complete development of both testicles.

TAIL Set on high on the line of the croup, it is not robust, but delicate and thin at the root, and is uniform throughout its length, except for the point, which is fine. Its length is 57 percent of the height at the withers, and it is considered long, although its point, when the dog is in normal stance, is very close to the point of the hock. The tail is carried as a saber tail, and is covered with very stiff hair on both upper and lower sides.

HINDQUARTERS Thigh Long, broad, covered with prominent muscles clearly separated from each other: its upper edge is very slightly curved, and the point of the buttocks is very

evident. Its length should not be less than ⅓ of the height at the withers, and therefore it is 33 percent of that height. Its direction is rather slanted from above to below and from behind forward; in respect to the vertical, it should be parallel to the medial plane of the body. **Legs** Covered with lean muscles, even in their upper parts: the furrow between the tendon and bone above the knee is well marked and evident, the outer saphenous vein is prominent. Its length is slightly less than the length of the thigh, and its slope is 40° from the horizontal. **Hocks** The hocks are considered to be low, since their distance from the point of the hocks to the ground should not be more than 27 percent of the height at the withers. Their sides cannot be too broad; the forward angle is closed, because of the accentuated slope of the tibia (40°): seen from behind, the backline which goes from the point of the hocks to the ground should lie on the vertical and on the extension of the buttock line. **Metatarsus** Robust and lean: its length depends on the height of the hocks; seen from behind or in

profile, it should be perfectly vertical. **Foot** Less oval than the forefoot, but otherwise with the same characteristics.

COAT Hair The coat of the Italian Segugio is found in two variants: short hair and normal; in both the difference in hair quality is the only difference. In the shorthaired variety, the hair should be dense and glossy, uniformly smooth, fine, and short both on head and ears, trunk, legs and tail. Its texture is hard. In the normal variety there may be a few coarse hairs scattered over the trunk, muzzle and even on the legs: such harsh hairs, which are usually isolated, do not constitute a fault, since they indicate only the presence of long-haired blood, and such crossing is not only not forbidden but is recommended, since the breed is a single one differentiated into two varieties only because of the nature of the coat. In the second variety, the hair is coarse on the head and ears, trunk, legs and tail. The length of the hair on the trunk should not be more than 2 inches. On the head, ears and muzzle, the hairs are generally less coarse than on the trunk and lips: their length, which however is limited, provides the so-called beard. On the supraorbital arches, the hairs should be of limited length, so as not to cover the eyes or to fall down over them. **Colors Permissible:** solid fawn in all of its gradations, from deep reddish fawn to very pale fawn; black and tan. The tan markings, as in all black and tan dogs, should be distributed over the muzzle, eyebrows, chest, perineum, legs (from the wrist to the foot and from the tarsus to the foot). The fawn variety may have white on the muzzle or skull (mask, symmetrical or unsymmetrical), neck, pasterns and metatarsi, feet and the tip of the tail; a white star on the chest. White, however, is not desirable: the less of it there is, the better. Black and tan may have a white star on the chest: in that case, the dog is called "tricolor." Brown (including coffee, liver) is not allowed. **Skin** Close-fitting all over the body; it should be thin and fine: in the coarsehaired variety, it is thicker. There should be no trace of dewlap; the head should not have wrinkles. The pigment of the lips, nose and eyelids, of the nails and the pads should be absolutely black. A black hard palate is desirable but not essential.

GAIT During the hunt, a gallop.

FAULTS Height over or under. **Head** Longitudinal cranial-facial axes parallel (a serious fault); is converging, disqualification. Hollow bridge (disqualification). Short or badly chiseled muzzle. Lips over developed below; flaccid and falling (disqualification). Skull broad at the zygomatic arches, not oval; supraorbital ridges too raised; absence of occipital protuberance; stop prominent and not sloping. **Eyes** Small or too prominent; light color; walleyes (disqualification). Eyes in frontal or subfrontal position; ectropion (a very serious fault); entropion. Partial depigmentation of the eyelids; total and bilateral (disqualification). **Pigmentation** Depigmentation of the nose and the edges of eyelids; total or major depigmentation of the nose and of the edges of the eyelids (disqualification). Diminishing of intensity of pigmentation (a serious fault). **Ears** Short; set on above the zygomatic arches; folded longitudinally, that is, from the base to the tip; curling; rounded tips. **Neck** Short, with dewlap; insufficiently detached from nape. **Forelegs** Straight, short, fleshy shoulder; points of scapulae wide apart. Forearm out of vertical; spongy; divergent or convergent elbow. **Wrist** With evident hypertrophy of the wrist bones, spongy; pisiform bone not sufficiently evident; short pastern; pastern too long, too extended or straight, or out of vertical. Round foot (cat-

foot); foot fat, with splayed toe; foot broad, crushed; insufficient arching of the toes; carried outward or inward: not in vertical; deficient in pigmentation of nails and pads. **Body** With longitudinal diameter greater than the height at the withers. Rib cage too low, too shallow, not of sufficient circumference; too narrow or too wide; decidedly carenated; xiphoid appendix curved inward; false ribs not sufficiently open. Backline broken at eleventh vertebra; saddleback (lordosis); roach back (kyphosis). Belly too drawn up or too low; flanks hollowed and long. Loins long, flat, narrow. Croup narrow, hollowed. Monorchidism (disqualification); cryptorchidism (disqualification); incomplete development of one or both testicles (atrophic) (disqualification). **Hindquarters** Thigh short, narrow, deviated from stifle area, too straight or too slanted. Leg with insufficient furrow between the tendon and bone above the knee; short; not sufficiently sloping. Hocks high, not broad; hock angulation open, or too closed because of the forward deviation of the metatarsus (beneath itself posteriorly); out of vertical. Metatarsus long, thin, out of vertical; dewclaws. **Foot:** As for the forefoot. **Tail** Too long, too short; lack of tail or brachyurism, either congenital or artificial (disqualification); set on too low or too far forward; tail thick at the root. In the shorthaired variety, the presence of hairs which are not short on the un-

derside of the tail; fringe in the rough variety. Carried curled over the back; lateral deviation; flaccid, hanging; mousetail. **Coat** Hair too long and hard in shorthaired variety, silky or woolly in rough variety. Slate or lead color (disqualification); streaked (disqualification); coffee, brown or liver (disqualification); prevalently white (disqualification). Thick skin in shorthaired dogs, overabundant skin; dewlap; wrinkles on the head; traces of depigmentation on the nose and eyelids; total depigmentation of the nose (disqualification); depigmentation of the edges of the eyelids; depigmentation of the vulva and vent. **Gait** Continuous ambling (disqualification); continuous trot during the hunt (disqualification).

SCALE OF POINTS

General appearance	20
Skull and muzzle	35
Eyes and eyelids	5
Ears	20
Shoulders	10
Rib cage	15
Loins and croup	10
Tail	10
Legs and feet	15
Coat and color	10
	150

RATINGS

Excellent: score not lower than	140
Very good	130
Good	120
Fairly good	110

ITALIAN SHORTHAIRED SEGUGIO

244

Photo: Fotostampa-Embrione.

ITALIAN SHORTHAIRED SEGUGIO

171 ITALIAN COARSE-HAIRED SEGUGIO

Segugio Italiano a pelo forte

ITALY

Except for his coat, this Segugio possesses the same psycho-physical attributes as those of the Italian Shorthaired Segugio.

ITALIAN COARSEHAIRED SEGUGIO

ITALIAN COARSEHAIRED SEGUGIO

245

Photo: Prato.

172 DUNKER
NORWAY

DUNKER

GENERAL CHARACTERISTICS The Dunker is a strong but not heavy dog of rectangular build. He should be built for staying rather than sprinting.

SIZE Height at the withers: 18½-21½ inches; especially well-built males may reach 22½ inches at the withers.

HEAD Should be clean-cut and of fair length, with no loose skin. It should not be wedge-shaped, nor carried too high. The skull should be slightly arched, the occipital protuberance should be clearly defined. The stop should be neither too sharp nor too large, yet should stand out in good definition. The muzzle should be rather long than short, its bridge straight and of uniform width. The nose should be black, with well-open nostrils. There should be no prominence in the cheeks. The teeth should meet in a scissors bite.

EYES Dark, rather large but not protruding. They should be clear, with a calm expression. The lids should be firm, not loose and hanging. China-blue eyes (clear blue) are permissible in blue merles.

EARS Should not be set on too high; exaggerated low placement is preferable to bring exaggeratedly high. They should be of medium width, soft to the touch, slightly rounded at the ends, carried flat and close to the head. The leather must not be too short and should reach the midpoint on the muzzle when drawn forward.

NECK Rather long, with no dewlap.

BODY The back should be straight, strong, and not too long. The loins should be broad and well muscled. The croup should be well muscled and slightly sloping. The chest should be spacious, with good spring of rib. The back ribs should be particularly long, giving a longer appearance to the chest. Depth of the chest should be one half the dog's height. The belly should not be drawn up.

TAIL Should reach to the hocks or a little beyond. It should be strong at the root and taper gradually to the point. It is carried with a gentle curve but not curled.

FOREQUARTERS Shoulders should be long and sloping, well muscled, fine at the withers and placed close to the chest. The forequarters should be well angulated, with straight legs and springy pasterns, not upright. **HINDQUARTERS** The hind legs should be well angulated, the thighs and second thighs broad and strong. The hock joint should be broad and close to the ground. Viewed from behind the hind legs should be perfectly straight. Dewclaws are not permissible. **FEET** Compact, well arched, the toes should have hair between them, and the pads should be thick and strong.

COAT Close, hard, straight, not too soft. The hind legs and tail may have more hair than the rest of the body. **Color** Black or blue merle, with fawn and white markings. Deep chestnut is objectionable; predominantly white with blue merle markings or liver should disqualify. ●

173 HALDENSTOVER
NORWAY

GENERAL CHARACTERISTICS A strong, long-bodied staying dog of medium size.

HEAD Medium size, well chiseled and well balanced. Skull slightly domed, with a slight occipital protuberance. The stop is clearly visible but not accentuated. The muzzle is in proportion to the entire head. The bridge of the muzzle is straight, lips not excessively pendant. The nose is black. Cheeks are flat. Teeth should be sound, with the upper teeth slightly overlapping the lower.

EYES Of medium size, brown, preferably dark, with a serene expression.

EARS Should be set neither too high nor too low. Extended, they should reach the midpoint of the muzzle.

NECK Rather long, well arched, lean, with no suggestion of throatiness.

BODY Deep chest, with good spring of ribs but not barreled; well ribbed up. The back should be straight and strong, the loins broad. The croup should be well developed, rounded and slightly sloping.

TAIL Should be set on neither too high nor too low and should approximately reach the hocks. It should be rather thick and should be carried rather low.

FOREQUARTERS Shoulders long and sloping, fine, not reaching above back. The forelegs are straight, lean and strong-boned. The elbows must be turned neither inward nor outward. Pasterns slightly sloping. **HINDQUARTERS** Thighs muscular and broad. The stifles are well bent, the hocks broad, lean, and well bent, turning neither inward nor outward. Dewclaws acceptable. **FEET** Preferably oval, but round feet are not a fault. Toes should be well arched and close together. Pads are to be strong and not spongy. Good growth of hair between the toes.

COAT Smooth, very dense, not too fine nor too short. The hind legs and tail may have more abundant hair than the rest of the body. **Color** White with black markings and brown shading on head and legs and between the white and black areas. Small black or brown spots are to be discouraged. Black must not predominate. Any other color or pattern is a disqualification. ●

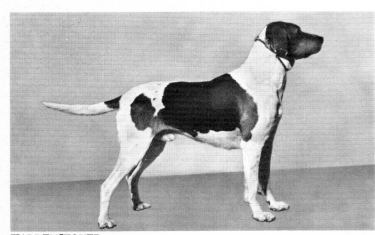

HALDENSTOVER

174 HYGENHUND
NORWAY

GENERAL CHARACTERISTICS Compact, solid, built for endurance; with a short, powerful back.

SIZE Height: males 18½-21½ inches; females slightly smaller. Deviations from these measurements acceptable in unusually good males up to 23½ inches.

HEAD Neither too big nor too small, yet somewhat broad without being heavy or long. Viewed from the front the skull is slightly domed; seen in profile it is well domed. The occipital bone is scarcely perceptible. The stop is well defined. The muzzle is clean, rather broad and deep, short rather than long. Bridge of muzzle straight, nose black. Clean lips, not pendant, falling away evenly to the corners of the mouth. Cheeks not protruding or full. The whole head is shaped like a blunt wedge. Viewed from the side, the front part of the muzzle should be rounded, not square. The jaws close in a scissors bite.

EYES Medium size, not protruding; dark or hazel depending on color of coat. The expression of the eyes is earnest and mild. The haw is not visible. Walleyes not permitted.

EARS Set neither too high nor too low; they should be moderately thick at the point of insertion. They do not hang close to the cheeks. They are broad and not long, reaching only halfway to the nose when extended. The leather is thin and soft, tapering and rounded at the tips.

NECK Medium length, strong, not excessively throaty.

BODY The chest should not be too broad nor too narrow; it should, however, be long, deep and spacious, well ribbed up, reaching down to the elbows. It must not be barrel-shaped. The belly is not drawn up. The back is short, straight and powerful. The loins are very strong and well muscled. The croup is long, broad, and slightly rounded.

TAIL Set on in line with the back. It should not descend below hocks. It is strong at the root, tapering to the tip. It is carried gaily but not curled over the back.

FOREQUARTERS The shoulders are long, strong and muscular, set obliquely, with the tops not above the backline. The legs are solid and sinewy, clean but not heavy. The forelegs are straight in bone and well angulated. Pasterns sloping and rather short. **HINDQUARTERS** Upper thighs broad and muscular, well angulated. Hocks deep, broad and clean, placed low. Seen from behind the hind legs should be perfectly straight. Dewclaws permitted, but double dewclaws are undesirable. **FEET** Toes well arched and close together. Soles strong, well covered with hair between the toes. The feet should be neither turned in nor turned out.

COAT Straight and preferably a little rough to the touch, dense, glossy, and not too short. A little feathering may be tolerated. **Color** Chestnut or yellow-red, with or without black shading; or black and tan. Both colors may be combined on white. White with tan to yellow markings or spots, or with black and tan markings. These colors are all acceptable. ●

HYGENHUND

HUNTING IN THE MAREMMA MARSHES ▶

Photo: E. Münch, A. Wintzell, M. Pedone.

175 LUNDEHUND
NORWAY

This breed has lived for centuries solely on two islands to the north of Norway where it is employed today for hunting puffins. For several decades it has not been possible to export Lundehunds from this region.

While other dogs have four toes and sometimes an atrophied fifth one, the Lundehund has five toes and an atrophied sixth one. Unlike other small-sized dogs with five toe cushions, the Lundehund has seven or eight.

By virtue of his small size and especially his five functional toes and toe cushions, he is able to climb steep rock walls and is an expert in scaling cliffs and in getting into rocky crevasses, where he very carefully removes the birds from their nests and brings them unharmed to his waiting master. Sometimes lively struggles take place when the dog makes contact with adult birds who try to drive him off by vigorously pecking at him.

This dog's ear has a peculiar feature worthy of mention. In the upper part the cartilage ends meet and can shut when the dog raises his ear halfway. This is evidently nature's protection against the infiltration of the constantly dripping water of the caves.

The tail is normally coiled over the back although not as definitely as is the case with the Elkhound. When the dog barks, when he is excited or following a trail, the tail hangs behind and is slightly bent back.

GENERAL CHARACTERISTICS A small Spitz with ears erect, tail curled over back, the head carried rather low, with a coat of medium length including a dense undercoat. Double dewclaws on all feet. Temperament alert and very active.

WEIGHT AND SIZE Weight: approximately 13-14 lb. Height: males 12½-14 inches; females 12-13½ inches.

HEAD Clean, wedge-shaped, the skull of medium breadth with protruding orbital ridges. The stop is pronounced, the nose bridge slightly convex. The skull should not be domed. The jaws meet in a scissors bite.

EYES Brown, fairly deep-set, not protruding.

EARS Carried erect, neither too big nor too small, rather broad at the base. The ears are carried with the openings forward, but they may be folded backward like rose ears so that the auditory passage is closed.

NECK Strong, clean-cut, of medium length.

BODY Strong, straight back; long, spacious chest; belly not drawn up. The whole body is rather long, with a short, straight croup.

TAIL Set on rather high, the tail has a short, dense coat but no flag.

FOREQUARTERS AND HINDQUARTERS The forelegs are straight and strong, the hindlegs are powerful and well angulated. **FEET** With toes arched; the pads are very large.

COAT Dense and rather rough to the touch but lying rather flat to the body. On the head and the front of the legs the coat is short and slick. On the front of the neck, the underside of the chest, the back side of the legs and on the tail the coat is longer. The coat consists of a comparatively long harsh top coat with dark tips on the hairs and a light, soft undercoat. **Color** Black, gray, brown in various shades combined with white. ●

MEDIUM-SIZED SHORTHAIRED PORTUGUESE PODENGO

176 MEDIUM-SIZED PORTUGUESE PODENGO
PORTUGAL

GENERAL CHARACTERISTICS A moderately long-lined dog, of medium size, well proportioned, with good bone and good muscling; this breed is characterized by great vivacity and intelligence; the dogs are good, reliable country dogs.

WEIGHT AND SIZE Weight: 35-44 lb. Height: 15½-22 inches.

HEAD The head is lean, its shape is that of a truncated quadrangular pyramid with a wide base; the end of the muzzle is fairly pointed. The nose is small with an obliquely cut tip. Fairly prominent, its color is darker than the coat. The bridge is rounded in width and straight in profile; it is shorter than the length of the skull; it is broader at the base than at the end. The teeth meet in a scissors bite; they are fine, firmly set, straight; the jaws are normal, the teeth are white. The stop is not pronounced. The upper cranial-frontal longitudinal axes are divergent. The skull is flat with a nearly straight profile. The supraorbital arches are prominent. The metopic suture is not prominent; the space between the ears is horizontal, and the occipital protuberance is accentuated.

EYES They have a lively expression, are not prominent, and the color varies from honey to brown depending on the color of the coat. The eyes are small and slanted. The eyelids are darker than the coat.

EARS Set on obliquely, they are of medium size, straight, highly mobile, vertical or slightly moved forward when the dog is alert. The ears are pointed, broad at the base, triangular in shape, fine, quite long (longer than they are wide at their base).

NECK Graceful, straight, long, in good proportion, strong, well muscled; there is no dewlap.

BODY The chest is not prominent but it is muscular. It is not very wide but well let down. The thorax is of medium thickness, deep, with the sternum sloped backward and upward. The backline is straight or slightly arched; the lower line of the trunk is slightly ascending to the rear. The ribs are oblique and not greatly sprung. The back is straight or slightly ascending and quite long. The loins are straight or slightly arched, broad, muscular. The belly and flanks are lean and slightly drawn up. The croup is of medium length, broad and muscular, straight or slightly sloping.

TAIL Set on rather high and is strong, thick, pointed and of medium length. In repose it is carried hanging and reaches to the hock, or else it is carried slightly curved; in action it is raised to the horizontal and carried

LUNDEHUND

MEDIUM-SIZED COARSEHAIRED PORTUGUESE PODENGO

Photo: A. Wintzell.

slightly curved or vertically as a saber tail, but never curled.

FOREQUARTERS The legs are vertical as seen both from in front and in profile, well muscled and lean. The shoulder and upper arm are long, sloped, strong and well muscled, with the shoulder angle well open. The forearm is straight, long and muscular, the wrists are lean and not prominent, the pasterns are strong, short and slightly sloped. **HINDQUARTERS** Vertical as seen both from behind and in profile, well muscled and lean; the thighs are long, of moderate width, and muscular. The hind legs are oblique, long, lean, strong and muscular. The hocks are at medium height, lean, strong, with obtuse angulation. The metatarsi are strong, short, oblique, without dewclaws. **FEET** Round, with long, strong and well-closed toes, which are well arched. The nails are short and sturdy, and preferably dark. The pads are hard and strong; the gait is light and fast.

COAT May be short or long and moderately heavy; it is smooth in shorthaired dogs, harsh in longhaired dogs; it is denser in the shorthaired variety than in the longhaired. In the latter variety the muzzle is also feathered with long hair. There is no undercoat. **Color** The predominant colors are: yellow and fawn in various tones (light, common and dark) and a rather dull black; solid or with white markings; or white with markings. **Skin** Fine and close-fitting; the lips, nose and eyelids are preferably pigmented with black or with a darker color than the coat.

FAULTS General appearance showing signs of Greyhound or hound blood; jaws meeting badly; teeth badly set; eyes of different coloring; ears not pointed, not straight; arched neck; backline greatly arched; belly excessively drawn up; croup excessively slanting; curled tail; dewclaws.

SCALE OF POINTS

General appearance	20
Head	20
Eyes	5
Ears	10
Neck	5
Trunk	15
Legs	15
Tail	5
Coat and color	5
	100

MEASUREMENTS AND WEIGHT OF A TYPICAL DOG

Head	inches
Length of skull	4½
Width of skull	3¾
Length of bridge	3⅛
Thorax	
Circumference	21¼
Width	5
Height	8
Backline	
Length	17
Width	4
Length	
Of the body	19
Of the tail	11¼
Height	
At the withers	18
Of the forelegs	9
At the croup	18½
Weight	40 lb

SMALL PORTUGUESE PODENGO

177 SMALL PORTUGUESE PODENGO

PORTUGAL

GENERAL CHARACTERISTICS A long-bodied dog, small in size, used particularly for hunting rabbits over rocky terrain. It differs from the medium Podengo in the following characteristics:

WEIGHT AND SIZE Weight: 10-12½ lb; height: 8-12 inches.

HEAD Skull may be domed, flat, or slightly domed.

BODY The length of the body is greater than its height.

FOREQUARTERS AND HINDQUARTERS The legs are short. The forearms are straight or very slightly curved inward and from top to bottom.

COAT Short hair, smooth and close.

DIMENSIONS OF A TYPICAL FEMALE

Head	inches	cm
length of skull	3.15	8
width of skull	2.95	7.5
length of bridge	2.17	5.5
Body		
circumference	15	38
width	6.29	16
height	4.72	12
Backline		
length	11.02	28
width	2.95	7.5
Length		
of body	12.59	32
of tail	6.29	16
Height		
at the withers	10.63	27
of the forelegs	5.32	13.5
at the croup	10.63	27
Weight	11 lb	5 kg

SMALL PORTUGUESE PODENGO

Photo: Jovane.

DREVER

178 DREVER
SWEDEN

The Schwedische Dachbracke, more commonly called Drever, is a hound of considerable qualities and very good for following fox, hare, or boar hunts. He has an excellent sense of smell and a good voice, a very important quality.

There is little information concerning the origin of this breed. It is evidently part of a Basset group prevalent more or less throughout Central Europe and the Scandinavian countries, different from the French-type Basset.

The standard was officially published in 1947 making it one of the younger Swedish breeds, although its origins are old. The Swedish Drever Club has always been active: more than 15,000 dogs of this breed are registered in the *Book of Origins* and more than 2,000 new entries are registered yearly.

GENERAL CHARACTERISTICS The Drever is a dog of moderate size. Seen in profile, he should have a rectangular body outline; moreover, the dog should be compact, well built and robust, and should have well-developed muscles. He should be clean and flexible, and the structural differences between males and females should be obvious.

SIZE Average height at the withers: males, 14 inches; females, 13½ inches. In any case, males should not exceed 15¾ inches nor be less than 12½ inches; maximum limits for females range from 15 inches down to 12 inches.

HEAD Large and long, but in good proportion; the greatest width is in the skull, between the ears: from that point the skull narrows progressively toward the muzzle. The nose is well developed, with well-open nostrils, preferably black. The bridge should be straight or very slightly arched. The lower edge of the upper lip should be close-fitting and only slightly elongated beyond the lower edge of the mandible. The muzzle is well developed and should not appear pointed, as seen either from above or in profile. The teeth are robust and the jaws close in a scissors bite. The stop is scarcely defined.

EYES Clear and very expressive; they should preferably be dark brown. They should be neither protruding nor excessively open. The eyelids are thin and close-fitting.

EARS Of medium length, broad, with the lower edge slightly rounded. They should be set on neither too high nor too low. When the dog is alert, their lower edge should rest against the head.

NECK Long and quite strong, the neck is gracefully fitted into the shoulders. The skin at the throat should be loose but sustained, and there should be no trace of a dewlap.

BODY The ribcage is well developed and oval in cross section; the lowest point of the thorax should definitely be below the elbows. The last back ribs should be well developed. The backline is straight and, seen in profile, slightly rounded toward the back of the loin. The back is robust and slopes slightly from the withers to the tail; the loins are robust and short in proper proportion. The croup is strong, broad and slightly sloping. The lower edge of the thorax merges gradually into the belly, which is slightly drawn up.

TAIL Long and thick at the root. It is preferably carried downward, but it may be carried slightly raised when the dog is in action. In no case should it be curled over the back.

FOREQUARTERS The shoulders are muscular, with long and slightly sloping scapulae, which should fit closely to the trunk. The points of the shoulders, moreover, should not emerge from the spinal apophysis of the withers. The forelegs are strong. Seen from in front, they are perfectly vertical and parallel. The upper arm is proportionately long, broad and well angulated with the scapula. The pastern is elastic and only slightly sloped. **HINDQUARTERS** Seen from behind, the legs are perfectly vertical and parallel. The thighs should be well muscled and broad in profile. The stifle and the hock are well angulated. The metatarsus is short and almost perpendicular to the ground. There should be no dewclaws. **FEET** Forefeet and hind feet should be solid, facing forward, with elastic and well-closed toes. The pads are well developed and hard.

COAT Thick, close-fitting, and flat over the entire body. On the head, ears, the lower part of the legs and on the upper part of the tail, it should be proportionately shorter; while on the neck, back and buttocks it is longer. The hair is bristly on the underpart of the tail, but it should not form a fringe. **Color** All colors are acceptable, but white should always appear and be well in evidence in front, on the side and behind. There should, moreover, be white markings, and preferably a white collar as well; the tip of the tail and the feet should preferably be white. The colors should be clean and the markings precise. ●

179 HAMILTONSTÖVARE
SWEDEN

The origins of this Swedish hound, whose standards have recently been published by the FCI, go back to a series of cross-breedings between the Holstein Beagle, the Hanover Beagle, the Kurland Beagle and the Foxhound. The breeder who fixed the points of this breed was Adolf Patrick Hamilton (from whom we get the name of Hamiltonstövare), and he later founded the Swedish Kennel Club.

GENERAL CHARACTERISTICS The dog should be well built, give an impression of strength and ruggedness and should have a tricolor coat.

SIZE Height: males, 22½ inches; females, 21 inches. Maximum and minimum variations permissible are: 23½ and 19½ inches for males; 22½ and 18 inches for females.

HEAD Long, rectangular and lean. The skull is moderately arched and broad; the occipital protuberance is not prominent. The stop is not pronounced. The nose is always black, fairly large and with wide nostrils. The bridge is straight and parallel to the line of the skull. The upper lips should be full but not excessively pendulous. The muzzle is robust, rectangular and quite long. The zygomatic arch should not be overly prominent. The teeth are strong and should be without any defect; they should close in a scissors bite.

EYES Light or dark brown, with a serene expression.

EARS Set on high. When the dog is alert they may be raised slightly above the occiput. They should be slightly shorter than the distance between the forward limit of their set-on and the midpoint of the nasal bridge. The cartilage is soft, and the ears hang flat, without folds or wrinkles.

NECK Long and powerful; it merges gracefully with the shoulders. The skin is close-fitting and without dewlap.

BODY The chest is well let down, and the ribs are moderately well sprung; the back ribs are proportionately long. The back should be straight and strong, with powerful loins. The croup slopes ever so slightly, and should be long and broad, with well-developed muscles. The belly is muscular and slightly drawn up.

TAIL Set on high, almost as a continuation of the backline; when down it should reach the hocks. Thick at the root, it tapers toward the tip; it should be carried straight out or slightly curved.

FOREQUARTERS The shoulders are muscular and long, well set and well joined to the trunk. The point of the scapula should not pass beyond the spinal apophysis of the vertebrae at the withers. The forearms should be vertical. The upper arm is long and well angulated with the scapula; the elbows are close to the body, and they should not be visible beneath the brisket. The pastern is elastic but with only a slight angulation with the forearm. **HINDQUARTERS** Seen from behind, they should be vertical well angulated at the stifle and at the hock; seen in profile, the thighs are muscular and broad. The metatarsus is short and lean, perpendicular to the ground when the dog is standing erect. **FEET** They should be strong and directed forward, with elastic and well-closed toes and large pads. Wolf feet are not desirable.

COAT The undercoat is short, thick and soft; it should be very dense, particularly in winter. The top coat is strong and dense. The hair may be fairly long on the underside of the tail, without however forming a fringe; the feet are well feathered between the toes. **Color** The upper part of the neck and back, the neck areas generally and the upper part of the tail should be black; brown on head, legs, lower part of the neck, thorax and tail. White should be present on the underside of the muzzle and neck, the chest, the tip of the tail and the legs. A mixture of black and brown hair is not desirable. ●

HAMILTONSTÖVARE

Photo: A. Wintzell

HAMILTONSTÖVARE

180 SCHILLERSTÖVARE

SWEDEN

This Swedish hound descends from dogs going back farther than the fifteenth century. The Schillerstövare were first shown by the breeder Per Schiller, whose name the breed bears.

It is particularly adapted for hunting in snow. The breed was officially recognized in 1952.

SCHILLERSTÖVARE

Photo: S. A. Thompson, A. Wintzell.

GENERAL CHARACTERISTICS Dogs of this breed should be lean, of noble aspect, light but robust, with a black and tan coat. Its build shows strength and energy.

SIZE Ideal height: males, 22½ inches; females, 21 inches. Upper and lower tolerances: males, 23½, 19½ inches; females, 22½, 22 inches. The head should be long and tapering toward the nose. The skull should be very broad between the eyes, and the upper cranial-facial lines are parallel. The stop is well defined. Seen from above, the head should appear to be wedge-shaped, but the muzzle should not be pointed. The nose is large, invariably black and with well-open nostrils. The bridge is straight. The lips and the commissure should be close-fitting to the jaws. The zygomatic arch is not prominent. The teeth are strong and well set; they close in a scissors bite.

EYES The eyes should be light or dark brown, with a fine, temperamental expression.

EARS Set on high; when the dog is alert, they may rise very slightly above skull level. They should be slightly shorter than the distance between the forward corner of the set-on and the midpoint of the muzzle; their texture is soft, and hang rather flat; their forward corners should not be folded.

NECK Long and powerful, merging gracefully with the shoulders; the skin should be thick and flexibly close-fitting to the underlying tissues.

BODY A straight and powerful back, with strong loins and a slightly sloping croup. The chest is well let down, the ribs moderately sprung, the hind legs proportionately long. The croup is gently sloping, long and broad, with well-developed muscles.

The belly is muscular and very slightly drawn up.

TAIL Set on high, almost on the prolongation of the backline. It should be carried straight or slightly curved; it should be thick at the root, tapering toward the tip; when hanging down it reaches the hocks.

FOREQUARTERS Muscular shoulders, with long, sloping scapulae, which are well joined to the thorax and back. The points of the scapulae should not emerge from the spinal apophysis of the withers. The forelegs are vertical. The upper arm is long and broad, well angulated with the scapula. The elbows should fit close to the body and not be visible below the brisket. The pasterns are elastic, but only slightly angulated toward the forearm. **HINDQUARTERS** Vertical as seen from behind, well angulated at the stifle and hock. The thighs are muscular and broad as seen in profile. The metatarsus is short and lean; it is perpendicular to the ground when the dog is standing. **FEET** The feet should be compact and directed forward, with elastic, well closed toes; the pads are robust. Harefeet are not desirable.

COAT It should consist of a heavy, smooth top coat which, especially in winter, is bolstered by a softer, thicker layer of undercoat. **Color** The upper part of the neck, the back, the upper part of the shoulders, the sides of the thorax, the loins, the croup and the upper part of the tail should be black; the head, throat, chest, lower shoulders, forelegs and hind legs (up to the flanks) and the underside of the tail should be tan. There may be a small white stripe on the chest and a little white on the toes. There should not be black markings on the tan areas of adult dogs; black markings on the supraorbital ridges are, however, permissible. ●

181 SMÅLANDSSTÖVARE
SWEDEN

Indigenous to Central Sweden, this hunting dog is light and elegant, endowed with an excellent sense of smell, and is employed for fox and rabbit hunting. His standard was first fixed in 1921 and was revised and finalized in 1952.

SMÅLANDSSTÖVARE

GENERAL CHARACTERISTICS A medium-sized dog, compact, light but of robust build, of noble aspect. The body outline should be square.

SIZE Desirable height: males, 19½ inches; females, 18 inches. The upper and lower limits of tolerance are, respectively: males, 21¼-17¾ inches; females, 19½-16½ inches.

HEAD Lean; the zygomatic arch should not be too obvious. The nose is always black, with well-opened nostrils. The bridge is straight and parallel to the skull line. The upper lip is slightly pendulous. The muzzle, well developed, should not be heavy or pointed. The teeth are strong, well set and close in a scissors bite.

EYES Clear and dark, with a serene, intelligent expression.

EARS Set on rather high; they should be slightly shorter than the distance from the forward angle of the set-on of the ear to the midpoint of the bridge. They should hang flat, rounded at the tips and without folds.

NECK Moderately long and robust; it should hold the head up gracefully and merge well with the shoulders. The skin should be soft, fairly thick and close-fitting to the underlying tissues.

BODY The chest is well let down, the ribs well sprung. The back is short, straight and powerful, with strong loins. The croup is gently sloped and should be long and broad, with well developed muscles. The belly is muscular and slightly drawn up.

TAIL The tail may be either of two types: (a) long, barely reaching the hocks, carried straight or as a saber tail; (b) short by birth and carried high.

FOREQUARTERS The shoulders are muscular, long and oblique, well joined to the thorax and the back. The points of the scapulae should not emerge from the spinal apophysis of the withers. The forelegs are vertical; the upper arm is long and broad, well angulated with the scapula. The elbows, which fit close to the body, should not be visible beneath the brisket. The pasterns are elastic and only slightly angulated toward the forearm. **HINDQUARTERS** Vertical and well angulated at the stifle and the hock. Seen in profile, the thighs are muscular and broad. The metatarsus is short and lean, perpendicular to the ground when the dog is standing. **FEET** Straight and directed forward, with elastic, closed toes; the pads are robust. Harefeet are not desirable.

COAT The top coat is thick, rather heavy and sustained, but always smooth and glossy; there is an undercoat. The hair on the back of the thighs and on the underside of the tail may be quite long; it should be abundant between the toes. **Color** Black with tan markings above the eyes, on the forefeet and pasterns, on the underside of the tail and around the vent. Chocolate brown dogs with tan markings are not eligible for inclusion in stud books, although they are acceptable for show. Permissible but not desirable are colors different from those specified in the standard, including abundant tan on the head or legs. White may appear only as an occasional small spot on the chest or toes. ●

182 SWISS HOUND
Schweizer Laufhund
SWITZERLAND

The origins of the Swiss Hound must be sought among the hunting dogs of the Nile introduced by the Phoenicians and the Greeks before the Christian era, first in the Mediterranean Islands and then on the Continent. From Southern Europe they spread to the coasts of Gaul and Britain and subsequently into Switzerland during the Roman rule. Their general characteristics have not varied since that era.

The presence of the Swiss Hound during the Middle Ages is confirmed by illustrations dating from the twelfth century in the Zürich cathedral which show deer being pursued by dogs. There also exists an exchange of letters between the Milanese Sforzas and the Dean Albrecht von Bonstetten which indicate that during the fifteenth century the Swiss hunting dog was much esteemed for his excellent sense of smell and his great tracking abilities.

As we have already mentioned in our remarks on the Porcelaine, some authors including Tschudy consider the handsome French hound to be of Swiss origin and should therefore be grouped with the Schweizer Laufhund.

GENERAL CHARACTERISTICS The general appearance of this Swiss breed should be that of a dog of medium size, fairly long, selected for vigor, resistance, nobility and general overall conformation; they are lively, intelligent, and have great enthusiasm for the hunt. The head is lean and long, with huge, folded ears which are set on low and back. The forelegs are strong and vertical, the hind legs powerful and well muscled, the back rather long, straight and muscular, the loins very muscular, the shoulders long and sloping, the rib cage deep. All these qualities indicate great powers of resistance. These dogs are excellent hunters, combining a number of fine talents, such as very keen sense of smell, utmost self-reliance in the field, with a powerful voice; they are, moreover, very good in the roughest terrain. All Swiss tracking hounds (except for those of the Bloodhound type) have the same general characteristics, differing only in color and coat.

SIZE Minimum height at the withers: 15¾ inches; most dogs are 17¾-21½ inches.

HEAD Lean, long, in good proportion to the overall size of the dog. The stop is well defined. The nose is black and fairly large, with broad, well-open nostrils. The bridge is slightly arched. The lips are not heavy. The muzzle is long, the jaws very strong, with well-adapted teeth; the jaws close in either a pincers or a scissors bite.

EYES As dark as possible, with a gentle expression.

EARS Set on low and back, with the base narrower than the maximum width of the ears. The ears are very long and fall in folds; they are well rounded at the tips and are narrow, light and covered with fine hair.

NECK Moderately long and powerful, with no appreciable dewlap.

BODY The chest is fairly well let down and not excessively broad; the rib cage is not greatly sprung. The back is of good length, straight and compact; the loins are solid.

TAIL Not too long, the tail should be carried horizontally or slightly curved; it should never be curled. Pointed at the tip, the tail should be well feathered, smooth in smoothhaired dogs and proportionately thicker in the coarsehaired dogs, without being tufted.

FOREQUARTERS Vertical, well boned, with lean, well developed tendons. **HINDQUARTERS** The hocks are moderately bent, the muscles are well developed; there should be no dewclaws. **FEET** Rounded, with hard and wrinkled pads and solid nails.

COAT Thick and abundant, short or hard according to the type; the hair is shorter and finer on the head and ears. The Lucerne dog is always shorthaired. Coarsehaired dogs should have a fine, very dense undercoat covered with sparse, coarse hair. The following varieties of Swiss hounds are recognized on the basis of the coat: (a) **Schweizer Laufhund-Rotschecken.** White coat, with more or less large markings of orange or yellow-orange. Dogs with red coats are admissible. An occasional small red spot is not to be considered a fault. (b) **Luzerner Laufhund-Blausprenkel.** The coat of this variety has a white background with gray or blue speckling and broad dark or black markings. It also has tan markings or yellow-brown areas of color on the head, body and feet. Similarly, beneath the white hair, the skin is speckled with more or less dark markings. When the coat is wet, the white disappears and the dog seems to be much darker, slate gray or blue. A similar coat distinguishes the Gascony Blues and the mottled-blue Harrier. (c) **Berner Laufhund-Schwarzschecken.** The coat is invariably tricolor: white, black and more or less intense tan markings. The background is white, with huge black markings and small black spots here and there. The tan markings are above the eyes, on the cheeks, on the inner part of the ears and at the root of the tail. (d) **Jura Laufhund (brown).** The coat may be solid brown-yellow or reddish brown, or it may have a huge black saddle on the back; or it may be black, with tan markings

SWISS HOUND

Photo: A. Wintzell, E. Münch.

above the eyes, on the cheeks and on the underparts of the body. Sometimes there is a white mark on the chest. (e) **Jura variety, Bloodhound type.** The coat has the same colors as the preceding variety; the Bloodhound type differs from the other in its somatic characteristics. (f) **Coarse-haired variety.** All colors are accepted, with the exception of black or chocolate solid color overall.

VOICE Sonorous, capable of being heard from a distance, without being either high-pitched or strident.

BROWN JURA HOUND BLOODHOUND TYPE

GENERAL CHARACTERISTICS This is the most massive of the Swiss hounds. The back is long and broad; the members are strongly boned. The dewlap, especially the heavy, massive head with its long muzzle, the lips, the wrinkles on the forehead, the eye with its profound and melancholy expression, ears set on low, long and folded—all these features distinguish this variety and have attracted attention to it.

SIZE Minimum at the withers: 15¾ inches.

HEAD Powerful and massive. The skull is broad and fully rounded. The forehead is wrinkled in a characteristic manner. The occipital protuberance is very pronounced.

EYES Dark, melancholy; the lower lids, slightly open, reveal a small section of the haw.

EARS Set on well back and low, in folds, always very large and heavy; they widen toward the middle, and are narrower below, and well rounded at the tips.

NECK Broad, long and powerful, with a dewlap.

BODY Strong ribs, broad and deep. The back is long and broad, always straight and compact; the loins are vigorous, broad and nervous.

TAIL Of medium length, ending in a pointed tip, strong and well feathered, but never tufted; it is carried rather high, without appreciable curving; it is never carried above the back.

FOREQUARTERS AND HINDQUARTERS Vertical, with extremely powerful bone. The thigh is muscular, the tendons are exceptionally well joined. There should be no dewclaws. The feet are rounded, well closed, with hard, wrinkled pads; the nails are strong and black.

COAT Very short and smooth. ●

BERNESE HOUND

183 LUCERNE HOUND
Luzerner Laufhund

SWITZERLAND

184 BERNESE HOUND
Berner Laufhund

SWITZERLAND

LUCERNE HOUND

BERNESE HOUND

Photo: Fotostampa-Embrione, E. Münch, M. Meerkämper.

185 JURA HOUND
Jura Laufhund

SWITZERLAND

186 ST. HUBERT TYPE JURA HOUND
Jura Laufhund type Saint-Hubert

SWITZERLAND

JURA HOUND

ST. HUBERT TYPE JURA HOUND

Photo: Buzzini, Fotostampa-Embrione.

187 SWISS COARSE-HAIRED HOUND

Rauhhaarlaufhund

SWITZERLAND

SWISS COARSEHAIRED HOUND

188 SMALL SWISS HOUND

Schweizer Niederlaufhund

SWITZERLAND

Of smaller dimensions than the regular Swiss Hounds, the Small Swiss Hounds are divided into several breeds which share the same standard.

GENERAL CHARACTERISTICS Typical Bloodhound in miniature; well proportioned despite smaller size. Voice must not be strident but a full and pleasantly resonant baying.
SIZE 12-15 inches in height.
HEAD Slightly domed, with only a moderate stop.
EYES Rather large, with close-fitting lids. The eyes must be dark.
EARS Long, reaching down at least to the level of the nose.
NECK Light, carried elegantly, if possible with no dewlap.
BODY Slender and lithe; the brisket must not reach beneath the elbow; back preferably short rather than long and well in proportion to the overall size of the dog. Broad, powerful loin, belly held up, with slightly sloping croup.
TAIL Medium length, set on not too low but neither too high, falling with no noticeable upward curve. At work the tail is carried slightly up. Pointed tip.
FOREQUARTERS Lean, short, robust.
HINDQUARTERS The angulation of the hock is slightly rearward **FEET** Short, closed toes with fine hair between toes. No dewclaws. ●

SMALL SWISS HOUND

189 SMALL BERNESE HOUND

Berner Niederlaufhund

SWITZERLAND

SMALL BERNESE HOUND

190 SMALL LUCERNE HOUND

Luzerner Niederlaufhund

SWITZERLAND

SMALL LUCERNE HOUND

191 SMALL JURA HOUND

Jura Niederlaufhund

SWITZERLAND

SMALL JURA HOUND

Photo: Fotostampa-Embrione, M. Meerkämper.

BASSET HOUND

192 BASSET HOUND
UNITED STATES

The popularity of this breed is a rather recent phenomenon. It must be remembered that less than fifteen years ago it was practically impossible to acquire a Basset puppy, so rare were specialized breeders. The Basset was imported into England about a century ago, a French breed developed in the seventeenth century based on the St. Hubert type, and considering the fact that this dog was the stock of other more modern hounds (Bloodhound, Foxhound, Harrier, etc.) the account of the above is equally applicable to the Basset.

The French-type Basset was selectively bred in England until its inscription in 1883 among the breeds recognized by the British Kennel Club. Immediately following this, disputes arose among English breeders between those who wished to develop the dog's aesthetic qualities and those who wished to bring out the hound characteristics. This dispute inhibited for some years the diffusion of the breed which acquired renown only when Americans, with careful breeding, made the Basset one of the foremost luxury and show dogs.

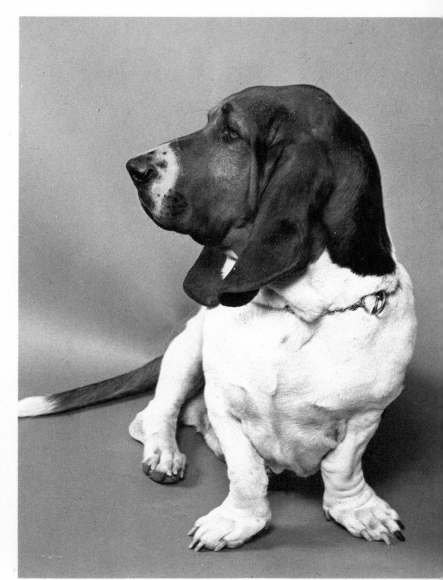

BASSET HOUND

BASSET HOUND

GENERAL CHARACTERISTICS The Basset Hound is especially equipped to follow a trail over the most difficult terrain. He is a short-legged dog, heavier in bone, size considered, than any other breed; and while his movement is deliberate, he is in no sense clumsy. His temperament is mild, never belligerent or timid. He is capable of great endurance in the field and his devotion is of the utmost.

SIZE His height should not exceed 14 inches. More than 15 inches at the highest point of the shoulder blade is a disqualification.

HEAD Large and well proportioned. Its length from occiput to muzzle is greater than the width at the brow. In overall appearance the head is of medium width. The skull is well domed, showing a pronounced occipital protuberance. A broad flat skull is a fault. The length from nose to stop is approximately the length from stop to occiput. The sides are flat and free from cheek bumps. Viewed in profile the toplines of the muzzle and skull are straight and lie in parallel planes; the stop is moderately defined. The skin over the entire head is loose, falling in distinct wrinkles over the brow when the head is lowered. A dry head and tight skin are faults. The muzzle is deep, heavy, and free from snipiness. The nose is darkly pigmented, preferably black, with large, open nostrils. A deep liver-colored nose conforming to the coloring of the head is permissible but not desirable. The teeth are large, sound

and regular, meeting in either a scissors or an even bite. A bite either overshot or undershot is a serious fault. The lips are darkly pigmented and pendulous, falling squarely in front and, toward the back, in loose-hanging flews.

EYES The eyes are soft, sad, and slightly sunken, showing a prominent haw; in color they are brown, preferably dark brown. A somewhat lighter-colored eye conforming to the general coloring of the dog is acceptable but not desirable. Very light or protruding eyes are faults.

EARS The ears are extremely long and low-set, and when drawn forward they fold well over the end of the nose. They are velvety in texture, hanging in loose folds with the ends curling slightly inward. They are set far back on the head at the base of the skull and, in repose, appear to be set on the neck. Ears set on high and flat ears are a serious fault.

NECK Powerful, of good length and well arched. The dewlap is very pronounced.

FOREQUARTERS The chest is deep and full, with prominent sternum showing clearly in front of the legs. The shoulders and elbows are set close against the sides of the chest. The distance from the deepest point of the chest to the ground, while it must be adequate to allow free movement when working in the field, is

not to exceed a third of the total height at the withers in an adult Basset. The shoulders are well laid back and powerful. Steepness in shoulders, fiddle fronts, and elbows that are out are serious faults. The forelegs are short, powerful, heavy in bone, with wrinkled skin. Knuckling over of the front legs is a disqualification. The foot is massive and very heavy, with tough, heavy pads which are well rounded; both feet are equally inclined a trifle outward, balancing the width of the shoulders. Feet down at the pastern is a serious fault. The toes should be neither pinched together nor splayed; the weight of the forepart of the body should be born evenly on each. Dewclaws may be removed.

BODY The rib structure is long, smooth, and extends well back. The ribs are well sprung, allowing adequate room for heart and lungs. Flat-sidedness and flanged ribs are faults. The topline is straight, level, and free from any tendency to sag or roach, which are faults.

TAIL The tail is not to be docked, and is set in continuation of the spine with but slight curvature, and carried gaily in hound fashion. The hair on the underside of the tail is coarse.

HINDQUARTERS Very full and well rounded, approximately equal to the shoulders in width. They must not appear slack or light in relation to

the overall depth of the body. The dog stands firmly on its hind legs, showing a well-let-down stifle with no tendency toward a crouching stance. Viewed from behind, the hind legs are parallel, with the hocks turning neither in nor out. Cowhocks or bowed legs are serious faults. The hind feet point straight ahead. Steep, poorly angulated hindquarters are a serious fault. The dewclaws, if any, may be removed.

COAT The coat is hard, smooth and short, with sufficient density to be of use in all weather. The skin is loose and elastic. A distinctly long coat is a disqualification. **Color** Any recognized hound color is acceptable; the distribution of color and markings is of no importance.

GAIT The Basset Hound moves in a smooth, powerful, and effortless manner. Being a scenting dog with short legs, he holds its nose low to the ground. His gait is absolutely true, with perfect coordination between the front and hind legs, and he moves in a straight line with hind feet following in line with the forefeet, the hocks well bent with no stiffness of action. The forelegs do not paddle, weave, or overlap, and the elbows must lie close to the body. Going away, the hind legs are parallel.

DISQUALIFICATIONS Height of more than 15 inches at the highest point of the shoulder blades. Knuckled-over front legs. Distinctly long coat. ●

257

Photo: T. Fall, Bonora, M. Pedone.

BASSET HOUND WITH PUPPIES

Photo: MARKA.

193 BLACK AND TAN COONHOUND

UNITED STATES

The Black and Tan Coonhound for hunting raccoons is a descendant of the old Talbot—therefore from the Bloodhound and the Foxhound. This breed was selectively bred and subsequently fixed in the United States by hunters who wished to develop a dog particularly adapted to hunting raccoons and possums. This breed has not yet been recognized by the F.C.I. Its standard was published in 1945 by the American Kennel Club.

GENERAL CHARACTERISTICS The Black and Tan Coonhound is first and fundamentally a working dog, capable of withstanding the rigors of winter, the heat of summer, and the difficult terrain over which he is called upon to work. Judges are asked by the club sponsoring the breed to place great emphasis upon these factors when evaluating the merits of the dog. The general impression should be that of power, agility, and alertness. His expression should be alert, friendly, eager, and aggressive. He should immediately impress one with his ability to cover the ground with powerful, rhythmic strides.

SIZE Measured at the shoulder: males 25-27 inches; females 23-25 inches. Height should be in proportion to general conformation, so that the dog appears neither leggy nor close to the ground. Dogs oversized should not be penalized when general soundness and proportion are in his favor. Judges should penalize the following defects: Undersize, elbows out at shoulder, lack of angulation in hindquarters, splay feet, sway back, roach back, flat-sidedness, lack of depth in chest, yellow or light eyes, shyness and nervousness.

HEAD Should be cleanly modeled, with medium stop occurring midway between occiput bone and nose. The head should measure 9-10 inches in males and 8-9 inches in females. Viewed in profile, the line of the skull is on a practically parallel plane to the foreface or muzzle. The skin should be devoid of folds or excess dewlap. The flews should be well developed, with typical hound appearance. Nostrils well open and always black. Skull should tend toward oval outline. Teeth should fit evenly with slightly scissors bite.

EYES Should be hazel to dark brown in color, almost round and not deeply set.

EARS Should be set low and well back. They should hang in graceful folds, giving the dog a majestic appearance. In length they should extend well beyond the tip of the nose.

BODY The neck should be muscular, sloping, of medium length, extending into powerfully constructed shoulders and a deep chest. The dog should possess full, round, well sprung ribs, avoiding flat-sidedness. The back should be level, powerful and strong, with a visible slope from withers to rump.

TAIL Strong, with base slightly below level of back line, carried free and, when in action, at approximately a right angle to the back.

FOREQUARTERS AND HINDQUARTERS The forelegs should be straight, with elbows well let down, turning neither in nor out; pasterns strong and erect. Feet should be catlike with compact, well-arched toes and thick, strong pads. Hindquarters should be well boned and well muscled. From hip to hock, long and sinewy; hock to pad, short and strong. Stifles and hock well bent and not inclining either in or out. When standing on a level surface the hind feet should set back from under the body, and the leg from pad to hock should be at right angles to the ground when viewed both in profile and from the rear. The stride of the Black and Tan Coonhound should be easy and graceful, with plenty of reach in front and plenty of drive behind.

COLOR Coal black, with rich tan markings above eyes, on sides of muzzle, chest, legs and breeching, with black pencil markings on toes.

FAULTS Dewclaws; white on chest or other parts of body is highly undesirable.

DISQUALIFICATION White on chest or other parts of the body more than 1½ inches in diameter. ●

BLACK AND TAN COONHOUND

194 RHODESIAN RIDGEBACK

SOUTH AFRICA

This breed, already prevalent in ancient times in its places of origin, is still little known in Europe except for certain breeding kennels in England and Italy. These dogs with their characteristic "dorsal crest" seem to be limited to only two places in the world: Southeast Asia and South Africa. The origins of the breed should be sought in the latter area from which the dog later came to Thailand. Bred by Africans, he remained pure-blooded to the present day. The breed found an enthusiastic supporter in South Africa in Cornelius van Rooyen, a hunter who considers the Rhodesian Ridgeback to have exceptional qualities. Among these qualities one should be especially noted as containing an element of danger: the dog barks at lions in order to attract them toward the hunter.

GENERAL CHARACTERISTICS The peculiarity of this breed is the dorsal ridge formed by hair growing in the opposte direction from the rest of the coat. A strong, muscular, and active dog, symmetrical in outline, capable of great endurance with fair speed. The ridge is the escutcheon of the breed; it should be clearly defined, tapering and symmetrical. It should start immediately behind the shoulders and continue to a point between the prominence of the hips; it should have two identical crowns opposite each other. The lower edge of the crown should not extend farther down the ridge than one-third.

WEIGHT AND SIZE The mature Ridgeback should be a handsome, upstanding dog. Males, 25-27 inches; females, 24-26 inches. Minimum bench standard, 25 and 24 inches for males and females, respectively. Desirable weights are 75 lb for males and 65 lb for females.

HEAD Should be of a fair length, the skull flat and rather broad between the ears. It should be free from wrinkles when in repose. The stop should be reasonably well defined and not in a single straight line from nose to occiput. The muzzle should be long, deep, and powerful; the jaws should be level and strong, with well-developed teeth, particularly the canines. The lips should be clean and closely fitting to the jaws. The nose should be black or brown, according to the color of the dog. No other color is permissible for the nose. A black nose should occur with dark eyes, a brown nose with amber eyes.

EYES Should be set moderately well apart and should be round, bright and sparkling, with an intelligent expression, the color in harmony with that of the dog.

EARS The ears should be set rather high, of medium size, fairly wide at the base and tapering to a rounded point. They should be carried close to the head.

NECK Fairly strong and free from throatiness. The shoulders should be sloping, clean, and muscular, attributes indicative of speed.

BODY The chest should not be too wide; it should be very deep and capacious, with moderately well-sprung ribs. The ribs should never be rounded like barrel hoops (indicative of lack of speed): the back should be powerful, loins strong, muscular, and slightly arched.

TAIL Strong at the point of insertion, generally tapering toward the end and free from coarseness. It should not be inserted too high or too low; it should be carried with a slight upward curve.

FOREQUARTERS The forelegs should be perfectly straight, strong, and heavy in bone, with the elbows close to the body. Shoulders oblique, well formed and muscular, indicative of the speed of which the Ridgeback is capable.

HINDQUARTERS The muscles should be clean, well defined, with hocks well down. **FEET** Compact, with well-arched toes, round, tough and elastic pads, which are protected by hair between pads and toes.

COAT Short and dense, sleek and glossy in appearance, neither woolly nor silky. **Color** Light wheaten to red wheaten. A little white on the chest and toes permissible, but excessive white here, on the belly, and above paws is undesirable.

SCALE OF POINTS

Ridge	20
Head and eyes	15
Neck and shoulders	10
Body, back, chest, loins	10
Legs and feet	15
Coat	5
Tail	5
Size, symmetry, general appearance	20
	100

RHODESIAN RIDGEBACK

RHODESIAN RIDGEBACK

Photo: Prato.

BALKAN HOUND

195 BALKAN HOUND
Balkanski gonič

YUGOSLAVIA

In Yugoslavia there exist hounds of very good quality which are always well bred. We offer below the standards starting with the Balkan Hound, the two Istrian Hounds (including the varieties of coarsehaired and shorthaired), the Posavatz, the Bosnian Hound, the Yugoslavian Tricolor, and the Yugoslavian Mountain Hound. As has been the case with many other European hounds, points have been fixed first by acclimatization, their particular task, their adaptation to the terrain, and then by selective breeding.

GENERAL CHARACTERISTICS A strong, fairly long-lined dog, with short, dense hair colored like that of a red fox, with a black top coat, more or less extended, on the upper part of the body. The head is long and bony. He is a tenacious tracking dog, energetic, with lively, easy movements; has a high-pitched voice, which under certain conditions may be very deep.

WEIGHT AND SIZE Weight: about 44 lb. Height at the withers: males, 18-21 inches; females, 17½-20½ inches.

HEAD Long, with a broad forehead, narrowing toward the muzzle. The bridge is straight and, in males, a little longer than the skull. The lips are well developed; the teeth meet in a scissors or a pincers bite; the premolars are strong. The stop is not pronounced. The eyebrows are well in evidence. The occipital protuberance is not highly developed.

EYES Generally brown, clear, with an intelligent expression.

EARS Of medium length, not very broad, rounded at the tips. They are not very fleshy, and they are set on fairly high and hang down flat.

NECK Of medium length and very strong; it widens toward the chest, without a dewlap.

BODY The chest is wide and in good proportion to the rest of the body, let down to the elbow and very deep. The ribs are well sprung; the withers are not pronounced; the back is broad, long, slightly sloping behind the shoulders. The loins are strong, slightly rounded; they are not very much in evidence; the croup is long, strong, muscular, slightly sloping. The belly is very slightly drawn up.

TAIL Short, not reaching below the hocks; not set on very high; thick at the base and tapers toward the tip. It is carried either straight or slightly curved in its second half.

FOREQUARTERS The shoulders are sloping, very muscular, close to the body, with good movement. The upper arm is sloping, muscular and firmly joined to the body in its upper part. The elbow is vertical, the forearm straight and strong. The wrist is not pronounced; the pasterns are strong and straight. The feet are strong, round, with well-closed toes and strong, exceptionally arched nails. The pads are large and hard. **HINDQUARTERS** The thighs are long and strong, well developed. The legs are sloping, long and strong. The hocks are strong, with a regular angulation. The metatarsi are almost straight, strong. The feet are similar to the forefeet.

COAT Dense, rather coarse, with an undercoat. At the withers the hair is longer than on the other parts of the body, except for the tail. **Color** Basically fox red or rust brown; the latter is, however, less desirable. On the upper part of the trunk there is a more or less broad area of black coat or a black saddle. This continues to the head, where a black spot is found on the two sides of the head at the temples. White is not acceptable except on the chest, in the form of a small star or marking. The lips, nose, eyelids and nails are of dark pigmentation.

FAULTS Broad muzzle; bad bite; underdeveloped canines; light eyes; ears with folds, pointed or erect; tail too short or not straight; legs not vertical; excessively long hair; partial depigmentation.

DISQUALIFICATIONS Insufficient or excessive height; disproportion between prescribed height and length; pointed nose; undershot jaw; monorchidism or cryptorchidism; colors different from those required by standard; total depigmentation of nose or eyelids.

MEASUREMENTS

	inches
Length of head	7¾-9½
Length of ears	4¾-5⅛
Length of neck	4¾-6¼
Length of trunk in excess of height at withers	2-3⅛
Circumference of trunk in excess of height at withers	4-4¾
Length of croup (value slightly larger in females)	5½-7

ISTRIAN COARSEHAIRED HOUND

196 ISTRIAN COARSE-HAIRED HOUND
Istrski resati gonič

YUGOSLAVIA

GENERAL CHARACTERISTICS A hound of medium weight, snow white, with yellow-orange markings, and long, coarse hair; the head is oblong, the body is compact, the bone structure is strong, the tail is solid and slightly curved upward. The eyebrows are thick; the expression is sober, sometimes melancholy. The breed is particularly successful in hunting hare, fox and roebuck; these dogs work equally well on a blood track. The voice is full, of medium pitch and sometimes very low-pitched.

WEIGHT AND SIZE Weight: 35-53 lb. The recommended weight for a normal dog is 44 lb. Height at the withers: 18-23 inches; females are usually slightly smaller.

HEAD In good proportion to the rest of the body and not too light, 8-9½ inches long. The nose is broad with well open nostrils, black or at least dark leather in color. A pinkish or flesh-colored nose is objectionable. Nasal bridge full. The lips should not be too thick or pendulous. The muz-

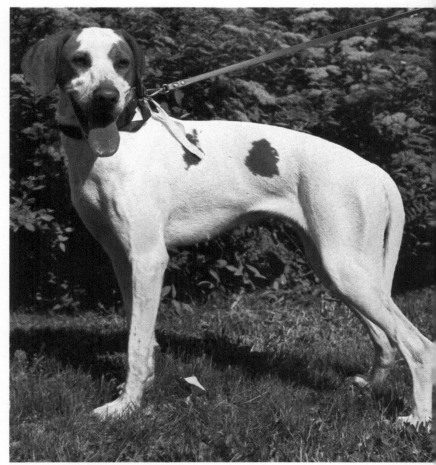

ISTRIAN SHORTHAIRED HOUND

Photo: Fotostampa-Embrione.

OFF TO THE HUNT

zle is strong, rectangular, not pointed, with thick moustaches. The forepart of the lower jaw is rounded, not squared off. The teeth are strong and close in a good scissors bite. The stop is not pronounced. The forehead is rather broad, narrower toward the eyes, slightly rounded; the occipital protuberance is well in evidence, as is the metopic suture, which is often covered with softer, longer hair.

EYES Dark-colored, full without being prominent; the haw is not visible; the expression is serious. The eyebrows are particularly bushy because of the long, tough hair of which they are composed.

EARS Not too thick, covered with shorter hair, set on slightly behind the eyes, but not too high on the skull: they widen toward the middle, hang along the cheeks without folds, and narrow and become rounded toward the tips; they are long enough to reach the nose or the canines; the minimum length should permit the ears to reach beyond the eyes. All three lengths are found—very long, long, semilong.

NECK The neck is 6-8 inches long, solid, without dewlap, with a visible depression behind the occiput.

BODY Oval chest. The thorax is broad, descending at least to the level of the elbows: its circumference ordinarily is some 4½-6 inches more than the height at the withers. The ribs are well sprung; the sternum is barely visible. The withers are not pronounced. The back is broad and straight; its length proportionate to the general size of the dog, its width diminishing toward the croup. The loins are full and short; the line of the belly rises gently from the sternum to the flanks, which must be neither relaxed nor drawn up; the belly is slightly tucked up. The croup is broad, especially in females, gently sloping, without, however, falling off greatly. The length of the trunk is 1-3 inches greater than the height at the withers.

TAIL Short; it reaches the hocks, or slightly beyond; set on not too high, thick at the base and slender at the tip; it is carried with a slight upward curve.

FOREQUARTERS The shoulders are long and sloping, well joined to the body and muscular; the scapula-humeral angle is 90 degrees; the elbows are close to the body. The forearm is straight and muscular. The wrist is not obvious; the pastern is vertical, short, only slightly inclined (no more than 10 degrees). The feet are narrow, compact, catfeet, with full, hard pads; the nails are strong. **HINDQUARTERS** Not greatly in evidence; the thighs are short, broad, muscular. The legs are longer, sloping and muscular. The hocks are big. The metatarsi are short and vertical. Dewclaws are acceptable, but not desirable. Hind feet like the forefeet, except that they are often longer.

COAT Hair The top coat is hard, and 2-4 inches long, not glossy, rough, ruffled without waves or curls. At least in winter there is an undercoat which is woolly but short. The top coat does not lie flat to the body: it should not be matted or feltlike (goat hair). The length and density vary from one part of the body to another and depend largely on climate, nutrition, care and the general conditions of the dog. **Color** Snow white. The ears are generally yellow-orange (mask); on the forehead there is often a star; the ears may be spotted with orange, and this is an indication of pureness of breed. More or less large markings (such as streaks, spots and points) may be found scattered over the whole body, most frequently at the root of the tail. Such markings, however, should never be so extensive as to dominate the basic color. Their color should be deep, that is, not pale or faded or brown, since these tones would indicate a mixture of blood. A third color is unacceptable, even if limited to a few hairs. **Skin** Pink; the lips, nose and eyelids are dark. The skin may also be uniformly white with no markings.

GAIT Regular.

FAULTS (a) **Of type:** height at the withers above or below standard; disproportion between height and length; muzzle too blunt, too pointed or puglike; glassy eyes, ears too short, too far from the head, set on too high or too low; tail curled or to one side; hair too long, soft, wavy, matted, curly; any color in markings besides orange, especially grayish or blackish. (b) **Anatomical:** undershot jaw; crooked forearm; elbows away from the body; pasterns too sloped; cryptorchidism. ●

197 ISTRIAN SHORT-HAIRED HOUND

Istrski kratkodlaki gonič

YUGOSLAVIA

This dog is common in Istria where he is also referred to as the Istrian Setter. The pure breed is of uniform type and has been prevalent in the area from the most ancient times. This handsome hound, of great endurance in broken and stony terrain, in pine thickets and heavy vegetation, is a favorite auxiliary of hunters who like to combine them into small packs when they hunt together.

He is equipped with an excellent sense of smell and is a good rabbit hunter, although he is not very well adapted for fox hunting.

GENERAL CHARACTERISTICS A distinguished hound, snow white, with yellow-orange markings and fine, short hair; the head is long, lean and narrow, and the body is agile. The tail is thin and slightly curved upward. This is an excellent tracking hound, especially good in working with hare and fox. Its voice is generally high-pitched, continuous and with a good timbre.

WEIGHT AND SIZE Weight: 31-44 lb; the normal weight is about 40 lb, although in a male it may vary. Height at the withers: 18-23 inches. Females are usually slightly smaller. Ideal height is about 20½ inches.

HEAD The length of the head measured from the occiput to the forepart of the nose is 8-9½ inches. The nose is black, or at least dark, with well open nostrils; any color but black is undesirable. The nasal bridge is full. The lips fit closely to the jaws, and are small and not pendulous. The muzzle is long, regular, not pointed and not puglike. The teeth are strong, meeting in a scissors bite. The stop is not pronounced, nor brusque. The forehead is long, rather narrow, and slightly rounded. The occiput is pronounced; the medial furrow is visible. There should be no wrinkles on the head.

EYES Oval in shape, open but not prominent, preferably dark. The haw should not be visible. The expression is wide-awake.

EARS Fine, broadly set on a little above eye level; they hang flat at the sides of the head, without folds, and are narrower at the ends and long enough to reach the canines (long ears), or to pass them (very long), or at least to pass the eyes (semi-long).

NECK From the occiput to the withers, the neck measures 6-8 inches. It is strong, slightly arched at the nape, with a visible depression behind the occiput. The neck is set on obliquely to the trunk. There is no dewlap.

BODY The chest is well rounded. The brisket is at least down to the elbows; the circumference behind the elbows is normally about 5 inches more than the height at the withers. The ribs are well sprung, the sternum barely visible. The withers are well marked but not pronounced, the back is broad and straight, neither arched nor saddled: the backline slopes gently from the withers to the croup. The loins are full and short. The croup, especially in females, is long and broad, straight or slightly sloping, but not greatly falling off. Its height is about ½ inch less than the height at the withers. The lower line of the belly slopes gently upward from the sternum to the flanks, which should neither be falling, which would give the dog a paunchy look, nor drawn up. The belly is slightly tucked up.

TAIL Of medium length, reaching not much below the hocks. It is set on high, it is thicker at the root and tapers toward the tip; it is carried slightly curved upward, but never curled or to one side. The more slender the tail, the more distinguished the dog.

FOREQUARTERS Long, sloping shoulders, with a scapula-humeral angle of 90 degrees; they are well joined to the rib cage and muscular; the elbows are close to the body. The forearm is entirely straight and muscular; the wrist is not greatly in evidence. The pasterns are vertical, short, occasionally slightly sloping (the permissible angle between pasterns and the vertical is at most 10 degrees). The feet are narrow, compact, rather catfeet than harefeet, with hard, full pads and strong nails. **HINDQUARTERS** Not greatly in evidence. The thighs are short but well filled out, broad and muscular. The stifle is high; the rotula is broad (the angle between femur and tibia is more than 120 degrees). The legs are long, sloping and muscular, and the hock is pronounced: seen from behind, the femur, tibia, Achilles tendon and metatarsus lie in a straight line. The metatarsi are short, vertical or perhaps only slanting (angle from 10 to 20 degrees). Dewclaws are not a fault but should preferably be removed. The hind feet, although a bit long, are otherwise similar to the forefeet.

COAT Short, of fine texture, dense, glossy and sometimes a bit longer on the thighs ("culottes") and on the tail, where it forms a fringe, although the fringe is not desirable. **Color** Snow white; the ears are usually yellow-orange; on the forehead there is often a star, or the ears are speckled with orange, this last condition being an indication of pure blood. Orange markings (streaked, spots and points), more or less large, may be found anywhere on the body, although they are generally seen at the root of the tail. They should never be so numerous as to predominate over the fundamental color. Their color should be strong, not pale or dull or brown, which would indicate mixed blood. A third color is not permissible, even if limited to a few spots. The coat may be solid white, that is, without markings. **Skin** Pink; the pigmentation of lips, nose and eyelids is deep.

GAIT The movements of this breed are quite free and lively.

FAULTS (a) **Of type:** height over or above standard; muzzle too blunt, pointed or puglike; walleyes; ears too short or too much off the head, set too high or too low; disproportion between height and length; tail curled or deviated to one side; hair too long; any color in the markings except orange, especially grayish or blackish. (b) **Anatomical:** undershot jaw; forearm short; elbows off the body; pasterns too sloped; cryptorchidism. ●

198 POSAVATZ HOUND

Posavaski gonič

YUGOSLAVIA

GENERAL CHARACTERISTICS A vigorous hound, of medium size, reddish, wheaten or fawn in color, usually with a white collar or at least white marking on the head, chest, neck and feet. The hair is short but dense, the head is long and narrow, the bone structure is solid, the tail is short and thick. A good tracking hound, with a high-pitched voice.

WEIGHT AND SIZE Weight: about 40 lb. Height at the withers: 18-23 inches; females are normally slightly smaller. The height at the croup is a little less, and thus the backline slopes from the head.

HEAD Measured from the dome to the forepart of the nose, the head is 8-9½ inches long. The nose is large, black or at least blackish. The bridge is slightly arched. The lips are not too heavy nor too pendulous. The muzzle is long, not pointed, regular in its development. The teeth are strong and meet in a scissors bite. The stop is well defined but not accentuated. The forehead is oblong, slightly rounded. The occiput is well in evidence.

EYES Well open but not prominent; dark in color, with a wide-awake expression.

EARS Hanging, rounded at the tips; long enough so that the ears, when extended, reach the canines.

NECK Long and muscular; there is a visible depression behind the occiput.

FOREQUARTERS Long and sloping shoulders, well joined to the body, muscular; the elbows are close to the body. The forearm is vertical and muscular. The wrist is not prominent. The pasterns are short, not bent. The feet are narrow and compact, catfeet rather than harefeet; the pads are full and hard, the nails strong.

BODY The length of the trunk is 1½-3 inches more than the height at the withers. The chest is well rounded and well let down, the brisket is at least at elbow level. The circumference of the body behind the elbows normally is about 4 inches more than the height at the withers. The ribs are well sprung, the sternum scarcely visible. The withers and back are strong without being prominent; the back is broad and straight, narrowing toward the croup. The loins are full and short. The belly line rises gently from the sternum to the flanks, which should not be loose nor drawn up. The croup is broad, especially in females, sloping but not falling off. The haunches are not prominent.

TAIL Short, not reaching below the hocks, set on at medium height; it is thicker at the base and tapers toward the tip. It is carried straight or curved upward; it should never have hard or bushy hair, although it may have a slight fringe.

HINDQUARTERS The thighs are short, broad and muscular. The stifle is high, the rotula is broad. The legs are long, sloping and muscular. The hocks are strong; the metatarsus is vertical and short. Dewclaws are permitted but should preferably be removed. The hind feet are similar to the forefeet.

COAT Dense, ¾-1½ inches, rather tough and not so fine as the Short-

ISTRIAN SHORTHAIRED HOUND

POSAVATZ HOUND

POSAVATZ HOUND

haired Istrian Hound's. The hair may be slightly longer on the belly, thighs and tail. **Color** The basic color is reddish; wheaten yellow with all the possible shadings, or decidedly fawn, but without darkening to deep brown (chocolate). A more or less wide, white collar is frequently found, as is a white stripe behind the occiput and on the muzzle, white markings on the chest, belly and feet, especially the latter. In any case, the white should not dominate the basic color. **Skin** Pink; lips, nose and eyelids dark.

GAIT Lively.

FAULTS (a) **Of type:** height at the withers over or above standard; disproportion between height and length; muzzle too blunt, too pointed or puglike; glassy eyes; ears too short, off the head, set on too high or too low; tail curled or deviated to one side; hair too long; all color in markings except white, especially grayish or blackish. (b) **Anatomical:** Undershot jaw; curved forearm; elbows falling away; curved pasterns; cryptorchidism. ●

199 BOSNIAN COARSE-HAIRED HOUND

Basanski ostrodlaki gonič-barak

YUGOSLAVIA

GENERAL CHARACTERISTICS A strong dog, with long, rough hair, a long head of medium width; thick, well marked eyebrows. The expression is serious, even severe, but playful. Full of temperament, courageous and persevering. The voice ranges from high to moderately low.

WEIGHT AND SIZE Weight: 35-53 lb; ideal weight, 44 lb. Height at the withers: 18-22 inches; ideal height 20 inches. Females are slightly smaller than males.

BASIC FORM The length of the trunk should be 10 percent more than the height at the withers.

HEAD The occiput is well marked, the forehead slightly protruding, the bridge straight. The skull has pronounced supraorbital ridges and a medial furrow which is accentuated to the touch. The stop is moderately accentuated. The muzzle is powerful and rectangular, with heavy moustaches and beard. Seen from above, the head is of medium width, narrowing toward the muzzle. The muzzle is slightly longer than the skull. The length of the head is 8-9½ inches. The muzzle narrows toward the nose, which is broad, with well developed nostrils; the nose is black or dull brown. The lips are rather fleshy and fit close to the jaws. The teeth are strong and close in a scissors bite.

EYES Large, oval, brown, with an intelligent and playful expression. **Ears** Set on at moderate height; they are of moderate length and height, and toward the end they narrow and become rounded; they are rather fleshy.

NECK Seen in profile, the insertion of the neck into the occipital region is well marked; the neck slopes into the trunk. Strong, of moderate width, it increases in depth toward the chest. The skin is close-fitting and elastic, and well covered with hair overall.

BODY General appearance: the backline slopes slightly from the withers to the croup. The withers are fairly prominent. The back is broad, compact and muscular; the flanks are short and muscular. The croup slopes gently and is broad (especially in females). The haunches are not pronounced. The thorax is long, fairly broad, slightly rounded, and the brisket is at least at elbow level. The chest is fairly broad. The belly and flanks are slightly drawn up.

TAIL Set on fairly high, the tail is thick at the root and tapers toward the tip. In length it reaches the hocks. It is carried slightly raised, and is well covered with hair.

FOREQUARTERS Regular as seen from in front or in profile. The shoulders are long, sloping and muscular. The humerus is long and muscular. The elbows are fairly close to the body. The upper arm and the scapula should form a 90-degree angle. The forearm is short, vertical and muscular, with good bone; the pasterns are fairly prominent and are either vertical or sloped up to 10 degrees; they are short. The forefeet are compact catfeet, with hard pads and dark nails.

HINDQUARTERS Seen from behind, or in profile, the hind legs are regularly positioned. The thighs are moderately long, broad and muscular. The shins are strong, long, sloping and muscular. The hocks are strong and well positioned. The metatarsus is vertical, short and strong. The leg from the hock to the ground is similar to the foreleg but slightly longer.

GAIT Sure and highly resistant.

SKIN Of medium thickness, elastic, close-fitting and well pigmented, well covered with hair.

HAIR Long, hard, wiry, with a dense undercoat.

COLOR The basic color is wheaten yellow, reddish yellow, gray, blackish. There are often white areas on the head, bridge, dewlap, chest, lower limbs and tip of the tail. The color may also be a combination of these colors. Bicolor or tricolor dogs are acceptable.

FAULTS Head too broad or heavy; eyelids lighter than nose and lips; pincers bite; ears wrinkled or away from head; insufficient dewlap; irregularities in positions and angulations; chest too wide and not sufficiently deep; slight saddleback or roach back; weak bone and muscle; harefeet, soft or open feet, dewclaws; slight disproportions among various parts of the body.

DISQUALIFICATIONS Lack of nobility in carriage of head; light eyes, fish eyes; lack of pigmentation on nose, lips and eyelids; height over or under standard; strong disproportion among the various parts of the body; legs strongly turning inward or outward; crooked, curled or inward-bent tail; bad teeth, bad jaws or abnormalities of the sexual organs; hair too long, soft, wavy or curly; any color besides those mentioned above, especially chocolate and black. ●

BOSNIAN COARSEHAIRED HOUND

Photo: Fotostampa-Embrione.

YUGOSLAVIAN TRICOLOR HOUND

YUGOSLAVIAN MOUNTAIN HOUND

200 YUGOSLAVIAN TRICOLOR HOUND

Jugoslavenski drobojni gonič

YUGOSLAVIA

GENERAL CHARACTERISTICS A medium long-lined dog on the basis of its shape, size and weight. The Yugoslavian Tricolor is well built, his body showing both strength and proportion. The colors are black, tan or yellow-and-white. Black dogs are commonest.

SIZE Height at the withers: 18-22 inches. Structurally perfect dogs may exceed or fall short of these limits by ¾ inch. The length of the trunk should be 2-3 inches more than the height at the withers.

HEAD Of medium length, in good proportion to the general size of the dog, 7-9 inches in length. The skull is quite flat, but rounded from one side to the other. The supraorbital ridges are not prominent, the medial furrow is not greatly marked and the occipital protuberance is well defined. The nose is fairly large and dark, preferably black. The bridge is straight, fairly long and broad, with a minimum stop. The lips are quite fine and firm; they are not pendulous, and the upper lip overhangs the lower very slightly.

EYES Dark in color, varying from brown to black, with a gentle expression.

EARS Set on above eye level, carried flat against the cheeks, rounded at the tips and not hanging below the back of the jaw.

NECK Well joined to the head and trunk, slightly sloping, moderately muscular: it widens toward the base, and its upper surface is wider than the lower.

FOREQUARTERS The shoulders are of moderate length and sloping, forming an angle of about 55 degrees with the horizontal; they are well muscled and close to the body. The upper arms are muscular, moderately long, with normal elbows; the forearm is straight, muscular and cylindrical. The wrist is not pronounced, the pasterns are straight, broad and not too long. The forefeet are rounded, with toes closed and arched with strong, dark nails. The pads are springy.

BODY The chest is broad and slightly rounded. The thorax is well developed in depth, height and width. The ribs are sloping and only moderately sprung. The back is rather short, straight and muscular. The loins are broad, short and well muscled. The belly is slightly drawn up, the flanks are slightly rounded. The croup is fairly long, broad and sloping.

TAIL Well set on; it is a prolongation of the loin line and when hanging it reaches the hocks; it is either straight or slightly curved (saber tail), held low in repose and slightly raised in action.

HINDQUARTERS The thighs are of medium length, broad and muscular. The legs are oblique, long and well muscled. The hocks are well developed as to height and width, with a fairly open angulation. The metatarsus is straight, almost vertical, long and without dewclaws. The foot is fairly rounded, the toes are closed with accentuated arching; the nails are strong, and the pads are solid.

COAT Short, dense and glossy, with an undercoat which should not be too abundant. Long hair on the underside of the tail is tolerated but not desirable. **Color** Three colors are obligatory. Black or yellowish black dominates, providing gloss to the coat. The black usually extends from the forehead to a part of the tail, covering the upper part of the neck and back. Pale yellow with shades deepening to tan is separated from the black on one side and from the white on the other; normally it surrounds the eyes, covers the inner face and the edges of the ears, the sides of the neck, the shoulders, the elbows, the legs and the hocks. White is found on the neck only as a stripe; it is seen in more or less extended markings on the throat, below the neck (where it forms a more or less regular color), on the chest, on the brisket, on the lower parts of the legs and the tip of the tail. White should cover about ⅓ of the body surface; it should not dominate and should not be present on the back. The lips, nose and eyelids should be dark and preferably black.

FAULTS All the faults common to hound breeds, and especially: bad proportion between height and length; short or rounded muzzle; muzzle too pointed or not straight; erect ears; depigmentation of eyes; coat too long; lack or excess of white markings.

DISQUALIFICATIONS One or more of the faults mentioned in the preceding paragraph, or: height above or below standard; overshot and undershot jaws; chest too narrow, too high; elbows badly joined; backline too long; saddleback; tail curled or carried above the backline; tail too curved to one side; legs turning inward or outward to a noticeable degree; pasterns too long or too sloping; monorchidism, cryptorchidism; exaggerated depigmentation of lips, nose or eyelids. ●

201 YUGOSLAVIAN MOUNTAIN HOUND

Jugoslavenski planinski gonič

YUGOSLAVIA

GENERAL CHARACTERISTICS A robust, shorthaired dog of medium size; black and tan coat and tan markings over the eyes, a characteristic of the breed. These dogs are calm and of good character. The body is elastic and rectangular in outline. It is a persevering hound when pursuing game.

SIZE Height at withers: 18-22 inches.

HEAD The skull is wide, narrowing progressively at the level of the eyes and ending in a strong, wedge-shaped muzzle. The head is in good proportion to the overall size of the dog, and in length measures 7-9 inches. The muzzle is a little shorter than the skull. The nose is black, of medium width, slightly rising above the line of the bridge, which is straight. The muzzle, broad and deep at the base, narrows gently toward the nose. The lips are well developed, close-fitting and black; the commissure is barely visible. Dentition is complete, and the jaws close in a scissors bite. The canines are strong. The stop is not prominent. The upper profile of the skull is straight or very slightly rounded. The supraorbital ridges are well in evidence, the medial furrow scarcely evident in its forward part. The occipital protuberance is not accentuated.

EYES Dark, with an intelligent expression. The eyelids are well pigmented and fit closely.

EARS Set on slightly low and, as a result, far apart from each other. They hang without folds, and have rounded tips. Extended, they reach the lower edge of the neck.

NECK The upper and lower sides of the neck diverge toward the trunk; the insertion of the neck into the head on one side and the body on the other are harmonious. Of medium length, oval, muscular, the neck widens toward the trunk. The skin is close-fitting, elastic, without folds or dewlap; it is covered with short hair.

FOREQUARTERS Seen from in front or in profile, they are normally vertical. In comparison with the height at the withers, they are relatively short. The shoulder is well joined to the body, long and sloping, forming with the horizontal an angle of about 50 degrees. The upper arm is long and slanted, forming an angle of approximately 60 degrees with the horizontal. The forearm is cylindrical, vertical, very strongly boned. The angulation of the elbow is rather open, the wrist is strong, the pasterns are lean and rather long; seen in profile, the pasterns from back to front form an angle of about 10 degrees with the vertical. The feet are strong, round, with well-closed toes; the pads are strong and elastic.

BODY The thorax is high, broad and deep. The brisket is beneath the elbow. The ribs are well sprung. The chest is broad. The upper line of the body is straight, slightly sloping toward the croup or horizontal. The withers are well defined but not prominent. They join the neck harmoniously, not abruptly. The back is broad and muscular; the backline continues the line of the withers toward the croup. The lumbar region is broad, strong, of medium length. The croup is on a level with the withers, slightly sloping, of medium length, broad, muscular. The haunches are barely apparent. The hollow of the flank is very slight.

TAIL Curved at the lower part, quite thick at the base; carried on a slant as a prolongation of the line of the croup. It reaches the hocks.

HINDQUARTERS Seen in profile, the vertical from the point of the ischium hits the ground slightly ahead of the toes. Seen from behind, the two legs are parallel. The thighs are long and muscular; the legs are strong and sloping; the metatarsus is oblique from back to forward (like the pasterns) and strong. The hind feet are similar to the forefeet and should not have dewclaws.

COAT The coat is thick, slightly coarse, flat, with an abundant undercoat. The hair is a little longer on the withers; on the head and the ears it is a little shorter than on the rest of the body. On the tail it is slightly longer but it does not form a brush. **Color** The background color is black, with red or rust-colored markings; over each eye there are hazelnut-shaped markings of the same color. A white spot, rather grayish, about 2 inches in diameter is admissible on the chest. **Skin** Soft, close-fitting and black.

GAIT The pace is sure, elastic and regular.

FAULTS Pointed or blunt muzzle; ears semierect; slight undershot condition; legs not properly vertical; height greater at the croup than at the withers.

DISQUALIFICATIONS All physical defects indicating degeneration; height above or below the standard; brush tail; light eyes; pronounced cow hocks or bow hocks; nontypical appearance; disproportion among the various parts of the body; any white marking other than that described in this standard. ●

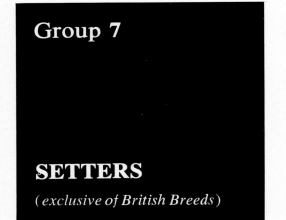

Group 7

SETTERS

(exclusive of British Breeds)

Firearms, social evolution, and the urban development of recent years, especially in the most industrialized nations, have profoundly modified the sport of hunting.

A feudal privilege once reserved for a select number of social categories, hunting has now become a popular pastime and, in the course of its development, has acquired features distinct from those of former times. Thus, for example, the laws governing it used to be left to the discretion of the gentry, who did not hesitate to promulgate stringent laws against whoever would kill, even in self-defense, wolves, bears, or other game. Legislation governing hunting is nowadays instituted by the state. But the greatest changes have occurred in the very methods of hunting. The great spectacular chase on horseback with packs of hounds in running pursuit of the game is the diversion today of only a very small number of devotees of the sport, and as a rule restricted by the scarcity of grounds available for it. The search for game with the help of a terrier has almost everywhere gone out of fashion.

Today hunting is done with an essential tool which is being continually perfected—the firearm, and the hunter, alone or with a few companions, moving on foot through fields, paths, woods, or swamp, no longer needs a dog that can run but one that can be of use when he hunts with a shotgun. Precisely such a dog is the setter.

What is a setter, and how does he work?

He can be defined as a dog trained to stop abruptly when he observes the presence of game after having carefully explored the grounds, covering either a small area (in which case it will be a trotting setter) or a large one (galloping setter). When he stops, this type of hunting dog remains as motionless as a statue, as though frozen or in a state of catalepsy, with nose "pointed," that is, turned in the direction of the scent.

To see such a dog when he stops in this manner is, according to experts, an exquisite aesthetic enjoyment: every muscle of the animal is tense, the vibrant tail signals his intent watch on the quarry as he awaits his master's shot.

Our contemporary dog lovers divide setters into two groups: those that are not British and which we shall presently review, and those that are native to the British Isles (pointer, setter, retriever, spaniel, and cocker) which we shall find in the eighth group.

Among the Continental setters, the Brach Hounds are outstanding. They are said to have originated from an ancient Italian dog called "dog of the net," which during the sixteenth century was much prized by avid bird hunters. The name "Brach" (in French *Braque* and Italian *Bracco*) comes from the German *brachacker*, meaning the uneven, uncultivated stretches of land which many breeds of Brach Hounds are especially well adapted to explore.

Another important group of setter breeds is the spaniel, beautiful dogs with a coat of soft, often curly, long hair. Even though the name suggests Spanish origin, this is by no means certain. All we know is that this is a very ancient breed of dogs of great agility, with excellent leaping and swimming aptitudes, often used in hunting waterfowl.

Finally, Griffons too have fine "stopping" aptitudes. They are akin to the Brach Hounds in size, shape, and origin but are distinguished by their often very rough coat.

202 KURZHAAR OR GERMAN SETTER

Deutscher kurzhaariger Vorstehhund

GERMANY

In the past this dog was considered heavy, tranquil, and slow, similar to the old Spanish Pointer. Today he is fast and elegant, and widely prevalent because of his many qualities which make him an excellent aid in quite different kinds of terrain.

There are many theories concerning his origins. Some think he is descended from local hounds, perhaps the old Bear Hound, while others, including French dog fanciers, believe he comes from the Italian Pointer which, crossed with indigenous German breeds, is thought to have produced the Kurzhaar. Still others consider that he descends from the Belgian Braque—a breed practically extinct today—or from the celebrated French "White

Dogs of the King," so esteemed in France in past centuries. The theory of his having descended from the Spanish Pointer is also worthy of consideration.

Not so long ago the German Setter had much grosser characteristics than he has today: he had abundant dewlaps, thick and pendulous lips, eyes which indicated conjunctivitis, a saddle back; he was rabbit-footed and had a massive aspect reminiscent of his Bloodhound strain. The field hunters who employed these setters had more patience and time than those of today, although there was then more feathered game available and they were quite satisfied with the help of these dogs which today seem to us not sufficiently adapted for this particular use. However, around 1970 sport hunters increased in some German regions and many English Setters were imported. Crossbreedings were carried out between them and the old Kurzhaar. The results were remarkable and were welcomed by the German field hunters, although not by the forest hunters. This was because the German-English dogs or "new Germans" as they were then called, could not perform satisfactorily in the kind of hunting the

Photo: W. Chandoha.

forest hunters preferred. Nevertheless, in view of the excellent qualities the dogs had acquired, the finer type of Kurzhaar was eventually given preference.

GENERAL CHARACTERISTICS The general appearance of the Kurzhaar is that of a distinguished and well-proportioned dog, whose structure is a guarantee of resistance, speed and strength. He should be neither small nor too big. Medium-sized dogs are preferred, for their short back permits them to cover a lot of ground. Heavy dogs, slow in movement, should be discarded; the first impression given by the dog should be that of a temperamental, energetic but not nervous animal, whose movements seem to be composed. The results of well-directed and intelligent breeding and refinement of the breed are shown not only in the bodily characteristics which are necessary for good movement, but also in the overall distinction of the dog, in the free outer lines, in the lean head, in the good carriage of the tail and in close-fitting skin. The shoulders should be long and sloping, the chest well let down, the loins muscular and the hindquarters robust; these characteristics are indications of speed. A high degree of resistance in the field is shown by good bone structure, a good spring of rib and well-marked muscling over the entire body.

SIZE The height at the withers should be 24½-25½ inches; the female is slightly shorter than the male but should never be less than 23 inches.

HEAD Lean, well defined, neither too light nor too heavy, of a size and length in good proportion to the rest of the body. The upper part of the skull is broad and flat; the medial furrow is not deep; the occipital protuberance is not so pronounced as in the Pointer. The nose is brown, and the larger the better; the nostrils are well open and mobile. Flesh-colored or spotted noses are not desirable, and are acceptable only with coats of light background. In profile the nasal bridge shows a slight arch which may vary from a distinct "Roman nose" effect to a barely perceptible arching of the straight line. This arching is generally more marked in males; a completely straight bridge is acceptable, but it is rare and less desirable. A concave bridge is undesirable. The nose is slightly protruding. The upper lips hang almost perpendicular to the point of separation, then extend in a slight curve to the commissure. The lips should not be excessively falling. The muzzle should be sufficiently robust and long to enable the dog to make a good and efficient retrieval of game. A pointed muzzle is unacceptable. Robust jaws, well-developed masseters. The jaws should not be overshot or undershot by more than 1/16 inch. The teeth are robust and sound, and the molars meet exactly; the upper incisors are exactly positioned over the lowers

(scissors bite). The stop is gentle; the supraorbital ridges, seen in profile, are pronounced.

EYES Of medium size, neither protruding nor excessively deep-set; the eyelids are close-fitting. The preferred color is deep brown; light yellow eyes (bird of prey) are undesirable.

EARS Moderately long, not too fleshy nor too fine; set on high; the hair on the ears is smooth; the ears are flat, without folds, and carried close to the cheeks. The tips are rounded. Their length enable them to reach the commissure.

NECK Of good length; muscular at the nape; slightly arched, the neck broadens gradually toward the shoulders; the skin at the throat should be as close-fitting as possible.

BODY In general, the chest should give the impression of being rather more let down than broad, but at the same time it should be in good proportion with the other parts of the body. The ribs should be well sprung, not flat as in the Greyhound, but never barrel-shaped; barrel ribs would not permit sufficiently deep breathing action. The back ribs should not be too far removed from the groin. The belly is slightly drawn up. The circumference of the trunk behind the elbows is from 3-4 inches more than the height at the withers. This circumference should be less than the circumference measured about 2 inches from the elbows, so that the humerus has sufficient moving space. A strong back is very important since it enables the dog to move energetically for long runs. Thus the back should be neither long nor arched. The loins are broad and slightly arched. The croup is broad, fairly long, neither raised nor sloping, and beginning at the level of the loins, with only a very slight slope to the root of the tail.

TAIL Set on high, thick at the root, the tail tapers gradually; it is of medium length. To avoid wounds during the hunt, the tail is docked to half or two-thirds of its original length. In repose it is carried down; in relaxed movement it is carried horizontally, neither high above the back nor greatly curved. During the hunt, the tail moves vigorously.

FOREQUARTERS The sloping shoulders are mobile and solidly muscled. The scapulae are flat, close-fitting to the body, with the humerus as long as possible. The elbows are set well back, neither too tight nor too loose to the body. The forearm is straight and lean, fairly muscular, well boned without coarseness, and the pasterns are only slightly sloped, nearly straight, never perpendicular.
HINDQUARTERS The pelvis is long, broad and roomy; the thighs are con-

GERMAN SETTER

268

GERMAN SETTER

GERMAN SETTER

sequently broad, well muscled and lean. There is a good angulation of leg and metatarsus (an excessive angulation is harmful to the dog's resistance). The metatarsus itself is of good bone, almost straight and almost vertical below the hocks. The hocks, seen from behind, should be turned neither inward nor outward. Dewclaws, if present, should be removed, since they impede the dog's work. The hind feet are robust, closed, either round or oval, with fairly well-arched toes and strong nails. The pads are solid and hard. Thin, weak bones are not desirable in a dog that must work in all kinds of terrain and must therefore have a great deal of strength. Here we are speaking not of the mass but of the structure of the bone: dogs with coarse bone lack mobility and speed. With good breeding procedures aimed at purifying the breed, the bones become in outer line finer but more compact, more solid overall, while coarse bone is porous and spongy.

COAT Short and thick, harsh and hard to the touch; on the underside of the tail it should not be excessively longer than on the rest of the coat. On the ears and head the hair is shorter and softer. **Color** The following are acceptable: (a) brown without markings; (b) brown with small white markings or spots on the chest and the legs; (c) dark roan, with brown head, and brown markings or spots. The basic color of this coat is not brown mixed with white or vice versa: the hair is an even mixture of brown and gray (white) producing the typical coat which is so useful in its work. On the inner side of the hind legs and on the tip of the tail the color is often lighter; in judging, the greater or lesser quantity of wholly brown markings should be considered: the fewer such markings there are, the better. The color of the head is generally brown; often, however, there is peppering on the bridge, occiput and lips; (d) light roan brown, with brown head and brown markings

or spots. In this coloring, the brown hairs are fewer and the white hairs dominate. Thus, dogs with this coat seem lighter; (e) white, with brown mask, markings and spots; (f) black in the same nuances, respectively of brown and brown roan. Yellow and tan is not considered a fault. **Skin** It should be close fitting, tight and not forming wrinkles or folds in any part of the body.

FAULTS (a) **Disqualifications.** Complete monorchidism or cryptorchidism; pronounced entropion or ectropion; undershot condition exceeding 1/16-⅛ inch; incomplete dentition, except for the first premolar on either side; serious faults of type. (b) **Faults excluding a rating above "Good."** Slight entropion or ectropion; pincers bite; first premolars lacking left and right; excessively heavy build or excessive massiveness of the hindquarters; loins too bent or too arched (roach back); serious faults in depth of thorax; elbows turned strongly outward; concave and spongy pasterns; gait with feet turned in or out; size more than ¾ inch above or below standard; cow hocks; open feet; "bird of prey" eyes, light yellow; hollowed bridge or excessively pronounced stop; loose shoulders; lack of expression in relation to sex; bad angulation of forelegs or hind legs. (c) **Faults excluding from rating as "Excellent."** First premolar lacking left or right, above or below; slight cow hocks; curved legs; feet slightly open; height at the withers slightly outside standard; loins excessively arched; sloping croup; forefeet turned outward (duck feet); very light eyes; too much or too little lip; slight insufficiency of shoulder; general appearance not very elegant or, when there are no other faults, a slight lack of expression in relation to sex of animal; faulty gait; tail carried too high above the backline and strongly bent. Dogs with natural tails and dogs with dewclaws are to be disqualified for not corresponding to the standard. ●

203 DRAHTHAAR (COARSEHAIRED)

Deutscher drahthaariger Vorstehhund

GERMANY

Almost sixty years ago three breeders left the Poodle Pointer Club to undertake the formation of the Drahthaar, a dog which could fulfill all hunting needs as practiced by professional or sport hunters. Such a dog would be of medium height, of undetermined color, and with a thick and stiff coat, physically strong and well balanced, and adapted to the general functions of a hunting dog. He would be a robust and well-formed dog, with a highly developed sense of smell, a quick intelligence, a lively temperament, and noble bearing. In a word: the old utility dog which would be able to carry out the demands of the hunter with absolute certainty.

Once the breed was fixed, the first entries in the Deutsch-Drahthaar Stud Book were made and soon reached a considerable number. During the years preceding World War II the entries reached a total of about 1,200 yearly.

A restrictive criterion concerning the Drahthaar's breeding consists in not listing more than six entries from a breeding, even if both parents are entered in the Drahthaar's Stud Book. The breeder is therefore obliged to make a first selection immediately, a method that may be questionable but which has concrete advantages regarding the stabilization of characteristics of a particular stock and the type in general.

Photo: S. A. Thompson.

GENERAL CHARACTERISTICS A Pointer of noble appearance, with hard hair which covers and protects the entire area of the skin. A lively temperament, and attentive and energetic expression. The dog's movement should be vigorous, broad, easy and harmonious. He is of very good proportons, lean, with joints, muscling and ligaments built in such a way as to give resistance, agility and speed to the dog's movements.

SIZE Height at the withers: males 23½-26½ inches; females 22-24½ inches. The length of the trunk and the height at the withers should be, if possible, equal; the former dimension may be ¾ inch more.

HEAD The dimensions of the head should be in good proportion to the overall size and the sex of the dog. The muzzle is broad, long and robust. The teeth should be complete, strong and closing in a scissors bite. The upper lip should not hang or descend over the lower lip.

EYES Not deep-set, clear, dark; the eyelids are well closed.

EARS Of medium size, set on high, broad and not turned.

NECK Of medium length, rather long and slender, with robust, lean muscling.

BODY The chest is prominent, the sternum prolonged toward the rear. The ribs are well sprung. The withers are well defined, long and muscular. The back is short, with a straight backline, which, however, slopes very slightly toward the muscular loin region. The belly is slightly drawn up, the flanks are free, short and high.

TAIL Set on as a continuation of the backline and, if possible, carried at the same height or slightly raised; not stiff, not too big and docked as required for hunting.

FOREQUARTERS AND HINDQUARTERS The shoulders are sloping and close to the body. The upper arm is rather long, the elbows should turn neither inward nor outward. The legs are robust, lean, perpendicular to the horizontal axis of the body; the angulations are such as to give good drive to the hindquarters. The pasterns are elastic and slightly bent. The thighs are of good width. **FEET** Round-oval, with compact toes and thick, hard pads. The gait is parallel to the horizontal axis of the body.

COAT Very tough and wiry, close-fitting and thick. The top coat is ¾-1½ inches long. The undercoat is long and thick. The surface of the body should not have excessively long hair since the hardness and thickness of the coat is supposed to provide good protection against rough weather and terrain. The lower parts of the legs, the lower part of the chest and the belly should have shorter hair (still providing a good covering, however); hair on the head and ears is shorter but thicker (not softer). The eyebrows should be accentuated, and there should be a robust

DRAHTHAAR (COARSEHAIRED)

beard, not too long, as coarse as possible, and which stresses the energetic expression of the muzzle. **Color** From dark brown to medium brown. It may also be roan-dark brown, roan-light brown, roan-black with or without markings. **Skin** Close-fitting, without wrinkles. ●

DRAHTHAAR (COARSEHAIRED)

Photo: E. Münch, S.E.F.

LANGHAAR (LONGHAIRED)

204 LANGHAAR (LONGHAIRED)

Deutscher langhaariger Vorstehhund

GERMANY

We have little information on the origins of this breed although it is evident that the physical and anatomical characteristics of these dogs are typical of spaniels. After passing through Spain, France, and England they arrived in Germany at an unknown time and were probably crossbred with indigenous breeds. The Langhaar has, in fact, preserved a great number of his ancestral qualities.

He has a keen sense of smell and is definitely not inferior to other spaniels in general qualities, as he is adapted to all kinds of hunting. He is gentle, very obedient, easy to train, and constant and tenacious in the hunt.

Despite his excellent qualities, this dog is disappearing. Apparently there are a few fanciers in Germany who favor it.

GENERAL CHARACTERISTICS A dog of robust, muscular build, but with a distinguished general appearance. The expression is one of intelligence and nobility, the character lively without nervousness.

SIZE The official German standard on the Langhaar gives no requirements for size. A good general estimate would be from 25-27½ inches.

HEAD Long, lean, quite broad, divided into equal length for skull and muzzle; the upper part of the head is slightly rounded. It is the head which gives import and distinction to the general appearance. The nose is flat, more or less deep brown in color; the bridge is fairly wide, with a slight arch; the lower jaw is robust; the teeth are complete and strong, with particularly robust canines and incisors, with no congenital or acquired fault. The stop is sloping. The foregoing refers to the head of the male; the head of the female should be narrower.

EYES Well closed, and the darker the better. They are symmetrically positioned.

EARS Broad-based, set on high, close-fitting and rounded at the tips, slightly wavy and hanging. Their length should be in good proportion to the size of the head and to the dog's general appearance.

NECK Robust but distinguished, merging gracefully with the chest and shoulders.

BODY The chest is deep, the brisket below the elbow, and wide in good proportion to the overall size of the dog. Thus the belly should be correspondingly drawn up. The back is solid, straight and short, the withers not pronounced. The loins are well made, the croup gently sloping. The length of the back should be in such proportion to the height at the withers that the overall body outline is square.

TAIL Well set on, carried horizontally, sometimes slightly curved upward, the tail may be slightly docked if it is too long or if it is out of proportion with the rest of the body; the long hair at the midpoint of the tail should be a good fringe.

FOREQUARTERS The shoulders should fit close to the body and not rise above the backline. The shoulder, upper arm, forearm, pastern and foot, seen from in front, are in a vertical line. The elbows are directed straight back, and only if the thorax is particularly robust are they slightly turned outward. In repose, the shoulder and upper arm form almost a right angle; the upper arm and forearm, a straight angle. **HINDQUARTERS** Seen from behind, the haunch, femur and tibia should form a vertical line; hocks and foot joints should be well angulated. Dewclaws should be eliminated. **FEET** Well closed, of moderate length, moderately round.

COAT A good coat is highly important in this breed. It should be that of a true Langhaar. On the back and flanks, 1¼-2 inches; on the underside of the neck, the chest and the belly, slightly longer. The legs should be well fringed; toward the feet the hair is shorter. On the head the hair is short, leaving intact the lean lines of the skull. As mentioned above, tail and ears should be feathered with good, faultless hair. The hair should be thick between the toes. ●

205 STICHELHAAR (WIREHAIRED)

Deutscher stichelhaariger Vorstehhund

GERMANY

Although considered the oldest of German Wirehaired Setters (he was first called the Hessischen Rauhbart) this direct ancestor of the Drahthaar was selectively bred at Frankfort-am-Main at a relatively recent date.

The first specimens were heavy, but not as heavy as the old hunting dogs then existing in Germany. They were very aggressive toward predatory animals and toward humans as well, an indication of blood strains from the old German sheep dogs. Subsequent selective breeding, not always performed with the necessary care, brought the breed to its present type. Today the breed is not very prevalent even in Germany.

GENERAL CHARACTERISTICS The overall appearance of this breed is robust but not heavy. The forequarters and hindquarters should be in good proportion to each other and to the rest of the body. When walking, the Stichelhaar holds head and neck slightly erect, with the tail almost always carried slanting upward; when hunting, the dog carries the tail more horizontally. The general impression is one of intelligence and seriousness. Because of the thickness of the eyebrows, the expression seems almost threatening. In this breed a general appearance of harmony is more important than detailed measurements.

SIZE Males 23½-26 inches; females slightly smaller.

HEAD Of medium size (length approximately 9-10 inches), not too heavy. The upper part of the skull is slightly rounded, broad; seen in profile, its highest part is in the middle. The occipital protuberance is not accentuated. The nose is broad, well open, well muscled; depending on the color of the dog, it may be dark or light brown. A double nose is inadmissible. The bridge is long, broad, straight, never hollowed; the muzzle should not be too short and should be rather square, never pointed; when the lips are closed they fall over the commissure and form a fold where they meet. The stop is not pronounced.

EYES Slightly oval, of medium size, clear, neither protruding nor deep-set; the eyelids are close-fitting; color, brown, and the eyes may be lighter in dogs with light coats, but they should never be yellow "bird of prey" eyes. The eyebrows are bushy, robust and thick, with the hair directed outward.

EARS Of medium length, not too wide in the upper part, slightly rounded at the bottom; they are set on high and are regular throughout their entire length; the ears should not be set back too far and, if possible, should be without folds. They hang flat and close to the head.

NECK Of medium length, robust, slightly arched at the nape, the neck broadens gradually toward the breadth of the chest. There should be no dewlap.

BODY Seen from the front, the chest is moderately broad; seen in profile, the thorax is deep, the ribs are well sprung and must never be flat. The back is broad and straight; the loins should be broad and short; both the back and the loins should be well muscled; the croup should not be too short and only gently sloping. The belly is compact, especially toward the flanks, and it is moderately drawn up.

TAIL Of medium length, straight, sometimes slightly curved upward, thick at the root, not set on too low; it tapers gradually toward the tip of the tail, which should not be too pointed. The tail may be moderately docked, but the remaining part should be at least as long as half the distance from the root of the tail to the hocks.

FOREQUARTERS Shoulders sloping, elbows turned neither in nor out; the forearm and pastern should be straight and well developed, the wrist should not be bent. The toes are well arched, closed; the foot, seen from in front, appears round. The nails are well arched. The pads are large and strong. **HINDQUARTERS** The thighs and hind legs are muscular; the hind leg forms a slight angle with the hock, which must not be too straight or too slanted, as in the Greyhound. The metatarsus is not too slanted but almost straight beneath the hock. Seen from behind, the hocks should appear perpendicular.

COAT The hair on the trunk should be about 1½ inches long, lightly

STICHELHAAR (WIREHAIRED)

Photo: E. Münch

close-fitting and directed from forward back, or from above down, straight, rather like bristles; immediately above the shoulders and in the lower part of the body, the hair is slightly longer from the throat down on the centerline of the chest and belly, in such a way that the longest hair, which is directed downward, forms a light fringe. Over the entire body there is often a barely visible undercoat, which is heavier in winter; in summer it is very light and often disappears entirely. On the muzzle the hair forms moderate moustaches, on the bridge the hair is short and hard, never long and soft and preferably falling. On the skull the hair is flat, short and hard; on the ears it is slightly harder and longer than in the shorthaired variety, but is not so harsh as on the skull. The head should have no soft, woolly or silky hair, except for moderate moustaches and eyebrows. The eyebrows are thick, robust, with the hair turned upward and the tips of the individual hairs slanting toward the outside. On the front part of the forelegs the hair is flat; on the back part it forms a small fringe which goes from the elbow to the wrist. There is also a light fringe on the hind legs, extending almost to the hocks. The tail is extremely well feathered. On the underside the hair is a little longer, without, however, forming a brush or fringe. The hair fits closely to the tail, so that even the longest hair on the underside of the tail does not interrupt the straight line. **Color** Brown and white, gray-brown mixed, or with larger, individual markings of brown.

FAULTS Heavy, awkward build or excessive height; head too large, the forepart of the skull wedge-shaped, excessive occipital protuberance; nose flesh-colored or black; imperfect fit of the eyelids (so-called "lachrymal sacs"); saddleback; forelegs not straight, loose elbows, feet turning out, flat feet, open toes; tendency of hair to divide on the back; soft or semisoft (goat hair) hair, with the exception of the moustaches and the eyebrows; predominant white coloring, if not truly a fault is at least not desirable; only limited tan markings—to different shades of brown—are acceptable, but the black hairs usually found with this color and yellow or fawn markings on the head and legs are faults. ●

206 LARGE MÜNSTERLÄNDER

Grosser Münsterländer

GERMANY

GOOD POINTS People once said, "Whatever is good is also beautiful"; today we could say, "Whatever is both good and beautiful is even better." Rigid specifications in Germany today insist on a well-defined type, distinguished, lean, with the height at the withers between 23 and 24½ inches. The color is white with black spots, or white with spots and speckling or black-and-white roan. A wholly black coat is less desirable; this coloring has thus far resulted from cross breeding with the German Langhaar, which in the future will not be permitted, since the best of the dogs produced by such cross breeding have already been accepted in sufficient numbers into the breed. Multicolored brown puppies will also not be accepted in the future. So far as build is concerned, the aim is the same as for any good dog and for all those qualities which do not detract from his work in the field and from his hardiness, to wit, a distinguished, long head; lean muzzle; ears of medium length, set on rather high and with good fringe; dark eyes, with uniform eye rims; and an intelligent expression. The chest must be of good depth in relation to breadth. The back should be straight and solid, the loins muscular, the croup moderately hollowed. The tail should be set on high, either straight or with a slight upward curve, well feathered (the tip should be docked from ¼ to ¾ inch on the third or fourth day after the birth of the puppy and the dewclaws should be removed from the hind legs). When the dog is standing, seen from in

LARGE MÜNSTERLÄNDER

LARGE MÜNSTERLÄNDER

207 SMALL MÜNSTERLÄNDER

Kleiner Münsterländer

GERMANY

Although the number of Brittany Spaniels in Westphalia in 1910 was not more than fifty, it was decided to form a local breed utilizing the surviving Brittany Spaniels as well as the numerous specimens of the Deutsch Langhaar (German Longhair). The breeding was so well performed that today the Small Münsterländer numbers several thousand dogs, all with uniform points.

The present efforts of breeders belonging to a very competent dog club (Verband für Kleiner Münsterländer) are united in their aim to eliminate as much as possible the incidence of Langhaar blood so as to obtain dogs typically spaniel in appearance.

front, the shoulder, upper arm, forearm and feet should be approximately a straight vertical line; the shoulder and upper arm, in profile, should form a right angle. Seen from behind, the pelvic bones, the femur, the tibia and the tarsus should lie in a straight, vertical line. The hocks and articulations of the feet should be well angulated, and the feet should be closed. The coat should be long, naturally smooth and slightly wavy. The back of the forelegs and hind legs should have a fringe.

FAULTS Too light eyes, eyes too open or with the nictitating membrane (third eyelid) visible; tough ear tips;

dewlap, loose skin; curly tail; harsh or excessively abundant hair, undistinguished or tangled coat, curly hair on head; drooling or undershot jaws; defects due to inferior kennel care (wrong diet, worming) such as barrel ribs or compressed rib cage; long back, saddleback; dog thrown forward or with forequarters higher than hindquarters; badly set shoulders; excessively acute angulations of forequarters; "French position" of forequarters, cowhocks in hindquarters; round feet (catfeet) or long feet (harefeet). Dogs with secondary sexual characteristics belonging to the opposite sex are to be considered as not promising for breeding. ●

GENERAL CHARACTERISTICS The Small Munsterlander is a working dog whose sharp intelligence, vigor and fidelity enable him to adapt quickly to any type of terrain or quarry which may be selected by his master, for whom he is a tireless and devoted companion and aid. At home the Münsterländer is an excellent guard dog and a good-natured companion. His virtues as a working dog include a diligent and meticulous tracking ability, maximum ruggedness and resistance (even to external forces), a solid pointing capacity, an infallible tenacity on the scent, a great love for retrieving and enthusiasm for working in water. He is easy to guide and re-

acts ferociously to predators. The smallest of German gun dogs, the Small Münsterländer is strongly built, of great resistance, very distinguished, and all in all ideally adapted to the requirements of his job in the field.

SIZE Height at the withers: males 19-22 inches; females 17½-20½ inches. Studs should be selected with a view to maintaining these standards.

HEAD Should be lean and distinguished. The nose is brown and should have no white or flesh-colored markings. The lips fit well over the gums and close tightly. The muzzle is long and not too heavy. The stop is not pronounced.

SMALL MÜNSTERLÄNDER

274

Photo: E. Münch, S. A. Thompson.

SMALL MÜNSTERLÄNDER

EYES Dark, well set into the eye rims. The eyes are an important distinguishing characteristic of the breed, setting it apart from any other group.

EARS Light, with good feathering. The tips are pointed.

NECK Slightly arched, very muscular, it gifes an impression or shortness.

BODY The chest is deep and broad, with well sprung ribs; the body has everything needed in a rugged, swift dog. The trunk is distinguished by a straight back that is exceptionally solid and robust. The croup is well developed, the loins well filled out.

TAIL Carried straight out, with a slight curve in the last third, with a magnificent white or grizzle flag. The dog uses his tail as an instrument of expression, and this signaling ability is highly useful in its work, particularly in water.

FOREQUARTERS AND HINDQUARTERS In judging the dog's build attention should be paid to sufficient angulation and close fitting of the shoulders. The forelegs should be solid and straight. The hindquarters should be well angulated, with well-muscled thighs. The metatarsi should be solid and the feet closed, these characteristics being the guaranty of a free and elegant movement.

COAT Smooth and close-fitting, forming a complete fringe on the tail, covering the edges of the ears with a slight wave and feathering the legs well. An excessive coat, strongly waved or tangled, hampers the dog's activity in the field and is therefore faulty. **Color** The basic coloring is white and brown; the head is covered with brown hair, almost always marked or tufted. Some strains have sporadic tan markings on the muzzle or above the eyes. Puppies are born white with brown markings or else with a brown coat; after 6 or 8 weeks the characteristic markings appear with white marbling on the brown. A few days after birth the pads of the feet darken. ●

SMALL MÜNSTERLÄNDER

208 PUDELPOINTER
GERMANY

As its name indicates, this breed represents a compromise between the Poodle and the Pointer. The idea of a dog of this kind started in Germany toward the end of the last century. It was desired to obtain a good general hunting dog, specialized in partridge hunting like the Pointer, good in marshes like the old Barbet Hound, in the woods like a Cocker, and also like a Retriever for the hunt.

The Pointer was chosen for his keen sense of smell, his fiery temperament, his speed, and the Poodle for his intelligence, obedience, adaptability, instinct for retrieving, fidelity, love of water, and aggressiveness toward the game (foxes, polecats, etc.).

Through judicious crossbreeding between excellent breeding dogs and by careful selective breeding, the product of an all-purpose dog was obtained, endowed with good structure and a resistant and hard coat with a soft undercoat, enabling him to meet all kinds of hunting conditions.

GENERAL CHARACTERISTICS The ideal type has a build similar to that of a heavy Pointer.

SIZE Breeders should endeavor to arrive at a height at the withers of 23½-25½ inches. Males below 22 inches and females below 21 inches should not be inscribed in pedigree books. The length of the trunk in respect to the height at the withers should be in the ratio of about 10:9.

HEAD Of medium length, broad, covered with rough hair, a beard and heavy, bushy eyebrows. The bridge should resemble the line and the direction of the Pointer's. The long, broad muzzle, not narrow and ending in a point like the muzzle of the Poodle, is to be preferred. The stop should be clean and perpendicular.

EYES Large, round, full of fire, with a "bird of prey" expression, with the color ranging from yellow to yellow-brown.

EARS Of medium size, flat, adhering to the size of the skull, neither thick nor fleshy; they are more pointed than rounded and are fairly well feathered.

NECK Of medium length, lean and muscular, arched at the nape. Breeding should strive to avoid flat necks that are not sufficiently muscled.

BODY The croup is long, moderately sloping, well muscled. The back is short and straight, with very muscular loins; the flanks are broad. The hocks are high, long and full. The chest is moderately broad and very deep. The ribs are well sprung. The belly is drawn up, lean and short in the loin section.

TAIL The tail is light, set on in a way similar to the Pointer's, and is carried horizontally; it does not have a harsh fringe and is covered with harsh hair. In puppies the tail should be docked for use in hunting, in such a way that in females it reaches the lower margin of the vagina and in males should be sufficiently long to cover the testicles.

FOREQUARTERS The shoulders are oblique, broad, long, close to the body and full. The muscling should be very apparent. The forelegs are straight, the bones of the upper arm and the forearm are long and covered with taut muscling. The articulation of the elbow is set far back, and the tendons are clearly visible. **HINDQUARTERS** The angulation of the bones is correct, the muscles are long, taut, robust and well developed in proportion to the overall physique. The hocks are rather far back, high and distinctly angulated. The forelegs and hind legs, seen from behind, are nearly vertical. **FEET** Round, with closed toes. The pads should be very robust. The hair covering feet and toes should be short.

COAT The ideal coat is of medium length, very hard, rough and thick. The lower part of the legs should be covered with short hair. **Color** Light brown or brown. Any white color, black or too light or streaked (unless such streaking is minimal) is not allowed. ●

PUDELPOINTER

Photo: S. A. Thompson, E. Münch.

209 WEIMARANER

GERMANY

Some authorities claim that the Weimaraner is derived from a cross ordered by the Grand Duke Charles Auguste of Weimar (whence the name) between a yellow Pointer and a bitch of an unspecified breed. Strebel, on the other hand, maintains that the breed always existed and that its present form is due to albinism.

The hypothesis supported by the German Weimaraner Association is more likely: the basic stock of the breed is the Leithund, considered in turn to be the descendant of the Bracken (an ancient German hound). Colonel De Mori, who has closely studied this breed, observes: "There exist genetic characteristics that lead one to suppose that there are marked relationships between the Bracken and the Weimaraner as, for example, the form of the skull, the rectilinear nose groove, the minimal frontal furrow of the nose, the moderately pendulous lips, the small labial seam, the way the tail is carried, etc."

The fact that these typical congenital particulars have been preserved through the centuries is a clear demonstration of the breed's inalterable qualities. At the same time it is possible that the breed has never been crossbred and that it must be accorded precedence over other German hunting breeds.

GENERAL CHARACTERISTICS A medium-sized gray dog, with fine, aristocratic features. The Weimaraner should present a picture of grace, speed, stamina, alertness and balance. Above all, the dog's conformation must indicate the ability to work with great speed and endurance in the field. The temperament should be friendly, fearless, alert, and obedient.

SIZE Height at the withers: males 25-27 inches; females 23-25 inches.

HEAD Moderately long and aristocratic, with moderate stop. Rather prominent occipital bone and trumpets well set back. Measurements from tip of nose to stop equal that from stop to occipital bone. The flews should be straight, delicate at the nostrils.

Skin drawn tightly. Neck clean-cut and moderately long. Teeth even; the upper teeth protrude over the lower teeth slightly, but not more than 1/16 inch. The nose is gray. Lips and gums are pinkish-flesh shades.

EYES Light amber, gray or blue-gray, set well enough apart to indicate good disposition and intelligence. When dilated in excitement the eyes may appear almost black.

EARS Long and lobular, slightly folded and set high. When drawn snugly alongside the jaw the ear should end approximately 2 inches from the point of the nose.

BODY The back should be moderate in length, set in a straight line, strong, and should slope slightly from the withers. The chest should be well developed and deep, with shoulders well laid back. Ribs well sprung and long. Abdomen firmly held; flank moderately tucked up.

TAIL Docked. At maturity it should measure approximately 6 inches, with a tendency to be light rather than heavy.

FOREQUARTERS AND HINDQUARTERS The forelegs are straight and strong, with the measurement from the elbow to the ground approximately equaling the distance from the elbow to the top of the withers. The hindquarters should have well-angulated stifles and straight hocks. The feet should be compact, webbed, toes well arched, pads closed and thick, nails short and gray or amber. Dewclaws should be removed.

COAT Short, smooth, and sleek. **Color** Solid, in shades of mouse gray to silver gray, usually blending to lighter shades on the head and ears. A small white marking on the chest is permitted, but should be penalized on any other portion of the body. A dis-

WEIMARANER

Photo: S. A. Thompson, E. Münch.

WEIMARANER

tinctly blue or black coat is a disqualification.

GAIT Should be effortless and indicate smooth coordination. When seen from the rear, the hind feet should be parallel to the forefeet.

FAULTS Minor faults: Tail too short or too long; pink nose **Major faults:** Doggy females, effeminate males; improper muscular condition; badly affected teeth; more than four teeth missing; back too long or too short; faulty coat; neck too short, thick or throaty; low-set tail; elbows in or out; feet east or west; poor gait; poor feet; cow hocks; faulty back, either roached or sway back; badly overshot or undershot bite; snipy muzzle; short ears. **Very serious faults:** White, other than a spot on the chest; eyes other than gray, blue-gray or light amber; black-mottled mouth; not docked tail; dogs exhibiting strong fear, shyness or extreme nervousness.

DISQUALIFICATIONS Deviation in height of more than 1 inch from standard either way. A distinctly long coat.

OBSERVATIONS The old standard for the Weimaraner permitted registration of longhaired dogs. In comparison with the shorthaired variety, the following points are of value: body sometimes slightly longer with a less impressive muscular system. A greater margin of tolerance in regard to height at the withers; dark flesh-colored nose, straight and often arched nasal bridge; muzzle seemingly longer because of the back position of the masseters. Minimal stop; rather light head, with a narrower skull and a slightly more pronounced nape. Light eyes, amber; expressive and intelligent expression (puppies have blue eyes); ears light, broad, alert, curled, rounded at the tips; set on high with narrow base. Legs thinner but with good tendon; hair softer and thicker; coat solely solid-colored in the following shades: silver gray, mouse gray, roebuck gray. Small white flecks. Faded tan markings are not desirable. Hair of the long variety, which is very rare, is eagerly sought. ●

WEIMARANER

277

Photo: MARKA, R. Kinne (Photo Res.).

GAMMEL DANSK HONSEHUND

BURGOS SETTER

210 GAMMEL DANSK HONSEHUND

DENMARK

GENERAL CHARACTERISTICS A powerfully built, rugged hunting dog. The length of the body is greater than the height at the withers.

SIZE Males, 20½-23 inches, with preference given to specimens over 21¼ inches; females, 19-21¼ inches, with preference given to those over 19¾ inches.

HEAD Relatively short and deep. Ample nose, with well-developed light or dark liver-colored nostrils. Deep muzzle, broad bridge. Lips slightly pendulous; scissors bite. The stop should not be too evident. Broad skull, pronounced occipital crest.

EYES Not too small; lower lids slightly relaxed. Color ranging from light to dark hazel.

EARS Of notable length and width, well rounded at the tips, set on rather low, pendant, with forward edge touching cheek.

NECK Strong, muscular, with dewlap, especially in the male.

FOREQUARTERS Powerful, oblique shoulders. Legs strong and straight. Round feet, with well-arched, closed toes. Tough soles.

BODY Well developed, deep and broad. Back muscular, straight; strong loin.

TAIL Of medium length, thick at the root, tapering gradually to the tip; set on rather high, the tail hangs straight, becoming raised in movement.

HINDQUARTERS Thighs should be muscular. Good angulation. The feet have the same characteristics as for the forequarters.

GAIT Free, elastic, rugged.

COAT Dense, short tight coat. **Color** White with light or dark liver markings. ●

211 BURGOS SETTER

Perdiguero de Burgos

SPAIN

The Burgos Setter or Perdiguero is an ancient Spanish hunting dog with excellent qualities. He is enduring, serious, gentle, easy to train, with a keen sense of smell either for the stop or for the retrieve. He is a dog for use on any kind of terrain. His resistance to bad weather and his ability with feathered as well as other game is much esteemed and make him the favored Spanish hunting dog. The care which has always been given to breeding him has served to preserve his original qualities, and today it is not difficult to find absolutely pure specimens. His ancestry is the same as that of other setters.

WEIGHT AND SIZE Weight: varies with the size of the dog; it should be 55-66 lb for males, slightly less for females.

HEAD Large, broad nose dark but not black; muzzle almost square; lips large but not excessively so and not pendulous. The forehead is rounded, the skull slightly domed; the profile is straight and perfectly outlined from the muzzle to the skull. The stop is at the midpoint between the occiput and the tip of the nose.

EYES Have an intelligent and melancholy expression; they are well protected by prominent supraorbital ridges, which are dark in color.

EARS Set on high. They are long and wide, hanging down in folds, and are pointed at the tips. The texture is soft.

NECK The neck is well proportioned, round and strong. The skin is slightly wrinkled at the dewlap.

BODY The chest is broad and strong, the rib cage strong with well-sprung ribs, giving power and resistance. The withers are slightly raised, the croup is well rounded, slightly hollowed and broad.

TAIL Thick at the root and tapering to the tip. Carried high and gaily. It should be docked to 1/3 of its length.

FOREQUARTERS Solid, with good free movement, as are the hindquarters. The shoulders are very muscular and strong, well filled out and short, which means that this breed does not have a very fast gait. **HINDQUARTERS** Broad thighs, muscular; the legs are long, vertical, turned neither inward nor outward. **FEET** Short and round (catfeet). The toes are arched, with strong, dark nails.

COAT May be one of two types: either predominately white, with liver markings or spotting, or more or less dark liver, with white speckling.

SCALE OF POINTS

General appearance	25
Head	12
Eyes	4
Ears	11
Body	18
Legs	18
Tail	4
Coat	8
	100

212 SPANISH HOUND

Sabueso Español

SPAIN

Spain too has a hound whose origins are common to those of other hounds that have become prevalent throughout Europe. The breed has been fixed in the Iberian Peninsula from such far-off times that today it is considered to be indigenous.

SPANISH HOUND

Photo: A. Wintzell, Barrachina.

BURGOS SETTER

GENERAL CHARACTERISTICS The general appearance is that of a strong dog, rather long and lean but not excessively so, of a serious but not sad expression (and the expression should not be suspicious). The dog may have a wrinkled forehead, which gives him an even more thoughtful appearance.

SIZE Males 20-22 inches; females 19-20½ inches.

HEAD Should be long, with a large and well-rounded skull. The curve from one ear to another over the occiput should be a rather elongated, pointed arch.

EYES The eyes are more or less dark chestnut, without abnormal markings in the iris; well covered by fine lids which do not hang, well pigmented and with fine hair and eyebrows.

EARS The ears are very long. They should reach the nose without stretching. They are fine and flexible and set below eye level.

NECK Strong; loose skin, forming wrinkles, should not be considered a fault.

BODY The chest is broad, high and deep, with well-sprung, strong ribs; the circumference of the thorax measured just behind the elbows should be at least 4½ inches more than the average height at the withers. The back is straight or slanted slightly forward when the dog does not have his hind-legs out in back; the loins are a little short and slightly rounded; in the pos-

terior part they are as high as the withers. The belly is compact and not drawn up.

TAIL Thick at the root and tapers to a point. Carried down, it should reach a little lower than the point of the hocks; it is set on rather low, and in repose it is carried down; it is curved upward in movement, but should never be curled.

FOREQUARTERS Straight, strong; the pasterns are vertical or slightly sloped forward, with strong but not stocky articulation. **HINDQUARTERS** The thighs are slanted and very muscular; the hocks are strong: their extremities should be vertical to the point of the buttocks; the lower legs are short and perpendicular to the ground. A small dewclaw is not a fault. **FEET** Regularly arched, long, tending to have a triangular print; they are not flat, but the toes are compact and do not separate much when the foot is on the ground. The pads are hard and surrounded by hair.

COAT Should be fine and with no fringe at any point. **Color** The coat should be generally white, with large round markings of more or less deep orange or black. **Skin** A little heavy but elastic and fairly loose.

SABUESO ESPANOL, LIGHT VARIETY

GENERAL CHARACTERISTICS The general appearance is that of an agile, light lively dog, which is nevertheless

not so mobile as the Perdiguero. Some dogs of this variety have a characteristic thoughtful expression.

SIZE The height should be less than 20 inches in males, less than 19½ in females.

HEAD Long, with a pigmented nose. The mouth is not large, and the lips, if at all pendulous, are only slightly so. The cheeks are lean, and the muzzle is less heavy than in the standard dog. The teeth are sound and well adapted. The skull is quite broad and well rounded.

EYES Brown, with no abnormal markings, with fine eyelids; the haw should not be visible.

EARS Longer than the muzzle, fine with rounded tips; they are set on low, as in the larger Sabueso.

NECK Not very long and without wrinkles in the skin.

BODY The chest is broad and deep, the ribs are well sprung. The circumference of the thorax should be at least 4½ inches greater than the height at the withers. The back is straight and horizontal; the loins are strong and rather filled out. The belly is straight, not falling, and with no sign of hernia.

TAIL Thin, with short, fine hair.

FOREQUARTERS Straight, with slightly prominent muscling. **HINDQUARTERS** Strong, very muscular. Perfectly vertical, with no trace of

twisting; the dewclaw is not a fault as long as it does not hamper the gait. **FEET** The toes are rather long and slightly arched; the pads are hard. Flat feet are not acceptable, nor are cat-feet.

COAT The coat is short, smooth and glossy. **Color** White with red or black markings, which may be so extensive as almost to cover the whole animal except for the neck, muzzle, chest and feet. **Skin** Fine and elastic.

SCALE OF POINTS

General appearance and symmetry	6
Head	10
Mouth, lips	2
Bridge and nose	7
Ears	3
Eyes	4
Neck	4
Back, shoulders, forequarters	10
of thorax	15
Croup and loins	10
Haunches and hindquarters	12
Feet	7
Tail	2
Coat and color	8
	100

NEGATIVE POINTS

Albinism, depigmented eyelids	20
Overshot or undershot jaw	10
Dental cavities	8
Tricolor coat, tan markings above eyes	10
Rickets	25
In small dogs, tumors, hernias, etc.	10

213 IBIZAN PODENCO
Podenco Ibicenco
SPAIN

This country dog comes from Ibiza in the Balearic Islands. He is very prevalent throughout the archipelago, especially on Mallorca where he is known by his original name "ca eivissenc." He is also found in Catalonia and in France, in Roussillon, and in Provence. His name changes in Mallorcan dialect according to region; Mallorcan Xarnelo, Charnegue, Charnigue, and Balearic dog. He exists in three varieties, smooth-coated, coarse-haired, and longhaired. He belongs to the Graioid family and shares common origins with all Mediterranean Greyhounds.

He is agile, resourceful, intelligent, gentle, and is capable of making great bounds from a standing start. He hunts more by his sense of smell and hearing than by sight, and when he sees or hears the quarry he makes a stop which he easily breaks. Among other things he is a very good retriever. He is used especially for rabbit hunting, either by day or by night, even in thick underbrush. Sometimes he is also used to hunt hares, partridges, and larger feathered game.

Females are used in the packs, never more than one male. In hunting they do not cooperate with each other and are rather quarrelsome. When a pack has hunted some thousands of rabbits it sometimes happens that some of the dogs are unwilling to hunt further or only return to the hunt after a long rest. There is a local name for this condition—"fed up with rabbits."

WEIGHT AND HEIGHT Weight: males about 49 lb; females about 42 lb. Height: males 23½-26 inches; females 22½-25 inches.

HEAD Long and narrow, wedge-shaped, lean; the stop is not pronounced, and the forehead is narrow. The nose is prominent, protruding in respect to the lower jaw, flesh-colored, in harmony with the color of the coat; nostrils well open. The bridge is slightly arched; the length of the bridge from the eye to the tip of the nose is equal to the distance between the eye and the occiput. The lips are thin and compact, the jaws are strong and dry, meeting in a level bite; white teeth, well set; long, flat skull; occipital protuberance prominent.

EYES Slanted and small, light amber in color, with a very intelligent, but not particularly noble, expression.

EARS Invariably rigid; normally directed forward, horizontally toward the sides, or back, toward the top when the dog is excited, and very mobile; the center of the base of the ears is at eye level, and has the form of an elongated rhomboid, truncated at a third of its longer diagonal; fine, rather short, without hair inside.

NECK Very lean, quite long, muscular and slightly arched.

BODY The withers are high. The chest is deep, narrow and well let down; the back is straight, the loins are arched and of medium breadth; the croup is raised, not broad. The stern forms a very acute and very prominent angle; the ribs are only slightly sprung, the belly is compact.

TAIL Long, set on rather low, tufted. In repose it is carried naturally low; when passed between the legs, it should reach at least the spinal column; in action, sometimes it is carried as a very closed sickle tail, at times straight; it should never be entirely curled.

FOREQUARTERS Slanted shoulders. **HINDQUARTERS** The thighs are long, strong, lean; the hocks are well bent, broad and near to the ground. **FEET** Harefeet; the space between the toes has abundant hair. The nails are very strong and generally white or some color harmonious with the color of the coat. The pads are very hard.

COAT Smooth, hard, long: where long, it should be harsh, thick, shorter on the head and ears, longer on the back part of the thighs and the lower part of the tail. **Color** The neck is white and red, white and fawn or solid: white, red, or fawn; red is to be preferred to fawn. Other colors are not acceptable.

DISQUALIFICATIONS Anything in the characteristics that reveals the admixture of Greyhound blood, since, although speed in racing is thus increased, the sensitivity of hearing is diminished, as is the agility of the standing jump and especially the sense of smell, which are the principal physiological qualities of this breed. There is moreover a noticeable lowering of the intelligence and judgment. Button ears; dark eyes; teeth which do not close in a precisely level bite; stern not pronounced; forefeet turning outward; broad loins; broad croup; rounded or broad thighs with swollen veins.

SCALE OF POINTS

General appearance, stature, gait	25
Head	10
Eyes	4
Ears	6
Neck	5
Body	20
Limbs	20
Tail	4
Coat and color	6
	100

SMOOTH-COATED IBIZAN PODENCO

IBIZAN PODENCO

Photo: Buzzini

214 ARIÈGE SETTER
Braque de l'Ariège

FRANCE

As this dog certainly comes from Ariège, he reminds one of the famous "White dogs of the King." The early type was modified about sixty years ago through crossbreedings with the Saint-Germain Setter.

GENERAL CHARACTERISTICS A dog of noble breed and of great size and dignity; elegant in spite of its size and stolidity.

SIZE Height: 23½-26½ inches.

HEAD The skull is rather more narrow than rounded, nevertheless it is fairly broad and convex; the occipital protuberance is well pronounced. The nose is pink or brown, light in color, with nostrils well open. The nasal bridge is long and straight, meeting the skull in a slightly sloping stop. The lips are fine and well let down, but not pendulous, and their size and shape are such as to give the muzzle an approximately square aspect.

EYES Tender, well open, with a frank and intelligent expression.

EARS Very fine, long with a fold, the ears are set on above the eye line and slightly back; they stand off from the head.

NECK Long, elegant yet quite strong, with a slight dewlap.

BODY The chest is broad and deep, reaching to the level of the elbow. The back is rather long and slightly arched. The loins are rather long, arched, muscular and fairly broad. The croup is slightly hollowed. The flanks are flat and fairly well let down.

TAIL Set on rather low, the tail is long; it is very often docked, as with most dogs in southern France.

FOREQUARTERS The shoulders are straight, slightly flat and broad; the forearm is straight and well boned; the elbow is vertical, the pasterns are fairly long and gently sloping. **HINDQUARTERS** The thigh is straight, well let down and muscular; the hocks are strong. **FEET** Of the type called "harefeet."

COAT Fine, white, not glossy. **Color** The coat is marked with orange, sometimes with brown or with light spotting of the undercoat. The major markings are never symmetrical. Some dogs have only the speckling. **Skin** Quite fine.

FAULTS Nose too dark, pug nose; nostrils not well open; short, excessively arched or excessively narrow bridge, with an abrupt stop; lips too fine, too close-fitting or forming an almost square muzzle; flat, narrow, too broad, too round skull; the haw must not be visible, nor should the lower eyelid be falling; small eyes with unpleasant expression; thick ears, flat ears, ears set on too high or carried forward; short, weak, excessively strong, excessively dewlapped neck; narrow chest or insufficiently let down; flat back, saddleback, short back; short, narrow, or flat loins; straight croup; flanks too high, tail set on high; narrow shoulders; too muscular or too oblique shoulders; thin forearm; elbows turned outward, pasterns too short; flat thighs, deviated hocks, narrow hocks, hocks too close or too far apart; round and not sufficiently lean feet; coarse, long or too many markings on coat; thick skin. ●

ARIÈGE SETTER

215 BLUE AUVERGNE SETTER
Braque bleu d'Auvergne

FRANCE

According to certain dog fanciers this is an indigenous breed or at least obtained through a series of crossbreedings with the old type of French Setter. According to others, on the contrary, this is an imported breed. This latter opinion has it that the Braque was introduced into Auvergne by the Knights of Malta when they returned to their country in 1798 during Napoleon's occupation when he decreed the dissolution of their order.

GENERAL CHARACTERISTICS A powerful dog with exceptionally robust legs, well boned without being massive or coarse. In spite of its hound type, this dog has a remarkable lightness and an air of elegance which is enhanced by the rich quality of the coat. The solidity of the tissues and the power of the muscular system are indicative of a highly active dog.

SIZE The ideal height for males is 22½-25 inches; females 21½-23½ inches.

HEAD The head should be rather long; the skull is oval in the back part; the forehead is developed but not excessively in comparison with the breadth; the supraorbital arches are well up. The nose is always black, brilliant, and well set onto the extension of the bridge. Quite strong, it also slightly overhangs the lip. The nostrils are well open. The lips are substantial, and shape out a good, square muzzle. The jaws are quite strong and of equal length; the teeth are strong and white. The stop is not pronounced.

EYES Of fair size, well set in the sockets, dark hazel in color, with an open and frank expression. The eyelids are black, the haw not visible.

EARS Set on low, at eye level and rather back, so as to show the roundness of the skull. They are finely textured, light and satin, slightly folded, long but not excessively so; they seem to be longer than actually because they are set on low; they frame the head nicely without being too far from the cheeks.

NECK Rather long, quite strong, especially at the point of insertion into the shoulders, and slightly arched; a slight dewlap is desirable.

BODY The chest is well let down, the brisket being at least at elbow level, moderately broad and in good proportion to its depth. The ribs are fairly well sprung but not excessively so. The withers are high. The back is short and straight, the loins are short, slightly arched, broad and muscular. The croup is broad, well boned and not too hollow; the flanks are flat and slightly raised.

TAIL Set on at about the back line, of medium size and carried horizontally. It should be docked at about ⅔ inches; the ideal length of the tail is 6-8 inches.

FOREQUARTERS The shoulders are sloped and muscular without heaviness, with excellent joints; the forearms are straight, strong, well muscled; the elbows should be firm. The pasterns are straight, short and robust; the joints are broad and strong. The bones are well developed. **HINDQUARTERS** The thighs are very muscular and strong, well fleshed out; the bones and the joints are robust; the hocks are strong but not bent. Overall, the hindquarters should be very robustly built. **FEET** Rather short, combining the qualities of both cat-feet and harefeet, compact, with toes well closed. The nails are heavy and short, the pads are hard and rugged. The feet should never be turned in or out.

COAT The coat should not be too fine, but glossy; short, never hard. **Color** (a) Light coat: a white background with or without black markings and more or less numerous spots; (b) dark coat: with a mixture of white and black or at least with a certain amount of black hair, giving a charcoal gray color to the coat. The coat to be sought in breeding is one with white background with markings of a blue-black shade: black markings are fairly numerous. Both the large markings as well as the smaller spots have a characteristic border with a bluish tint, which is provided by the mixture of black and blue hairs in the white

BLUE AUVERGNE SETTER

Photo: Studio Pierre, Prato.

ARIÈGE SETTER

coat. The head should be normally marked in such a way that the eyes are surrounded by black. Between the eyes there is a white or bluish stripe. **Skin** Quite fine, rather loose but not excessively so, peppered with white and black.

FAULTS Head too short, cheeks too full (a frequent fault), head too broad; nose of indefinite color, with depigmented spots, small, pointed, set on too high or rising; double nose, bridge too short or arched; pointed muzzle; stop insufficiently or excessively pronounced; lips too fine or too heavy or too short; overshot or undershot jaws; teeth badly set and decayed; narrow flat or excessively broad skull; parietals excessively developed; eyes too small, too protruding, too light, too deep set; eyelids lacking pigmentation; visible haw; white eyebrows; ears set on too high, flat, thick, too short, carried too far back or too close to the head, ears carried forward, ears without folds; chest too broad or too narrow; chest insufficiently deep with brisket above elbow level; flat ribs and false ribs not sufficiently long; back too long, hollowed, flat loins, saddleback, weak back; croup too straight, too hollowed, weak, too open, not sufficiently muscular; points of haunches too prominent; tail carried vertically, set on too high or too low, too thick, docked too short (a natural tail is not a serious fault, it is nevertheless preferable for it to be docked in the proper way); weak forelegs; elbows turning out; legs not properly vertical; long pasterns, curved, turning in or out; flat or weak thighs, lacking in muscle; long metatarsi; hocks too bent or too straight, hocks too close together; thighs open and carried outside in action; broad flat feet with toes excessively long, too open or too fine; feet turning out or in during action; hair too fine, too thick, too long; coat too white; lack of markings; head with irregular markings, with an eye surrounded by white; skin too thick, too thin, too close-fitting.

DISQUALIFICATIONS Double nose; short tail or tail lacking; dewclaws, indicating an admixture of Pointer blood; tan markings, markings of the type called **"pain brule"** on the cheeks; dogs with strongly tanned markings should be eliminated from judging with no credits; those which have only the appearance of **"pain brulè"** markings are eligible for mention, if the type and quality of the dog are sufficiently strong, but such dogs are not to be awarded prizes. ●

BLUE AUVERGNE SETTER

Photo: Buzzini, DIM.

TRAINING

216 BOURBONNAIS SETTER

Braque du Bourbonnais

FRANCE

The Bourbonnais Setter is almost always born without a tail. This peculiarity explains his being called the "Short-Tailed Setter."

BOURBONNAIS SETTER

GENERAL CHARACTERISTICS A fairly light, although compact, dog with the appearance of a cob.

SIZE The average height is about 21½ inches.

HEAD The skull is long and fairly domed; the parietals are rounded and join the bridge at an obtuse angle, thus forming a head which is not too square. The nose is brown or light brown, broad, hanging slightly below the level of the chin. The bridge is long, straight and quite wide; the nostrils are well open, the lips are rather heavy, slightly pendulous.

EYES The eyes are large and dark amber in color, well set into their sockets; their expression is frank and kindly.

EARS Rather fine, not too broad, quite close to the head, set on rather low, slightly folded; in normal position they extend slightly below the throat.

NECK Heavy, rather short, well muscled, solidly set into the shoulders. There is a slight dewlap.

BODY The chest is deep and broad, let down at least to the elbow. The ribs are long and prominent, the back is slightly arched. The loins are short, arched, broad and muscular; the croup is rounded. The flanks are flat and slightly let down.

TAIL Very short (rudimentary), set on rather low; it forms a cone 1-2 inches long; at its maximum the tail should never be more than about 3 inches long.

FOREQUARTERS The shoulders are strong, long, sloping, well closed at the point of juncture with the spinal column. The forelegs are straight, well boned, and the elbows are perfectly vertical. The pasterns are short and

slightly sloped toward the front, but without turning either inward or outward. **HINDQUARTERS** The thighs are straight, descending and very muscular. The hocks are broad, straight, without deviations; the metatarsi are rather long and vertical. **FEET** Catfeet, small, vertical; the toes are closed, and the pads are lean.

COAT Dense and short, slightly oily, not glossy. **Color** White and light brown, forming a color which is like wine dregs or slightly fawn, without large markings but with very small spots fused into the white and spread uniformly over the entire body. **Skin** Quite fine.

FAULTS Nose black or pointed; bridge short, too arched or too narrow; lips too fine, too short or forming a muzzle which is excessively square; flat, narrow, flat-sided skull, meeting the bridge with too obtuse an angle; eyes too light, too superficially set, too little, too deep-set, with a suspicious or mean expression; ears excessively thick or fine, flat or set on too high or too low or carried too far forward; slender, excessively long or short neck, with too much dewlap; chest not sufficiently descended or narrow; ribs flat or too close; flat or arched back; flat or narrow loins; excessively hollowed or excessively straight croup; flanks too high or too low; tail too short, too long or hooked; forelegs weak, elbows turning out, long and straight pasterns, sloping back, turned in or out; flat thighs; hocks turning in or out, narrow, too far apart, too close together; metatarsi sloping from back to front, or turning east or west; broad feet, feet turning out, toes too wide apart, fleshy pads, thick skin; fine, brilliant coat, or white coat; coat with colors not properly melded; coat black or with large markings. ●

Photo: M. Pedone

Another story claims that the Dupuy Setter is the result of a cross between a very beautiful Poitou Setter and a Greyhound. Numerous experts, however, do not agree with this theory, since it seems improbable that a Greyhound was used, as his pure blood would have a negative effect on the keen sense of smell.

Paul Mégnin claims, on the other hand, that the breed is one of the most ancient forms of the French Setter of which only a few survivors were saved during the Revolution through the efforts of a game warden of the Abbey d'Argensois, named Dupuy.

GENERAL CHARACTERISTICS A good-sized dog, elegant, noble, with a high degree of distinction; a mixture of lightness, elasticity and strength. The males are generally leaner than the females, especially in the hindquarters.

SIZE Large and streamlined, males may measure as much as 26½ or 27 inches; females 25½-26 inches.

HEAD Fine, long, narrow and lean. The skull is narrow, long and rounded out; the occipital protuberance is pronounced, the forehead is prominent and the cheeks are flat. The nose is dark brown, broad, with well open nostrils; it is slightly pointed. The bridge is long, narrow, slightly arched; the lips are fine, small, lean, light, closed; the upper lip covers the lower without being coarse or pendulous. The jaws meet cleanly, and the teeth are powerful. The stop is not accentuated.

EYES Open, golden or brown in color; the expression is gentle and dreamy.

EARS Small, narrow, rather longer than short, very fine and soft; they are nicely folded and carried slightly back, and the point of insertion is at eye level.

NECK Very long, rounded, light, fine, with no trace whatever of dewlap; the neck issues well from the shoulders, narrowing harmoniously toward the head.

BODY The chest is deep and well let down, the ribs are long and flat; the sternum is large, strongly accentuated before the shoulders. The withers are free, the back well sustained; the loins are slightly arched, powerful, muscular, rather short and in good proportion to the overall size of the dog. The flanks are slightly hollowed. The haunches are long, sloping and powerful, sometimes slightly drawn up.

TAIL Set on neither too high nor too low, of medium size, often fairly well feathered; it is carried low, straight, or very slightly curved; it is quite long, reaching the hocks when down.

FOREQUARTERS Shoulders long, sloped, muscular, the forelegs well vertical, strong, bony, good tendons; the forearm is very powerful; the elbows are close to the rib cage. The pasterns are of good length, straight or slightly sloped from back to front.

HINDQUARTERS The thighs are long, flat, muscular, well let down and broad. The hocks are very wide and lean, slightly bent; the metatarsi are fairly long, strong and vertical.

FEET Long, very lean, with well closed toes (harefeet); the nails are strong and quite long; the tips of the nails touch the ground when the dog is in repose.

COAT Invariably smooth, quite short, except on the head and ears, where it is very fine and very short; the hair is rather hard to the touch, especially on the back and loins. **Color** White and dark brown. The background should be a good white with more or less broad markings or a brown saddle with or without flecking or streaking of brown. The latter should be invariably found on the legs, especially the forelegs. There should be no tan or faded brown on the eyebrows, lips or buttocks. **Skin** Very fine all over the body, especially on the head and ears. ●

217 DUPUY SETTER
Braque Dupuy

FRANCE

It is said that at the beginning of the nineteenth century a hunter from Poitou, Pierre Dupuy, owned a magnificent setter bitch named Leda, white and chestnut colored. After Leda was mated with Mylord, breed unknown, the first Dupuy was born.

DUPUY SETTER

218 FRENCH SETTER
Braque Français

FRANCE

All breeds of French Setter come from the same stock: the old Setter simply classified as French. French dog fanciers are mostly in agreement that the old setter dog that gave birth to the Saint-Germain, Ariège, Bourbonnais, Dupuy, and Auvergne Setters is indigenous to the southwest of France. In the opinion of qualified naturalists, the center for the formation of shorthaired setters was the Italian Peninsula where the racing Segugio might have encountered the Mastiff. From Italy the shorthaired setter spread to many countries, including France.

However, another theory holds that the old French Setter came from the Spanish Setter, although this would change nothing concerning the primitive origins of the Setter. Many experts claim that the Spaniards got their dogs in France, although it seems much more probable that the dogs came directly to Spain from Italy.

England quickly became interested in the old French dog, and it is from this fact that the modern English Pointer owes his origins. This formation was probably created in France and perfected in England. The old French Setter crossed with the Quail Setter might also have seen the origin of the old form of setter.

SMALL-SIZED FRENCH SETTER

219 SMALL-SIZED FRENCH SETTER
Braque Français de petite taille

FRANCE

The present lightweight French Setter is the product of long and careful selective breeding. He has been used in the hunt for many years because of his small size and tremendous activity. He is a country dog of great endurance and ideal for all hunters and all types of hunting: on the plains, the mountains, and even in the swamps.

He is lively and intelligent and differs considerably from the heavy French Setter by his size and the delicacy of his legs. Up to the end of the last century he was exported to many countries, and there is no doubt that he was used for crossbreedings with other breeds, bettering them considerably and making them lighter and more agile. This factor indicates the age of the breed.

He obviously originated in the regions where his qualities as a tracker would offer the greatest possibilities of his service, that is, in regions where a dog is needed that can follow very faint trails.

He was formerly very prevalent throughout France but today he is particularly employed in the southwestern part, where he is much esteemed for his tendency to be "born trained," in the literal sense of the word, and for his good nature, his perfect sense of smell, the natural force of the stop, his ability to retrieve, and by the homogeneity of his offspring.

GENERAL CHARACTERISTICS A hound of noble presence, powerful yet not heavy, robust and strong-limbed.

WEIGHT AND SIZE Weight: about 54-69 lb; height at shoulder: 22¾-26 inches.

HEAD Not too heavy, although weighty enough. The skull should be almost flat or very slightly arched, with a lightly marked central ridge. The occipital protuberance is not strongly pronounced. The stop is evident but not accentuated. The muzzle is straight, massive, rectangular, with the lips well dropped and the joining of the lips wrinkled. The nose is broad and brown in color. The nostrils are well open.

EYES Well open and well set in their sockets; brown or deep yellow in color, they have a pensive, affectionate expression.

EARS Of average length, set at eye level. They should not be too big at the point of insertion. They should frame the head well, with a slight fold and a slight rounding at the tip. One or two vertical wrinkles should be visible on the cheeks, at the level of or slightly below the ear attachment.

NECK Of good length, slightly arched on the nape; it presents a rather thick impression because of the mandatory dewlap.

BODY The chest is broad when viewed from the front, deep when viewed in profile, let down to elbow level. The ribs are rounded but not excessively so. The back is substantial, straight, occasionally a little long but always strong and firm. The loins are short, muscular, lightly arched. Buttocks slightly slanting off the line of the back. Haunches well out.

TAIL Usually docked, it continues the curve of the buttocks; a tail of any length, if well carried, should not be counted as a fault.

FOREQUARTERS The shoulders are very muscular and moderately sloping. The forelegs are straight, broad and muscular. The elbow is well placed, the pasterns are strong. **HINDQUARTERS** The thighs are robust but not always with much angulation. Hocks broad, with moderate angulation, set low to the ground. **FEET** Compact, nearly round or slightly oval, with thick pads and strong nails.

COAT Rather thick and smooth, finer on the head and ears. Skin supple and fairly slack **Color** White, with more or less dark brown flecking with or without troutlike speckling or entirely speckled; brown-speckled and sometimes brown-speckled without patches. Traces of pale tan above the eyes, on lips, on legs.

FAULTS Head too short; cheeks too heavy; facial wrinkles exaggerated; speckling on nose and eyelids; pointed muzzle; excessively wide or narrow skull; light eyes; mean expression; ears set too high or badly carried; ears too long, excessively folded; excessive delicacy of shoulders and ribs; feet with insufficient spread.

DISQUALIFICATIONS A black nose; double nose; black specks or black hairs in the coat; dewclaws or traces thereof. ●

GENERAL CHARACTERISTICS The small-sized French setter has the same general characteristics as the standard strain, with reduced dimensions and an overall lightness which differentiates it from the standard. Its general appearance is that of a country dog, quite muscular but without heaviness.

WEIGHT AND SIZE Weight: 37-55 lb; height: 18½-22 inches, with the limits of 19½ and 21½ inches recommended as ideal.

HEAD The skull of the miniature is shorter than that of the standard Braque. The lips are less pendant, giving the muzzle a less rectangular appearance, however, without seeming pointed. The bridge may be slightly arched.

EYES The description for the standard breed is applicable to the miniature.

EARS Set higher than on the standard; slightly shorter, barely folded.

NECK There is little or no dewlap.

BODY The back is shorter than is the case with the standard Braque. The belly is more drawn up.

FOREQUARTERS AND HINDQUARTERS The legs are leaner and harder. The thigh is less oblique. **FEET** Leaner, more compact than the standard Braque.

TAIL The tail is thin and should be docked or short at the base.

COAT The hair is finer and shorter than on the standard Braque. **Color** The following are allowed: (1) White with more or less dark brown spots, with or without trout-speckled spots; (2) entirely banded (like the tabby among cats) and trout-brown; (3) all brown or with brown on the head, chest, and extremities; (4) white with cinnamon spotting and, occasionally, all cinnamon. Some marks of a paler color must show over the eyes, on the cheeks and legs, with similar spotting on the belly or brisket.

FAULTS Heavy head; heavy-edged cheeks; big or narrow skull; pointed muzzle; light eyes; mean expression; mealy spotting on nose and eyelids; long or short ears; badly set or badly carried ears; flat shoulders, flanks or thighs; slack skin; underweight or overweight.

DISQUALIFICATIONS Black nose or double nose; traces of black in the coat; dewclaws or marks of dewclaws. ●

FRENCH SETTER

SMALL-SIZED FRENCH SETTER

Photo: Buzzini.

FRENCH SETTER

220 ST. GERMAIN SETTER
Braque Saint-Germain

FRANCE

This beautiful Pointer, also known as the Compiègne Setter, is reminiscent of the Pointer from which he derived many characteristics. He was already much esteemed in the first half of the last century, although then less refined than he is today.

In regard to his origins, we quote from De La Rue's book *Les Chiens d'Arrêt Français et Anglais*: "The two Pointers Miss and Stop, which the Count de Girardin had bought in England for King Charles X, had yellow spots [white-orange] of large size; graceful, the ears attached high on the head, with black palate and nose, these two types had great elegance of form.

They are excellent in the woods for rabbit and pheasant—in the open they were mediocre, disobedient and disagreeable. These dogs were given to the Baron de Larminat, who was inspector of the forest of Compiègne. Stop died a short time later and the Baron de Larminat sent the bitch to the Count de l'Aigle at Tracy, as he had a handsome pointer named Zamor. Miss produced seven puppies and four of these were given to the Compiègne forest wardens: the latter, transferred to Saint-Germain, took their dogs with them. Their elegance was pleasing to the hunters of Paris." From that time on the white-orange dog was called the "Saint-Germain dog."

GENERAL CHARACTERISTICS   A beautiful, well-made and well-proportioned dog, but with the musculature lighter than in the Pointer, so that the framework is less developed; stop is less strongly shown, the muzzle more tapering or receding; ears longer; buttocks more sunken or drooping; tail set lower; lastly, the foot must be outstretched and never rounded. In his general appearance, heavy movement and more limited

Photo: Buzzini.

ST. GERMAIN SETTER

sense of smell, the St. Germain Setter (Brach) can be compared with a Pointer only as a mongrel can be compared with a thoroughbred; the differences show his origin.

SIZE Height at the withers: males 20-25 inches; females 21-24 inches. In judging, the specimens nearest these figures will be preferred over others.

HEAD Skull projecting, domed occiput; the foreskull is broad but not excessively so. The stop is well defined but not too accentuated. Forehead long, straight or slightly curved. Muzzle strong, of average length, with strong white teeth. Nose deep pink, large, projecting a little toward the front of the lips. Nostrils wide. Lips thin, a little dipped, pink inside as well as on the palate.

EYES Large in size and well set; the color is golden yellow, with a clear, open, frank and sweet expression.

EARS Shorter than those of the old Braque but longer than those of the Pointer, set on at eye level; standing well away from the head and forming a dropping angle; skin must be thin and supple.

NECK Strong, well muscled, long, a trifle arched; a slight droop is allowed.

BODY Chest broad, deep, descending to the level of the elbows; ribs long. Back must be short and straight; loins slightly arched and fairly short. The croup is bony, with the tip of the rump slightly protruding and drooping a little.

TAIL Set on in line with the back, but not going beyond the tip of the hock; large at the root and tapering, to a very thin tip; must be carried horizontally.

FOREQUARTERS Shoulders strong, long, slightly slanting, well muscled and graceful. Forelegs straight, strongly boned, elbows perfectly upright; short, straight pasterns. **HINDQUARTERS** Straight thighs, well-dropping hams, strong-limbed; large straight hocks, not curving inward or outward; lower part of leg short and perpendicular; curving hocks, narrow, not too wide or too close together; lower part of leg long and slanting,

not too bent or too straight. Dewclaws. **FEET** Long, narrow, close toes, upright, pads tough and strong.

COAT Hair short, not too fine, yet never harsh. **Color** Off-white with orange specks; the orange may be blended with a few white hairs; some spotting is allowed but is not desirable. **Skin** Fine and supple.

FAULTS Over- or undersize indicated above; forehead short, raised or arched; skull narrow, flat, bulging or curved at the sides, or with a supraorbital arch at a right angle to the forehead, bones too prominent; eyes small, too light in color, a wild or vicious expression, squinting eyes; thin eyelashes and inverted eyelids (black eyes are a disqualification); ears set too high or too low, close to the head, flat, carried backward or too curled; jaws undershot or overshot; teeth badly set; spotted nose; pinched nostrils, dry or scaly-looking; black nose; lips thick or short below the nose; black, brown or dark hard palate; neck short, puffy, too light, too drooping; shoulders short, too slanting, or widening at the top; thin legs; chest narrow, lacking in depth, sunken under the armpits, flat or rounded ribs; narrow, long, flat or hollow back; too straight or too falling croup; elbows close or turned outward, pasterns slanting, upright on fetlock joints; flat thighs; feet rounded, curving outward or inward, broad or too big or too thick; toes crushed or narrow; thick, slack tissues; hair too short, long and bushy; bright color, the orange too light or too deep. ●

221 BRITTANY SPANIEL
Épagneul Breton

FRANCE

Less speedy than the setter, the Brittany Spaniel is, on the other hand, effective in all sorts of terrain in all seasons. His tracking is of wide range, he is tireless and fast, and his sense of smell is acute. He can be defined as belonging to an indigenous breed of Brittany whose origins go back to the ancient "agasse." The classic poet Oppianus wrote in the first stanza of his *Hunt*: "The savage people of Brittany, who paint their body in various colors, carefully bred this animal, which they call in their language "agasse." The dog is slender and provided with a thick coat. It is principally by its acute sense of smell that it is superior to other dogs . . ."

Formerly the original type of the Brittany Spaniel was prevalent almost solely within the inaccessible Argoat forests, in the peninsula formed by the Arrée and the Black Mountains.

BRITTANY SPANIEL

BRITTANY SPANIEL

Photo: Buzzini, O. Langini.

GENERAL CHARACTERISTICS A small dog, elegant but vigorous, both compact and stocky. The movement is energetic, the expression intelligent, the general look of a fine spaniel.

SIZE Height: maximum 20½, minimum 18¼ inches; ideal for males 19¼-20 inches; for females 18¾-19¾ inches.

HEAD Skull of average length, rounded, hollow stop sufficiently obvious although lightly falling in or sloping. Forehead shorter than the larger axis of the skull. Straight or slightly curved, in 3:2 proportion to the skull. Nose a deep shade according to the color of the dog; white and orange, white and maroon, black and white. Well open, a little angular. Lips thin, receding, under lip slightly overlapping the lower.

EYES Deep amber, consistent with the coat, alive and expressive.

EARS Set on high, short rather than long, slightly rounded, slightly fringed, although the ear can be well furnished with wavy hair.

NECK Of average length, although well away from the shoulders and without dewlap.

BODY Chest deep, let down to the level of the elbow, ribs well sprung. Back short, withers definitely protruding, never saddlebacked. Loins short, big and sturdy. Flanks raised, but not excessively.

TAIL Straight or drooping, if the animal is not in action; always short, about 4 inches; often a trifle crooked and endirg in a tuft.

FOREQUARTERS Front legs very straight, the pasterns slightly slanting, thin and muscular, slightly fringed and wavy. **HINDQUARTERS** Haunches lower than the withers, protruding, reaching height of back. Buttocks slightly receding. Hind legs big and well dropped, very muscular, hock and tip of buttocks in line. The metatarsus perpendicular to the hock and not too bent. **FEET** Closed toes, with a little hair between the toes.

COAT Hair on body fine and thick, but not excessively; rather flat or very slightly wavy. **Color** Orange and white, maroon and white, black and white, tricolor or marked with one or the other of these colors.

FAULTS Nose tight, wheezy; lips thick or drooping; forehead too short or too long; skull square, pointed or straight; excessively accentuated stop; ears set low, drooping, big or frizzy; eyes too light; haggard or wild expression; neck too long or too slender, too near the shoulders or too heavy; shoulders straight or excessively sloping; legs puffy or thin; narrow body let down or flat-sided chest; long or hollow back; long, narrow or weak loins; narrow, straight or receding buttocks; fleshy or fallen flanks; excessively long tail; pasterns too straight or too slanting, lack of fringe; hind legs too straight or too slanting, no fringe; feet big, long, flat, too rounded or open; thick or slack skin; fuzzy or silky hair; albinism; monorchidism. ●

MORNING IN THE FOREST ▶

PICARDY SPANIEL

222 FRENCH SPANIEL
Épagneul Français

FRANCE

The origins of all spaniels must be sought in the ancient Quail Setter which represents one of the first forms derived from the crossbreeding, in prehistoric times, of the peat-bog dog (*Canis palustris*) and the Bronze Age dog. We are unable to ascertain exactly where the breed was formed and from where it spread. Many think that the Quail Setter came from Spain and that the word "spaniel" is proof of its Spanish descent, yet the breed would have proliferated at a fairly recent time especially in France, England, and Germany. Each of these nations produced, by selective breeding and crossbreeding, new breeds with points fairly distant from the early type, such as the French and English Spaniels, the German Longhaired Setter (Langhaar), as well as the Wachtelhund.

GENERAL CHARACTERISTICS A spaniel built on good lines, well muscled and active, with great endurance and tenacity in hunting, an excellent gun dog.

SIZE Height: males 22-24 inches at the withers, with a tolerance of an additional inch; females 21¾-23½ inches.

HEAD Strong, but free of any clumsiness and fairly long, the skull slightly curved and not flat. The occipital protuberance marked but without exaggeration. The muzzle should be rather long and fairly broad, the back cheekbones not very marked. The forehead should be of good length, slightly arched. The stop should be well marked but not overly accentuated. The nose is well developed and open, well aligned with the forehead; it should invariably be brown, with no light areas. The lips should be of average thickness, not too sloping. slightly curved in such a way as not to present a square profile like that of the English Setter.

EYES Of medium size, dark amber in color, they are impressive for their gentle, intelligent expression. The haw is not visible. Yellow, light "bird of prey" eyes make dogs eligible merely for mentions.

EARS Long, framing the head, set on low, either at eye level or lower, hanging slightly to the rear without showing the inner side. The ears are well furnished with wavy, silky hair to the tips, which should be rounded, not pointed.

NECK Well rounded, free from heaviness, the neck should have a length in good proportion to the length of the head and body.

BODY The chest is deep, fairly broad, well ribbed up, the rib cage descending to elbow level. It must be neither flat nor excessively rounded. The back should be of medium length and well proportioned. The loins must be straight and short, with well-developed muscles, rather arched sides, strong and elegant.

TAIL Set on rather low, in many dogs slightly long and carried horizontally and obliquely, with a slight S-curve. It is covered with long silky hair which begins about 1 inch from the root and gets progressively longer up to the middle, then shorter to the tip.

FOREQUARTERS Long, sloping shoulders, with well-developed muscles and a marked angulation. **HINDQUARTERS** Sloping rump, with the buttocks slightly prominent. The thighs are broad, well muscled, definitely curved and well joined to the hock. The hock should be slightly bent, the metatarsus should be straight. No dewclaws. **FEET** Oval, firm, compact, with hard pads, close toes with abundant hair between them. The hare-foot is objectionable.

COAT The hair is long and supple, either flat or slightly wavy, thick, short on the head. Curly hair is allowable only on the ears, neck, paws, and the root of the tail. **Color** Invariably white with brown markings, with or without spots, which must, however, never be too numerous. The setter's liver coat and the Picard Spaniel's roan coat are not acceptable. Tan on the cheeks or about the eyes is a disqualification. ●

223 PICARDY SPANIEL
Épagneul Picard

FRANCE

This spaniel has long been known in Picardy and the Somme Valley. He shares common origins with the old French Spaniel. He is both elegant and robust, equally skilled in swamp hunting as in a flat and covered terrain.

Toward the turn of the century the breed threatened to degenerate completely since hunters in the small countries did not control breeding properly and failed to attach importance to certain disastrous crossbreedings. Conscientious breeders intervened to rescue the breed. Among these was Rattel, who, through proper selection, reestablished the true type of the breed and, during the years 1902, 1903, and 1904 showed his dogs at the Paris show alongside French Spaniels. Thereupon, thanks to the efforts of other capable breeders, a special club was formed and the breed was accepted among those recognized by international dog associations.

FRENCH SPANIEL

PICARDY SPANIEL

Photo: Buzzini, DIM.

GENERAL CHARACTERISTICS This dog has a strong back, with a gentle and highly expressive face, a gay and striking carriage of the head, with especially well-developed forequarters and powerful limbs.

SIZE Height at the withers 22-24 inches, with a tolerance for the male up to 25 inches.

HEAD Skull big and domed, with a prominent occiput, flat cheekbones, and the stop slanted rather than perpendicular. The forehead is long, of good width, shortening from the brow to the muzzle with a slight arch toward the middle. The nose should be brown, of average size and nicely rounded. The lips are of average thickness, not too pendant but slightly drooping.

EYES Deep amber in color, well open, with a frank, expressive look.

EARS Sufficiently low-set to frame the head, covered with beautiful wavy and silky hair.

NECK Well placed and very muscular.

BODY Deep and fairly broad, well let down, reaching elbow level. The back should be of average length, with a slight depression just behind the withers. The haunches should be slightly flatter than the withers. Straight loin, not too long, but rather wide and thick. The haunches are projecting and curve down to the level of the back and loins. The rump should be very slightly slanting and rounded. Flanks are flat and deep, the belly is well drawn up.

TAIL The tail forms two slight curves, one concave, the other convex. It must not be too long, and it should be somewhat profusely covered with hair.

FOREQUARTERS The shoulders should be rather long, straight and well muscled. The forelegs are muscular and straight. The elbows are let down straight and are well furnished with hair. **HINDQUARTERS** Straight thighs, well let down, broad and muscular, with a fair profusion of hair down to the hocks. The metatarsal bones should be straight, the hocks should be only slightly bent. **FEET** Round, broad and close, with moderate hair between the toes.

COAT Heavy, not too silky, rather finer on the head than elsewhere, slightly wavy on the body. **Color** Mottled gray, with brown marks on the various parts of the body, almost always with some tan extending to head and feet. The skin is fine and soft.

FAULTS Pear-shaped head; pointed nose, closed nose, double nose; nasal bridge too short, too arched, too fine; lips too thick or too drawn up; square skull, too straight, narrow or short; eyes too light, too protruding, too sunken, not open or with a mean expression; ears too narrow, short, set too high, too curly or insufficiently silky; neck too long, too thin or too short; chest too narrow or not sufficiently deep; back too long or roached; loins too long, too narrow or too weak; haunches too low, too high, or too narrow; rump too slanting; forelegs too thin or lacking in hair; shoulders short, too straight, or too oblique; elbows turned too much inward or outward; hindquarters with narrow or insufficiently hairy thigh; hocks turned inward or outward; feet too narrow, too close or splayed; saber tail, too curled, too long, set on too high or too low; coat too fine, too silky, too wavy or too short; coat with exaggeratedly large brown markings, white spots; skin too thick. ●

224 PONT-AUDEMER SPANIEL

Épagneul de Pont-Audemer

FRANCE

This dog has excellent qualities for the hunt, especially in swamps. He is probably descended from the old French Spaniel crossbred with the Irish Water Spaniel.

GENERAL CHARACTERISTICS A compact, vigorous dog.

SIZE The average size is 20½-23 inches.

HEAD The skull is round and well developed on top, with a prominent occipital protuberance and rather rounded parietals which join the nasal bridge in a rather weak angle, although the stop is accentuated. The forehead is raised toward the topknot, which should be very curly and set on the dome of the skull, leaving the forehead itself free of long hair. The nose is brown, rather pointed and noticeably protruding above the lip. The nasal bridge is long and slightly arched. The lips are thin and slightly let down, so as to give a rather pointed appearance to the muzzle.

EYES Rather small and set well into their sockets, dark amber; the expression is kindly and frank.

EARS Of medium thickness, flat, long and set on rather low; they have very curly, rather long fringes, which join the characteristic topknot, in such a way as to form a fine curly frame to the head.

NECK Muscular, lean, slightly arched; it is solidly joined to the shoulders and delicately to the head.

BODY The chest is broad and deep, with the brisket well down to elbow level. The ribs are long and prominent, with the last back rib close to the haunch. The back is straight or slightly arched. The loins are broad, solid, muscular and quite short; they may be raised, reaching the level of the backline. The croup is very slightly inclined. The flanks are flat and slightly drawn up.

TAIL Set on approximately at the level of the loins, carried rather straight. Usually it is docked at 1/3 its length. Thick at the root, it is well feathered with curly hair, which should surround the tail completely. A natural tail should be of medium length and slightly curved.

FOREQUARTERS Strong, long, sloping shoulders, closed at the point where they join the spinal column; the upper arm is strong and muscular. **HINDQUARTERS** The thighs are

COARSEHAIRED GRIFFON

straight, well let down and muscular; the point of the buttock is prominent. The hocks are broad and straight, turned neither inward nor outward; the metatarsi are rather short, feathered, especially on the backside, with a curly fringe. The thighs should be well fleshed out and with culottes. Dewclaws are undesirable. **FEET** Round, directed straight, with long, curly hair between the toes. The legs should be rather short, because the dog must seem close to the ground (but not as much as the Cocker).
COAT Curly and slightly ruffled.
Color Brown, brown and gray (better if distinctly agate), with dull brown flocking.
FAULTS Nose black, pale, depigmented, round; bridge short or excessively arched; thick or pendulous lips; excessively abrupt stop; skull flat at the parietals; forehead parallel to the bridge; lack of topknot; topknot reaching the supraorbital arches or made up of hanging hair;

eyes light, insufficiently or excessively deep-set; unfriendly or mean expression; thick ears, folded, too short, set on too high, carried too much forward or back; neck too heavy, flat in its upper part; thorax insufficiently let down, not well open or hollowed; ribs flat or too close together; back long, narrow, saddleback; loins long, narrow or flat, low; croup sloping, too straight; flanks fleshy and excessively let down; tail set on too high or too low, too curved, carried as saber tail or with flag; shoulders short, straight, turned out at the top; upper arm too lean; thighs flat; hocks deviated, straight, too far apart or too close together; metatarsi long, slanting from back forward, turned east or west, without fringe; feet narrow, too large, too hairy; fleshy pads; hair too flat, too curly; topknot not curled and hanging as in the Poodle; topknot too hard or too fine; black, black and white coat; presence of tan markings. ●

225 WOOLLYHAIRED GRIFFON

Griffon à poil laineux—Boulet

FRANCE

In 1872, Emmanuel Boulet, a rich merchant of Elbeuf, decided to reestablish the handsome Woollyhaired Griffon breed (the issue of a curious crossbreeding of a sheep dog, a Poodle, and an old coarsehaired Griffon). The breed had been sadly neglected and had seemingly entered a definite decline.

He used several males in his possession and finally found a female that seemed to have as many as possible of the points he wanted to transmit to the offspring. He commenced the breeding

PONT-AUDEMER SPANIEL

WOOLLYHAIRED GRIFFON

Photo: R. Kinne (Photo Res.), Buzzini.

with enthusiasm and expertise. The first litter were white and chestnut or white and black. Boulet, during his frequent hunts in the forests of Londe in the company of his Braque Setter, often noticed that the too bright color of his dog often caused a premature flight of the game and it therefore occurred to him to give to the breed he was regenerating a coat of such color as would blend in with the terrain. A uniform "dead leaf" color was chosen which has become the unmistakable characteristic color of the Boulet Griffon.

The unified color of the coat for this breed was arrived at after ten years of selective breeding; and to this aim hundreds of individuals which did not fulfill the requirements were sacrificed. In 1886 the Boulet dogs won numerous prizes including field trials.

In the opinion of some dog fanciers this is a good all-around dog, robust, with a keen sense of smell, able to endure fatigue and heat, and intelligent although somewhat difficult to train. Others do not share this opinion. Among these, the very competent Mégnin states that the breed is not prevalent today and is more suitable as a pet than as a hunting dog.

WOOLLYHAIRED GRIFFON

SIZE Males, 21½-23½ inches; females, 19½-21½ inches.

HEAD Bushy, with a long, broad muzzle, well set with big moustache. Nose more or less dark (brown), with strong, well-separated nostrils.

EYES Intelligent, with bushy eyebrows which, however, do not cover the eye entirely but only veil it slightly. Color of eyes invariably yellow.

EARS Pendant, put on rather low, slightly volute, well furnished with smooth or wavy hair.

NECK Rather long.

BODY Chest broad and deep, powerful loins which are slightly arched.

TAIL Straight, carried well, well covered with hair but not plumed.

FOREQUARTERS Oblique shoulder, but not exaggeratedly so; strong legs, muscular, with long hair down to the feet. **HINDQUARTERS** Long-boned thigh, well let down, hocks more bent than opened. **FEET** Rather elongated, nails covered with hair.

COAT Slightly silky, not shiny, smooth or wavy, never curly. **Color** Leaf brown, with or without white markings. Large white spots unacceptable. ●

226 COARSEHAIRED GRIFFON

Griffon à poil dur—Korthal

FRANCE

SIZE Height: males, about 22-24 inches; females 20-22 inches.

HEAD Large, long, with rough tufted hair, thick but not too long, very pronounced moustache and eyebrows, skull not too wide, muzzle long, strong and square, facial angle not too pronounced, nose invariably brown.

COARSEHAIRED GRIFFON

Photo: R. Kinne (Photo Res.).

COARSEHAIRED GRIFFON

EYES Large, overhung but not concealed by eyebrows. The eyes, yellow or brown, have a very intelligent expression.

EARS Medium size, not set too low, lying flat and not curling. The ears are covered by short hair more or less mixed with long hair.

NECK Fairly long; there must be no dewlap.

BODY Deep, not very broad chest. The flanks are slightly bulging, the back is strong with the crupper very stoutly formed.

TAIL Carried horizontally or with the tip slightly raised; the hair abundant but not plumed. Usually it is docked to a third or a quarter of its length.

FOREQUARTERS The shoulders are fairly long and very oblique. The forelegs are straight, strong, supple at the shoulders; they are covered with tufted hair. **HINDQUARTERS** Long and well muscled in the thighs. The hocks are well bent. The hind legs are well covered with tufted hair. **FEET** Round and solid, the toes close and webbed.

COAT Hard and coarse, reminiscent of the European wild boar, never woolly or curled. Beneath the top coat there is a thick undercoat of fine hair; this undercoat is obligatory. **Color** Preferably steel gray with chestnut markings or uniformly reddish chestnut or roan. White and chestnut and white and orange are also acceptable. ●

227 DRENTSE PATRIJSHOND

THE NETHERLANDS

The Dutch Setter, although little known and even less prevalent outside his land of origin, is the perfect hunter on land as well as in the water. He has an acute sense of smell, great perseverance for raising the game, and is a valuable aid to the hunter.

He is somewhat close to the Langhaar, the principal difference being his shorter head and his muzzle, square without being heavy.

The great spirit of initiative which is one of his characteristics make him an easy dog to train. His attractive and harmonious appearance, his good nature, and his intelligence bring him high esteem as a pet.

GENERAL CHARACTERISTICS Well proportioned, this breed has a body which is longer than the height at the withers. Although the hair is not long on the body, it gives the impression of being so because of the fringe on the neck, ears, legs and tail. An excellent hunting dog. A good companion because of his intelligence and character.

HEAD The skull is rather broad and flat; the stop is scarcely defined. The passage from skull to muzzle should be gradual, with no sudden transition whether seen from in front or in profile. The occipital protuberance is not accentuated; the masseters are very slightly pronounced; the supra-orbital ridges are well developed. The nose is large and brown; the nasal bridge is straight, neither arched nor hollowed; a slight arching is allowable, while a pug nose is absolutely unacceptable. The lips are thin and close-fitting; the muzzle is wedge-shaped and cut blunt at the end. The teeth are strong, with an efficient bite.

EYES Set rather far apart, neither too deep-set nor too prominent, with the gentle and intelligent expression characteristic of hunting dogs. The color is amber; the eyelids are close-fitting.

EARS Set on high, not too heavy and hanging close to the cheeks, without wrinkles or folds; in length they reach to within an inch of the tip of the nose; they are broad at the set-on, they are pointed at the tips (more than the ears of the Langhaar). On their outer side they are covered with abundant, wavy hair, while the auricle is covered with shorter hair; they should be feathered with a good fringe.

NECK Powerful, not too long or, better, short rather than long; it marks a flowing line between head and body. An excessively long neck, although it may contribute to the elegance of the dog, does so at the expense of that impression of power which is so necessary in this breed. The neck should be clean, with no trace of dewlap.

BODY The chest is deep, the brisket

HUNTING IN A SWAMP

DRENTSE PATRIJSHOND

shaped. The identifying characteristic of the breed is the hair, which at the base of the ears is long and on the lower part (1/3 of the ear has very short hair) should be smooth; the coat may be slightly wavy, but not curly.

NECK Short and cylindrical; it forms an obtuse angle with the back, in such a way that the head is generally carried low; the neck is slightly arched and without dewlap.

BODY Strong. Seen from in front, the thorax is quite broad; it is deeper than it is let down, and consequently the forelegs are not close to each other. The sternum is not pointed and does not reach below the elbows. The ribs are well sprung and well developed in the back part. The back is straight, quite long; the croup slopes very slightly. The loins are strong, the belly only slightly drawn up.

TAIL Long, reaching to the hocks. It is set on at medium height, hangs straight, with the last third turned upward. In action, the tail is raised. It is covered all around with long hair, which is neither curled nor wavy and not too thick.

FOREQUARTERS The shoulders are carried close to the body; sloping, they form an angle of about 110 degrees with the humerus. The forearm is strong and straight; the forefeet are set on the vertical, and are rounded, with well-developed, well-arched toes. They should not be catfeet nor harefeet. The pads are strong. **HINDQUARTERS** Strong and with good coxal-femoral and femural-tibial angulations. The metatarsus is not too long, hence the hocks are "close to ground." **FEET** The hind feet are round, with strong pads.

COAT Long and smooth; a slight wave is permitted only on the croup. On the head the hair is short. It is quite long on the back of the forelegs and hind legs; it is long on the buttocks. Curly hair indicates cross breeding, and consequently dogs with curly coats should not be admissible to the Staby-Houn breed. **Color** Dappled black, dappled blue, dappled brown, dappled orange. ●

at elbow level. Seen from in front the ribs appear to be well sprung; a narrow, flat thorax is a fault. The ribs are long; the back ribs are well developed, although they should not be barrel-shaped. The back is powerful, neither too long nor too short; its overall appearance is one of good build. The loins are compact, broad. The croup is rather long and slightly sloping.

TAIL Natural, not docked; set on rather high. In length it reaches the point of hock. Carried low or as a saber tail. When the dog is in action, the tail is carried almost horizontally with the final third turned upward. A characteristic of the Patrijshond is that when he wags his tail, it moves in a circle, especially when the dog has caught the scent of game; it is never carried over the back. The fringes which begin at the set-on of the tail should be abundant, growing shorter toward the tip.

FOREQUARTERS The shoulders are well set (at about 90 degrees), with flat scapulae which are well inserted into the body. The forelegs are straight, muscular; the elbows are close to the body without, however, inhibiting their free movement. **HINDQUARTERS** Parallel, with short metatarsi and hocks which are neither turned in nor out. The feet are round or oval, with well-closed toes and well-developed pads.

COAT Dense, of medium length on body; longer on the chest and the neck; the ears should be covered with long, wavy hair and they should have good fringe, as indeed should the legs and the tail. The spaces between the toes are well feathered. **Color** White background, with brown or orange markings. ●

228 STABY-HOUN
THE NETHERLANDS

GENERAL CHARACTERISTICS A simple, robust Pointer, whose body is longer than it is high; he should appear neither too massive nor too fragile. The skin, well stretched over the frame, has no folds or wrinkles. In character the Staby-Houn is faithful, docile, a gentle companion, intelligent, obedient, tranquil, alert, and never menacing.

SIZE The maximum height at the withers for males is 19½ inches; females are slightly smaller.

HEAD Lean, of a size in good proportion to the rest of the body, longer than it is broad. The skull and muzzle are of equal length. The skull is slightly rounded, not narrow; nevertheless it should not give the impression of great breadth; it descends to the cheeks with a slight rotundity; the muscles of the cheeks are not highly developed; the stop is minimal.

The nose is black for brown and orange dogs. It is not divided; the nostrils are well open and large. The bridge is broad and straight; seen in profile, it is neither arched nor hollowed. The muzzle is strong, narrowing gradually toward the tip of the nose, without, however, coming to a point. The lips are close-fitting; the teeth are strong.

EYES Set horizontally, of medium size, round, with close-fitting eyelids, which do not show the haw; they should be neither prominent nor deepset. They are dark brown in dogs with black or blue markings and a little lighter in dogs with brown or orange markings; they should never be of the "bird of prey" type.

EARS Set on relatively low, with a rather small auricle which means that they bend well without turning too much against the head. They are of moderate length, and trowel-

229 DUTCH SPANIEL
Wetterhoun
THE NETHERLANDS

GENERAL CHARACTERISTICS A modest dog which, many years ago, was used as an Otter Hound. The dog is of solid build, without being either coarse or heavy. In general appearance he seems stronger, more compact than the Staby-Houn. His skin fits closely to the body without forming any wrinkles, not even at the throat. The lips are not pendulous. The temperament is much more aggressive than that of the Staby-Houn. He is courageous on the attack, and is highly prized as a fine guard dog.

SIZE Height at the withers: males about 21½ inches; females are slightly smaller.

HEAD Lean, strong, the size in good proportion to the body. The skull and muzzle are of equal length. The skull is slightly rounded and gives the impression of being wider than it is long; it merges well with the cheeks, the muscles of which are of normal development. The nose is large, with well open nostrils; it is black in black or black-and-white dogs, brown in brown dogs; it is not cleft. The muzzle is strong and narrows gradually toward the nose without being pointed; actually rather blunt. The nasal bridge is straight, and thus, seen in profile, it is neither arched nor hollowed; it is broad as seen from above. The lips are close-fitting, not pendulous. The teeth are strong and meet in a scissors bite. The stop is not accentuated; the passage from skull to muzzle is gradual.

EYES Of medium size, oval in shape, with well fitting eyelids. The haw is not visible. The eyes are set obliquely and should not appear either too prominent or too deep-set; because of its position in the head, in combination with the minimal stop, the eyes are the most important part of the muzzle and are of greater importance than in the Staby-Houn. The eyes are dark brown in black or black-and-white dogs, brown in brown dogs.

EARS Set on rather low, not too thick, they turn toward the head, without twisting or forming folds. Heavy ears which cannot turn easily at the base or which do not turn at all are to be faulted. The ears are of medium length, shaped like a spatula. The hair on the ears is a characteristic of the breed—wavy, quite long at the base, becoming shorter and shorter toward the tip, so that the lower third is covered only with short hair.

NECK Short, strong, meeting the back with a very slight angulation, which accounts for the very low carriage of the head. The neck is slightly arched and without wrinkles in the skin.

BODY The chest is broader than it is high, and this causes the forelegs to be quite far apart. The brisket is not below the elbows. The trunk is very strong, with well-developed and well-sprung ribs. The back is short and straight. The croup slopes very slightly. The loins are strong; the belly is moderately drawn up.

TAIL Set on at moderate height, curled in a spiral, curled over the

STABY-HOUN

DUTCH SPANIEL

Photo: E. Münch, G. Smits.

croup. The spiral is the chief ornament and typical of the breed.

FOREQUARTERS Shoulders close to the body; scapula sloping, forming an angle of about 110 degrees with the upper arm; the forearms are straight, strong; the feet are round, with well-developed and well-arched toes; the pads are strong. **HINDQUARTERS** Strong, normally angulated in regard to tibia, fibula, tarsus and metatarsus. This last should not be too long. The hocks are low; therefore the metatarsus is short. **FEET** Well rounded, with well developed pads.

COAT The entire body is covered with thick, curly hair, except for the head, where the hair is thick and close; sparse curls or curls made of excessively fine hair give a woolly aspect which is a serious fault. Coarse-textured, the hair should seem oily to the touch. **Color** Black, brown-white, blue-white. ●

230 VIZSLA
Hungarian Shorthaired Setter
HUNGARY

This dog probably descends from a German Setter (the Weimaraner?) and a Pointer. In the *Magiar Ebtenyesztok Orzagos Egyesulete* one may read: " ... from the point of view of use one can do no better than compare it to the other setters. The Pointer has a more rapid method of searching and a better-developed sense of smell, but he is not good at retrieving and his use is limited. The German Setter hunts more slowly, has a sufficiently developed sense of smell, retrieves well, keeps the trail well, and can be used in different ways. The Hungarian Setter, on the other hand, is quick in the hunt and obedient, has a very delicate sense of smell, retrieves perfectly, and keeps the trail. In a word, this is a dog that combines in himself all the good qualities of the breeds which we have quoted above."

GENERAL CHARACTERISTICS A medium-sized hunting dog of quite distinguished appearance. Robust but rather lightly built. His short coat is an attractive rusty gold. He is a dog of power and drive in the field and a tractable and affectionate companion in the home. His temperament is that of the natural hunter endowed with a good nose and above-average ability to take training. Lively, gentle in manner and demonstratively affectionate; fearless, with well-developed protective instinct.

SIZE Males 22-24 inches; females 21-23 inches at the highest point of the shoulders. Any dog measuring over or under these limits shall be considered faulty, the seriousness of the fault depending on the extent of the deviation. A dog measuring more than 2 inches over or under these limits shall be disqualified.

HEAD The head is lean but muscular. The skull is moderately wide between the ears, with a medial furrow down the forehead. Stop moderate. The muzzle is a trifle longer than the skull and, although tapering, is well squared at its end. Jaws strong, with well-developed white teeth meeting in a scissors bite. The lips cover the jaws completely, but they are neither loose nor pendulous. Nostrils slightly open, the nose brown. A black or slate-gray nose is objectionable.

VIZSLA

Photo: R. Kinne (Photo Res.).

VIZSLA

EYES The eyes are medium in size and depth of setting, their surrounding tissue covering the whites, and the iris harmonizing with the shade of the coat. A yellow eye is objectionable.

EARS Thin, silky, and proportionately long, with rounded tips; set fairly low and hanging close to the cheeks.

NECK The neck is strong, smooth, and muscular; moderately long, arched, and devoid of dewlap. It broadens nicely into shoulders, which are well laid back.

BODY Strong and well proportioned. The back is short, the withers high, and the topline slightly rounded over the loin to the set-on of the tail. Chest moderately broad and deep, reaching down to the elbows. Ribs well sprung; the underline is slightly tucked up beneath the loin.

TAIL The tail is set just below the level of the back, thicker at the root and docked one third.

FOREQUARTERS AND HINDQUARTERS The forelegs are straight, strong, and muscular, with elbows close. The hind legs have well-developed thighs, with moderate angulation at stifles and hocks. Too much angulation at the hocks is as faulty as too little. The hocks, which are well let down, are equidistant from each other from the hock joint to the ground. Cow hocks are faulty. **FEET** Catlike, round and compact, with close toes. Nails are brown and short, the pads thick and tough. Dewclaws, if present, are to be removed. Harefeet are objectionable.

COAT The coat is short, smooth, dense and close-lying, without woolly undercoat. **Color** Solid. Rusty gold or rather dark sandy yellow in different shades, with darker shades preferred. Dark brown and pale yellow undesirable. Small white spots on chest or feet are not faulted.

GAIT The gait is far-reaching, light-footed, graceful and smooth.

DISQUALIFICATION Deviation in the height of more than 2 inches from standard either way.

SCALE OF POINTS

Skull	10
Muzzle, nose, lips, teeth	15
Eyes and ears	5
Trunk and belly	10
Neck, rib cage, shoulders	10
Legs	10
Feet	10
Tail	15
Coat and color	10
Overall distinction and balance	5
	100

VIZSLA

Photo: R. Kinne (Photo Res.)

231 HUNGARIAN COARSE-HAIRED SETTER

Drotszörüvizla

HUNGARY

The Hungarian Coarsehaired Setter is a breed that was formed spontaneously from the Hungarian Shorthaired Setter and then by crossbreeding the latter with the German Coarsehaired Setter.

GENERAL CHARACTERISTICS A medium-sized hound, of noble appearance, with lean muscling; strong bone, powerful tendons, lean feet. This breed is characterized by vigor and intelligence. The coat is tough, dark yellow in color.

WEIGHT AND SIZE Weight: 48½-66 lb. Height: males 22½-25½ inches; females 21-23½ inches.

HEAD The head is lean and noble. The skull is broad, slightly rounded, well muscled, with a pronounced metopic suture. The supraorbital ridges are only slightly developed. The stop is a moderate curve. The occipital protuberance is moderate. The nose is large, wide, with well open nostrils. The bridge, in all directions, is rounded and not pointed; it is straight and forms an angle of 30-35 degrees with the skull. The lips and cheeks are moderate, lean, not pendulous. The jaws are powerful; the incisors, in normal dentition, meet in a scissors bite.

EYES Neither protruding nor deepset. The expression is lively and intelligent, the eyelids fit well so that the whites and the haw are not visible. The color of the eyes is invariably darker than the color of the coat. Black eyes and light eyes are not inadmissible.

EARS Set on at medium height; they have thin skin and are not fleshy; they are V-shaped and hanging, rather longer than average.

NECK Of medium length, moderately arched and muscular. There is no dewlap.

BODY The withers are long and pronounced; the back is straight, short and very muscular. The loins are of moderate length, solid, broad and muscular. The croup is straight but not horizontal, and it is well muscled. The chest is well rounded, of moderate width, very well muscled. The thorax is deep and long and not too wide; the ribs are moderately well sprung. The belly is slightly drawn up, and the flanks are slightly hollowed.

TAIL Set on rather low, of medium thickness. It should be docked to 2/3 of its natural length. When so altered it reaches the stifle. When the dog is in motion, the tail is usually held in a horizontal position.

FOREQUARTERS The scapula is close to the body and very well muscled; it is sloping. The elbows are set on the longitudinal axis of the body, neither turning inward nor outward. The forearm is long, the pastern short. The feet are round and closed, the pads well filled out and elastic. The nails are short and strong, darker in color than the coat. **HINDQUARTERS** Set at a rather open angle and long. The thigh and the leg are both long. The femural-tibial angle is about 110-120 degrees. The hocks are low. Dewclaws are a fault. The feet are well closed, the pads well filled out and elastic.

COAT The hair on the nasal bridge is short and hard and produces a beard of perhaps ¾ of an inch at the chin. The hair on the head is short, hard, smooth and not glossy. On the ears the hair is slightly longer, like that of the Vizsla, but even finer. The eyebrows are thick and hard; they stand up obliquely and forward. On the neck and the trunk the hair is harsh, hard and not glossy, fitting loosely on the rest of the body. There is an undercoat, evident in winter. The hair on the forequarters is smooth; it forms a brush on the back part of the forelegs. On the hind legs this brush is seen down to the hocks. The hair is shorter and softer between the toes. The hair is dense, longer on the lower part, without forming a fringe. **Color** Dark yellow, without markings. **Skin** Taut, without wrinkles. The lips and eyelids are deep brown.

GAIT The movement is lively, elegant, graceful. It is a classical gait of perfect form.

FAULTS Tail badly docked or twisted; hair longer than 1½ inches, soft, silky, curly, or similar to that of the Griffon; soft and woolly hair on the head; mane along the spine.

HUNGARIAN COARSEHAIRED SETTER

ITALIAN SETTER

DISQUALIFICATIONS Height at the withers less than 22 inches or more than 25½ inches in males; less than 20½ or more than 24½ in females; lack of type; black or spotted nose; falling eyelids; pendulous, slavering lips; overshot, undershot jaw more than ⅛ inch at the incisors; coat marked or speckled; a marking on chest of more than 2 inches in diameter; white feet; brown or faded color.

MEASUREMENTS Bodily proportions expressed as percentage of height at the withers:

	percent
Length of trunk	100
Depth of thorax	44
Amplitude of chest	33
Circumference behind the elbows	117

Length of the nasal bridge is 46 percent that of the head; length of the ears is 76 percent that of the head ●

232 ITALIAN SETTER

ITALY

The setter has been mentioned in a general way in very old documents and this is an indication of how far back its origins go. Egyptian drawings depict it as a rather graceful dog, somewhat similar to the Greyhound, with hanging ears and a tail carried in the same way as present-day setters. This ancient physical structure of the setter probably was derived from crossbreeding between the Segugio Racing Hound and the Assyrian Mastiff.

The setter was destined to develop, especially in Italy, where he was prevalent in ancient ties together with the Segugio and the Mastiff.

Actually it is not known whether the Egyptian Setter was brought to Europe. Probably he was formed there through crossbreeding between hounds and mastiffs descended from the Asiatic Mastiff. The theory that the Italian setters were formed in Europe seems one which merits the most consideration.

According to many dog experts the Italian Setter is among the oldest setters and it is probable that he is the ancestor of all setters of European origin.

At present, Italian setters are subdivided by dog associations into two distinct varieties: the white-orange and the roan chestnut. Of the two, the elder is probably the white and orange, although this in no way prevents the roan chestnut from being a first-class dog with no need to envy the other—especially since he has the same physical characteristics.

Some authorities are inclined to think that the white-orange originated in Piedmont and the roan in Lombardy, although both came from the same stock. Others, however, believe that the roan is a cross between the Italian Brown and Orange Setter (imported into Germany and Austria) and the Black and Brown St. Hubert Bloodhound.

Photo: H. József.

Photo: M. Pedone.

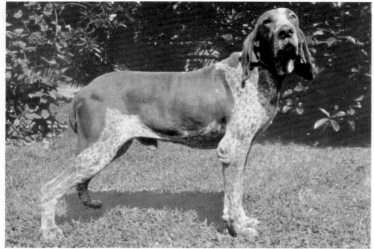

ITALIAN SETTER

GENERAL CHARACTERISTICS A powerful, well-proportioned dog, of vigorous aspect; the gait is loose, the trotting pace is ample and fast; while hunting, this dog carries its head relatively high, with the nose slightly above the backline. The facial expression is serious, gentle and intelligent; a docile dog, diligent in hunting, the Italian Setter is highly resistant and well adapted to all types of hunting. The best dogs are lean-limbed, powerfully muscled and with that sensitive expression of the head which indicates true distinction.

WEIGHT AND SIZE Both of these criteria vary between fairly wide limits, but mutually in good proportion. Height at the withers, 21½-26½ inches; weight, 55-88 lb. Weight and height above or below these limits does nothing for the dog and are considered faults.

HEAD Dolichocephalic, angular, slightly depressed at the mastoid-temporal region. The nose is large, more or less pink or flesh-colored, or brown, depending on the coat; it overhangs the lips somewhat; the nostrils are large and well open. The nasal bridge is either straight or slightly arched. The upper lips are well developed, fine and falling, but not flaccid; they cover the front part of the lower jaw and pass beyond it at the sides. Seen from in front, the lips form an inverted V, starting from slightly below the nose at an acute angle and becoming rounded at the front, lower edge. The commissure should be accentuated, but not excessively falling in the corner. The muzzle is rather square as seen from the front, rounded at the end as seen in profile; if its upper line is prolonged, it should pass above or tangentially to the occipital protuberance, never below it. A head is considered to be well proportioned when, measured from the occiput to the point of the nose, the midpoint falls on the most forward point of the eye. The forepart of the muzzle should be sufficiently broad to cover, as seen from the front, the sides of the muzzle. The profile of the forward edge of the lower jaw is slightly receding; the upper and lower teeth meet cleanly. The stop is not pronounced. The occipital protuberance is definitely pronounced; the sinuses and supraorbital arches are well marked.

EYES The eyes have a good-natured expression, and are neither protruding nor deep-set. They should be well open, oval in shape, with close-fitting eyelids. Their color is yellow or ocher, depending on the color of the coat.

EARS Well developed, long enough to reach the lower edge of the nose; they are set on rather far back, with a narrow insertion beneath the line from the upper edge of the nose to the eye, or, more precisely, set on the zygomatic line; they have little erectile power. A flexible ear, folded at the front, with the forward inner volute well marked, and close to the cheek. The lower edge is slightly rounded, with a suggestion of a graceful backward fold.

NECK Strong, relatively short but of good proportions; it is well distinguished from the nape. There is a dewlap, but an undivided, excessively abundant dewlap is considered a fault.

FOREQUARTERS The shoulder should be strong, with good muscles, long and sloping, free in its movements. The humerus is sloping, fitting

ITALIAN SETTER

RETURNING HOME

Photo: O. Langini.

ITALIAN SETTER PUPPIES

ITALIAN SETTER

close to the body; the forearms are robust, vertical, with the back tendons strong and well separated; the point of the elbow should lie on a perpendicular from the point of the scapula. The pasterns are of good proportions, lean, of fair length and slightly bent; both short- and long-coupled pasterns are considered faults, as are those out of vertical. The feet are robust, large and round, with slightly long toes, covered with fine, short hair; they are well closed and should never be open. Strong, curved nails, white, ocher or brown of more or less intense shade depending on the coat, as are the pads, which should be lean and elastic. The absence of dewclaws, simple or double, is not a fault.

BODY The thorax is ample, deep, with the brisket at elbow level, not carenated and with ribs which are more rounded below than above. The chest should be large in proportion to the size of the body. The withers are high, with the scapulae well out from the body. The upper line of the trunk is composed of two segments: one is almost straight, sloping from the withers to the eleventh dorsal vertebra; the other is curved, slightly sloping from the croup to the same vertebra and joining the line of the loins. The lower edge of the trunk is almost horizontal in the thoracic region and slightly curved upward in the abdominal region; it rises, curving broadly, toward the forward point of the sternum. A drawn-up belly is considered a very serious fault. The lumbar region is broad, muscular, rather short and arched, especially in the male. The croup is well muscled, rather short, with a very slight suggestion of slope; the pelvis is ample, especially in the female.

TAIL Thick at the root, straight, with a slight tendency to taper; it must not be shaggy. The tail is carried horizontally or slightly down or up on the march and at the hunt; it is carried low in repose. It should be docked to 6-10 inches. A tail curving upward is a fault, as is a lack of tail.

HINDQUARTERS The thighs are rather long, not spreading, well muscled and with the back edge tending toward a straight line. The legs are strong, with broad and not excessively bent hocks, which are well in vertical; the leg is set rather forward in the femur-rotula-tibia articulation. The metatarsi are short and lean; long metatarsi, those turning outward or inward are considered faulty. The hind feet are similar to the forefeet.

COAT Short, thick and glossy; it is finer and much shorter on the head, ears, shoulders, thighs, and on the forepart of the legs and feet. Long hair and wavy hair are faults, even when limited to the croup and tail, or to the fringe in the region between thigh and belly, on the buttocks and on the back edge of the thighs. **Color** White; white with more or less large orange or more or less deep amber markings; white with more or less large markings of brown; white speckled with pale orange; white speckled with brown (roan brown). Faults include large, dull spots, very dark brown, solid colors; a warm brown color with metallic reflections is highly prized. The following are not permitted: black, black and white, tricolor, fawn, solid hazel, black and tan. A symmetrical facial mask is preferable; the absence of a mask is not a fault. **Skin** Should be consistent but flexible; it is thinner on the head, throat, underarm areas and lower parts of the trunk. Lips, nose and eyelids should be pigmented in keeping with the color of the coat, but they should never be speckled with black. The inner mucous areas of the mouth are pink; in roan or white-brown dogs there may be a bit of brown or pale brown inside the mouth. An excessive dewlap is a defect, as are several wrinkles on the head; although when the head is held down, a slight fold is admissible between the outer corner of the eye and falling along the cheek.

FAULTS (Of the head) Excessively protruding zygomatic arches; overshot or undershot jaws; medial division of nose (double nose) is a disqualification; lips too abundant and flaccid; commissure excessively overturned; light or too dark eyes, lower eyelid falling, almond-shaped eyes; ears too small or too large, flat, erectile, triangular, wide at root, set on high; thick ears; broadly folded tips of ears. ●

Photo: O. Langini, Prato.

233 ITALIAN SPINONE
Spinone Italiano

ITALY

ITALIAN SPINONE

Opinions vary widely concerning the origins of this dog. Some believe that he is descended from the same stock as the setter and that climate alone has affected the development of his thick coat. However, since relatively ancient times, we find the setter and the Spinone prevalent in the same areas, and for this reason this theory becomes unacceptable.

Other commentators believe the Spinone stemmed from the Coarsehaired Segugio, well known throughout the Piedmont. Nevertheless, some writers claim that the Spinone was prevalent beyond the Piedmont, in Venetia, Dalmatia, Istria, and as far as the Danube, which would support the theory that the Spinone came from the East. Talé, a dog expert, states that about a hundred years ago the Roan Spinone was especially well-known in Lombardy and Venetia, and that this variety with longer hair than the classic Spinone and with silky hair on the ears and forehead is still extant. Although some experts are convinced that the Spinone is a cross with the Griffon, he is probably the true Spinone of the Julian and Graie Alps which, having come from Russia, later spread into Lombardy and Venetia.

All this is in opposition to Tschudy's statements with which we also agree, namely, that during the Roman era the setter was developed in Italy.

The Italian Coarsehaired Setter had origins comparable to the Pointer in Italy, where Greek traders and others from the western Adriatic coast brought Coarsehaired Setters in ancient times. The Coarsehaired Setter was called the Spinone. This breed was formed by crossbreeding an imported Coarsehaired Setter and a white Mastiff of those already prevalent along the coasts of Italy.

GENERAL CHARACTERISTICS Scientific classification places the Spinone in the braccoid group (according to the classification of Pierre Mégnin). As a working dog he is classed as a hunting dog and a Pointer. Purely Italian in origin: Xenophon, Grattius Faliscus, Nemesianus, Seneca, Arrianus—all mentioned this dog twenty centuries ago or more. The general structure is that of a modified mesomorph (submesomorph), whose body outline is square, harmonious in regard to form and disharmonious in respect to profiles. A solid, vigorous country dog, with strong bone and well developed muscles, the Spinone is characterized by its excellent, fast trotting gait. He is an expert hunter on every type of terrain and in all seasons, but especially in swampland and in the woods; he is docile, patient and sociable. His facial expression is intelligent and reveals power and courage. The eyes are expressive, with a markedly sweet, almost human expression. He is exceptionally hardy and enters nonchalantly into brambles and deep, cold water; for such work he is protected by his thick skin and hard,

ITALIAN WHITE AND ORANGE SPINONE

ITALIAN WHITE AND ORANGE SPINONE

thick coat. He is an excellent retriever by instinct and a fine swimmer.

WEIGHT AND SIZE Weight: Males 70-82 lb; females 62-71 lb. Height at the withers: males 23½-27½ inches; females 23-25½ inches.

HEAD Dolichocephalic, with its total length 40 percent of the height at the withers, and the length of the muzzle should measure half the total length of the head. Half this length lies on the horizontal line joining the two inner corners of the eyes. The width of the skull should not exceed half of the total length of the head, preferably less. The total cephalic index should not exceed 50, and the ideal is about 45. The upper longitudinal axes of the skull and muzzle are divergent, which means that prolonging the upper line of the nasal bridge, it should pass before or tangentially to the occipital protuberance and never beneath it.

Nose Generous, on the same line as the nasal bridge, spongy in appearance, with the top surface very large and quite rounded. The pigment is fleshy red in white dogs, a little deeper in white-orange dogs, brown in the brown roans. In profile, the nose protrudes over the forward vertical line of the lips; the nostrils should be large and well open. **Nasal Bridge** Slightly arched or straight. (For its length and direction in relation to the axis of the skull, see HEAD.) The width, measured at the midpoint, should be 1/5 to 1/6 of the total length of the head, or 1/3 of the length of the nasal bridge itself. **Lips** The upper lips are rather thin; they begin beneath the nose at a wide angle and, becoming rounded in their lower forward extremity, they cover the lower lips and reach the commissure in a visible fold, in such a way that the lower lateral profile of the muzzle is provided by the profile

Photo: A. P. Rossi.

formed by the upper lips, which have the commissure as the lowest part of the profile itself. **Muzzle** The lateral faces of the muzzle should be parallel; the lower one should be square. **Jaws** Strong in appearance, the jaws are of normal development, with the teeth meeting in a perfect scissors bite. The teeth are sound. The two sides of the lower jaw should be very slightly curved at the midpoint of their length. **Stop** Gently sloping, be-

cause of the divergence of the upper cranial-facial longitudinal axes. **Skull** The length is approximately equal to the length of the muzzle; it should not be more than the width of the skull or half the total length of the head (see HEAD). Oval-shaped, the skull has an exceptionally developed occipital protuberance and a marked inter-parietal crest, in such a way that the lateral walls of the skull, along their upper edge and particularly in the

posterior region are gently sloping and very slightly rounded: therefore the upper part should not be flat. The sinuses are not overly developed in their fore part and upper part and are rather receding toward the back, and the supraorbital ridges are not greatly raised. The medial furrow is pronounced.

EYES Large and well open, the eyes

tend to be round; the eyelids should be close-fitting, and the lower lid should never be ectropionic. The eyes are neither protruding nor deep-set, and the line joining the outer and inner corners lies at an angle of 15-20 degrees with the center plane of the head. The color is deep yellow in white and white-orange dogs; ocher in brown roans. The pigmentation of the eyelids is the same as that of the nose.

ITALIAN ROAN AND CHESTNUT SPINONE

EARS Triangular in shape. In length, they are not more than 2 inches longer than the lower line of the throat (in normal stance); in width, they are equal to the distance from the head-neck line to the midpoint of the zygomatic arch. The base of the ears is rather narrow; it should lie on the line of the zygomatic arch, in its upper part. The ears fall with the forward edge close to the cheek, not folded, but with an inside volute. It should be carried low at practically all times, and should have little erectile power. Its point is slightly rounded, the cartilage is fine; the skin is covered with thick, short hair, mixed with a longer, sparser down, which is thicker at the edges.

NECK Strong and muscular, clearly distinguished from the nape, it merges gently into the shoulders, with a harmonious line. Its length is about 2/3 of the total length of the head; its circumference is 1/3 of the height at the withers. The skin at the throat should be normal, with a slight, divided dewlap, in such a way that the channels of the jaws and throat are clearly distinguishable.

FOREQUARTERS Shoulders Should be strong, with well-developed muscles and free and easy in their movements; the length is about 1/4 that of the height at the withers, and it is inclined to the horizontal at an angle of 50-60 degrees. In respect to the center plane of the body, the points of the shoulders are not very close together or, rather, well set apart. **Upper Arm** Should be sloping to the horizontal, but at a lower slope than that of the shoulder (65 degrees); it is well muscled, and is directed al-

most parallel to the axis of the body. The scapula-humeral angle is 125 degrees, with a slope of the shoulder of 60 degrees. **Forearm** Straight and vertical; it is strongly boned. In cross section it is oval; the back tendon is strong and detached (the tendon of the cubital flexor muscle of the wrist), in such a way that the furrow between tendon and bone is well in evidence. Its length is slightly more than 1/3 of the height at the withers, that is, 35.4 percent of such height. The height of the entire foreleg to the elbow (point) is 50 percent of the height at the withers. The elbows are covered with soft, loose skin and should lie in a plane which is parallel to the center plane of the body. The point of the elbow should be slightly forward of the perpendicular from the posterior point of the scapula. **Wrist** Follows the vertical line of the forearm; it is extremely mobile, covered with fine, thin skin and with the pisiform bone prominent. **Pasterns** Should be flat from forward back and follow, when seen from in front, the straight, vertical line of the forearm. They are lean, slightly less than 1/6 the height of the leg at the elbow, and slightly extended as seen in profile. **Feet** Compact round, with well-closed toes which are well arched and covered with short, thick hair, including the spaces between the toes; the pads are hard and lean, more or less pigmented depending on the color of the coat. The nails are strong and arched; in white and white-orange dogs the nails may be more deeply pigmented, and in brown roans the pigment should be dark but never black.

BODY The length of the body is equal to the height at the withers.

Chest Broad and open, with well-developed pectoral muscles. Its width, which is directly proportional to the width of the thorax, between its lateral limits (upper forward edges of the arms) should be 30 percent of the height at the withers. The anterior segment of the sternum should be positioned slightly below the level of the point of the shoulders, and the closer it is to the horizontal line of the sternum, the better. That is, the chest should be well let down. **Thorax** Roomy; the brisket should be at least at the level of the elbows. The thorax is deep and well rounded at the midpoint of its height, where its cross diameter is maximum, and noticeably narrows from there to the sternum, but it should not form a carena, in such a way that the rib cartilage remains rounded. The ribs should be well open. The profile of the sternum area should be basically horizontal. In a Spinone measuring 25½ inches at the withers, the thorax should have the following dimensions: circumference behind the elbows, 31 inches; circumference around the ribs, 27 inches; depth, 15¼ inches; height, 10¼ inches; cross diameter, 8⅔ inches. Thus, the thoracic index should not be more than 6, and preferably even lower. **Ribs** Well sprung, sloping, with extended space between the ribs. The back ribs (false ribs) should be long, sloping and well open. **Back** The withers are raised above the backline and are widened by the separation between the points of the shoulders. The upper profile of the back is made up of two lines—one, almost straight, slopes at 15 degrees from the withers to the eleventh dorsal vertebra; the other, slightly arched, rises from this vertebra to

the croup, joining with the line of the loins. The length of the back is 38 percent of the height at the withers. **Loins** Follow the line of the second part of the back, with which they are well fused; they are slightly convex in profile, and are well muscled in their width. Their length is a little less than 1/5 of the height at the withers, their width is close to the length, in the ratio of 14.5:16. **Belly and Flanks** The lower line of the belly, from the profile of the sternum, ascends perhaps 2 inches upward toward the flank. The flanks should be approximately equal in length to the lumbar region; the hollowing should be minimum. **Croup** Broad, robust and muscular. The cross diameter between the haunches should be, therefore, 1/7 of the height at the withers. Its length is about 1/3 of the height at the withers and, more exactly, 29 percent. Its inclination to the horizontal is 15-20 degrees; the slope of the coxa is 35-40 degrees; thus the croup is sloping. **Sexual Organs** Normal and complete development of the testicles.

TAIL Thick at the base and set on as a continuation of the croup line; it is carried horizontally or down; it should be docked at 6-10 inches from the root.

HINDQUARTERS Thigh long, broad and muscular, with a slight arch to the back edge. Its length should not be less than 1/3 of the height at the withers. Its outer side, from one edge to the other, should be ¾ of its length; its direction is slightly oblique from the upper part downward and from the back part forward, and it should be parallel, in respect to the vertical to the center plane of the body. **Hind leg** With strong bone and lean muscling in the upper part; the furrow between, the tendon and the hock is well marked and plainly visible. The length of the leg is in a ratio of 23:25 to the length of the thigh; its slope varies from 55-60 degrees to the horizontal. **Hocks** The distance from the soles of the foot to the point of the hock is a little more than ¼ of the height at the withers; the wider the surfaces of the hocks, the better. The angulation of the hocks is open, because of the slight slope of the tibia (150 degrees). Seen from behind, the backline from the point of the hocks to the ground should lie on the vertical and on the extension of the buttock line. **Metatarsus** Lean and robust; its length depends on the height at the withers; there is a simple dewclaw on the inner side. **Hind foot** Slightly more oval than the forefoot, but otherwise with all the characteristics of the latter.

COAT Hair Tough, thick, slightly wiry and rather close-fitting to the body, which is entirely covered with hair. The average length of the hair on the body is 1½-2½ inches, it is less long on the nasal bridge, ears, and head and even shorter on the front sides of the legs and on the feet; on the back sides of the legs the hair is a rough brush, but not long enough to constitute a fringe. In shedding, the hair may be mixed with shorter hair and a fine down, close (not to the point of predominating over the tough hair), uniform, as an undercoat. Longer, stiffer hair makes up the eyebrows, and even longer hair, though softer, covers part of the cheeks and the upper lips, where it forms moustaches and beard, giving to the head its typical expression of "good-natured grouch." **Color** Permissible colors include: white; white with orange markings; solid white peppered with orange; white with brown markings; white speckled with brown hairs (brown roan), with or without larger brown markings. **Skin** Close-fitting to the body, the skin should be thick, heavy and leathery; it covers the body with barely a suggestion of folds beginning at the lower jaw and disappearing at the first half of the neck (dewlap); there is also a fold, barely visible when the head is held down, which descends from the outer corner of the eye over the cheek, followed by a tuft of hair. The pigment of the skin varies with the markings of the coat. The lips, nose and eyelids should be pigmented according to the coat's color. There should never be black markings (disqualification), nor depigmentation.

GAIT In the hunt the gait is loose

ON THE HUNTING TRAIL ▶

Photo: Pedone.

ITALIAN WHITE AND ORANGE SPINONE

and easy, an ample, fast trot; when first on the track or when not strictly tracking, or on the return, the dog may gallop a few paces now and then.

FAULTS Height at the Withers Deficient or in excess. **Head** Upper cranial-facial longitudinal axes parallel; if convergent, it constitutes a disqualification. **Nose** Rising above the level of the bridge; small; with pigment which is too dark in comparison with the color of the coat; specklings of depigmentation; total depigmentation (disqualification); black pigmentation (disqualification). **Nasal Bridge** Short, narrow, with lateral lines converging; hollowed (disqualification). **Lips and Muzzle** Lips excessively large, extending beneath beyond the horizontal line of the commissure; lips deficient in development or flaccid; excessively accentuated commissure, commissure falling or turned back, commissure lacking; convergence forward of the lateral lines of the muzzle, that is, pointed muzzle. **Jaws** Delicate; undershot; overshot (disqualification); sides of the lower jaw too curved; horizontal erosion of the teeth. **Skull** Flat on top and broad on the sides; underdeveloped dome; excessively developed sinuses; metopic suture not marked; too pronounced or abrupt stop. **Eyes** Small (excessively small eyes constitute a disqualification); light eyes; walleyes (disqualification); almond-shaped; ectropion; entropion; eyes too close together; shifty, suspicious eyes; partial depigmentation of the eyelids; total depigmentation (a very serious fault); total bilateral depigmentation is a disqualification; black pigmentation on edges of eyelids (disqualification);

cross eyes: bilaterally crossed eyes are a disqualification. **Ears** Thick, short; base too wide, set on too high and too far back; base too narrow or too low; absence of longer, fine hair; curling of the leather; broadly rounded tips. **Neck** Thin, too short, with undivided and too obvious dewlap. **Shoulder** Straight, short, with badly developed muscling; bound in its movements; points of the scapulae too close together or too far apart. **Upper Arm** Too slanting or too straight; deficient in muscular development. **Forearm** Out of vertical; weak bone, spongy; elbows out or in. **Wrist** Evident hypertrophy of the wrist bones; spongy, small; jaded condition. **Pasterns** Short, thin, too long, too extended or straight or out of vertical. **Feet** Long, broad, open toes; flat feet; lack of toughness in pads; deficiency of pigmentation in nails or, in the brown roans, in pads; black nails (disqualification); black pads (disqualification). **Body** Longer than height at the withers. **Chest** Narrow, insufficiently let down; badly developed muscles; manubrium of sternum too high. **Thorax** Lacking in height, depth and circumference, narrow or carenated; xiphoid appendage curved inward; rib arches insufficiently open. **Ribs** Not well sprung, back ribs short and not open; back short, saddleback (lordosis), without break at eleventh vertebra; low withers, roach back (kyphosis). **Loins** Long, flat and narrow. **Belly and Flanks** Belly excessively drawn up, flanks too long and too hollowed. **Sexual Organs** Monorchidism (disqualification); cryptorchidism (disqualification); incomplete development of one or both testicles (disqualification). **Croup**

Narrow, too short, not sloping. **Tail** Lack of tail (disqualification); congenitally short tail; set on too low or too high; tail carried vertically; tail with feathering forming fringe. **Thighs** Short, with insufficient muscular development, narrow or deviated from the area of the second thigh. **Leg** Weak bone, shortness, excessive or insufficient slope; furrow between tendon and bone above hock not well defined. **Hocks** High, narrow, or with angulation excessively open or closed; out of vertical. **Metatarsus** Long, thin, out of vertical; absence of the dewclaw. **Hindfoot** As for forefoot. **Hair** Soft, silky (disqualification), waviness (disqualification), woolly (disqualification), curly (disqualification); too short, sparse; tending to form fringe on back sides of legs and underside of tail. **Color** Tricolor coat (disqualification); black markings (disqualification); solid-colored coats (disqualification), except for white. **Skin** Fine or too plentiful; traces of depigmentation on the nose and eyelids; total bilateral depigmentation of the eyelids (disqualification); total depigmentation of the nose (disqualification); black mucous areas (disqualification). **Gait** Continued ambling (disqualification); predominantly galloping gait in hunt (disqualification).

SUMMARY OF DISQUALIFICATIONS Height at the Withers Above 28¼ inches or more than ¾ inch below the minimum. **Head** Convergence of the upper cranial-facial longitudinal axes. **Nose** Total depigmentation, black pigmentation, even partial. **Nasal Bridge** Concave. **Jaws** Overshot condition; undershot condition if it harms the outward appearance of the muzzle.

Eyes Walleyes; eyelids with black pigment; total bilateral depigmentation of the eyelids. Bilaterally crossed eyes. **Sexual Organs** Cryptorchidism, monorchidism; incomplete development of one or both testicles. **Feet** Black nails; black pads. **Tail** Lack of tail. **Hair** Silky, wavy, woolly, curly. **Color** Solid color, except for white; tricolor; black markings; coat of color other than specifications of standard. **Skin** Black mucous areas; total depigmentation of the nose; total bilateral depigmentation of the eyelids. **Gait** In field tests, continuous gallop in hunt.

SCALE OF POINTS

Height and general appearance	20
Skull and muzzle	30
Ears	5
Eyes and eyelids	10
Shoulders	10
Backline and belly line	10
Thorax	10
Loins and croup	15
Legs and feet	20
Coat and color	15
Tail	5
	150

RATINGS

Excellent: points at least	140
Very good	130
Good	120
Fairly good	110

N.B. In judging at a show, if any body area directly concerned with type is given the rating "zero," judges should disqualify the dog, even if the dog is otherwise excellent. ●

234 PORTUGUESE SETTER
Perdigueiro Português
PORTUGAL

The origins of the Portuguese Setter are probably related to those of the Italian Setter, as happens with all closely related breeds.

He is a tenacious hunter and is active on the trail. He searches the ground with the skill and perseverance of an explorer. He is a good worker and a faithful helpmate of the hunter with whom he works in perfect harmony. Silently, and with the speed that comes naturally to him, he is always successful in showing the attentive hunter by his attitude, expression, position of his tail, and the way he advances, the knowledge he has gained through his sense of smell. A good Portuguese Setter invariably shows his determination to hunt intelligently and with surprising skill. His "stay" position is always associated with a particular psychic state: a set expression, fixed gaze, ears poised for listening, head immobile, tail horizontal, and one paw raised. At such moments he is oblivious to his surroundings.

He is not self-centered and shares with evident joy his master's pleasure in hunting, no matter what the temperature is and over all sorts of terrain. His utmost desire is to fulfill his function completely, and once the quarry is brought down his greatest reward consists in retrieving it and presenting it to his master.

PORTUGUESE SETTER

GENERAL CHARACTERISTICS A medium-sized dog, with straight lines, braccoid in type. This breed is extremely sociable and sometimes aggressive toward other dogs. He has a calm and lively temperament, graceful in his movements. His body is in good proportion, with a shape indicative of a solid build which, however, imparts no trace of coarseness.

WEIGHT AND SIZE Weight: Males 44-60 lb; females 35-49 lb. Height at the withers: males, 20½ inches; females, 20½ inches. A difference of 1½ inches over or above these figures is acceptable.

HEAD In good proportion to the body, the head gives the impression of being larger than it really is. It should be neither bony nor coarse. The skin is loose but without wrinkles. Seen from in front, the head is square: in profile, it is rectilinear. It is well set onto the neck, with which it merges well, permitting ease and energy of movement. It is of good shape, proportional and harmonious in its dimensions, and when seen from in front there is a clear separation between the nasal bridge and the skull. **Nose** The nostrils form a perfect right angle with the bridge and the upper lip; they should be large and well shaped, well open. They should be black in chamois dogs, or nearly so; preferably light brown or dark brown in brown dogs. **Nasal Bridge** Long, straight and of good width, flat on all four sides. **Jaws** Of moderate size and well adapted. The mouth is of moderate size, the coloring of the mucous areas indefinite; it should close well, permitting the natural fall of the upper lips, which are loose but not excessively so, not too fleshy, and hanging without wrinkles. They meet rather loosely with the lower lips, so that the corners of the mouth seem slightly falling. The condition of the teeth at birth and the development of them during the dog's life must be good, because the entire development and closure of the mouth depends on good dentition. **Stop** Well defined (forming a cranial-facial angle of 100 degrees), the stop is positioned closer to the nose than to the occipital crest. **Skull** Seen from in front, the forehead is almost flat, high, broad and symmetrical; in profile it is slightly arched. The occipital protuberance is barely perceptible.

PORTUGUESE SETTER

EYES Full, symmetrical and large; they may be of various shades of chestnut, but dark shades are preferable. They are oval, horizontal and not deep-set. They have fine, well-open lids, close-fitting and easy in movement. The eyelids are pigmented black or brown, consistent with the coloring of the nose. The expression is lively, especially in adult dogs. The supraorbital ridges are prominent but not excessively so, since that would make the head look bony.

EARS Of medium length and width (6 inches long, 4½ inches wide); they should be thin, soft, covered with fine, very short hair, and much larger at the base than at the tips, in a ratio of approximately 2½:1. The tips of the ears are rounded and the auricles are like an inverted triangle. The ears, moreover, have an almost flat surface. They are set on high, they are hanging and parallel; on the outer side, when the dog is surprised, one or two small lengthwise furrows of variable depth and width may be seen, though never accentuated.

NECK Straight, not very thick, rather long and having a short dewlap. It is joined harmoniously to the head and, sloping almost at 90 degrees, it should join the thorax without appreciable interruption, thus achieving a perfect harmonious whole.

BODY Thorax High and broad, indicating plenty of heart and lung room; it should be higher and deeper than it is wide, and the brisket should be at elbow level. The cross section should be horseshoe-shaped. The withers should not be too high. The back should be short, broad and straight, moving horizontally into the lumbar region without any obvious interruption. **Loins** The loins should be short, quite broad and well muscled, slightly curved and well joined to the croup. In length the croup is in good proportion to the loins, of harmonious shape and slightly sloping. **Belly Line** From the sternum to the groin, the lower line of the body slopes upward from front to back, following the natural outline of the abdomen. The belly is of moderate capacity, and the flank is short and well filled out.

TAIL The tail is generally docked at the third joint. If not docked, it should not reach below the hocks and should preferably be much shorter. It should be straight, set on at moderate height and thick at the root, tapering gradually and without exaggeration toward the tip. It is in continuation with the median line of the croup. Its shape and carriage should contribute to the gracefulness of the body outline. In repose the tail is carried down, along the thighs (never between the legs); when the dog is in action, the tail is raised to the horizontal, sometimes slightly above it but never vertical, never curved. In the hunt, the dog moves the tail laterally, synchronized with his pace.

FOREQUARTERS AND HINDQUARTERS When the dog is standing, the forelegs are perfectly vertical as seen from in front (although the general appearance of the dog is slightly open); the same applies to the hind legs as seen from behind. Forelegs and hind legs should, moreover, be perfectly parallel to the center plane of the body. Seen in profile, the legs are normally vertical. Overall, there is a great stability of stance as well as great ease of movement. **Forequarters** The shoulders are long, sloped, well set, slightly filled out. The upper arm is well joined to the body, as are the shoulders: the length of the upper arm should be in proportion to the distance separating the withers from the scapula-humeral articulations, and its slope to the slope of the shoulders. The forearm is well away from the body, long, straight and clearly perpendicular to the ground. The elbows are well out from the body, and should turn neither inward nor outward. The wrists are a perfect continuation of the forearm; the pasterns are broad, slightly sloping and of normal length. **Hindquarters** The thighs should preferably be long, broad, heavy but not coarse. The curve of the buttocks is more or less accentuated from the root of the tail to the tendon of the hocks; their length depends on the comparative length and slope of the thighs. They should preferably be long and slightly in relief. The second thigh is positioned slightly below but not far from the abdomen. It is slightly rising and slightly directed outward. The legs have good direction and are of a length proportionate to the thighs. The slope of the legs should be well coordinated with the slope of the croup. The hocks are normally open and well positioned, broad and heavy. The metatarsi are short, vertical, almost cylindrical, lean and of normal thickness. The articulations should clearly be well developed in both width and thickness and formed in such a way as to allow great facility and freedom of movement. All angulations should be such as to permit a regular gait. **Feet** In good proportion to the length of the legs and the size of the dog. They should preferably be rounded rather than long, but without being catfeet. The toes are well formed and arched; they separate slightly when bearing the weight of the dog. The pads are black, wrinkled and hard, highly resistant. The nails are well set, hard and preferably black.

COAT Short, strong, well distributed, dense and not soft; it covers the entire body uniformly. It is fine and very short on the head, especially on the ears, which have a velvety feel. There is no undercoat. **Color** Yellow and brown, solid or with markings.

GAIT The movements are normal. At work, the dog's normal gait is a broad trot, easy and rhythmic.

DISQUALIFICATIONS Weight not in conformance with standard; size too much above or below the standard; nontypical head; depigmented nose, nonblack nose in solid black or solid white dogs; overshot or undershot condition; total or partial loss of sight; eyes different in shape or size; atypical ears, badly set on, too large, fleshy, excessively folded or curled; deafness; lack of tail, rudimentary tail, completely docked tail, nontypical carriage of tail when natural; dewclaws; nontypical coat; albinism.

SCALE OF POINTS

	M	F
General appearance (harmony of form, gait, build, sexual characteristics)	25	25
Head (carriage, skull, ears, eyes, nasal bridge, stop, nose)	25	25
Neck, withers, shoulders, forequarters	10	10
Chest, loins, upper and lower body lines	15	10
Croup, pelvis, hindquarters	10	15
Feet, toes, nails	5	5
Tail (carriage, shape, insertion)	3	3
Coat (texture, color, density)	7	7
	100	100

235 CZECH COARSE-HAIRED SETTER

Ceský Fousek

CZECHOSLOVAKIA

The Czech Coarsehaired Setter almost completely disappeared from his native land almost immediately after World War I—and because of it. However, thanks to the few specimens which had preserved the type and the considerable blood strain of other setters, it was possible to regenerate and modernize the breed; that is, to make it more suitable to modern hunting needs. The F.C.I. published its standards in 1963.

The modern type is sometimes noticeably different from the original. The dog has increased his speed in the search without, however losing his ancient and excellent qualities for hunting in the woods and in the water. As for efficiency, he compares favorably with other setters, as he has shown by his many victories in the most important Czechoslovakian field trials.

Today breeders are able to produce many specimens of the Czech Coarsehaired Setter which are much esteemed and, in their own country, preferred to foreign shorthaired setters, that had previously enjoyed great popularity.

GENERAL CHARACTERISTICS A medium-sized hunting dog, short-haired, with hereditary qualities for working in the fields and in the woods. In spite of his natural aggressiveness toward interlopers, he is easily led and is devoted to his master. The Czech Setter is a noble dog whose general appearance indicates ruggedness and strength.

SIZE Height at the Withers: males 23½-26; females 23-24½.

WEIGHT Males 62-75 lb; females 48½-62 lb.

HEAD The head is lean, quite narrow, long and carried erect. The skull is very slightly rounded, slightly broader in males than in females. The stop is fairly pronounced, particularly at the forehead. The supraorbital ridges are clearly defined, and give an angular appearance to the head. The eyes are deep-set. The occipital protuberance is not accentuated. The nose is wide, with sensitive and well-open nostrils. Color of the nose should invariably be dark brown; the nasal bridge is slightly arched; the muzzle, which is a little longer than the skull, narrows from the eyes to the nose. The lips are of medium size; they fit closely over the jaws. The upper lip overlaps slightly the lower. The jaws are powerful, perfectly coordinated and muscular. The teeth are robust and the bite is of the scissors type. Dentition is complete.

EYES Deep-set, from dark amber to dark brown. The lids are close-fitting, well developed and gray-black. The eyes are almond-shaped, the expression kindly.

EARS Set on very high, broad at the base, pointed toward the tip; their length is about 2/3 that of the cheek; the tips are slightly rounded; the ears are carried close to the head.

NECK Of moderate length, with well-developed muscles, very lean and set on high over the withers; it is arched to an average extent.

FOREQUARTERS The scapula is well raised, with well developed muscles. The shoulders are properly sloped, forming an obtuse angle with the upper arm. The elbow is strong and well muscled. The forearm is vertical and straight, with lean and well-developed muscle. The pasterns are relatively short, very close to the vertical or slightly sloped forward. **Feet** Well closed, spoon-shaped; the toes are well arched, with strong, dark

CZECH COARSEHAIRED SETTER

Photo: J. Jaros.

CZECH COARSEHAIRED SETTER

gray or black nails. The pads are thick and hard, completely pigmented. There is a curious, vestigial remnant of membrane between the toes.

BODY Seen from in front, the chest and the scapula are lyre-shaped. The thorax is oval in cross section, its length in good proportion to the overall build of the dog. The brisket should be at least at elbow level; the thorax is well developed at the chest; seen in profile, the sternum should be clearly forward. The ribs are well sprung and in good proportion throughout the entire length of the rib cage. The back is short and compact, gently sloping from withers to croup. The loins are short, relatively broad and slightly arched. The belly should be slightly drawn up, so as to permit free movement, yet with no suggestion of skinniness. The croup is slightly sloped, quite broad and long. The sacral bone should be set in so that its muscles do not influence the carriage of the tail, which should be horizontal or slightly raised.

TAIL Set on so as to form a prolongation of the backline. It is moderately thick, and should be docked to 40 percent of its length.

HINDQUARTERS The pelvis is in good proportion to the body, the femur is broad and well muscled. The hind legs are sloped toward the back, with good angulation allowing easy movement. The articulation of the hind feet should not be too high, but lean, with the points of the hocks slightly protruding. The metatarsus is very close to vertical, short and relatively strong. **Feet** Similar to the forefeet. Dewclaws, if present, should be eliminated.

COAT Three types of hair make up the coat: (a) a soft, dense undercoat, about ¾ inch long, which protects the skin from humidity; in summer it disappears almost entirely; (b) the top coat, measuring from 1 to 1½ inches, is hard and rough, close-fitting; (c) a certain amount of bristly hair, 2-2½ inches long, particularly straight and harsh, especially on the chest, on the backline, at the groin and on the shoulders. On the forelegs and hind legs the hair is shorter and harder on the front, while on the back part it is longer and

may form a tuft. The tail should not have a fringe on the underside. The lower part of the cheeks and the lips are feathered with a longer, softer hair which forms a beard which is characteristic of the breed. The eyebrows are composed of hair which stands up obliquely. The forehead and the upper part of the head and cheeks are covered with short, tough hair. The hair on the ears is short, soft and close-fitting. **Color** Permissible colors include: dirty white, with or without brown markings; brown with honey-colored markings on the chest and the lower forelegs; brown without markings.

GAIT When the dog is walking or trotting, the movement is quite regular; the backline is virtually motionless; and when the dog trots the footprints coincide.

FAULTS Short, conical or rounded head; protruding eyes; coloring other than that provided by the standard; ears too long or set on too low; neck too long or too thick, with loose skin; thorax underdeveloped in front, sternum insufficiently evident; withers badly defined; bad proportion be-

tween height and width; croup too rigid; splayed toes; fine hair, hair too long or too short; noncharacteristic lack of beard and eyebrows; lack of pigmentation; predominance of white hair (streaked markings are not allowed); excessively hairy feet.

MEASUREMENTS	M		F	
Weight	75	lb.	55	lb.
Height at withers	25	in.	23¾	in.
Length of head	11	in.	9	in.
Length of skull	5½	in.	4¼	in.
Breadth of skull	4¾	in.	4	in.
Length of muzzle	5	in.	4¼	in.
Breadth of ribcage	7¾	in.	7	in.
Height of thorax	10	in.	9	in.
Length of trunk	22	in.	21	in.
Circumference behind elbows	31½	in.	28¼	in.
Circumference at last rib	28¼	in.	25¼	in.

ANGULATION OF LEGS

Scapula-humeral	110°
Humeral-radial	135°
Coxal-femoral	110°
Femural-tibial	125°
Tibial-tarsal	135°

313

Photo: J. Jaros.

The eighth group of breeds recognized by the F.C.I. includes British hunting dogs except terriers (which we noted in the third group) and hounds (included in the fifth and sixth groups). We may therefore state that British (English, Scottish, Welsh, and Irish) dogs whose descriptions and standards are given in the following pages do not include all the hunting breeds of these areas but only those employed in the "modern" hunt, that is, with firearms.

Among the English dogs we first have the setter breeds: the Pointers and setters which are famous throughout the world. Then there is a group of typically British breeds, the Retrievers. These famous Retrievers specialize in bringing back game shot down by their master, often (in England almost always) working as a pair, with a setter or a Pointer.

Next come the spaniels, descendants of various spaniels from the continent. The Cockers are related to the spaniels and are very good for hunting. However, because of their beauty and their friendly nature, they often become pet dogs, as is the case with the Cocker Spaniel and the American Cocker.

236 POINTER
GREAT BRITAIN

Much has been said and written about the Pointer's origins but, as usual, opinions and conclusions are not always in agreement.

Mégnin states that the Pointer's ancestry must be sought in the old Spanish Setter that came to the British Isles in the fourteenth century. Others share this opinion but specify that the Spanish Setter arrived in England only in 1713, after the Peace of Utrecht.

The famous English authority Arkwright, in his *History of the Pointer,* claims that the breed came from the Italian Setter and states that it is the source of an entire group of setters. What appears to be the most reliable hypothesis is that the English simply perfected the Pointer and attained the modern type, which was already present for some time in France and which was the origin of all French shorthaired setters. By the beginning of the eighteenth century the French had already obtained from their old Pointer an intermediate type which had attained a remarkable degree of perfection as well as excellent structural characteristics and general qualities.

This result was arrived at through crossbreedings effected in England using the Foxhound, the Bull Terrier and the Bulldog, with careful application of the different strains. Stonehenge believes that the Pointer has Greyhound blood, which might be possible, although contested by Faelli, the Italian expert, who states that such a strain would have weakened the Pointer's well-known keen sense of smell. It appears also that the Bloodhound has also contributed in forming the Pointer. Cetain writers limit outside blood strains to the Foxhound. Others are inclined to think that the Pointer was arrived at exclusively from the setter through selective breeding. Arkwright admits to different blood combinations, but all with negative results.

In any case, it is evident that the result, however obtained and by whatever method, has crowned the efforts of English breeders with success: 130 years ago they produced the splendid Pointer with the ability for sudden stops.

The first "perfected" Pointers made their appearance at the end of the nineteenth century in France, Italy, and other European countries.

Photo: S. A. Thompson.

POINTER

GENERAL CHARACTERISTICS The Pointer should be symmetrical and well built all over. Alert, with the appearance of strength, endurance and speed.

HEAD The skull should be medium in breadth and in proportion to the length of the foreface; the stop well defined, pronounced occipital bone. Nose and eye rims dark but may be lighter in a lemon-and-white-colored dog. The nostrils wide, soft and moist. The muzzle somewhat concave, and ending on a level with the nostrils, giving a slightly dish-faced appearance. The cheekbones should not be prominent. Well-developed, soft lips. Mouth should have scissors bite, neither undershot nor overshot.

EYES The same distance from the occiput as from the nostrils. A slight depression under the eyes, which should be bright and kindly in expression, not staring or bold, and not looking down the nose. Irises are either hazel or brown, according to color of coat.

EARS Should be set on fairly high and lie close to the head; they should be of medium length and inclined to be pointed at the tips.

NECK Long, muscular, slightly arched, springing cleanly from the shoulders and free from throatiness.

BODY Well-sprung ribs, gradually falling away at the loins, which should be strong, muscular, and slightly arched. The couplings should be short. The haunch bones well spaced and prominent, but not above the level of the back. The general outline from head to tail is a series of graceful curves, giving a strong but lissome appearance.

TAIL Medium length, thick at the root, growing gradually thinner to the point. It should be well covered with close hair and carried on a level with the back, with no upward curl. With the dog in motion, the tail should lash from side to side.

FOREQUARTERS The shoulders long, sloping, and well laid back. The chest just wide enough for plenty of heart room. The brisket well let down, to a level with the elbows. The forelegs straight and firm, of oval bone, with the back sinews strong and visible. The knee joint should be flat with the front of the leg, protruding very slightly on the inside. Pasterns lengthy, strong and resilient. **HINDQUARTERS** Well-turned stifles. The hocks should be well let down and close to the ground. A good expanse of thigh, which should be muscular, as should also the second thighs. **FEET** The feet oval, with well-knit, arched toes, well cushioned underneath.

COAT Should be fine, short, hard and evenly distributed, perfectly smooth and straight, with a decided sheen. **Color** The usual colors are lemon and white, orange and white, liver and white, and black and white. Self colors and tricolors are also correct.

N.B. The foregoing is a summary of the information contained in the official British standard. In 1953, after many years of study, the eminent Italian authority on the Pointer wrote a detailed account amplifying the standard. This work was published by the E.N.C.I., and because of its success in England it has been included here.

GENERAL CHARACTERISTICS Scientifically the Pointer is classified in the braccoid group (according to the classification of Pierre Mégnin); these are rectilinear, shorthaired dogs (according to the classification of Déchambre). As to function, these dogs are classed as hunting pointers. English origin. The general conformation is mesomorphic, the body outline being square. The Pointer is a game dog par excellence. His physique is that of an extremely agile, vigorous dog; each separate part of the body shows maximum power joined to maximum facility of movement. The Pointer is a tireless galloper, impetuously enthusiastic, gifted with a superlatively keen sense of smell. His light build is perfect for a continuous, swift and light gait. His muscles are long and extremely well toned. He is an ideal dog for work in vast, open countryside, where his galloping gait can be developed to the full. He is somewhat hampered in the woods, and is not the ideal breed for work in covered terrain. The characteristics of his way of working are a sudden, pointing stop and subsequent guiding. The hunter should beware of Pointers that work on the ground, especially those that guide in English Setter style, because such methods suggest the likelihood of cross breeding, evident in a working style not typical of the breed. The type characteristics of the Pointer are: a head with upper cranial-facial longitudinal axes converging; a very pronounced stop; eyes in subfrontal position; a square muzzle with a raised nose; well-developed lips, with a distinctly visible commissure; ears set on high, flat and triangular, which barely reach the lower edge of the throat; an elegant neck, well arched; a tail thick at the root and narrowing to a fine point at the end; fine skin, very short hair, glossy; muscles and tendons very much in evidence; a visible network of veins; and, finally, a well-chiseled head.

WEIGHT AND SIZE: Weight: 44-46 lb. Height at the withers: males, 21½-24½ inches; females, 21¼-23½ inches.

HEAD The Pointer's head seems to be sculptured in marble; it expresses good mettle and a high degree of intelligence, together with energetic will and lively temperament. It is clean-cut and is always carried high, with the eyes blazing as he looks at man. The basic lines of the head and the expression of the eyes make it practically the opposite of that of the Bloodhound. The Pointer is dolichocephalic; the total length of the head is 2/5 of the height at the withers; the length of the muzzle should equal half the total length of the head, and thus the midpoint of the head lies on the line joining the two inner corners of the eyes. The width of the skull should be less than half the total length of the head; therefore the total cephalic index should not be above 45. The directions of the upper longitudinal axes of the skull and muzzle are convergent, and the prolongation of the upper line of the nasal bridge should pass through the head under the occipital protuberance. The head should be altogether free of wrinkles, and the skin should be close-fitting over the underlying tissues, smooth and taut. In other words, the head should be totally lean. **Nose** Seen in profile, the nose is slightly raised above the top line of the bridge, like the edge of a plate, and does not extend beyond the forward vertical line of the lips; the forepart of the nose is on the same vertical plane of the foreface as the muzzle. It should be large, wet and cool, with well open, mobile nostrils. The nasal pinnae should not be fleshy, but thin, and the upper and lateral sides of the nose should form with the forepart a nonrounded edge, but decidedly at a right angle. The pigmentation should be of the same color as the dark markings of the coat; but in white-orange dogs, the mucous and sclerotic areas may be either flesh-colored or black. Slight marbling of the nose is not, however, a fault. **Nasal Bridge** Straight. For length and direction relative to the cranial axis, see above. Its width, measured from the midpoint of its length, should be 20 percent of the total length of the head, or 40 percent of the length of the nasal bridge itself. **Lips and Muzzle** The upper lips, seen from in front, form a semicircle at their lower edge, specifically at the point where they meet; they are full, and therefore the forepart of the muzzle is well developed as to height. This forepart should, moreover, be broad and flat. The lower, lateral profile of the muzzle before the commissure is delineated by the lips, while at the level of the commissure it is determined by the fold of the skin of the commissure itself. The anterior-inferior-lateral profile of the muzzle is a semicircle of a fairly closed chord. When the muzzle is held horizontal, the lowest point of this semicircle, on the lower-forward line of the lips, should never extend beyond the level of the commissure, which should be the lowest point of the lower profile of the muzzle. The commissure itself should be pronounced, with the inner part clearly visible. The position of the commissure should be as oral as possible. The *rima oris*, that is, should be short. A characteristic feature of the commissure in Pointers is a fold of skin which begins immediately behind the commissure, directed almost horizontally toward the parotid region and the neck, like a fascia above the lower part of the head, determining almost a hollowing out of the lower part of the cheeks. The lips should be fine-textured and thin, not pendulous, heavy or loose. The height of the muzzle, measured at the level of the commissure, should be 4/5 of its length. The length of the muzzle is equal to the length of the nasal bridge. The suborbital region should be well chiseled. The lateral faces of the muzzle are parallel, and thus the forepart of the muzzle, as mentioned above, is square. **Jaws** Not robust in appearance, of normal development and meeting in a scissors bite. The lower jaw is straight throughout its entire length, well developed in front and never receding, so that it forms a support for the upper lips at their conjunction. The teeth are white, regular, complete as to development and number. **Stop** Should be a rather abrupt slope, very pronounced. The frontal bone drops sharply, almost perpendicularly, on the nasal and maxillary apophyses, and, together with the well-developed sinuses, determines the accentuation of the stop. The stop should be at a 90-degree angle with the bridge and a 120-130-degree angle with the forehead. **Skull** The length should be equal to that of the muzzle, and its width should be less than half of the total length of the head (see above); the lateral walls of the skull are, therefore, flat. Seen from in front, the skull is spheroid; in profile, it is nearly so except between the bases of the ears, where it is rather flat. In profile the skull rises from the stop to the occiput in an accentuated slope, with the upper longitudinal axis being convergent in respect to the axis of the nasal bridge. The sinuses should be greatly developed in height, width and length. The medial furrow is well marked. The occipital protuberance should be clean-cut and prominent without being exaggerated, and should be clearly visible; it should be short longitudinally.

EYES Extraordinarily challenging and confident. The eyes should be large, round, shining and—because of the great development of the sinuses—in a subfrontal position. The inner corner of the eyelids should be equidistant from the forward edge of the nose and from the extreme outer point of the occipital protuberance. The eyes are globular, neither deep-set nor protruding. The color should be dark ocher; in white-orange dogs, the color may be lighter ocher, which, however, must never be a really light color. The eyelids are normally close-fitting, and the shape is round, not almond. The pigmentation of the edges of the eyelids should be of the same color as the dark markings of the coat; in white-orange dogs it should be black or nearly so. The direction of the axes of the eyelids, or, more specifically, the straight line joining the two corners of the *rima palpebrarum*, intersects the center plane of the head at an angle of 10 degrees.

EARS The ears should be hanging, soft, thin, almost triangular in shape and flat, in such a way that they adhere for their entire length to the cheeks and the parotid region; the base of the ears is wide, and the point of insertion is considerably above the zygomatic arch, specifically on the upper part of the temporal muscles, and so the upper lateral profile of the skull is provided by the insertion of the ears. The posterior limit of the insertion has for its limit the point at which the head and neck are joined; the forward limit is at the midpoint of the skull. The tips of the ears should be sharply pointed and never broadly rounded. The cartilage should be thin and covered with extremely fine skin, in which the network of veins is clearly visible on the outer side, which should be covered with extremely short and very fine hair. When pointing or when excited, the dog raises the base of the ears slightly, and the edge performs a rotatory movement sufficient to detach the ears from the parotid region. When the dog is standing normally and in repose, the ears should at most reach the lower edge of the the throat—that is, equal to the length of the muzzle; this means that in a Pointer 23⅝ inches high at the withers, with a head 9½ inches long, the ear should not be more than 4¾ inches long.

Photo: Fotostampa.

POINTER

NECK The length of the neck, measured at its full extension, from the nape to the forward edge of the withers, is equal to the length of the head, that is, it should be 2/5 of the height at the withers. The insertion of the head and neck should provide a clear division from the nape; the neck should also merge with the body in harmonious fusion with the shoulders. The carriage of the neck is erect when the dog is in normal stance and horizontal when the dog is galloping. Its circumference at the midpoint of its length, in a dog 23⅝ inches, should be 15¾ inches, that is, 3/5 more than its own length; in proportion to the height at the withers, the circumference should be 2/3 (66.67 percent). The neck, therefore, should be well wrapped in muscle, lean, long and light. Its upper line should be a curve which starts immediately after the nape line and disappears toward the meeting with the withers. The lower line should not be marred by loose skin, and the throat should be absolutely free of dewlap.

FOREQUARTERS **Shoulders** Very free in movement, long, sloping, with long, well-developed muscles which are well separated from each other. Their length is slightly more than ¼ of the height at the withers, and, in a dog 23⅝ inches high, the scapula should measure not less than 6¼ inches. Its slope is 45-55 degrees to the horizontal. In respect to the center plane of the body, the points of the shoulders, with the dog in normal stance, should be very close to each other, with no more than ½ inch between them. **Upper Arm** Well joined to the body in their upper 2/3; they should have long, strong, clean muscles and robust bone. The slope, less than that of the shoulders, is 60-70 degrees to the horizontal, and the length is about 30 percent of the height at the withers. The scapula-humeral angle is 110 degrees, considering the scapula as having a slope of 45 degrees. Its direction is almost parallel to the center plane of the body. In its lower part, the upper arm stands away from the body, and thus the underarm region should be high. **Forearm** Straight, vertical, of strong bone; its cross section is oval; it has a strong, separate posterior tendon (the tendon of the flexor-cubital muscle of the wrist), in such a way that the furrow between bone and tendon should be well in evidence. Its length is equal to the length of the humerus and slightly less than 1/3 of the height at the withers. The height of the entire foreleg to the elbow is 50.87 percent of the height at the withers; that is, in a Pointer 23⅝ inches high at the withers, the height of the foreleg to the elbow is about 12 inches. In other words, it might be said that the elbow is situated at the midpoint between ground and withers. The elbows, which are covered with soft, loose skin, should be set in a plane parallel to the center plane of the body. This means that they must not be turned inward nor outward. The point of the elbow should be slightly ahead of the perpendicular drawn from the back of the scapula. **Wrists** Follow the vertical line of the forearm; they are very mobile and lean, covered with fine, thin skin, and with a pronounced pisiform bone. **Pasterns** Should be flat from the front backward and, as seen from in front, they follow the vertical line of the forearm; they are thinner than the forearm, and should be lean and covered with fine, thin skin, with a minimum of tissue beneath, so that the four wrist bones are well in evidence beneath the skin. Their length should not be less than 1/6 of the height of the entire foreleg to the elbow. Seen in profile, the pasterns should be rather extended. **Feet** Oval (harefeet), with well-closed and well-arched toes, covered with short, thick hair; the pads are lean, hard and dark. The nails are strong, curved and also dark.

BODY The length of the trunk, measured from the point of the shoulder (scapula-humeral angle) to the point of the buttock (posterior point of the ischium), is equal to the height at the withers. **Chest** Wide and well open, with well-developed pectoral muscles. Its width varies according to the width of the rib cage, and should be equal to 25 percent of the height at the withers. The manubrium of the sternum should be located at the level of the point of shoulder.

Photo: S. A. Thompson.

Rib cage Ample, descending to elbow level or slightly below; it is deep and well rounded at the midpoint of its height. The cross diameter, which is greatest at the midpoint of the height, narrows appreciably toward the sternum, but not so much as to form a carena. The ribs are therefore long and well sprung, and the rib arches should be well open; the spaces between the ribs are extended. The last back ribs are close to the forward edge of the thighs. The region of the sternum is long, and its outline is a semicircle which ascends gradually toward the abdomen. The circumference of the rib cage should be about ¼ more than the height at the withers, and its cross diameter should be at least 30.83 percent of the height at the withers. In a Pointer measuring 23⅝ inches at the withers, the rib cage should have the following measurements: circumference behind the elbows, 29 inches; circumference around the ribs, 25 inches, depth, 12 inches; height, 11½ inches; cross diameter, 7¼-7¾ inches. The thoracic index should therefore not be more than 8, preferably less. **Back** The withers are raised above the backline and narrowed by the closeness of the scapula points. The backline is straight. The length of the back is about 31 percent of the height at the withers, which means that in a Pointer measuring 23⅝ inches at the withers, the back is about 7¼ inches. **Loins** The loins are well fused to the backline and are slightly arched when seen in profile. The muscles are well developed in breadth. The length is slightly more than ¼ the height at the withers; the width is very nearly equal to the length, in a ratio of 14.5:16. **Belly and Flanks** The belly line, from the sternum, ascends toward the flank so as to make the belly lean, though not to an exaggerated degree. In a Pointer 23⅝ inches high at the withers, the belly should ascend 2¼-3⅛ inches from the lowest part of the sternum. The flanks should be almost equal in length to the loins, and the hollow in the flanks should be minimum. **Croup** Continues the arched line of the loins; it should be broad, robust and muscular, and the cross diameter between the haunches should be 1/7 of the height at the withers. The haunches should be prominent, reaching the topline of the lumbar region. The length of the croup is about 1/3 (28-30 percent) of the height at the withers. Its slope from the haunches to the root of the tail is about 10 degrees to the horizontal, and thus the Pointer's croup is technically called horizontal.

TAIL The tail is set on even with the croup. It is thick and robust at the root, narrowing toward the tip, which should be extremely fine. The tail should be covered with fine, very short hair all around, its length not more than 53 percent of the height at the withers, and not longer than the height of the foreleg to the elbow. A tail sufficiently long so as to reach the hocks when the dog is in normal stance is acceptable. The correct carriage of the tail may be (a) rigid, when the tail is straight for its entire length, whether held horizontal or down; (b) in "pumphandle" style, if the tail in its first third or first half describes a curve which is convex on the upper edge and in the second half a slight curve which is the opposite of the first, that is, with the convexity at its lower edge; (c) in a single broad curve, if throughout its length there is a single convexity with a very broad chord at its upper edge.

HINDQUARTERS Thighs Long. broad covered with pronounced muscles which are clearly separated from each other; the posterior edge is arched, and the point of the buttock is well in evidence. Its length should not be less than 1/3 of the height at the withers, that is, 33 percent. The outer side, from one edge to the other, should be ¾ of its length; therefore, in a Pointer 23⅝ inches at the withers, the width of the thigh should be very close to 6 inches. Its direction is slightly sloped from the top downward and from the back forward, and in respect to the vertical it should be parallel to the central plane of the body. **Legs** Strongly boned, with lean muscling all over. The furrow between the bone and the tendon above the hocks is pronounced, and the external saphenous vein is so near the surface that it seems like a tendon. Their length is slightly inferior to the length of the thigh, that is, 32.5 percent of the height at the withers; its slope is about 38 degrees from the horizontal. **Hocks** The distance from the ground to the point of the hock should not be more than 26.93 percent of the height at the withers; therefore, in a Pointer 23⅝ inches high at the withers, the height of the hock should be about 6½ inches. The wider the face of the hocks, the better. The forward angle is closed because of the accentuated slope of the tibia (38 degrees); seen from behind, the backline from the point of the hock to the ground should be vertical and a prolongation of the line of the buttock. **Metatarsus** Robust and lean. The length depends on the height at the withers; seen from behind and in profile, it should be vertical. In profile it should also appear behind the perpendicular from the point of the buttock to the ground, at least 1½ times the length of the hind feet. **Feet** Less oval in shape than the forefeet, but otherwise similar to them.

COAT Hair The hair should be dense, of equal length all over, uniformly smooth, fine, short and glossy, with no hint of a fringe, not even the slightest, at any point on the trunk, legs or tail. The texture is very hard. The length of the hair is about 2/5 inch and should in no case be longer than 3/5 inch. **Color** Permissible colors are: white, black, black and tan, orange, fawn, red, brown, burnt brown, in all of their shadings. All of these colors may be solid or combined with white. The shape of the markings is not important, nor is that of the mask. **Skin** Close-fitting to the body in every part. It should be thin and fine, to the point where the network of veins is visible, especially on the auricles and the forelegs. The neck should have no dewlap or wrinkles, nor should the head. The pigmentation of the lips, eyelids and nose should be black or brown, depending on the color of the dark markings of the coat. In white-orange dogs, it should be black or blackish, although flesh color is admissible. The pigment of the nails and pads should be dark.

POINTER

POINTER

GAIT A fine galloping gait when hunting.

FAULTS **General Characteristics** Undistinguished overall appearance, heavy, lymphatic; light bone, lack of symmetry. **Height at the Withers** Over or above standard. **Head** Upper cranial-facial axes parallel; even slightly divergent axes (very serious fault). **Nose** Below topline of nasal bridge; protruding beyond forepart of muzzle; nostrils not well open; small nose or with upper edges greatly rounded; of spongy appearance; deficient in pigment, traces of depigmentation on or in nostrils; total depigmentation (disqualification). **Nasal Bridge** Short, narrow, arched (disqualification); hollowed; lateral lines converging. **Lips and Muzzle** Short and insufficiently chiseled muzzle; lips overly developed and hanging below line of commissure; deficient in development; flaccid; thick, fleshy; commissural fold pronounced, too falling or lacking; receding labial profile; forward con-

vergence of lateral walls of muzzle, that is, pointed muzzle, and its effect on the forepart of the muzzle; upper lips meeting in an inverted V; bad chiseling in the suborbital region. **Jaws** Thin; undershot condition if it harms the general aspect of the muzzle; overshot condition: if for lack of length in lower jaw, disqualification; if caused by crooked teeth, a fault; sides of lower jaw too curved; teeth irregular or not complete; horizontal erosion of teeth. **Stop** Not pronounced, receding. **Skull** Small, short, round, too narrow at the parietals; exaggeratedly flat above and broad on the sides, that is, at the level of the zygomatic arches; supraorbital arches flat; masseter muscles overly developed; occipital protuberance absent or overdeveloped; sinuses underspaced or overdeveloped; medial furrow not pronounced; exaggerated convergence of cranial-facial axes. **Eyes** Small or too prominent; light eyes or too light in white-orange dogs; walleyes (disqualification); almond-shaped or slanting; ectropion

(very serious fault); entropion; shifty, suspicious gaze, cross eyes; partial depigmentation of the eyelids; if total, such depigmentation is a very serious fault, if bilaterally total it is a disqualification. **Ears** Thick, long or too short; with narrow or longitudinally folded insertion; set on at the zygomatic arch or above and behind in respect to it; rigid because of excessive thickness; curled; rounded points; hair not sufficiently short. **Neck** Thin, or massive and heavy, short; dewlap; neck cylindrical or flat at the sides; insufficiently arched; insufficient detachment from nape and lack of fusion with shoulders. **Shoulders** Straight, heavy, short; insufficiently developed muscles; not free in movement; points of the shoulders separated. **Upper Arm** Too slanting or too straight; short; deficient in muscular development; weak bone. **Forearm** Weak bone, spongy, round bone; out of vertical; elbows in or out; underarm area low; absence of furrow at wrist. **Wrists** With evident hypertrophy of the wrist bones;

spongy, small; pisiform bone not pronounced. **Pasterns** Short, weak, too long or too extended, or straight and out of vertical. **Feet** Round (catfeet); splayed toes; broad, crushed feet; insufficient arching of toes; feet carried out or in, that is, not in vertical; fleshy pads; thinly textured soles; deficient pigment in nails and pads; bad placement of pads; feet too long or crushed. **Body** Length greater than height at withers. **Chest** Narrow, badly let down; insufficiently developed muscle; manubrium too low. **Rib cage** Not high enough, not deep enough, circumference too small; narrow or too large; decidedly carenated; xiphoid appendage curved inward; sternum short; rib arches not sufficiently open. **Ribs** Not sufficiently sprung; interrib spacing too close; back ribs short and insufficiently sprung, not open and low. **Back** Short: interruption of backline at eleventh vertebra; saddleback (lordosis), roach back (kyphosis); low withers. **Loins** Long, flat, narrow. **Belly and Flanks** Belly drawn up too little or too much; flanks excessively hollowed and long. **Sexual Organs** Monorchidism (disqualification); cryptorchidism (disqualification). **Croup** Narrow, too short, sloping. **Tail** Too long or too short; lack of tail or rudimentary tail, whether congenital or acquired (disqualification); tail set on too low or too far forward; not thick at the root; hair not sufficiently short on underside; tail carried above loin line; lateral deviation; sickle tail; tail carried over back (disqualification); tail carried up; exaggerated "pumphandle" effect; flaccid, pendulous; mousetail. **Thighs** Short, insufficiently developed as to muscle, that is, flat; narrow; separated from the stifle; too straight or too sloping. **Legs** Weak bone; furrow between bone and tendon above hocks not sufficiently evident; short or insufficiently sloped. **Hocks** High, not broad; angulation open or too closed because of forward deviation of metatarsus; out of vertical. **Metatarsus** Long, weak, out of vertical; dewclaws (disqualification). **Feet** Similar to the forefeet. **Hair** Too long or hard. **Color** Slate or lead (disqualification); streaked (disqualification). **Skin** Thick, overabundant; dewlap; wrinkles on the head; traces of depigmentation on the nose and edges of the eyelids; total depigmentation of the nose (disqualification); depigmentation of the edges of the two eyelids of both eyes (disqualification); depigmentation of the vulva and vent. **Gait** Amble (disqualification); continued trotting during hunt (disqualification).

DISQUALIFICATIONS **Height at the Withers** Above 26 inches or more than 3/4 inch below minimum of standard. **Head** Accentuated divergence of the upper cranial-facial longitudinal axes. **Nose** Total depigmentation. **Nasal Bridge** Decided arch. **Jaws** Overshot condition, if caused by underdevelopment of lower jaw; accentuated undershot condition if it harms the general appearance of the muzzle. **Eyes** Walleyes; total bilateral depigmentation of the eyelids; bilaterally crossed eyes. **Sexual Organs** Cryptorchidism, monorchidism. **Tail** Lack of tail or rudimentary tail, either congenital or acquired; tail carried over the back. **Legs** Presence of dewclaws on hind legs. **Color** Slate, lead, streaked. **Skin** Total depigmentation of the nose and total bilateral depigmentation of the eyelids. **Gait** Ambling; in field tests, continued trotting during hunt.

SCALE OF POINTS

General appearance	20
Skull and muzzle	30
Eyes and eyelids	10
Ears	5
Shoulders	10
Rib cage	15
Loins and croup	10
Legs and feet	20
Tail	25
Coat and color	5
	150

Photo: S. A. Thompson.

237 ENGLISH SETTER
GREAT BRITAIN

Three varieties (not different breeds, since their physical points are identical) of English setters are distinguished by the color of the coat. The Lemon Belton has a white coat with orange spots, the Blue Belton has black spots and streaks which tend to look blue, and the Liver Belton has chestnut spots. The Blue Belton sometimes has russet spots under the eyes, in which case he is called a tricolor.

This Setter is also called a Lawerack, although improperly, as the Laweracks were an important variety some time ago but have now almost disappeared. Originally the Setter was white with black and red spots and had in addition a rather massive build. Some breeders, including Lawerack, undertook the task of refining the beautiful dog and applied themselves sedulously to this work. Lawerack was of humble origin, and first worked as a shoemaker. Later he inherited a large fortune from a distant relative, which allowed him to devote himself to his passion— the hunt. The Setter then prevalent around Shropshire did not possess the physical and aesthetic qualities he desired in a dog. Since he had acquired two white-coated blue spotted dogs (Blue Belton), he began selective breeding. He spent his whole life in the task and succeeded in creating a truly superb dog. At the age of seventy-three he published a book, *The Setter*, which is among the most interesting of its kind. However, as we have mentioned, Lawerack limited himself to selectively breeding a line of setters which, though remarkable, were surpassed by others, and above all by the individuals which Llewellin, Lawerack's successor, brought to a high degree of perfection. Even to this day specimens from this lineage (the Llewellin Setter) are much esteemed. They too have been modified by constant selective breeding.

GENERAL CHARACTERISTICS An engagingly friendly and quiet-natured dog with a keen game sense. Of medium height, clean in outline, elegant in appearance and movement.

WEIGHT AND SIZE Males, 60-66 lb, height 25½-27 inches; females, 56-62 lb, height 24-25½ inches.

HEAD Should be long and reasonably lean, with a well-defined stop. The skull oval from ear to ear, showing plenty of brain room, and with a well-defined occipital protuberance. The muzzle moderately deep and fairly square; from the stop to the point of the nose should equal the length of skull from occiput to eyes; the nostrils wide and the jaws of nearly equal length; flews not too pendulous; the color of the nose should be black or liver, according to the color of the coat. Mouth to be level.

EYES Bright, mild, and intelligent, and of a dark hazel color, the darker the better.

EARS Moderate length, set on low, and hanging in neat folds close to the cheek. The tip should be velvety, the upper part clothed in fine silky hair.

NECK Rather long, muscular, and lean, slightly arched at the crest and clean-cut where it joins the head; toward the shoulder it should be larger and very muscular, not throaty or pendulous below the throat, but elegant in appearance.

BODY The body should be of moderate length, the back short and level, with good, round, widely sprung ribs and deep in the back ribs, i.e., well ribbed up.

FOREQUARTERS The shoulders should be well set back or oblique; the chest deep in the brisket and of good depth and width between the shoulder-blades. The forearm big and very muscular, with rounded bone, and the elbow well let down. Pasterns short, muscular, round and straight. **HINDQUARTERS** The loins should be wide, slightly arched, strong and muscular, with defined second thigh. Stifles well bent and rugged, thighs long from hip to hock **FEET** The feet should be very close and compact and well protected by hair between the toes.

TAIL Should be set on, almost in line with the back, medium length, not curly or ropy; a slight curve is permissible, the flag or feather hanging in long, pendant fringes. The feather should not commence at the root but slightly beneath, and increase in length to the middle, then gradually taper off toward the end; the hair long, bright, soft and silky, wavy but not curly.

COAT The coat from the back of the head in a line with the ears ought to be slightly wavy, long and silky; so also the coat generally; the breeches and forelegs, nearly down to the feet, should be well feathered. **Color** May be either black and white, lemon and white, liver and white, or tricolor— that is, black, white, and tan; preferably without heavy patches of color on the body, but flecked all over.

FAULTS Coarse lumpy shoulders, short foreface tapering to nose, lack of stop, light or obliquely set eyes, ears placed high, loose elbows from bad shoulder placement, flat ribs, too long loin, wide feet, weak pasterns, straight stifles, narrow quarters, gay flag, lightness of bone, mouth undershot or overshot, lack of freedom of action.

N.B. The following material is an amplification of the British standard, prepared by Fabio Cajelli, official judge of the E.N.C.I.

GENERAL CHARACTERISTICS In the classification devised by Pierre Mégnin the English Setter is assigned to the braccoid group. Its practical classification is that of a sporting dog trained as a pointer. English origin. The Setter is a light mesomorph, whose body outline is rectangular and whose forelegs, from the ground to the elbow, are shorter than from the elbow to the withers. A fine English Setter today should combine power without weight and elegance of form. He should be eager to work, with great ease of movement; the muscles should be long, the bone good but not excessively heavy, the transverse diameter not highly pronounced. It can never be too strongly urged that breeders should abandon those mastodonic English Setters, with heavy skin and enormous heads, which, beside not being typical, are slow and of low resistance. The upper cranial-facial longitudinal axes are parallel; the stop is pronounced, the eyes are expressive, with a gentle quality; the lips are neat, not flaccid; the ears are set on low. The hair is silky and long.

WEIGHT AND SIZE Weight: 44-66 lb. Height at the withers: males, 22-24½ inches; females, 21¼-23½ inches.

HEAD Dolichocephalic; its total length is 2/5 of the height at the withers. The length of the skull is equal to the length of the muzzle, and the midpoint of the total length of the head is on the horizontal line joining the two inner corners of the eyes. The total cephalic index should not be above 45, that is, the width should be less than half the total length of the head. The directions of the upper longitudinal axes of the skull and of the muzzle are parallel. The head is long, lean, light but not excessively so; the stop is pronounced; the lips, decisively marked in front, should terminate at the jaws, neither flaccid nor pendulous. Lawerack in his book on the English Setter, claims that a large and heavy head indicates laziness and indolence. **Nose** Large, broad, wet, cool and shiny, black or dark brown; the brown pigmentation is found, in general, in white-yellow and liver dogs. A flesh-colored nose is not a disqualification. The nose should be on the same line as the nasal bridge and, seen in profile, its forepart should be on the same forward vertical plane of the lips. Open, mobile nostrils, thin nasal pinnae. **Nasal Bridge** Straight, long, broad; measured at the midpoint of its length, its width is 40 percent of its length. For its length and direction in relation to the cranial axis, see above. **Lips and Muzzle** The lips should not be big, but only sufficiently large to cover the lower jaw at the sides. They are very soft, neither flaccid nor pendulous. The anterior-inferior-lateral profile of the muzzle is a broad-chorded semicircle. Therefore in the English Setter the lower edge of the muzzle is marked by the lips, contrary to the case of the Irish Setter. The commissure is not pronounced, although it is readily visible. The length of the muzzle is the same as that of the nasal bridge, and its lateral planes are parallel; the forepart should be high and flat, that is, square. The length of the muzzle should be half the total length of the head. The directions of the upper longitudinal axes of the skull and muzzle are parallel. The suborbital region should have several prominent places. **Jaws** The upper and lower jaw are of equal length, with the sides of the lower jaw tending to be straight throughout their entire length; they meet in a perfect scissors bite. The teeth are sound, complete in development and number. **Stop** Accentuated but not abrupt. **Skull** The length of the skull is equal to the length of the muzzle. The total cephalic index should not be above 45, that is, the width of the skull should be less than half the total length of the head. The skull is slightly domed, as seen in profile; the back of the skull should be oval, and the occipital protuberance should be definite. The skull, not so broad between the ears as that of the Gordon Setter, less rounded behind than the skull of the Pointer, is a more elongated oval. The side walls are flat throughout. The sinuses are not greatly developed. The medial furrow is marked.

EYES Large, brilliant, gentle, expressive, indicative of intelligence; they are in a semilateral position; they should be hazel, as dark as possible; although the color may be slightly lighter in white and white-orange dogs. The supraorbital ridges should be clearly separated from the forehead. The eyelids should conceal the haw and should be close-fitting over the eyes; the pigmentation of the eyelids is brown or black.

EARS Set on low, at the level of the zygomatic arch or, even better, below and behind the arch. The ears are of moderate length, always less than 2/3 of the total length of the head. When the dog is in normal stance, with the head in a horizontal position, the tips of the ears are about 1 to 1¼ inch below the throat line. They should hang close to the cheeks and should not show the inner side. They should not be wide; that is, they should not be spread out to their entire width, as is the case with the Pointer. The ear of the English Setter is folded upon itself longitudinally (that is, with the length of the ear), and this fold is possible precisely because of the soft, thin skin and cartilage which characterizes it. The fine, silky fringes which cover the outer side of the auricle should become shorter in the lower part, in such a way that the tip of the auricle, which is an inch more or less at the most, should be covered with very short, velvety hair. The tips of the ear should be slightly rounded.

NECK The length of the neck is about the same as the length of the head. It should be 2/5 of the height at the withers. Its circumference at the midpoint of its length in a Setter 23⅝ inches high at the withers should be 15¾ inches. The neck should be lean and muscular, slightly arched in the upper half. Its meeting with the head is clearly marked, so that the back part of the skull is free. The neck should broaden harmoniously, and its muscles should reach peak development at the point where the neck merges with the shoulders, but

ENGLISH SETTER

ENGLISH SETTER

this must be without coarseness and always with elegance. There should be dewlap, and the fringes should be clean-cut, forming a light collar at the lower edge.

FOREQUARTERS A vertical line from the scapula-humeral articulation (point of shoulder or of upper arm) should, when it reaches the ground, touch the tips of the toes of the forefeet; a vertical angle from the humeral-radial articulation should divide into two almost equal parts (the greater is the forward part) the forearm, the wrist, the pastern and the foot. The distance from the ground to the elbow is less than the distance from the elbow to the withers. This reduced length of the lower part of the foreleg is caused by the shortness of the forearm, which in other Setter breeds is longer than the upper arm. This peculiarity of the English Setter is what made possible the original stealthy movement for which the Setter was famous. **Shoulders** The length of the shoulders is ¼ the height at the withers (greater length is desirable), sloped at 45-55 degrees to the horizontal, with well-developed muscles which are free in their movements. The points of the shoulders, when the dog is in normal position with its neck carried erect, should be very close together (not more than 2/3 inch apart). **Upper Arm** Like the shoulders, the upper arm is very well muscled and of strong bone. It is sloped at 65 degrees to the horizontal, and its length (greater than the length of the forearm) is about 33 percent of the height at the withers. Its direction is almost parallel to the center plane of the body. **Forearm** Strongly boned, the forearm is straight and vertical; its cross section is oval; unlike other Setters the English Setter has the forearm shorter than the upper arm. In an English Setter measuring 23⅝ inches at the withers, the elbow is 11¼ inches above the ground. If the forearm were shorter, the whole foreleg would be too short, and the dog would be exaggeratedly close to ground, a condition which is negative for appearance, gait and speed. The elbows should lie in a plane parallel to the center plane of the body and should be turned neither in nor out. The point of the elbow should lie slightly forward of the perpendicular dropped from the rear point of the scapula. **Wrists** Seen from in front, the wrists lie on the vertical of the forelegs. They are mobile and lean, with a prominent pisiform bone. **Pasterns** Flat from the front back; they follow the vertical line of the forearm as seen from in front; seen from the side, they should be extended to a point such that a vertical dropped from the humeral-radial articulation would divide the forearm and the wrist in half and emerge at the midpoint of the pastern. Its length is a little more than 1/6 of the height of the foreleg to the elbow. **Feet** Oval (harefeet), with well-closed, well-arched toes, covered with rather long hair, even between the toes. The pads are hard, the nails are curved, strong and dark.

BODY The length of the trunk, measured from the point of the shoulder (scapula-humeral articulation) to the point of the buttock (posterior point of the ischium) should be greater than the height at the withers. The amount by which the trunk is longer should not exceed 1/20 of the height at the withers or, at most, 1/18. The body outline should be rectangular. **Chest** Broad, well open, with well-developed pectorals. Its width is in direct proportion to the width of the rib cage, and should be 25 percent of the height at the withers, if measured between the upper arms. The manubrium is at the level of the point of the shoulders. **Thorax** It should descend to the elbow in depth, and preferably extend perhaps ¾ inch beyond. It is deep, with long and well-sprung ribs. The back ribs are close to the front edge of the thighs; the transverse diameter of the thorax, which is greater at the midpoint of

ENGLISH SETTER IN ACTION

Photo: MARKA.

the height of the rib cage, decreases gradually toward the sternum, without, however, forming a carena. The sternum region is long, gently rising toward the abdomen. The circumference of the rib cage should be ¼ greater than the height at the withers, and its transverse diameter should be 39 percent of the height. In an English Setter 23⅝ inches at the withers, the rib cage should have the following dimensions: circumference behind the elbows, 29 inches; circumference at the rib arches, 25¼ inches; depth, 13 inches; height, 12-1/3 inches; transverse diameter, 7½ inches. **Back** The withers are raised above the backline, and they are narrowed by the closeness of the points of the shoulders. The backline is straight. The length of the back should be in proportion to the depth of the thorax: for each spinal vertebra there is a corresponding rib. **Loins** Well muscled, the loins are well fused with the backline and well arched, as seen in profile. Their length is a little less than 1/5 of the height at the withers, and their width is close to the length.

Belly and Flanks The belly should be slightly but not excessively drawn up. It should not be tucked up like that of a Greyhound. The flanks are almost as long as the loins, with minimal hollowing. **Croup** Broad, muscular, horizontal (with a slope of about 10 degrees to the horizontal). Its length is about 1/3 of the height at the withers, and the width is 1/7 of the height. **Sexual Organs** The testicles should be equally developed and contained naturally within the scrotum.

TAIL Set on high; thick and robust at the root, it narrows toward the tip. Its length should be about 1¼ inch more than the length of the foreleg at the elbow. It is carried low rather than high, not deviated to either side, slightly curved. The fringes should not begin at the root but only about an inch below, and the length of the hair increases to the midpoint of the tail and then decreases gradually toward the tip, to the point where it achieves the shape of an isosceles triangle. The hair should fall in straight or slightly wavy fringes, not thick, never kinky or curly.

HINDQUARTERS The vertical from the point of the buttock should touch the point of the toes, since the metatarsus should always be in a vertical position. Seen from behind, the same vertical should divide the hock into two equal parts, the metatarsus and the foot. **Thighs** Broad, long and muscular, arched at the back; they slope downward and forward (75 degrees), and, in respect to the vertical, they are parallel to the center plane of the body. The length should not be less than 1/3 of the height at the withers, and the outer faces should be at least ¾ of the length. **Legs** Strongly boned, well muscled, with a well-marked furrow between the bone and the tendon above the hock. The length of the leg is slightly less than the length of the thigh, and its slope is about 38 degrees to the horizontal. **Hocks** The facing of the hocks should be very wide; the forward angulation should be closed, because of the accentuated slope of the tibia. The distance from the point of the hock to the ground should be about 27 percent of the height at the withers. A vertical from the point of the hock to the ground should be an extension of the vertical from the point of the ischium. **Metatarsus** Should always be in a vertical position, and the length of the metatarsus in a Setter 23⅝ inches high at the withers is about 6½ inches. It is robust, lean, without dewclaws; seen in profile, it should be behind the vertical drawn from the point of the buttock at a distance slightly more than the length of a foot. **Feet** The hind feet are slightly less oval than the forefeet, but otherwise resemble them closely.

COAT Hair Fine, long; throughout its entire length, which is 2-2½ inches, it is a straight line, with no deviation from its axis. The texture is silky. The hair is very short on the head, except for the outer side of the ears (upper part) and the forward edge of the sides of the forearm, tarsus and metatarsus. There are fringes which are not thick on the underside

Photo: R. Kinne (Photo Res.).

ENGLISH SETTER

ENGLISH SETTER

of the neck, the sternum, the back of the legs, the buttocks and the tail. The feet are well feathered, especially between the toes. In winter, but only then, there is an abundant undercoat. **Color** Highly variable: white and black, close to blue (blue belton); white and orange (lemon belton); white and brown (liver belton); tricolor (white with black spots and tan markings). These are the preferred coats. Coats that are entirely white, liver, orange, black and black with tan are not particularly desirable. Flecks may be more or less numerous, and the markings may be more or less extensive. The preferred coat is that with a white background. **Skin** Thin, with limited subcutaneous connective, and consequently close-fitting to the body in all parts; there should be no dewlap at the neck, and the head should have absolutely no wrinkles. The lips, nose and eyelids should be black or brown, as also the nails and the pads.

GAIT When hunting, a good gallop.

ENGLISH SETTER PUPPY

FAULTS General Characteristics Overall appearance heavy, undistinguished, coarse, not indicative of maximum speed, ease and freedom of movement. **Height at the Withers** Over or under the standard. **Head** Short, heavy, with skin not close-fitting to the underparts; upper cranial-facial axes divergent or convergent (an accentuated condition is a disqualification). **Nose** Raised above the top line of the nasal bridge; small, with traces of depigmentation (total depigmentation is a disqualification); overhanging in front; nostrils not well open. **Nasal Bridge** Short, narrow; lateral lines converging; arched, hollowed (serious defect). **Lips and Muzzle** Lips too large or flaccid; underdeveloped lips, to the point where the profile of the muzzle is indicated by the underjaw rather than the lips; depigmentation of lip edges; receding lip profile; fold of the commissure too pronounced or not visible; anterior convergence of lateral muzzle walls, that is, pointed muzzle, resulting in nonflat forward surface; lack or deficiency in chiseling; short muzzle; upper lips meeting in inverted V. **Jaws** Crooked or deficient teeth; sides of lower jaw excessively curved; horizontal erosion of teeth or, worse, transversal; undershot condition (minor fault), if it does not harm the general appearance of the muzzle; overshot condition: a disqualification if the result of a short underjaw; if caused by cooked teeth, slight fault. **Skull** Short, small, round, massive; too narrow at the parietals; broad at the sides, that is, at the level of the zygomatic arches; not domed as seen in profile, flat on top; excessively developed masseters; absence of occipital protuberance; medial furrow not marked; accentuated or brusque stop as in the Pointer; wrinkles. **Eyes** Small or too prominent; light eyes; wall eyes (disqualification); almond-shaped; ectropion, entropion; eyes too close together; shifty or suspicious gaze; partial depigmentation of the eyelids: if total, a very serious defect and if bilaterally total, a disqualification; cross eyes: if bilateral, disqualification. **Ears** Thick, short or too long; set on too low or too high; broad ears; tips covered with long hair rather than very short hair. **Neck** Thin, short, massive, not arched, not sufficiently distinguished from nape; dewlap; lack of collar on lower side. **Shoulders** Short, straight, with insufficiently developed muscles; not free in movement; points of scapulae wide apart. **Upper Arm** Short; too slanted or too straight; weak bone; deficient in muscular development. **Forearm** Thin bone, spongy; round bone; long; out of vertical; elbows out or in. **Wrists** Evident hypertrophy of the wrist bones; wrist spongy or small; pisiform bone not well defined; stubbiness. **Pasterns** Short, too long, too extended or straight; weak, out of vertical. **Feet** Broad, long; splayed; flat, crushed, round, thin pads; lack of pigmentation in nails and pads; feet carried outward or inward; flat or crushed feet, a serious fault. **Body** Longitudinal diameter equal to the height at the withers or more than 1/18 over it; distance from elbow to top of withers equal to or less than the height of the elbow from the ground. **Chest** Narrow, too large, not well let down; insufficiently developed muscles; manubrium too high. **Rib cage** Lacking in height and depth; lack of spring of rib; carenated, too broad; sternum region short; xiphoid appendage curved inward; ribs badly spaced. **Ribs** Insufficiently sprung; back ribs short, not open; limited space between ribs. **Back** Short, saddle back, roach back; withers low. **Loins** Long, flat, narrow. **Belly and Flanks** Belly excessively or insufficiently drawn up; flanks excessively hollowed and long. **Sexual Organs** Monorchidism, cryptorchidism (both disqualifications); testicles not contained in the scrotum, insufficiently developed or unequally developed. **Croup** Narrow, short, sloping. **Tail** Lack of tail (disqualification); rudimentary tail, whether congenital or acquired (disqualification); too long or too short, set on low; carried vertically, or over the back (in this case, disqualification); fringe beginning at root of tail, not in shape of isosceles triangle; hair wrapping tail rather than forming fringe. **Thighs** Short, insufficient muscular development, narrow; deviated in region of second thigh; too straight or too sloping. **Legs** Weak-boned; furrow between bone and tendon above hock not well defined; short, excessively or insufficiently sloped. **Hocks** High, narrow; angulation too open or

Photo: R. Kinne (Photo Res.), S.E.F.

too closed; out of vertical. **Metatarsus** Long, weak, out of vertical, sloped forward; dewclaws (disqualification). **Feet** As for forefeet. **Hair** Soft, wavy, short, too thick; not stretched out; flocked or curled (disqualification). **Color** Mottled black, black and tan. **Skin** Thick, loose; wrinkles on the head; traces of depigmentation on the nose and the edges of the eyelids; total bilateral depigmentation of the eyelids and total depigmentation of the nose (disqualification). **Gait** Ambling, or continuous trot while at work.

DISQUALIFICATIONS **Height** Over 25¼ inches or more than ¾ inch below the minimum prescribed by the standard. **Head** Divergence or accentuated convergence of the upper cranial-facial longitudinal axes. **Nose** Total depigmentation. **Nasal Bridge** Excessively arched or hollowed. **Jaws** Accentuated overshot or undershot condition. **Eyes** Total bilateral depigmentation of the eyelids; bilaterally crossed eyes. **Sexual Organs** Cryptorchidism or monorchidism. **Tail** Lack of tail or rudimentary tail, whether congenital or acquired; tail car-

ried over the back. **Legs** Dewclaws. **Gait** Continuous trotting in field tests; ambling.

N.B. In judging, whenever any part of the body which involves type is rated as zero, the dog must be disqualified even if the other parts of the body are excellent.

SCALE OF POINTS

General appearance	30
Skull and muzzle	20
Eyes and eyelids	10
Ears	5
Shoulders	10
Rib cage	10
Loins and croup	15
Legs and feet	20
Tail	15
Coat and color	15
	150

RATINGS

Excellent: score at least	140
Very good	130
Good	120
Fairly good	110

IRISH SETTER

Photo: MARKA.

238 IRISH SETTER
GREAT BRITAIN

Some time ago the Irish Setter was white with red spots, showing his common origins with the English Setter. Breeders then attached more importance to a good structural adaptation to the task at hand, to the sense of smell, gait, and endurance than to the color of the coat. When the dog's appearance became important, the red spots were spread and the color of the Irish Setter was changed to a warm red with large white spots which were subsequently reduced to even smaller surfaces. The work of outstanding dog fanciers such as Major Hutchison, Colonel Cooper, and Dr. Hone contributed to the perfection of the breed, and toward the middle of the last century the form was fixed. The first dogs entered in the breed's studbook were Bob, born in 1859; Ranger, born in 1864; Plunket, born in 1868; and Dak, born in 1870.

The Irish Setter possesses excellent hunting qualities, such as great speed, endurance, and extraordinary sense of smell. He is perhaps more difficult to train than other setters because of his independent spirit and his irresistible desire for open spaces.

GENERAL CHARACTERISTICS Must be racy, full of quality and kindly in expression.

HEAD Should be long and lean, not narrow or snipy, and not coarse at the ears. The skull oval (from ear to ear), having plenty of brain room and with well-defined occipital protuberance. Brows raised, showing a stop. The muzzle moderately deep, and fairly square at end. From the stop to the point of the nose should be long, the nostrils wide, and the jaws of nearly equal length, flews not pendulous. The color of the nose: dark mahogany, dark walnut, or black. Mouth not overshot or undershot.

EYES Should be dark hazel or dark brown and not too large.

EARS Should be of moderate size, fine in texture, set on low, well back, and hanging in a loose fold close to the head.

NECK Moderately long, very muscular, but not too thick; slightly arched, free from tendency to throatiness.

BODY Should be proportionate, the ribs well sprung, leaving plenty of lung room. Loins muscular, slightly arched.

TAIL Of moderate length, proportionate to the size of the body, set on rather low, strong at roots, and tapering to a fine point; to be carried as nearly as possible on a level with or below the back.

FOREQUARTERS The shoulders should be fine at the points, deep and sloping well back. The chest as deep as possible, rather narrow in front. The forelegs should be straight and sinewy, having plenty of bone, with elbows free, well let down, not inclined either in or out. **HINDQUARTERS** Should be wide and powerful. The hind legs from hip to hock should be long and muscular; from hock to heel short and strong. The stifle and hock joints well bent, and not inclined either in or out. **FEET** Should be small, very firm, toes strong, close together and arched.

COAT On the head, front of the legs, and tips of the ears should be short and fine, but on all other parts of the body and legs moderately long, flat, and as free as possible from curl or wave. The feather on the upper portion of the ears should be long and silky; on the back of forelegs and hind legs should be long and fine; a fair amount of hair on the belly, forming a nice fringe, which may extend on the chest and throat. Feet well feathered between the toes. Tail to have a nice fringe of moderately long hair, decreasing

in length as it approaches the point. All feathering to be as straight and as flat as possible. **Color** Should be rich chestnut, with no trace whatever of black; white on chest, throat, or toes, or small star on the forehead, or narrow streak or blaze on the nose or face should not disqualify.

N.B. The following is an elaboration of the standard written by Fabio Cajelli, official judge of the E.N.C.I.

GENERAL CHARACTERISTICS The Irish Setter, according to the classification of Pierre Mégnin, belongs to the braccoid group. It is a hunting dog, capable of working as a Pointer. Origin: the name of Irish Red Setter comes, of course, from the name of his country of origin and the color of his coat. This breed is the true type of the light mesomorph, with long muscles and an extremely sensitive nervous system. The general conformation is that of an agile, vigorous animal, with a square body outline. The type characteristics in the Irish Setter are: solid, golden mahogany, glossy coat; perfectly parallel cranial-facial longitudinal axes; lower line of the muzzle established by the lower jaw, with the commissure not visible; the withers are greatly raised, the eyes are oval, the height at the withers is equal to the length of the trunk, the feet are small and oval in shape. The general build is lean, with fine but strong bone.

WEIGHT AND SIZE Weight: 44-66 lb. Height at the withers: males 22-25¼ inches; females 21¼-24½ inches. Because the Irish Setter works at a vigorous gallop, some breed associations have declared that excessive size is negative and that an ideal height is perhaps 24½ inches.

HEAD Dolichocephalic; light, lean, clean, with no wrinkles on the skull. The head is long rather than wide; its total length should be about 2/5 of the height at the withers; the width of the skull should not be more than half of the total length of the head, and may well be less. The total cephalic index should not be more than 50; the ideal index is perhaps 45. The length of the muzzle should be equal to the length of the skull, which means that the midpoint of the total length of the head falls on the line joining the two inside corners of the eyes, as above. The directions of the longitudinal axes of the skull and muzzle are perfectly parallel; this is characteristic of the breed. **Nose** The nostrils should be well open, large, mobile; the nose should be on a line with the nasal bridge, and seen in profile, the forepart should not overhang the front vertical of the lips.

The pigmentation is black. **Nasal Bridge** Straight; for the length and direction in relation to the skull axis, see above. Its width, at the midpoint of its length, should be slightly more than 1/3 the length. **Lips and Muzzle** The upper lips are thin, close-fitting to the jaw, and divided beneath the nose, forming a semicircle as seen from in front. The height is barely sufficient to cover the lower teeth, and thus the underline of the muzzle is provided by the lower jaw, not lean and dry. The lateral walls of the muzzle are parallel, and the muzzle is squared off in front. **Jaws** Of normal development, tending toward a straight line, meeting in a perfect scissors bite. The teeth are sound, complete in number and of normal development. **Stop** Well defined but not pronounced, because the sinuses are not greatly developed forward and upward but are developed toward the back. **Skull** The length of the skull is equal to the length of the muzzle; for the width, see above. Oval in shape, it is lean and dry, with thin skin fitting closely; the upper part is oval in shape. The occipital protuberance is well marked; the sinuses are longer than they ae high; the medial furrow is well marked.

EYES The eyelids are close-fitting. The shape of the eye is oval, and the eye is neither prominent nor deep-set. The eye should be large, well open, in a semilateral position. The expression should be gentle. The color is brown or deep hazel; the pigmentation of the eyelids is the same as a of the nose—black.

EARS Hanging, of roughly triangular shape; they are thin, fine to the touch, set on at the level of the zygomatic arch, flat; when the head is held horizontal, they should not extend more than ¾ inch beyond the lower line of the throat. The outer side of the auricle is covered with long, silky hair, down to 2/3 of its length; the tip of the ear is covered with short hair.

NECK Its length is 2/5 of the height at the withers, that is, equal to that of the head. The neck is not coarse, arched, lean, without dewlap, and clearly separated from the nape. It merges harmoniously with the shoulders. It should give an impression of slenderness, and its circumference should be slightly less than 2/3 the height at the withers.

FOREQUARTERS The vertical from the scapula-humeral articulation (point of shoulder or upper arm) should pass through the foot just behind the tips of the toes; the vertical from the humeral-radial articulation should divide the forearm and wrist in two approximately equal parts (the greater is the forward part), emerging behind on a level with the midpoint of the pastern. Seen from in front, the vertical from the scapula-humeral articulation (point of shoulder or upper arm) should divide in

two approximately equal parts the forearm, the wrist, the pastern and the foot. **Shoulders** Long, about ¼ of the height at the withers, well sloped and with an inclination of 45-55 degrees (ideal 45 degrees) to the horizontal; they are strong, free in their movements, covered with long muscles which are clearly differentiated. The points of the scapulae, in respect to the center plane of the body, are close to each other. **Upper Arms** Slightly longer than half the height of the foreleg to the elbow; its slope is less than that of the shoulders (60-70 degrees to the horizontal). The direction is almost parallel to the center axis of the body. **Forearms** Strong-boned, oval in cross section; they are vertical, and their length is equal to that of the upper arm; the wrist furrow is well in evidence. The elbows should lie in a plane parallel to the center plane of the body. The height of the forelegs to the elbows is 50 percent of the height at the withers, and consequently, in an Irish Setter 23⅝ inches high at the withers, the height of the foreleg at the elbow is 11-2/5 inches. **Wrists and Pasterns** The wrist follows the line of the forearm, as do the pasterns, seen from in front; seen from the side, the pasterns should be extended. The length of the pasterns is about 1/6 or a little more of the height of the leg to the elbow. **Feet** Oval (harefeet), small, lean, with well-closed and well-arched toes and hard, tough pads, pigmented with black; the nails are strong and curved, and they should be black.

BODY The backline is straight, rounded at the region of the loin. The under line of the trunk is almost straight for the length of the sternum region (which should be long, not perfectly straight, but slightly filled out); after the xiphoid appendage, the outline is provided by the belly line, which ascends gently upward. Thus the lower line of the trunk follows the topline fairly well. The length of the trunk, measured from the point of the shoulder or upper arm (scapula-humeral articulation) to the point of the buttock (point of the ischium) is equal to the height at the withers. In other words, the body outline is square. **Chest** The typical Irish Setter is rather narrow in the chest, and thus at first sight he might seem weak. The width, measured between the upper arms, should not be more than 1/5 of the height at the withers or half the length of the head. In a dog 23⅝ inches high at the withers, the chest should measure 4¾ inches. The manubrium is on a level with the point of shoulder. **Thorax** Well let down, extending about an inch below elbow level. It is deep and slightly carenated, arched in its upper part. The rib arches should be well open. In an Irish Setter 23⅝ inches high at the withers, the thorax should have the following dimensions: circumference behind the elbows, 29½ inches; circumference at the rib arches, 25¼ inches; depth, 12½ inches; height, 12½ inches; transverse diameter, 7 inches. The thora-

IRISH SETTER

Photo: R. Kinne (Photo Res.).

IRISH SETTER

cic index should not be more than 8, and a lower value is preferable. **Ribs** Well sprung, sloping, with good space between the ribs; back ribs long, sloping and well open. **Back** The withers are exceptionally raised above the backline, narrow because of their length and the nearness to each other of the scapula points. The length of the back is about 31 percent of the height at the withers, and the backline is straight. **Loins** Short, well supplied with muscle and merging harmoniously with the backline; they appear arched as seen in profile. The length of the loins is a little less than 1/5 of the height at the withers, the width a little less than the length. **Belly and Flanks** The belly line ascends slightly, and thus the belly does not seem to be greatly drawn up. The length of the flanks should be almost equal to the length of the loins. **Croup** Long, muscular, broad and sloping, but not excessively so. That is, its slope should not exceed about 20 degrees above the horizontal. Its length is 1/3 of the height at the withers, while the transverse diameter between the two haunches is 1/7 of the height at the withers. **Sexual Organs** Of normal development and position. The testicles should be equally well developed, and contained in the scrotum.

TAIL Because of the conformation of the croup, the tail is set on low and carried either horizontally or down. It may follow almost a straight line throughout its entire length, with a slight concavity along the upper edge, or it may be a saber tail, that is, with a more accentuaed curve. Thick at the root, it tapers toward the point. Its length is equal to the height of the foreleg to the elbow or it may exceed this measurement by ½ or ¾ inch. It has a fine fringe shaped like an isosceles triangle, of the same color as the coat; this fringe should begin about an inch down from the root of the tail.

HINDQUARTERS Seen in profile, the vertical drop from the point of the buttocks should touch the tips of the toes, since the metatarsus is in a vertical position. Seen from behind, this vertical should divide the hock metatarsus and foot into two equal parts. **Thighs** Well muscled, slightly arched to the rear; in a dog 23⅝ inches high at the withers, its length is about 8 inches, its width about 6 inches; its direction is slightly sloped from the back forward and from above downward, with an angulation of about 75 degrees above the horizontal; in respect to the vertical, it is positioned parallel to the center plane of the body. **Legs** Well boned and well supplied with lean, long muscles; the furrow between the bone and tendon above the hocks is well marked. The slope is about 40 degrees to the horizontal, and its length is slightly less than the length of the thigh. **Hocks** The sides of the hocks should be broad, the angulation should be closed, because of the 40-degree slope of the tibia. The distance from the ground to the point of the hock should not be more than 27 percent of the height at the withers. Seen from behind, the backline from the point of the hock to the ground should lie on the vertical and on the prolongation of the buttock line. **Metatarsus** Robust and lean; for the length of the metatarsus, see above under "Hock." Seen from behind and in profile, it should lie on the vertical. Its inner face should be free of dewclaws. **Feet** Less oval than the forefeet, but otherwise quite similar.

COAT Hair 2-2¼ inches long, silky in texture, well drawn, with rich fringes which are light, not thick. The hair is long on the body and on the outer, upper part of the auricle; it forms a fringe on the back of the legs, on the sternum, throat and tail. It is short and fine on the head, on the sides and foreparts of the legs and on the tips of the ears. There should be plenty of hair between the toes. The undercoat is abundant only in winter. **Color** Solid, golden mahogany, brilliant and without the least trace of black, the same color extending to the fringes on the legs and tail. A small white marking on the chest and, according to some specialists, on the forehead or toes as well, is not a disqualification although it is not desirable. Some breeders have claimed that a blood red and white coat was originally as pure as solid red. Sir Edward Laverack considers such a coat to be older and purer. **Skin** Thin and fitting closely to the underlying tissues; neck and throat without dewlap; the head should have no wrinkles. The lips, nose and eyelids, the nails and the pads of the feet should be black. Any partial depigmentation of the lips, nose or eyelids is a fault; if extensive, such depigmentation is a disqualification.

GAIT Galloping when hunting.

FAULTS **General Characteristics** Undistinguished overall appearance; coarseness, heaviness, sluggishness; heavy or light bone; lack of symmetry. **Height** Over or above standard. **Head** Short, not light; upper cranial-facial axes divergent or convergent (very serious defect which, when accentuated, amounts to disqualification). **Nose** Not uniformly black, small, raised above the line of the nasal bridge or below; extending beyond the front of the muzzle; total or extensive depigmentation (disqualification). **Nasal Bridge** Short, narrow, hollowed (disqualification), arched (if slightly arched, a serious fault; if accentuated, disqualification); convergent lateral lines. **Lips and Muzzle** Lips overly developed, extending beyond the lower jaw (very serious fault); visible commissure (very serious fault if accentuated); flaccid lips, thick or fleshy; convergence of lateral lines of muzzle (pointed muzzle, not square); short muzzle. **Jaws** Undershot condition (if accentuated, disqualification); overshot condition (disqualification); incomplete dentition, extensive horizontal erosion of teeth. **Stop** Too pronounced. **Skull** Short, flat on top and wide at the sides; occipital protuberance insufficiently or excessively developed; medial furrow not marked. **Eyes** Small or prominent; round; light eyes, walleyes (disqualification); ectropion or entropion; suspicious gaze; cross eyes (if bilaterally, disqualification); eyes in frontal, lateral or ultralateral position; partial depigmentation of the edges of the eyelids (if total, disqualification). **Ears** Long or too short; set on too high or too low; stiff or curled, with broadly rounded tips. **Neck** Coarse, short, with dewlap, not arched, not well fused with shoulders. **Shoulders** Straight, short, with insufficiently developed muscles; points of the scapulae not close together. **Upper Arm** Too sloping, short, not muscular; too strongly boned. **Forearm** Weak bone, too strongly boned, coarse or spongy; round bone; out of vertical, with elbows in or out; wrist furrow not evident. **Wrists** Hypertrophy of wrist bones, small wrists, spongy or hollowed. **Pasterns** Short, thin or too long, straight or too extended, out of vertical. **Feet** Round, large, splayed toes, flat or with toes not arched; out of vertical; nails and pads not black. **Body** Outline not square; longitudinal diameter greater than the height at the withers. **Chest** Broad or too narrow; muscles insufficiently developed; manubrium too low. **Thorax** Insufficiently let down, shallow and deficient in circumference; short sternum, xiphoid appendage turned inward; barrel-shaped, too broad. **Ribs** Not sprung or sprung in middle of thorax, excessively sprung; rib arches too closed; back ribs short, not open. **Back** Short, saddleback, roach back; low withers. **Loins** Long, flat; insufficiently developed muscles. **Belly and Flanks** Belly drawn up, flanks long and turning in. **Croup** Short, narrow, not properly sloped. **Sexual Organs** Monorchidism, cryptorchidism (disqualification); testicles not contained in the scrotum and unequally developed. **Tail** Lack of tail or rudimentary tail (disqualification); tail set on too high or too low, too long or too short, straight up or over back (disqualification), flaccid, hanging, deviated to one side. **Thighs** Short, excessively or insufficiently sloped, with deficient muscular development, carried away from the second thigh. **Legs** Short, insufficiently sloped, thin or too strongly boned; furrow between bone and tendon above the hocks not evident. **Hocks** Out of vertical, high, narrow sides, angulation too closed or too open. **Metatarsus** Long, too bony or thin, out of vertical; dewcaws (disqualification). **Feet** Same as for forefeet. **Hair** Short, wavy, curly (disqualification), not silky. **Color** Not mahogany red and not glossy, brown or liver (disqualification), presence of black hairs; light, discolored fringes. **Skin** Coarse, thick, not close-fitting; dewlap, wrinkles on the head; total or extensive depigmentation of the nose or of the edges of the eyelids of both eyes (disqualification). **Gait** Continued trotting during work, ambling (disqualification).

SCALE OF POINTS

General appearance	25
Skull and muzzle	25
Eyes and eyelids	10
Ears	5
Shoulders	10
Upper and lower profile of trunk	10
Thorax	10
Loins and croup	10
Legs and feet	15
Coat and color	25
Tail	5
	150

RATINGS

Excellent: score at least	140
Very god	130
Good	120
Fairly good	110

A PAIR OF GOLDEN RETRIEVERS WITH THEIR PUPPIES ▶

Photo: Y. Lanceau, S. A. Thompson.

239 GORDON SETTER

GREAT BRITAIN

This is the heaviest and therefore the slowest among the setters, although he is also the strongest. He is able to hunt on almost any terrain and even in the water, where he shows his excellent swimming ability.

Charles II, who reigned in England from 1660 to 1685, is reported to have had several specimens of massive black-and-red setters. It is said that he esteemed them so much that he wanted them by his side when he posed for official portraits.

Professor Pollacci, a famous Italian breeder of Scottish Setters, writes of this breed: "In the region of Scotland north of Fochabers, near the Spey River, and located some miles from the sea, shepherds prior to 1800 had dogs which, although they were used for guarding flocks, were capable of finding game a great distance off and following its trail. These dogs gave proof of an extraordinary sense of smell and an instinct for the stop superior to that of other hunting breeds then extant. Duke Alexander IV of Gordon, who died in 1827 at the age of 84, often borrowed these dogs from shepherds for his hunting parties. Among these there was a female who distinguished herself by her exceptional sense of smell and her ability for the stop, and it is to this humble bitch that we probably owe the famous hunting qualities fixed in the stock of Gordon Setters raised by the Duke of Gordon, as he had her covered by one of his best setters which produced the present black-and-red setter."

Some experts, including Stonehenge, maintain that there was a Bloodhound strain in the old black-and-red setter. This theory might be supported by the relatively heavy skeleton and by the marked development of the lips.

GENERAL CHARACTERISTICS A sylish dog, built on galloping lines, having a thoroughbred appearance consistent with its build, which can be compared to a weight-carrying hunter. Must have symmetrical conformation throughout, showing true balance. Strong, fairly short and level back. Shortish tail. Head fairly long, clearly lined and with intelligent expression, clear colors, and long flat coat.

WEIGHT AND SIZE Height at shoulder: males, 26 inches; females, 24½ inches; weight: males, about 65 lb; females, about 56 lb. These values for show condition.

HEAD Deep rather than broad, but definitely broader than the muzzle, showing brain room. Skull slightly rounded and broadest between the ears. The head should have a clearly indicated stop, and length from occiput to stop should be slightly longer than from stop to nose. Below and above the eyes should be lean and the cheeks as narrow as the leanness of head allows. The muzzle should be fairly long, with almost parallel lines and not pointed, as seen from above or from the side. The flews not pendulous but with clearly indicated lips. Nose big and broad, with open nostrils and black in color. The muzzle should not be quite as deep as its length. Mouth must be even and neither undershot nor overshot.

EYES Of fair size, not too deep nor too prominent but sufficiently under the brows to show keen and intelligent expression. Dark brown and bright.

EARS Set low on the head and lying close to it, of medium size and thin.

NECK Long, lean and arched to the head, and without throatiness.

BODY Of moderate length, deep in brisket, with ribs well sprung. Deep in back ribs, i.e., well ribbed up. Loins wide and slightly arched. Chest not too broad.

FOREQUARTERS Shoulders should be long and slope well back, with wide flat bone and fairly close at withers; should not be loaded, i.e., too thick, which interferes with liberty of movement. Elbows well let down and showing well under the body, which gives freedom of action. Forelegs big, flat-boned and straight, with strong upright pasterns, well feathered. **HINDQUARTERS** Hind legs from hip to hock should be long, broad, and muscular; hock to heel short and strong, stifles well bent; hocks straight, not inclined either in or out. Pelvis should tend to the horizontal, i.e., opposite goose rump. **FEET** Oval, with close-knit, well-arched toes, with plenty of hair between. Full toe pads and deep heel cushions.

TAIL Fairly short, straight, or slightly scimitar-shaped; should not reach below hocks. Carried horizontal or below line of back. Thick at the root, tapering to a fine point. The feather or flag, which starts near the root, should be long and straight, growing shorter uniformly to the point.

COAT On the head and front of legs and tips of ears should be short and fine, but on all other parts of the body and legs moderately long, fairly flat, and free as possible from curl or wave. The feather on the upper portion of the ears should be long and silky, on the back of the hind legs long and fine; a fair amount of hair on the belly, forming a nice fringe whch may extend on chest and throat. All feathering to be as flat and straight as possible. **Color** Deep, shining, coal-black, with no sign of rustiness, with tan markings of a rich chestnut red, i.e., color of a ripe horse chestnut just out of the shell. Tan should be lustrous. Black penciling allowed on toes and also black streak under jaw. **Tan markings** two clear spots over the eyes, not over ¾ inch in diameter. On the sides of the muzzle, the tan should not reach above the base of nose, resembling the stripe around the end of the muzzle from one side to the other. On the throat: two large, clear spots on the chest. On the inside of the hind legs and inside the thighs, markings can show down the front of the stifle, broadening out to the outside of the hind legs from the hock to the toes. They must not, however, completely obliterate the black back of the hind legs. Tan markings also appear on the back of the forelegs up to the elbows, to the knees, or a little bit above in front of the knees, and around the vent. A white spot on chest is allowed, but the smaller the better.

FAULTS General impression: unintelligent appearance. The Bloodhound look, with heavy and big head and ears and clumsy body; the Collie look with pointed muzzle and curved tail. The head: pointed, snipy, upturned or downturned muzzle, too small or large mouth. The eyes: too light in color, too deep set or too prominent. The ears: set too high or unusually broad or heavy. The neck: thick and short. Shoulders and back: irregularly formed. The chest: too broad. The legs and feet: crooked legs. Outturned elbows. The toes scattered, flatfooted. The tail: too long, badly carried or hooked at the end. The coat: curly, like wool, lusterless. Color: yellow or straw-colored tan, or without clearly defined lines between the different colors. White feet. Too much white on the chest. There should be no tan hairs among the black.

N.B. The following is an elaboration of the standard written by Fabio Cajelli, official judge of the E.N.C.I.

GENERAL CHARACTERISTICS In the classification of Pierre Mégnin, the Gordon Setter belongs to the braccoid group. He is a hunting dog trained to work as a Pointer. Of Scottish origin. The general conformation is that of a mesomorph, with the body outline square (height at the withers equal to the length of the trunk, measured from the scapula-humeral articulation—point of shoulder or upper arm, to the posterior point of the ischium—point of buttocks). The Gordon Setter is of powerful build; extremely strong-boned, with fairly short muscles, heavier than the English Setter and Irish Setter; the chest is rather broad. The Gordon is less impetuous than the English and Irish Setters, but he hunts at the gallop, although the gallop is less intense than in the others because of his general build and nervous system. The typical Gordon should have a general build unlike either of the other two Setters. The bone is strong, the muscles relatively short, the head rather large, with the lower profile of the muzzle provided by the upper lip; the eye has a gentle, good-natured expression, neither staring nor fiery; the skull is fairly domed, the coat is a brilliant black verging on blue, with mahogany flecking but without black markings.

WEIGHT AND SIZE Weight: 44-66 lb. Height at the withers: males 23-25¼ inches; females 22-24½ inches, with a tolerance of ¾ inch above or below.

HEAD Dolichocephalic; its total length is 2/5 of the height at the withers. The length of the skull is equal to the length of the muzzle, and the midpoint of the total length of the head lies on the horizontal line joining the two inner corners of the eyes. The total cephalic index should not be more than 50, and therefore the width of the skull should not exceed half the total length of the head. The directions of the upper longitudinal axes of the skull and muzzle are parallel. The head is rather large and not light, in good proportion with the general build, which is relatively heavy. There should be no wrinkles on the skull, and the skin should be close-fitting ot the underlying tissues. **Nose** Should be large, cool and wet, with well open, large and mobile nostrils, on the line of the nasal bridge and, seen in profile, the forepart is on the same vertical plane as that of the lips. The coloring is black. **Nasal Bridge** Straight; it is as long as the skull, and its longitudinal axis is parallel to the longitudinal axis of the skull. Its width, at the midpoint, is 40 perecnt of its length. **Lips and Muzzle** The upper lips are thin, neither pendulous nor loose, fitting closely over the jaw; seen from in front, the lower part forms a semicircle; they are fairly fleshy; the forepart of the muzzle should be flat (squared muzzle). The upper lips cover the lower jaw. This profile is interrupted by the commissure, which is visible but not excessively so. The anterior-inferior-lateral profile of the muzzle is a semicircle with a rather open chord. **Jaws** Of normal development, the lower jaw is quite straight; the jaws meet in a perfect scissors bite. The teeth are sound, completely developed and complete in number. **Stop** Very pronounced, but not sloping abruptly. The sinuses are neither high nor greatly developed forward. **Skull** Its length is equal to the length of the muzzle, its width should be less than half the total length of the head. Seen in profile and in front, it is a spheroid. This shape is more accentuated at the crest, where the skull is arched in the form of a cupola. Its upper longitudinal axis is parallel to the axis of the nasal bridge. The medial furrow is pronounced; the occipital protuberance is clearly marked but not exaggerated. The

GORDON SETTER

Photo: S. A. Thompson.

sinuses are not greatly developed in height, although they are fully developed in length and width. The skin is close-fitting without wrinkles.

EYES Large, with gentle expression; rather rounded, with the eyelids close-fitting. They should be neither protruding nor deep-set and should be in the subfrontal position. The color is dark brown, while the pigmentation of the edges of the eyelids should be the same as that of the nose—black.

EARS Hanging, fine to the touch, soft, triangular, with the tips slightly rounded, flat, close to the cheeks; they are set on at the level of the zygomatic arch. In normal stance and with the head held horizontally, their length extends about 1-1¼ inches below the throat. The skin on the outside is covered with silky hair which extends about ¾ inch beyond the tips of the ears.

NECK Lean, without dewlap, muscular, well differentiated from the nape; it merges harmoniously with the shoulders. Its length is 2/5 of the height at the withers (in a dog 23⅝ inches high at the withers, the length of the neck will be about 9½ inches); its circumference is 2/3 of the height at the withers. It is arched. The lower profile of the neck shows no loose skin.

FOREQUARTERS As seen in profile, the vertical drop from the scapula-humeral articulation (point of shoulder or upper arm) should touch the tips of the toes as it reaches the ground; the vertical from the humeral-radial articulation should divide the forearm and wrist into two almost equal parts (the greater is the forward part), emerging at the level of the pastern midpoint. Seen from in front, the first of these verticals should divide the forearm, wrist, pastern and foot into two equal parts. The length of the foreleg from the ground to the elbow is equal to half the height at the withers. **Shoulders** The shoulders are about ¼ of the height at the withers, sloped at 45-55 degrees to the horizontal, with well-developed muscles and free in movement. The points of the scapulae are close together. **Upper Arms** Like the shoulders, the upper arms have well developed muscles and strong bone. They are sloped at approximately 65 degrees to the horizontal and their length is approximately 30 percent of the height at the withers. Their direction is practically parallel to the center plane of the body. **Forearms** Strongly boned; seen from in front, they should follow the vertical from the point of the scapula-humeral articulation. In cross section the forearm is oval, and its length is the same as that of the upper arm. The elbows should lie in a plane parallel to the center plane of the body. **Wrists and Pasterns** Seen from in front, they follow the vertical line of the forearms. The pasterns, seen in profile, should be extended in such a way that the vertical from the humeral-radial articulation divides the wrist into two nearly equal parts and emerges at the midpoint of the length of the pastern. The pastern itself is about 1/6 the height of the foreleg to the elbow. **Feet** Oval, with well-closed and well-arched toes, covered with thick hair. The pads are hard, the nails are strong, curved and black.

BODY The length of the trunk, measured from the point of the shoulder or of the upper arm to the point of the buttock is equal to the height at the withers (this means that the body outline is square). The backline is straight and slightly curved at the loin. The lower profile of the trunk follows approximately the backline; it is nearly straight all along the sternum region, which should be long; the profile is not absolutely straight, but slightly curved. After the xiphoid appendage, the profile is given by the belly and ascends slightly to the rear. **Chest** Broad, open and supplied with well-developed muscles. Its width between the upper arms should be a little more than 27 percent of the height at the withers. The manubrium is on a level with the point of the shoulders. **Thorax** Well filled out at half its height, descending to ½ or ¾ inch below the elbows; the curve of the ribs diminishes gradually toward the sternum, without forming a carena. From the side, the sternum is seen to be long, ascending gradually toward the abdomen. In a dog 23⅝ inches high, the measurements of the thorax are: circumference behind the elbows, approximately ¼ of the height at the withers, i.e., 29½ inches; circumference at the rib arches, 25½ inches; depth, 11-2/5 inches; height, 12-1/5 inches; transverse diameter, 7½ inches. The thoracic index should not be more than 7. **Ribs** Well sprung, sloping, with good room between the ribs; back ribs long, sloping and well open. **Back** The withers are raised above the backline, which is straight. The length of the back is slightly less than 1/3 the height at the withers. **Loins** Arched, with well-developed muscles. The length is a little less than 1/5 the height at the withers, and the width is slightly less than the length. **Belly and Flanks** The lower line of the trunk should ascend toward the flanks, but just slightly. The flanks should be almost as long as the loins. **Croup** The width is 1/7 the height at the withers. The croup is muscular, its length 1/3 the height at the withers; its slope is approximately 10 degrees to the horizontal; it is consequently a basically horizontal croup. **Sexual Organs** Normally developed and with the testicles equally developed and contained within the scrotum.

TAIL Set on high. Thick and robust at the root, it narrows gradually to the tip. Its length should be equal to the height of the forelegs to the elbows, or slightly longer. It is carried horizontally and should be nearly straight throughout its length; a saber tail, however, is acceptable. It has a fringe in the shape of an isosceles triangle, beginning about one inch from the root.

HINDQUARTERS Seen from the side, the vertical from the point of the buttocks should touch the tips of the toes, and the metatarsus should always be vertical. Seen from behind, the vertical should divide the point of the hock, the metatarsus and the foot into two equal parts. **Thighs**

GORDON SETTER

Muscular, long and broad, arched at the back edge; the direction of the thigh is sloping from above downward and from behind forward (75 degrees), and, in respect to the vertical, is parallel to the center plane of the body. The length should not be less than 1/3 the height at the withers, and the width of the outer face should be ¼ the height at the withers. **Legs** Strong-boned and muscular, lean in the upper part; the furrow between the bone and the tendon above the hock is well marked. They are slightly shorter than the thighs, and their slope is approximately 40-45 degrees to the horizontal. **Hocks** The sides of the hocks should be very broad, the angulations relatively close The line from the point of the hock to the ground should lie on the vertical and be a prolongation of the line of the buttock. The distance from the point of the hock to the ground should be about 27 percent of the height at the withers. **Metatarsus** Robust, lean. For the length, see above. The metatarsus should always be vertical. Seen in profile, it is considered in normal position if the vertical from the point of the buttock touches the tips of the toes. There should be no dewclaws. **Feet** Less oval than the forefeet, but otherwise similar.

COAT Hair Of silky texture, 2-2¼ inches long, slightly wavy, with rich but not thick fringes. The hair is long on the body and the ears; it forms a fringe on the back of the legs, chest, throat and tail. It is short and fine on the head, on the sides and forepart of the legs. There is plenty of hair between the toes. The undercoat is thick only in winter. **Color** Brilliant black, with blue tint and mahogany markings in certain well-determined parts. These markings should be solid, without bright flecks, and should be distributed as follows: two clearly defined spots above the eyes, no more than ¾ inch in diameter; on the sides of the muzzle, no higher than the base of the nose; on the throat; two broad markings on the chest; on the forelegs, almost to the elbows on the inner sides, and slightly above the wrists on the front (on the inner side of the thighs, they may extend to the hocks and the outer edge of the metatarsus; the fringe of the metatarsus should, however, be black); on the feet; around the vent. A small white mark on the chest is acceptable. **Skin** Thin, close-fitting in every part of the body; there should be no dewlap at the throat and no wrinkles on the skull. The lips, nose and eyelids should be black, as should also be the nails and the pads.

GAIT A fairly vigorous gallop.

FAULTS General Characteristics Undistinguished overall appearance; lightness, heaviness, sluggishness; light bone; lack of symmetry. **Height** Over or above standard. **Head** Light, like Irish Setter, short; upper cranial-facial longitudinal axes divergent or convergent (disqualification). **Nose** Small, lacking in pigment, above or below line of nasal bridge; extending past front vertical of muzzle; total depigmentation (disqualification). **Nasal Bridge** Short, narrow, arched (serious fault), hollowed (disqualification); lateral lines convergent. **Lips** Too large, hanging below commissure, flaccid, fleshy. **Muzzle** Short, insufficiently developed, pointed, not square in front. **Jaws** Overshot condition (disqualification); undershot condition (if harming the general appearance of the muzzle, disqualification); crooked teeth, teeth lacking; extensive horizontal erosion of teeth. **Skull** Short, small, flat on top, broad at the sides; stop receding or too prominent; occipital protuberance too marked; absence of medial furrow. **Eyes** Small, prominent; oval; light eyes; walleyes (disqualification); ectropion or entropion; suspicious gaze; frontal, lateral or ultralateral position; partial depigmentation of the eyelids (if total and bilateral, disqualification); cross eyes (if bilaterally crossed, disqualification). **Ears** Too long or too short; set on

Photo: Palnic

CURLY-COATED RETRIEVER

too high or too low; rigid, thick or curled; broadly rounded tips. **Neck** Thin, short, with dewlap, not arched, too thick. **Shoulders** Straight, short, insufficiently muscled; insufficiently close to body. **Upper Arms** Too sloping; light bone; insufficient muscling. **Forearms** Out of vertical; light or spongy bone; elbows out or in; wrist furrow little evident. **Wrists** Out of vertical, bulging or hollowed, small, with hypertrophy of wrist bones. **Pasterns** Short, straight, too extended, too long, thin, out of vertical; spongy bone. **Feet** Round, broad, flat, toes too closed, out of vertical; nails and pads not black. **Body** Not square in outline, that is, with the longitudinal diameter greater than the height at the withers. **Chest** Too broad or narrow; manubrium too low; deficient muscling. **Thorax** Lacking in height, depth and circumference, carenated; xiphoid appendage turned inward; short sternum. **Ribs** Badly sprung; too close together; back ribs not sprung, short and not open. **Back** Short, saddleback or roach back; withers too low. **Loins** Long, flat, narrow. **Belly and Flanks** Belly tucked up; flanks hollowed and long. **Croup** Short, narrow, sloping. **Sexual Organs** Monorchidism or cryptorchidism (disqualification); abnormal or unequal development of the testicles; testicles not within the scrotum (disqualification). **Tail** Too long or too short, carried straight up or over the back (disqualification), carried to the side, hanging, flaccid, set on too low; lack of tail or rudimentary tail (disqualification). **Thighs** Short, insufficiently muscled, too straight or too sloping,

carried away from the stifle. **Legs** Short, weak-boned, insufficiently sloped; furrow between bone and tendon above hock not sufficiently evident. **Hocks** High, narrow, out of vertical; angulation not closed or excessively closed. **Metatarsus** Out of vertical, long, thin; dewclaws (disqualification). **Feet** Same as for forefeet. **Hair** Too wavy, curly (disqualification), not silky, short, not glossy. **Color** Any color other than brilliant black tending to blue; markings not clearly defined, of any color other than mahogany red. **Skin** Coarse, thick, not fitting close to the underlying tissues; total depigmentation of the nose or the edges of the two eyelids (disqualification); dewlap; wrinkles on the head. **Gait** Continued trotting during hunt; ambling (disqualification).

SCALE OF POINTS

General appearance	25
Skull and muzzle	25
Eyes and eyelids	10
Ears	5
Shoulders	10
Thorax	10
Upper and lower profile	10
Loins and croup	10
Legs and feet	15
Coat and color	25
Tail	5
	150

RATINGS

Excellent: score at least	140
Very good	130
Good	120
Fairly good	110

240 CURLY-COATED RETRIEVER

GREAT BRITAIN

This dog is perhaps a cross between the Labrador and the Irish Water Spaniel. Certain experts believe that the setter and the Poodle have also contributed to this breed.

CURLY-COATED RETRIEVER

Photo: S. A. Thompson, T. Fall.

GENERAL CHARACTERISTICS A strong, smart, upstanding dog, showing activity, endurance, and intelligence.

WEIGHT AND SIZE 70-80 lb; height approximately 26 inches.

HEAD Long and well-proportioned skull, not too flat, jaws strong and long but not inclined to snipiness. Nose black in the black-coated variety, with wide nostrils. Teeth strong and level.

EYES Black or brown but not yellow, rather large but not too prominent.

EARS Rather small, set on close-lying to head and covered with short curls.

NECK Should be moderately long, with shoulders well laid back and free from bossiness.

TAIL Moderately short, carried fairly straight and covered with curls tapering toward the point.

FOREQUARTERS Shoulders should be very deep, muscular and obliquely placed. **HINDQUARTERS** Strong and muscular, hocks low to the ground, with moderate bend to stifle and hock. **FEET** Round and compact, with well-arched toes.

COAT Should be one mass of crisp curls all over; a slightly more open coat not to be severely penalized, but a saddleback or patch of uncurled hair behind the shoulders should be penalized; a prominent white patch on the breast is desirable, but a few white hairs in an otherwise good dog is allowable. **Color** Preferably black or liver.

FAULTS Wide skull, light eyes, curled tail, bad movement.

N.B. *The standard of the British Kennel Club does not include a description of of the body.* ●

241 FLAT-COATED RETRIEVER

GREAT BRITAIN

This is a relatively recent breed which appears to have derived from the crossbreeding of the old Spanish dog with the Newfoundland. The breed takes its general appearance from the Newfoundland although differing from it in its general dimensions. On the other hand, some authorities consider that the Flat-Coated Retriever is descended from the Curly-Coated Retriever crossed with the Labrador. Finally it appears that the setter has also contributed to the formation of this excellent Retriever.

GENERAL CHARACTERISTICS A bright, active dog of medium size with an intelligent expression, showing power without lumber and raciness without weediness.

WEIGHT 60-70 lb.

HEAD Should be long and nicely molded, the skull flat and moderately broad. There should be a depression or stop between the eyes, slight and in no way accentuated, so as to avoid giving either a down- or dish-faced appearance. The nose of good size, with open nostrils. The jaws should be long and strong, capable of carrying hare or pheasant.

EYES Should be of medium size, dark brown or hazel, with a very intelligent expression (a round, prominent eye is a disfigurement); they should be obliquely placed.

EARS Should be small and well set on, close to the side of the head.

NECK The head should be well set in the neck, with the latter long and free from throatiness, symmetrically set and running well into the back to permit easy trail-seeking.

BODY The fore ribs should be fairly flat, showing a gradual spring and well arched in the body, but rather lighter toward the quarters. Open couplings are to be severely condemned. The back should be short, square, and well ribbed up.

TAIL Should be short, straight and well put on; carried gaily but not excessively over the back.

FOREQUARTERS The chest should be deep and fairly broad, with a well-defined brisket, on which elbows should work cleanly and evenly. The legs are of the greatest importance. The forelegs should be perfectly straight, with bone of good quality carried right down to the feet, and when the dogs is in full coat the legs should be well feathered. **HINDQUARTERS** Should be muscular. The stifle should not be too straight or too bent, and the dog must neither be cow-hocked nor move too widely behind; in fact, he must stand and move true on legs and feet all around. The legs should be well feathered. **FEET** Round and strong with toes close and well arched; the soles should be thick and strong.

COAT Should be dense, of fine quality and texture, as flat as possible. **Color** black or liver. ●

FLAT-COATED RETRIEVER

Photo: T. Fall, S. A. Thompson.

FLAT-COATED RETRIEVER

GOLDEN RETRIEVER

242 GOLDEN RETRIEVER
GREAT BRITAIN

GENERAL CHARACTERISTICS Should be a symmetrical, active, powerful dog, with an even movement, sound and well put together, with a kindly expression, neither clumsy nor long in the leg.

WEIGHT AND SIZE The average weight for dogs in good hard condition should be: males 65-70 lb; females, 20-22 inches.

HEAD Broad skull, well set on a clean, muscular neck; muzzle powerful and wide, not weak-jawed, with a good stop. Teeth even, neither undershot nor overshot.

EYES Dark and set well apart, very kindly in expression, with dark rims.

EARS Well proportioned, of moderate size and well set on.

NECK Clean and muscular.

BODY Well balanced, short-coupled, deep through the heart. Ribs deep and well sprung.

TAIL Should not be carried too gay nor curled at the tip.

FOREQUARTERS The forelegs should be straight, with good bone. Shoulders should be well laid back and long in the blade. **HINDQUARTERS** The loins and legs should be strong and muscular, with good second thighs and well bent stifles. Hocks well let down, not cow-hocked. **FEET** Round and cat-like, neither open nor splayed.

COAT Should be flat or wavy with good feathering; the undercoat should be dense and water-resistant. **Color** Any shade of gold or cream, but neither red nor mahogany. The presence of a few white hairs on chest is permissible. White collar, feet, toes, or blaze should be penalized. Nose should be black. ●

GOLDEN RETRIEVER

GOLDEN RETRIEVER

338

Photo: R. Kinne (Photo Res.), A. Wintzell, S. A. Thompson.

GOLDEN RETRIEVER

GOLDEN RETRIEVER

339

Photo: A. Wintzell.

243 LABRADOR RETRIEVER

GREAT BRITAIN

This dog is indigenous to the region from which he takes his name. He was imported into the county of Dorset and raised and trained there for retrieving game by the Count of Malmesbury, the Duke of Buccleuch, the Count of Home, and Lord Scott. The breed was kept pure for a long time and then was submitted to different crossbreedings which resulted in other varieties of Retrievers. However, some fanciers have succeeded in preserving, up to the present day, the original type while perfecting its appearance and its abilities.

LABRADOR RETRIEVER

GENERAL CHARACTERISTICS The general appearance of the Labrador Retriever should be that of a strongly built, short-coupled, very active dog, broad in the skull, broad and deep through the chest and ribs, broad and strong over the loins and hindquarters. The coat close, short, with dense undercoat and free from feather. The dog must move neither too wide nor too close in front or behind: he must stand and move true all around on legs and feet.

SIZE Desired height: males 22-22½ inches; females 21½-22 inches.

HEAD The skull should be broad, with a pronounced stop so that the skull is not in a straight line with the nose. The head should be clean-cut without fleshy cheeks. The jaws should be medium in length, powerful and free from snipiness. The nose should be wide, the nostrils well developed. Teeth should be sound and strong, the lower just behind but touching the upper.

EYES Medium size, expressing intelligence and good temper; they should be brown or hazel.

EARS Should not be large and heavy; close to the head; set rather far back.

NECK Should be clean, strong, and powerful.

BODY The chest must be of good width and depth, with well-sprung ribs. The back should be short-coupled.

TAIL A distinctive feature of the Labrador, it should be very thick toward the base, gradually tapering toward the tip. It should be of medium length and practically free from feathering, but it should be clothed thickly all round with the Labrador's short, thick, dense coat, presenting that peculiar rounded appearance which has been described as "otter tail." The tail may be carried gaily.

FOREQUARTERS The shoulders should be long and sloping, the forelegs well boned and straight from the shoulder to the ground when viewed from front or side. **HINDQUARTERS** The loins must be wide and strong with well-turned stifles; well developed and not sloping toward the tail. The hocks should be slightly bent. **FEET** Should be round and compact with well-arched toes and well-developed pads.

COAT Short, dense and without wave, with a weather-resistant undercoat; it should give a hard feeling to the hand. **Color** Generally black, liver, or yellow, although a small white spot on the chest is allowable. The coat should be of a whole color, not flecked.

FAULTS Undershot or overshot mouth, lack of undercoat, bad action, feathering, snipiness on the head, large or heavy ears, cow hocks, tail curling over back. ●

LABRADOR RETRIEVER

LABRADOR RETRIEVER

Photo: S. A. Thompson, A. Wintzell, B. Young (Photo Res.).

UNDERWATER VIEW

Photo: R. Kinne (Photo Res.).

244 CHESAPEAKE BAY RETRIEVER

UNITED STATES

There are opposing theories concerning the origins of this breed. The most creditable is the following: In 1807 an English ship foundered in the sands of the Maryland coast. The crew was saved by the American ship *Canton*, and with the crew were two young Newfoundland dogs, a dark red male named Sailor and a black female subsequently named Canton in honor of the rescue ship. These two dogs were given to the people of the vicinity who had aided the shipwreck victims, and it was found that they had great qualities as retrievers. Many local Retrievers were crossed with Sailor and Canton, but these two dogs were not mated. However, some think that there were infusions of Otter Hound blood, which is doubtful because the Chesapeake has no ability for the search. It is more logical to think that the long-haired and curlyhaired Retriever shared in the formation of this breed, if in effect there were crosses. What is certain is that the points were fixed in 1885 and that the Chesapeake Retriever spread in great numbers because of his excellent general qualities and his endurance.

CHESAPEAKE BAY RETRIEVER

GENERAL CHARACTERISTICS Should show a bright and happy disposition and have an intelligent expression, with general outlines impressive and indicative of a good worker. The dog must be well proportioned, have a good coat, and be well balanced in other points rather than excelling in some and deficient in others. Texture of coat is a prime requisite, since the dog is used for hunting in all kinds of weather, often in ice and snow. The oil in the harsh outer coat and the woolly under-coat, is well adapted to keeping the

CHESAPEAKE BAY RETRIEVER RETRIEVING

Photo: S. A. Thompson, C. R. Meyer (Photo Res.).

CHESAPEAKE BAY RETRIEVER DURING TRAINING

frigid water away from the skin and helps in drying quickly. The coat should resist water like the feathers of a duck. When the dog emerges from the water and shakes himself, he retains no water at all but is merely moist. Color and coat are both of prime importance, since the dog is used for duck hunting. The color must be as nearly that of his surroundings as possible. Thus, color and texture of coat must be given every consideration when judging on the bench or in the ring. Courage, willingness to work, alertness, nose, intelligence, love of water, quality in general, and, above all, disposition should be given primary consideration in the selection and breeding of the Chesapeake Bay Retriever.

WEIGHT AND SIZE Weight: males 65-75 lb; females 55-65 lb. Height: males 23-26 inches; females 21-24 inches.

HEAD Skull broad and round, with medium stop; nose medium; muzzle pointed but not sharp. Lips thin, not pendulous.

EYES Medium size, set wide apart, yellowish in color and very clear.

EARS Small, set well up on head; they should hang loosely and be of medium leather.

NECK The neck should be of medium length, strongly muscular in appearance and tapering to shoulders.

BODY Chest should be strong, deep and wide. The barrel should be round and deep. The body must be of medium length, neither cobby nor roached, but approaching hollowness. The flanks should be well tucked up. The hindquarters should be as high or slightly higher than the shoulders and should be at least as powerful as the forequarters. There should be no tendency to weakness in either forequarters or hindquarters. The latter should be especially powerful to supply the drive for swimming. Back should be short, well coupled and powerful.

TAIL Tail should be of medium length, in the male 12-15 inches, in the female 11-14 inches. It should be fairly heavy at the root. Moderate feathering on tail and stern permissible.

FORELEGS AND HIND LEGS Legs should be of medium length, straight, showing good bone and muscle, with well-webbed harefeet of good size. Toes well rounded and close, the pasterns slightly bent. Both pasterns and hocks are of medium length, and the straighter the legs the better. Dewclaws on forelegs permissible, but they may be removed. Dewclaws on hind legs disqualify.

COAT Thick and short, nowhere over 1½ inches long, with a fine, dense undercoat. Hair on face and legs should be very short and straight, tending to waviness on the shoulders, neck, back, and loins only. A curly coat or coat tending to curl not permissible. **Color** Any color varying from dark brown to faded tan or dead-grass color of any shade from tan to dull straw. Solid color preferred, although white spot on breast (the smaller the better) permissible.

SCALE OF POINTS

General appearance	12
Head, incl. lips, ears, eyes	16
Neck	4
Shoulders and body	12
Back quarters and stifles	12
Elbows, legs, feet	12
Color	4
Stern and tail	10
Coat and texture	18
	100

APPROXIMATE MEASUREMENTS

	Inches
Head, nose to occiput	9½-10
Girth at ears	20 -21
Muzzle below eyes	10 -10½
Length of ears	4½-5
Width between eyes	2½-2 ¾
Girth neck close to shoulder	20 -22
Girth of chest to elbows	35 -36
Girth at flank	24 -25
Length from occiput to tail base	34 -35
Girth forearms at shoulder	10 -10½
Girth upper thigh	19 -20
From root to root of ear (over skull)	5 -6
Occiput to top shoulder blades	9 -9 ½
From elbow to elbow over the shoulders	25 -26

245 ENGLISH COCKER SPANIEL

GREAT BRITAIN

Present-day spaniels—we are speaking of dogs used for search and retrieval—come directly from the British Isles but are descended from spaniels which, having been imported in far-off times, have undergone important modifications during the course of complex and carefully carried out breedings. In a word, the English used the old spaniel or Quail Setter, a product of crossbreeding the Peatbog Dog with the Bronze Age Dog, to create different types, each one suited to a special task. It is among these that we find the magnificent setters and the graceful toy spaniels.

The Cocker is a very well-known spaniel. The modern type originated in Wales or Devonshire and is distinctly different from the primitive type that was quite similar to the present Springer. He is often used for woodcock with which he matches wits and always triumphs. He is a very good auxiliary to the hunter since, because of his small size, he can easily move among briars and brambles and in all kinds of terrain where thick vegetation makes it difficult for a setter to penetrate. He has an acute sense of smell, is energetic and untiring, and flushes the quarry and raises it while keeping close to his master who is waiting to fire. He returns the game even over a great distance with extreme care and without ever damaging the feathers or flesh.

Villar, a great authority on this breed, says: "There is no more pleasant dog nor one more affectionate or lively than the Cocker. His well-developed psychology makes him extremely interesting. The qualities of intelligence, goodness and cunning are all tied together within him. He obeys not through servility but by sharing ideas with his master, whose slightest intention he is able to guess. He is most faithful, and also an excellent guard dog, wary of any suspicious sound and, if necessary, confronts an intruder with courage."

Photo: C. R. Meyer (Photo Res.).

Photo: S. A. Thompson.

WHITE AND ORANGE ENGLISH COCKER SPANIEL

BLACK ENGLISH COCKER SPANIEL

GENERAL CHARACTERISTICS The English Cocker Spaniel has the appearance of an active, merry sporting dog. It does not follow in the lines of the larger Field Spaniel (See No. 247) either in lengthiness, lowness, or otherwise, but is shorter in back and rather higher on the legs.

WEIGHT AND SIZE Weight: males 28-34 lb; females 26-32 lb. Ideal height at withers: males 16-17 inches; females 15-16 inches. Deviations to be severely penalized but should not disqualify the dog.

HEAD A nicely developed square muzzle and level jaw, with distinct stop. Skull and forehead should be well developed, with plenty of brain room, cleanly chiseled and not cheeky. Nose sufficiently wide and well developed to ensure the exquisite scenting power of the breed. Teeth should be even and set squarely.

EYES Full but not prominent, hazel or brown, harmonizing with color of coat, with a general expression of intelligence and gentleness, decidedly wide-awake, bright and merry.

EARS Lobe-shaped, set on low; leather-fine and not extending beyond the nose; well clothed with long silky hair, which should be straight; no distinct curls or ringlets.

NECK Should be long and muscular, neatly set on to fine sloping shoulders.

BODY Compact and firmly knit, giving the impression of a concentration of power and untiring activity. Short in back. Immensely strong and compact in proportion to the size and weight of the dog; slightly drooping toward the tail.

TAIL Set on to conform with the topline of the back. Merry in action. It should be docked, neither too short nor too long, to allow for its flashy action.

FOREQUARTERS The shoulders should be sloping and fine, chest deep and well developed but not too wide and round to interfere with the free action of the forelegs. The legs must be well boned, feathered and straight; they should be sufficiently short for concentrated power, but not so short as to interfere with the tremendous exertions expected from this grand little sporting dog. **HINDQUARTERS** Wide, well rounded and very muscular. The legs must be well boned, feathered and straight, and should be sufficiently short for concentrated power but not so short as to interfere with its full activity. **FEET** Should be firm, round and catlike, not too large nor spreading or loose-jointed.

COAT On head, short and fine; on body, flat or slightly wavy and silky in texture. Should be of medium length with enough undercoating to give protection. The English Cocker should be well feathered but not so profusely as to hide the true lines or interfere with his field work.

FAULTS Muzzle too short or snipy, jaw overshot or undershot, lips snipy or pendulous, skull too flat or too rounded, cheeky or coarse; stop insufficient or exaggerated; light, round, or protruding eyes, conspicuous haw, ears set or carried too high, insufficiently feathered ears; short thick neck, dewlap or excessive throatiness; too long or too shallow chest, insufficient spring of rib, barrel rib; loose shoulders, elbows turned in or out, legs bowed or too close or too far apart; excessive angulation of hindquarters; white feet in self-colored specimens. ●

ENGLISH COCKER SPANIEL

346

Photo: S. A. Thompson, T. Fall.

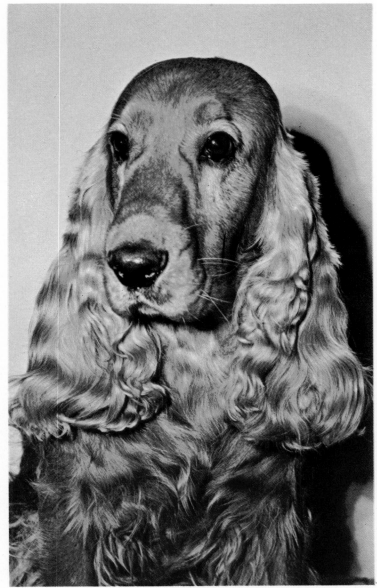

GOLDEN ENGLISH COCKER SPANIEL

BLACK AND RED ENGLISH COCKER SPANIEL

246 CLUMBER SPANIEL

GREAT BRITAIN

This dog gets his name from Clumber Castle in Nottingham-shire. Stonehenge believes that this breed comes originally from France and more specifically from the kennels of the Duke de Noailles who, in the reign of Louis XIV, is said to have offered two of these dogs to the Duke of Newcastle. These dogs then bred in great number. This is the longest, largest, and lowest slung of all spaniels. In England he is frequently employed in teams of five to ten dogs, which in practice take the place of beaters.

GENERAL CHARACTERISTICS Appearance should be that of a heavy, massive, but active dog with a thoughtful expression.

WEIGHT Males 55-70 lb; females 45-60 lb.

HEAD Large, square, and massive, of medium length, broad on top with a decided occiput; heavy brows with a deep stop; heavy muzzle with well-developed flew, level jaw and mouth. Nose square and flesh-colored. The mouth should be neither undershot nor overshot.

EYES Dark amber, slightly sunk. Full or light eyes are very objectionable.

EARS Large, shaped like a vine leaf, well covered with straight hair, hanging slightly forward; the feather should not extend below the leather.

NECK Fairly long, thick and powerful, well feathered underneath.

BODY Long and heavy, near the ground, with well-sprung ribs. Back straight, broad, and long.

TAIL Set low, well feathered and carried about level with the back.

FOREQUARTERS Shoulders strong, sloping and muscular; chest deep. Legs short, straight, thick and strong.

HINDQUARTERS Very powerful and well developed. Loin powerful, well let down in flank. Hocks low, stifles well bent, set straight. **FEET** Large and round, well covered with hair.

COAT Abundant, close, silky and straight; legs well feathered. **Color** Plain white, with lemon markings; orange permissible but not desirable; slight head markings and freckled muzzle, with white body preferred. ●

CLUMBER SPANIEL

347

CLUMBER SPANIEL

FIELD SPANIEL

247 FIELD SPANIEL
GREAT BRITAIN

This dog has the same origins as the Cocker with which he is often confused, although he is lower slung and more robust. Black spaniels, which were in style in 1900, are merely a variety of this breed as can be seen on the standard which admits different-colored specimens. The Field Spaniel is principally employed to hunt on hard ground. He barks on the trail but not as much as the Sussex.

GENERAL CHARACTERISTICS Appearance is that of a well-balanced, noble, upstanding sporting dog, built for activity and endurance, combining beauty and utility, and unusually docile.

WEIGHT AND SIZE Weight 35-50 lb. Height, approximately 18 inches at shoulder.

HEAD The head should be characteristic, like that of the Bulldog or the Bloodhound. Its very stamp and countenance should at once convey the impression of high breeding, character, and nobility. Skull well developed, with a distinct occipital protuberance, which gives the character mentioned above. Not too wide across the muzzle, long and lean, neither snipy nor squarely

348

Photo: S. A. Thompson, T. Fall.

cut, and in profile curving gradually from nose to throat. Lean beneath the eyes; thickness here gives coarseness to the whole head. The great length of muzzle gives surface for the free development of the olfactory nerve and thus secures the highest possible scenting powers. Nose well developed, with good open nostrils. Mouth level and strong, neither overshot nor undershot.

EYES Not too full, but not small, receding, or overhung; color, dark hazel or brown, or nearly black according to the color of the coat. Grave in expression showing no haw.

EARS Moderately long and wide, sufficiently clad with nice setterlike feather and set low. They should fall in graceful folds, the lower parts curling inward and backward.

NECK Long, strong, and muscular to enable the dog to retrieve game without undue fatigue.

BODY Should be of moderate length, well ribbed up to a good strong loin, straight or slightly arched, never slack. The chest deep and well developed but not too round and wide. Back and loins very strong and muscular.

TAIL Well set on and carried low, if possible below the level of the back, in a straight line or with a slight downward inclination, never elevated above the back, and in action always kept low, nicely fringed with wavy feather of silky texture.

FOREQUARTERS The shoulders should be long and sloping and well set back, thus giving great activity and speed. The forelegs should be of fairly good length, with straight, clean, flat bone and nicely feathered. Immense bone is not desirable. **HINDQUARTERS** Strong and muscular. The stifles should be moderately bent and not twisted either in or out. **FEET** Not too small; round, with short, soft hair between the toes; good strong pads.

COAT Flat or slightly waved, never curled. Sufficiently dense to resist the weather and not too short. Silky in texture, glossy and refined without duffleness, curliness, or wiriness. On the chest, under the belly, and behind the legs there should be abundant feather, but never too much, especially below the hocks, and the feather should be of the right type, i.e., setterlike. **Color** The Field Spaniel should be self-colored, black, liver, golden liver, mahogany, red, roan, or any of these colors but with tan over the eyes and on the cheeks, feet, and pasterns. Other colors, such as black and white, liver and white, red or orange and white, etc., are to be considered a fault, although not a disqualification. ●

248 IRISH WATER SPANIEL

GREAT BRITAIN

His rather obscure origin is not very old; in fact, the Irish Water Spaniel was probably created after 1800. Some authorities maintain that he comes from a cross between the Poodle and the Irish Setter, the Poodle having given him his coat, his intelligence, his perseverance, and his great love for the water (in describing the Poodle, we will tell how he was formerly used in France to hunt ducks); and the Irish Setter having given him other valuable qualities along with his determination and the color of his coat.

GENERAL CHARACTERISTICS The peculiar gait of the Irish Water Spaniel differs from that of any other spaniel. In general appearance, the Irish Water Spaniel is a gun dog bred for work in all types of shooting and particularly suited for wildfowling. His fitness for this purpose should be evident in his appearance. He is a strongly built, compact dog, intelligent, enduring and eager.

WEIGHT AND SIZE Males 55-65 lb; females 45-58 lb. Height; males 22-24 inches; females 21-23 inches.

HEAD The head should be of good size, the skull high in dome, of good length, and sufficiently wide to allow adequate brain capacity. The muzzle should be long, strong, and rather square, with a gradual stop. The face should be smooth, the skull covered with long curls in the form of a pronounced topknot growing in a well-defined peak to a point between the eyes. Nose large and well developed, dark liver in color. There should be an impression of fineness. The teeth should be regular and meet in a normal bite.

EYES Comparatively small, medium to dark brown in color, bright and alert.

EARS Very long and lobe-shaped in the leather, low set, hanging close to

IRISH WATER SPANIEL

IRISH WATER SPANIEL

the cheeks and covered with long twisted curls.

NECK Strongly set into the shoulders, powerful, arching, and long enough to carry the head well above the level of the back. The back and sides of the neck should be covered with curls similar to those on the body. The throat should be smooth, with the smooth hair forming a V-shaped patch from the back of the lower jaw to the breast bone.

BODY Should be of good size. The back short, broad and level, strongly coupled to the hindquarters; ribs carried well back; loins deep and wide. The body as a whole should be so proportioned as to give a barrel-shaped appearance accentuated by the springing of the ribs.

TAIL Peculiar to the breed, the tail should be short and straight, thick at the root and tapering to a fine point. It should be set low, carried straight and below the level of the back; in length it should not reach the hock joint; 3 to 4 inches of the tail at the root should be covered by dense curls that end abruptly; the remainder should be bare or covered with straight fine hairs.

FOREQUARTERS The shoulders should be powerful and sloping. The chest deep and of large girth, with ribs so well sprung behind the shoulders as to give a barrel-shaped appearance to the body but with normal width and curvature between the forelegs. The forelegs should be well boned and straight, with arms well let down and carrying the forearm at elbow and knee in a straight line with the point of the shoulder. **HINDQUARTERS** Powerful, with long, well bent stifles and hocks set low. **FEET** Should be large, round and spreading; well covered with hair over and between the toes.

COAT Should be composed of dense, tight, crisp ringlets and free from woolliness. The hair should have a natural oiliness. The forelegs covered with feather in curls or ringlets down to the feet. The feather should be abundant all around, though shorter in front so as to give a rough appearance. Below the hocks the hind legs should be smooth in front but feathered behind down to the feet. **Color** A rich dark liver having the purplish tint or bloom peculiar to the breed and sometimes referred to as puce-liver. ●

349

ENGLISH SPRINGER SPANIEL

ENGLISH SPRINGER SPANIEL

249 ENGLISH SPRINGER SPANIEL

GREAT BRITAIN

This is a very ancient breed and represents the stock from which, except for the Clumber, all English hunting spaniels descended.

Originally he flushed and raised game for his master's net, the falcon, or the Greyhound. Today he is employed exclusively to flush and bring the game back to the hunter armed with a gun. The Springer has a characteristic gait: foremembers whose motion comes from the shoulder, moves in line with it; the feet are brought back under the trunk, and the action of the rear members is synchronized with that of the front. When many Springers move slowly they seem to amble, a feature typical of this breed.

Photo: S. A. Thompson.

ENGLISH SPRINGER SPANIEL PUPS

Photo: L. H. Newman.

ENGLISH SPRINGER SPANIEL

GENERAL CHARACTERISTICS The general appearance of the modern Springer is that of a symmetrical, compact, strong, upstanding, merry and active dog, built for endurance and activity. He is the highest on the leg and raciest in build of all land spaniels.

WEIGHT AND SIZE Weight of the Springer should approximate 50 lb; height should approximate 20 inches.

HEAD The skull should be of medium length and fairly broad and slightly rounded, rising from the foreface and making a brow or stop, divided by a fluting between the eyes which gradually vanishes along the forehead toward the occipital bone, which should not be peaked. The cheeks should be flat, that is, not rounded nor full. The foreface should be of proportionate length to the skull, fairly broad and deep and square in flow, but not exaggerated to such an extent as would interfere with comfort when retrieving. Nostrils well developed, underjaw strong, and level mouth, that is, neither overshot nor undershot.

EYES Neither too full nor too small but of medium size, not prominent nor sunken but well set in (not showing haw), of an alert, kind expression. A mouselike eye without expression is objectionable, as also is a light eye. The color should be dark hazel.

EARS Lobe-shaped, set close to the head, of good length and width, but not exaggerated. The correct set should be in a line with the eye.

NECK Should be strong and muscular, of nice length and free from throatiness, well set in the shoulders, nicely arched and tapering toward the head, this making for great activity and speed. A ewe neck is objectionable.

BODY Strong and of proportionate length, neither too long nor too short, the chest deep and well developed, with plenty of heart and lung room, well-sprung ribs, strong and muscular loins, and with a slight arch and well coupled; the thighs should be broad and muscular and well developed.

TAIL The stern should be low and never carried above the level of the back, well feathered and with lively action.

FOREQUARTERS The forelegs should be straight and nicely feathered, elbows set well to body and with proportionate substance to carry the body; pasterns should be strong and flexible.
HINDQUARTERS The hind legs should be well let down from hip to hocks. Stifles and hocks moderately bent, inclining neither inward nor outward. Coarseness of hocks objectionable.
FEET Tight, compact, well rounded, with strong, full pads.

COAT The coat should be close, straight, and weather-resistant without being coarse. **Color** Any recognized land spaniel color is acceptable, but liver and white, black and white, or either with tan markings is preferred. ●

352

250 SUSSEX SPANIEL
GREAT BRITAIN

In the spaniel group the Sussex occupies an intermediate position between the Clumber and the Cocker. He is a native of England and particularly of the county of Sussex, as indicated by his name. Until recently he was quite prevalent in the south of the country; but today, although he is a proven hunter, with an excellent sense of smell, great endurance, an ardent hunter and intelligent, he is eschewed by hunters because of the color of his coat, which is too easily lost against the terrain. Although his origins are very old he obtained official recognition only in 1885.

He is quiet while resting, but when working he is lively and active, skillful in hunting over relatively easy terrain.

SUSSEX SPANIEL

GENERAL CHARACTERISTICS Massive and strongly built. An active, energetic, strong dog, whose characteristic movement is a decided roll, unlike that of any other spaniel.

WEIGHT AND SIZE Ideal weight: male 45 lb; female 40 lb. Height: 15-16 inches for both.

HEAD The skull should be wide and show a moderate curve from ear to ear, neither flat nor apple-headed, with center indentation and a pronounced stop. Occiput decided but not pointed. Nostrils well developed and liver colored. A well-balanced head. Mouth strong and level, neither overshot nor undershot, with a scissors bite.

EYES Hazel, fairly large, not too full, with a soft expression; haw not overly apparent.

EARS Thick, fairly large and lobe-shaped, set moderately low but above eye level. Should lie closely; hair soft and wavy, but not too profuse.

NECK Long, strong and slightly arched, not carrying the head much above the level of the back. Not much throatiness but with a well-marked frill.

BODY Chest deep and well developed, neither too round nor too wide. Back and loin well developed and muscular, both in width and in depth. The back ribs must be deep. Whole body should be strong and level with no hint of "waistiness."

TAIL Set low and not carried above level of the back. Free-actioned, thickly clothed with hair but without feather. Docked—5-7 inches in length.

FOREQUARTERS The shoulders should be sloping and free, with the arms well boned as well as muscular. Knees large and strong, pasterns short and well boned. Legs rather short and strong, moderately well feathered.
HINDQUARTERS The thighs must be strongly boned as well as muscular; hocks large and strong, legs rather short and strong with good bone, moderately well feathered. The hind legs should not appear shorter than the forelegs or be excessively bent at the hocks so as to give a setterlike appearance, which is objectionable. The hind legs should be well feathered above the hocks, but without much hair below the hocks. **FEET** Circular, well padded, well feathered between toes.

COAT Abundant and flat, with no tendency to curl, and ample undercoat for weather resistance. **Color** Rich golden liver, with hair shading to gold at the tips, the gold predominating. Dark liver or puce is objectionable. ●

SUSSEX SPANIEL

SPANIEL IN ACTION

251 AMERICAN COCKER SPANIEL

UNITED STATES

This breed was attained in the United States through conscientious selective breeding, with the English Cocker Spaniel as a base. The American Cocker differs from him in certain physical characteristics such as the size, color of coat, ears, etc. The American Cocker has always been popular. He is affectionate and faithful, even more so than his English counterpart. He adapts easily to family life and is considered one of the finest pet dogs. Nevertheless, on the hunting ground he proves himself to be a good hunter. He conducts a persistent search and is quite resistant to fatigue.

GENERAL CHARACTERISTICS A highly attractive dog with finely chiseled head, standing on straight legs and well up at the shoulders, of compact body and wide, muscular quarters. The Cocker Spaniel's sturdy body, powerful quarters and strong well-boned legs show him to be capable of considerable speed combined with great endurance. Above all he must be free and merry, sound, well balanced throughout, and in action show a keen inclination to work; equable in temperament with no suggestion of timidity.

HEIGHT The ideal height at the withers for an adult dog should be 15 inches; for an adult female, 14 inches. The maximum height at the withers for a male is 15½ inches; for a female, 14½ inches. A male or female whose height exceeds the specified maximum shall be disqualified. **NB:** Height is determined by a line perpendicular to the ground from the top of the shoulder blades, the dog standing naturally with forelegs and lower hind legs parallel to the line of measurement.

HEAD Well developed and rounded with no tendency to flatness or pronounced roundness of the crown (dome). The forehead smooth, the eyebrows and stop clearly defined, the median line distinctly marked and gradually disappearing until lost somewhat more than halfway up to the crown. The bony structure surrounding the socket of the eye should be well chiseled; there should be no suggestion of fullness under the eyes or prominence in the cheeks which, like the sides of the muzzle, should present a smooth, clean-cut appearance. To attain a well-proportioned head, which above all

should be in balance with the rest of the dog, the distance from the tip of the nose to the stop, at a line drawn across the top of the muzzle between the front corners of the eyes, should approximate half the distance from the stop at this point up over the crown to the base of the skull. The muzzle should be broad and deep, with square, even jaws. The upper lip should be of sufficient depth to cover the lower jaw, presenting a square appearance. The teeth should be sound and regular and set at right angles to the jaw. The relation of the upper teeth to the lower should be that of scissors, with the inner surface of the upper in contact with the outer surface of the lower when the jaws are closed. The nose of sufficient size to balance the muzzle and foreface, with well-developed nostrils, and black in the blacks and black and tans; in the reds, buffs, livers, particolors and roans, it may be black or brown, the darker coloring being preferable.

EYES The eyeballs should be round and full and set in the surrounding tissue to look directly forward and give the eye a slightly almond-shaped appearance. The eye should be neither weak nor goggled. The expression should be intelligent, alert, soft and appealing. The color of the iris should be dark brown to black in the blacks, black and tans, buffs, and creams, and in the darker shades of the particolors and roans. In the reds, dark hazel; in the livers, particolors and roans of the lighter shades, not lighter than hazel and the darker the better.

EARS Lobular, set on a line no higher than the lower part of the eye, the leather fine and extending to the nostrils, well clothed with long, silky, straight or wavy hair.

NECK The neck sufficiently long to allow the nose to reach the ground easily, muscular and free from pendulous "throatiness." It should rise

strongly from the shoulders and arch slightly as it tapers to join the head.

BODY Its height at the withers should approximate the length from the withers to the set-on of tail. The chest deep, its lowest point no higher than the elbows, its front sufficiently wide for adequate heart and lung space, yet not so wide as to interfere with straightforward movement of the forelegs. Ribs deep and well sprung throughout. Body short in the couplings and flank, with its depth at the flank somewhat less than at the last rib. Back strong and sloping evenly and slightly downward from the withers to the set-on of tail. Hips wide with quarters well rounded and muscular. The body should appear short, compact and firmly knit together, giving the impression of strength.

TAIL Set on and carried on a line with the topline of the back; when the dog is at work, its action should be incessant.

FOREQUARTERS The shoulders deep, clean-cut and sloping without protrusion and so set that the upper points of the withers are at an angle which permits a wide spring of rib. Forelegs straight, strongly boned and muscular, and set close to the body well under the scapulae. The elbows well let down and turning neither in nor out. The pasterns short and strong. **HINDQUARTERS** The hind legs strongly boned and muscled with well-turned stifles and powerful, clearly defined thighs. The hocks strong, well let down and parallel both in motion and at rest. **FEET** Compact, not spreading, round and firm, with deep, horny pads and hair between the toes; they should turn neither in nor out.

COAT On head, short and fine. On body, flat or slightly wavy (never curly), silky in texture, of medium length, with enough undercoating to give protection. The ears, chest, ab-

Photo: R. Kinne (Photo Res.), Palnic, S. A. Thompson.

AMERICAN COCKER SPANIEL

domen and posterior sides of the legs should be well feathered, but not so excessively as to hide the Cocker Spaniel's true lines and movement or affect his appearance and function as a sporting dog. Excessive coat or feathering shall be penalized. **Color** Blacks should be jet black; shadings of brown or liver in the sheen of the coat shall not disqualify but shall be penalized. A small amount of white on the chest and throat shall not disqualify, but shall be penalized; however, white in any other place shall disqualify. Solid colors other than black should be of a sound shade. Lighter color of the feathering, while not favored, does not disqualify.

In particolor dogs, two definite colors appearing in clearly defined markings, distinctively distributed over the body, are essential. Primary color which is 90 percent or more of the specimen shall disqualify; secondary colors which are limited solely to one location shall disqualify. Roans are classified as particolors and may be of the accepted roan patterns of mottled appearance or alternating colors of the hairs throughout the whole coat. Black and tan, shown under the variety of "any solid color other than black," should have definite tan markings on a jet black body, with clearly defined lines between the two colors. The tan markings should be distinct and plainly visible, and the shade of the tan markings may be from the lightest cream to the darkest red. The quantity and location of the tan markings are the essence of this description. The amount of tan markings is restricted to 10 percent or less of the color of the specimen; tan markings in excess of 10 percent shall disqualify. A mere semblance of tan markings at the specified locations does not disqualify, but is severely penalized; the total absence of tan markings at any of the specified locations shall disqualify. The marking should be located as follows: (1) A clear spot over each eye; (2) on the sides of the muzzle and on the cheeks; (3) on the undersides of the ears; (4) on all feet and legs; and extend upward toward the knees and (5) under the tail. Tan on the muzzle which extends up and over and joins, or tan on the cheeks which is solid, or tan on the feet which does not extend upward toward the knees and

hock joints does not disqualify, but is penalized. Black hairs and penciling on the tan markings are not penalized, but tan markings which are "brindled" are penalized. A small amount of white on the chest and throat does not disqualify, but is penalized. However, white in any other location shall disqualify.

DISQUALIFICATIONS Color and markings: Blacks, white markings except on chest and throat; particolors, 90 percent or more of primary color, secondary color or colors limited solely to one location: black and tans, tan markings in excess of 10 percent; total absence of tan markings at any of the specified locations; white markings except on chest and throat. Height: males over 15½ inches, females over 14½ inches.

SCALE OF POINTS

Skull	8
Muzzle	10
Teeth	4
Eyes	6
Ears	3
Neck and shoulders	15
Body	15
Legs	9
Feet	6
Stern	3
Coat	6
Color and markings	3
Action	12
	100

WELSH SPRINGER SPANIEL

AMERICAN COCKER SPANIEL

252 WELSH SPRINGER SPANIEL
GREAT BRITAIN

In all probability the Welsh Springer Spaniel was developed by selective breeding, using other breeds of spaniels with the aim of obtaining a dog skillful in hunting on Welsh terrain.

GENERAL CHARACTERISTICS A symmetrical, compact, strong, merry, very active dog; not stilty; obviously built for endurance and hard work. A quick and active mover, displaying plenty of push and drive.

WEIGHT AND SIZE Weight: 34-45 lb; height: male not to exceed 19 inches, female not to exceed 18 inches.

HEAD Skull proportionate, of moderate length, slightly domed, with clearly defined stop and well chiseled below the eyes. Muzzle of medium length, straight, fairly square; the nostrils well developed and flesh-colored or dark. A short chubby head is objectionable. Strong jaws, neither undershot nor overshot.

EYES Hazel or dark, medium in size, not prominent nor sunken; no haw visible.

EARS Set moderately low and hanging close to the cheeks, comparatively small and gradually narrowing toward the tip; shaped somewhat like a vine leaf, covered with setterlike feathering.

NECK Long and muscular, clean in throat, neatly set into long, sloping shoulders.

BODY Not long; strong and muscular, with deep brisket, well-sprung ribs; length of body should be proportionate to length of leg and very well balanced; muscular loin slightly arched and well coupled up.

TAIL Well set on and low, never carried above the level of the back; lightly feathered and lively in action.

FOREQUARTERS Forelegs of medium length, straight, well boned, moderately feathered. **HINDQUARTERS** Strong and muscular, wide and fully developed with deep second thighs. Hind legs and hocks well let down; stifles moderately bent (neither twisted in nor out), moderately feathered. **FEET** Round, with thick pads. Firm and catlike, not too large or spreading.

COAT Straight or flat and thick, of a nice silky texture, never wiry nor wavy. A curly coat is highly objectionable. **Color** Rich red and white only.

FAULTS Coarse skull, light bone, long or curly coat, bad shoulders, poor movement. ●

253 AMERICAN WATER SPANIEL
UNITED STATES

Although not an ancient breed, the American Water Spaniel is of uncertain origin. Experts set his place of origin in the American Middle West. The color and type of his coat and his physical conformation suggest that he is a descendant of the Irish Water Spaniel and the Curly-Coated Retriever.

The American Kennel Club officially recognized the breed in 1940. For years the American Water Spaniel has been considered an excellent hunting dog. He is much esteemed for his work in the water. He is steady in the stop, but once the game has been flushed he acts like a Springer in raising it.

Today the breeding of the American Water Sapniel is carried out by a special American association with the principal aim of refining certain physical points without changing the extraordinary psychic qualities of the breed.

GENERAL CHARACTERISTICS Medium in size, of sturdy, spaniel character, with a curly coat; an active, muscular dog, with emphasis on proper size and conformation, correct head properties, texture of coat and color. The American Water Spaniel is of amicable disposition, and his demeanor indicates intelligence, strength and endurance.

WEIGHT AND SIZE Weight: males 28-45 lb; females 25-40 lb. Height at the shoulder: 15-18 inches.

BODY Well developed, sturdily constructed but not too compactly coupled. General outline is a symmetrical relationship of parts. Shoulders sloping, clean and muscular. Strong loins, lightly arched, and well furnished, deep brisket but not excessively broad. Well-sprung ribs. Legs of medium length and well boned, but not so short as to handicap for field work. **Legs and Feet** Forelegs powerful and reasonably straight. Hind legs firm with suitably bent stifles and strong hocks well let down. Feet to harmonize with size of dog. Toes closely grouped and well padded. **Tail** Moderate in length, curved in a slightly rocker shape, carried slightly below level of back; tapered and covered with hair to tip, action lively.

COAT The coat should be closely curled or have marcel effect; it should be of sufficient density to protect against weather, water, or punishing cover, yet not coarse. Legs should have medium short, curly feather. **Color** Solid liver or dark chocolate, a little white on toes or chest permissible.

HEAD Moderate in length, skull rather broad and full, stop moderately defined but not too pronounced. Forehead covered with short smooth hair and without tuft or topknot. Muzzle of medium length, square and with no inclination to snipiness; jaws strong and of good length, neither undershot nor overshot; teeth straight and well shaped. Nose sufficiently wide and with well-developed nostrils to ensure good scenting power. **Eyes** Hazel, brown or of dark tone to harmonize with coat; set well apart. Expression alert, attractive, intelligent. **Ears** Lobular, long and wide, not set too high on head, but slightly above the eyeline. Leather extending to end of nose and well covered with close curls. **Neck** Round and of medium length, strong and muscular, free of throatiness, set to carry head with dignity, but arch not accentuated.

FAULTS Cow hocks; rat tail or shaved tail; coat too straight, soft, fine or slightly kinked; very flat skull.

DISQUALIFICATION Yellow eyes. ●

WELSH SPRINGER SPANIEL

AMERICAN WATER SPANIEL

Photo: S. A. Thompson, T. Fall, M. Pedone.

PET DOGS

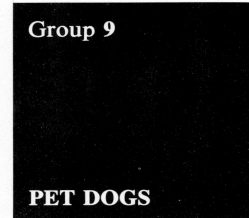

Group 9

PET DOGS

PLAYMATE

AFFENPINSCHER

254 AFFENPINSCHER
GERMANY

In his country of origin this dog is also called "Zwergaffenpinscher" (*zwerg* means "dwarf" and *affen* means "monkey"); in France he is sometimes called "diablotin moustachu" (small-moustached devil)—a name that fits him very well. It is difficult to establish the origins of the first typical specimen. Some believe that the breed is a miniaturization of the Zwergschnauzer (a small German coarsehaired terrier), while others think that he is linked to the Belgian Griffon, and still others hold that the Affenpinscher is the source of the Griffon. In any case, the most logical hypothesis is perhaps the first, since the other theories lose much of their value if one considers that the conformation of the skull and the other characteristics of the Affenpinscher are typical of terriers and not of Griffons. The origin, however, is clearly German.

He is very gentle and affectionate, despite what is sometimes said about him; a great ratter (the terrier strain), and he is also, in spite of his small size, an excellent watchdog.

GENERAL CHARACTERISTICS A small, lively, intelligent dog, hairy, mustached and bearded, well constructed. He is of the terrier type, with many terrier characteristics in addition to the typical terrier skull.

SIZE Height, 10-11 inches.

HEAD Large, round, with a rounded skull. The head is covered with long, coarse hair, irregular and tangled, with an abundant mustache and sizable beard. The expression is rather monkeylike. The nose is short and well feathered, as is the entire face. The muzzle is short and strong. The jaws are of unequal length, the lower being the longer; yet the teeth must not be visible. The stop is pronounced.

EYES The eyes are round, large, prominent, dark in color and with an intelligent expression. The eyelids are well penciled with black, the brows are bushy, but they must not hang down over the eyes.

EARS Invariably set on straight, the ears are pointed and set rather far apart. They are clad in thick short hair.

NECK Exceptionally short and well arched.

BODY Compact and well built. The chest is quite broad, the back is straight, the belly is only slightly drawn up.

TAIL Invariably docked to two thirds of its length; it should be carried high. The hair on the tail is shorter than on the body.

FOREQUARTERS AND HINDQUARTERS The legs are of medium length, straight and well boned. They should be well covered with hair. The feet are short and round, with arched toes which are well feathered.

COAT Long, dense, hard and coarse to the touch, very dry and without glossiness. The undercoat is soft and slightly curled. **Color** Grayish black, bluish gray, yellow-red with numerous variations in shading. Light-colored dogs often have a black mask. ●

AFFENPINSCHER

359

HARLEQUIN PINSCHER

255 HARLEQUIN PINSCHER

Harlekinpinscher

GERMANY

This dog has the same origins as the German Shorthaired Pinscher. He is somewhat smaller and, according to the standard, his ideal size is between the Great Pinscher and the Dwarf Pinscher.

GENERAL CHARACTERISTICS With a square but not stocky outline, the Harlequin Pinscher is lean and muscular, with an agile body; he is quick in his movements, his whole appearance lively and alert. An ideal house dog in crowded quarters such as a city apartment, he is affectionate and obliging.
SIZE The ideal height is between that of the Standard Pinscher and the Miniature Pinscher, i.e., about 12-14 inches.
HEAD The head should be in good proportion to the structure of the body, neither long and narrow nor short and broad, and with good features. The skull and muzzle must be in good proportion to each other, with the former broad and full and merging with the latter to form a harmonious whole. The nose is black. The teeth are good and if possible should be a full complement. Overshot or undershot jaw, if the condition is pronounced, is a fault. An excessively robust skull ending in a short, narrow muzzle is also a fault.
EYES Well set and adequately proportioned to the shape and size. They must not be too full or round, nor should they be too small or too slanted. They should be as dark as possible but of a shade harmoniz-

ing well with the color of the coat and not spoil the pleasant and affectionate expression natural to the breed.
EARS Small, carried erect, with the tips either barely folded over or wholly erect.
NECK Lean and without dewlap, the neck is broad at the point of insertion into the shoulders and slightly arched at the nape.
BODY Sufficiently robust to provide a good base for the shoulders and upper arms. The ribs are not overly sprung and are rather flat. The back is sturdy and powerful, with well-developed loins terminating uniformly in the tail. The belly line is moderately tucked up from the belly to the groin.
TAIL Set on high and carried high and straight. In most dogs it is docked short.
FOREQUARTERS AND HINDQUARTERS Regular throughout their entire length. The forelegs are straight, rather flat at the wrist and pastern. The hind legs are well angulated, parallel and freely moving.
COAT Short and flat, dense, close-fitting and glossy. It covers the body uniformly. **Color** White or light coat with markings; gray with black or dark markings; streaked, with or without tan markings. ●

256 KROMFOHRLÄNDER

GERMANY

GENERAL CHARACTERISTICS An elegant dog, of medium size, faithful, devoted and vigilant. The length of the trunk is slightly more than the height at the withers. There are three varieties, distinguished by different qualities of the coat: the shorthaired rough coat, the rough coat and the longhaired rough coat. Of these, the most desirable is the one with the rough coat covering a robust body. He is used as a companion, a house dog, a guard dog, and for defense.
SIZE Height at the withers: 15-18 inches (males and females).

HEAD Seen in profile the head appears long, but seen from above it appears wedge-shaped and of medium width. The muzzle is of medium size.
Nose Of medium size, well open, black; a brown nose is accepted but is not desirable. **Nasal bridge** Straight, moderately broad, rounded at the tip of the nose. **Lips** Close-fitting and not excessively large; the commissure is well closed and black. **Jaws** Meeting well, with no prominence in cheeks. A scissors bite is preferred; a pincers bite is acceptable but not desirable. The stop is well

KROMFOHRLANDER

defined. **Skull** Flat, slightly rounded, without a prominent forehead and with the medial furrow barely visible; the head is in good proportion to the overall size of the body; the occipital protuberance is not pronounced.
EYES Dark eyes are preferable and may even be deep brown; light eyes are undesirable. The eyes are oval and of medium size, somewhat slanted.
EARS Set on high, of medium thickness, triangular, with rounded tips. They fit flat against the head and should not be like those of a terrier. Ears carried on the side and slightly flapping are admissible.
NECK Sloped, the neck is slightly arched and without dewlap. Its length is half the length of the back, of moderate thickness and rounded, with good muscling at the point of insertion. The skin is close-fitting, with no folds or wrinkles.
FOREQUARTERS Seen from in front, the forequarters are vertical and always in good proportion to the overall size of the dog. **Shoulders** Moderately long, in good proportion to the size of the dog, very muscular and sloping. **Upper arm** Well muscled and approximately of the same length as the scapula, with which it forms a right angle. **Forearm** A little longer than the upper arm; it should be perpendicular at the elbows and well muscled; the bone is of sufficient strength for the structure of the body. In females the bone is normally lighter. **Angulation of the elbows** Slightly open, if not actually a right angle. **Wrist** Well developed, not too massive. **Pasterns** The length of the pasterns is 1/3 that of the forearm. They are of moderate size and inclined slightly backward (never in the position seen in the Fox Terrier). **Feet** Slightly arched, with well-closed toes, with strong and preferably black nails. The pads are well developed and dark in color. Light nails are not a fault and are accepted.
BODY Rather long and harmonious in its proportions. The brisket is at elbow level, the thorax is roomy and deep; the ribs are moderately sprung. The sternum is slightly accentuated. **Withers** Well in evidence, joining the neck smoothly. **Back** Powerful within proper limits, slightly narrowing toward the loins, which are well developed and slightly raised. **Croup** Slightly sloping toward the tail, moderately broad and well muscled.

Belly From the brisket the belly merges harmoniously into the well-developed loins; it is slightly drawn up.
TAIL Of medium length, the tail is carried with a slight curve or even curled. Thick at the root, it tapers toward the tip. It is well supplied with hair, which should match the coat.
HINDQUARTERS Seen from behind, the hind legs should be vertical to the ground, with the hocks turning neither in nor out; they are robust and in good proportion to the rest of the dog. **Thigh** Muscular and well angulated, about the same length as the forearm. It is slanted from the back forward, in the same direction as the elbow. **Haunches** Not too open. **Legs** Muscular, robust in the bone. **Leg joints** The legs should form an angle varying from obtuse to right angle with the thighs; the same is true for the articulation of the stifle. **Articulation of the hocks** More or less angulated, depending on how the dog is posed; it should, however, be robust and developed in good proportion. **Metatarsus** Similar to the pastern. **Feet** The hind feet should be free of dewclaws; otherwise they are similar to the forefeet.
COAT From short and rough to long and rough; preferably a rough coat of medium length which, being thick, is easily kept clean. There is an undercoat. **Color** The basic color is white, with markings ranging from light brown to dark brown on the head, or the head is brown with a white star. The more regular the markings on the head, the better. On the body there are large markings forming a saddle (and it is better if such markings are separate rather than forming an uninterrupted area). **Skin** Close-fitting, without visible folds or wrinkles. The pigmentation of the skin may vary with the color of the coat.
FAULTS Brown markings too pale, lack of markings on back; asymmetrical markings on the head which harm the dog's expression; light eyes (dogs with this fault merit the rating "Very Good" only if they are of exceptional build and appearance).
DISQUALIFICATIONS Missing teeth (more than 2 molars or more than 3 premolars); slanting teeth or irregular incisors; overshot or undershot condition; monorchidism or cryptorchidism. ●

257 PINSCHER

GERMANY

The origins of this dog go far back in time, as is proven by many ancient drawings. Today, however, specimens of this breed have become somewhat rare. At the beginning of the present century there began to appear among litters coarsehaired

Photo: A. Wintzell.

PINSCHER

and shorthaired specimens with coats of various kinds. The club then decided that no shorthaired specimen would be entered if it did not descend from at least three generations of shorthaired dogs. The *Book of Origins* does not accept specimens which do not fulfill these conditions. This selective breeding gave such effective results that today one rarely sees specimens of the two varieties within the same litter.

GENERAL CHARACTERISTICS The Pinscher is an extremely mobile dog, with a very elegant and sober general appearance. He is of medium size and square build, with robust muscling and a good deal of tendon. His anatomy and characteristic qualities are similar to those of the Schnauzer. He is courageous and attentive, although his disposition is docile; he is an excellent guard dog for the house, the barnyard, the automobile and his master's property. He is highly suspicious of strangers. His hair is short and clean, and these factors help to make him an excellent dog for city apartment living. His requirements are modest.

SIZE 15¾-19 inches. The lower figure is for females, the higher for males.

HEAD Long, narrow, flat on the underside, with a slight stop. The total length of the head is approximately half that of the back. The bridge is straight; the upper cranial-facial axes are parallel. Any tendency toward filled out or heavy cheeks is undesirable, and the absence of a stop is a fault. Other faults include a short, pointed muzzle and a big, wide skull. The teeth are normal and close in a vigorous scissors bite.

EYES Dark, of medium size, full and oval in shape. A small, slanting terrier eye is a fault.

EARS Set on high, docked according to regulations.

NECK Long, nobly arched, lean; it is robust at the nape.

BODY Square in build. The ribs are flat, the thorax is deep and moderately broad. The chest is well developed. The belly is moderately drawn up. The build of the Pinscher, with its fine muscling which is visible beneath the short coat, gives the dog a rather more noble appearance than the Schnauzer. Good construction of the trunk is to be greatly valued in judging. Weak details constitute faults, as do those that are too massive.

TAIL Set on high, of medium size, carried vertically, docked at the third joint.

FOREQUARTERS The shoulders should be sloping; serious faults include straight shoulders, a terrier front, forelegs close together. The forearm and the pastern are as straight as a column. **HINDQUARTERS** Good angulations in the hindquarters give the Pinscher a long, elastic gait. A jumpy or rigid gait is a fault. **FEET** Small, round compact catfeet, with well-closed, curved toes.

COAT Short, hard to the touch, strong, smooth, glossy, close-fitting to the body, which is entirely covered. **Color** Black, with the more tan markings the better; solid black; roebuck brown to stag red; brown; chocolate; blue-gray with red to yellow markings; silver gray (salt and pepper).

N.B. For other details see the standard for Schnauzer, with appropriate modifications. ●

PINSCHER

Photo: S. A. Thompson, E. Münch.

258 GREAT SPITZ
GERMANY

The basic stock must be sought in the Peatbog Dog (*canis familiaris palustris*) whose fossils from Neolithic times indicate characteristics very similar to those of the present day Spitz. It is quite difficult to establish the center from which the breed spread inasmuch as remains of dogs similar to the present Spitz are found in great numbers among prehistoric remains in the Asiatic north, south, and east, in the Pacific Islands as far west as Madagascar; and Max Siber has even found some in the interior of Africa. Keller has identified the type of Spitz in Egyptian drawings from the time of the pharaohs. Kraemer has found contemporaneous representations in ancient Mycenae in Greece and also in Italy, and further osteological remains have been discovered in the Celtic settlement of Siggenthal and the Roman colony of Vindonissa. Many naturalists have identified in the most varied locations remains which indicate that the Spitz was prevalent everywhere.

Although the Peatbog dog gave birth to various breeds that are more or less different from the primitive breed, only the Spitz has preserved his original characteristics just as they were depicted in ancient artifacts.

The two types of German Spitz, large and small (Grossspitz and Kleinspitz) differ among themselves only in size with all the other characteristics being similar.

GENERAL CHARACTERISTICS The Spitz has an extraordinarily beautiful coat, sustained by an abundant undercoat. Around the neck there is a rich mane. The head is similar to that of the fox, with bright, intelligent eyes, small, pointed ears which are set on rather close together, and a tail which is dashingly curled over the back forming a huge hairy bush. These details give the Spitz its typical courageous and vivacious expression. There

GREAT SPITZ

are many qualities which have made the Spitz popular as a guard dog and companion; these include his mistrust of strangers, his absolute faithfulness, his total lack of interest in the vagabond life or the wild life and, not least, his proverbial vigilance.

HEAD Of medium size and, seen from above, with a broad skull which narrows like a wedge to the tip of the nose. The nose is round and small and preferably flat. Its color should be pure black; in the brown Spitz it should be dark brown. The lips should not overlap, nor should they be wrinkled at the commissure. The color of the lips and of the eyelids is black in the white Spitz. The muzzle is not too long and should be in good proportion to the upper part of the head and to the length of the forehead. Seen from the side, the head shows a fairly accentuated stop.

EYES Of medium size, rather long, set in with a slight slant, invariably dark.

EARS Small and pointed, set on very close together (the ears should be as close together as possible). They are triangular, set on very high and always carried erect, with rigid tips.

NECK Of medium length.

BODY The back should be as short as possible, completely straight, but sloping from the withers to the croup. The chest is well let down, the ribs well sprung; the belly is moderately tucked up.

TAIL Of medium length, naturally perpendicular at the root and bent forward over the back, then turned laterally to right or left, thus taking the form of a circle lying close to the back or curled directly over the back.

FOREQUARTERS AND HINDQUARTERS Of medium length, in comparison with the overall dimensions of the body. On the hindquarters the hocks are only very slightly bent. The feet should be as small as possible, rounded and with curved toes (cat-feet). Dewclaws should be removed within 3 or 4 days after birth.

COAT The hair is thick and short on the muzzle, ears, feet, outer and inner sides of the forelegs and hind legs. The rest of the body is covered with abundant long hair. The characteristic feature of the Spitz's hair is that, on the neck and around the shoulders, it stands away from the body, soft and smooth, without matting or curling. On the back the hair is not parted but broadens out softly and freely along the whole body. The greatest length is at the throat and on the tail. The back side of the forelegs has a well-developed fringe from the elbows to the wrists. On the hind legs the fringe does not quite completely cover the hocks, so that the bottom part down to the feet is shorthaired.

COLOR VARIANCE Wolfsspitz: The Wolfsspitz is silver gray, with almost black coloring on the points of each single hair. The hair on the muzzle, the area around the eyes, the legs, the belly and the tail is slightly lighter. **Schwarzer Grossspitz:** In the Black Spitz both the top coat and the undercoat must be dark in color, while on the surface the color of the coat should be a good blue-black, with no trace of white or any other color. **Weisser Grossspitz:** The coat should be pure white, with no variation, especially that yellowish color which tends to appear, particularly on the ears. **Brauner Grossspitz:** The brown should be uniform, solid and deep.

VARIATIONS IN SIZE Wolfsspitz: These dogs are distinguished from other Spitzes not only by color but by their greater height. The height at the withers should be at least 17¾ inches; any variation above this is acceptable if the general appearance of the dog is not spoiled.

STANDARD SPITZ

(a) Schwarzer Grossspitz: Should be similar to the Wolfsspitz except in color and should be at least 15¾ inches high at the withers; **(b) Weisser Grossspitz:** Should also be similar to the Wolfsspitz except in color and should measure 15¾ inches at the withers; **(c) Brauner Wolfsspitz:** Like the preceding dogs, these should be similar to the Wolfsspitz except in color and should measure at least 15¾ inches at the withers.

SMALL SPITZ

The Small Spitz is a replica of the Standard Spitz except for size. They measure 11 inches maximum at the withers and should not weigh more than 7½ lb. The following color variants are recognized:
(a) Schwarzer Kleinspitz: Black Small Spitz.
(b) Weisser Kleinspitz: White Small Spitz.
(c) Brauner Kleinspitz: Brown Small Spitz.
(d) Oranger Kleinspitz: Orange Small Spitz.
(e) Wolfsfarbiger Kleinspitz: Wolf-Gray Small Spitz.

FAULTS Flat or apple head; nose, eyelids or lips flesh-colored; undershot or overshot condition; eyes too big or too light, teary; ears too long, set on too far apart or folded at the tips; monorchidism; tail not well settled on the back, too long or hanging to one side; hair curly or divided; in wolf-gray dogs an excessively dark mask is a fault, as is the presence of white markings. ●

GREAT BLACK SPITZ

Photo: E. Münch, Fotostampa-Embrione.

GREAT WOLF GRAY SPITZ

SMALL SPITZ PUPPIES

Photo: S. A. Thompson.

SMALL SPITZ

SMALL SPITZ

259 SMALL SPITZ
GERMANY

Except for the size and the orange color allowed for the Small German Spitz, the standard is the same as for the Great Spitz.

SMALL SPITZ

260 SHORTHAIRED DWARF PINSCHER

Zwergpinscher

GERMANY

SHORTHAIRED DWARF PINSCHER

GENERAL CHARACTERISTICS A well-built dog, robust, compact and elegant; he shows no defects ascribable to dwarfism, to the head or to the legs. His lines are harmonious throughout the body. Well typed, with well-distributed muscling, the Dwarf Pinscher is sound, lively, quick and eager in his bearing, attentive and full of temperament.

SIZE Height at the withers: 9½-11½ inches.

HEAD Tends to be long rather than short; it is narrow and with little cheek. The skull is flat, merging gradually into the muzzle. The nose is black. In the fawn variety, which is known as Rehpinscher, in brown dogs, and in other varieties the nose should be of a color compatible with the coat. The muzzle is rather more robust than delicate and should be in good proportion with the skull. The teeth meet in a scissors bite. The upper jaw meets the lower nicely. The stop is not exaggerated.

EYES Rather rounded, of medium size, the eyes are well adapted to the muzzle—neither too full nor too rounded, neither too small nor too slanted. They should invariably be dark, almost black.

EARS Well set on, clipped and pointed.

NECK Lean, without dewlap, issuing cleanly from the shoulders. Rather more robust than delicate, it joins the nape in a gentle curve.

BODY The thorax is well formed, deep and well let down, serving as a good support for the shoulder all the way down to the elbow, not rounded but rather flat on the sides. The back is robust and straight, its length approximately equal to the height at the withers. In females it is slightly longer, in keeping with the maternal function. The belly is moderately tucked up.

TAIL Robust, set on high, docked, the tail is carried gaily.

FOREQUARTERS Sound and robust in bone structure, soild in their joints. The forequarters are straight and in line with the vertical of the forearm. **HINDQUARTERS** Well bent, well directed backward, meeting the ground with good separation. **FEET** Compact, with well-arched toes and black nails.

COAT Short, close-fitting, dense, glossy, distributed evenly over the body with no bare spots. **Color** (a) Glossy black, with markings which may vary frcm reddish tan to yellow beneath the chin, over the eyes, on the cheeks, lips, throat, chest (two spots), toes and half of the hind feet, the inner part of the hind legs and around the vent; (b) solid yellow, fawn and stag color (Rehpinscher); (c) brown, blue, in all their shades, with red or yellow tan markings like those described above.

FAULTS Excessively heavy skull; short, pointed muzzle (apple head); teeth not meeting properly in bite; large, protruding eyes (cow eyes); saddle back or roach back; chest too broad or too narrow; thorax too high; sloping croup; crooked legs, cow hocks; excessively light bone; straight shoulders, elbows turned out; hind legs too close together, "under the dog," or forming an X; white spots on the toes, chest, forehead or elsewhere; light (yellow-white) spotting or dark spotting. ●

TOY TERRIER AND ENGLISH BRED SHORTHAIRED DWARF PINSCHER

DWARF SCHNAUZER

261 DWARF SCHNAUZER
Zwergschnauzer

GERMANY

This is the dwarf variety of the Schnauzer, whose temperament he shares. His small size has in no way diminished the ardor and sportive qualities of this dog. He is well adapted to our era; he likes to follow his master into the car and is no trouble, not only because he is little but because he stays put.

Vigilant and attentive, he makes a good watchdog. He is very popular and appreciated everywhere.

GENERAL CHARACTERISTICS The Dwarf Schnauzer is the smaller form of the Standard Schnauzer and should conform as strictly to the larger as possible and also have all the good points of character and personality of the Standard. He differs from the larger dog only in size and carriage, in which he should reveal his typical temperament.

DWARF SCHNAUZER

367

Photo: S. A. Thompson, A. Roslin-Williams.

DWARF SCHNAUZER

Flanders and Brabant canals in great number and is their devoted friend. He is an excellent guard for barges and boats, a persistent hunter of rats that try to get aboard, and his liveliness offers entertaining diversion to boatmen during the long lonely voyages. The Schipperke attained great popularity after 1888 when a fad for this strange tailless dog developed in England and America. There was such a great demand for the Schipperke that every dog more or less resembling the authentic Schipperke was exported. This was the cause of the transformation of the breed, which is quite different in its characteristics from one country to another. For example, we find round-eyed and blue and brown Schipperkes in England, although the Belgian standard established rather oval eyes and absolutely black coat.

SIZE Height for both males and females ranges from 12 to 14 inches. Breeders should endeavor to obtain dogs of about 13 inches. Height above 14 or below 12 inches constitutes a fault.

HEAD Long and without any prominence of the cheeks. Its total length (from the tip of the nose to the peak of the occiput) is to the length of the back (from the withers or the first spinal vertebra) in an approximate ratio of 1:2. The skull is flat and parallel to the muzzle. The nose is well developed, the muzzle is strong, the teeth are strong and normal and meet in a scissors bite. The stop is only moderately accentuated.

EYES Dark, oval, not prominent but well adapted to the head.

EARS Set on high, the ears should be as nearly identical as possible in size and shape.

NECK Long, elegantly arched, robust and carried erect. It should never be too thick, too short or carried horizontally. A dewlap is a fault.

BODY The chest is of moderate width and well developed. The ribs are flat but well developed, so that the brisket is below the elbows. The back is slightly arched. The length of the trunk is about equal to the height at the withers. The loins are strong, the croup is slightly rounded. The belly is moderately drawn up. The Dwarf Schnauzer is of harmonious proportions, powerful, compact, and well constructed.

TAIL Set on high; it should be docked at the third joint.

FOREQUARTERS The shoulders are sloping, the elbows are close to the body. The legs should appear straight as seen from any point. The pastern should be straight and vertical. **HINDQUARTERS** Well angulated, permitting an ample, robust gait. **FEET** Catfeet are preferred.

COAT The harder and coarser the better. The eyes are shaded with bushy, bristly eyebrows. The beard is bristly. The hair on the head and legs is also tough in texture. **Color** Salt and pepper or solid black.

N.B. All other details are to be taken from the description of the Standard Schnauzer, with due allowance made for the difference in size. ●

262 SCHIPPERKE
BELGIUM

This dog is particularly attractive because of his frisky and sometimes rather petulant nature, his very black coat and his lack of tail. He was long raised by the boatmen who travel the

SCHIPPERKE

SCHIPPERKE

Photo: S. A. Thompson.

GENERAL CHARACTERISTICS An excellent and faithful guard dog, suspicious of strangers. Active, agile, indefatigable, continually occupied with what is going on around him, watchful of things that are given him to guard, very kind with children, knows the ways of the household; always curious to know what is going on behind closed doors or about any object that has been moved, betraying his impressions by his sharp bark and upstanding ruff; he seeks the company of horses and is a hunter of moles and other vermin; can be used to hunt game and is a good rabbit dog.

WEIGHT AND SIZE Weight: for small dogs, 6½-11 lb; for large dogs, 11-20 lb. Dogs weighing less than 6½ lb are classified as Miniature Schipperkes.

HEAD Foxlike, fairly wide, narrowing at the eyes, seen in profile slightly rounded, tapering muzzle not too elongated nor too blunt; not too much stop. Nose small and black. Teeth meeting evenly. A tight scissors bite is acceptable.

EYES Dark brown, small, oval rather than round, neither sunken nor prominent. They should have a questioning expression, sharp and lively, but not mean or wild.

EARS Very erect, small, triangular, placed high, strong enough not to be capable of being lowered except in line with the body.

NECK Strong and full, slightly arched, rather short.

BODY Short, thickset and cobby. Broad behind the shoulders, seeming higher in front because of ruff. Shoulders muscular and sloping. Chest broad and deep in brisket. Back strong, short, straight and level or slightly sloping down toward rump. Ribs well sprung. Loins muscular and well drawn up from the brisket but not to such an extent as to cause a weak and leggy appearance of the hindquarters.

TAIL Lacking.

FOREQUARTERS Forelegs straight under body, with bone in proportion, but not coarse. **HINDQUARTERS** somewhat lighter than the foreparts, but muscular, powerful, with rump well rounded, tail docked to no more than 1 inch in length. **FEET** Small, round and tight (not splayed), nails straight, strong and short.

COAT Abundant and slightly harsh to the touch, short on the ears and on the front of legs and on the hocks, fairly short on the body, but longer around the neck beginning back of the ears, and forming a ruff and cape; a jabot extending down between the front legs, also longer on rear where it forms a culotte, the points turning inward. Undercoat dense and short on body, very dense around neck making ruff stand out. Culotte should be as long as the ruff. **Color** Black.

FAULTS Light eyes; large round prominent eyes; ears too long or too rounded; narrow head and elongated muzzle; domed skull; smooth short coat with short ruff and culotte; lack of undercoat; curly or silky coat; body coat more than 3 inches long; slightly overshot or undershot; swayback; Bull Terrier-shaped head; straight hocks; straight stifles and shoulders; cow hocks; feet turning in or out; legs not straight when viewed from front; lack of distinction between length of coat, ruff and culotte.

DISQUALIFICATIONS Any color other than solid black. Drop or semi-erect ears. Badly overshot or undershot jaw. ●

263 BELGIAN GRIFFON

Griffon Belge

BELGIUM

Belgian Griffons are divided into three varieties which are considered by modern dog associations to be three separate breeds whose standards are given below. Belgian Griffons are attractive pet dogs, very intelligent and also very interesting.

As with many other dogs, their origins are little known or hazy, especially since they are claimed by different countries. However, everything would lead to the conclusion that the first Griffon, with characteristics very similar to the present one, was born in Belgium and is justifiably called Belgian Griffon, Brussels Griffon, or Small Brabançon.

According to the Dutch, its origins should be sought among the descendents of the Smonshondje, a breed that has almost disappeared. Germans consider the Griffon a variety of Small German Griffon—the Affenpinscher.

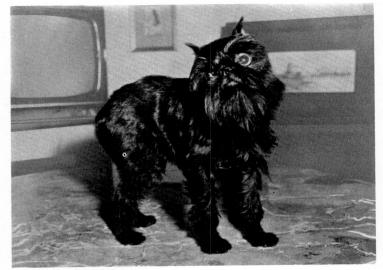

BELGIAN GRIFFON

BELGIAN GRIFFON

COAT Rough, wiry and dense. The head should be covered with wiry hair slightly longer around the eyes, nose, cheeks, and chin, thus forming a fringe.

Color Black and reddish brown mixed, usually with black mask and whiskers; or solid black. ●

264 SMALL BRABANÇON GRIFFON

Griffon Brabançon

BELGIUM

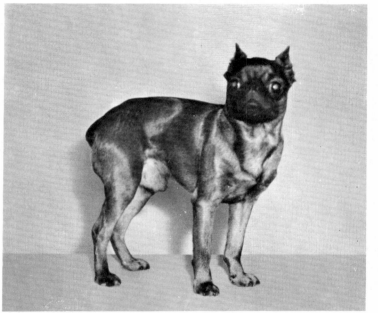

SMALL BRABANÇON GRIFFON

265 SMALL BRUSSELS GRIFFON

Griffon Bruxellois

BELGIUM

BELGIAN GRIFFON

GENERAL CHARACTERISTICS A toy dog, intelligent, alert, sturdy, with a thick-set short body, a smart carriage and set-up, attracting attention by an almost human expression.

WEIGHT (a) Small dogs: not over 6½ lb; (b) large dogs: males 6½-11 lb; females 6½-10 lb. Tolerance of ¼ lb is allowed.

HEAD Skull large and round, with a domed forehead. Nose very black, extremely short, its tip being set back deeply between the eyes so as to form a lay-back. The nostrils large, the stop deep. Lips edged with black, not pendulous but well brought together, giving a clean finish to the mouth. Chin must be undershot, prominent and large, with an upward sweep. The incisors of the lower jaw should protrude over the upper incisors, and the lower jaw should be rather broad. Neither teeth nor tongue would show when the mouth is closed. A wry mouth is a serious fault.

EYES Should be set well apart, very large, black, prominent, and well open. The eyelashes long and black. Eyelids edged with black.

EARS Small and set rather high on the head. May be shown cropped or natural. If natural they are carried semierect.

NECK Medium length, gracefully arched.

BODY Brisket should be broad and deep, ribs well sprung, back level and short.

TAIL Set on and carried high; docked to about one-third.

FORELEGS Of medium length, straight in bone, well muscled, set moderately wide apart and straight from the point of the shoulders as viewed from the front. Pasterns short and strong.

HINDLEGS Set true, thighs strong and well muscled, stifles bent, hocks well let down, turning neither in nor out.

FEET Round, small, and compact, turned neither in nor out. Toes well arched. Black pads and toenails preferred.

SMALL BRUSSELS GRIFFON

SMALL BRUSSELS GRIFFON

CURLYHAIRED BICHON

266 CURLYHAIRED BICHON FRANCE

Bichon à poil frisé

CURLYHAIRED BICHON

This breed was obtained from the fifteenth-century Maltese. The name Bichon seems to be derived from *barbichon* or "goatee," doubtless because of the curly coat feature of this attractive dog.

GENERAL CHARACTERISTICS A small, gay, playful dog, with a lively gait, a muzzle of moderate length, long hair in a corkscrew curl. The hair is very slack and is something like that of the Mongolian goat. The head is carried proudly and high, the dark eyes are vivacious and expressive.

SIZE Height at withers: must not go beyond 12 inches, the small size being an element of success in show.

HEAD The skull is longer than the muzzle in the ratio of 8 to 5; the circumference of the skull is approximately equal to the height at the withers. The nose is rounded, definitely black, smooth and glossy. The lips are thin, fairly lean, although not quite like the Schipperke *(q.v.),* falling just far enough to cover the lower lips but never heavy or pendulous. The lips are normally black; the lower lip must not be heavy or obvious, nor can it be slack. The inner area must not be visible when the mouth is closed. The mouth is neither undershot nor overshot, the jaws meeting in a scissors

bite. The muzzle should be neither thick nor heavy, but it must not be pinched. The cheeks are flat, not very muscular. The skull is rather flat to the touch, although the coat gives it a rounded appearance.

EYES Dark as possible, with dark eye rims. They are rather rounded, not almond-shaped. They are lively and set straight, i.e., not obliquely. The whites do not show. The eyes are lively but are neither large nor prominent as in the Brussels Griffon or the Pekingese. The socket does not bulge, nor do the eyes.

EARS Drooping, well furnished with crisp, long hair carried rather forward on alert, but in such a way that the fore edge touches the skull. They should not reach the tip of the nose when extended, as in the Poodle, but should go just about halfway. Besides, they are not as wide and fine as a Poodle's.

NECK Fairly long and carried high and proudly. Round and slender near the skull, it broadens gradually and

372

Photo: Buzzini, DIM, E. Münch, S. A. Thompson.

fits smoothly into the shoulders. Lengthwise, it measures about a third of the body.

BODY The chest is well developed, the sternum is pronounced. The back ribs are rounded and do not terminate abruptly, thus giving a substantial horizontal depth to the chest. The flanks are well tucked up at the belly; the skin at that point is thin. The loin is wide and well muscled, slightly arched. The pelvis is wide, the rump slightly rounded.

TAIL Normally the tail is carried high and gracefully curved in line with the spine without actually being rolled up. It is not docked and must not be close to the back, although the hair may fall against the backline. It is set on slightly lower than in the Poodle.

FOREQUARTERS The shoulder is fairly slanting, not prominent, and gives the appearance of being about the same length as the forearm (about 4 inches). The foreleg is not turned outward from the body, especially at the elbow. The legs, viewed from the front, must be straight and finely boned; in profile they are very slightly slanting. **HINDQUARTERS** The thighs are wide, well muscled and with the legs well slanted. The hock is also more angulated than is the case with the Poodle. **FEET** Black nails are preferred, although this ideal is hard to attain.

COAT The hair is fine, silky and crisply curled, 3-4 inches long, and neither flat nor ropy. **Color** The ideal is pure white, although tan or dark gray markings are permissible on the ears and body. The dog may be shown with only the feet and muzzle clipped. **Skin** The pigmentation beneath the coat is preferably dark, and if so the genitals are either black, bluish, or beige, depending on the body markings.

FAULTS Pigmentation extending into the hair and forming spots; flat, wavy, roped or too short hair; monorchidism; overshot or undershot jaw; failure to meet standards for height and length.

DISQUALIFICATIONS Undershot or overshot jaw to the extent that incisors do not touch; pink nose; flesh-colored lips; pale eyes; cryptorchidism; tail rolled up or spiraled; black spots on coat. ●

LITTLE LION DOG

267 LITTLE LION DOG
Bichon petit chien lion

FRANCE

This dog differs from the Bichon in that his coat is short on his body and part of his tail. On the other hand, the hair on his head, shoulders, the lower part of his legs and tail is as long as that of the Bichon.

This small dog is very prevalent in France but is rarely found elsewhere.

GENERAL CHARACTERISTICS A very small dog, intelligent and affectionate, with a lively gait. Combines in a single dog many of the typical qualities of the small nonsporting dog. The coat is clipped in classical Poodle style, and the tail is also clipped to end in a plume, which contributes much to the leonine appearance of this breed. **WEIGHT AND SIZE** Weight: About 4½-9 lb. Height at the withers: 8-14 inches.
HEAD Short, with a rather broad skull. Black nose, well placed at the tip of the muzzle.

EYES Round and dark colored, rather large and with an expression of lively intelligence.

EARS Long, hanging, and furnished with a profuse fringe.

BODY Short and well proportioned.

TAIL Medium length. It should be clipped at the base so that a tuft is left at the tip forming a fine plume.

FORELEGS AND HINDLEGS Straight and fine. The feet are small and round.

COAT Quite long and wavy, but not curly. **Color** All colors are acceptable, both solid and marked; the colors most sought are white, black, and lemon yellow.

FAULTS Excessive head length, insufficient breadth of skull; nose not wholly black as specified or pug-like; small or almond eyes; globular, light, wild or unfriendly eyes; short ears, ears without fringe or with slight fringe; body too long, too slack, badly coupled; tail too long or short; cow hocks or bowlegs; flat feet, long feet, open toes; short coat, straight hair, curly hair instead of long wavy hair; unclipped dogs not eligible for judging in show. ●

268 FRENCH BULLDOG
Bouledogue Français

FRANCE

The French Bulldog's origins are uncertain. According to N. M. Martin, the dog expert, this is a French breed obtained from crossbreeding a little known variety common in certain districts of Paris with breeds imported from Belgium. By virtue of careful selective breeding specimens were eventually obtained which made it possible to fix the breed.

The French Bulldog may then be an ancient breed of French origin, although he has existed in his present form for only a

FRENCH BULLDOG

FRENCH BULLDOG

dog with the aid of a terrier strain that would keep the many Bulldog traits and be a good ratter.

Tron, who was a well-known breeder of English Bulldogs and also a connoisseur of the French Bulldog, agrees entirely with this English theory. He maintains that this small dog is not indigenous to France but derives from the "miniature" Bulldog with added strains from other breeds, inducing psycho-physical modifications and making a noticeable difference between the two types.

hundred years. In the last century no porter, coachman, or butcher in the slums of Paris was without his Bulldog. The favorite pastime of these people consisted of staging bloody contests between their dogs in rings designed for the purpose.

British writers, however, think the French Bulldog descends from the English Bulldog. This hypothesis which would also explain the fact that *bouledogue* is simply phoneticized French for "Bulldog," is based on the following facts: In the breeding of bulldogs practiced in England there were often specimens of true type but of very small size and extremely light weight (22–26 lb) called miniatures and which constituted a separate variety. These small dogs were exported principally to Normandy. There they were bred for a utilitarian purpose in order to develop a

GENERAL CHARACTERISTICS The French Bulldog is classed as a companion, guard dog and pleasure dog. This breed is powerful, even if small. The lines are short, of compact proportions, short-haired and with a short, snub-nosed face. The ears are erect and the tail is naturally short. The French Bulldog should be active, intelligent, very muscular, of compact build and solid bone.

WEIGHT AND SIZE The weight should not be less than 17½ lb nor more than 31 lb; in healthy dogs, the size is proportional to the weight.

HEAD Very strong, broad and square. The skin on the head forms almost symmetrical folds and wrinkles. The head is characterized by a contraction of the maxillary-nasal region. The skull has broadened as it has lost in length. The occipital protuberance is not visible. The facial contraction explains certain characteristics which are described below. **Nose** Broad, very short, puglike. The nostrils are regular and well open, slanting from the bottom upward and from the forepart to the back. The disposition of the nostrils and of the snub nose should, however, permit normal breathing; pointed noses are a detriment; they provoke chronic snoring. **Nasal Bridge** Short, broad, with concentric, symmetrical folds falling on

the upper lip. **Lips** Thick, rather loose, black; the upper and lower lips meet at the center, completely covering the teeth, which should never be visible. Nor should the tongue ever show. The profile of the upper lip is descending and rounded. **Jaws** Broad, square, powerful. The angle of the lower jaw should be open to permit the forward projection of the mandible following a broad curve, and the lower jaw should terminate in front of the upper jaw, which is thus practically surrounded by the lower jaw. The prominence of the undershot lower jaw and the curve of the sides of the lower jaw toward the upper incisors are necessary if serious faults are to be avoided, such as a too short lower jaw (overshot condition), or a too long lower jaw (excessive undershot condition). The arch of the incisors should be rounded to avoid crossing of the teeth, and at the same time it should lie on a horizontal plane to avoid lateral deviations of the canines, which are the cause of protrusion of the tongue. The distance between the two incisor arches is not strictly fixed; an essential condition is that the lower lip and the upper lip meet to hide the teeth completely. The masseters are well developed but not pronounced. **Stop** Very pronounced, a characteristic of short-coupled dogs. **Skull** Broad, almost flat, with a bulging forehead. The

FRENCH BULLDOG PUP

FRENCH BULLDOG

FRENCH BULLDOG

brow arches are prominent and separated by a deep furrow between the eyes. This furrow should not extend to the forehead, as in the English Bulldog. The occipital protuberance should not be apparent.

EYES Lively in expression, set rather low, quite far from the nose and especially from the ears; they are dark, quite large, very round and slightly protruding; no white should be visible when the dog is looking straight ahead. The eyelids must be black.

EARS Of medium size, broad at the base and rounded at the tips. They are set on high but not too close together and are carried erect. Seen from in front, the auricle looks like a single unit. The leather should be thin and soft to the touch.

NECK Short, slightly arched, without dewlap.

FOREQUARTERS Shoulders and Upper Arm Short, thick; the muscles are solid and very evident. The upper arm should be short, the elbows should be close to the body to ensure proper movement. Elbows away from the body give faulty legs. **Forearms** Short, well separated, straight and muscular. **Wrists and Pasterns** Solid and short; otherwise the dog would be too close to the ground or excessively on the pasterns. The legs should be regular as seen from the front and in profile. **Feet** Round, small (catfeet), well set on the ground

and slightly turned outward. The toes are compact, the joints high, the nails short, thick and well separated. The pads are hard, thick and black. In dogs with streaked coats, the nails should be black; in dogs with the type of coat known as *caillé* (see COAT), dark nails are preferable, although no penalty is incurred for lighter colors (including horn color).

BODY Chest Broadly open, with a cylindrical rib cage, well let down. **Thorax** Barrel-like, with well-sprung, rounded ribs. It is essential that there be plenty of room for heart and lungs; this is why the ribs must be exceptionally well sprung and of the barrel type. **Back** Broad and muscular. **Loins** Short and robust. The profile of the back and loin region rises gradually to the level of the loins and then slopes rapidly toward the tail. This conformation, which is to be sought, implies short loins. **Belly and Flanks** Drawn up, but not excessively so. **Croup** Sloping.

TAIL Short, set on low, close to the buttocks, thick at the root, naturally twisted or knotted, pointed at the tip; it should always be carried below the horizontal, even in action. In some dogs, the vestigial joints of the coccyx causes shortening of the tail and a deforming ankylosis. The tail may therefore appear excessively shortened, but never so as to cause total disappearance of the tail (lack of a tail is a disqualification). Some tails are set into a cavity in the croup; this condition should be considered a

fault, although it may be the result of overbreeding. From another point of view, a relatively long tail (which should never pass the point of the hock), broken and pointed at the tip, may be a less desirable type. Judges should bear in mind, however, that this malformation is the classical one called for by the standard.

HINDQUARTERS Thigh Muscular, solid and compact. **Legs** The hind legs are strong and muscular. They are slightly longer than the forelegs, and thus cause a slight rise of the hindquarters. The hind legs are regular, as seen both from behind and in profile. **Hocks** Rather let down; straight hocks thrown forward must be absolutely avoided, as are cow hocks. **Tarsi and Metatarsi** Solid and short; puppies should be born without dewclaws. **Feet** Not quite so round as the forefeet.

COAT A very short, thick, glossy and soft coat. **Color** Two colors are recognized: streaked (brindled) and *caillé*. The streaked coat is a mixture of black and red (not too dark) hairs. Some white is permissible on the chest and head. A streaked dog, if there is too much white, will suffer in showing, since the coat is not strictly standard. Since by definition the streaked coat is a mixture of black and not excessively dark red, judges should oppose the current tendency to tolerate the progressive invasion of black as a predominating color and the disappearance of recessive red.

The type of coat known as *caillé* has a white background and streaked markings. Dogs which are entirely white are not classified in this group. The eyebrows and eyelids should be black; there should be no trace of depigmentation on the muzzle. If a *caillé* dog has a very dark nose and dark eyes with dark eyelids, a slight depigmentation of the muzzle can be tolerated. The background of a *caillé* coat should not be speckled, but a slight speckling of the white should not be penalized. All other considerations being equal, dogs with the purest coats should be preferred.

GAIT Correct and easy.

FAULTS Narrow or pointed nose; bad teeth; light eyes; dewlap; tail carried too high, excessively long or fleshy tail; long hair; speckled coat or excessively black coat.

SERIOUS FAULTS Underweight or overweight condition; teeth visible; tongue visible; depigmented spots on the muzzle; abnormal or "drum-beating" gait.

DISQUALIFICATIONS Nose any color besides black; harelip; overshot jaw; excessively undershot jaw; eyes of two different colors; walleyes; ears not carried straight; mutilation of ears, tail or dewclaws; lack of tail; cryptorchidism, anorchidism, monorchidism; dewclaws on hind legs; black, black and tan, coffee, mouse gray, brown coat. ●

376

Photo: S. A. Thompson.

269 GIANT POODLE

Grand Caniche

FRANCE

The Poodle's characteristic is to perfectly imitate what he sees others do, especially his master. Thus he performs the most varied tasks with ease, which is why the famous trained circus dogs are almost always Poodles. His intelligence, greater than that of other dogs, establishes him as one of the most interesting as well as the most prevalent breeds.

His beauty and originality cannot be separated from the qualities just mentioned. He is physically well constructed and attractive and, because of his characteristic grooming, clearly distinguishable from all other breeds.

Precise information about his origins is lacking. While the French insist that he is indigenous to France, the Germans also insist that he is indigenous to the north, particularly to Germany, a belief shared by Brehm, the famous naturalist. Others believe that he originated in Piedmont, an opinion Sélincourt shares based on the fact that there were formerly such beautiful

GIANT POODLE

Poodles in Italy that many English tourists brought them back to England.

The most logical hypothesis, however, is perhaps that sup-

THREE VARIETIES OF POODLE

Photo: Fotostampa-Embrione, A. Wintzell.

ported by the French, according to which the modern Poodle is descended from the Barbet, a French Setter that has almost disappeared, and which was characterized by his curly, woolly coat. It is suggested that the Poodle inherited his hunting instinct from the Barbet. The French word *caniche* (Poodle) comes from *canard* (duck), as the poodle used to be an ardent and successful hunter of wild ducks.

GENERAL CHARACTERISTICS The French Poodle is classified as a companion dog. Its hair is curly or ropy, clipped on the hindquarters and legs. The Poodle is an intelligent dog, always alert, active and harmoniously built, giving an impression of elegance and pride. The gait is light and springy; the Poodle should never walk with a long, sliding step. He is famous for his fidelity and willingness to be trained, traits that make him a particularly pleasant companion.

SIZE The French standard mentions three sizes—large, medium and miniature. The American standard recognizes the Standard Poodle and the Miniature Poodle. (1) large: 17¾-21½ inches at the withers; (2) medium: 13¾-17¾ inches; (3) miniature: less than 13¾ inches at the withers.

HEAD Distinguished, rectilinear, in good proportion with the body; its length should be a little more than 2/5 of the height at the withers. **Nose** Pronounced, highly developed, with vertical profile and open nostrils; the nose is black in black, gray, and white poodles, and brown in brown poodles. **Lips** Not heavy, rather dry, of moderate thickness; the lower lip is close-fitting, the upper lip overlaps it without falling. The lips are black in black, gray, and white dogs, and pigmented in brown dogs. **Muzzle** Straight; its length is about 9/10 the length of the skull; it is solid, elegant but not pointed. The cheeks are not prominent, fitting close to the bone. **Jaws** Normally meeting in a scissors bite; the sides of the lower jaw are almost parallel. The teeth are solid. **Stop** Not pronounced. **Skull** Well modeled; its width is less than half the length of the head (the axes form a 16-19 degree angle). The supraorbital ridges are moderately pronounced and covered with long hair. The medial furrow is broad between the eyes and narrows toward the occiput, which is very pronounced (it may be less so in miniatures).

EYES The expression is alert and intelligent. The eyes are set at the level of the stop and are slightly slanted. They are black or brown and are very dark in black, gray, and yellow dogs; they may be dark amber in brown dogs.

EARS Quite long, hanging at the cheeks; they are set onto the prolongation of a line from the nose passing underneath the outer corner of the eye. They should be flat, broadening after the roots, and rounded at the tips. They are covered with very long, wavy hair.

NECK Solid, slightly arched after the nape, of medium length and in good proportion, without dewlap. The head should be carried high and proudly.

FOREQUARTERS Shoulders and Upper Arms The withers are moderately developed. The shoulders are sloping and muscular. The scapula and upper arm form an angle of 90-100 degrees. The length of the upper arm is equal to that of the scapula. **Forearms** Perfectly straight and parallel, elegant, well muscled, with good bone. The height of the elbow from the ground is 5/9 of the height at the withers. **Wrists** Continue the forward line of the forearm. **Pasterns** Solid, not massive, and almost straight when seen in profile. **Feet** Rather small, closed, oval. The toes are well arched, compact, palmate, and the pads are hard and thick. The nails are black in black or gray dogs, black or brown in brown dogs. In white dogs the nails may be colored or very light, consistent with the pigmentation.

BODY The general appearance of the body is that of a well-proportioned dog; its length is slightly more tha the height at the withers. **Chest** Normal, with the point of the sternum slightly prominent and high, a condition which causes a more erect, easier and noble carriage of the head. **Thorax** Its breadth is equal to 2/3 of its height (from the spinal column to the sternum). The brisket is at elbow level. **Rib cage** Oval and broad in the back section. **Back** Short, with a harmonious backline. **Loins** Solid and muscular. **Belly and Flanks** Drawn up, but not excessively so. **Croup** Rounded, not falling.

TAIL The tail is set on quite high, at loin level. It should be cropped to 1/3 or ½ of its length in dogs with curly coats. A long tail, however, is not a fault if well carried; the natural tail may be left in dogs with corded coats. In action the tail is raised obliquely.

HINDQUARTERS The thighs are muscular and robust. The hind legs are parallel as seen from behind, with well developed and very evident muscles. The hocks should be well angulated. **Tarsi and Metatarsi** Vertical. **Feet** Similar to the forefeet.

COAT In curly-coated dogs, the hair is abundant, of fine, woolly texture, very curly, elastic and resistant to the pressure of the hand. It should be heavy and very thick, of uniform length, forming consistent curls, which are usually combed. The other dogs have abundant hair, of fine, woolly texture, dense, forming characteristic ropelike strands of even length, no shorter than 8 inches. The longer the hair, the better. The hair at the sides of the head can be caught up in a knot above the ears, and those on the body parted on each side, so as not to give the impression of a disordered coat. **Color** Black, white, brown, gray in both kinds of coat. **Skin** Soft, not loose, pigmented. In white poodles a silver color is desirable; there are white dogs whose skin is light and spotted, not only on the inner parts, which is very frequent, but over the entire body. Black, brown or gray dogs should have a corresponding pigmentation of the skin.

CLIP "Lion Clip" Clipping of the hindquarters is done in both varieties of Poodle; the clipping should be done up to the ribs. Also shaved are: the muzzle, both above and below, from the lower eyelids; cheeks; forelegs and hind legs, except for bracelets on the hind legs and puffs on the forelegs and the optional decorations on the hindquarters; the tail is shaved except for a round or oblong pompom at the tip. Leaving moustaches is recommended for all dogs; trousers may be left on the forelegs. "1960" **Type** In Europe another style of clip is permitted which leaves hair on the forelegs, provided the following standards are respected: (1) the following are shaved: (a) the lower part of the forelegs, beginning from the nails to the point of the dewclaw; the lower part of the hind legs to an equivalent height; machine clipping is permitted provided it is limited to the toes; (b) the head and the tail, according to the regulations already given. In this style of clip the following are exceptionally allowed: the presence of short hair beneath the lower jaw, not surpassing, however, the thickness of 2/5 inch, with the lower line cut parallel to the jaw itself (the so-called "goat's beard" is not acceptable); absence of the pompom on the tail (this, however, will diminish slightly the rating for coat texture). (2) shortened hair on the body, in such a way as to give a more or less long marbling on the backline of the thickness of at least 2/5 inch. The length of the hair shall be progressively increased about the ribs, on the shoulders and thighs. (3) "Regularized" hair: (a) on the head, which should have a casque of reasonable height; on the neck, descending behind the nape to the withers; in the forward region, continuously down to the shaven part of the foot, following a slightly sloping line from the point of the sternum. On the upper part of the ears, and at most to 1/3 of their length, the hair may be shortened with scissors or shaved in the direction of the hair. The lower part of the ears shall be left covered with hair of a length which increases progressively from the lower part upward, ending in fringes which may be regularized; (b) on the legs, trousers marking a clean separation from the shaven part of the feet. The length of the hair increases gradually upward, until it reaches on the shoulders and the thighs a length of 1½-2¾ inches, measured with the hair straightened, proportionately to the size of the dog, but avoiding puffs. The trousers of the hindquarters should clearly reveal the typical angulation of the Poodle. All other fancy clips which do not comply with these standards are disqualifying. Whatever standard silhouette is obtained by the clip should have no effect on the classification in show, since all dogs of a given class should be judged and rated together. All other characteristics being equal, preference shall always be given to dogs with leonine clips.

GAIT See GENERAL CHARACTERISTICS.

FAULTS Anatomical: arched nasal bridge; a slight overshot condition is a fault; an undershot condition makes the dog ineligible for first prize; teeth yellowed by distemper do not constitute a fault if they are otherwise correct; badly set teeth or missing teeth constitute a fault of irregularity; too short or too narrow ears. Of type: light nose, with insufficient general pigmentation; spotted; eyes insufficiently dark or with reddish tints; tail curved over the back; dull or soft coat; incisive color. A little white is acceptable on the chest; white hair on the feet constitutes a serious fault; dogs that have it cannot be awarded any prizes.

DISQUALIFICATIONS Monorchidism, cryptorchidism; lack of tail; dewclaws or traces of dewclaws on the hind legs; white spots; nonsolid coat. Poodles which are not clipped in conformity with the standard cannot be judged for ratings in shows or other official functions until clipped in such a manner. They are not, however, disqualified for stud. ●

POODLE

Photo: S. A. Thompson.

MEDIUM-SIZED POODLE

270 MEDIUM-SIZED POODLE
Caniche moyen   FRANCE

POODLE

POODLE WITH A PUPPY

Photo: Fotostampa-Embrione, S. A. Thompson.

MINIATURE POODLE

271 MINIATURE POODLE
Caniche nain

FRANCE

MINIATURE POODLE

MINIATURE POODLE

Photo: F. Grehan (Photo Res.), S. A. Thompson.

272 CONTINENTAL TOY SPANIEL WITH HANGING EARS

Phalène

FRANCE

It is difficult to speak of the long history of Continental Toy Spaniels without mentioning the historic personages, especially ladies, of whom they were the inseparable companions. In ancient times they were already held in great favor, and were so prevalent as pets of noble families that many considered that the Toy Spaniel originated in Italy.

The breed was exported to France and Belgium and was perfected through selective breeding until the present type became standard.

CONTINENTAL TOY SPANIEL WITH HANGING EARS

CONTINENTAL TOY SPANIEL WITH HANGING EARS

GENERAL CHARACTERISTICS A Toy Spaniel of normal, harmonious build, with long hair, a moderately long muzzle shorter than the skull, of lively personality, graceful and at the same time robust, with a proud, easy and elegant gait. Although the skeleton is of the square type, the dog seems to be a little longer than high because of the abundance of hair which is differently directed about the rump and beneath the throat.

WEIGHT AND SIZE Weight: (1) less than 5½ lb for both males and females; (2) 5½-10 lb for males; 5½-11 lb for females. The minimum weight is 3-1/3 lb. Height: maximum, about 11 inches.

HEAD In normal proportion to the body and even, proportionally, lighter and shorter than in the medium and standard spaniel. The skull is not excessively rounded, neither as seen from in front. or in profile; in some dogs there is a slight trace of the medial furrow. The nose is small, black and round, slightly flattened on top. The muzzle, shorter than the skull, is fine, pointed and never pug-like. The nasal bridge is straight, the stop is accentuated. In larger dogs the stop is less evident, but still well defined; in very small dogs the stop is clearly marked but not steep. The lips are strongly pigmented, thin and closed. The teeth are quite strong and close normally. The tongue should not be visible; if it is constantly visible and is not drawn in when touched, it constitutes a disqualification.

EYES Rather large, well open, broadly almond-shaped; they are set rather low in the face and are not prominent. The inner corner is at the meeting point of skull and muzzle. They are dark in color and very expressive. The eyelids are strongly pigmented.

EARS Quite fine, but rugged. In dogs with erect ears and with drop ears, the cartilage should not terminate in too sharp a point. The ears are set on rather far back on the head, well apart from each other, so as to reveal clearly the rounded shape of the occiput. (a) Hang-eared variety (called Phalène). In repose, the ear is set on high, considerably higher than eye level, and is hanging but at the same time quite mobile. It is feathered with wavy hair, which may reach a considerable length and gives a charming appearance. (b) Erect-eared variety (Papillon). The ears are set on high, with the auricle well open and turned to the side; the inner edge of the auricle forms an angle of approximately 45 degrees with the horizontal. In no case should the ear point upward, that is, it should not be a Spitz-type ear, which would be disqualifying. The inner part of the auricle is covered with fine, wavy hair, with the longest hairs extending slightly beyond the edge of the ear. The outer face, on the contrary, is covered with long hair which forms hanging fringes extending beyond the edges of the ears. Crossbreeding of the two varieties often produces semi-erect ears, with dropped tips. This mixed form of ear carriage constitutes a serious fault.

NECK Of moderate length, slightly arched at the nape.

BODY The thorax is broad, fairly well let down, with well-sprung ribs. The circumference of the body measured at the two last ribs should be approximately equal to the height at the withers. The back is quite long and straight (neither arched nor saddled), without however being flat; the loins are moderately curved and solid. The belly is slightly drawn up.

TAIL Set on quite high, rather long with a rich fringe which forms a fine flat. In action the tail is carried at the backline and curved; the tip may touch the back, but it should not curl or lie on the back.

FOREQUARTERS AND HINDQUARTERS The shoulders and upper arms are well developed, of equal length, normally angulated and well joined to the trunk. The legs are straight and fairly delicate. The dog should not appear to be raised up. In profile, the wrist is apparent, the hocks are normally angulated. Seen either from in front or from behind. the legs are parallel. **FEET** Quite long, harefeet, vertical to the soles. The nails are strong, preferably black, lighter in subjects with brown or white coats (white nails in white dogs or in dogs with white feet do not constitute a fault if the dogs are otherwise well pigmented). The toes are well muscled, with rugged pads and with fine hair extending beyond the tips of the feet and forming a point.

COAT The top coat, without undercoat, is abundant, glossy, wavy (not curly), not soft but slightly resistant to the touch; it has a silky quality here and there. The hairs are inserted flat, they are quite fine and slightly curved by the wave. The appearance of the coat is much like that of the Toy Spaniel of England, but differs sharply from the coat of the Spaniel and the Pekingese. At the same time it should have no similarity to the coat of the Spitz. The hair is short on the face, muzzle, the lower part of the legs and above the hocks. It is of medium length on the body, slightly longer around the neck, forming a collar and a jabot which descends in waves on the chest; it forms fringes at the ears and the back part of the forelegs; at the backside of the thighs it forms a culotte of soft hair. There may be small tufts between the toes and they may even extend slightly beyond the tips of the toes, provided they do not give a heavy appearance to the foot but rather give it a more delicate appearance by lengthening it. Typical dogs in good condition have hair 3 inches long at the hocks and fringes of 6 inches on the tail. **Color** Every color is acceptable; all dogs, including white, should have pigmented lips, eyelids, and especially nose.

GAIT Proud, with a free, easy and elegant stride.

FAULTS Flat skull, apple-shaped or convex as in Toy Spaniel; stop excessively or insufficiently marked; nasal bridge arched or hollowed; small eyes, too round, prominent, light in color, showing the whites when the dog looks straight ahead; nose not black; depigmentation at the edges of the eyelids and on the lips; overshot or, especially, undershot jaws; forelegs arched, with knotty wrist; hind legs out of vertical at the rotula, hocks or feet; weak hindquarters; feet turned outward or inward; nails which do not touch the ground; simple or double dewclaws on the hind legs; tail curled, resting on the back, falling to the side (that is, the bone, not the fringes which, because of their length, fall to the side); poor, soft or inconsistent coat; hair planted straight or not waved, woolly, or with undercoat which indicates cross breeding with the Spitz; saddleback or roach back.

DISQUALIFICATIONS (a) Pink or pink-spotted nose; (b) excessive undershot or overshot condition, to the point where the incisors do not touch; (c) paralyzed tongue or tongue constantly visible. ●

◀ A PAIR OF CHIHUAHUAS

Photo: M. Pedone, Buzzini.

CONTINENTAL TOY SPANIELS

Photo: S. A. Thompson.

273 CONTINENTAL TOY SPANIEL WITH UPRIGHT EARS

Epagneul nain Continental à oreilles droites—Papillon   FRANCE

CONTINENTAL TOY SPANIEL WITH UPRIGHT EARS

EARS Small, triangular, carried erect and slightly to the fore.

NECK Thick and robust.

FOREQUARTERS A well-developed and quite oblique shoulder. The forearms are straight, the elbows close to the body. The pasterns are very slightly inclined. The forefeet are round, with close toes. The pads are hard, the nails hard and black.

BODY The chest is deep, the ribs well rounded. The back is short and straight. The loins are wide and powerful. The belly is slightly drawn up; the genitals must be without abnormality.

TAIL Thick and strong, the tail is curled and carried as a sickle tail. It is long enough to reach the hocks when straight.

HINDQUARTERS Thighs and legs well developed. The hock is well directed. The feet, nails, and pads are the same basically as in the forequarters.

COAT Hard and straight, with a fine undercoat. **Color** Red, salt and pepper, red-peppered, black-peppered, black, black-brown, brindle, or white.

GAIT Light, lively and energetic.

FAULTS (a) Not serious: nose different in color from coat; slight overshot condition; teeth marked by distemper; pale eyes; long hair. (b) Serious faults: Distinctly overshot jaw; more than 5 teeth missing; confusion of sexual characteristics; timidity; monorchidism.

DISQUALIFICATIONS Flat ears, cryptorchidism; naturally pendant tail; short tail.

SCALE OF POINTS

General appearance	20
Character and temperament	10
Head	20
Back, loins	10
Torso, belly	10
Forequarters and hindquarters	10
Coat	10
Gait	10
	100

274 SHIBA INU

JAPAN

This dog is prevalent in the prefectures of Fukushima, Nagano, Gumma, Yamanashi, Gifu, Niigata, Tottori, and Shimane. He is of very ancient origin and it is believed that he migrated from Southern Asia in early times. Bones belonging to this dog have been found in ruins of the Jōman era (500 B.C.). His name means "Little Dog" in the Nagano dialect. He is a good guard dog and is also used for hunting small game.

GENERAL CHARACTERISTICS A small dog, well shaped, compact and muscular, with more of a rustic look about him than elegance. Gifted with great agility, the Shiba Inu is a graceful and friendly dog, lively and gay but also obedient, faithful, sensitive and attentive.

SIZE Height at the withers: males 15-16 inches; females 13¾-15 inches. These size limits should be observed as strictly as possible. Larger dogs are acceptable only when in exceptional form.

HEAD The forehead is wide, the median furrow pronounced; cheeks well formed; muzzle pointed, neither too short nor too long. The nose is dark-colored, with a straight bridge. The teeth are solid, neither undershot nor overshot. The stop is well defined but not exaggerated.

EYES Small, triangular in shape, dark brown.

SHIBA INU

275 JAPANESE SPITZ

JAPAN

This dog has the same origins as the Nordic Spitz. He was imported to Japan in ancient times and rapidly became acclimated and spread throughout the country. He is intelligent, lively, and courageous, but unfriendly and distrustful with strangers.

GENERAL CHARACTERISTICS The body is covered with a rich coat of pure white. The muzzle is pointed, the ears are erect and pointed. The tail, richly fringed, falls on the back. The tail is robust and elastic. The forequarters and hindquarters are well proportioned and fairly ample. The structural details are compact and make up a handsome, harmonious overall appearance. The Japanese Spitz is characterized by great courage. Its face is distinguished, intelligent and cheerful. The height at the withers is 10/11 of the total length of the dog.

SIZE Males 12-16 inches; females 10-14 inches.

HEAD Of moderate size for the body, pointed, relatively broad and slightly rounded. The occiput is very broad; the cheeks are fairly filled out. The forehead is not prominent. The stop is not pronounced. The nose is round, small and black. The lips are well closed. Black pigmentation of the lips is desirable. The muzzle is pointed, neither too broad nor too long, in good proportion to the skull. The teeth are white, regular, solid and meet in a scissors bite.

EYES Quite large, oval, slightly slanted, not too close together nor too far apart, dark in color. The eyelids are preferably black.

EARS Small, well erect, pointed at the tips and set on high. They are quite close together and turned forward.

NECK Of medium length, well muscled.

BODY The chest is broad and deep, the ribs are powerfully sprung. The withers are prominent and short. The back is short and straight, the loins broad and well sustained. The croup is relatively long and slightly arched. The belly is fairly drawn up. The sexual organs should be perfect.

TAIL Moderately long, set on high and carried curled on the back. It is covered with long hair.

FOREQUARTERS The shoulders are sloping, the forelegs straight. The elbows are close to the body. The pasterns are slightly sloped. The feet are small, round, well closed (catfeet); the pads are thick and dark in color, the nails are hard and preferably dark if not black. **HINDQUARTERS** The legs are parallel and well musceld. The second thighs and the hocks are well angulated. The metatarsi are straight. The feet, pads and nails are practically identical with those of the forequarters.

COAT Straight and not falling; it is short on the head, ears and the frontside of the legs, as well as beneath

JAPANESE SPITZ

Photo: S. A. Thompson.

the hocks. The other parts of the body are covered by a rich, very long fur; in particular, the hair about the neck, on the chest and shoulders is exceptionally long. The undercoat is short, soft and abundant. **Color** Pure white.

GAIT Light, gentle, lively.

FAULTS Serious Faults Excessively undershot jaw; monorchidism. **Light Faults** Slight undershot condition; hair too short.

DISQUALIFICATIONS Naturally flat ears; cryptorchidism; tail not naturally curled.

SCALE OF POINTS

General appearance	20
Character	10
Head	15
Back, loins	10
Thorax, belly	10
Legs	10
Coat	15
Gait	10
	100

276 BOLOGNESE
ITALY

This breed is probably descended from the Maltese, which it closely resembles. We have no further record on this subject since Italian and other literature make little mention of this attractive toy dog. In any case, it is certain that his country of origin is Italy and, more precisely, the city of Bologna from which he gets his name. His origins are very old and we know that as far back as the eleventh and twelfth centuries he was much esteemed for his grace and beauty.

In 1668 Cosimo de' Medici sent eight of these little Bolognese dogs to Belgium and ordered a Colonel Alamanni to give them to a leading personage of Brussels in his name. This is an additional proof of how highly the Bolognese was valued in former times: In diplomatic circles he represented a distinguished, refined, and very fashionable gift.

Several famous paintings depict dogs very similar to the present Bolognese with the difference that formerly his color was always white and black whereas now the white coat is mandatory.

GENERAL CHARACTERISTICS The Bolognese is classified scientifically as belonging to the braccoid group (according to the classification of Pierre Mégnin). He is further classed as a nonsporting dog, a companion. Italian origin. The general conformation is mesomorphic. The body outline is square. A very serious dog, not vivacious, extremely intelligent, devoted to his master, almost to the point of abnegation. The pure white coat is beautiful and makes him a popular dog in stylish homes.

WEIGHT AND SIZE Weight: 5½-9 lb. Height: Males 10½-12 inches; females 10-11 inches.

HEAD Mesocephalic; the total length of the head is 1/3 of the height at the withers; the length of the muzzle should be 2/5 of the total length of the head.

The width of the skull is more than half the total length of the head, which means that the total cephalic index is 60. The upper longitudinal axes of the skull and the muzzle are parallel. **Nose** On the same line as the nasal bridge. Seen in profile, the forepart of the nose is on the vertical. The nose should be sizable, wet and cool, and absolutely black; no other color is acceptable. **Nasal Bridge** Straight. For the length, the total cephalic index and its direction in respect to the cranial axis, see above. **Lips and Muzzle** The upper lip is not high, to the point where it leaves the lower jaw uncovered. The lower line of the muzzle is thus provided by the lower jaw. The sides of the muzzle are parallel, giving the forepart a rather square appearance. The suborbital region is well chiseled. The lips, like the entire muzzle, are covered with long hair, which is slightly less long on the bridge. **Jaws** Of normal development, with upper and lower teeth meeting perfectly. The sides of the lower jaw are straight throughout their entire length. The teeth are white, regular, complete in development and number. **Stop** Fairly accentuated; the sinuses are well developed. **Skull** The length of the skull exceeds that of the muzzle by 2/5 of the total length of the head. Its breadth is equal to its length. It is very slightly ovoid. The occipital protuberance is fairly marked. The upper part of the skull is flat. The medial furrow is not accentuated. For the direction of the upper longitudinal axis, see above. The walls of the skull are rather convex.

EYES Well open, round, larger than the normal, with an intelligent expression. Seen from in front, the haw should not be visible. The edges of the eyelids should invariably be pigmented with black, and the color of the iris is deep ocher.

EARS Long and hanging, set on high, above the zygomatic arch. The base is rather rigid, keeping the upper part separated from the skull, thus giving a broader appearance to the head. The ears, like the entire head, is covered with long, flocked hair.

NECK The length of the neck is equal to the length of the head. There is no dewlap.

FOREQUARTERS Shoulders The length of the shoulders is ¼ the height at the withers. They are free in movement. The scapulae tend to be vertical in respect to the center plane of the body and are quite oblique in respect to the horizontal. **Upper Arm** Almost as long as the shoulder, well joined to the trunk; it is less sloped than the shoulder. **Forearms** They follow a straight vertical, their length equal to that of the humerus; the elbows lie in a plane parallel to the center plane of the body. **Wrists and Pasterns** Seen from in front, they follow the straight vertical of the forearm; seen in profile, the pasterns are slightly bent. The forearms, wrists and pasterns are covered with thick, flocked hair. **Feet** Oval, covered with long hair; the nails are black, the pads are hard and also black.

BODY The length of the trunk, measured from the point of the shoulder (outer scapula-humeral angle) to the point of the buttock (the back of the ischium) is equal to the height at the withers. The manubrium of the sternum is not pronounced. **Rib cage** Ample; the brisket is at elbow level. The ribs are well sprung. The depth of the chest is almost half the height at the withers. **Back** The withers are slightly raised above the backline and are rather broad because of the distance which separates the point of the scapulae; the backline is straight. **Loins** Well integrated with the backline; the loins are slightly arched and merge harmoniously with the croup. **Flanks** The length of the flanks is almost equal to that of the lumbar region; they are very slightly hollowed. **Croup** Broad and very slightly sloping. **Belly** From the sternum the lower line of the body ascends slightly toward the belly. **Sexual Organs** The testicles are of normal development, both within the scrotum.

TAIL Set on at the level of the croup and carried curved over the back; it is well feathered with long, flocked hair.

HINDQUARTERS Thighs Long, measuring 1/3 of the height at the withers; the thighs slope from above downward and from back forward and, in respect to the vertical, parallel to the center plane of the body. **Legs** Somewhat longer than the thighs, the legs are covered with long, flocked hair, rather like the thighs, but not fringed. **Metatarsus** The distance from the points of the hocks to the ground is 27 percent of the height at the withers. The angulation of the hocks is not particularly closed; seen from behind, the backline which goes from the point of the hocks to the ground should be vertical and a prolongation of the line of the buttocks. The metatarsus, seen both from behind and in profile, should lie on the vertical. It is covered, like the rest of the leg, with long, flocked hair which does not fringe. **Feet** Less oval than the forefeet but otherwise similar.

COAT Hair Long, flocked; it does not lie close to the underparts. It covers the entire head, the trunk and the feet. It is shorter on the nasal bridge. **Color** Pure white without markings, not even simple shading. **Skin** The lips, eyelids and nose should absolutely be pigmented with black.

GAIT Normal.

FAULTS General Characteristics Undistinguished overall appearance; short, nonflocked coat; lack of symmetry. **Height** Under or over the standard. In males height below 10 inches or above 13 inches is a disqualification; the respective figures for females are 8¾ and 12½ inches. **Head** Upper longitudinal axes convergent or divergent. Total cephalic index above 60 or below 50 (disqualification). **Nose** Small nose; traces of depigmentation, even if they are only in the nostrils; total depigmentation (disqualification); any color besides black (disqualification). **Nasal Bridge** Short or too long, arched or hollowed; if decidedly arched, disqualification. **Lips** Overly developed. to the point where they cover the lower jaw. **Jaws** Undershot condition: if it spoils the outer appearance of the muzzle, it is a disqualification; decided overshot condition (disqualification); sides of lower jaw curved; irregular teeth, any teeth lacking; horizontal erosion of the teeth. **Skull** Small, spheroid (serious fault) and not flat; underdeveloped sinuses; occipital protuberance too pronounced; medial furrow pronounced or lacking; convergence or divergence of the upper longitudinal cranial-facial axes. **Eyes** Small or too prominent; light eyes; wall eyes (disqualification); almond-shaped and oblique, that is, not in a subfrontal position; entropion, ectropion, cross eyes; partial depigmentation of the eyelids; total depigmentation is a very serious fault; total bilateral depigmentation is a disqualification; bilaterally crossed eyes (disqualification). **Ears** Short, relaxed at the base, short hair. **Neck** Massive and short; dewlap; hair of insufficient length. **Shoulders** Lacking in freedom of movement. **Upper Arm** Too sloping, too straight, too short. **Forearm** Spongy bone; elbows out or in; insufficient length of hair. **Wrists** Evident hypertrophy of the wrist bones; sponginess; insufficient length of hair. **Pasterns** Out of vertical, spongy; insufficient length of hair. **Feet** Catfeet; broad, crushed feet; pointed outward or inward. **Body** Longitudinal diameter greater than height at the withers. **Rib cage** Too narrow, not sufficient height, not sufficient depth; xiphoid appendage curved inward; ribs insufficiently sprung. **Back** Short, saddleback (lordosis); roach back (kyphosis). **Loins** Long and narrow. **Croup** Sloping. **Belly** Drawn up. **Flanks** Excessively hollowed. **Sexual Organs** Monorchidism (disqualification), cryptorchidism (disqualification); incomplete development of one or both testicles, which are consequently too small (disqualification); testicles out of natural position (disqualification). **Tail** Not curved over the back, hanging; lack of tail or rudimentary tail, whether congenital or acquired (disqualification); tail insufficiently feathered, hair insufficiently long. **Thighs** Carried away from stifle; lack of hair. **Legs** Excessively or insufficiently sloping; deficiency of hair. **Hocks** Too high; angulation too open or too closed through forward deviation of metatarsus; out of vertical. **Metatarsus** Too long, out of vertical; dewclaws; lack of hair. **Feet** As for the forefeet. **Hair** Not dense, not long, not flocked. **Color** Any color besides

BOLOGNESE

white; markings of another color, even if minimum (disqualification). **Skin** Dewlap; traces of depigmentation on nose and eyelids; total depigmentation of the nose (disqualification); depigmentation of the edges of the eyelids of both eyes (disqualification); depigmentation of the vulva and vent; deficiency of pigment in nails and pads; total depigmentation of the pads (very serious fault). **Gait** Ambling (very serious fault).

DISQUALIFICATIONS **Height:** Males, below 10 or above 13 inches; females, below 8¾ or above 12½ inches. **Head** Accentuated divergence or con-

vergence of the upper cranial-facial longitudinal axes; total cephalic index over 62 or under 50. **Nose** Total depigmentation; any color besides black. **Nasal Bridge** Accentuated arch. **Jaws** Overshot condition; accentuated undershot condition if it spoils the outer appearance of the muzzle. **Eyes** Walleyes; total bilateral depigmentation of the eyelids; bilaterally crossed eyes. **Body** Longitudinal diameter above 1¼ inches over the maximum allowed by the height at the withers. **Tail** Lack of tail or rudimentary tail, either congenital or acquired. **Sexual Organs** Monorchidism, cryptorchidism; incom-

plete development of one or both testicles; testicles not in natural position. **Hair** Very short, curly. **Color** Any color or besides white; markings, even if very small. **Skin** Total depigmentation of the nose; total bilateral depigmentation of the eyelids. In judging, whenever a given somatic region involving in any essential way the type of the breed is rated zero, the dog is immediately disqualified, even when the other regions are to be rated excellent.

SCALE OF POINTS

General appearance	20
Skull and muzzle	25
Eyes	10
Ears	10
Shoulders	5
Rib cage	10
Loins and croup	5
Legs and feet	10
Tail	20
Coat and color	35
	150

RATINGS

Excellent: points not less than	140
Very good	130
Good	120
Fairly good	110

MALTESE

277 MALTESE
ITALY

The Bichon dogs include the Maltese, the Bolognese, the Curly-Coated Bichon, and the Havanese. They are a group of breeds related to one another and are of very ancient origin, which Darwin himself places at 6000 B.C. The Maltese was formerly called the "Roman Ladies' Dog," as they esteemed and valued him so highly. His long and immaculate coat makes him very attractive, and his intelligence, affectionate disposition, and liveliness make him one of the most perfect pet dogs.

There are differences of opinion about his origins. Strabo, the writer on geography who lived in the first century B.C. describes a Maltese dog, defining him as *Canis melitoeus* or "dog of Melita," the Latin name for the island of Malta from which according to

Robin, "he departed to conquer the world." Many specialists believe that the Maltese of today is the exact descendant of the Maltese mentioned by Strabo. Others, however, do not agree. Among these is Baron Houtart, a well-known specialist in European toy breeds. He states: "The ancient peoples of the southern Mediterranean had a dwarf breed called Melitoeus. It originated on the island of Malta or Melitz, near Sicily. I would call these dogs Malita dogs rather than Maltese so as not to confuse them with the modern Maltese dogs which are absolutely different from the ancient ones."

The origins of the modern Maltese, on the contrary, should be sought in the crossing of the miniature Spaniel with the miniature Poodle or with the Cayenne dog. These are the sources from which the Barbichon, later called the Bichon, originated. It appears that the Bichon originated in Italy, proof of which can be found in numerous early pictorial representations.

Photo: S. A. Thompson.

GENERAL CHARACTERISTICS The Maltese is scientifically classified in the braccoid group, miniature type (according to the classification of Pierre Mégnin); a nonsporting dog of extremely old origin, Italian and probably Maltese (cf. Pliny, Strabo and Columella, all of whom called it *Canis melitensis*). The general conformation is that of a small dog, whose trunk exceeds in length the height at the withers. The body should give the overall impression of being narrow and long. The Maltese is an elegant dog with head, trunk, tail and legs covered (on all sides) with silky, very white, highly glossy hair long enough to be almost excessive. The Maltese is intelligent, of vivacious personality and devoted to his master. The rich, pure white coat makes a most highly preferred companion.

WEIGHT AND SIZE Weight: 6½ to 9 lb. Height: males 8¼-10 inches; females 7¾-9 inches. The upper limit may be increased by 2/5 inch in dogs of exceptional beauty.

HEAD Mesocephalic; its total length is 6/11 of the height at the withers. The length of the muzzle is ⅓ of the total length of the head, i.e., 3.7/10. The naso-cephalic index is therefore 37.46 and should never be above 40 or below 35. The width of the skull should never be more than 3/5 of the total length of the head, giving a total cephalic index of 60.06. The directions of the upper longitudinal axes of the skull and of the muzzle are parallel. **Nose** On the same line with the nasal bridge; seen in profile, the forepart of the nose is on the vertical. It should be large compared with the volume of the head, wet and cool, with the nostrils well open. It is round and absolutely black. No other color is permissible. **Nasal Bridge** Straight. For the length of the nasal bridge and its direction relative to the skull axis and for the naso-cephalic index, see above. Its width, measured at the midpoint, should be 72 percent of its length, or 26 percent of the total length of the head. The nasal bridge has extremely long hair, which mingles with the hair of the beard. **Lips and Muzzle** The upper lip, seen from in front, has the shape of a semicircle with an extremely long chord. The lips do not appear high as seen from in front and in profile; therefore the commissure is not visible. The edges of the lips must absolutely be black. The edges of the upper lip, moreover, meet the edges of the lower lip over their entire length; this means that the lower profile of the muzzle is supplied by the mandible. The medial furrow is pronounced. The muzzle should be in height 77 percent of its length; the sides are parallel, but the forepart of the muzzle is not perfectly flat

and square since its sides join the sides of the muzzle itself in a gentle curve. The suborbital region should be well chiseled. The lips and the entire muzzle are covered with extremely long hair similar to that found on the ears. **Jaws** Light in appearance and of normal development; the upper and lower teeth meet in a scissors bite. The edges of the lower jaw are straight throughout their entire length. The lower jaw itself is normal, that is, neither prominent nor receding. The teeth are white and irregular, 42 in number and completely developed. The stop is very pronounced, because the profile of the apophyses of the nasal bones and upper jaws rises toward the frontal bone with an accentuated slope. The sinuses are well developed. The angle of the stop is 90 degrees. **Skull** The length should exceed the length of the muzzle by 3/11 of the total length of the head. Its width is almost equal to its length. The average difference between length and width of the skull is about 1/10 inch. Its shape is very slightly ovoid, the occipital protuberance is very slightly marked. The back part of the forehead should be flat. The height of the sinuses and the supraorbital ridges accentuate the stop. The medial furrow is almost nonexistent. For the direction of the upper longitudinal axis of the skull, see above. The parietals are somewhat convex.

EYES The expression is vivacious and intelligent. The eyes should be well open and rather larger than normal. The shape tends to be round. The eyelids are close-fitting. The eyes are slightly protruding and should never be deep-set. They are set well up on the forehead. Seen from in front, the eyes should show no haw. The color is deep ocher, the pigmentation of the eyelids is black, identical to that of the nose.

EARS Triangular and flat. Their length is slightly more than 1/3 of the height at the withers. In a dog measuring from 8½-9¾ inches at the withers, the length of the ears is 3-3½ inches. The base is broad and the ears are set on high, considerably above the zygomatic arch. They hang close to the sides of the head, as close as the abundant hair permits. Although set on very high, the ears have little erectile power because of the weight of the hair. They are entirely covered with long, thick and nonwavy hair reaching at least to the shoulders and, preferably, beyond. They are further covered by the hair falling from the crest of the skull.

NECK In spite of the abundant hair, the forward and upper lines of the nape should be clearly visible. The length of the neck is approximately

MALTESE

MALTESE

Photo: S. A. Thompson.

equal to half the height at the withers, that is, approximately the same length as the head, and with a circumference equal to or greater than the height at the withers, when the neck is normally feathered. The throat and jaws should not have loose skin, meaning that there is no dewlap. The neck is carried erect, giving the impression that the head is thrown back.

FOREQUARTERS **Shoulders** Should be 1/3 as long as the height at the withers; its inclination to the horizontal varies from 60-65 degrees. In a dog 8¾ inches high at the withers, the scapula is about 3 inches long. The shoulders should be free in their movement, and their direction in relation to the center plane of the body is slightly inclined at the point, which means that the scapulae tend to a vertical position. **Upper Arm** Well joined to the trunk in its upper two-thirds. The inclination to the horizontal is about 70 degrees, and its longitudinal direction is almost parallel to the center plane of the body. Its length, greater than that of the scapula, is 40.45 percent of the height at the withers. **Forearm** Straight and vertical, lean, well boned, with few muscles; the bone is quite strong considering the size of the dog. The length of the forearm is less than that of the humerus (33 percent of the height at the withers), and the height of the entire foreleg to the elbow is 54.54 percent of the height at the withers, which means that in a dog measuring 8¾ inches at the withers, the height of the foreleg at the elbow is about 4¾ inches, that is, slightly more than half the height at the withers. The elbows should lie in a plane parallel to the center plane of the body. This means that they should not be too close to the ribs, thus eliminating the armpit, nor should they be turned outward. The forearm, from the elbow to the lower end of the pastern, is covered all around with long hair, which in general is flocked, forming a fringe on the backside of the foreleg. **Wrists** Follow the vertical line of the forearm. They are very

mobile, should not be knotty, and covered with thin skin. The wrist is covered on all sides by long, thick hair. **Pasterns** Follow the vertical of the forearm and, like the wrists, should be lean and covered with fine hair. The pasterns are short and straight and covered, like the forearms and the wrists, with long, thick hair in every part. **Feet** Round, with closed toes, well arched, covered with long, thick hair; there is also long, thick hair between the toes. The pads are black, and the nails are black or at least dark.

BODY The length of the trunk, measured from the point of the shoulder (external scapula-humeral angle) to the point of the buttock (posterior point of the ischium), exceeds on the average the height at the withers by 3 inches, or more precisely, for every inch of height at the withers there corresponds 1.38 inch of length in the trunk. **Rib cage** Roomy, reaching beyond elbow level, with moderately sprung ribs. The sternum region is long, its outline being a semicircle of very large radius which ascends slightly toward the belly. The circumference of the rib cage should be 2/3 more than the height at the withers, and its diameter should be 36.88 percent of the height at the withers. The depth of the thorax should be 65 percent of the height at the withers, or at least half the length of the trunk, and it is better if it exceeds it. In a dog 9 inches high at the withers, the rib cage should have the following dimensions: circumference (behind the elbows), 14½ inches; depth, 6 inches; height, 4½ inches; diameter, 3-1/3 inches. **Back** The withers are slightly raised above the backline, which is straight. The backline goes from the withers to the root of the tail. The length of the back is about 65 percent of the height at the withers; that is, in a dog 9 inches high at the withers, the back is close to 6 inches long. **Loins** Perfectly joined with the backline, the loins continue its outline. The muscles are well developed. The length is 1/3 of the height at the withers, and the width

is the same. **Belly and Flanks** The belly is rather low, ascending very little from sternum to flank. The flanks should be almost equal in length to the loins. The hollow of the flanks should not be pronounced. **Croup** Continues the straight backline. It is broad, and its width should be 1/3 of the height at the withers, its length about ¾ inch greater than its width in a dog measuring 9 inches at the withers. The inclination to the horizontal, from the haunch to the root of the tail, is always less than 10 degrees. **Sexual Organs** The testicles should be perfectly developed.

TAIL Set on level with the croup, it is very thick at the root and fine at the tip. In a dog measuring 9 inches at the withers, the tail should measure 5½ inches. The tail is correctly carried in a single large curve, with the tip touching the croup between the haunches. A tail curved over to one side is tolerated. The tail is covered with very long, abundant hair, which falls entirely on one side of the body, that is, on the flank and thigh, rather like the branches of a weeping willow. The hair on the tail should be long enough to reach the hocks.

HINDQUARTERS **Thighs** The thighs are covered with hard muscle; the back edges are arched. The length of the thighs is 39 percent of the height at the withers. The direction of the thighs is somewhat sloped downward and forward and, in respect to the vertical, it should be parallel to the center plane of the body. In a dog measuring 9 inches at the withers, the width of the thighs is about 1¼ inches less than its length. They are covered with long hair which forms a fringe at the back edge. **Legs** Extremely well boned for a dog of this size; the furrow between the bone and the back tendon is not pronounced. The legs are slightly longer than the thighs; their inclination to the horizontal is 55 degrees. The legs are covered on all sides by long hair which is generally flocked and fringed on the back surface. **Hocks** The distance from the soles to

the points of the hocks is a little more than 1/3 of the height at the withers. The forward angulation is 140 degrees. Seen from behind, the line from the point of the hock to the ground should be on the vertical and on the prolongation of the buttock line. **Metatarsus** The length depends on the height at the withers; it should lie on the vertical, as seen both in profile and from behind. It is covered all around by long hair, generally flocked, which forms a limited fringe on the backside. **Feet** Round like the forefeet and otherwise similar.

COAT **Hair** Dense, glossy, heavy, very long; its texture is silky. The hair is straight throughout its length. The average length of the hair on the body should be a little less than 8¾ inches, that is, the longest hair should be equal to or slightly more than the height at the withers. Such long hair should cover the entire body—trunk, forequarters, tail, neck, ears, skull and muzzle. Besides being glossy, long and white, the thick mass of hair on the Maltese should fall heavily to the ground, like a solid mantle fitting close to the trunk, and the hair should be without flocks or tufts (except on the forelegs from the elbows to the feet and on the hind legs from the stifle to the feet, where tufted hair is permitted). The entire mass of hair should be superlatively glossy. The coat should reveal only the principal curves and projections of the body. There is no undercoat. **Color** Pure white; a pale ivory shade is permitted. Very limited pale orange tints are tolerated, but they constitute a fault. Decided markings, even if very small, are not acceptable. **Skin** Close-fitting to the body at all points. The head (skull and muzzle) should have no wrinkles; there should be no dewlap. The skin is in part or over the whole body pigmented with dark spots; when the hair is parted, the skin color, especially on the back, should be of a more or less intense wine red. The pigment of the lips, nose and eyelids should be black. The pads must be black; the nails also should be black or at least dark.

GAIT The trotting gait consists of short, very rapid steps, giving somewhat the impression of rolling. The gait should in no way resemble that of the Pekingese.

FAULTS **General Characteristics** Undistinguished overall appearance; heavy appearance; dull or coarse coat; lack of symmetry. **Height at the Withers** Over or above standard. **Head** Upper longitudinal cranial-facial axes divergent or convergent; naso-cephalic index above 40 or below 35 (disqualification). **Nose** Lower than the line of the bridge; protruding over the vertical line of the forepart of the muzzle; nostrils not well open; small nose; deficient pigmentation; traces of depigmentation on the nostrils; total depigmentation (disqualification); any color besides black (disqualification). **Nasal Bridge** Short; narrow; converging sidelines; arched; hollowed. If decidedly arched, disqualification. **Lips and Muzzle** Short or excessively long muzzle; lips too large, to the point where they cover the lower jaw; deficient in development; forward convergence of the sides of the muzzle, that is, pointed muzzle; forepart of the muzzle not broad; conjunction of two halves of upper lip form an inverted V; lack of chiseling in the suborbital region. **Jaws** Undershot: if this condition harms the appearance of the muzzle, disqualification; overshot: if for insufficient length of underjaw, disqualification; if caused by crooked teeth, fault; sides of lower jaw curved;

MALTESE

Photo: M. Pedone.

teeth irregular or not full complement; horizontal erosion of teeth. **Skull** Small, short, too narrow at the parietals; spheroid (very serious fault); skull not flat; supraorbital ridges flattened; sinuses insufficiently developed; occipital protuberance excessively pronounced; medial furrow pronounced; stop insufficiently accentuated or receding; convergence or divergence of the upper cranial-facial longitudinal axes. **Eyes** Small or too prominent; light eyes, walleyes (disqualification); slanting, almond eyes; ectropion; entropion; eyes too close; cross eyes; partial depigmentation of the eyelids; total depigmentation is a very serious fault; total bilateral depigmentation is a disqualification. **Ears** Thick, too short; narrow base; rigidity caused by excessive thickness; curling; short hair. **Neck** Massive and short; insufficient arching; lack of definition in nape; dewlap; hair too short. **Shoulders** Lacking in freedom of movement; straight. **Upper Arm** Too sloping or too straight; short. **Forearm** Spongy bone; arching at outside of radial (very serious fault); deviation from vertical; elbows in or out; short hair. **Wrists** Evident hypertrophy of the wrist bones; short hair. **Pasterns** Out of vertical; spongy; short hair. **Feet** Oblong; splayed; broad, crushed; carried inward or outward, that is, not vertical; bad arrangement of pads; deficiency of pig-

mentation in nails and pads; lack of hair between toes and on toes. **Body** Longitudinal diameter greater than the required length or shorter. **Chest** Manubrium of the sternum not pronounced. **Rib cage** Deficient in height, depth and circumference; too narrow; decidedly carenated; xiphoid appendage curved inward. **Ribs** Insufficiently sprung. **Back** Short; breaking of the backline at the eleventh vertebra; saddleback (lordosis); roach back (kyphosis). **Loins** Narrow, too long, arched. **Belly and Flanks** Belly insufficiently or excessively drawn up; flanks excessively hollowed. **Croup** Narrow, sloping. **Sexual Organs** Monorchidism or cryptorchidism (disqualification); incomplete development of one or both testicles (disqualification). **Tail** Too long or too short; lack of tail or rudimentary tail, either congenital or acquired (disqualification); tail set on low; not thick at the root; not curved over the back (carried horizontally or hanging: a very serious fault); tail carried curved on one side of trunk; tail curled; lack of feathering, short hair. **Thighs** Carried away from stifle region: insufficiently feathered. **Legs** Insufficiently sloped; lack of hair. **Hocks** Too high; angulation too open or too closed because of forward deviation of metatarsus; out of vertical. **Metatarsus** Too long; out of vertical; dewclaws; lack of hair. **Feet** Similar

to forefeet. **Coat** Hair not dense, dull, not long; woolly texture; mass of hair soft and fluffy, light; hair tufted or flocked; mass of hair not close-fitting to trunk; curly hair (disqualification); wavy hair (serious fault). **Color** Any color besides white (disqualification), with the exception of pale ivory; pale orange tint; well-defined markings, even if very small (disqualification). **Skin** Wrinkles on the head; dewlap; traces of depigmentation on the nose and eyelids; total depigmentation of the nose (disqualification); depigmentation of the edges of both eyelids of both eyes (disqualification); depigmentation of the vulva and vent; lack of pigmentation in the nails and pads; total depigmentation of the pads (very serious fault). **Gait** Ambling (very serious fault); Pekingese gait (disqualification).

DISQUALIFICATIONS Height at the Withers In males, over 10¼ inches or more than ¾ inch less than the minimum; in females, more than 10 inches or more than ¾ inch less than the standard. **Head** Accentuated divergence or convergence of the upper cranial-facial longitudinal axes; naso-cephalic index over 40 or under 35. **Nose** Total depigmentation; any color besides black. **Nasal Bridge** Definite arch. **Jaws** Overshot condition if caused by shortness of the

lower jaw; accentuated undershot condition if it harms the appearance of the muzzle. **Eyes** Walleyes; total bilateral depigmentation of the eyelids; bilaterally crossed eyes. **Body** Longitudinal diameter ¾ inch over the maximum standard for height at the withers. **Sexual Organs** Monorchidism, cryptorchidism; incomplete development of one or both testicles. **Tail** Lack of or rudimentary, whether congenital or acquired. **Coat** Short hair, curly hair. **Color** Any besides white, with the exception of pale ivory; definite markings, even if very small. **Skin** Total depigmentation of the nose; depigmentation of the edges of both eyelids on both eyes. **Gait** Pekingese gait.

N.B. In judging in a show, when any part of the body involving type is rated zero, the dog is disqualified, even if the other parts are excellent.

SCALE OF POINTS

General appearance	20
Skull and muzzle	20
Eyes and eyelids	10
Ears	10
Shoulders	5
Rib cage	10
Loins and croup	5
Legs and feet	10
Tail	20
Coat and color	40
	150

Photo: S. A. Thompson.

278 ITALIAN SPITZ
Volpino Italiano
ITALY

The Italian, German, and Pomeranian Spitz have so many points in common that they may easily be confused. However, in the Italian breed the eye is slightly larger, the ear longer, and the skull rounder. It is difficult to establish whether the Italian Spitz descends from the German or vice versa. In any case, the Italian Spitz was always very prevalent in Italy, especially in Tuscany where he was called "the Florence Spitz" and in Rome where he was called "the Quirinal Dog."

One must consider, concerning the origins of the miniature form of Spitz, which has been prevalent since ancient times, that whereas many breeds, for purposes of performance, were bred for larger size, there was also a tendency to breed for smallness. This resulted in small or even dwarflike animals which would be objects of curiosity, comparable to the jesters and dwarfs who enlivened the princely courts. These dwarf dogs are represented by the Spitz, Dwarf Pinscher, Small Italian Greyhound, Toy Spaniels, Toy Terriers, and so on.

GENERAL CHARACTERISTICS Scientifically the Italian Spitz is classified as belonging to the lupoid group, according to the classification of Pierre Mégnin. As to use, he is a nonsporting, companion dog. Italian origin. The general conformation is that of a small dog, mesomorphic, with a square body outline. A very compact dog, with neck, body and tail covered with extremely long hair. The Italian Spitz is intelligent and lively, devoted to his master and all that belongs to him. Thus he is a splendid and fearless guard dog.

SIZE Males 10½-12 inches; females 9¾-11 inches.

HEAD Submesocephalic, with the shape of a horizontal pyramid. Its length is 3.8/10 of the height at the withers; the length of the muzzle should be slightly less than half of the total length of the head (muzzle 5, head 11.5). The width of the skull is greater than half the total length of the head; therefore the total cephalic index is 63. The directions of the upper longitudinal axes of the skull and muzzle are slightly convergent. **Nose** Seen in profile, the nose lies on the horizontal line of the nasal bridge. It does not extend beyond the vertical of the forepart of the lips. It should be wet and cool, with well open nostrils; its pigmentation is always black, both in dogs with white coats and red coats. **Nasal Bridge** For the length and direction of the nasal bridge, see above. **Lips and Muzzle** The sides of the muzzle are convergent. The two parts of the upper lip, seen from in front, determine at their lower edge a straight line; therefore at the point where they meet there is neither an inverted V nor a semicircle. Because of the convergence of its sides, the muzzle is pointed. Its lower line is given by the lower jaw, and the commissure is not visible. The lips are therefore very short. The edges of the lips should be absolutely black. The muzzle is covered with red hair. **Jaws** Not of robust appearance, normally developed, with dental arches meeting perfectly in front. The sides of the lower jaw are straight, while the body of the jaw itself is not greatly developed. White teeth, regular, complete in number and development. **Stop** Rather accentuated; the sinuses are large, falling almost perpendicularly onto the apophyses of the nose and upper jaws. **Skull** The length of the skull exceeds that of the muzzle, in a ratio of 6.5:5. Its width is 63.5 percent of the total length of the head. Its shape is ovoid; the occipital protuberance is only slightly marked, the sinuses well developed. The medial furrow is not accentuated. For the direction of the longitudinal axis of the skull, see above. The skull is covered with flat hair of moderate length.

EYES Well open and of normal size, the eyes reveal the vivacious character and the intelligence of the Italian Spitz. Their position is subfrontal, and the opening of the eyelids is approximately round. The eyelids are close-fitting. Seen from in front, the eyes should not show any haw. The color is deep ocher, the pigmentation of the eyelids is black, that is, the same as for the nose.

EARS Short and triangular; they are carried erect, with the auricle directed forward and with rigid cartilage. They are set on high, well above the zygomatic arch, very close to each other. The length of the ear is half the total length of the head, but it seems to be much shorter, because its base is hidden by the relatively long hair on the head. The hair on the ears is very fine and very short.

NECK The neck is almost as long as the head. It is always carried erect. It is covered with very long, dense, rigid hair. There should be no dewlap.

FOREQUARTERS Shoulders The length of the shoulders should be equal to ¼ the height at the withers; the inclination to the horizontal is 60 degrees. **Upper Arms** The upper arms are slightly longer than the scapula, and the inclination to the horizontal is 65 degrees. The longitudinal direction is almost parallel to the center plane of the body. **Forearm** Fine-boned and vertical. Its length at the elbow is slightly greater than half the height at the withers. The elbows should lie in a plane which is parallel to the center plane of the body; this means that they should be turned neither inward nor outward. The forearms and feet are covered with short hair. The backside of the forelegs has a fringe. **Wrists and Pasterns** They continue the vertical line of the forearm. The pasterns are slightly bent. **Feet** Oval, with well-closed toes, covered with short hair. The pads are black, and the nails are black in both white and red dogs.

BODY The length of the trunk, measured from the point of the shoulder (outer scapula-humeral angle) to the point of the buttock (posterior point of the ischium), is equal to the height at the withers. **Rib cage** Deep, extending to elbow level, with well-sprung ribs; the sternum is long. Its vertical diameter is 3.8/10 the height at the withers, while the cross diameter is 1/3 of the height at the withers. **Back** The withers are slightly raised above the backline, which is straight. **Loins** Slightly arched as seen in profile; the loin region is short. **Belly and Flanks** The lower line of the belly rises slightly from the sternum to the flank. The flanks should be about the same length as the loins and slightly hollowed. **Croup** Follows the line of the loins, and its slope from the haunches to the root of the tail is 10 degrees from the horizontal. **Sexual Organs** Perfect and complete development of the testicles, which should be in their natural position in the scrotum.

TAIL Set on at the level of the croup. In a dog 11¾ inches high at the withers, the tail is 5½ inches long. It is well feathered and is carried curled over the back, to the point where the closer the flag is to the neck, the better.

HINDQUARTERS Thighs Are 1/3 the height at the withers; they are trousered. **Legs** The length of the legs is slightly less than that of the thighs. The bone is light, inclined at 55-60 degrees to the horizontal. The legs are fringed at the back, and the front side is covered with short hair. **Hocks and Metatarsi** The points of the hocks are about 3⅛ inches above the ground. The metatarsus should lie on the vertical, as seen both in profile and from behind. The backside has a very limited fringe, negligible in certain dogs. **Feet** Oval and otherwise similar in every way to the forefeet.

COAT Thick, very long and essentially straight. The straightness of the hair is a corollary of its hard texture. Even when not thick, the hair should be straight and not falling. It is very long, covering the neck and trunk, giving the impression of a muff. **Color** Solid white or solid red. Honey color is accepted, but not desirable. Slight pale orange tints are tolerated on the ears; such coloring does, however, constitute a fault.

GAIT Normal trot, not jerky; normal gallop.

FAULTS General Characteristics Undistinguished overall appearance; long body; dull, falling, short coat. **Height at the Withers** More than 1⅛ inch above or below standard (disqualification). **Head** Upper cranial-facial longitudinal axes parallel; if divergent, disqualification. **Nose** Lower than the topline of the bridge; extending over the vertical line of the forepart of the muzzle; insufficient pigmentation; traces of depigmentation in the nostrils; total depigmentation (disqualification); any color besides black (disqualification). **Nasal Bridge** Too long or too short; arched (disqualification). **Lips** Too large, to the extent of covering the lower jaw. **Skull** Too broad, that is, with a total cephalic index above 63; underdeveloped sinuses; medial furrow prominent. **Eyes** Small or too prominent; light eyes; walleyes (disqualification). **Ears** Too long; half-hanging; entirely hanging (disqualification); ears covered with long hair and with fringe. **Neck** Insufficiently abundant hair; soft, hanging hair. **Shoulders** Lacking in freedom of movement. **Forearms** Spongy bone; deviation from vertical; elbows out or in; short fringe. **Wrists** With evident hypertrophy of the wrist bones. **Feet** Broad, crushed; splayed toes; feet carried inward or outward; deficient pigmentation in nails and pads. **Body** With longitudinal diameter greater than the height at the withers. **Rib cage** Insufficiently developed; xiphoid appendage curved inward; insufficient spring of rib. **Back** Interruption of backline at eleventh vertebra; saddleback (lordosis), roach back (kyphosis). **Loins** Long, narrow, weak. **Belly** Excessively or insufficiently tucked up, hollowed loins. **Croup** Narrow or falling off. **Sexual Organs** Monorchidism (disqualification), cryptorchidism (disqualification); incomplete development of one or both testicles; small testicles (disqualification); testicles not contained in scrotum (disqualification). **Tail** Too long or too short; lack of tail or rudimentary tail, whether congenital or acquired (disqualification); tail not curved over back; permanently and decidedly hanging between the hind legs (disqualification); poorly feathered tail, short hair on tail. **Thighs** Carried away from the stifle region; lack of hair. **Legs** With insufficient fringe. **Hocks and Metatarsi** Too long, out of vertical; dewclaws; lack of hair. **Feet** As for the forefeet. **Hair** Not thick, dull, not long; woolly texture (very serious fault); hair not straight, flocked; excessively hanging hair (disqualification). **Color** Any color besides white or red (both of these to be solid); decided markings, even if small, of other color (disqualification); pale orange tint on ears. **Skin** Dewlap; traces of depigmentation on the nose

ITALIAN SPITZ

CHIHUAHUA PUPPIES

and eyelids; total depigmentation of the nose (disqualification); depigmentation of tne edges of the two lids of both eyes (disqualification); depigmentation of the vulva and vent; lack of pigmentation in nails and pads; total depigmentation of the pads (very serious fault). **Gait** Continual ambling (very serious fault); Spanish gait.

DISQUALIFICATIONS Height at the Withers More than ⅝ inch above or below the standard. **Head** Upper cranial-facial longitudinal axes divergent. **Nose** Total depigmentation; any color besides black. **Nasal Bridge** Arched. **Eyes** Walleyes. **Ears** Completely hanging. **Sexual Organs** Cryptorchidism, monorchidism; insufficient development of one or both testicles; testicles not contained in scrotum. **Tail** Lack of tail or rudimentary tail, whether congenital or acquired; tail decidedly and permanently hanging between the hind legs. **Hair** Falling and adhering to trunk. **Color** Any color besides white or red; red or other markings on white background; black

markings on red background. **Skin** Total depigmentation of the nose; depigmenation of the edges of both eyelids on both eyes.

SCALE OF POINTS

General appearance	20
Skull and muzzle	25
Eyes and eyelids	10
Ears	10
Shoulders	5
Rib cage	10
Loins and croup	5
Legs and feet	20
Tail	20
Coat and color	25
	150

RATINGS

Excellent: points not lower than	140
Very good	130
Good	120
Fairly good	110

N.B. In judging in a show, when any part of the body involving type is rated zero, the dog is disqualified, even if the other parts are excellent. ●

279 CHIHUAHUA
MEXICO

Among the few indigenous American breeds, the Chihuahua is the oldest and the best known. In spite of his small size the Chihuahua is relatively strong and robust and a good hunter of small rodents.

Few small-sized dogs can be compared to the Chihuahua. Considered as a show dog or toy dog, he possesses all the diverting gracefulness and lightness of the terrier. As guard dog he is always on the alert and is always interested in what is going on around him. And when one has gained his confidence he will be faithful unto death. This breed is perhaps the smallest extant. Adult specimens weighing no more than 2 lb are not unusual. Although Mexico is his country of origin, he is also bred with good results in parts of the United States and Canada where the climate is more severe.

Photo: R. Kinne (Photo Res.).

CHIHUAHUA PUPPIES

Photo: S. A. Thompson.

CHIHUAHUA

MEXICAN HAIRLESS

GENERAL CHARACTERISTICS This breed is differentiated from all others by many particular characteristics, of which the most obvious is its very small size. Some Chihuahuas weigh less than 2 lb, while others reach 7¾ lb; the average weight is 2¾-4 lb. In the United States, a show dog should never exceed 6 lb. Small as he is, the Chihuahua is ever alert, lively, very intelligent and fast moving. He is courageous, capable of standing up to much larger dogs. He is very loyal to his master and impatient with strangers, and this makes him a good guard dog because he barks angrily and gives the alarm at the least suspicious movement.

WEIGHT The smallest Chihuahuas weigh just under 2 lb; the largest weigh 7¾ lb, but these are exceptions; normally they weigh 2¾-4 lb. In judging between two dogs of equal quality, the preference is to be given to the smaller.

HEAD It is the head which gives the Chihuahua its extraordinary appearance. The beauty of the dog lies in the correctness of its form. It should be round, the so-called apple head, with fine cheeks and an accentuated stop. Another difference between the Chihuahua and other dogs is in the fontanelle, which persists in adults. A very black nose is desirable. In light-colored dogs, the nose may be black or light, and even pink is allowed. In blue-coated, chocolate, or mole dogs it can be the same color as the coat. The bridge is quite short and rather pointed. The jaws should be neither large nor prominent, but thin and equipped with fine teeth, set regularly. A slight undershot condition is acceptable, but the teeth should never be visible.

EYES Brilliant, full, not too prominent and set well apart. They may be black, brown, blue, ruby or luminous. In light-colored dogs, light eyes are acceptable.

EARS Large and set far apart. They should be erect when the dog is alert. They are sloped at 45 degrees.

NECK Round, well proportioned, gracefully descending to the withers.

BODY Compact, longer than high, cylindrical or, better, slightly tucked up, a characteristic which gives this small dog his graceful, quick gait.

TAIL Moderately long and carried curved over the back or slightly on the side. The hair on the tail should harmonize with the hair on the body, and should be thicker if possible; however, even a hairless tail is acceptable.

FOREQUARTERS The shoulders are fine-boned. The articulations are high and elastic to permit good use of the thorax. The legs should be moderately high and straight although slightly short and bowed legs are permitted. The pasterns are slender.

HINDQUARTERS The thighs are muscular, the hocks are well separated and vertical. In action, the hindquarters should be free-moving, a condition which gives the Chihuahua a light gait when walking, running or trotting. The metatarsi are slender. **FEET** small, with the toes well apart, the pads round. The nails are long and curved.

COAT In respect to coat, there are two types of Chihuahua (1) longhaired, wavy: such dogs are rare; (2) shorthaired, with the coat close-packed and glossy. Dogs of the latter type are much more numerous. A small collar is always desirable; the hair on the neck may be a bit sparser than on the rest of the body. **Color** All colors and mixtures of colors are permitted, this being a matter of taste. The commonest colors and those considered most desirable are: fawn or brown, chocolate, grizzle, white, cream, silver fawn, silver gray, black and tan, black.

DISQUALIFICATIONS Clipped or falling ears; docked or broken tail; lack of hair (in this case the Chihuahua resembles the Mexican Hairless).

RATINGS Given on the basis of weight, head, body, legs, color and tail, in that order.

LONGHAIRED CHIHUAHUA

The differences between longhaired and shorthaired dogs are the following:

EARS The ears may be held less erect than in the case of the shorthaired dog, because of the length of the hair. In neither case, however, should they hang.

TAIL Should be long and well feathered.

COAT Of soft texture, either flat or slightly curly, with undercoat preferred. Ears fringed (heavily fringed ears may be tipped slightly, never down), feathering on feet and legs, and pants on hind legs. Large ruff on neck desired and preferred. ●

280 MEXICAN HAIRLESS
Xoloitzcuintli

MEXICO

This is a hairless breed, especially prevalent in Mexico but also found in greater or lesser numbers in Argentina, Chile, and other Central and South American countries. The Mexican Hair-

less' origin is very old; before the Spanish Conquest the Indians used its flesh for food which they esteemed highly. The dog was also considered the representative of the god Xolotl (from which his name is evidently derived), a divinity who was supposed to guide the souls of the dead toward their eternal resting place. In tombs recently discovered in Colima, Mexico, amusing clay effigies have been found depicting dogs very similar to the present Mexican Hairless.

MEXICAN HAIRLESS

Photo: A. Roslin-Williams, B. Frances, Buzzini.

BODY The chest is deep but fairly narrow, descending as far as the elbows. The thorax is well developed but must not impede the movement of the forelegs. The belly is muscular and well drawn up. The back is straight but supple, ending in a distinctly rounded rump. Swayback and roach back are undesirable. The body is rather thin compared to its height, in an approximate ratio of 9:10.

TAIL Set on low; smooth and rather long, reaching at least to the hocks and tapering to a fine point (for hair on tail see below).

FOREQUARTERS AND HINDQUARTERS When viewed from in front or behind the legs should be straight and well proportioned. They must be sufficiently long to permit a long and elegant gait in relation to the dog's size. Elbows should not protrude. The angle between the shoulder blade and the humerus should be 45 degrees. The thighs are strong and well muscled. **FEET** The Mexican Hairless has harefeet, with retracted toes. The nails are black in dark animals, lighter in those with unpigmented feet.

COAT There is usually a tuft of short, coarse, not very dense hair on the skull, although this should never have the length or softness of the mane of the Chinese Crested Dog. A wisp of similar hair is usually found near the tip of the tail, but it should not be so profuse as to alter the profile of the tail. Total absence of hair is not penalized. **Color** A uniform color of dark bronze, elephant gray, grayish black, or black is to be preferred, though pink and brown spots (which are really those without pigmentation) are acceptable. Exaggeration of this lack of pigmentation is undesirable. The hair on head and tail, when present, should be black for dark animals and any harmonizing color for lighter animals. **Skin** Smooth and soft to the touch, particularly in those areas which are less exposed to the sun. Scars on the skin resulting from normal wear and tear are not to be penalized, since this dog's skin is naturally very sensitive. The skin feels hot to the touch, since the Mexican Hairless' normal temperature is about 104°F (40°C); this extraordinarily high temperature is one of the distinguishing characteristics of this breed. Since it perspires profusely through its skin, particularly in the underparts, it rarely or never pants following exertion as most dogs do.

FAULTS Timid character; ears not entirely erectile; hair elsewhere than as specified above; exaggerated lack of pigmentation; excessively loose skin with folds and creases; dewclaws.

DISQUALIFICATIONS Hanging, hound-like ears, clipped ears not conforming with above description; cut or broken nails; albinism; cryptorchidism and monorchidism.

N.B. A good adult animal will usually be rather quiet and reserved, barking and growling only under provocation. This does not imply a cowardly or unhappy disposition. On the contrary, the Mexican Hairless should be gay and intelligent, yet dignified and not belligerent. Young puppies are snub-nosed and short-legged for some time and noisier and more mischievous than adults. They do not conform to the description given above until fairly late in their development.

MINIATURE MEXICAN HAIRLESS

Measures less than 12 inches at the withers. The standard has not yet been published by the Asociación Canofilia Mexicana, the Kennel Club of Mexico. ●

281 DALMATIAN
YUGOSLAVIA

The Dalmatian's harmonious lines, his engaging liveliness and, above all, his spotted coat, make him a valued luxury and pet dog noted for his great qualities of intelligence and fidelity. He has always shown a tendency to follow his master whether the latter travels by carriage, on horseback, or on a bicycle. In England, around the turn of the century, it was considered very stylish to have this dog follow one's elegant carriage and for this reason he was called a "coach dog." More recently, in the United States one frequently catches glimpses of him riding on fire engines. He has become the traditional mascot of firemen to the point that many firehouses have their own beautiful Dalmatian.

Many authors have written about the origins of this dog but very few are in agreement. His name should indicate his origin but this is not the case. The breed appears to be quite ancient, since the friezes discovered in Greece and the Middle East dating back to remote periods show dogs similar in lines and coat to the present Dalmatian.

Some authorities think that he came from Denmark, a theory supported by the fact that he is called Dane in some countries. He is quite prevalent today in Denmark. Buffon believes that he is descended from the Mastiff which, after having passed from England to Denmark and then to warmer climes, presumably produced the Turkish Dog. Besides these theories there are many others, all different, all somehow plausible, but none certain, while Angliola Denti di Pirajno, a well-known expert on the breed, states: "The hypothesis which seems to rest on the most solid base indicates that the Dalmatian has an Eastern origin."

The Dalmatian formerly had a highly developed sense of smell and was used as a hunting dog. And, although he barks very little, he is also considered an excellent guard dog for the home.

DALMATIAN

GENERAL CHARACTERISTICS In build and stature this breed is comparable to the larger Manchester Terriers. Almost rangy, it has a harmonious general aspect and graceful movements, with well-proportioned slender legs.

SIZE Minimum height at the shoulder is 12 inches, although the best strain as of 1961 measured almost 20 inches.

HEAD The skull is broad, with a tapering muzzle longer than the lengthwise dimension of the skull. The muzzle forms an almost continuous line with the skull, with little stop. The zygomatic arch is scarcely noticeable. The nose is dark in dark animals, pink or brown in less pigmented animals. The lips should adhere as closely as possible to the gums and teeth. There should be no flews—no wrinkles in the lips. The jaws should be neither overshot nor undershot, the teeth meeting in a scissors bite. The absence of all premolars is normal, and the absence of one or more of the incisors is not to be penalized, although animals having all their incisors are preferable.

EYES Should be of medium size, neither excessively close nor wide apart, neither deep-set nor protruding. They are slightly almond-shaped and in color vary from yellow to black; dark eyes are to be preferred. Both eyes must be of the same color. The expression should be intelligent, alert. Rims are dark, but in animals with less pigmentation on the face they may be pink or pinkish.

EARS Elegant, large and expressive. Up to 4 inches in length, they should be thin and delicate in texture, somewhat reminiscent of bats' ears. They are set on rather laterally and when the animal is alerted should be held rigid and obliquely erect, their axis between 50 and 80 degrees from the horizontal.

NECK Carried high, proportionately long, flexible, and slightly arched, it is a graceful neck, rather like an antelope's, free of wrinkles or any suggestion of a dewlap. It is slender at the point where it joins the head and broadens gradually toward the shoulder.

Photo: M. Pedone.

DALMATIAN

DALMATIAN

DALMATIAN

GENERAL CHARACTERISTICS A balanced, strong, muscular, active dog of good demeanor. Symmetrical in outline, free from coarseness and lumber, the Dalmatian is capable of great endurance with a fair amount of speed.

WEIGHT AND SIZE Weight: males approximately 55 lb; females approximately 49½ lb. Ideal height: males 21½-24 inches; females 19½-23 inches.

HEAD Of fair length, the skull flat and reasonably broad between the ears but refined, moderately well-defined at the temples; that is, showing a moderate amount of stop, not in one straight line from nose to occiput. The dog must be wholly free from wrinkles. The muzzle should be long and powerful, never snipy, and the lips should be clean, fitting the jaw moderately closely. In the black-spotted variety the nose should always be black, and in the liver-spotted variety it should invariably be brown. The jaws should close in a scissors bite.

EYES Set moderately well apart and of medium size, round, bright and sparkling. with an intelligent expression. The color depends on the markings and color of the dog. Eyes should be dark in the black-spotted dogs and amber in the liver-spotted variety. The rim around the eyes should be complete, following the same variations in color as those noted above—black for black, liver for liver.

EARS Set on rather high, of moderate size, rather wide at the base and tapering to a rounded tip. Fine in texture, the ears should be carried close to the head. Markings should be well broken up, preferably spotted.

NECK Fairly long, nicely arched, light and tapering, entirely free from throatiness.

FOREQUARTERS The shoulders should be moderately oblique, clean and muscular. Elbows close to the body, forelegs perfectly straight, with strong round bone down to the feet, with a slight spring at the pastern joint.

BODY The chest should not be too wide, but it should be deep and capacious, with plenty of lung and heart room. The ribs should be well sprung and have well-defined withers and a powerful, level back: the loins should be strong, clean, muscular, and slightly arched.

TAIL Should reach approximately to the hocks. It should be strong at the root and taper gradually to the point; must not be set on too low or too high, and it should be free of coarseness. It is carried with a slight upward curve but never curled; preferably spotted.

HINDQUARTERS Rounded, muscles clean, with well developed second thigh, good turn of stifle and hocks well defined. The feet are compact with well arched toes (catfeet) and round, tough elastic pads. Nails black or white in the black-spotted type, brown or white in the liver-spotted variety.

COAT Should be short, hard and dense, sleek and glossy. **Color** The ground color should be pure white. Black-spotted dogs should have dense black spots, liver-spotted dogs should have liver-brown spots. They should not run together but be round and well defined, measuring in diameter ½-1½ inches and be as well distributed as possible. Spots on forefeet and hind feet should be smaller than those on the body.

FAULTS Patches, black and liver spots on the same dog (tricolor); lemon spots; blue eyes; bronzing and other faults of pigmentation. ●

398

Photo: J. Cooke (Photo Res.).

282 CHOW CHOW
DIFFERENT AREAS OF ORIGIN

(no official decision)

This magnificent breed invariably arouses the greatest interest when exhibited in shows. Public admiration is inevitably excited by its noble and proud aspect, its lionlike look, the outstanding beauty represented by its perfect physical configuration and its unusually colorful coat.

Those who are familiar with the Chow Chow are aware, however, that besides these external qualities he possesses others which make him a valuable aid to man whatever the locality. He is an excellent guard for the house or boat, a courageous hunter of wolves or game, a vigorous and tireless sled dog, and an important factor in the economy of the Orient, since his fur is much esteemed, even in Europe. Unfortunately, one must regretfully mention that in many areas of Asia this breed is raised for food; the flesh is considered a delicacy. One would think that its keen intelligence would merit more consideration from human beings.

CHOW CHOW

GENERAL CHARACTERISTICS Leonine in appearance, with a proud, dignified bearing, the Chow Chow is loyal but aloof, and unique in his stilted gait and in blue-black tongue. An active, compact, short-coupled and well-balanced dog, well knit in frame and with the tail carried well over the back.

SIZE The minimum height for this breed is 18 inches, but in show balance should be the main criterion and height should be left to the judges' discretion.

HEAD Skull flat and broad, the stop not accentuated, well filled out under the eyes. Muzzle moderate in length, broad from the eyes to the point (and not pointed at the end like a fox's). The nose should be black, invariably wide (with the exception of cream-and-white dogs, which may have a light-colored nose; and of blues and fawns, which may have a self-colored nose); but in all colors the black nose is to be preferred. Teeth should be strong and level, with a scissors bite. The tongue is blue-black; the flews and the hard palate are black. Gums preferably black.

EYES Dark and small, preferably almond-shaped (in blues or fawns a light color is permissible).

EARS Small, thick, slightly rounded at the tips, carried stiffly erect but set on well forward over the eyes and wide apart, giving the dog the peculiar scowl which is characteristic of the breed.

NECK Strong, full, set well on the shoulders and slightly arched.

BODY The chest is broad and deep; the back is short, straight and powerful. The loins are well muscled and strong.

TAIL Set on high and carried well over the back.

FOREQUARTERS Shoulders are muscular and sloping. The forelegs are perfectly straight, of moderate length and of good bone. **HINDQUARTERS** The hind legs are muscular, the hocks are well let down and perfectly straight, a characteristic which is essential to the dog's stilted gait and the desired "double-jointed hocks." **FEET** Small, round catfeet, standing well on the toes.

COAT Abundant, dense, straight and standing off. The top coat is rather coarse in texture, the undercoat soft and woolly. **Color** Whole-colored black, red, blue, fawn, cream or white, frequently shaded but not in patches or particolored (the underpart of the tail and the back of the thighs are frequently of a light color).

FAULTS Drop ears; tongue splashed or patchy; tail not carried over the back; particolor; off-black nose except in the colors specified above.

VARIETIES The standard for the smooth variety is the same as for the dog described above except for the smooth coat. ●

CHOW CHOW

CHOW CHOW

Photo: S. A. Thompson.

PEKINGESE

Photo: S. A. Thompson.

283 PEKINGESE

DIFFERENT AREAS OF ORIGIN

(no official decision)

The early form of the Pekingese could be found in the Toy Spitz of Southeast Asia which in turn comes from the Peatbog Dog, like all Spitzes.

In any case, we do not exactly know the origins of this dog. It is certain, however, that he made his appearance in the distant past, perhaps coincidentally with the Celestial Empire.

A curious Chinese legend relates that once upon a time a lion fell in love with a little she-monkey and wished to marry her. To do this he first had to appear before the god Hai Ho, who said to the lion: "If you are willing to sacrifice your size and your power to your love for the little she-monkey, then I give you my consent." The lion accepted willingly and the fruit of their union was the Pekingese, which combined the proud and noble expression of the King of Beasts with the grace and sweetness of the little she-monkey.

The Pekingese was introduced into Europe and, more specifically, into England in 1861 after the fall of Peking and the destruction of the Summer Palace by the Anglo-French expeditionary force. British officers brought several specimens back with them and gave one as a gift to Queen Victoria. European breeders therefore obtained their first subjects and breeding was so well conducted that incomparably beautiful specimens were obtained. In its native land, however, the breed unexpectedly deteriorated to such an extent that studs and bitches had to be imported from Europe and Australia! This state of affairs caused increasingly marked modifications in the dimensions and general and physical characteristics of the breed, proof being the comparison between the Oriental standard of twenty years ago and the European standard. Today we do not know what the breeding situation is in China.

PEKINGESE

Photo: S. A. Thompson.

PEKINGESE WITH PUPPY

PEKINGESE

GENERAL CHARACTERISTICS Should be a small, well-balanced, thickset dog of great dignity and quality. He should carry himself fearlessly in the ring with an alert, intelligent expression.

WEIGHT AND SIZE As a guide, the ideal weight to be 7-11 lb for males, 8-12 lb for females. The dog should look small but be surprisingly heavy when picked up. Heavy bone and a sturdy, well-built body are essentials of the breed.

HEAD Head massive, skull broad, wide and flat between the ears, not domed; wide between the eyes. Nose very short and broad, nostrils large, open and black; muzzle wide, well wrinkled, with firm underjaw. Profile should look quite flat with nose well up between the eyes. Deep stop. Level lips; teeth or tongue not visible.

EYES Large, clear, dark and lustrous. Prominent but not bolting.

EARS Heart-shaped, set level with the skull and carried close to the head. Long, profuse feathering on ears. Leather not to come below the muzzle.

NECK Rather short and thick.

BODY Short but with broad chest and good spring of rib, falling away lighter behind; leonine, with distinct waist, level back; the body is slung well between the legs, rather than on top of them.

TAIL Set high, carried tightly, slightly curved over back to either side. Long feathering.

FOREQUARTERS Short, thick, heavily boned forelegs; bones of forelegs bowed but firm at shoulder. Absolute soundness essential. **HINDQUARTERS** Hind legs lighter but firm and well shaped. Close behind but not cow-hocked. Absolute soundness essential. **FEET** Large and flat, not round. The dog should stand well up on feet, not on pasterns. Front feet turned slightly out. Absolute soundness essential.

COAT Long and straight, with profuse mane extending beyond the shoulders forming a cape or frill around the neck; top coat rather coarse, with thick undercoat. Profuse feathering on ears, legs, thighs. tail, and toes. **Color** All colors and markings are permissible and equally good, except albino or liver. Particolors should be evenly broken. ●

Photo: S. A. Thompson, T. Fall.

284 SHIH TSU

DIFFERENT AREAS OF ORIGIN

(no official decision)

"Shih tsu" means "lion" in Chinese. In the Buddhist religion of Tibet the lion is considered an attribute of divinity and in ancient paintings Buddha himself is sometimes represented as a lion. Since there are at present no more lions to be found in China or Tibet, perhaps that is why these small lionlike dogs are so esteemed by the people of these countries.

They were doubtless formed at the Court of the Celestial Empire through the crossbreeding of the small sacred Tibetan dogs with the ancestors of the present-day Pekingese. They were first imported into England in 1930 and, since then, many specimens have been bred in Europe.

SHIH TSU

GENERAL CHARACTERISTICS Very active, lively and alert, with a distinctly arrogant carriage.

WEIGHT AND SIZE Weight range, 10-18 lb, with ideal weight 10-16 lb; height at withers not more than 10½ inches; type and breed characteristics are of the utmost importance and are not to be sacrificed to size alone.

HEAD Broad and round, wide between the eyes. Shock-headed, with hair falling well over the eyes. Good whiskers and beard. The hair growing upward on the nose gives a distinctly chry-santhemum-like effect. Muzzle square and short, but not wrinkled like a Pekingese's; rather, it is flat and hairy. Nose black preferably, with about 1 inch from tip to stop. Mouth level or slightly underhung.

EYES Large, dark and round, but not prominent.

EARS Large, with long leathers, carried drooping. Set slightly below the crown of the skull. So heavily coated that they appear to blend with the hair of the neck.

BODY Between withers and root of tail, body should be longer than height at withers; well coupled and sturdy; chest broad and deep, shoulders firm, back level.

TAIL Heavily plumed and curled well over back; carried gaily, set on high.

FOREQUARTERS Legs short and muscular, with ample bone. The legs should look massive because of the abundance of hair. **HINDQUARTERS** Legs short and muscular, with ample bone. They should look straight when viewed from the rear. Thighs well rounded and muscular. Legs should look massive because of abundance of hair. **FEET** Firm and well padded. The abundant hair should make them look big.

COAT Long and dense but not curly, with good undercoat. **Color** All colors permissible, but a white blaze on the forehead and a white tip to the tail are highly prized. Dogs with liver markings may have dark liver noses and slightly lighter eyes. Pigmentation on muzzle as unbroken as possible.

FAULTS Narrow head, pig jaws, snipiness, pale pink nose or eye-rim coloring, small or light eyes, legginess, sparseness of coat. ●

SHIH TSU

285 TIBETAN TERRIER
DIFFERENT AREAS OF ORIGIN

(no official decision)

The Tibetan religion accepts the transmigration of the soul and for this reason animals (and dogs in particular) and plants are considered on a par with human beings. Small dogs are therefore called "small persons," and are devotedly cared for.

Professor C. J. Stelzer writes on the subject: "For centuries the peoples of Asia, including the Tibetans, sent tribute to the Emperor of China. Every year convoys left for the Potala, the Palace of the Dalai Lama, bringing tribute to China which included Tibetan Terriers (always male) which were often given as a gesture of thanks to village chieftains who offered lodgings or other services. These dogs were considered as sacred talismans and if they did not reproduce their kind, the happiness and prosperity of the village would be threatened. For this reason the villagers crossbred them with the only small-sized breed available: the Tibetan Spaniels. The products of this crossbreeding closely resembled the male ancestors. When rebellions later broke out in Tibet, the nation's sacred dogs, the Tibetan Terriers, were led from the capital city into valleys in the interior of the country. Later, these very small longhaired dogs which are known today by the name of Lhasa Apso ("Longhaired Dog of Lhasa") spread considerably, having been also obtained by crossbreeding the Tibetan Terrier with the Tibetan Spaniel. In effect, if the Lhasa Apso has the hair of the Tibetan Terrier, he also has the longer body of the Tibetan Spaniel; even his slightly shorter muzzle bears witness to his spaniel strain."

TIBETAN TERRIER

GENERAL CHARACTERISTICS Alert, intelligent and game, not fierce or pugnacious. Chary of strangers. The Tibetan Terrier is a medium-sized terrier, in its general appearance not unlike a miniature Old English Sheepdog.

SIZE Height at shoulders: males 14-16 inches; females slightly smaller.

HEAD Skull of medium length, not broad or coarse, narrowing slightly from ear to eye, not domed but absolutely flat between the ears. The malar bones are curved but should not be overdeveloped to the extent of bulging. There should be a marked stop in front of the eyes, but this must not be exaggerated. The head should be well furnished with long hair falling forward over the eyes. The lower jaw should carry a small but not exaggerated amount of beard. Jaws between the canines should form a distinct curve. The length from eye to tip of nose should be equal to the length from eye to base of skull. Head not broad or massive. Nose black.

EYES Large, dark, neither prominent nor sunken; should be set fairly wide apart. Eyelids dark.

EARS Pendant, not too close to head, V-shaped, not too large, heavily feathered.

BODY Compact and powerful. Length from point of shoulder to root of tail equal to height at withers. Well ribbed up. Loin slightly arched.

TAIL Medium in length, set on fairly high and carried in a gay curl over the back. Very well feathered. There is often a kink near the tip.

FOREQUARTERS Legs straight and heavily furnished. **HINDQUARTERS** Heavily furnished, hocks well let down. **FEET** The feet should be large, round, heavily furnished with hair between the toes and pads. The dog should stand well down on its pads.

COAT Double-coated, the undercoat fine wool, the top coat profuse, fine, but not silky or woolly; long, either straight or waved. **Color** White, golden, cream, gray or smoke, black, particolor, and tricolor; in fact, any color except chocolate.

FAULTS Mouth extremely undershot or overshot; a weak, snipy foreface should be penalized. ●

286 LHASA APSO
DIFFERENT AREAS OF ORIGIN

(no official decision)

As we have already mentioned regarding the Tibetan Terrier, the Lhasa Apso was formed by crossbreeding the Tibetan Terrier with the Tibetan Spaniel. Because of his small size, his agreeable nature, and his physical beauty, he rapidly found wide acceptance as a perfect toy dog. In his country of origin he lived in the monasteries, at least until the annexation by the Chinese People's Republic. The most beautiful and most esteemed kinds (and this is true for the three small Tibetan breeds) were to be found in the Potala, the Palace of the Dalai Lama, and within the dwellings of ministers and other high personages. It was impossible to obtain a specimen for money, as they were presented to people in special circumstances as a mark of beneficence.

The above-mentioned Professor C. J. Stelzer writes: "A Tibetan Lama told me that the specimens of little value wander in the villages and eat whatever people give them. The more valued specimens are considered like precious jewels. The Lhasa Apso is not used for any work whatever. He has an acute sense of hearing and notices faint and far-off sounds and gives the alarm with his characteristic clear and piercing bark. It is for this reason that he is called in Tibetan 'apso seng kye,' which means 'the sentry dog with the bark of a lion.' "

TIBETAN TERRIER

Photo: S. A. Thompson.

They were extremely welcome at the Imperial Court of China where they were brought as tributary gifts from Tibet and they contributed to the formation of the Shih Tsu breed.

GENERAL CHARACTERISTICS Gay and assertive but chary of strangers; free and jaunty movement.

SIZE Ideally 9 or 10 inches at shoulder for males; females slightly smaller.

HEAD Heavy head furnishings with good fall over the eyes, good whiskers and beard, should be dark. Skull moderately narrow, falling away behind the eyes in a marked degree; not quite flat, but not domed or apple-shaped; straight foreface of fair length. Nose black, about 1½ inches long, or the length from tip of nose to eye to be roughly one third of the total length from nose to back of skull. Mouth should be level; but slightly undershot preferred to overshot. Muzzle of medium length; a square muzzle is objectionable.

EYES Dark, not large and full or small and sunken.

EARS Pendant, heavily feathered; dark tips an asset.

NECK Strong, well covered with a mane which is more pronounced in males than in females.

BODY The length from point of shoulders to point of buttocks longer than height at withers. Well ribbed up, strong loin, well-developed quarters and thighs. Well-balanced and compact type is to be preferred.

TAIL Well feathered, should be carried well over back. There is often a kink at the end. Low carriage of tail is a serious fault.

FOREQUARTERS Forelegs straight and heavily furnished with hair. **HINDQUARTERS** Heavily furnished with hair. **FEET** Well feathered, should be round and catlike, with good pads.

COAT Heavy, straight, hard, not woolly or silky, of good length. Dense undercoat. **Color** Golden, sandy, honey, dark grizzle, slate, particolor, black, white, or brown. This being the true Tibetan Lion-dog, golden or leonine colors are preferred. ●

287 TIBETAN SPANIEL
DIFFERENT AREAS OF ORIGIN

(no official decision)

We know little about the origins of this small Oriental Spaniel and can only offer hypotheses. As was mentioned before, the people of Tibet used to send gifts each year to the Celestial Emperor in Peking. It must be assumed that the Emperor responded by sending back Chinese dogs no less precious. These were perhaps the Happa, considered by some to be the ancestors of the Pekingese, and the Carlin, which would therefore have had some part in the formation of the Tibetan Spaniel.

A dog similar to the Tibetan Spaniel was also known in the Silla Kingdom at the beginning of the eighth century A.D. Southern Korea had relations with Japan, and several dogs of this type were offered as gifts to the Emperor of Japan by envoys from the Royal House of Silla in the year 732 A.D. The Japanese Spaniel (the Chin) apparently descended from these dogs. Certain experts claim that these Chins are the dogs of the Shinra region of Korea, sent as gifts to the Emperor of Japan. One may assume that the differences developed at this time contributed towards the modern type of Chin. We may assume from this that the Tibetan Spaniel is the ancient form of the Chin.

LHASA APSO

Photo: S. A. Thompson.

TIBETAN SPANIEL

GENERAL CHARACTERISTICS Gay, intelligent, aloof with strangers.

WEIGHT AND SIZE The ideal weight is 9-15 lb. The height is about 10 inches.

HEAD Small in proportion to body and carried proudly. Skull slightly domed. Stop slight but defined. Black nose preferred. The mouth is ideally slightly undershot. Full dentition desirable. Teeth must not show when mouth is closed.

EYES Dark brown, oval in shape.

EARS Medium in size, pendant, well feathered in the adult and set fairly high. They may have a slight lift from the skull but should not "fly."

NECK Moderately short, strong and well set on.

BODY Slightly longer from point of shoulder to root of tail than the height at the withers, well ribbed.

TAIL Set high, richly plumed and carried in a gay curl over the back when moving.

FOREQUARTERS The bones of the forelegs slightly bowed but firm at shoulder. Moderate bone. Shoulder well placed. **HINDQUARTERS** Well made and strong, hocks well let down and straight when viewed from behind. Stifle well developed, showing moderate angulation. **FEET** Harefooted, small and neat. White markings allowed.

COAT Double coat, silky in texture. Should not be overcoated; females tend to carry less coat and mane than males. **Color** All colors allowed.

FAULTS Large full eyes, broad flat muzzle, overshot mouth, extremely bowed or loose front, straight stifle, cow hocks, nervousness, catfeet, coarseness of type, mean expression, liver or putty pigmentation, light eyes, protruding tongue, cryptorchidism.

TIBETAN SPANIEL

288 HAVANESE BICHON
DIFFERENT AREAS OF ORIGIN

(no official decision)

This small dog is not very prevalent and little is known about his origins. Apparently long ago some peasants from Emilia, a suburb in Italy, took some Bolognese dogs to Argentina, crossbred them with a small poodle, and created a new type of Bichon. When this dog reached Cuba he was called the Havanese. European varieties would thus be reimported products.

The hypothesis advanced by Dechambre is different: the Havanese is descended from the Maltese, brought to the West Indies by the Spaniards. In some countries he is called the "Havana Silk Dog."

Photo: S. A. Thompson, A. Roslin-Williams.

HAVANESE BICHON

JAPANESE SPANIEL

GENERAL CHARACTERISTICS A small breed descended from a cross between Bolognese dogs and a South American Poodle.

WEIGHT The Havanese Bichon should not weigh more than 13¼ lb (6 kg).

HEAD The nose is invariably black, muzzle fairly slender, cheeks very flat; the jaws must meet closely in a scissors bite. The skull is broad and flat, the forehead not imposing.

EYES Rather large, very dark, and preferably black. The rim is almond-shaped.

EARS Rather pointed and falling in such a way that they assume a slight fold. They are slightly raised. They must not be directed toward the flanks, nor should they frame the cheeks.

BODY Slightly longer than high, with rounded ribs, flanks well drawn up. The backline leads to a noticeably slanting rump.

TAIL Carried high, curled, and covered with long silky hair.

FOREQUARTERS AND HINDQUARTERS Straight, quite lean. **FEET** Slightly elongated, with lean toes.

COAT Rather flat, quite soft, with tufts tending toward the extremities. The hair around the muzzle may be slightly shortened, but it is preferable to leave it natural. **Color** Rarely pure white; it may be beige, more or less dark, or "Havana," gray or white broadly marked by those colors. ●

with fine bone; well feathered to the thighs behind. **FEET** Should be long and harelike, also feathered.

COAT Should be long, profuse, and straight, free from curl or wave and not too flat; it should have a tendency to stand out, more particularly at the frill, with profuse feathering on the tail and thighs. **Color** The males should be either black and white or red and white, i.e., particolored. The term "red" includes all shades of sable, brindle, lemon, and orange, but the brighter and clearer the red the better. The white should be clear and the color, whether black or red, should be evenly distributed as patches over the body, cheek, and ears.

FAULTS "Flying" ears, narrow muzzle, excessive length of nose, tongue showing, light eyes, long back, excessively short legs, drooping tail, uneven markings, rounded and short feet, wavy or curly coat, narrow chest, undershot or overshot mouth, weakness in hindquarters. ●

289 JAPANESE SPANIEL
Chin

JAPAN

The Japanese Spaniel is of Asiatic origin. In Japan he is considered a luxury and pet dog, much esteemed by ladies who carried him in their hands as a "muff" or "sleeve" dog.

Information brought to us by European travelers of the seventeenth century tells how well the Japanese dogs were cared for. In certain areas of the empire there existed numerous dogs that lived undisturbed on the edges of roads. Shelters were constructed especially for them and the inhabitants of neighboring villages would bring them food. As we mentioned with regard to the Tibetan Spaniel, which seems to be an ancestor of the Chin, the breed probably came from the Shinra region of Korea. It is small breed, and the only Japanese breed quite prevalent in Europe, where it seems to have been present since the seventeenth century when Portuguese navigators offered some puppies to Princess Catherine of Braganza.

GENERAL CHARACTERISTICS A lively, high-bred little dog of dainty appearance, with a smart, compact carriage, clothed in a profuse coat. These dogs should be essentially stylish in movement, lifting the feet high when in motion, carrying the heavily feathered tail proudly, curved or plumed over the back.

WEIGHT AND SIZE Classes should be established for animals over and under 7 lb. Wide variation in size, but the smaller the better, provided type and quality not sacrificed. Males average about 12 inches.

HEAD Head should be large for the size of the dog, with a broad skull, rounded in front. Muzzle very short and wide, and well cushioned, i.e., the upper lips rounded on each side of the nostrils, which should be large and black except in the case of red-and-white dogs, in which brown noses are as common as black. Mouth should be wide and neither undershot nor overshot.

EYES Should be large, dark, set far apart. It is desirable that the white shows in the inner corners (it is this characteristic which gives the Japanese Spaniel its look of astonishment, sometimes wrongly called "squint", and which should not be lost).

EARS Should be small, set wide apart and high on the dog's head. They are V-shaped and should be carried slightly forward.

NECK Should not be too long.

BODY Should be squarely and compactly built, wide in chest, cobby in shape. The length of the dog's body should be about equal to its height.

TAIL Should be well plumed and carried proudly over the back.

FOREQUARTERS The legs should be straight and with fine bone, well feathered to the feet. **HINDQUARTERS** The hind legs should be straight and

JAPANESE SPANIEL

Photo: Prato.

JAPANESE SPANIEL PUPPY

290 KING CHARLES SPANIEL

GREAT BRITAIN

Until the last few years the different toy spaniels were classed according to color. In this way there was the King Charles Spaniel proper, that is to say, black and red-brown, then the ruby-chestnut—one color, the white Blenheim with chestnut spots and a little spot on the skull called a "beauty spot," and finally the Prince Charles tricolor. At present all these varieties have been regrouped into a single type: the King Charles Spaniel.

The method of constant crossbreeding consists of breeding the black and red-brown with the ruby, and the Blenheim with the tricolor. With such crossbreeding one succeeds, first of all, in reducing the mahogany color of the black and red-brown and of enriching the red of the ruby, as well as obtaining a longer coat and thicker fringes. The occasional use of the Blenheim is necessary in the crossing of the tricolor in order to fix the mahogany spots which otherwise might completely disappear; conversely, the tricolor blood is sought for the Blenheim to guarantee its rich color and to preserve the best points of the head. If one breeds the Blenheim with other Blenheims for many generations the white spots become lighter, the eyes and nose become paler, and the head becomes less bulging. Among the best dogs, a great number have been obtained by the union of the Blenheim with the black and red-brown.

Photo: S. A. Thompson.

KING CHARLES SPANIEL

KING CHARLES SPANIEL

GENERAL CHARACTERISTICS Compact and cobby, on refined lines, chest wide and deep, legs short and straight, back short and level. Tail well flagged, not carried over the level of the back. Movement free, active and elegant.

WEIGHT AND SIZE The most desirable weight is 8-14 lb.

HEAD Skull massive in comparison to size, well domed and full over the eyes. Nose should be black with large, wide-open nostrils, very short and turned up to meet the skull. The stop between skull and nose should be well defined. Muzzle square, wide, deep, well turned up; lower jaw wide, lips meeting exactly. Cheeks well cushioned up, not falling away under eyes.

EYES Very large and dark, set wide apart, with eyelids square to face line; pleasing expression.

EARS Set on low, hanging quite flat to cheeks, very long and well feathered.

FORELEGS Shoulder not too straight.

Legs medium-boned, straight. **HINDQUARTERS** Legs medium-boned, straight. **FEET** Compact, well fringed.

COAT Long, silky and straight, a slight wave allowed, not curly. The legs, ears, and tail should be profusely feathered. **Color** a) **Black and tan:** A rich, glossy black, with bright mahogany tan markings on muzzle, legs, chest, linings of ears, under tail, and spots over eyes. b) **Tricolor:** Ground pearly white and well distributed black patches, brilliant tan markings on cheeks, linings of ears, under tail, and spots over the eyes. A wide white blaze between the eyes and up the forehead. c) **Blenheim:** A ground of pearly white with well-distributed chestnut-red patches. A wide clear blaze, with the "spot" in center of skull. The spot should be a clear chestnut-red mark about the size of a dime in center of skull. d) **Ruby:** Whole-colored, a rich chestnut red.

FAULTS The presence of a few white hairs on the chest of a black-and-tan or ruby coat is undesirable, but a white patch is a major fault. ●

CAVALIER KING CHARLES SPANIEL WITH PUPPIES

410

Photo: A. Roslin-Williams, S. A. Thompson.

291 CAVALIER KING CHARLES SPANIEL

GREAT BRITAIN

The Cavalier King Charles Spaniel is probably a recent breed. It constitutes a variety of toy which has probably never been crossed with others.

GENERAL CHARACTERISTICS An active, graceful, and well-balanced dog. Absolutely fearless and sporting in character and very gay and free in action.

WEIGHT AND SIZE Weight varies from 12 to 18 lb; a small, well-balanced dog well within these limits is desirable.

HEAD Almost flat between the ears, without dome. Stop shallow. Length from base of stop to tip about 1½ inches. Nostrils should be well developed, the pigment black. Muzzle well tapered. Lips well covered but not houndlike. Face should be well filled out beneath the eyes. Any snipy tendency is undesirable. Mouth should be level; a scissors bite is preferred.

EYES Large, dark and round, but not prominent. They should be spaced well apart.

EARS Long and set high, with plenty of feather.

NECK Of moderate length, slightly arched.

BODY Short-coupled with plenty of spring of rib. Back level. Chest moderate, leaving ample heart room.

TAIL Docked tail is optional. No more than one-third to be removed. The length of the tail should be in balance with the body.

FOREQUARTERS Shoulders well laid back, legs moderately boned and straight. **HINDQUARTERS** Legs with moderate bone; well-turned stifle, with no tendency to cow hocks or sickle hocks. **FEET** Compact, cushioned, and well feathered.

COAT Long, silky and free from curl. A slight wave is permissible. There should be plenty of feather. **Color** a) **Black and tan:** Raven black with tan markings above eyes, on cheeks, inside ears, on chest, legs and underside of tail. The tan should be bright. b) **Ruby:** Whole-colored, rich red. c) **Blenheim:** Rich chestnut marking, well broken up on a pearly-white ground. The markings should be evenly divided on the head, leaving room between the ears for the greatly valued lozenge mark or spot (unique in the breed). d) **Tricolor:** Black and white well spaced and broken up, with tan markings over the eyes, on cheeks, inside ears, inside legs, and on underside of tail. Black and white permissible but not desirable.

FAULTS Light eyes, undershot or crooked mouth, pig jaws, white marks on whole-colored dogs, coarseness of type, putty nose, flesh marks, nervousness. ●

CAVALIER KING CHARLES SPANIEL

Photo: A. Wintzell.

BOSTON TERRIER

292 BOSTON TERRIER

DIFFERENT AREAS OF ORIGIN

(no official decision)

It is almost certain that three European breeds have contributed to the formation of this dog: the Bulldog, the Bull Terrier, and probably the Boxer.

GENERAL CHARACTERISTICS The general appearance of the Boston Terrier should be that of a lively, highly intelligent, smooth-coated, short-headed, compactly built, short-tailed, well balanced dog of medium size, brindle color, and evenly marked with white. The head should be in proportion to the size of the dog; the body rather short and well knit; the limbs strong and neatly turned; tail short; no feature to be so prominent that the dog appears badly proportioned. The dog should convey an impression of determination, strength and activity, with style of a high order; carriage easy and graceful. The gait of the Boston Terrier is that of a sure-footed, straight-gaited dog, forelegs and hind legs moving straight ahead in perfect rhythm, each step indicating grace and power.

WEIGHT Should not exceed 25 lb, according to the following classes: lightweight, under 15 lb; middleweight, 15 to just under 20 lb; heavyweight, 20 to just under 25 lb.

HEAD Skull square, flat on top, free from wrinkles; cheeks flat; brow abrupt, stop well defined. Muzzle short, square, wide and deep; it should be in good proportion to the skull, free from wrinkles, shorter in length than in width and depth, not exceeding about a third of length of skull; width and depth carried out well to end; the muzzle from stop to end of nose on a line parallel to the top of the skull; nose black and wide with well-defined line between nostrils. Jaws broad and square, the chops of good depth but not pendulous, completely covering the teeth when mouth is closed. Teeth short and regular, bite even, or sufficiently undershot to square muzzle.

EYES Wide apart, large and round, dark in color, expression alert but kind and intelligent. The eyes should set square in the skull, and the outside corners should be on a line with the cheeks as viewed from the front.

EARS Carried erect; small and thin; situated as near corner of skull as possible.

NECK Of fair length, slightly arched and carrying the head gracefully; neatly set into the shoulders.

BODY Deep, with good width of chest; shoulders sloping, back short; ribs deep and well sprung, carried well back to loins; loins short and muscular; rump curving slightly to set-on of tail; flank very slightly cut up. The body should appear short but not chunky.

TAIL Set on low, the tail should be short, fine and tapering, straight or screw, devoid of fringes or coarse hair, and not carried above horizontal.

FOREQUARTERS Legs set moderately wide apart and on a line with the point of the shoulders; straight in bone and well muscled; pasterns short and strong. Elbows standing neither in nor out. **HINDQUARTERS** Legs set true, bent at stifles, short from hocks to feet; hocks turning neither in nor out; thighs strong and well muscled. **FEET** Round, small and compact, turned neither in nor out; toes well arched.

COAT Short, smooth, bright and fine in texture. **Color** Brindle with white markings; brindle must show distinctly throughout the body; black and white markings are permissible, but brindles with white markings are preferred. The ideal color is one in which the brindle coloring is evenly distributed throughout the body. Ideal markings: white muzzle, even white blaze over head, collar, breast, part of whole of forelegs and hindlegs below hocks.

FAULTS Solid black, black and tan, liver or mouse color; Dudley nose; docked tail. Skull domed or inclined; furrowed by a medial line; skull too long for breadth, or vice versa; stop too shallow; brow and skull too slanting; eyes small or sunken, too prominent, light color or walleye, showing too much white or haw; muzzle wedge-shaped or lacking depth; downfaced; too much cut out below the eyes; pinched or wide nostrils; butterfly nose; protruding teeth, weak lower jaw, showing "turn-up"; ears poorly carried or out of proportion to the head; ewe-neck; throaty, short or thick neck; flat sides, narrow chest, long or slack loins, roach back, swayback, too much cut-up in flank; loose shoulders or elbows, hind legs too straight at stifles, hocks too prominent, long or weak pasterns, splay feet; tail long or gaily carried, extremely gnarled or curled against body (**NB:** The preferred tail should not exceed in length approximately half the distance from the set-on to hock); color and markings all white, absence of white markings, preponderance of white on body without proper proportion of brindle and white on head; any variations detracting from the general appearance; long or coarse coat, coat lacking in luster. ●

BOSTON TERRIER

Photo: R. Kinne (Photo Res.), H.P.F.

293 CARLIN

DIFFERENT AREAS OF ORIGIN

(no official decision)

The Carlin is an example of many breeds which formerly enjoyed great popularity and which seem to have been put aside but not completely forgotten. The Carlin was very prevalent in the past, especially in Italy. According to Buffin, the Carlin is also called the "small mastiff," and was derived from the German Mastiff and the small Dane. Cornevin defines him as a miniature Bordeaux Mastiff. Reul believes that the breed is a Mastiff reduced to small proportions and modified in certain characteristics, and this hypothesis is perhaps the most plausible. It appears that his origins are the same as those of the Mastiff, both coming from the same very ancient Asiatic source, despite their great difference in size. In ancient times, along with the giant forms there also existed dwarf forms, which were preserved as they were: one of these is the Carlin, that has the Mastiff's characteristics along with accentuated signs of dwarfism. The name Carlin was employed for the first time in France because of the dog's amusing aspect, both curious and frowning at the same time, caused by the folds and unique pigmentation of his face. In the eighteenth century the dog was given the name of a famous actor who played Harlequin because he resembled the actor with his round and ridiculous face partly covered by a black mask.

Various specimens exist in Germany, imported from Holland, called "mops" from the verb *moppen*, which means "to have an angry look." The English named him "pug" or "pug dog," meaning "miniature dog."

CARLIN PUP

GENERAL CHARACTERISTICS A decidedly square and cobby dog, the Pug should be *multum in parvo*—a lot of dog in little space. This compression should be shown by compactness of form, well-knit proportions, and hardness of developed muscle.

WEIGHT Desirable weight for both males and females is 14-18 lb.

HEAD Large, massive, round but not apple-headed, with no indentation of the skull. Muzzle short, blunt, square, but not upfaced. Wrinkles large and deep.

EYES Dark, very large, bold and prominent, globe-shaped, soft and solicitous in expression, very lustrous and, when the dog is excited, full of fire.

EARS Thin, small, soft, resembling black velvet. There are two kinds of ears—so-called rose ears and button ears. Preference should be given to the latter.

BODY Short and cobby, wide in the chest and very well ribbed.

TAIL A twist tail, curled as tightly as possible over the hip. The double curl is considered perfection in the Pug.

FOREQUARTERS Legs very strong, straight, of moderate length, set well under the body. **HINDQUARTERS** Legs very strong, straight, of moderate length, set well under. **FEET** Neither so long as the foot of the hare nor so round as that of the cat; toes well split, with black nails.

COAT Fine, smooth, soft, short and glossy, neither hard nor woolly. **Color** Silver, apricot fawn, or black. Each should be clearly decided, to render complete the contrast among color, trace, and mask. **Markings** Should be clearly defined; the muzzle or mask, ears, cheek moles, thumbmark or diamond on forehead, and the trace should be as black as possible. **Mask** The mask should be black, the more intense and well defined the better. **Trace** A black line extending from the occiput to the tail.

FAULTS Leanness, legginess, shortness of leg, and lengthiness of body. ●

CARLIN

CARLIN

Photo: A. Wintzell, S. Salmi.

294 BLACK AND TAN TOY TERRIER

GREAT BRITAIN

This dog caused a sensation in the latter part of the nineteenth century, and even today, although not very prevalent, is still esteemed for his highly developed intelligence as well as for his miniature dimensions which make him look like a toy. The Manchester Terrier is obviously the ancestor of the Toy Terrier, although the former is much larger, since they share the same physical characteristics. In spite of his small size the Toy Terrier is not deficient in force or courage. In the curious competitions of rat hunting which still take place in certain countries, it is not unusual to see, among the large terriers, this Toy Terrier that bravely competes with larger adversaries, who win simply because they're stronger, although very often the Toy hunts the rodents with great agility, catching and killing them—a really amazing feat considering the small difference in size between the hunter and the hunted.

GENERAL CHARACTERISTICS A well balanced, elegant and compact toy with terrier temperament and characteristics. It must be borne in mind that in the past the breed was often required to acquit itself ably in the rat pit. Therefore present-day specimens should be sleek and cleanly built, giving an appearance of alertness combined with speed of movement but with nothing of the Whippet type. This being a toy with terrier characteristics, unduly nervous specimens cannot rank as altogether typical representatives of the breed. It is recommended that judges bear this in mind.

WEIGHT AND SIZE Ideal weight: 6-8 lb. Ideal height at shoulders: 10-12 inches. For weight, judges are encouraged to use scales in an effort to establish uniformity in the breed.

HEAD Should be long and narrow with a flat skull, wedge-shaped without emphasis of cheek muscles and well filled up under the eyes. The upper and lower jaws should be held tightly together within compressed lips. Close inspection of the foreface should reveal a slight stop. The foreface then tapers gently to provide a wedge-shaped impression in profile, just as when seen from in front. Although an illusion of being overshot can result, any suggestion of a snipy appearance is undesirable. The nose is black. Teeth should be level and strong; the upper front teeth should close slightly over the lower front teeth, the latter to lean forward fractionally, thus establishing the correct level bite.

EYES Very dark to black, without light shading from the iris. They should be small, almond-shaped, obliquely set and sparkling.

EARS "Candleflame" shape, slightly pointed at the tips, placed high upon the back of the skull and proportionately close together. A guide to the proper size can be obtained by bending the ear forward. It should not reach the eye. From 9 months of age, the ear carriage must be erect. The entire inside of the ear should face forward. The leather of the ear should be thin. "Cat ears" are objectionable.

NECK Long, graceful and slightly arched. The shoulders should be well laid back and not straight. The neckline flows into the shoulders and then slopes off elegantly. Throatiness is undesirable.

BODY The body is compact, the head and legs in good proportion, thus producing correct balance. The back curves very slightly from behind the shoulder to the loin and then falls again to the root of the tail. The chest should be narrow and deep, with the ribs well sprung to a well-cut-up loin. The buttocks should be gently rounded.

TAIL Thick at the root, tapering to a point, set low and not reaching beyond the hock.

FOREQUARTERS The chest should be narrow and deep, the legs falling straight from the shoulders, with the elbows close to the chest providing a straight front. Loose elbows and

BLACK AND TAN TOY TERRIER

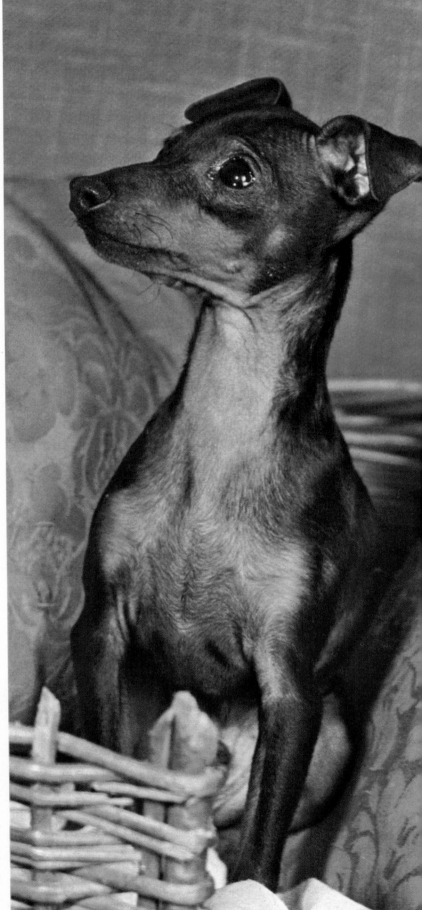

BLACK AND TAN TOY TERRIER

Photo: M. Pedone, T. Fall, S. A. Thompson.

wide front are faults. Fine bone is eminently desirable. The ideal fore movement is akin to the "extended trot"; hackney action is not desirable. Equally to be discouraged is a shuffling gait. **HINDQUARTERS** A well-rounded loin leading to a good turn of stifle is required. The hocks should be well let down. A "tucked under" appearance is undesirable. Hind action should be smooth and suggest ease and precision combined with drive. There should be a flowing quality to give true soundness. **FEET** Dainty, compact, split up between the toes and well arched, with jet black nails; the two middle toes of the front feet rather longer than the others and the hind feet shaped like those of a cat.

COAT The texture should be thick, close, smooth and of glossy appearance. Dense, short hair is required. **Color** Black and tan. The black should be ebony, and the tan can be likened to the color of a new chestnut, deeply rich. These colors should not run or blend into each other but should meet abruptly, forming a clear and well-defined line of color division. Forelegs tanned to the knee in front, the tan then continuing inside and at the back of the foreleg to a point just

below the elbow. A thin black line up each toe (penciling) and a clearly defined black "thumb mark" on the center of each pastern and under the chin. The hind legs should be well tanned in front and the inside, with a black "bar" dividing the tan at the center of the lower thigh. Each toe should be penciled. Heavy tan on the outside of the hindquarters ("breeching") is a fault. On the head the muzzle is well tanned and the nose is black, the black continuing along the top of the muzzle and curving below the eyes to the base of the throat. There should be a tan spot above each eye and a small tan spot on each cheek. The underjaw and throat are tanned; the lip line is black. The hair inside the ears is tanned (tan behind the ears is a fault). Each side of the chest is slightly tanned, as are the vent and the area under the root of the tail.

FAULTS Light, large or round eyes; protruding or disproportionately wide or narrow distance between eyes; large of flapping ears; roach back, camel back, dead flat back; harefeet; excessive gay carriage of tail; sparse, weak coat; white patches anywhere on coat. ●

295 HAIRLESS DOG
DIFFERENT AREAS OF ORIGIN

(no official decision)

Hairless dogs have been known for a very long time, although in Europe specimens have been rare because of the difficulty in adapting to temperate and cold climates. The center of spread for certain of these hairless dogs should be sought in Central Africa from where they may have been exported to different warm countries where they would have developed certain physical differences. They are known by different names: Chinese dogs, Mexican dogs (Xoloitzcuintli), Guatamalan dogs, West Indian dogs, Small African Greyhounds, and Nubian dogs. Although there were no such dogs in China and Japan, a substantial number existed in the other countries just mentioned. As far as the origin of the Hairless Dog is concerned, the case of the Xoloitzcuintli is especially perplexing, because his very ancient origins are ascertainable, leading one to suppose the possibility of indigenous and not African formation. He nevertheless has the same characteristics, especially regarding the absence of hair, and his teeth which show the consequences of modifying factors of hot countries: heat and humidity.

HAIRLESS DOG

The total absence of hair on the Hairless Dogs—except for some silky tufts on the skull, around the mouth, and on the tail —in certain secondary breeds probably occurred progressively because of the torrid and humid climate of equatorial lands. The type was therefore definitely fixed when all individuals began to produce hairless progeny.

The naturalist Pichot states that in the crossbreeding of hairless dogs with other breeds the absence of hair persists for many generations, and among the descendents this special characteristic of hairlessness is sometimes prolonged indefinitely. The rare and hard hairs found on the skull, around the mouth, and on the tail of the Hairless are later replaced in the descendents by hair similar to that of the breed with which the cross was made. This significant example of the predominance of certain characteristics is in accord with Mendel's theory of heredity. The absence of hair represents a certain advantage in cleanliness and the absence of parasites, although it also represents serious drawbacks for these dogs in temperate zones; they catch cold easily and their life span is generally short. Another reason for the scanty diffusion of these dogs in Europe seems to be, according to many reports, their characteristically unpleasant odor.

GENERAL CHARACTERISTICS This dog resembles in a general way both the Italian Greyhound and the Manchester Terrier. An elegant dog, fine-boned yet robust.
WEIGHT AND SIZE Weight 9-17½ lb; height 10-16 inches at the withers.
HEAD Nicely chiseled, with normal jaws and regular teeth. The incisors do not have the characteristic "fleur-de-lis."
EARS The dog is rose-eared or with ears erect, depending on the type.
BODY Lean, elegant, robust.

TAIL Of medium length; sometimes it has a few hard, sparse hairs.
FOREQUARTERS AND HINDQUARTERS Fine, correct, robust.
COAT The skin is bare and smooth. Sometimes there is sparse, bristly hair on the skull, around the mouth, on the tail and backline. **Color** Varies with different strains from elephant gray to slate gray; gray with pinkish markings (depigmentation) is found also, as well as flesh color with gray or black markings. Season and temperature influence skin color. ●

296 YORKSHIRE TERRIER
GREAT BRITAIN

This truly phenomenal dog is a small zoological marvel. Imagine a moving muff made of silky hair of a golden color shaded by steel and lead. This beautiful toy dog is very prevalent in Great Britain and he represents one of the most recent luxury and pet breeds.

He is derived from crossbreedings between the Black and Tan, the Skye Terrier, and the Dandie Dinmont. It also appears that a typically Italian dog, the Maltese, also had a role in the mixture. Formerly this dog was called the Scottish Terrier, although today this name is used to designate another breed of much greater size and different characteristics. This dog was then called a miniature longhaired terrier. For the last sixty years he has been called the Yorkshire Terrier. The first breedings were conducted by workmen in the mining region of Yorkshire County. Their actual intention was to obtain a small dog for underground hunting, and this quality, at first keen, later disappeared. The new breed attracted the attention of practical breeders who, thanks to well-conducted selective breeding, soon attained varieties of great distinction.

Admirers soon appeared, and today in Europe as well as in America the Yorkshire Terrier finds many shows happy to greet this miniature house pet.

GENERAL CHARACTERISTICS The general appearance of the Yorkshire should be that of a long-coated toy terrier, with the coat hanging quite straight and even down each side, with a parting extending from the nose to the end of the tail. The animal should be very compact and neat, with a very upright carriage conveying an air of importance. The general outline should convey the impression of a vigorous, well-proportioned body.

WEIGHT Up to 7 lb.

HEAD Should be rather small and flat, not too prominent nor round in the skull, not too long in the muzzle,

Photo: H.P.F.

YORKSHIRE TERRIER

Photo: Comet.

YORKSHIRE TERRIER

with a perfect black nose. The fall on the head must be long, of a rich golden tan, deeper in color at the sides of the head about the ear roots and on the muzzle, where it should be very long. On no account must the tan on the head extend onto the neck, nor must there be any sooty or dark hair intermingled with any of the tan. Teeth should be perfectly even, as sound as possible; an animal having lost teeth through accident not to be faulted provided jaws are even.

EYES Medium-sized, dark and sparkling; intelligent expression; eyes placed so as to look directly forward. They should not be prominent. The edge of the eyelids should be dark in color.

EARS Small, V-shaped, carried erect or semi-erect, not widely separated. They should be covered with short hair, a deep rich tan in color.

BODY Very compact, with a good loin. The backline must be level.

TAIL Docked to medium length, the tail should have plenty of hair, darker blue than the rest of the body, especially at the end of the tail. The tail is carried a little above the level of the backline.

FOREQUARTERS Legs quite straight, well covered with hair of a rich golden tan, slightly lighter at the ends than at the roots, and on the forelegs, does not extend above the elbow. **HINDQUARTERS** Legs straight, well covered with hair of a rich golden tan, slightly lighter at the ends than at the roots, and not extending higher on the hind legs than the stifle. **FEET** As round as possible, with black nails.

COAT The body hair is moderately long and perfectly straight, not wavy; it should be glossy as silk and of a fine silky texture. **Color** A dark steel blue (not silver blue) extends from the occiput to the root of the tail, and on no account must this blue be mixed with fawn, bronze, or dark hairs. The hair on the chest is a rich, bright tan. All tan hair must be darker at the roots than in the middle, shading to a still lighter shade at the tips. ●

YORKSHIRE TERRIER WITH PUPPIES

418

Photo: H.P.F., MARKA.

Category IV

GREYHOUNDS

Group 10

GREYHOUNDS

Companion of princes and crowned heads for centuries, the Greyhound, by the superb elegance of his form, has always constituted the aristocracy of the canine breeds. In this regard Noël Du Foil wrote in *Stories of Europe* in the sixteenth century: "Just as the Mastiff does not like the Greyhound, so the peasant dislikes the gentleman." And, as if he clearly wished to show his difference from all other dogs, his sense of smell is weak and he hunts by sight, without using his scent as does the humble hound.

It is thought that the French name for Greyhound (*lévrier*) comes from *lièvre* (hare) either because the Greyhound can run as fast as the hare or because hare hunting was, in past days, a function typical of this dog.

In any case, it is certain that the Greyhounds were among the first dogs trained by man for the hunt, and the Greyhounds of Gaul were much esteemed by the Romans.

The origins of this group of breeds are most ancient, and the theories concerning them are naturally extremely varied. Some of the following seem the most reliable.

Studer, for example, believes that the Greyhound group has two sources (polyphyletic origin): one in the north away from the *Canis familiaris leineri*, to which he connects the English Greyhounds which presumably were formed in Brittany or northeastern Gaul. The other southern group would be connected with the Indian Pariah dog, whose wild form is probably represented by the African jackal.

Another specialist, Hilzheimer, is more or less of this opinion, designating the Greyhound as a descendent of *Canis familiaris leineri*, thus making the wolf prevalent in the southwestern areas of Europe the ancestor of the European group.

Other naturalists have different opinions. Keller thinks all Greyhounds descended from a common source and indicates Ethiopia as the area of formation and the original wild form as the *Canis simensis*, or Abyssinian wolf. The ancient Greyhound, according to this theory, spread first to Egypt (Egyptian representations of Greyhounds are attributed to eras going back to 2000 B.C.) and, from there, throughout southern Africa. In Egyptian hieroglyphics the Greyhound with tail raised represents courage and victory, whereas with lowered tail it means fear and defeat.

The Greyhound would have spread to Europe and Asia during the Pharaonic period and there evolved its different types and breeds. Having crossed the Black Sea and migrated toward the north, it was transformed into the Russian longhaired Greyhound. In this regard the zoologist Antonios claims, and probably correctly, that a cross was made with the ancient Russian shepherd, which would have given the Borzoi its long coat.

Other experts indicate Asia as the Greyhound's formation area; it is well known that different breeds of Greyhounds exist in Asia which have been there since very ancient times. Kallmeyer Belin states: "On archaeological artifacts of the Assyrian era, a period that goes back 7,000 years, we find pictorial representations of Greyhounds. Some are held on a chain and others are running free in the desert sands."

But whether they descend from a single source or from various sources, all Greyhounds possess the same characteristics—a graceful body, long legs, long muzzle, deep and narrow chest, retracted belly, and powerful muscles: in a word, a perfect racing machine. Today, although they are much esteemed as pet and show dogs, certain breeds are still used for hunting and racing.

297 AFGHAN HOUND
Tazi

DIFFERENT ORIGINS

(no official decision)

The Afghan Hound (Tazi) exists in three varieties in his country of origin: a) shorthaired; b) fringehaired (Saluki type); c) long- and thickhaired (the true Afghan mountain dog).

The types found near the northeastern frontier, that is, adjacent to Iran, are tall and clearly demonstrate their relationship to the Persian Greyhound (Saluki) whose points predominate. The same phenomenon exists with the dogs from the lower plains, which are shorter, hairier, and perhaps formed through breeding with local shepherd dogs. People say that this variety of Afghan can be seen during the goat festival, when the shepherds come down from the mountains accompanied by their dogs which are adorned with flowers.

AFGHAN HOUND

Photo: S. A. Thompson, A. Roslin-Williams.

According to Professor Cornelia Jutta Stelzer, an experienced breeder of Afghans and specialist of this breed, the Afghan mountain dog is an exceptional hunter and also still gives proof of his instinct for the flock, a sign that shepherd blood still flows in his veins. As the two main types carry out different tasks, it is possible to clearly distinguish between them by their physical makeup: the Fringed Afghan (Saluki type), living in the desert and on the steppes, runs great distances and has a longer body and rather straight hind legs—a typical trotter. The mountain Afghan, a smaller dog, displays better footing over rocks; his back is shorter and the hind legs have a pronounced angulation, enabling him to make remarkable bounds—he is a galloping type.

There is yet another variety, the Kirghis Tajgan of Russia, of which there scarcely exist a thousand purebred specimens.

BLACK AND RED AFGHAN HOUND

AFGHAN HOUND

GENERAL CHARACTERISTICS The Afghan Hound should be dignified and aloof, with a certain keen fierceness. The Eastern or Oriental expression is typical of the breed: the Afghan looks at and through one. Gait should be smooth, springy, distinctly stylish. The whole appearance should give the impression of strength and dignity combining speed and power.

SIZE Ideal height: males 27-29 inches; females 2-3 inches smaller.

HEAD The skull is long, not too narrow, with a prominent occiput. The foreface is long, with punishing jaws and a slight stop. The skull is well balanced and has a long topknot. The nose should be black, preferably, but liver is not held a fault in light-colored dogs. The mouth is level.

EYES Preferably dark, but golden eyes are not barred. They are nearly triangular, slanting slightly upward from the inner corner to the outer.

EARS Set on low and well back; they are carried close to the head and are covered with long silky hair.

NECK Long and strong, ensuring proud carriage of the head.

BODY The back is level, of moderate length, well muscled and falling slightly away to the stern. The loin is straight, broad, and rather short. The hip bones are rather prominent and wide apart. There is a fair spring of ribs and a good depth of chest.

TAIL Must not be too short. It is set on low, with a ring at the end. In action the tail is raised. It is sparsely feathered.

FOREQUARTERS The shoulders are long and sloping, set well back. They are strong and well muscled with no loading, however. The forelegs are straight and well boned, straight to the shoulder and with the elbows held well in. **HINDQUARTERS** Powerful, well-bent and well-turned stifles. Great length between hip and hock, with comparatively little distance between hock and foot. Dewclaws may stay or be removed, as the breeder prefers. **FEET** The forefeet are strong and very large in both length and breadth; they are covered with long, thick hair. The toes are arched; the pasterns are long and springy, especially in the forelegs. Pads are well down on the ground. The hind feet are long but less broad than the forefeet. They are covered with long, thick hair.

COAT Long and with very fine texture on the ribs, the forequarters, the hindquarters, and flanks. From the shoulder backward and along the saddle, the hair should be short and close in mature dogs. Hair is long from the forehead backward, with a distinct silky topknot. On the foreface the hair is the same length as on the back. Ears and legs well clad. Pasterns may be bare. The coat must be allowed to develop naturally. **Color** All colors are acceptable.

FAULTS Any appearance of coarseness; skull too wide and foreface too short; weak underjaw; large, round or full eyes; neck too short or too thick; back too long or too short. ●

Photo: S. A. Thompson.

AFGHAN HOUND

BORZOI

Photo: S. A. Thompson.

298 BORZOI
USSR

The Borzoi, like all Greyhounds, is of very ancient origin. He was formerly used in Russia solely to protect his master from the wolves that infested the more desolate areas, while later, with the encouragement of the rulers and nobles, the wolf hunt became a favored pastime.

Borzois were rather late in spreading to the countries of Western Europe, and it was only after 1860 that breeding was begun. Queen Victoria owned several specimens that aroused considerable interest. Thereafter important breeding kennels were established in France, the Netherlands, Belgium, Germany, and elsewhere. In England, production became of immediate importance because of the difficulties of importation, and the creation of a local type was progressively arrived at. This was a highly refined type, considerably different from the classic Greyhound of Russian origin.

In Europe, with rare exceptions, the Borzoi was considered a special pet, as he is today. As he was kept completely inactive, he soon lost the combative instincts of his ancestors in their native regions. He was occasionally used for fox and rabbit hunting for which he showed little aptitude, inasmuch as the small game was not suited to the great size and physical powers of the Borzoi.

GENERAL CHARACTERISTICS A very distinguished and noble breed, harmonious in body and movements. The general appearance should be the chief indication of pureness of breed, and thus it should never be sacrificed for perfection in other points, no matter how important.

SIZE Height: males, 29¾ inches; females, 28 inches. The largest dogs are rarely more than 32¼ inches. As a general rule, the greater size is preferred provided it does not compromise symmetry.

HEAD Long and narrow, extremely lean and finely chiseled. The skull should be as long and narrow as possible, but in good proportion with the rest of the body. In the ideal head the angle formed between skull and nasal bridge should be as obtuse as possible. The nose should be black; the nostrils overlap the lower jaw. The muzzle is long, narrow and lean, with a very slight arch just before the nose. The muzzle should not be pointed. The teeth close regularly, with no overshot nor undershot condition.

EYES Quite close together and set midway between the top of the skull and the end of the muzzle. They are oblong in shape and dark, set normally, neither prominent nor deepset. The eyelids are black.

EARS Highly mobile, set on high and ending in a point; they should lie back on the neck. When the dog is alert, they are sometimes erect like a horse's ears or, preferably, erect with the tips slightly dropped forward.

NECK Of medium length, without dewlap.

BORZOI

BORZOI

BODY The chest is rather narrow, with great depth of brisket, reaching elbow level. The ribs are only slightly sprung, but they are very deep, allowing room for heart and lungs. The back is quite short in males and curves gradually toward the loins, thus forming a long and graceful curve without seeming humpbacked. In the females the back is less arched than in the male; a flat back does not constitute a fault. The loins are quite long, very muscular, arched and passing in a curved line toward the croup, so that the curve of the back continues to the loins and croup, finishing in the hindquarters. The croup is long and broad, and there should be a good 2 inches between the bones of the haunches. The belly is tucked up to the point where it disappears behind the flanks. The groin is minimal in males, slightly longer in females. The flanks are strong and seem stretched to the touch, broader in females than in males.

TAIL One of the characteristic features of the breed. It is carried low in repose, in a graceful curve. The tail is very soft and should be as long as possible. A curled-up tail or one carried higher than its root is faulty.

FOREQUARTERS The shoulders are flat, well shaped and not too slanted. The scapulae meet close to the withers. The forelegs should be absolutely straight, with flat and lean bone, in no sense rounded. Seen from in front, they are narrow, and seen in profile they are wider toward the shoulders, narrowing gradually down to the feet. The elbows should not be turned out, but they are still clearly off the body. **HINDQUARTERS** Broader than the forequarters. The thighs are flat, very broad-boned, with extremely developed muscles which are flat, long and close to the body. The hocks are clean and well let down. The thighs should neither be too wide nor too long. The metatarsi are short. The hind legs should not be too straight. **FEET** Long harefeet, with well-closed toes. The weight of the dog seems to rest more on the nails than on the feet.

COAT Long, not woolly, silky; flat, wavy or rather curly. On the head, ears and front of legs it should be short and smooth; on the neck the frill should be profuse and rather curly. Feathering on hindquarters and tail, long and profuse, less so on chest and back of forelegs. Short hair is a serious fault, and even small curls constitute an esthetic fault. **Color** Preferred colors are: solid white, white marked with yellow, orange, red, streaked and gray. Coats of solid color are often found in all of the foregoing. If the dog is colored, such color tends to become lighter toward the feet. Colored markings should not be too distinctly delineated against a white background. White with black markings and solid black are not preferred. Black with tan markings, with or without white, is a serious fault. ●

BORZOI

Photo: DIM.

299 DEERHOUND

English Coarsehaired Greyhound

GREAT BRITAIN

The Deerhound is intelligent, gentle, affectionate, more timid than aggressive, obedient, calm almost to the point of indolence, although this indolence sometimes, especially in the fresh morning hours, is apt to explode in energetic outbursts of joy, including wild gallops and long bounds. Another quality of this breed is its extraordinary good sense and its ability to keep calm in any circumstance.

This dog has a very agreeable temperament and becomes attached to everyone in the family. He does not fight with other dogs and does not bite. As he has no particular value as a guard dog, he is used mainly as a racing dog and a sight hunter. He makes an excellent companion, preferably for someone living in the country. Left to himself, he does not stray far from home, but when he is sent after a hare (if nothing better is available) his long-legged, hell-for-leather, ground-burning gallop and speed, like an arrow in flight, is truly spectacular.

He is gradually coming back into style in Great Britain, the United States, Canada, and Australia, in a dual role of pet and sporting dog. Deerhound owners have periodic meetings and organize competitions among themselves in areas where there are hares (principally in Great Britain, which lacks big game), coyotes, or other smaller wild life. The Deerhounds proceed to flush these, pursue them, and finally capture them through their agility and speed, which almost rivals the English Greyhound's.

GENERAL CHARACTERISTICS An elegant dog, more robust than the greyhound, even in the bone. An identifying characteristic is the roughness of the coat.

WEIGHT AND SIZE Weight: Males 85-105 lb; females 65-80 lb. Height of males not to be less than 30 inches at the shoulder, females less than 28 inches.

HEAD Broadest at the ears, tapering slightly to the eyes, with the muzzle tapering more decidedly to the nose. The muzzle should be pointed, but with level lips. The head should be long; the skull, flat rather than round, with a very slight rise over the eyes, which is not strictly speaking a stop. The skull should be coated with moderately long hair, softer than the rest of the coat. The nose should be black (though in some blue-fawns the color is blue) and slightly aquiline. In lighter-colored dogs, a black muzzle is preferable. There should be a good moustache of rather silky hair and a fair beard. Teeth to be level.

EYES Dark; generally they are dark brown or hazel. A very light eye is not desirable. The eye is moderately full, with a soft look in repose but with a keen, distant look when the dog is aroused. Eyelid rims should be black.

EARS The ears should be set on high and, in repose, folded back like those of the Greyhound, although they are raised above the head in excitement without losing the fold; in some cases they may become semi-erect. A prick ear is bad, and a big thick ear hanging flat to the head or heavily coated with long hair is the worst of faults. The ear should be soft, glossy, and like a mouse's coat to the touch. The smaller it is the better. It should have no long coat or long fringe, but there is often a silky, silvery coat over the extent of the ear and tip. Ears should be black or dark, no matter what the general coat color.

NECK The neck should be long, as befitting the Greyhound character of this breed. Excessive length is not necessary nor desirable, and the mane, which every good Deerhound should have, detracts from the apparent length of the neck. The Deerhound needs an extraordinarily strong neck in order to hold a stag. The nape should be prominent where the head is set on; the throat should be prominent and clean-cut at the angle.

BODY The body and general formation are like the bigger, larger-boned Greyhound's. The chest is deep rather

DEERHOUND

427

Photo: C. M. Cooke, S. A. Thompson, R. Kinne (Photo Res.), T. Fall.

DEERHOUND

than broad, but it must not be too narrow nor flat-sided. The loin must be well arched and drooping to the tail. A straight backline is not good, since this formation is ill suited to going uphill.

TAIL The tail should be long, thick at the root and tapering; it should reach to within 1½ inches from the ground. In repose, the tail is dropped perfectly straight down or curved. In motion it should be curved when the dog is excited, but in no case to be lifted out of the line of the back. It should be well covered with hair, thick and wiry on the inside and longer on the underside; toward the tip a slight fringe is not objectionable. A curled or ring tail is highly undesirable.

FOREQUARTERS The shoulders should

be well sloped, the blades well back without too much width between them. Loaded and straight shoulders are very bad faults. The forelegs should be straight, broad and flat, and a good broad forearm and elbow are desirable. **HINDQUARTERS** Drooping, as broad and powerful as possible, the hips set wide apart. The hind legs should be well bent at the stifle, with great length from the hip to the hock, which should be broad and flat. **FEET** should be close and compact, with toes well arranged. Nails strong.

COAT The hair on the body, neck, and quarters should be harsh and wiry and 3-4 inches long. The hair on the head, breast, and belly is much softer. There should be a slight hairy fringe on the inside of the forelegs

and hind legs, but nothing approaching the feather of a Collie. The Deerhound should be a shaggy dog but not excessively coated. A woolly coat is bad. Some good strains have a mixture of silky and hard coat, and this is better than a woolly coat; but the proper sort is a thick, close-lying, ragged coat, harsh or crisp to the touch. **Color** A matter of preference, to a great degree, but the dark blue-gray is without doubt the most preferred, since quality tends to be found together with this color. Next comes the lighter and darker grays or brindles, with the darkest generally preferred. Yellow, sandy-red or red-fawn, especially with black points (ears and muzzle) are equally esteemed, since such are the colors of the oldest known strains (the McNeil and Cheethill

Menzies). White is condemned by all the old authorities, but a white chest and toes, found in many of the darkest dogs, are not so insistently objected to; but the less white the better, as the Deerhound is ideally a self-colored dog. A white blaze on the head or a white collar should be heavily penalized. In other cases, though tolerable, an attempt should be made to breed out white markings. A slight white tip to the stern occurs in the best of strains.

FAULTS Thick ear hanging flat to the head or heavily coated with long hair, curl or ring tail, light eye, straight back, cow hocks, weak pasterns, straight stifles, splayed feet, woolliness of coat, shoulders loaded and straight, white markings. ●

428

GREYHOUND

300 GREYHOUND
English Smooth-Coated Greyhound

GREAT BRITAIN

The Greyhound is a true masterpiece obtained through the persevering skill of English breeders who wished to create a beautiful, brave, and extremely fast dog. The name Greyhound is a corruption of "Greek Hound," whose lines and general appearance recall, although roughly, the points of the modern Greyhound. This Greek Hound was very prevalent in Ancient Greece. He was brought westward by Phoenicians, Celts, and Croatians.

The Greyhound combines an aristocratic and haughty appearance with exceptional skill and remarkable speed which enables him to pursue the hare in open terrain or chase mechanical ones on race tracks. The latter sporting event is especially popular in England and America, attracting crowds of sometimes 100,000 filling the stands of White City, London. Public enthusiasm for these fast contestants never seems to wane, especially since it is whetted by the possibility of winning money.

There are no official dog tracks in France, where they were abolished because of competition with horseracing. However, Greyhound races are held in England and the United States where phenomenally fast times are being recorded continually.

GENERAL CHARACTERISTICS A dog of remarkable stamina and endurance; his straight-through, long-reaching movement enables him to cover ground with great speed. In general appearance the typical Greyhound is a strongly built, upstanding dog of generous proportions, muscular power, and symmetrical formation. He has a long head and neck, clean, well-laid shoulders, deep chest, capacious body, arched loins, powerful quarters, sound legs and feet, and a suppleness of limb, all of which emphasize to a marked degree its distinctive type and quality.

WEIGHT AND SIZE Weight: males 65-70 lb; females 60-65 lb. Ideal height: males 28-30 inches; females 27-28 inches.

HEAD Long, moderate width, flat skull, slight stop. The jaws are well cut and powerful. The teeth should be white and strong, and the incisors of the upper jaw should clip those of the lower jaw.

EYES Bright and intelligent, dark in color.

EARS Small, rose-shaped, of fine texture.

NECK Long and muscular, elegantly arched, well set into the shoulders.

BODY Chest deep and capacious, providing adequate heart room. Ribs deep, well sprung and carried well back. Flanks well cut up. Back rather long, broad and square, well muscled. Loin powerful and slightly arched.

TAIL Long, set on rather low, strong at the root and tapering to the point; carried low and slightly curved.

FOREQUARTERS Shoulders oblique, well set back, muscular without being loaded, narrow and cleanly defined at the top. Forelegs long and straight, bone of good substance and quality. Elbows should be free and well set under the shoulders. Pasterns of moderate length and slightly sprung. Elbows, pasterns, and toes should incline neither inward nor outward.
HINDQUARTERS Thighs and second thighs should be wide and muscular, demonstrating great propelling power. Stifles should be well bent and the hocks well let down, inclining neither outward nor inward. Body and hindquarters features should be of ample proportions and well coupled, making it possible to cover adequate ground when standing. **FEET** Of moderate length, with compact, well-knuckled toes and strong pads.

COAT Fine and close. **Color** Black, white, red, blue, fawn, fallow, brindle, or any of these broken by white. ●

GREYHOUND

Photo: Fotostampa-Embrione, A. Wintzell.

GREYHOUND RACING

430

301 IRISH WOLFHOUND
GREAT BRITAIN

It is claimed that the formation of this breed goes back to 1863 when a certain Captain Graham crossbred the Deerhound with the German Mastiff. Another theory holds that its origins go back much further, since fighting dogs of great size and muscular strength were known in Ireland since ancient times.

The naturalist E. C. Ash does not consider that the breed's origins go back further than the fourteenth century, although he refers to Irish hounds of great size but claims these were only German Mastiffs, Mastiffs, or Greyhounds.

During the past few years the Wolfhound has been coming back into style in Great Britain and the United States. In both countries its numbers have increased and its psychological qualities have considerably improved.

Despite his gigantic size and hairy appearance, the Wolfhound, although conscious of his strength, is nevertheless quite gentle. He is good-natured and devoted, patient with everyone and particularly with children. It is difficult to find a safer dog in this respect.

He is very intelligent and reflective rather than lively. He is also resourceful and in such good esteem that anyone who has ever had him as a companion rarely chooses another breed.

He is a good guard dog, brave, energetic, and rarely bites. He limits himself to barking and keeping his eye on the intruder until his master arrives. However, if trained for attack, he can be very dangerous, since with his unusual strength he is capable of killing a man.

Although he is affectionate with all members of the family, he has a marked tendency to attach himself to a single individual. When he does so, his devotion knows no bounds and he will never transfer it to another.

It is not advisable to keep him in the city. He suffers from the heat and is more comfortable outdoors than in the house. Provided he keeps close to his master, he can adapt himself to any surroundings, but lack of liberty and space could have a deleterious effect on his health and temperament.

GENERAL CHARACTERISTICS The Irish Wolfhound should not be quite as heavy or as massive as the Great Dane but more so than the Deerhound, which he should otherwise resemble in general type. Of great size and commanding appearance, very muscular, strongly though gracefully built, movements easy and active; head and neck carried high; the tail carried with an upward sweep and with a slight curve toward the tip.

WEIGHT AND SIZE Minimum weight: males 120 lb; females 90 lb. Minimum height: males 31 inches; females 28 inches. Weights and heights below these minima should be severely penalized. Great size, including height at shoulder and proportionate length of

IRISH WOLFHOUND

Photo: Fotostampa-Embrione.

IRISH WOLFHOUND

body is the desideratum to be aimed at, and it is desired to establish a breed that should average 32-34 inches in males, with the requisite power, activity, courage, and symmetry.

HEAD Long, with the frontal bones of the forehead very slightly raised and with very little indentation between the eyes. Skull not too broad; muzzle long and moderately pointed.

EYES Dark.

EARS Small and carried like those of the Greyhound.

NECK Rather long, very strong and muscular, well arched, without dewlap or loose skin about the throat.

BODY Chest very deep; breast wide; back rather more long than short; loins arched; belly well drawn up.

TAIL Long and slightly curved, of moderate thickness and well covered with hair.

FOREQUARTERS Shoulders muscular, giving breadth of chest, and set sloping. Elbows well under, turned neither inward nor outward. Leg and forearm muscular, with the whole leg

strong and quite straight. **HIND-QUARTERS** Muscular thighs and second thighs; long and strong as in the Greyhound, with hocks well let down and turning neither inward nor outward. **FEET** Moderately large and round, turned neither inward nor outward. Toes well arched and closed. Nails very strong and curved.

COAT Rough and hardy on the body, legs and head; especially wiry and long over eyes and under jaw. **Color** The recognized colors are gray, brindle, red, black, pure white, fawn, or

any color that appears in the Deerhound.

FAULTS Head too light or too heavy, too highly arched frontal bone; large ears, ears hanging flat to the face; short neck; full dewlap; too narrow or too broad a chest; sunken, hollow or quite straight back; bent forelegs; overbent fetlocks; twisted feet; spreading toes; too curly a tail; weak hindquarters and a general lack of muscle; too short in body; pink or liver eyelids; lips and nose any color other than black; very light eyes. ●

Photo: S. A. Thompson.

302 WHIPPET
GREAT BRITAIN

Formerly called a "snap dog" because of the way he bounds after hares, the Whippet may be described as a miniature Greyhound. He is extremely fast and can attain a speed of about 45 miles an hour. In Great Britain today he is used for racing.

He is intelligent, affectionate, very obedient, and is more timid than aggressive. He is neither a fighter nor given to biting. Although he looks delicate, he is really exceptionally robust, able to resist the elements, and rarely becomes ill.

He is clean and does not have an offensive odor. His very short coat does not require particular attention. If he lives in the country he cleans himself by rolling in the grass.

He adapts easily to a city apartment (he loves to sleep on his master's bed), although it must be remembered that the Whippet likes to run at liberty, and that a garden of somewhat small dimensions is not enough for him. If a Whippet is kept in the city he should be taken to the country at least two or three times a week.

WHIPPET

GENERAL CHARACTERISTICS Should convey an impression of beautifully balanced muscular power and strength, combined with great elegance and grace of outline. Symmetry of outline, muscular development, and powerful gait are the main considerations. Since the dog is built for speed and work, all exaggerations should be avoided. The dog should possess great freedom of action, the forelegs should be thrown forward and low over the ground like a thoroughbred horse, not in a hackneylike action. Hind legs should come well under the body, giving great propelling power; general

WHIPPET

Photo: Prato.

SPANISH GREYHOUND

movement not to look stilted, high-stepping, or in a short-paced or mincing manner.

SIZE Ideal height for males is 18½ inches, for females 17½ inches. Judges should use their discretion and not unduly penalize an otherwise good specimen.

WHIPPET

HEAD Long and lean, flat on top, tapering to the muzzle; rather wide between the eyes; the jaws powerful and clean-cut; nose black (in blues a bluish cast is permitted and in livers a nose of the same color; in whites or particolors a butterfly nose is permissible). Mouth should be level, the teeth in the upper jaw fitting closely over the teeth in the lower.

EYES Bright, with a very alert expression.

EARS Rose-shaped, small and finely textured.

NECK Long and muscular, elegantly arched.

BODY Chest very deep, with plenty of heart room; brisket deep and well defined; back broad, firm, rather long and showing, definite arch over the loin but not humped, the loin giving the impression of strength and power; ribs well sprung; well muscled on back.

TAIL No feathering. Long, tapering; when in action, carried in a delicate upward curve but not over the back.

FOREQUARTERS Shoulders oblique and muscular, the blades carried up to the spine and closely set together at the top. Forelegs straight and upright, front not too wide, pasterns strong with slight spring, elbows well set under body. **HINDQUARTERS** Strong and broad across the thighs; stifles well bent; hocks well let down; second thighs strong, enabling the dog to stand over a lot of ground and show great driving power. **FEET** Very neat, well split up between the toes; knuckles highly arched, pads thick and strong.

COAT Fine, short, as close as possible in texture. **Color** Any color or mixture of colors.

FAULTS Front and shoulders: Weal; sloping or too straight pasterns; pigeon toes; tied elbows; loaded or bossy shoulders wide on top and with straight shoulderblades; flat sides. An exaggerated narrow front not to be encouraged. Head and skull: apple skull, short foreface or downface. Ears: Pricked or tulip. Mouth: overshot or undershot. Neck: Throatiness at the joining of neck and jaw or at base of neck. Body and hindquarters: a short-coupled or cramped stance, an exaggerated arch or a camelback or humped back (with the arch starting behind the shoulderblades), an excessively short or long loin; straight stifles, poor muscular development of thighs and second thighs. Feet: splayed, flat or open. Tail: gay, ringed or twisted, short or docked. Coat: wire- or broken-coated; coarse or woolly coat; coarse, thick skin. ●

434

Photo: Buzzini, T. Fall.

303 SPANISH GREYHOUND

Galgo Español

SPAIN

HUNGARIAN GREYHOUND

This Greyhound has many similarities to the English Greyhound and the Slughi, but on close observation certain important differences become apparent: the back is less arched and the head is narrower.

A variety called the Anglo-Spanish exists in which the English strain is so predominant that it could easily be confused with the Greyhound except for its darker eyes and longer tail.

WEIGHT AND SIZE Weight about 67 lb, height 25½-27½ inches. Females are slightly smaller.

HEAD Long and narrow, truncate-conical in shape. Prominent nose overhanging the lower jaw, the color varying with the coat. Well-opened nostrils. Jaws lean and strong, lips finely cut. Overshot and undershot teeth not acceptable. The nasal bridge is slightly convex. Distance from eyes to nose and distance from eyes to occipital chest approximately equal. The skull is broad, flat, with pronounced occipital apophysis. Very little stop.

EYES Dark, bright, vivacious.

EARS Falling back, rose type.

BODY The back is long and nearly straight; the rump is higher than the withers, but when the dog is erect this characteristic is not noticeable. Belly drawn up.

TAIL Very long, carried low, slightly sabered.

FOREQUARTERS Oblique shoulders, legs straight. **HINDQUARTERS** Very rugged and muscular, with broad thighs and good angulation. Hocks low.

COAT Close, shiny, short (no longer than ½ inch on the shoulder). **Color** Tawny with black mask, or black; generally streaked with light undercoat, with white muzzle, belly, and feet. ●

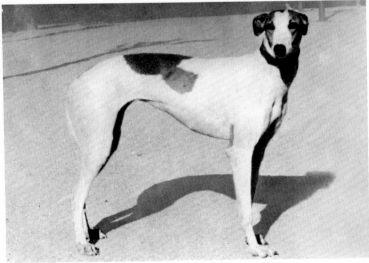

SPANISH GREYHOUND

304 HUNGARIAN GREYHOUND

Magyar Agár

HUNGARY

During the ninth century, Magyar invaders burst into Pannonia, Transylvania, and the middle Danubian valley, bringing with them Greyhounds from the western Carpathians. According to contemporaneous accounts, these people, so devoted to the hunt, pursued it with true Greyhounds whose lineage became mixed during the passing centuries with other Greyhound breeds from both the West and the East. They encountered Turkish and Asiatic Greyhounds between the fifteenth and seventeenth centuries, besides Salukis, Tazis, and the African Greyhound, and probably perfected the breed during the nineteenth century by crossing it with the English Greyhound, resulting in a dog capable of great speed. The Hungarian Greyhound is a first-class dog of easy temperament, faithful and loving. He is also well adapted to guard his master's home. His sense of smell is less keen than that of other dogs; in fact, one might say that this is the only hunting dog whose olfactory sense is actually deficient. He is used to capture hares in the running hunt, and among the most expert of these dogs are some that are capable of killing the fox.

GENERAL CHARACTERISTICS A fast-moving dog, used precisely for his principal gift, speed. In appearance the Magyar Agár is impressive for the singular harmony of power and attitudes. Some parts of the body have become, through specialization, disproportionately long—streamlined, so to speak. Beneath the short hair and the fine skin, the muscling is visible for certain lengths. The articulations are lean, the rib cage is deep and flat. The form of the body itself is long. The teeth are well developed. The Magyar Agár is found in various colors.

WEIGHT Adult weight ranges from about 59½-68 lb for males, about 10 lb less for females.

HEAD Very long. The nose is black. The muzzle is short in newborn puppies and grows to a Greyhoundlike point only after weaning. The stop is very gradual, as in the Greyhound and in another Hungarian breed, the Kuvasz.

EYES Of medium size. The expression is open and frank.

EARS Small, button type; when the dog is alert the ears are half-raised but never become erect.

NECK The Magyar Agár's neck is long.

FOREQUARTERS The forelegs are long and lean, perpendicular to the ground. The joints are lean, toes long. Dewclaws should be removed from dogs meant for hunting; this should be done 2 or 3 days after birth. The reason is that they might become injured and in that case convalescence is long.

BODY Long, flat and deep, withers practically nonexistent. The loins are strongly muscled and well adapted to racing; they are gently rounded but flatter than in the Greyhound. The rump is slightly concave. The belly is well tucked up.

TAIL Rather long, thin and twisted. The tip is sometimes curved to right or left. When the dog is excited the tail is lifted to the horizontal, especially in males. The tail is used in making sudden changes in direction or stopping abruptly, being rapidly agitated.

HIND LEGS The pelvis and thigh are very lean and well muscled. The structure is of good bone, well coupled and with good angulation.

COAT Short and smooth, to the point where the dog suffers from the cold and often shivers. If the dog is kept outdoors in winter the coat becomes noticeably longer. **Color** Black, Isabella, gray, brindle, ash, piebald, rarely white. The tip of the tail is often white, a white spot is often seen on the chest, but these do not change the basic color classification of the coat. A white collar and blaze puts the dog into the piebald class. **Skin** Very fine. The nose, inner lips, and in general the free surfaces of the skin are black. The tongue is bright red. In dogs with gray or Isabella coats the nose may be the same color or black.

GAIT The gait is elastic. In place of a short gallop (as, for example, when working as a coach dog) the dog will trot for miles. His gallop is similar to the "belly to ground" gallop of a thoroughbred horse, except that the back is more arched. The Magyar Agár is capable of a show of strength, speed, and dash, of elegance and flexibility, which is truly remarkable. If he stumbles and falls at full speed he is capable of continuing his run with no loss of stride. Speed has been clocked at better than 36 mph. Puppies are inclined to run aimlessly in a circle for the pure joy of running. On the trail of a rabbit, the Magyar Agár runs constantly at full speed, and on good terrain can maintain maximum speed for more than 4 minutes without flagging. Such activity may sometimes bring the dog to a state of total exhaustion. The biggest dogs or bitches in heat may even be subject to heart attacks. In brief, the Agár is more tenacious but not quite as fast as the Greyhound.

FAULTS Prick ears, exaggerated stop, straight back, sloping hindquarters, excessively angulated hind leg below hock, too harsh or too long hair on hindquarters and tail, nails too long or badly curved. ●

305 PHARAON HOUND

DIFFERENT ORIGINS

(no official decision)

Buffon claims that all breeds have more or less preserved their primitive characteristics according to the surroundings where they have lived, the tasks assigned to them by man, the climatic conditions, and especially, their degree of isolation.

PHARAON HOUND

SALUKI

We have mentioned in the case of Greyhounds how these dogs were probably products of a single stock, most likely Asiatic, and how the Egyptian Greyhound himself is an intermediate type between the primitive stock and the so-called European Greyhound. The Asiatic or African Greyhounds were exported for trade by the Phoenicians to Greece, Sicily, and Brittany and, possibly, to the Balearic Islands. While in other areas they seem to have undergone considerable modifications through acclimatization, crossbreeding, and residence, they seem to have preserved their purest characteristics in the Balearics. On the island of Ibiza one finds dogs which are closest to the Greyhounds of antiquity, kept so by total isolation. Nor has its task changed: it is still used for hunting hares.

These Balearic Greyhounds, or Pharaon Hounds, are supposed to have given birth to the Podenco and the Ibizan Podenco which, in turn, spreading to France, became the Charnigue, much used by French poachers and eventually forbidden.

In any case, these two varieties are entirely similar to the Pharaon Hound, tending to prove the theory that all of them are from the same stock.

GENERAL CHARACTERISTICS The Pharaon Hound is the same type as the Greyhounds depicted among the relics of ancient Egypt. The dog has a triangular head, large erect ears, a frequently curved tail, long muscles, a streamlined profile, and short, fine hair. The outline is approximately square and the lines generally are lean. The Pharaon Hound is capable of great speed and outstanding elasticity of movement; he is a phenomenal jumper. Pleasant and docile in character, he also displays an obvious love for the hunt. He loves to play and has a great need for activity and movement.

SIZE Height at the withers: males 25-27½ inches; females 22½-26 inches.

HEAD Viewed both from above and in profile the head is triangular, with a flat, relatively broad skull. The nose is either flesh or light fawn. The muzzle is wedge-shaped. Skull and muzzle are of equal length. The jaws are powerful and meet in a scissors bite. The cheeks are firm, the stop is minimal. The back of the skull is slightly raised.

EYES Quite small and deep-set; they may be amber or light brown.

EARS Broad, large, set on high, straight, light fawn in color. The tips of the ears point in opposite directions.

NECK Slender, rather long and very well muscled.

BODY Slender, flat, well muscled. The thorax is narrow, with fine, well-sprung ribs. The chest is less let down than in the Greyhound. The back is straight, with a long curve of loin which is well muscled but not arched. The croup is quite long and slightly falling. The belly is neat and fairly tucked up, but rather less so than in other Greyhound breeds.

TAIL Curved, long enough to reach the hock; it may be carried high when the dog is excited.

FOREQUARTERS AND HINDQUARTERS The forequarters are long, lean, well muscled and with flat bone. The legs should be straight and parallel, with the elbows well in to the body. The pasterns are rather short and straight. The same applies basically to the hindquarters. The stifle is slightly bent, the second thigh well developed. The muscles are less well developed than in the Greyhound. The hocks should be parallel, strong and well angulated. **FEET** Strong, with close toes. The pads and toes are light-colored.

COAT Short, fine and glossy. **Color** White with chestnut or rich tan or yellow tan markings. Chestnut self-coloring is also found. Other colors are not allowed. **Skin** Soft. ●

306 SALUKI
Persian Greyhound

DIFFERENT ORIGINS

(no official decision)

For a time between the thirteenth and seventeenth dynasties Egypt was under the domination of the Hyksos, a nomadic and warlike Asiatic people. The first Saluki stock appears to have come from a cross between the Asiatic hunting dogs (Greyhounds) and Egyptian Greyhounds that followed these nomads. There are now only Slughis but no Salukis in Egypt; on the other hand, but for the hair, the two breeds have many points in common; perhaps the crossbreeding occurred only in the areas near the Euphrates River, close to the Persian frontier. Toward the end of the seventeenth dynasty, after the war of liberation, the victorious Egyptians extended their borders to the Euphrates, and this may account for the crossbreeding between the Asiatic and Egyptian Greyhounds. Some experts, however, consider that the Saluki derives from the Tazi (Afghan Greyhound) that lived during the time of Genghis Khan and Tamerlane.

The Saluki of today is a direct descendant of the most ancient racing dogs in the world which were perhaps the first dogs trained by man for the hunt.

In England the Saluki is used largely on hares and regular coursing meets are held. The judging is based on the dog's ability to turn quickly and overtake the hare in the best possible time. The Saluki hunts largely by sight, although he has a fair nose.

The American Kennel Club describes the Saluki as possessing "the beauty of the thoroughbred horse—symmetry of form; clean-cut; short silky hair except on the ears, legs and tail; slender, well-muscled neck, shoulders and thighs; arched loins; and a smooth and shining coat with long fringes on the tail, ears, and flanks." All of these attributes facilitate in the showing of the dog as it needs very little grooming when being shown.

GENERAL CHARACTERISTICS The overall appearance of the Saluki gives an impression of grace and symmetry and of great speed and endurance, along with strength and activity sufficient to run down gazelle or other quarry over deep sand or rocky mountain terrain. In the Arab world there are several distinct types of Saluki.

WEIGHT AND HEIGHT Weight: 50-66 lb. Height: males 23-28 inches; females are smaller but must not be less thas 21¼ inches at the withers.

HEAD Long, narrow and lean. Viewed from above or in profile, the head is wedge-shaped. The nose is black in dark-coated dogs, and in light-colored dogs the nose may be liver. Straight or slightly raised nostrils. The muzzle is long, lean, powerful. The lower jaw is robust and with complete dentition. The stop is minimal. The top of the skull is flat, broadening toward the ears. The occipital protuberance is pronounced.

EYES Relatively large but not prominent; brilliant, with coloring ranging from dark to light brown. The shape is oval, with eye rims which should be

Photo: S. A. Thompson, Fotostampa-Embrione.

SALUKI

SALUKI

black, especially in dogs with dark coats. The expression is one of great dignity, gentle, and as if looking far off. On the alert, the Saluki's expression is one of penetrating curiosity.

EARS Set on rather high, framing the face and clad in long silky hair, sometimes slightly wavy. At the base the width is about 3 inches, the length from 4-5½ inches. When alert, the dog tends to prick up his ears and move them forward.

NECK Long, flexible and elegant; the muscling not too evident.

FOREQUARTERS The angulations are rather wide; the shoulders are let down straight and are long, powerful, and muscular and kept close to the body. The elbows are compact to the brisket. The forearm is long, straight, lean and muscular. The pastern is relatively short. The feet are solid, with fairly long toes which are close and curved.

BODY Long, with a flat, very deep chest. The ribs are well rounded and usually visible. The withers are pronounced; the back is straight, with a slight hollow behind the withers. Back and loin are relatively broad and powerfully muscled; the loins are well shaped because of the muscling. The bones of the stern are pronounced and set well apart. The rump slopes slightly, the belly is well drawn up.

TAIL Long, reaching at least to the hock. It is set on low and is thick at the root, tapering to the tip, carried either straight or slightly curved. The end of the tail may be curved into a ring. When excited or in full action the tail may be carried higher. In the lower part the tail is well feathered with long, silky hair.

HINDQUARTERS Well-marked angulations, but without exaggeration. The thigh is powerful, lean and muscular. The hind legs are long but with no sign of weakness. The hocks are lean. The metatarsus and the feet are very like the forequarters counterparts.

COAT Short, soft, glossy. Sometimes long hair, woolly or soft and silky, may feather the shoulders and the thighs or, more rarely, the chest and flanks; this longer coat may be slightly wavy. The ears, particularly at their edges, also have long, silky, possibly wavy hair. The hindparts of the forelegs and thighs also have similar hair, and it may also grow between the toes. The tail has an abundant fringe, which, however, should never be woolly or tufted; this hair may grow in a number of ways. One type of Saluki has short hair entirely, that is, with no fringes and with no woolly growth. On all other points this variety conforms to the basic standard.

Color White, cream, fawn, golden red, grizzle and tan, tricolor (white, black and tan) and black and tan, or variations thereof. In short, practically all colors are found.

GAIT Dynamic, elastic, fast. ●

438

SLUGHI
Arabian Greyhound
DIFFERENT ORIGINS

(no official decision)

The Arabs give the Slughi every possible care and protection, although they detest other dogs. They treat the Slughi as if he were a member of their own family, and sometimes this affection goes beyond bounds. It sometimes happens that the death of a dog, especially if he has attained considerable fame, is a greater source of sorrow to the tribe than the death of a human member.

The peoples of North Africa, particularly the nomads, use this dog sometimes for hunting and sometimes as a guard dog. The eminent naturalist Hilzhelmer, who spent some time in Kordofan, tells us that in the village of Melbess he saw beautiful Greyhounds in front of each house. They were especially vigilant and protected the village from the hyenas and leopards that dared to approach, and were hesitant only in attacking the lion. They became active at nightfall, climbing up to the straw roofs of buildings and standing watch from these observation posts. As soon as a predator approached (which happened nightly), whether a hyena, leopard, or wild dog, the first dog to see the enemy immediately leapt down from his post, and in a moment all the other dogs jumped down as well, formed a pack, and routed the intruders, killing some of them. Thereupon they quickly went back to their sentry posts and resumed their watch while their masters slept. There is little to add to what we have already said about their origins from the Greyhound group. The ancestor of the Slughi should be sought in the ancient Egyptian Greyhound, which is seen on the monuments of the Pharaonic era.

SLUGHI

GENERAL CHARACTERISTICS The general appearance of the Slughi is that of a very racy dog, with a frame outstanding for its muscular leanness and the delicacy of tissue.

SIZE Height at the withers is 22-30 inches.

HEAD Without being heavy, the head is a little weightier than that of the Greyhound. The Slughis' lines are less marked than those of the English Greyhound. The skull is flat, rather wide, distinctly rounded at the back and curving harmoniously inward on the sides. The orbital arches are scarcely projecting. The muzzle is wedge-shaped and almost in a straight line with the slope of the skull, to which it is roughly equal in length. There is virtually no stop. The nose is black, with open nostrils. The lips are thin and either black or very deep brown. The jaws are neither undershot nor overshot.

EYES Large, dark, deep-set in their sockets and slanting. The expression is gentle but slightly sad, as if homesick. Light-colored individuals (off-white, sable, fawn) have a velvety black eye with very dark eyelashes, much like the large liquid eye of the gazelle. Dark-coated Slughis have eyes the color of burnt topaz.

EARS Drooping, set well to the head and either at eye level or slightly above. The ear is not excessively wide; it is flat, triangular, and slightly rounded at the tips. Some dogs carry their ears slightly off the skull, sometimes slightly thrown back, although this is not desirable. Ears carried like those of a Greyhound are also objectionable.

NECK The neck must be absolutely lean, with no muscling apparent. The relaxed skin beneath the throat forms slight wrinkles.

BODY The Slughi's chest should not be too wide; in depth it reaches to the level of the elbow. It is well developed, with fairly long back ribs. The belly is fairly tucked up, but not so much as in the Greyhound. The backline is quite straight, and the back is relatively short. The loins are lean, wide, and slightly arched. The buttocks are bony and very slanting; the haunches are well out or projecting.

TAIL Thin and without fleshiness, fringes, or long hair. It has an accentuated curve at the tip and should be long enough to reach the tip of the hocks. When moving, the Slughi should not carry the tail higher than the backline.

FOREQUARTERS AND HINDQUARTERS The shoulders should be flat, lean, and with a moderate slope. The thighs are well dropped and slightly flat. The forelegs and hind legs are lean, without fleshiness, with flat bones and well-separated tendons. The hocks are close to the ground but not abruptly bent. **FEET** Lean, long oval in shape, and lighter than the Greyhound's feet. The nails are strong and either black or very dark color.

COAT The hair is smooth and close. **Color** Sable or all shades of fawn, with or without a black mask; a mantle is also allowed; off-white, brindle, black with reddish marks on lower part of the head, on the paws, and occasionally on the chest. Solid black or white is permissible but not desirable. Dark-colored dogs someimes have a few white hairs on the chest.

FAULTS Light eyes, mealiness, overshot or undershot jaw, knotty muscles.

DISQUALIFICATIONS Definite mealiness, ears straight or button ears, Greyhound ears, harsh coat, coarse coat, long coat, fringes on legs or tail, piebald coat. ●

SALUKI

Photo: Fotostampa-Embrione, S. A. Thompson.

308 SMALL ITALIAN GREYHOUND

Piccolo Levriero Italiano

DIFFERENT ORIGINS
(no official decision)

One cannot speak of this dog without mentioning the great popularity it enjoyed during the seventeenth and eighteenth centuries when it was always present in noble salons, carried in the arms, or standing beside aristocratic ladies.

Charles I of England, Frederick the Great, and the Emperor Frederick III had a special fondness for this beautiful little dog. Frederick the Great had more than fifty of them in his kennels, cared for by a selected and very competent personnel. He loved to take walks accompanied by two or three of his small friends.

This dog's characteristic movements, easy and graceful, his lively intelligence, his unsurpassed fidelity, the perfection and elegance of his features, the symmetry of his body, and the softness of his coat all contribute to making the Small Italian Greyhound a true "model of grace and distinction," a phrase that appears in his description within the Italian standard.

In spite of his delicate appearance, this dog is actually robust and well built for racing. In Great Britain he is called "Italian Greyhound" because he is a perfect replica in miniature of the English breed.

As far as his origins are concerned, and although literature is unanimous in stating that he comes from Italy, still no proof exists nor has any theory been offered. Certainly the presence of Small Greyhounds in Italy is incontestable since the Roman era when a great many of these miniature animals were highly esteemed guests in patrician households. As we have already mentioned concerning the larger Greyhounds, it seems logical to seek the origin of all Greyhounds in a single Asiatic stock imported into Europe by the Phoenicians.

GENERAL CHARACTERISTICS Scientifically the Small Italian Greyhound is classified as belonging to the graioid group, according to the classification system of Pierre Mégnin. Italian origin. This dog is a dolichomorph, with square body outline. In miniature, it is very similar to the Greyhound, and particularly to the Slughi, whose finesse and elegance are accentuated in the present breed —an elegance which is increased by the Italian dog's movements and graceful pose. Agile, intelligent and affectionate, the Italian Greyhound is a model of grace and distinction.

WEIGHT AND SIZE Maximum weight, 11 lb. Height: minimum, 12½ inches; maximum, 15 inches.

HEAD Dolichocephalic; the total length may reach 2/5 of the height at the withers. The skull and muzzle are of equal length. The upper longitudinal axes of the skull and muzzle are parallel. The skin is smooth and close-fitting. The nose is dark and preferably black. The muzzle is pointed, with the lips well pigmented and dark; the inner lip is not visible at the commissure. The lips are thin and close-fitting. The teeth are sound, complete in number and meet in a scissors bite. The stop is not pro-

SMALL ITALIAN GREYHOUND

SMALL ITALIAN GREYHOUND

SMALL ITALIAN GREYHOUND

nounced. The skull is flat. The sub-orbital region is well chiseled.

EYES Large, expressive, neither protruding nor deep-set; there is neither ectropion nor entropion. The color is dark, the eyelids are dark in pigmentation.

EARS Set on high, small, with thin cartilage. The tips of the ears are dropped. The ears are carried back, over the nape and the upper part of the neck, so as to reveal the auricle. When the dog is attentive, the first part of the ear is carried horizontally. This position is commonly called "roofed."

NECK As long as the head, with a slightly arched upper line, and with an abrupt insertion at the withers. It is lean, without dewlap and at the thyroid level, it is slightly bulging.

FOREQUARTERS Shoulders Slightly sloping, covered with clean, prominent muscle. **Upper Arms** The scapula-humeral angle is very obtuse, the direction is parallel to the center plane of the body. **Forearms** Extremely light-boned, straight and vertical, as seen from in front or in profile. The elbows are turned neither in nor out. The height from the ground of the elbows is slightly more than the distance from the elbows to the withers. **Pasterns** Seen in profile, the pasterns should be slightly bent; they continue the vertical line of the forearm and have a minimum of subcutaneous tissue. **Feet** Small,

extremely lean, almost oval, with well-closed and well-arched toes covered with extremely short, fine hair. The pads are dark, preferably black. The nails are black or dark, depending on the coat and whether there is any white on the feet. Such white is acceptable.

BODY The length of the trunk is slightly less, or perhaps equal to, the height at the withers. The chest is narrow, the brisket is at elbow level. The backline is straight, and the dorsal-lumbar region is arched. The lumbar arch merges harmoniously with the croup. The belly is extremely drawn up. The croup is deeply sloped. There should be full development of both testicles, which should be contained in the scrotum.

TAIL Set on low; although very slender at the root, the tail tapers to the tip. It is covered with extremely short hair. The first half is straight, the second half is curved. Its length should be such that, when extended toward the haunches, it goes slightly beyond.

HINDQUARTERS Thighs Long, lean, with well separated muscles; not large. **Legs** Fine-boned, with the furrow between the bone and tendon above the hocks pronounced and greatly sloped. **Hocks and Metatarsi** Should lie along the vertical and on the prolongation of the line of the buttocks. **Feet** Less oval in shape than the forefeet, but otherwise similar.

COAT Hair Very short and fine. **Color** Solid black, slate gray, isabella, in all shades. White is acceptable on chest and feet. **Skin** Thin, close-fitting in all parts of the body, except at the elbows, where it is loose.

GAIT Springy and elegant.

FAULTS General Characteristics Heavy bone, undistinguished overall appearance, lack of symmetry. **Height at the Withers** Over or above standard. **Weight** More than 11 lb. **Head** Upper cranial-facial bones diverging or converging. **Nose** Lacking in pigmentation. **Lips and Muzzle** Short muzzle, lacking in chiseling; lips large and covering lower jaw; accentuated fold of the commissure; cheekiness; partial depigmentation of the eyelids and lips. **Jaws** Robust; defective or missing teeth; undershot or overshot condition. **Skull** Domed, round; accentuated stop. **Eyes** Small or bulging; light eyes; almond-shaped and oblique eyes, that is, not in the proper subfrontal position; ectropion, entropion. **Ears** Carried erect (very grave fault). **Neck** Short, insufficiently arched, with dewlap. **Shoulders** Heavy, excessively large muscles, not free in movement. **Upper Arm** Sloped, short and heavy. **Forearm** Heavy-boned (very serious fault), diverging or converging, deviated from the vertical. **Wrists** Evident hypertrophy of the wrist bones; pasterns out of vertical, too short, too long and too extended. **Feet** Round, out of vertical; deficiency of pigmentation in nails

and pads; splayed toes. **Body** Longitudinal diameter greater than the height at the withers. **Back** Saddle-back or roach back; interruption of the backline. **Loins** Long or flat. **Sexual Organs** Incomplete development of one or both testicles. **Tail** Too long or too short; thick and with hair too long. **Thighs** Short, too fleshed out, carried away from the stifle, too straight or too sloped. **Legs** Insufficient slope, strong bone. **Hocks and Metatarsi** Out of vertical; high hocks; angulation too open. **Hair** Not short. **Color** White markings except on chest and feet. **Skin** Not thin, partially depigmented (nose, eyelids and lips). **Gait** Not springy.

DISQUALIFICATIONS Height at the Withers More than 15 inches for both males and females or less than 12½ for males and 12¼ for females. **Head** Accentuated convergence or divergence of the upper cranial-facial longitudinal axes. **Nose** Above the top line of the bridge; depigmentation of half or more of its surface. **Nasal Bridge** Arched or hollowed. **Jaws** Overshot or undershot condition. **Eyes** Walleyes; total depigmentation of the eyelids. **Sexual Organs** Cryptorchidism, monorchidism; incomplete development of one or both testicles. **Tail** Carried over the back; lack of tail and rudimentary tail, either congenital or acquired. **Metatarsi** Dewclaws. **Color** Not solid color; presence of white, except in those parts indicated in the standard. **Gait** Continuous ambling. ●

THE TWO FRIENDS ▶

Photo: M. Pedone, Sabatini-MARKA.

INDEX

The number in heavy type indicates the number according to classification on pages 34-35. The number in Roman type indicates the first page of each standard; the number(s) in italics refers to the pages with illustrations of specimens of each breed.

AFFENPINSCHER **254** 359, *359*
AFGHAN HOUND **297** 421, *421, 422, 423*
AINU DOG **54** 115, *115*
AIREDALE TERRIER **82** 150, *150*
AKITA DOG **56** 117, *117, 118*
ALASKAN MALAMUTE **74** 137, *137*
AMERICAN COCKER SPANIEL **251** 354, *354, 355, 356*
AMERICAN FOXHOUND **135** 207, *208*
AMERICAN WATER SPANIEL **253** 356, *356*
ANGLO-FRENCH TRICOLOR **159** 231, *231*
ANGLO-FRENCH WHITE AND BLACK **160** 231, *231*
ANGLO-FRENCH WHITE AND ORANGE **161** 231, *231*
APPENZELLER CATTLE DOG **63** 124, *125, 126*
ARDENNES BOUVIER **10** 54, *54*
ARIÈGEOIS **148** 221, *221*
ARIÈGE SETTER **214** 282, *282*
ARTOIS HOUND **149** 222, *222*
ATLAS DOG **58** 118, *118*
AUSTRALIAN TERRIER **102** 167, *168*
AUSTRIAN COARSEHAIRED HOUND **143** 217, *217, 218*
AUSTRIAN HOUND **141** 216, *216*
AUSTRIAN SHORTHAIRED PINSCHER **47** 105, *105*
BALKAN HOUND **195** 261, *261*
BASENJI **106** 170, *171*
BASSET HOUND **192** 257, *256, 257, 258, 259*
BAVARIAN MOUNTAIN HOUND **138** 214, *215*
BEAGLE **166** 235, *234, 235, 236, 237*
BEAGLE HARRIER **165** 234, *234*
BEARDED COLLIE **30** 79, *79*
BEAUCE SHEPHERD **3** 46, *47*
BEDLINGTON TERRIER **83** 151, *151, 152*
BELGIAN GRIFFON **263** 369, *369, 370*
BELGIAN SHEEPDOG **2** 43, *44, 45, 46*
BERGAMESE SHEPHERD **19** 64, *64, 65, 66*
BERNESE CATTLE DOG **64** 127, *127*
BERNESE HOUND **184** 253, *253*
BILLY **118** 191, *191, 193*
BLACK AND TAN COONHOUND **193** 259, *259*
BLACK AND TAN TOY TERRIER **294** 415, *415*
BLACK FOREST HOUND **133** 204, *205*
BLUE AUVERGNE SETTER **215** 282, *282, 283*
BLUE GASCONY BASSET **156** 228, *228*
BOBTAIL **33** 83, *83*
BOLOGNESE **276** 386, *386, 387*
BORDEAUX MASTIFF **51** 108, *109*
BORDER TERRIER **84** 152, *152*
BORZOI **298** 425, *424, 425, 426*
BOSNIAN COARSEHAIRED HOUND **199** 264, *264*
BOSTON TERRIER **292** 412, *412*
BOURBONNAIS SETTER **216** 284, *284*
BOUVIER DES FLANDRES **8** 51, *51*
BOXER **37** 89, *89, 90, 91*
BRAZILIAN GUARD DOG **42** 97, *97*
BRAZILIAN TRACKER **112** 185, *185*
BRIARD **4** 47, *47, 48*
BRITTANY SPANIEL **221** 288, *288*

BULLDOG **76** 140, *140,* **141,** *142*
BULLMASTIFF **77** 142, *143*
BULL TERRIER **85** 152, *153*
BURGOS SETTER **211** 278, *278, 279*
CAIRN TERRIER **87** 154, *154, 155*
CANAAN DOG **43** 97, *98*
CARLIN **293** 413, *413*
CASTRO LABORIERO DOG **60** 120, *120*
CATALONIAN SHEPHERD **11** 54, *54*
CAVALIER KING CHARLES SPANIEL **291** 411, *410, 411*
CHARPLANINATZ **27** 75, *75, 76*
CHESAPEAKE BAY RETRIEVER **244** 343, *343, 344*
CHIHUAHUA **279** 393, *382, 393, 394, 395*
CHOW CHOW **282** 399, *399*
CIRNECO DELL'ETNA **169** 239, *239, 240, 241*
CLUMBER SPANIEL **246** 347, *347, 348*
COARSEHAIRED GRIFFON **226** 293, *292, 293, 294*
CONTINENTAL TOY SPANIEL WITH HANGING EARS **272** 383, *383*
CONTINENTAL TOY SPANIEL WITH UPRIGHT EARS **273** 385, *384, 385*
CROATIAN SHEPHERD **29** 77, *77*
CURLY-COATED RETRIEVER **240** 335, *335*
CURLYHAIRED BICHON **266** 372, *372*
CZECH COARSEHAIRED SETTER **235** 312, *312, 313*
CZECH TERRIER **104** 168, *169*
DACHSBRACKE **136** 211, *210, 211*
DALMATIAN **281** 396, *396, 397, 398*
DANDIE DINMONT TERRIER **88** 154, *155*
DEERHOUND **299** 427, *427, 428*
DOBERMAN **38** 92, *92, 93*
DRAHTHAAR (COARSEHAIRED) **203** 270, *271*
DRENTSE PATRIJSHOND **227** 294, *296*
DREVER **178** 250, *250*
DUNKER **172** 246, *246*
DUPUY SETTER **217** 285, *285*
DUTCH SHEPHERD **13** 56, *57*
DUTCH SPANIEL **229** 296, *297*
DWARF SCHNAUZER **261** 367, *367, 368*
ENGLISH COCKER SPANIEL **245** 344, *345, 346, 347*
ENGLISH SETTER **237** 322, *322, 323, 324, 325, 326, 327*
ENGLISH SPRINGER SPANIEL **249** 350, *350, 351, 352*
ENTLEBUCHER CATTLE DOG **65** 127, *128*
ESKIMO **69** 133, *133*
FIELD SPANIEL **247** 348, *348*
FINNISH HOUND **145** 219, *219*
FINNISH SPITZ **144** 219, *218, 219*
FLAT-COATED RETRIEVER **241** 336, *336, 337*
FOXHOUND **134** 207, *180, 181, 196, 197, 206, 207, 208, 209*
FRENCH BULLDOG **268** 373, *373, 374, 375, 376*
FRENCH SETTER **218** 285, *286, 287*
FRENCH SPANIEL **222** 290, *290*
FRENCH TRICOLOR **119** 193, *186, 193*
FRENCH WHITE AND BLACK **120** 193, *192, 194*
FRENCH WHITE AND ORANGE **121** 195, *186, 194, 195*
GAMMEL DANSK HONSEHUND **210** 278, *278*

GERMAN DACHSHUND **107** 172, *173, 174, 175, 176, 177, 178*
GERMAN DWARF DACHSHUND **108** 179, *179*
GERMAN HUNTING TERRIER **105** 170, *170*
GERMAN MASTIFF **44** 98, *99, 100, 101, 102*
GERMAN SHEPHERD DOG **1** 39, *39, 40, 41, 42, 43*
GERMAN SPANIEL **137** 213, *212, 213*
GIANT POODLE **269** 377, *377, 378*
GOLDEN RETRIEVER **242** 338, *331, 338, 339*
GORDON SETTER **239** 332, *332, 333, 334*
GREAT ANGLO-FRENCH TRICOLOR **123** 196, *196*
GREAT ANGLO-FRENCH WHITE AND BLACK **124** 197, *197*
GREAT ANGLO-FRENCH WHITE AND ORANGE **125** 197, *197*
GREAT GASCON OF SAINTONGE **115** 188, *188, 189*
GREAT GASCONY BLUE **114** 187, *187, 188, 220*
GREAT PORTUGUESE PODENGO **130** 200, *200*
GREAT PYRENEES **50** 108, *108*
GREAT SPITZ **258** 362, *362, 363*
GREAT SWISS CATTLE DOG **66** 128, *128*
GREAT VENDEAN GRIFFON **122** 195, *195, 196*
GREENLAND DOG **71** 134, *135*
GREYHOUND **300** 429, *429, 430, 431*
HAIRLESS DOG **295** 416, *416*
HALDENSTOVER **173** 246, *246*
HAMILTONSTÖVARE **179** 250, *250, 251*
HANOVER HOUND **110** 181, *181, 183*
HARLEQUIN PINSCHER **255** 360, *360*
HAVANESE BICHON **288** 406, *407*
HELLENIC HOUND **168** 238, *238*
HOKKAIDO DOG **53** 114, *114*
HOVAWART **39** 94, *94*
HUNGARIAN COARSEHAIRED SETTER **231** 299, *299*
HUNGARIAN GREYHOUND **304** 435, *435*
HYGENHUND **174** 246, *246*
IBIZAN PODENCO **213** 280, *280*
IRISH SETTER **238** 329, *328, 329, 330*
IRISH TERRIER **89** 156, *156*
IRISH WATER SPANIEL **248** 349, *349*
IRISH WOLFHOUND **301** 431, *431, 432*
ISTRIAN COARSEHAIRED HOUND **196** 261, *261*
ISTRIAN SHORTHAIRED HOUND **197** 263, *261, 263*
ITALIAN COARSEHAIRED SEGUGIO **171** 245, *245*
ITALIAN SHORTHAIRED SEGUGIO **170** 242, *242, 243, 244, 245*
ITALIAN SETTER **232** 299, *299, 302, 304*
ITALIAN SPINONE **233** 305, *305, 306, 307, 309, 310*
ITALIAN SPITZ **278** 392, *392*
JÄMTHUND **131** 200, *200*
JAPANESE FIGHTING DOG **55** 115, *115*
JAPANESE SPANIEL **289** 407, *407, 408*
JAPANESE SPITZ **275** 385, *385*
JURA HOUND **185** 254, *254*
KANINCHEN DACHSHUND **109** 179, *179*
KARELIAN BEAR DOG **113** 185, *185*
KARST SHEPHERD **28** 76, *76, 77*
KERRY BLUE TERRIER **90** 157, *157*
KING CHARLES SPANIEL **290** 408, *409, 410*

KOMONDOR **14** 58, *58, 59*
KROMFOHRLÄNDER **256** 360, *360*
KURZHAAR OR GERMAN SETTER **202** 267, *267, 268, 269, 270*
KUVASZ **15** 59, *59, 60*
LABRADOR RETRIEVER **243** 340, *340, 341, 342*
LAKELAND TERRIER **91** 158, *158*
LANDSEER **73** 136, *136*
LANGHAAR (LONGHAIRED) **204** 272, *272*
LAPLAND SPITZ **24** 72, *72*
LAPPONIAN HERDER **12** 56, *56*
LARGE MÜNSTERLÄNDER **206** 273, *273, 274*
LEONBERG **46** 104, *105*
LEVESQUE **116** 189, *189*
LHASA APSO **286** 404, *405*
LITTLE LION DOG **267** 373, *373*
LUCERNE HOUND **183** 253, *253*
LUNDEHUND **175** 248, *248*
MALTESE **277** 388, *388, 389, 390, 391*
MANCHESTER TERRIER **92** 158, *159*
MAREMMA SHEEPDOG **29** 66, *52, 66, 67*
MASTIFF **78** 143, *144*
MEDIUM-SIZED POODLE **270** 377, *379, 379, 380*
MEDIUM-SIZED PORTUGUESE PODENGO **176** 248, *248*
MEXICAN HAIRLESS **280** 395, *395*
MINIATURE BULL TERRIER **86** 154, *154*
MINIATURE POODLE **271** 377, *380, 381*
MODERN HARRIER **163** 232, *232, 233*
MUDI **16** 60, *60*
NEAPOLITAN MASTIFF **52** 110, *110, 111, 112*
NEWFOUNDLAND **70** 134, *134*
NIVERNAIS GRIFFON **151** 225, *225*
NORFOLK TERRIER **93** 160, *159, 160*
NORMAN ARTESIEN BASSET **155** 227, *277*
NORRBOTTENSPETS **68** 132, *132*
NORWEGIAN ELKHOUND (BLACK) **128** 198, *198*
NORWEGIAN ELKHOUND (GRAY) **127** 198, *198, 199*
NORWEGIAN SHEEPDOG **21** 70, *70*
NORWICH TERRIER **94** 160, *160*
OTTER HOUND **167** 237, *237, 238*
PEKINGESE **283** 401, *400, 401, 402*
PHARAON HOUND **305** 435, *436*
PICARDY SHEPHERD **7** 50, *50, 51*
PICARDY SPANIEL **223** 290, *290*
PINSCHER **257** 360, *361*
POINTER **236** 315, *314, 315, 316, 317, 318, 319, 320, 321*
POITEVIN **117** 190, *190, 191*
POLISH HOUND **129** 199, *199*
PONT-AUDEMER SPANIEL **224** 291, *291, 292*
PORCELAINE **150** 222, *223, 225*
PORTUGUESE MOUNTAIN DOG **9** 53, *53*
PORTUGUESE SETTER **234** 311, *311*
PORTUGUESE WATER DOG **62** 123, *123*
POSAVATZ HOUND **198** 263, *263, 264*
PUDELPOINTER **208** 275, *275*
PULI **17** 62, *62, 63*
PUMI **18** 63, *63*

PYRENEAN MASTIFF **49** 106, *106*
PYRENEES SHEPHERD **5** 48, *48, 49*
PYRENEES SMOOTH-FACED SHEPHERD **6** 50, *50*
RAFEIRO DO ALENTEJO **61** 122, *122*
RHODESIAN RIDGEBACK **194** 260, *260*
RIESENSCHNAUZER **41** 95, *96*
ROTTWEILER **40** 95, *94, 95*
ROUGH COLLIE **31** 80, *80, 82, 85*
SALUKI **306** 436, *436, 437, 438, 439*
SAMOYED **72** 135, *135, 136*
SAN SHU **57** 118, *118*
SCHILLERSTÖVARE **180** 251, *251*
SCHIPPERKE **262** 368, *368*
SCHNAUZER **45** 103, *103, 104*
SCOTTISH TERRIER **95** 161, *161*
SEALYHAM TERRIER **96** 162, *162*
SERRA DA ESTRELA DOG **59** 120, *120*
SHETLAND SHEEPDOG **34** 84, *84, 85*
SHIBA INU **274** 385, *385*
SHIH TSU **284** 403, *403*
SHORTHAIRED DWARF PINSCHER **260** 366, *366*
SIBERIAN HUSKY **75** 138, *138, 139*
SILKY TERRIER **103** 168, *168, 169*
SKYE TERRIER **97** 163, *162, 163*
SLOVAKIAN CHUVACH **26** 74, *75*
SLUGHI **307** 439, *439*
SMÅLANDSSTÖVARE **181** 252, *252*
SMALL ANGLO-FRENCH **162** 232, *232*
SMALL BERNESE HOUND **189** 255, *255*
SMALL BLUE GASCONY GRIFFON **153** 226, *226*
SMALL BRABANÇON GRIFFON **264** 370, *370*
SMALL BRUSSELS GRIFFON **265** 370, *370, 371*
SMALL GASCON OF SAINTONGE **147** 221, *221*
SMALL GASCONY BLUE **146** 220, *220*
SMALL ITALIAN GREYHOUND **308** 440, *440, 441, 443*
SMALL JURA HOUND **191** 255, *255*
SMALL LUCERNE HOUND **190** 255, *255*
SMALL MÜNSTERLÄNDER **207** 274, *274, 275*
SMALL PORTUGUESE PODENGO **177** 249, *249*
SMALL-SIZED FRENCH SETTER **219** 286, *286*
SMALL SPITZ **259** 365, *364, 365*
SMALL SWISS HOUND **188** 255, *255*
SMOOTH-COATED FOX TERRIER **80** 147, *147,* **148**
SMOOTH COLLIE **32** 82, *82*

SOFT-COATED WHEATEN TERRIER **98** 163, *163, 164*
SOMERSET HARRIER **164** 234, *234*
SPANISH GREYHOUND **303** 435, *434, 435*
SPANISH HOUND **212** 278, *278*
SPANISH MASTIFF **48** 106, *106*
STABY-HOUN **228** 296, *296*
STAFFORDSHIRE BULL TERRIER **99** 164, *164,* **165**
ST. BERNARD **67** 129, *129, 130, 131*
STEINBRACKE **140** 216, *216*
ST. GERMAIN SETTER **220** 287, *288*
ST. HUBERT BLOODHOUND **111** 183, *183, 184*
ST. HUBERT TYPE JURA HOUND **186** 254, *254*
STICHELHAAR (WIREHAIRED) **205** 272, *272*
SUSSEX SPANIEL **250** 353, *353*
SWEDISH GRAY DOG **132** 202, *202*
SWISS COARSEHAIRED HOUND **187** 255, *255*
SWISS HOUND **182** 252, *252*
TATRA SHEPHERD **22** 70, *71*
TAWNY BRITTANY BASSET **158** 230, *230, 231*
TAWNY BRITTANY GRIFFON **154** 226, *226*
TIBETAN MASTIFF **79** 144, *144*
TIBETAN SPANIEL **287** 405, *406*
TIBETAN TERRIER **285** 404, *404*
TRANSYLVANIAN HOUND **126** 198, *198*
TYROLEAN HOUND **142** 217, *216, 217*
VALÉE SHEPHERD **23** 72, *72*
VÄSTGÖTASPETS **25** 73, *74*
VENDEAN GRIFFON BASSET **157** 229, *229*
VENDEAN GRIFFON BRIQUET **152** 226, *226*
VIZSLA **230** 297, *297, 298*
WEIMARANER **209** 276, *276, 277*
WELSH CORGI CARDIGAN **35** 86, *86, 87*
WELSH CORGI PEMBROKE **36** 87, *87*
WELSH SPRINGER SPANIEL **252** 356, *355, 356*
WELSH TERRIER **100** 166, *166*
WEST HIGHLAND WHITE TERRIER **101** 166, *166, 167*
WESTPHALIAN BASSET **139** 215, *215*
WHIPPET **302** 433, *433, 434*
WIREHAIRED FOX TERRIER **81** 148, *148, 149*
WOOLLYHAIRED GRIFFON **225** 292, *292, 293*
YORKSHIRE TERRIER **296** 416, *417, 418*
YUGOSLAVIAN MOUNTAIN HOUND **201** 265, *265*
YUGOSLAVIAN TRICOLOR HOUND **200** 265, *265*